International Handbook of
Social Anxiety

International Handbook of Social Anxiety
Concepts, Research and Interventions Relating to the Self and Shyness

Edited by
W. Ray Crozier
Cardiff University, UK and
Lynn E. Alden
University of British Columbia, Canada

JOHN WILEY & SONS, LTD
Chichester · New York · Weinheim · Brisbane · Singapore · Toronto

WB

Other Wiley Editorial Offices

John Wiley & Sons, Inc., 605 Third Avenue,
New York, NY 10158-0012, USA

WILEY-VCH GmbH, Pappelallee 3,
D-69469 Weinheim, Germany

John Wiley & Sons Australia Ltd, 33 Park Road, Milton,
Queensland 4064, Australia

John Wiley & Sons (Asia) Pte Ltd, 2 Clementi Loop #02-01,
Jin Xing Distripark, Singapore 129809

John Wiley & Sons (Canada) Ltd, 22 Worcester Road,
Rexdale, Ontario M9W 1L1, Canada

Library of Congress Cataloging-in-Publication Data
International handbook of social anxiety : concepts, research, and interventions relating to the self and shyness / edited by W. Ray Crozier and Lynn E. Alden.
    p.   cm.
    Includes bibliographical references and index.
    ISBN 0-471-49129-2 (cased)
    1. Social phobia.   2. Bashfulness.   I. Crozier, W. Ray, 1945–   II. Alden, Lynn E.
RC552.S62 .I58 2001
616.85′225—dc21

2001026857

British Library Cataloguing in Publication Data

A catalogue record for this book is available from the British Library

ISBN 0-471-49129-2

Typeset in 10/12 pt Times by Best-set Typesetter Ltd., Hong Kong
Printed and bound in Great Britain by Biddles Ltd, Guildford and King's Lynn
This book is printed on acid-free paper responsibly manufactured from sustainable forestry, in which at least two trees are planted for each one used for paper production.

8/13/03

Contents

About the Editors   ix

List of Contributors   xi

Preface   xix

Chapter 1   The Social Nature of Social Anxiety
                 W. Ray Crozier and Lynn E. Alden   1

SECTION ONE **ORIGINS AND DEVELOPMENT**

Introduction   Origins and Development
                 W. Ray Crozier and Lynn E. Alden   23

Chapter 2   Biological and Environmental Contributions to
                 Childhood Shyness: A Diathesis–Stress Model
                 Louis A. Schmidt, Cindy P. Polak, and Andrea L.
                 Spooner   29

Chapter 3   Behavioral Inhibition: Physiological Correlates
                 Peter J. Marshall and Joan Stevenson-Hinde   53

Chapter 4   Positively Shy! Developmental Continuities in the
                 Expression of Shyness, Coyness, and Embarrassment
                 Vasudevi Reddy   77

Chapter 5   Origins of the Self-conscious Child
                 Michael Lewis   101

Chapter 6   Children's Conceptions of Shyness
                 Nicola Yuill and Robin Banerjee   119

Chapter 7   Behavioral Inhibition, Social Withdrawal,
                 and Parenting
                 Kim B. Burgess, Kenneth H. Rubin, Charissa S. L.
                 Chea, and Larry J. Nelson   137

Chapter 8   Shyness in the Classroom and Home
                   Mary Ann Evans   159

SECTION TWO   **SOCIAL AND PERSONALITY FACTORS**

Introduction   Social and Personality Factors
                   W. Ray Crozier and Lynn E. Alden   187

Chapter 9   Shyness and Social Interaction
                   Monroe A. Bruch   195

Chapter 10   Shyness and the Self: Attentional, Motivational,
                   and Cognitive Self-processes in Social Anxiety
                   and Inhibition
                   Mark R. Leary   217

Chapter 11   Relational Schemas: The Activation of Interpersonal
                   Knowledge Structures in Social Anxiety
                   Mark W. Baldwin and Patricia Fergusson   235

Chapter 12   Evolution and Process in Social Anxiety
                   Paul Gilbert and Peter Trower   259

Chapter 13   Shyness and Embarrassment Compared: Siblings in
                   the Service of Social Evaluation
                   Rowland S. Miller   281

Chapter 14   Blushing
                   Robert J. Edelmann   301

SECTION THREE **CLINICAL PERSPECTIVES AND
                   INTERVENTIONS**

Introduction   Social Anxiety as a Clinical Condition
                   Lynn E. Alden and W. Ray Crozier   327

Chapter 15   Social Anxiety, Social Phobia, and Avoidant
                   Personality
                   Thomas Widiger   335

Chapter 16   Social Anxiety and Depression
                   *Rick E. Ingram, Wiveka Ramel, Denise Chavira,
                   and Christine Scher*   357

Chapter 17   Interpersonal Perspectives on Social Phobia
                   Lynn E. Alden   381

Chapter 18   A Cognitive Perspective on Social Phobia
                   David M. Clark   405

Chapter 19   Shyness as a Clinical Condition: The Stanford Model
                Lynne Henderson and Philip G. Zimbardo   431

Chapter 20   Cognitive-Behavioral Group Treatment for
                Social Phobia
                *Meredith E. Coles, Trevor A. Hart, and Richard
                G. Heimberg*   449

Chapter 21   Psychopharmacological Treatments: An Overview
                Sean D. Hood and David J. Nutt   471

Chapter 22   Social Phobia in Children and Adolescents: Nature
                and Assessment
                Ronald M. Rapee and Lynne Sweeney   505

Chapter 23   Social Phobia in Children and Adolescents:
                Psychological Treatments
                Lynne Sweeney and Ronald M. Rapee   525

Author Index   539

Subject Index   555

About the Editors

W. Ray Crozier (PhD) is Reader in Psychology in the School of Social Sciences, Cardiff University. He is a Fellow of the British Psychological Society. He has published extensively on shyness and embarrassment as well as the psychology of art and decision-making, and is the author of *Understanding Shyness* (Palsgrave, 2001) and editor of *Shyness: Development, Consolidation and Change* (Routledge, 2000). He organized the International Conference on Shyness and Self-consciousness held in Cardiff in 1997.

School of Social Sciences, Cardiff University, Glamorgan Building, King Edward VII Avenue, Cardiff CF10 3WT, UK

Lynn E. Alden (PhD) is a Professor in the Department of Psychology at the University of British Columbia. She also holds an appointment as clinical supervisor in the psychology internship program at Vancouver General Hospital. She has served as Director of Clinical Training at UBC, as President of the Canadian Council of Professional Psychology Programs, and is a Fellow of the Canadian Psychological Association. Dr. Alden is currently an Associate Editor of *Cognitive Therapy and Research*. She has published extensively on cognitive-interpersonal perspectives of social anxiety, social phobia, and avoidant personality disorder.

Department of Psychology, University of British Columbia, Vancouver, BC, Canada V6T 1Z4, Canada

List of Contributors

Mark W. Baldwin (PhD) is an Associate Professor in the Department of Psychology at McGill University in Montreal. His research has examined the cognitive representation and activation of interpersonal knowledge. In particular, his publications have focused on security and insecurity in adult attachment and self-esteem.
Department of Psychology, McGill University, 1205 Dr. Penfield, Montreal, Quebec, Canada H3A 1B1

Robin Banerjee (DPhil) is a British Academy Postdoctoral Fellow at the University of Sussex. He has published research on various aspects of social-cognitive development, and has a particular interest in the links between self-conscious cognition and emotion in primary school children.
COGS, University of Sussex, Brighton BN1 9QH, UK

Monroe A. Bruch (PhD) is at the Department of Educational and Counseling Psychology, University of Albany, State University of New York.
Department of Educational and Counseling Psychology, ED 217, University at Albany, 1400 Washington Av., Albany NY 12222-0001, USA

Kim Burgess (PhD) is Assistant Research Professor in Developmental Psychology at the University of Maryland, College Park. Her research focuses on child psychosocial adjustment, peer relationships, and parent–child relationships. She also studies the behavioral and emotional processes of individuals and dyads via observation.
Department of Human Development, 3304 Benjamin Building, University of Maryland College Park, MD 20742-1131, USA

Denise A. Chavira (PhD) is a research fellow in the Anxiety and Traumatic Stress Disorders Clinic at the University of California San Diego. She is currently studying the effectiveness of combined pharmacological and psychoeducational treatments for social anxiety in children and adolescents, as well as prevalence rates and clinical correlates of social anxiety disorder in paediatric healthcare settings.

Department of Psychology, Doctoral Training Facility, San Diego State University, 6363 Alvarado Ct., #103, San Diego, CA 92120-4913, USA

Charissa Cheah is a senior doctoral student in the Department of Human Development, University of Maryland. Her research interests are the contributions of child disposition, parental beliefs and practices, and peer relationships to children's development. She also studies the role of sociocultural factors in parent–child relationships.

Department of Human Development, 3304 Benjamin Building, University of Maryland College Park, MD 20742-1131, USA

David M. Clark (DPhil) is Professor of Psychology, Institute of Psychiatry, London University, and a Fellow of the Academy of Medical Sciences. He has served as President of the International Association of Cognitive Psychotherapy Therapy and Chair of the British Association of Behavioural and Cognitive Psychotherapies. Dr. Clark has extensive publications addressing theoretical formulations and treatment of anxiety disorders.

Department of Psychology, Institute of Psychiatry, King's College London, De Crespigny Park, London SE5 8AF, UK

Meredith E. Coles is a doctoral student in clinical psychology at Temple University. Her research focuses on the role of information-processing biases in the development and maintenance of anxiety. She is also interested in the development and implementation of empirically supported treatments for the anxiety disorders.

Social Phobia Program, Department of Psychology, Temple University, Weiss Hall, 1701 North 13th Street, Philadelphia, PA 19122-6085, USA

Robert J. Edelmann (PhD) is Honorary Visiting Professor at the University of Surrey, Roehampton; he works in private practice with Psychologists at Law Group and Powell Campbell Edelmann. For many years Professor Edelmann's research has focused on aspects of embarrassment and blushing, most recently combining this with his clinical interests in social phobia. He has published two books and many papers on these topics.

School of Psychology and Counselling, University of Surrey Roehampton, Whitelands College, West Hill, London SW15, UK

Mary Ann Evans (PhD) received her doctorate from the University of Waterloo and is currently Professor of Psychology at the University of Guelph. She is a Fellow of the Canadian Psychological Association, and a registered psychologist.

She currently co-directs a program for university students with learning disabilities and does research in the areas of shyness and reading.

Department of Psychology, University of Guelph, Guelph, Ontario N1G 2W1, Canada

Patricia Fergusson (PhD) is a Psychologist in the Department of Clinical Health Psychology, Health Sciences Centre, Winnipeg, Manitoba. She is also a research associate with the Manitoba Centre for Health Policy and Evaluation, Department of Community Health Sciences, University of Manitoba. In addition to her interests in relational schemas and social anxiety, Dr. Fergusson is also involved in research exploring the psychosocial determinants of health status and health care utilization.

Department of Clinical Health Psychology, Faculty of Medicine, University of Manitoba, 771 Bannatyne Avenue, Winnipeg, Manitoba Canada R3E 3N4

Paul Gilbert (PhD) is Professor of Clinical Psychology at the University of Derby and Director of the Mental Health Research Unit at Kingsway Hospital. He is a Fellow of the British Psychological Society. He has published extensively on depression, anxiety, social phobia, and shame, and has written and edited several books.

Mental Health Research Unit, Kingsway Hospital, Derby DE22 2JX, UK

Trevor Hart is a doctoral student in clinical psychology at Temple University. His research and clinical interests lie in the areas of anxiety disorders and behavioral medicine.

Social Phobia Program, Department of Psychology, Temple University, Weiss Hall, 1701 North 13th Street, Philadelphia, PA 19122-6085, USA

Richard G. Heimberg (PhD) is Professor of Psychology and Director of the Adult Anxiety Clinic of Temple University. Dr. Heimberg is well known for his work in the development and evaluation of cognitive-behavioral treatments for social phobia. He has published more than 175 papers on various aspects of the diagnosis, assessment, and treatment of social phobia and the other anxiety disorders.

Social Phobia Program, Department of Psychology, Temple University, Weiss Hall, 1701 North 13th Street, Philadelphia, PA 19122-6085, USA

Lynne Henderson (PhD) is Director of the Shyness Clinic, and Co-Director of the Shyness Institute. She is a visiting scholar and lecturer in the Psychology Department at Stanford and a clinical faculty member in Counseling Psychology.

The Palo Alto Shyness Clinic, 4370 Alpine Rd., Suite 204, Portola Valley, CA 94028, USA

Sean D. Hood (MBBS) is a Clinical Research Fellow in the Psychopharmacology Unit of the University of Bristol. His research interests include investigating the neurobiology of Panic Disorder and Social Anxiety Disorder. Dr. Hood currently lives in Perth, Australia.

Psychopharmacology Unit, University of Bristol, School of Medical Sciences, University Walk, Clifton, Bristol BS8 1TD, USA

Rick E. Ingram (PhD) is a Professor of Psychology at Southern Methodist University. He is currently the Editor of *Cognitive Therapy and Research*, and serves on the Editorial Boards of the *Journal of Abnormal Psychology*, the *Journal of Consulting and Clinical Psychology*, and the *Journal of Social and Clinical Psychology*. He is co-author of *Cognitive Vulnerability to Depression*, and co-editor of the *Handbook of Psychological Change*. In 1990 he received the Distinguished Scientific Award of the American Psychological Association for Early Career Contributions to Psychology, and in 1987 he received the New Researcher Award, Association for the Advancement of Behavior Therapy.

Department of Psychology Southern Methodist University, Dallas, TX 75275, USA

Peter J. Marshall (PhD) obtained his doctorate from Cambridge University in 1997, with a dissertation on the cardiac correlates of behavioral inhibition in young children. Since then he has been a Research Associate in the Department of Human Development at the University of Maryland.

Center for Children, Relationships and Culture, 1108 Benjamin Building, University of Maryland, College Park, MD 20742-1131, USA

Mark Leary (PhD) is Professor in the Department of Psychology, Wake Forest University. He has published extensively on self-processes, social motivation and emotion, and interfaces of social and clinical psychology. He is author of *Understanding Social Anxiety: Social, Personality, and Clinical Perspectives*, *Social Anxiety* and *The Social Psychology of Emotional and Behavioral Problems: Interfaces of Social and Clinical Psychology* (both with Kowalski), and *Selfhood: Identity, Esteem, Regulation* (with Hoyle, Kernis, & Baldwin). Dr. Leary is editor of the journal *Self and Identity*.

Department of Psychology, Wake Forest University, Winston-Salem, NC 27109, USA

Michael Lewis (PhD) is University Distinguished Professor in the Institute for the Study of Child Development, Robert Wood Johnson Medical School, University of Medicine and Dentistry of New Jersey. He has published extensively on children's cognitive, social and emotional development, including self-consciousness, visual self-recognition, pride and shame. He is author of *Shame, The Exposed Self, Altering Fate: Why the Past does not Predict the Future, Social Cognition and the Acquisition of Self (with Brooks-Gunn)*, and co-editor (with Haviland) of *Handbook of Emotions*.

Institute for the Study of Child Development, Robert Wood Johnson Medical School, 97 Paterson Street, New Brunswick, NJ 08903, USA

Rowland S. Miller (PhD), a Professor of Psychology at Sam Houston State University in Huntsville, Texas, won the Newman Award for Excellence in Research from Psi Chi and the American Psychological Association for his work on empathic embarrassment. He is an Associate Editor of the *Journal of Social and Clinical Psychology*, and is the author of *Embarrassment: Poise and Peril in Everyday Life*.
Department of Psychology and Philosophy, Sam Houston State University, Huntsville, TX 77341-2447, USA

Larry Nelson is a senior doctoral student in Human Development at the University of Maryland, and instructor in the School of Family Life at Brigham Young University. His research interests include the role of non-social behaviors, peers, and parents in the development of the self-system.
Department of Human Development, 3304 Benjamin Building, University of Maryland College Park, MD 20742-1131, USA

David J. Nutt (DM, MRCP, FRCPsych) is Professor of Psychopharmacology and Head of the Department of Clinical Medicine at the University of Bristol. Professor Nutt is the editor of the *Journal of Psychopharmacology* and President of the British Association for Psychopharmacology.
Psychopharmacology Unit, University of Bristol, School of Medical Sciences, University Walk, Clifton, Bristol BS8 1TD, UK

Cindy P. Polak is a doctoral student in human development at the University of Maryland, College Park. Her research focuses on the psychophysiological correlates of individual differences in temperament.
Institute for Child Study, University of Maryland, College Park, MD 20742, USA

Wiveka Ramel is currently a graduate student in the Doctoral Program in Clinical Psychology at San Diego State University and University of California San Diego. Under the guidance of Drs. John McQuaid and Rick Ingram, she is examining how cognitive variables in individuals with affective disorders change with cognitive-behavioral therapy and mindfulness-based stress-reduction treatment.
Department of Psychology, Doctoral Training Facility, San Diego State University, 6363 Alvarado Ct., #103, San Diego, CA 92120-4913, USA

Ron Rapee (PhD) is currently Professor in the Department of Psychology, Macquarie University, Sydney, Australia. He has published extensively in the areas of child and adult anxiety and has written and edited several books.
Department of Psychology, Macquarie University, Sydney, 2109 Australia

Vasudevi Reddy (PhD) is currently a lecturer in the Department of Psychology, University of Portsmouth. Her research, which includes studies of early communication, humour and shyness, focuses on issues related to the infant's developing understanding of minds.
Department of Psychology, University of Portsmouth, King Henry Building, King Henry I Street, Portsmouth PO1 2DY, UK

Kenneth H. Rubin (PhD) is Professor of Human Development and Director, Center for Children, Relationships and Culture at the University of Maryland. His research is focused on social and emotional development and on the relations between parent-child and peer relationships. He is currently President of the International Society for the Study of Behavioral Development and an Associate Editor of *Child Development*.
Department of Human Development, 3304 Benjamin Building, University of Maryland College Park, MD 20742-1131, USA

Christine D. Scher (PhD) recently received her Ph.D. in clinical psychology from San Diego State University and the University of California, San Diego. Dr. Scher's research interests focus on developmental vulnerability to anxiety and depression, particularly how attachment relationships differentially predict these forms of psychological distress.
Department of Psychology, Doctoral Training Facility, San Diego State University, 6363 Alvarado Ct., #103, San Diego, CA 92120-4913, USA

Louis A. Schmidt (PhD) is an Assistant Professor of Psychology at McMaster University. He has published extensively on the biological origins and developmental outcomes of extreme fear and shyness in children and has recently co-edited *Extreme Fear, Shyness, and Social Phobia: Origins, Biological Mechanisms, and Clinical Outcomes* published by Oxford University Press.
Department of Psychology, McMaster University, Hamilton, Ontario Canada L8S 4K1

Andrea L. Spooner is a doctoral student in applied developmental psychology at the University of Guelph. Her research interests lie in the areas of shyness and social anxiety in children.
Department of Psychology, University of Guelph, Guelph, Ontario, Canada N1G 2W1

Joan Stevenson-Hinde (PhD) obtained her doctorate from Brown University in 1964. Since then she has been pursuing research at Cambridge University within the Sub-Department of Animal Behaviour, where she is now a Senior Research Fellow. In addition, since 1966 she has been a Fellow of New Hall, where she is currently Vice-President, Tutor and Director of Studies in Psychology.
Medical Research Council Group on the Development and Integration of Behaviour, Madingley, Cambridge CB3 8AA, UK

Lynne Sweeney (PhD) is a clinical psychologist whose research and clinical interests include the prevention and treatment of internalizing problems in young children and the epidemiology and treatment of chronic headaches in children and adolescents. Dr. Sweeney is a clinical lecturer at Sydney University and is in private practice.

Department of Psychology, Macquarie University, Sydney, 2109 Australia

Peter Trower (PhD) is Senior Lecturer in Clinical Psychology at Birmingham University and Consultant Clinical Psychologist in Birmingham Mental Health Trust. He has published extensively on cognitive-behavioural theory, research and practice in schizophrenia and anxiety, and has a particular interest in paranoia, voices and social phobia.

School of Psychology, University of Birmingham, Edgbaston, Birmingham B15 2TT, UK

Thomas Widiger (PhD) is a Professor of Psychology at the University of Kentucky. He was a member of the DSM-IV Committee for personality disorders and has published extensively on the diagnosis, assessment, and conceptualization of personality disorders. He currently serves as Associate Editor of the *Journal of Abnormal Psychology* and the *Journal of Personality Disorders*.

Department of Psychology, 012-H Kastle Hall, University of Kentucky, Lexington, KY 40506-0044, USA

Nicola Yuill is a senior lecturer in developmental psychology at the University of Sussex. Her research focuses on social-cognitive development in school-age children, and particularly on children's understanding of motivations for action. She is also interested in the role of language in social cognition, and the development of reading comprehension.

COGS, University of Sussex, Brighton BN1 9QH, UK

Philip Zimbardo (PhD), Professor of Psychology at Stanford University, is internationally recognized as an innovative researcher in social psychology, as well as an award-winning distinguished teacher, writer, and media personality. His book, *Shyness: What it is, What to do about it*, currently in its sixth printing, is translated into 10 languages.

Department of Psychology, Building 420 Room 246, Stanford University, Stanford CA 94305, USA

Preface

The *International Handbook of Social Anxiety* comprises a set of chapters specially written by distinguished researchers to give an account of what each regards as important in his or her specialist area. It aims to provide an account of the "state of the art" in the field of social anxiety. There is growing recognition among psychologists that problems of extreme shyness and social phobia are prevalent in the population, and recent years have seen a surge of research into these issues. The structure of the *Handbook* recognizes that social anxiety is a broad field encompassing the study of child development, the physiology of anxiety, the social psychology of shyness and interpersonal relationships, and clinical approaches to the diagnosis and treatment of social phobia. Chapters provide critical, yet accessible reviews of what they take to be the key issues and practices in their fields. They also include novel ideas and original syntheses of research where these promise to be seminal in the field. The volume is organized into three sections, concentrating respectively on the origins and development of social anxiety, its implications for social encounters and interpersonal relationships, and clinical interventions designed to reduce anxiety and enhance social functioning.

We are grateful to Mike Coombs at Wiley for his advice at every stage in the development of the *Handbook* and to Jonathan Cheek for his help in the planning stages. Ray Crozier thanks Sandra, John, and Beth Crozier for their support throughout the project and the Research Committee and School of Social Sciences at Cardiff University for granting a period of study leave to work on the book. Lynn Alden thanks Raymond and Sarah Andersen for their support throughout this project and Tanna Mellings and Andrew Ryder for their editorial assistance. We are grateful to John Crozier for help with the author index.

Table 13.1 in Chapter 13 is adapted from Miller, R. S. (2001) "Embarrassment and social phobia: Distant cousins or close kin?", in S. G. Hofmann & P. M. DiBartolo (Eds.), *From Social Anxiety to Social Phobia: Multiple Perspectives*, with permission from Allyn & Bacon.

The diagnostic criteria for Avoidant Personality Disorder that are included in Chapter 15, Table 15.1, are reprinted with permission from *the Diagnostic and*

Statistical Manual of Mental Disorders, Fourth Edition. Copyright 1994 American Psychiatric Association.

Figure 18.1 in Chapter 18 is adapted from Clark, D. M. and Wells, A. (1995) "A cognitive model of social phobia", in R. Heimberg, M. Liebowitz, D. A. Hope, & F. R. Schneier (Eds.), *Social Phobia: Diagnosis, Assessment and Treatment*, page 72, with the permission of Guilford Press.

Chapter 1

The Social Nature of Social Anxiety

W. Ray Crozier *and* **Lynn E. Alden**

THE PREVALENCE OF SOCIAL ANXIETY
THE SOCIAL CONTEXT OF SOCIAL ANXIETY
The Self-presentation Perspective
The Evolutionary Perspective
MATTERS OF DEFINITION
State Anxiety
Trait Anxiety
Traits and Situations
Unfamiliar Situations
Evaluative Situations
CONCLUSION
REFERENCES

This introductory chapter has three aims. First, it draws attention to the high prevalence rates of social anxiety in the general population and as a clinical condition. Second, it considers two frameworks in which explanations of prevalence can be located. Finally, it considers definitions of social anxiety. Questions of definition are always central to scientific investigation, and they are particularly important in a volume such as this, which draws together research carried out in different branches of a discipline, developmental psychology, social and personality psychology, psychiatry and clinical psychology. Our goal of facilitating communication among these branches requires a shared vocabulary.

International Handbook of Social Anxiety: Concepts, Research and Interventions Relating to the Self and Shyness. Edited by W. Ray Crozier and Lynn E. Alden.
© 2001 John Wiley & Sons Ltd.

THE PREVALENCE OF SOCIAL ANXIETY

As we write the introduction to this *Handbook* in the early months of a new millennium it is difficult to resist the temptation to reflect on the dramatic changes that have taken place in the human condition since the beginning of the previous millennium or even, indeed, the previous century. Without glossing over the poverty and hardship that still blight life in many countries, it is a truism that the world has been transformed since the year 1000. Advances in technology, in economic and financial systems, and in communications, education, sanitation, and awareness of the conditions that foster good health have, among other changes, brought about marked improvements in health, life expectancy, and the quality of life. Even in the past one hundred years there have been dramatic developments that impact on people's prosperity and well being. While many people in wealthy regions like North America or Western Europe still live in poverty, few experience the squalor and absolute deprivation that characterized life in the slums of the large cities at the end of the nineteenth century—for example, the London documented by Henry Mayhew, Charles Dickens, and others (Porter, 1996).

Although the general health of modern societies has improved alongside their growing prosperity (and indices of these are highly correlated) the incidence of problems of mental health is high. This is so despite considerable changes over the past century in society's attitudes to mental illness and an enormous amount of speculation, theory, and clinical research dedicated to identifying and classifying psychological problems, understanding their causes, and developing methods of treatment. In particular, there are high levels of anxiety about social interactions and interpersonal relationships. We can draw upon three strands of evidence to support this assertion.

Shyness is the concept in ordinary English language that captures many of the characteristics of social anxiety, as it is linked to notions of wariness, timidity, and psychological discomfort in interaction with other people. It is used to describe transient feelings ("I was suddenly overcome with shyness") and more stable individual characteristics ("I am basically a shy person"; "my life has been crippled by shyness"). Zimbardo and associates at Stanford University (see Pilkonis & Zimbardo, 1979; see also Henderson & Zimbardo, *Chapter 19*) initially surveyed a sample of 817 high school and college students and asked them whether they considered themselves as shy and whether they regarded shyness as a problem. Over 40% of respondents characterized themselves as shy, and of those who thought of themselves as currently shy, 63% endorsed an item asking whether their shyness was a problem for them. Subsequent research has replicated these findings and has also shown that self-attributed shyness is common in all of the many countries that have been surveyed (Pines & Zimbardo, 1978). The incidence in these studies ranged from 24% among a sample of Jewish Americans to 60% among respondents in Hawaii and Japan. More recent surveys suggest that there has been a trend over several years for the incidence of self-attributed shyness to increase. The figure has apparently risen in the USA from 40 to over 50% (Carducci & Zimbardo, 1997). The Stanford Survey also asks respondents whether they have ever been shy (now or in the past). A large majority of respondents endorse this item (a median value across studies of 84%) and there is little cross-cultural variation in these responses: the proportion of endorsements in different countries ranges from 66 to 92% of respondents—most young adults throughout the developed world have experienced shyness at one time or another.

Obviously there are problems in inferring from these data that rates of shyness are increasing. There is no information about the reliability of the single "yes–no" item or of the small set of shyness-related items comprising the Survey. In addition, tendencies to endorse the items will be influenced by growth in public awareness of shyness, a trend that becomes more likely as articles written by shyness researchers appear in popular magazines and it is covered in the media. Nevertheless, it is clear that a substantial number of people report that they are shy and that their shyness is undesirable and causes a problem for them.

A second strand is represented by a series of studies that were carried out within the framework of a behaviourist approach to the management of anxiety symptoms. In order to assess levels of anxiety and fears, self-report questionnaire measures have been constructed, for example, the Fear Survey Schedules devised by Lang and colleagues (Lang & Lazovik, 1963; Wolpe & Lang, 1964) and submitted to factor analysis. Two social fear factors emerge from these studies: one with highest loadings on items referring to fear of being with a member of the opposite sex or of speaking before a large group, and one loading on items referring to fear of criticism or of appearing foolish. Mean ratings on these social fears items are consistently high.

A third strand relates to epidemiological studies of social phobia. A clinical syndrome of social phobia has been recognized as a diagnostic category since its inclusion in the third edition of the *Diagnostic and Statistical Manual* (DSM-III) of the American Psychiatric Association published in 1980. This edition identified three types of phobias: agoraphobia, social phobia, and simple phobia. Social phobia was characterized as a persistent fear of situations where the individual might be subject to scrutiny by others and anticipates that his or her behaviour will lead to embarrassment or humiliation. This causes the individual a significant amount of distress because he or she recognizes that the fear is excessive.

Epidemiological surveys suggest that the incidence of social phobia in the general population is high. For example, Kessler et al. (1994) reported the findings of the National Comorbidity Study (NCS), a survey of a very large (over 8,000 respondents) national sample in the USA. Trained staff carried out structured interviews; the diagnostic interview included social phobia items that reflected the DSM-III-R criteria. The Survey reported a 12-month prevalence of 7.9% and a lifetime prevalence of 13.3%. These data imply that social phobia is the third most common psychiatric disorder in the United States, after major depression (17% lifetime prevalence) and alcohol dependence (14%). There is also evidence that social phobia is a "chronic and unremittent disorder" (DeWit, Ogborne, Offord, & MacDonald, 1999, p. 569). Their survey of retrospective accounts of social phobia showed that the median length of illness was reported to be 25 years and in some cases lasted up to 45 years.

These investigations have been criticized by some commentators for overestimating the prevalence of these anxieties, for example, by their reliance on survey approaches rather than clinical records, and by effectively extending the definition of phobia to embrace everyday social anxieties (Cottle, 1999). Of course, this objection begs the question why social anxieties are "everyday" or why there are individual differences in self-reported anxiety such that some people claim to be much less confident and more fearful than others do.

Cross-cultural studies of social phobia also show high prevalence rates across different cultures. There seems to be a somewhat lower incidence in East Asian countries although this conclusion must be qualified by the methodological problems of this research (these issues are discussed by Ingram, *Chapter 16*).

THE SOCIAL CONTEXT OF SOCIAL ANXIETY

Despite possible limitations of each of these lines of evidence they do converge on a picture of widespread psychological discomfort in routine social situations. When these reactions are commonplace as opposed to idiosyncratic, they raise questions about the social conditions that foster them. That is, analysis of social anxiety might fruitfully begin, not with the reasons why particular individuals are shy or anxious, but with investigation of cultural influences on patterns of social interaction, intragroup behaviour and intergroup behaviour. What is the nature of a society that produces widespread social unease among its members? This is a question that Zimbardo, Pilkonis, and Norwood (1975) raised in the context of the Stanford Survey findings. They argued (p. 27) that "the problem of shyness is not essentially a personal problem. It is really a social problem. Certain kinds of social and cultural values lead people to imprison themselves within the egocentric predicament of shyness." They went on to speculate that, "Shyness in America . . . is a consequence of cultural norms that overemphasise competition, individual success, and personal responsibility for failure" (p. 27). A similar point is made by Burgess, Rubin, Chea and Nelson (*Chapter 7*) who point to differences in the meaning of shyness between Western individualistic cultures and Eastern collectivist cultures. They write that "shyness and behavioral inhibition are positively evaluated in Chinese cultures because these behaviors are considered to reflect social maturity and understanding".

An alternative interpretation of social anxiety is that it is a response to threats to social status or reputation (Nesse, 1998). It is related to emotions of pride and shame, and to claims to entitlement to honour, dignity, and respect. These can be powerful motives for behaviour, as exemplified in the political slogan, "Death before dishonour". All societies have means for indicating social status, for example, through forms of appearance and dress or rules governing how one approaches and addresses an individual of high status. Social interactions are constrained by unwritten but widely acknowledged rules and conventions, such as "etiquette", "manners", and "taste". Failure to recognize or comply with these forms and rules can lead to punishment or to internalized forms of punishment, notably feelings of shame or guilt. These feelings can constitute a potent means for bringing about social conformity by encouraging self-regulation of behaviour (Scheff, 1988). Nevertheless, there is cultural diversity in how status and reputation are marked. Sennett (1976) has argued that there has been a historical shift in Western societies away from rigid demarcation of status and infrequent interactions between individuals of different status to more fluid boundaries and increasing encounters. For example, rules for appropriate forms of dress for people of different status were once rigidly enforced; while such rules undoubtedly still exist they are now less strictly observed and there is greater tolerance for deviations from norms. The onus is now on individuals to assert their own identity rather than rely upon, say, their accent, uniform, or the design of a tie.

The Self-presentation Perspective

These notions were brought to the attention of social scientists through the seminal writings of Erving Goffman (1972). He paid particular attention to the role of embarrassment in the regulation of social encounters: "Goffmanian men and women are driven by the need to avoid embarrassment" (Schudson, 1984, p. 634). According to Goffman, embarrassment is closely linked with individual claims to identity in the eyes of others. As Silver, Sabini, and Parrott (1987, p. 48) summarize this position:

> Participants need a working consensus about each other's qualities (natures, selves, or characters will do just as well). This working consensus specifies which qualities are relevant to the interaction at hand. It includes the qualities that each actor can be expected to display (and be sanctioned for not displaying) and, therefore, the qualities that each interactant is entitled to treat others (and herself) as having.

Embarrassment ensues when at least one interactant perceives that the consensus cannot be sustained and this brings the interaction to a halt, leaving the participants uncertain what to do next. Typically this breakdown is brought about by a specific unforeseen event or when there is a sudden loss of poise. For example, a child discomfits his parents when they are visiting acquaintances by making a frank remark about their hostess's appearance or by spilling his orange juice over her new carpet. This approach can also accommodate individual differences. Social discomfort can ensue when an individual senses, rightly or wrongly, that he or she lacks the qualities necessary to sustain a social encounter. Goffman regards the routine social encounters of everyday life as a series of negotiations where the social identities of interactants are claimed, accepted, or challenged. These negotiations require that interactants should have certain competencies and, perhaps of particular relevance to social anxiety, confidence in their competencies. Finding himself in the company of distinguished social anxiety scholars, a psychologist who lacks confidence in his own grasp of the subject may become tongue-tied and self-conscious. This represents the approach to shyness taken by Goffman (1972, p. 107):

> Various kinds of recurrent encounters in a given society may share the assumption that participants have attained certain moral, mental, and physiognomic standards. The person who falls short may everywhere find himself inadvertently trapped into making implicit identity-claims which he cannot fulfil . . . And, if he only imagines that he possesses a disqualifying attribute, his judgment of himself may be in error, but in the light of it, his withdrawal from contact is reasonable.

An individual's shyness might not be noticed by other interactants or it might be interpreted in other ways. Nor might it make much impact upon the social encounter, which may carry on without his or her active contribution. Nevertheless, there is evidence that an individual's shyness can and does influence other people's interpretations of his or her qualities and, in the longer term it can be a significant factor in shaping social relationships. Bruch (*Chapter 9*) assesses this evidence. More generally, understanding the relationship between shyness and embarrassment, whether in specific situations or in predispositions to react in these ways in social encounters, has proved problematic and has been conceptualized in various ways. Miller (*Chapter 13*) addresses this issue. Blushing provides a specific example of this uncertainty. This ubiquitous phenomenon has proved difficult to understand at both psychological and physiological levels. Paradoxically, the blush draws attention to the individual just at the time when he or she least wants to be visible. It is a characteristic expression of embarrassment yet does not always accompany it. It can be the presenting problem of individuals who are diagnosed with social phobia. However, research has not managed to produce a consensus about its role in social anxiety. Thus, some, but not all theorists would argue that it is an expression of shame and shyness as well as embarrassment. Edelmann (*Chapter 14*) surveys this research.

The major legacy of Goffman's writings has been social psychological explorations of the notions of impression management and self-presentation. Theories of self-presentation have been applied to a range of psychological phenomena. Goffman's notion of *preventive practices* has given rise to theoretical analysis and empirical investigations of impression management strategies (Shepperd & Arkin, 1990). There are similarities between these strategies, the self-protective behaviours that characterize many social phobics (Alden, *Chapter 17*), and the "safety behaviours" adopted by the socially anxious (Clark, *Chapter 18*). Schlenker and Leary (1982) produced a highly influential theory of social anxiety, which conceptualizes it as the motivation to create a desired impression in others combined with a lack of confidence in the ability to do so. This theory has been applied to shyness, embarrassment, blushing, and social phobia. Leary (*Chapter 10*) provides a review of this research.

Goffman's account of embarrassment has been criticized on a number of grounds, for example, that it describes social relationships as they are located within a particular, capitalist social order, or that it overemphasizes the significance of embarrassment. After all, many people often seem oblivious to the impression that they are creating in others and most interactions proceed without any breakdown in consensus (Schudson, 1984). Nevertheless, embarrassment, shyness and other forms of social discomfort do seem to be universal. For example, although research based on the Stanford Survey identified a significant degree of cultural variation in the incidence of self-attributed shyness, this was found to characterize a sizeable proportion of respondents in all the countries sampled. An alternative approach to social anxiety focuses on this universality and positions individual concerns with status and reputation within a biological perspective.

The Evolutionary Perspective

Evolutionary psychology has provided analyses for a range of human behaviours. It takes as central to its approach the adaptive significance of behaviour. This is not adaptation in the more common sense in psychological theory, in terms of the individual's adjustment to his or her environment, including the social environment. Adaptation is defined "as traits shaped by natural selection that serve functions that increase net reproductive success" (Nesse, 1998, p. 398). Analysis of social anxiety begins with recognition that the human is a social species, evolved, like many other such species, to live in hierarchically organized groups. Belonging to the group is adaptive in the sense outlined above, whereas social exclusion is maladaptive and makes it less likely that the individual will survive and pass on its genes. Hierarchical organisation is an effective arrangement of social life, facilitating group living while minimizing intragroup competition for mates and resources and its contingent aggression. Fear (and anxiety) has evolved because it is adaptive in a number of important ways, for example in anticipating danger and facilitating avoidance and escape. Nesse (1998) argues that although anxiety is typically thought of as maladaptive, in the sense that for the individual it is a painful experience and can be disruptive, restrictive, and overwhelming, its important feature—and the reason that it has not become extinct over time—is its adaptive significance for reproductive success.

Gilbert and associates (Gilbert & McGuire, 1998; Gilbert & Trower, 1990; see Gilbert & Trower, *Chapter 12*) have pioneered the application of an evolutionary perspective to social anxiety. Their approach is based on analysis of different forms of group living in the service of reproductive success. Humans, like members of other group living species, compete with one another for resources and seek to appear attractive to conspecifics, sexually or otherwise. The approach draws upon the thesis (Chance, 1988) that the organisation of living in groups can be classified into two forms. The agonic (threat based) mode is characterized by dominance hierarchies of power and rank. The hedonic (affiliation based) mode is characterized by mutual dependence and reciprocal relationships. Group members have developed appraisal systems that enable them to be alert to social threats of attack, exclusion, rejection, and loss of status, and have also developed competencies for selecting appropriate responses. Anxiety relates to these appraisals and responses. It can arise from the inappropriate activation of the defensive system that is responsive to threat to social status, for example, the individual tends to treat social interactions as potentially threatening. It can result from a failure to recruit the safety system which permits the individual to feel safe in the presence of others, or from fear of appearing unattractive to others.

The model offers an account of the universality of social anxiety and tries to show why social situations are threatening even when they involve little risk of physical danger. It provides an explanation of its pervasiveness, where individuals experience anxiety even though "objectively" they know that it is uncalled for or they try without success to control it. It also gives insight into specific characteristics of social anxiety. For example, lowering the eyes and gaze aversion is a typical response in shyness, embarrassment, and shame (see Reddy, *Chapter 4*). This is frequently interpreted as a social gesture, intended to signal submissiveness or appeasement (Keltner, 1995). It is sometimes construed in terms of shutting out information. For example, Barrett (1995, p. 41) writes that, in addition to communicating submission or deference, gaze aversion, along with lowering the head and hiding the face, serves to "distance" the ashamed individual from important others, and removes the face from their evaluation. This is similar to the interpretation offered within an evolutionary framework by Dixon (1998) who argues that "cut-off" acts and postures are used by animals when their escape from the threatening situation is blocked and they reduce the visual information emanating from the source of threat. This interpretation draws attention to a function of gaze aversion that could be explored in social anxiety research, it can assist in the self-regulation of arousal and gives the organism some "space" in which to seek an alternative strategy.

Explanations of social anxiety in terms of evolutionary psychology or the social psychology of impression management agree in asserting that anxiety is an inherent feature of social life. Although the aversive quality of the experience is more usually the focus of attention, it is salutary to recognize that anxiety serves useful functions. It helps to regulate social life while minimizing the risks of aggression or an irreparable breakdown in the group's activity. It is also functional at the individual level in helping the individual to acquire self-knowledge, in enhancing awareness of standards for behaviour, and in encouraging processes of self-regulation. Nevertheless, there are individual differences in propensity to anxiety and, for many people, this comes to dominate and restrict their social encounters and relationships—shyness is often described as "crippling" or a "handicap". Much of this volume is directly concerned with this individual variation.

MATTERS OF DEFINITION

Thus far we have been shy of offering a formal definition of social anxiety, but we hope that our use of the term anxiety has been uncontroversial since it corresponds to usage in both the lay and the psychological vocabulary, for example, as defined by *The Penguin Dictionary of Psychology*, "A vague, unpleasant emotional state with qualities of apprehension, dread, distress and uneasiness". Leary (1983, p. 15) has offered a formal definition of anxiety as: "a cognitive-affective syndrome that is characterized by physiological arousal (indicative of sympathetic nervous system arousal) and apprehension or dread regarding an impending, potentially negative outcome that the person believes he or she is unable to avert". By social anxiety, we mean that this anxiety is triggered by the prospect or reality of certain kinds of social situations, as opposed to anxiety associated with, say, insects, heights, enclosed spaces, blood, death, and so on. Empirical research can identify the range of social situations that tend to elicit anxiety (meeting new people, going on a date, public speaking, answering the telephone, etc.) while clinical case studies can identify the specific kinds of situations that trouble individuals.

So far we have treated shyness in its everyday usage as a word that refers to apprehension and uneasiness about social situations while recognizing that it has further connotations of timidity and wariness. It would be a task for sociolinguistic analysis to tease out these connotations. However, some psychologists have also used the term in a technical sense, as a label for a specific emotional state or as a summary of a trait that is called upon to help explain social difficulties. This inevitably raises questions about the relationship between shyness and social anxiety (Cheek & Briggs, 1990) or between shyness and social phobia (Turner, Beidel, & Townsley, 1990). It is particularly important for this volume, which aims to bring together research into the origins and development of social anxiety, its implications for social interactions and relationships, and its potential for change. This research is often published in separate scholarly journals, and it is essential to establish connections among these. Our approach to these problems of definition is based on two assumptions. The first is that it is useful in research into anxiety to distinguish between a state and a trait. The second is that it is important to consider that experiences like shyness and anxiety are complex, that they can be construed as having cognitive, somatic, and behavioural dimensions, and may not be reduced to only one of these dimensions.

State Anxiety

The greatest confusion seems to occur at the state level. Psychologists have investigated a number of emotions that are distinguished in everyday vocabulary, particularly shame, guilt, embarrassment, shyness, and anxiety. Some, for example, Buss (1980), have defined these as different forms of social anxiety, but this has proved problematic. It is not obvious that they are all anxiety states—for example, they do not all show the characteristic pattern of heightened sympathetic nervous arousal as indexed, say, by heart rate measures. Others have argued that they constitute distinct emotions: for example, Miller (1996) argues that embarrassment meets all the accepted criteria for identification as a basic emotion in its own right; it has quick onset, brief duration, involuntary, relatively automatic appraisal process, universal antecedent events, distinctive physio-logical responses, distinctive emotional display, and is found in other species. (See also, Lewis, *Chapter 5*, and Miller, *Chapter 13*, for discussion of shyness and embarrassment.) Whether or not it is a distinct emotion, embarrassment shares with shyness, shame, and guilt at least one component—namely, self-consciousness; indeed, these have been labelled as the "self-conscious emotions" (Tangney & Fischer, 1995). Self-focused attention is also a characteristic of anxiety; for example, there has been considerable research in the test anxiety literature into the detrimental effects of self-preoccupation upon task perfor-mance (Sarason, Pierce, & Sarason, 1996).

Buss (1980) had argued that self-attention was the essential element shared by different forms of social anxiety and subsequent research has established its key role in shyness, shame, embarrassment, blushing, and social phobia. For example, shy individuals spend more time in self-focus during a social encounter than the less shy (Melchior & Cheek, 1990). Improvements in social phobia following cog-nitive behaviour therapy are associated with reductions in self-focused attention (Woody, Chambless, & Glass, 1997). The self, and self-consciousness in particular, plays a key role in current conceptualizations of social anxiety and is addressed throughout this volume (for example: Lewis, *Chapter 5*; Yuill & Banerjee, *Chapter 6*; Leary, *Chapter 10*; Miller, *Chapter 13*; Ingram, Ramel, Chavira, & Scher, *Chapter 16*; Clark, *Chapter 18*; Coles, Hart & Heimberg, *Chapter 20*).

These states reflect the individual's concern with threats to his or her reputa-tion or standing in the eyes of others, and self-consciousness may be a key element because it forms part of the appraisal process whereby the individual monitors how his or her conduct appears to others. Leary and Downs (1995; also see *Chapter 10*) have postulated an executive process, the *sociometer*, which is credited with such an appraisal function, although they also consider that it can operate outside conscious awareness. Clark (*Chapter 18*) also refers to the detailed self-monitoring that is triggered when the anxious individual senses that he or she is in danger of being negatively evaluated by others. Anxiety also makes individuals alert to cues of threat from the environment. Coles et al. (*Chapter 20*) discuss this in terms of hypervigilance for social threats and cues about poten-tially negative social outcomes. Baldwin and Fergusson (*Chapter 11*) and Clark (*Chapter 18*) review evidence on biases in processing social cues.

At our current level of understanding it may be more fruitful to consider these states as sharing a family resemblance rather than claiming that they are discrete emotions or that they share a single underlying factor like "social anxiety". (We note the title of *Chapter 13* where Miller considers shyness and embarrassment as "siblings in the service of social evaluation".)

There are circumstances in which experiences are more likely to be labelled in one way than in another. To consider one example, Jane is *anxious* while she is waiting to go on stage in a musical produced by her university drama group. Unfortunately, when she performs her first number, her singing is off key and below the standards of everyone else. Jane might feel *embarrassed* about her performance, attributing it to first night nerves or to the discomfort of the stage lighting and her costume. She might feel *ashamed* of herself for having let everyone down or *guilty* at having taken a part that could have been played by a better singer. She might feel *shy* at the prospect of talking about the show afterwards with the other cast members or with her friends in the audience. Members of the audience could be *embarrassed* for her, empathizing with her predicament, but they could also be *embarrassed* by her performance, unsure how to react. They could be *ashamed* of her, for letting down the university, *guilty* for giving her the part, and so on. They could feel any of these even if Jane is blissfully unaware of how her performance is being received. It is an important goal of research to tease out the various experiences that can occur in social situations like these. This example suggests that the context in which emotions are elicited is an important consideration in deciding which member of a family of emotions is experienced.

Differences among states are not simply a matter of labelling. Some situations may elicit a blush and reduced heart rate whereas others that superficially are similar may produce pallor and elevated heart rates. Some experiences are recurrent, they evoke intense reactions or are difficult for an individual to assimilate to her self-image and cause her problems or predispose her to seek professional help. For example, most people blush; for many, this occurs frequently or with intense colour, and some find it unbearable. All of these states fall within the domain of social anxiety, since they are all instances of uneasiness and discomfort produced by social situations, even though it is a question for research whether they are indeed forms of anxiety.

Trait Anxiety

The primary problem at the trait level is the comparative meaning of a number of related constructs, specifically, shyness, behavioural inhibition, withdrawn behaviour, social anxiety, and social phobia. There are important distinctions to be drawn. First, social phobia is not a type of temperament or a personality trait but is a category within a diagnostic classification scheme. Whether or not an individual is assigned to this category is, in part, a function of factors that influence his or her decision to seek help (hypothetically, the same level of anxiety can lead one person but not another to seek professional help) or determine access to clinicians who recognize the condition (some physicians may decide the individual is suffering from generalized anxiety or from a condition that is comorbid with social phobia, such as depression or alcohol abuse). It is possible that specific temperaments (behavioural inhibition) or traits (shyness, social anxiety, extraversion or neuroticism, see Widiger, *Chapter 15*) predispose people either to develop extreme fears or to seek help for their problems, but this is a matter for research to establish. Any scheme and its categories evolve as understanding of social anxiety develops. Thus, the defining criteria for social phobia have changed with successive editions of the DSM. DSM-IV introduced a distinction between social phobia and avoidant personality disorder. This distinction may stand the test of time or it may be redrawn in the light of accumulating evidence (see Widiger, *Chapter 15*). Research suggests that distinctions can also be made among generalized social phobia, where a range of situations produce anxiety, non-generalized social phobia, where anxiety is restricted to a small number of types of situations, and phobia about public speaking (e.g., Westenberg, 1998).

Turner et al. (1990) have provided a summary of similarities and differences between shyness and social phobia. These share several features: negative cognitions in social situations; heightened physiological reactivity; a tendency to avoid social situations; and deficits in social skills. Negative cognitions include fear of negative evaluation, self-consciousness, devaluation of social skills, self-deprecating thoughts, and self-blaming attributions for social difficulties. Social phobia is distinct from shyness in that it has a lower prevalence in the population, follows a more chronic course, has more pervasive functional impairment, and a later age of onset. There are problems with these kinds of comparisons. It is not clear in what sense "shyness" is being used, whether as a lay term (e.g. drawing upon findings from the Stanford Survey) or as tied to personality measures, and the sense in which it is used will affect, for example, estimates of the prevalence of shyness. Different kinds of information are used to assess the characteristics of social phobia; for example, interview data are used for prevalence rates whereas clinical evidence is the source for inferences about its chronic and unremitting nature. Nevertheless, it seems reasonable to conclude that individuals who present with the problems that attract a diagnosis of social phobia share many characteristics with individuals who describe themselves as shy and report their shyness as a serious problem. It may be that the differences between them are quantitative rather than qualitative. For example, there are parallel sets of findings between clinical samples of social phobics and samples of students obtaining high scores on measures of shyness or social anxiety (see Clark, *Chapter 18*, for examples of this research).

Factor analysis has been the preferred method in personality research for bringing order to trait concepts. In practice, the intercorrelations among shyness scales are substantial and a factor analysis of sets of items tends to yield one common factor (Briggs, 1988). Shyness measures are also highly correlated with measures of social anxiety (Pilkonis, 1977a) so that it would be difficult to construct a shyness scale that did not correlate significantly with social anxiety scales, and *vice versa*. These findings imply that shyness and social anxiety are not discrete phenomena. Notwithstanding these findings, research has more generally found it valuable to treat anxiety as multidimensional, and to distinguish cognitive, somatic, and behavioural dimensions. Anxiety is associated with worry, self-preoccupation and self-deprecatory thinking, heightened sympathetic system arousal, and behaviours that are expressive of heightened arousal (pallor, trembling) or function to cope with threat (escape, aggression). It seems sensible to maintain these distinctions in the case of social anxiety since research has also identified these dimensions although they take specific forms. For example, self-consciousness is a significant element of the cognitive dimension, blushing of the somatic dimension, and gaze aversion and reticence of the behavioural dimension (these reflect the particular nature of social threats and ways of coping with them, given the difficulty of escaping most potentially threatening situations). Furthermore, some research has shown that shy individuals vary in the emphasis they place on these dimensions of their experience (Pilkonis, 1977a; Cheek & Watson, 1989; Cheek & Krasnoperova, 1999). Finally, keeping the distinction in mind also helps to resolve disagreements in definition. Cheek and Briggs (1990, p. 321) defined shyness as "the tendency to feel tense, worried, or awkward during social interactions, especially with unfamiliar people" whereas Leary (1986, p. 29) argued that the term is best reserved to describe a specific syndrome that involves inhibited behaviour as well as anxiety. The difference here is on the emphasis that is paid to the various dimensions. It is important that research studies are explicit about the measures of shyness that they use; without this information it is difficult to compare studies and accumulate evidence.

Traits and Situations

One key issue with regard to trait anxiety is the relative role of trait and situational influences on social anxiety. Social life consists of a diverse range of encounters with other people, from brief transactions with unfamiliar people, for example, those who serve in supermarkets, garages, restaurants, and so on, to recurrent but superficial encounters with neighbours and acquaintances, to exchanges with colleagues in the work environment, to time spent with partners, friends and family members. By definition, social interactions involve more than one person and they are rewarding, productive, satisfactory, or otherwise depending on the degree of "meshing" between individual goals and styles of interaction. The Stanford Survey established that shyness was more likely when social encounters were unfamiliar, involved power or status differences, gender differences, or the presence of large numbers of people. The prospect of being evaluated by others is an important element in the situations that elicit shyness. This implies a statistical interaction between trait and situation effects, where individual variation is most pronounced in certain types of situations. Unfamiliar and evaluative situations have been most emphasized.

Unfamiliar Situations

The role of novelty has been a constant theme in research into social anxiety. Its influence can be direct, eliciting behavioural inhibition (Kagan, 1998) or shyness (Asendorpf, 1989). It can also be indirect, serving as a potential trigger of the combination of conditions that, according to the Schlenker–Leary theory, produces social anxiety, namely social evaluation concerns and lack of self-confidence (Schlenker & Leary, 1982).

Although children are social creatures from birth and the quality of their early social relationships is widely regarded as a significant influence upon adult personality, there is a long course of development before the individual takes his or her place in the adult social world. Social anxiety in childhood is an important topic for investigation, both for the evidence it provides about the antecedents of adult social anxiety, and because it can create a problem for children's adjustment (Burgess et al., *Chapter 7*; Evans, *Chapter 8*; Rapee & Sweeney, *Chapters 22* and *23*). Research has received an enormous impetus from the study of behavioural inhibition in childhood (see Schmidt et al., *Chapter 2* and Marshall & Stevenson-Hinde, *Chapter 3*). Kagan (1998, p. 212) regards "shyness with strangers, whether peers or adults, as only one feature of a broader temperamental category called inhibition to the unfamiliar". In the initial research carried out by his group at Harvard, parents were interviewed by telephone about their child's shyness and a sample of these children were invited to the laboratory for detailed investigation, where they were exposed to a range of unfamiliar situations. Children were identified as inhibited on the basis of their tendencies to be upset, to be hesitant in approaching a stranger or a new toy, and to be little involved in spontaneous interaction. A longitudinal investigation has provided evidence for the relative stability of inhibition and has shown differences on physiological measures between inhibited and uninhibited children that are consistent with the thesis that behavioural differences are mediated by anxiety (see Schmidt et al., *Chapter 2*, and Marshall & Stevenson-Hinde, *Chapter 3*).

Although this temperament relates to reactions to all forms of novelty and not just to unfamiliar social situations, it has clear connections with shyness, and the term "inhibition" is often used interchangeably with shyness. Although inhibition has typically been assessed on the basis of systematic observations of behaviour, ratings by parents, teachers and psychologists have also been frequently used, for example, in such rating scales as the EAS Temperament Survey or Colorado Child Temperament Inventory (Buss & Plomin, 1984) or the Child Behavior Questionnaire (Rothbart, Ahadi, & Hershey, 1994).

Similar patterns of behaviour are to be found among shy and inhibited children. Thus, reticence, more specifically the timing and frequency of speech acts, has consistently differentiated between shy and less shy adults and children, and between inhibited and less inhibited children. In comparison with their less shy peers, shy adults take longer to produce their first utterance in conversation with an unfamiliar person; they are slower to break a silence in conversation, and they speak for a smaller proportion of the time (Pilkonis, 1977b; Cheek & Buss, 1981; Bruch, Gorsky, Collins, & Berger, 1989; see also Bruch, *Chapter 9*). Similar trends emerge in studies of children. For example, Kagan et al. (1988) reported that 7-year-old children who had originally been identified as inhibited when they were 21 months old took significantly longer to produce their first spontaneous comment during a test session with an adult experimenter than did non-inhibited children. Eisenberg et al. (1998) reported a similar delay in reaching a criterion number of spontaneous utterances among a sample of children who were rated by their parents as shy. Asendorpf and Meier (1993) reported a similar trend, but their research demonstrates the importance of taking situational factors in shyness into account. In their observational study, children who had been rated as shy by their parents were more reticent in interactions with strangers but there was no comparable trend when they were interacting with those with whom they were familiar.

In addition to contemporaneous correlations, children who have been identified as inhibited in childhood are at somewhat greater risk for subsequent anxiety disorders (Hirschfeld et al., 1992; Turner, Beidel, & Wolff, 1996) and for shyness and reduced social effectiveness (Gest, 1997). Among adults admitted to an anxiety disorders clinic, significant correlations have been reported between measures of social phobia, shyness, and retrospective self-report of behavioral inhibition in childhood (Van Ameringen, Mancini, & Oakman, 1998). The moderate size of the relationship between behavioural inhibition and subsequent social anxiety may reflect a number of factors (over and above questions about the reliability of the measures of inhibition or temporal changes in inhibited status). First, inhibition may predispose an individual to the disorder by making him or her more vulnerable to stressful experiences; it is not a sufficient precondition, and not all inhibited children will develop social anxiety. Second, there may be alternative routes to social anxiety and one clue to this is the contribution of self-evaluative concerns.

Individual variation in childhood shyness can be detected at an age when it is unlikely that children have any well-developed sense of themselves as social actors or a very sophisticated awareness that they can be the object of negative evaluation by other people. It is possible that individuals who were not inhibited at a younger age become shy only when they do develop the capacity to reflect upon their behaviour from another perspective. One can speculate that a predisposition to this may not simply be a matter of temperament but also of the self-schemata that have been constructed out of attachment experiences or other parent–child interactions (Burgess et al., *Chapter 7*; Alden, *Chapter 17*).

Evaluative Situations

Currently there is debate among researchers whether there are distinct forms of shyness—one appearing earlier than the other and related to fear of strangers, and another appearing later, related to social-evaluative concerns (Lewis, *Chapter 5*; Yuill & Banerjee, *Chapter 6*). Asendorpf has provided evidence implying that a distinction between types of shyness is also apparent in adulthood, and argues, "the same observable shy behavior can arise from two different inhibitory processes. According to this view, abnormal shyness with strangers and abnormal shyness due to social-evaluative concerns may be quite different disorders although they share the same overt behavior" (Asendorpf, 1993, p. 1071). Establishing the validity of this distinction has obvious implications for treatment since greater refinement of categories can lead to interventions targeted at specific concerns.

A detailed analysis of the situations that elicit shyness or social anxiety also plays an important role in psychotherapeutic approaches designed to help people overcome social anxieties. It forms the basis for identifying the belief systems that give rise to, and serve to maintain, anxiety. It assists in the development of approaches to treatment, whether this is systematic exposure to feared situations, the planning of appropriate homework exercises, or the construction of challenges to the coping strategies (or safety behaviours—Clark, *Chapter 18*) that clients have relied upon to help them to deal with particular classes of situation. It has potentially an important role to play in the evaluation of treatment programmes, including pharmacological regimens. Although clinician reports or client self-reports are common outcome measures in evaluation research (Hood & Nutt, *Chapter 21*) the situational nature of social anxiety implies the necessity to assess individuals in the specific situations that concern them.

Social anxiety is evidently a function of social situations as well as of temperament or personality characteristics. Shy individuals can be comfortable in some situations but ill at ease in others. Although research has identified features of social encounters that seem to be important for inducing anxiety, it should be recognized that the shift from confidence to discomfort can be produced by quite subtle changes in the nature of the situation. Furthermore, it is misleading to consider situational and personal factors as independent since it is the individual's interpretation of the situation that is crucial. This has long been recognized in research into anxiety; for example, manipulation of experimenter instructions can be sufficient to encourage a test-anxious individual to perceive an upcoming assessment as ego-involving and threatening or can induce a less threatening attribution. Nevertheless, it is a fundamental assumption of theories of social anxiety that individuals bring something to social situations, whether this is an inhibited temperament, self-schemata, mental representations of recurring social situations, learned habits, or coping behaviours.

CONCLUSION

Social anxiety is prevalent in the population, whether in terms of self-reported shyness or social fears or symptoms of social phobia. Understanding its prevalence will require contributions from many academic disciplines; and we have argued that it is a social phenomenon as well as an individual one. Psychological research has developed along three fronts. One approach (the focus of Section Three) examines social phobia from a clinical perspective, aiming to refine diagnostic criteria or to test psychotherapeutic or pharmacological forms of treatment. A second approach (the focus of Section Two) investigates the causes, correlates and consequences of trait shyness or social anxiety. Focus here has been on individual differences in behaviour in social settings and in the quality of social relationships. A third approach has investigated shyness in childhood, and a particularly influential construct has been behavioral inhibition.

This research, which is the focus of Section One, has been characterized by the extensive (and welcome) use of longitudinal methods.

Issues of definition remain a preoccupation in research into social anxiety. Clearly there is an onus on researchers to be explicit about the terms that they use, to provide details on the measures that operationalize the definition, and to be particularly careful when mixing lay and technical uses of terms. Social anxiety is neither a simple nor an unambiguous concept, yet we hope that this volume illustrates how investigations have found regularities in the patterns of cognitions, affective reactions and behaviours of individuals who are identified as inhibited, shy, socially anxious, or social phobic.

Despite differences in definitions and measures, common threads have emerged and are the focus of much of this volume, and we finish this chapter by alluding to some of these. One is that social anxiety is associated with heightened self-consciousness and with self-deprecation, particularly of the anxious individual's own social competence. A second is that anxious individuals have a heightened sensitivity to cues of social threat. A third is that anxious individuals adopt coping styles that can be counter-productive and function to reinforce rather than alleviate their social difficulties or anxiety. A fourth is evidence of psychophysiological differences between anxious and less anxious individuals, and developments in research here are associated with growing sophistication in measurement techniques. A challenge for the future is to connect this research programme with another strand of research, which is currently undertaken in a different branch of psychology and is represented in the clinical section of this volume. This could result in greater understanding of the neurochemical bases of pharmacological approaches to treatment of social anxiety (reviewed in detail by Hood & Nutt, *Chapter 21*).

We hope that researchers, teachers and practitioners will learn much from this volume, that they will not only find considerable interest and reference value in those chapters more directly relevant to their specialist concerns but will also find the chapters dedicated to other, perhaps less familiar aspects of social anxiety, exciting and useful. We hope, too, that our endeavour to bring together the findings of research from different perspectives and frameworks will stimulate the development of the study of social anxiety and of interventions that can alleviate this common and distressing condition.

REFERENCES

Asendorpf, J. B. (1989). Shyness as a final common pathway for two different kinds of inhibition. *Journal of Personality and Social Psychology*, *57*, 542–549.

Asendorpf, J. B. (1993). Abnormal shyness in children. *Journal of Child Psychology and Psychiatry*, *34*, 1069–1081.

Asendorpf, J. & Meier, G. (1993). Personality effects on children's speech in everyday life: Sociability-mediated exposure and shyness-mediated reactivity to social situations. *Journal of Personality and Social Psychology*, *64*, 1072–1083.

Barrett, K. C. (1995). A functionalist approach to shame and guilt. In J. P. Tangney & K. W. Fischer (Eds.), *Self-conscious emotions: The psychology of shame, guilt, embarrassment and pride* (pp. 25–63). New York: Guilford Press.

Briggs, S. R. (1988). Shyness: Introversion or neuroticism? *Journal of Research in Personality, 22*, 290–307.

Bruch, M. A., Gorsky, J. M., Collins, T. M., & Berger, P. A. (1989). Shyness and sociability reexamined: A multicomponent analysis. *Journal of Personality and Social Psychology, 57*, 904–915.

Buss, A. H. (1980). *Self-consciousness and social anxiety*. San Francisco: Freeman.

Buss, A. H. & Plomin, R. (1984). *Temperament: Early appearing personality traits.* Hillsdale, NJ: Erlbaum.

Carducci, B. J. & Zimbardo, P. G. (1997). Are you shy? In M. H. Davis (Ed.), *Annual editions: Social Psychology 1997/98* (pp. 35–41). Guilford, CT: Dushkin/Brown & Benchmark.

Chance, M. R. A. (1988). Introduction. In M. R. A. Chance (Ed.), *Social fabrics of the mind* (pp. 1–35). Hove, Sussex: Erlbaum.

Cheek, J. M. & Briggs, S. R. (1990). Shyness as a personality trait. In W. R. Crozier (Ed.), *Shyness and embarrassment: Perspectives from social psychology* (pp. 315–337). New York: Cambridge University Press.

Cheek, J. M. & Buss, A. H. (1981). Shyness and sociability. *Journal of Personality and Social Psychology, 41*, 330–339.

Cheek, J. M. & Krasnoperova, E. N. (1999). Varieties of shyness in adolescence and adulthood. In L. A. Schmidt & J. Schulkin (Eds.), *Extreme fear, shyness, and social phobia: Origins, biological mechanisms, and clinical outcomes* (pp. 224–250). New York: Oxford University Press.

Cheek, J. M. & Watson, A. K. (1989). The definition of shyness: Psychological imperialism or construct validity? *Journal of Social Behavior and Personality, 4*, 85–95.

Cottle, M. (1999). Selling shyness. *The New Republic, 221*, 5 (August 2), 24–29.

De Wit, D. J., Ogborne, A., Offord, D. R., & MacDonald, K. (1999). Antecedents of the risk of recovery from DSM-III-R social phobia. *Psychological Medicine, 29*, 569–582.

Dixon, A. K. (1998). Ethological strategies for defence in animals and humans: Their role in some psychiatric disorders. *British Journal of Medical Psychology, 71*, 417–445.

Eisenberg, N., Shepard, S. A., Fabes, R. A., Murphy, B. C., & Guthrie, I. K. (1998). Shyness and children's emotionality, regulation, and coping: Contemporaneous, longitudinal, and across-context relations. *Child Development, 69*, 767–790.

Gest, S. D. (1997). Behavioral inhibition: Stability and associations with adaptation from childhood to early adulthood. *Journal of Personality and Social Psychology, 72*, 467–475.

Gilbert, P. & McGuire, M. T. (1998). Shame, status, and social roles: Psychobiology and evolution. In P. Gilbert & B. Andrews (Eds.), *Shame: Interpersonal behaviour, psychopathology, and culture* (pp. 99–125). Oxford: Oxford University Press.

Gilbert, P. & Trower, P. (1990). The evolution and manifestation of social anxiety. In W. R. Crozier (Ed.), *Shyness and embarrassment: Perspectives from social psychology* (pp. 144–177). New York: Cambridge University Press.

Goffman, E. (1972). *Interaction ritual*. Harmondsworth, England: Penguin.

Hirschfeld, D. R., Rosenbaum, J. F., Biederman, J., Bolduc, E. A., Faraone, S. V., Snidman, N., Reznick, J. S., & Kagan, J. (1992). Stable behavioral inhibition and its association with anxiety disorder. *Journal of the American Academy of Child and Adolescent Psychiatry, 31*, 103–111.

Kagan, J. (1998). Biology and the child. In N. Eisenberg (Ed.), *Handbook of child psychology, 5th edition, Volume 3: Social, emotional, and personality development* (pp. 177–235). New York: John Wiley.

Kagan, J., Reznick, J. S., Snidman, N., Gibbons, J., & Johnson, M. O. (1988). Childhood derivatives of inhibition and lack of inhibition to the unfamiliar. *Child Development*, *59*, 1580–1589.

Keltner, D. (1995). Signs of appeasement: Evidence for the distinct displays of embarrassment, amusement and shame. *Journal of Personality and Social Psychology*, *68*, 441–454.

Kessler, R. C., McGonagle, K. A., Zhao, S., Nelson, C. B., Hughes, M., Eshleman, S., Wittchen, H.-U., & Kendler, K. S. (1994). Lifetime and 12-month prevalence of DSM-III-R psychiatric disorders in the United States. *Archives of General Psychiatry*, *51*, 8–19.

Lang, P. J. & Lazovik, A. D. (1963). Experimental desensitization of a phobia. *Journal of Abnormal and Social Psychology*, *66*, 519–525.

Leary, M. R. (1983). *Understanding social anxiety: Social, personality, and clinical perspectives*. Beverly Hills, CA: Sage.

Leary, M. R. (1986). Affective and behavioral components of shyness: Implications for theory, measurement, and research. In W. H. Jones, J. M. Cheek, & S. R. Briggs (Eds.), *Shyness: Perspectives on research and treatment* (pp. 27–38). New York: Plenum.

Leary, M. R. & Downs, D. L. (1995). Interpersonal functions of the self-esteem motive: The self-system as a sociometer. In M. Kernis (Ed.), *Efficacy, agency, and self-esteem* (pp. 133–144). New York: Plenum.

Melchior, L. A. & Cheek, J. M. (1990). Shyness and anxious self-preoccupation during a social interaction. *Journal of Social Behavior and Personality*, *5*, 117–130.

Miller, R. S. (1996). *Embarrassment: Poise and peril in everyday life*. New York: Guilford Press.

Nesse, R. (1998). Emotional disorders in evolutionary perspective. *British Journal of Medical Psychology*, *71*, 397–415.

Pilkonis, P. A. (1977a). Shyness, public and private, and its relationship to other measures of social behavior. *Journal of Personality*, *45*, 585–595.

Pilkonis, P. A. (1977b). The behavioral consequences of shyness. *Journal of Personality*, *45*, 596–611.

Pilkonis, P. A. & Zimbardo, P. G. (1979). The personal and social dynamics of shyness, In C. Izard (Ed.), *Emotions in personality and psychopathology* (pp. 133–160). New York: Plenum Press.

Pines, A. & Zimbardo, P. G. (1978). The personal and cultural dynamics of shyness: A comparison between Israelis, American Jews and Americans. *Journal of Psychology and Judaism*, *3*, 81–101.

Porter, R. (1996). *London: A social history*. London: Penguin Books.

Rothbart, M. K., Ahadi, S. A., & Hershey, K. L. (1994). Temperament and social behavior in childhood. *Merrill–Palmer Quarterly*, *40*, 21–39.

Sarason, I. G., Pierce, G. R., & Sarason, B. R. (1996). Domains of cognitive interference. In I. G. Sarason, G. R. Pierce, & B. R. Sarason (Eds.), *Cognitive interference* (pp. 139–152). Mahwah, NJ: Lawrence Erlbaum.

Scheff, T. J. (1988). Shame and conformity: The deference-emotion system. *American Review of Sociology*, *53*, 395–406.

Schlenker, B. R. & Leary, M. R. (1982). Social anxiety and self-presentation: A conceptualization and model. *Psychological Bulletin*, *92*, 641–669.

Schudson, M. (1984). Embarrassment and Erving Goffman's idea of human nature. *Theory and Society*, *13*, 633–648.

Sennett, R. (1976). *The fall of public man*. Cambridge: Cambridge University Press.

Shepperd, J. A. & Arkin, R. M. (1990). Shyness and self-presentation. In W. R. Crozier (Ed.), *Shyness and embarrassment: Perspectives from social psychology* (pp. 286–314). New York: Cambridge University Press.

Silver, M., Sabini, J., & Parrott, W. G. (1987). Embarrassment: A dramaturgic account. *Journal for the Theory of Social Behaviour, 17*, 47–61.

Tangney, J. P. & Fischer, K. W. (Eds.) (1995). *Self-conscious emotions: The psychology of shame, guilt, embarrassment and pride.* New York: Guilford Press.

Turner, S. M., Beidel, D. C., & Townsley, R. M. (1990). Social phobia: Relationship to shyness. *Behaviour Research and Therapy, 28*, 497–505.

Turner, S. M., Beidel, D. C., & Wolff, P. L. (1996). Is behavioral inhibition related to the anxiety disorders? *Clinical Psychology Review, 16*, 157–172.

Van Ameringen, M., Mancini, C., & Oakman, J. M. (1998). The relationship of behavioral inhibition and shyness to anxiety disorder. *Journal of Nervous and Mental Disease, 186*, 425–431.

Westenberg, H. G. M. (1998). The nature of social anxiety disorder. *Journal of Clinical Psychiatry, 59*, Supplement 17, 20–26.

Wolpe, J. & Lang, P. J. (1964). A fear survey schedule for use in behaviour therapy. *Behaviour Research and Therapy, 2*, 27–30.

Woody, S. R., Chambless, D. L., & Glass, C. R. (1997). Self-focused attention in the treatment of social phobia. *Behaviour Research and Therapy, 35*, 117–129.

Zimbardo, P. G., Pilkonis, P. A., & Norwood, R. (1975). Shackles of shyness. *Psychology Today, U.K. edition, 1* (6), 24–27.

Section One

Origins and Development

Origins and Development

Introduction

Origins and Development

W. Ray Crozier *and* Lynn E. Alden

BIOLOGICAL BASES OF INHIBITION AND SHYNESS
Temperament
The Emergence of Self-consciousness
FAMILY INFLUENCES ON SHYNESS
CONCLUDING REMARKS
REFERENCES

The considerable amount of attention that is currently paid to shyness in the child development literature owes much to the significant programme of longitudinal research into the temperamental category of behavioural inhibition undertaken by Jerome Kagan and his associates at Harvard. In itself, this programme has yielded considerable insights into the origins and development of shyness. In addition, it has stimulated important research in other laboratories, for example, by Fox and his colleagues at Maryland (see *Chapter 2*) and Stevenson-Hinde and her co-workers at Madingley, Cambridge, in the United Kingdom (see *Chapter 3*). However, other research traditions within developmental psychology have also contributed to our understanding of shyness and social anxiety. In this brief introduction to Section One we consider some of these contributions and also draw attention to links that are currently being made between them and the temperamental approach. These include: links with attachment theory (Marshall & Stevenson-Hinde, *Chapter 3*; Burgess et al., *Chapter 7*), styles of parenting (Schmidt et al., *Chapter 3*; Burgess et al., *Chapter 7*; Evans, *Chapter 8*); cognitive development (Lewis, *Chapter 5*; Yuill & Banerjee, *Chapter 7*); emotional development (Reddy, *Chapter 4*; Lewis, *Chapter 5*).

International Handbook of Social Anxiety: Concepts, Research and Interventions Relating to the Self and Shyness. Edited by W. Ray Crozier and Lynn E. Alden.
© 2001 John Wiley & Sons Ltd.

BIOLOGICAL BASES OF INHIBITION AND SHYNESS

Temperament

Explanations of individual differences in terms of temperament were neglected in psychology for many years, in tune with a zeitgeist where the emphasis was placed on environmental factors as the predominant influence on human development. This position reflected to a large extent the widespread distaste with biological explanations that followed controversies about race and intelligence. Yet there was much evidence to show that individual differences among babies are evident at birth, and a major investigation (the New York Longitudinal Study) led by Thomas, Chess, and their colleagues, sought to identify a small set of basic temperaments that might underlie this diversity. This research has been largely descriptive and has sought to find order in individual variation, establish the extent of temporal stability of basic temperament dimensions, and investigate their ability to predict child and adult personality and adjustment.

Kagan's programme has been developed within this biological framework, concentrating on a temperament labelled *behavioural inhibition to the unfamiliar*, defined by Kagan, Reznick, and Snidman (1985; cited by Marshall & Stevenson-Hinde, *Chapter 3*) as referring to "the child's initial behavioral reactions to unfamiliar people, objects, and contexts, or challenging situations". Despite the wide range of types of situation that can be unfamiliar, and hence provoke these reactions, there has been an emphasis in the literature on the links between inhibition and shyness. Encounters with unfamiliar adults or children play a large part in the assessment of inhibition. Outcome measures in empirical studies include the child's reticence and hesitation in making spontaneous contributions to conversation and his or her tendency to hover at the edge of social situations, in addition to ratings of shyness made by parents or by observers of the child's behaviour. The programme design has been longitudinal and has addressed issues such as cross-situational consistency in inhibition, the stability of the temperament over time, and prediction of personality and behaviour in later childhood and adolescence. Kagan has been explicit about the value of treating temperament as a category rather than a dimension, and hence stability is gauged in terms of the likelihood of changes of category membership rather than quantitative differences on criterion measures.

A distinctive feature of the research has been its aim to account for variation, not simply to describe it. Kagan's explanation is in terms of individual differences in reactivity to threat and he assigns a central role to limbic structures, particularly the amygdala and its projections (Kagan, 1994). The psychophysiological model has been tested by making predictions about peripheral response systems, based mostly on measures of heart period and heart period variability, although other measures have been used, such as cortisol levels. The theory has connected with accounts that focus on the role of hemisphere asymmetry in processing negatively charged emotional information (see Schmidt et al., *Chapter 2*, for a summary of this research; also Schmidt & Schulkin, 1999). Marshall and Stevenson-Hinde (*Chapter 3*) provide a thorough review of research into the physiological correlates of behavioural inhibition, and conclude that despite some inconsistent findings, there is substantial support for the proposition that the physiological model has made significant contributions to understanding behavioural inhibition. Physiological correlates of shyness have also been traced in studies of susceptibility to allergies and various medical conditions, for example, susceptibility to Parkinson's Disease (Bell et al., 1995). Evans (*Chapter 8*) reviews this literature, and also reports a significant tendency for shy children to be more likely to be absent from school due to illness, particularly gastro-intestinal conditions.

Longitudinal studies have demonstrated a degree of temporal stability in inhibition, and stability over time in measures of behaviour or in physiological assessments is more characteristic of a smaller sample of inhibited children who are consistently inhibited. Similarly, these children are at greater risk of later adjustment problems. However, consistency is a complex matter, even after taking into account the issue of whether measures made at various ages are strictly comparable. The social worlds of infants, toddlers, children, and adolescents make very different demands, and the same category of temperament will find different expression in these life periods.

The Emergence of Self-consciousness

One telling observation has been that shyness or social anxiety in later childhood or adulthood is associated with concerns with how one appears to others and the judgements that may be made about the self. The capacity to think about the self in these ways is certainly absent in the early years and this inevitably raises questions about the relationship between infant temperament and later social concerns. Buss (1986) made an influential distinction between early appearing and fearful shyness on the one hand, and later appearing or self-conscious shyness on the other. It is tempting to equate the early appearing form with the pattern of social behaviours identified by Kagan as an aspect of the inhibited temperament. Lewis (*Chapter 5*) has also noted similarities between inhibition and a form of embarrassment that does not require self-evaluation. Furthermore, he identified an interaction between scores on a measure of temperament, the capacity for self-consciousness (see below), and embarrassment. The interaction takes the form that temperament only contributed to embarrassment when self-consciousness was attained and was not evident beforehand.

The distinction between fearful and self-conscious forms of shyness has come to be widely accepted, although there is as yet little evidence to support it, Yuill and Banerjee (*Chapter 6*) have explored it by means of the study of children's conceptions of shyness, arguing that these could be expected to reflect pre-dominant forms of shyness at a given age. They do identify a shift in children's cnceptions from about 5 years of age, which they relate to the child's growing

appreciation of other people's perspectives of the self as well as to developments in the awareness of self-presentational concerns. Reddy (*Chapter 4*) and
Lewis (*Chapter 5*) also consider the development of distinct forms of shyness and
embarrassment. Future research will surely be aided by a measure of inhib-
ited/wary and self-conscious/anxious forms of social withdrawal recently constructed by Younger et al. (2000).

One of the key investigations of children's cognitive social development has
been the series of experiments carried out by Michael Lewis and his associates
into children's awareness of the self as assessed by the visual self-recognition
paradigm. In the classic mirror rouge test, a dab of rouge is surreptitiously placed
on the child's face and the child's reaction to seeing his or her face in a mirror is
evaluated. However, children's reactions to their mirror image, with or without
this manipulation, are of great interest, and it has been shown that from an early
age facial expressions of coyness and embarrassment can be recognized in the
child's reaction. Lewis has drawn upon this research to produce a theory of the
development of self-consciousness, and this is reviewed in Chapter 5. Lewis
regards the emergence of self-consciousness in the middle of the second year as
the key event in the development of the emotions. Initially it facilitates the development of "exposure-embarrassment" (the form closer to shyness, according to
Lewis), where embarrassment is only observed in those children who do touch
their nose in the rouge mirror test. Towards the third year of life, children are
also able to judge their behaviour relative to standards, and this enables the
development of shame, pride, guilt, and forms of embarrassment associated with
failure to behave appropriately (making a faux pas, loss of poise, behaving out
of role, and so on).

Reddy (*Chapter 4*) provides a thorough overview of research into the distinctive facial expressions of shyness, coyness and embarrassment. She emphasises
ambivalence, the combination of approach (gaze, smiling) with avoidance (gaze
and head aversion, covering the mouth with the hand). Reddy argues that expressions of coyness and ambivalent shyness (e.g., shy or coy smiles) can be identified in children in early infancy, long before visual self-recognition emerges.
Careful empirical studies are providing insights into the development of shyness
and embarrassment in the first year of life, and the theorizing of Lewis and
evidence reviewed by Reddy imply that previous conceptualizations of the
emergence of self-awareness have not dealt adequately with its complexity.

FAMILY INFLUENCES ON SHYNESS

Shyness is a social phenomenon, linked to self-appraisals and expectations about
the reactions of others to the self, and it is scarcely surprising that early social
relationships have been proposed as factors in the development just as, for
example, they have been argued as important in shame and guilt. Freud's theory,
and the work of his followers who specialized in childhood (Anna Freud, Melanie

Klein, John Bowlby, and others), have had a profound influence on the study of child development. This has been achieved not only by their writings and the professional institutions of psychoanalysis but also through the growth of child psychiatry more generally. Their direct influence on the developmental psychology of shyness has not been great, but Bowlby's attachment theory is attracting growing interest. His concept of the mother as a "secure base" from which the child can explore the world and the operationalization of his theoretical concepts in the Ainsworth Strange Situation Test strike obvious chords with shyness researchers. The tentativeness and ambivalence of the shy child implies that he or she lacks the security to explore the social world. The Strange Situation is similar in many (but not all) respects to the assessment of inhibition in Kagan's laboratory.

The relationship between temperament and attachment is treated in various ways in this section. Marshall and Stevenson-Hinde (*Chapter 3*) propose that attachment status, as assessed by the Strange Situation, interacts with inhibition and heart period. They argue that securely attached children are free to express their emotions in a more open manner whereas those who are insecurely attached are likely to develop strategies for dealing with their emotions. They report findings from their own laboratory supporting this hypothesis. Schmidt, Polak and Spooner (*Chapter 2*) refer to research linking secure attachment with children's social competence. Rubin and colleagues (see Burgess, Rubin, Cheah, & Nelson, *Chapter 7*) have proposed a developmental pathway where infants who are temperamentally reactive and who receive insensitive parenting come to develop an insecure-ambivalent attachment relationship with their primary caregiver.

Research into parenting has itself more than one parent, so to speak, and sociological and social psychological perspectives on cultural and individual differences in child-rearing practices have also shaped enquiries into the antecedents of personal capacities for forming social relationships. These perspectives are having an influence on studies of shyness. Rubin and his associates have conducted extensive studies of shyness, withdrawn behaviour, and parenting. The edited volume by Rubin and Asendorpf (1993) on these themes made a key contribution to the expansion of developmental research. Rubin and co-workers (*Chapter 7*) also provide an up to date review of the literature on relationships between parental beliefs and practices and inhibition and social withdrawal and examine how these relationships may be modified by gender and broader cultural factors. Schmidt, Polak, and Spooner (*Chapter 2*) also review findings on parental sensitivity and maternal personality. Evans (*Chapter 8*) offers an alternative to the emphasis of research into interactions with strangers by bringing together and evaluating the scattered literature on the impact of shyness on the child at home and at school. She examines the link between shyness and academic achievement and suggests ways in which the teacher can help the shy student. She cautions against over-interpretation of findings about the influence of parental styles on shyness, warning that the causal relationships may be complex.

CONCLUDING REMARKS

The set of chapters in this section of the *Handbook* provides a picture of a field of research in robust health, characterized by creative theorizing and vigorous research programmes. Biological and environmental factors, and the interactions between them, have been implicated in the development of inhibition, shyness, and social anxiety. Seemingly intractable problems about the emergence of self-consciousness are being addressed by empirical methods. Research has been programme driven and findings from different laboratories and countries can be compared, rather than the isolated studies that have characterized this field in the past. Investigators have drawn effectively upon longitudinal designs and have been prepared to marry psychological and physiological approaches to measurement. Of course, the psychology of child development and of the origins of individual differences is complex, and much research yet needs to be undertaken.

REFERENCES

Bell, I. R., Amend, D., Kaszniak, A., Schwartz, G. E., Peterson, J. M., Stini, W. A., Miller, J. W., & Selhub, J. (1995). Trait shyness in the elderly: Evidence for an association between Parkinsons Disease in family members and biochemical correlates. *Journal of Geriatric Psychiatry and Neurology, 8,* 16–22.

Buss, A. H. (1986). A theory of shyness. In W. H. Jones, J. M. Cheek, & S. R. Briggs (Eds.), *Shyness: Perspectives on research and treatment* (pp. 39–46). New York: Plenum.

Kagan, J. (1994). *Galen's prophecy.* London: Free Association Books.

Rubin, K. H. & Asendorpf, J. (Eds.) (1993). *Social withdrawal, inhibition and shyness in childhood.* Hillsdale, NJ: Erlbaum.

Schmidt, L. A. & Schulkin, J. (Eds.) (1999). *Extreme fear, shyness, and social phobia: Origins, biological mechanisms, and clinical outcomes.* New York: Oxford University Press.

Younger, A. J., Schneider, B. H., Wadeson, R., Guirguis, M., & Bergeron, N. (2000). A behaviour-based peer-nomination measure of social withdrawal in children. *Social Development, 9,* 544–564.

Chapter 2

Biological and Environmental Contributions to Childhood Shyness: A Diathesis– Stress Model

Louis A. Schmidt, Cindy P. Polak, *and* **Andrea L. Spooner**

GENETIC AND BIOLOGICAL CONTRIBUTIONS
Neural Circuitry of the Fear System
Genetic Variation in the Fear System: Animal, Behavioral, and Molecular
    Evidence
  Studies of inbred animal strains
  Studies of behavioral genetics
  Studies of molecular genetics and complex traits
On the Biology of Human Shyness
  Infant behavioral and physiological predictors
  Childhood behavioral and physiological correlates
  Adult behavioral and physiological correlates and outcomes
Summary
ENVIRONMENTAL CONTRIBUTIONS
Parental and Familial Relationships
  Mother–child attachment
  Parental sensitivity
  Maternal beliefs
  Maternal personality
Summary
A DIATHESIS–STRESS MODEL OF SHYNESS
CONCLUSIONS

International Handbook of Social Anxiety: Concepts, Research and Interventions Relating to the Self and Shyness. Edited by W. Ray Crozier and Lynn E. Alden.
© 2001 John Wiley & Sons Ltd.

ACKNOWLEDGEMENTS
REFERENCES

The question of how nature or nurture, biology or environment, contributes to the formation of personality can be traced to the early Greeks and is an issue that continues to be a major focus in contemporary fields of personality and developmental psychology as we begin the third millennium. Perhaps one personality trait that captures the very essence of this debate is that of human shyness. For example, one line of thinking is that the etiology of shyness in some people is very much determined by their biology. Much of the work of Jerome Kagan (see Kagan, 1999, for a review, and described later in this chapter) over the last decade on infant temperamental predictors of shyness embodies this belief, as does the earlier work of Buss and Plomin (1984). A second school of thought, while not dismissing the former, argues that environmental causes such as early mother–infant attachment and parental sensitivity contribute significantly to the development of shyness. The work of Joan Stevenson-Hinde (see this volume, *Chapter 3*) is very much rooted in this tradition. While many theorists and researchers working on human shyness often align themselves with one of these camps more than the other, most agree that it is probably an interaction of the two—biology and environment—that plays a role in the development of shyness. In this chapter, we review the importance of these two different perspectives concerning the origins of human shyness and provide an integrative model that incorporates the interplay of biology and environment.

Human shyness is a ubiquitous phenomenon that over 90% of the population have reported experiencing at some point in the lives (Zimbardo, 1977). Shyness reflects a preoccupation of the self during real or imagined social situations (Jones, Briggs, & Cheek, 1986) and is accompanied by feelings of negative self-worth (Crozier, 1981). There are, in addition, a number of distinct behavioral and physiological correlates and outcomes associated with shyness in children and adults (see, e.g., Hirshfeld et al., 1992; Rubin, Stewart, & Coplan, 1995; Schmidt & Fox, 1999). In terms of its conceptual underpinnings, some have argued that shyness reflects an emotion elicited by feelings of shame and embarrassment (e.g., Crozier, 1999) that leads to social inhibition, while others have viewed shyness from a trait perspective, with shyness serving as a dimension of personality (e.g., Cheek & Krasnoperova, 1999). Although the focus of that debate is beyond the scope of this chapter, we view shyness as an enduring personality trait in some people that is linked to an inability to regulate negative emotion in response to social stress, and we focus on the biological and environmental contributions and their interaction in determining shyness.

This chapter comprises three major sections. In the first section, we provide a review of the current literature that argues primarily from a biological perspective. Here, we discuss evidence that suggests that the origins of shyness in some people may be linked to a dysregulation of some components of the fear system that appears to have a genetic basis. In the second section, we review and discuss the role of environment in the development of shyness, focusing on familial and extra-familial relationships. In the third section, we attempt to combine the literature reviewed in the previous sections and propose an interactionist (i.e., diathesis–stress) model that encompasses both biological and environmental contributions in an attempt to understand the origins of shyness in some people.

GENETIC AND BIOLOGICAL CONTRIBUTIONS

Neural Circuitry of the Fear System

Current thinking suggests that the origins of shy behavior may be linked to the dysregulation of some components of the fear system (LeDoux, 1996, Nader & LeDoux, 1999). Fear is a highly conserved emotion that is seen across mammals, and it is the study of this emotion that has produced the most reliable evidence to date concerning the neuroanatomical circuitry of emotion. There also appears to be considerable variability across humans and animals in fear responses.

There is a rich and growing literature from studies of conditioned fear in animals that suggest that the frontal cortex and forebrain limbic areas are important components of the fear system. The frontal cortex is known to play a key role in the regulation of fear and other emotions. This region is involved in the motor facilitation of emotion expression, the organization and integration of cognitive processes underlying emotion, and the ability to regulate emotions (see Fox, 1991, 1994). The frontal region also appears to regulate forebrain sites involved in the expression of emotion. The amygdala (and central nucleus) is one such forebrain/limbic site and functional anatomical connections have been demonstrated between the amygdala and the frontal region. The amygdala (and the central nucleus) receives input from neocortical sites, in particular, the frontal cortex. There are also links between the amygdala (and the central nucleus) and lower brainstem nuclei used in the regulation of autonomic output. The central nucleus of the amygdala receives visceral projections from the solitary and parabrachial nuclei in the lower brainstem, projecting directly to these regions in addition to other areas of the brainstem intimately involved in arousal (see Schulkin, McEwen, & Gold, 1994, for a review of the neuroanatomical connections of the amygdala).

The amygdala (particularly the central nucleus) is known to play a significant role in the autonomic and behavioral aspects of conditioned fear (LeDoux, Iwata, Cicchetti, & Reis, 1988). For example, electrical stimulation of the central nucleus facilitates fear-potentiated startle responses (Rosen & Davis, 1988), while lesions to the amygdala and the central nucleus disrupt conditioned fear (Gallagher, Graham, & Holland, 1990; Hitchcock & Davis, 1986; Kapp, Frysinger, Gallagher, & Haselton, 1979; LeDoux, Sakaguchi, Iwata, & Reis, 1986). Still others have shown that electrically kindling the amygdala, but not the dorsal hippocampus, facilitates fear responses in rats (Rosen, Hamerman, Sitcoske, Glowa, & Schulkin, 1996). The amygdala also appears to be involved in the attentional aspects related to the recognition of changes in negatively valenced environmental stimuli (Gallagher & Holland, 1994).

Interestingly, the amygdala is known to be more reactive in defensive rather than nondefensive cats (Adamec, 1991). These behaviors are analogous to those seen in extremely fearful and shy children. There also appears to be considerable individual variation in the behavioral and physiological expression of fear and stress responses seen across mammalian species (e.g., Boissy, 1995; Suomi, 1991). It is this variation and its genetic susceptibility to which we will now turn.

Genetic Variation in the Fear System: Animal, Behavioral, and Molecular Evidence

The notion that there may be a genetic basis to individual differences in temperament is an idea that dates from the time of the early Greeks to issues of contemporary personality research. Much of the scientific legitimacy for this notion can be traced to evidence produced by three disparate literatures (see, e.g., Eley & Plomin, 1997), two of which have been reliable and convincing sources for years and a third which has only emerged within the last decade. The first literature involves studies of domesticated and laboratory animals in which there is strong evidence in support of a genetic basis to temperament. For example, as noted earlier, it has long been noted that inbred strains of animals can be produced that are highly fearful, defensive, aggressive, and subdued (see Plomin, DeFries, McClearn, & Rutter, 1997). A second body of work concerns findings derived from longstanding behavioral genetics studies of human twins. In such studies, it has been noted that monozygotic twins appear temperamentally more similar than dizygotic twins and adopted children (see Plomin, 1989). A third source concerns recent findings from the rapidly emerging field of molecular genetics in the study of human personality (see Cloninger, Adolfsson, & Svrakic, 1996; Hamer & Copeland, 1998; Plomin & Rutter, 1998). Here, a number of studies involving human adults have noted associations between genes that regulate specific neurochemical systems and complex human traits. Overall, these three sources are beginning to converge to provide the strongest evidence to date that there may be a genetic etiology underlying some complex human personality traits (see Cloninger et al., 1996; Plomin, 1989; Plomin et al., 1997; Plomin & Rutter, 1998, for excellent reviews of these literatures).

Studies of Inbred Animal Strains

There is a long and substantial animal literature that demonstrates a susceptibility to stress among inbred animal strains (see Blizard, 1989, and Boissy, 1995, for extensive reviews). As Blizard (1989) noted, genetic contributions to individual differences in the behavioral and psychophysiological reactivity to stress seem to be more of the rule rather than the exception. These genetic individual differences have been noted on the multiple fear-related psychophysiological measures implicated in the fear system. For example, strain differences in cardiac reactivity to stress have been noted among inbred mice (Blizard & Welty, 1971); strain differences in the startle amplitude and corticosterone reactivity in response to stress have been demonstrated in rats (Glowa, Geyer, Gold, & Sternberg, 1992); and studies of human twins have noted a genetic contribution to heart rate reactivity to stress (Carroll, Hewitt, Last, Turner, & Sims, 1985).

In addition to these genetic contributions to stress-related psychophysiological responses, other studies have noted strain differences in stress-related behavioral responses. For example, strain differences in active avoidance behavioral responses have been noted among mice (Collins, 1964) and rats (Harrington, 1981). Also, genetic contributions to emotionality (i.e., covariation in activity and defecation in a novel environment) among mice have recently been noted using behavioral and quantitative trait loci linkage strategies (Flint et al., 1995). Flint et al. (1995) suggested that this animal model of individual differences in emotionality may extend to understanding susceptibility to anxiety or neuroticism in humans. As we will see shortly, temperamentally shy children exhibit an analogous pattern of behavioral and physiological reactivity in response to stress to those seen in some inbred strains of animals.

Studies of Behavioral Genetics

There has been a long history of the use of human twins to study the heritability of personality in children and adults (Jang, Livesley, & Vernon, 1996; Matheny, 1989; Plomin & Rowe, 1979). Twin studies have demonstrated that shy behavior and timidity towards unfamiliar people and situations is heritable in children and adults (Matheny, 1989; Plomin, 1986). These include studies utilizing parental ratings and observational methods (Cohen, Dibble, & Grawe, 1977; Plomin & Rowe, 1979). The Louisville Twin Study reported genetic influences on inhibited behavior and timidity in 12- to 30-month-old children, with changes and stability in behavior being more concordant in monozygotic twins than in dizygotic twins (Matheny, 1989).

Studies of Molecular Genetics and Complex Traits

There have been a number of recent studies which have begun to examine associations of genes that code for the regulation and transportation of neurotransmitters with complex human traits such as shyness. The molecular genetic basis of individual differences in temperament/personality was sparked largely by the publication of three papers implicating a molecular genetic basis to complex human traits in adults. Two of these studies demonstrated an allelic association between novelty seeking and a functional polymorphism in the dopamine D4 receptor gene (Benjamin et al., 1996; Ebstein et al., 1996). Adults with longer-repeats (6–8) self-reported higher novelty seeking scores compared to adults with shorter repeats (2–5). Dopamine has been implicated as a major neuromodulator of novelty seeking because of the role it plays in inducing euphoria in humans and approach behavior in animals (Cloninger, 1987). The shorter alleles code for a receptor that is apparently more efficient in binding dopamine compared with the larger alleles (see Plomin & Rutter, 1998). A third paper noted an allelic association of a polymorphism in a gene that codes for the transportation of serotonin (5-HTT) with anxiety-related traits. Lesch et al. (1996) reported that adults with one or two copies of a short allele in the serotonin transporter gene self-reported higher levels of neuroticism, anxiety, and depression compared to adults with two copies of a long allele. The short allele reduces efficiency of serotonin promotion and results in reduced serotonin expression. Serotonin has been implicated as a major neurotransmitter of anxiety and withdrawal because of its effects on regulating mood and emotional states (see Westenberg, Murphy, & den Boer, 1996).

While these three papers provide an initial view of the role of genes in personality, it is important to note that other studies have failed to replicate the DRD4–novelty seeking and serotonin–neuroticism associations in adults. For example, Goldman et al. (1996), using a small unselected sample of Finnish adults and American Indians, were not able to replicate the DRD4 and novelty seeking association, nor was a recent study by Jonsson et al. (1997) with Swedish adults, although the trend was in the predicted direction. Plomin and his colleagues (Ball et al., 1997) attempted to extend the findings of Lesch et al. (1996) by using, in addition to self-report measures, peer-ratings of neuroticism and an extreme group design. Plomin's group failed to replicate the allele association in the serotonin transporter gene with neuroticism, as have two other recent studies (e.g., Deary et al., 1999; Kumakiri et al., 1999).

Although there have been relatively few studies of the molecular genetics of complex human personality traits in children, two recent studies (LaHoste et al., 1996; Swanson et al., 1998) noted an association of the DRD4 receptor gene with attention deficit hyperactivity disorder (ADHD). Children with ADHD differed from controls in that the 7-fold repeat form of the DRD4 occurred more frequently than in the control group. Two other very recent studies have noted a similar association of the DRD4 gene and attention-related problems in normally developing pediatric populations. Associations of DRD4 long alleles with less sustained attention in 12-month-old infants (Auerbach, Benjamin, Faroy, Geller, & Ebstein, 2001) and maternal report of attention problems in 4- and 7-year-old children (Schmidt, Fox, Perez-Edgar, Lu, & Hamer, 2001) have been noted in non-clinical samples. Another recent study has noted a gene–gene interaction in determining neonatal temperament (Ebstein et al., 1998). Neonates with the short serotonin transporter promoter, and who lacked the long form of the DRD4, had a lower orientation score on the Brazelton neonatal assessment scale compared to other neonates. In sum, the notion that there may be a molecular genetic basis to complex human traits is not a foregone conclusion, but it may provide a convergent piece of evidence in attempting to understand the origins of shyness.

On the Biology of Human Shyness

Infant Behavioral and Physiological Predictors

One of the most striking behavioral features in early human development is the ease with which some, but not all, infants become aroused and distressed to the presentation of novel stimuli. These differences in behavioral reactivity, which most likely reflect individual differences in sensory and perceptual thresholds, are seen across mammals (see, e.g., Boissy, 1995, and Schmidt & Schulkin, 1999) and are clearly heritable.

Kagan and his colleagues (Kagan & Snidman, 1991a, b) have argued that the origins of shyness in some children may be linked to individual differences in early infant reactivity. For example, infants who exhibit a high degree of motor activity and distress in response to the presentation of novel auditory and visual stimuli during the first four months of life exhibit a high degree of behavioral inhibition and shyness during the preschool and early school age years. There is, in addition, evidence to suggest that there may be a genetic etiology to inhibited behavior. Kagan's group (DiLalla, Kagan, & Reznick, 1994) noted in a behavior study of 157 24-month twin pairs that monozygotic twins showed stronger intra-class correlations of inhibited behavior to unfamiliar stimuli than dizygotic and non-twin siblings. Kagan and Snidman (1991b) have speculated that the locus of behavioral inhibition may be linked to hypersensitivity in forebrain limbic areas, particularly the central nucleus of the amygdala.

We have used measures of frontal EEG activity and the startle eyeblink response to test Kagan's speculation (see Schmidt & Fox, 1999). These two measures are thought to index forebrain limbic and frontal cortical areas involved in the regulation of emotion. In a series of studies with human infants, Fox and his colleagues (see Fox, 1991) have noted that the pattern of frontal EEG activity distinguishes different types of emotion. Infants exhibit greater relative right frontal EEG activity during the processing of negative emotion (e.g., fear, disgust, sadness) and greater relative left frontal EEG activity during the processing of positive emotions (e.g., happiness, joy, interest). In a series of studies with human adults, Davidson and his colleagues (see Davidson & Rickman, 1999, and Schmidt & Trainor, 2001) have noted similar relations between the pattern of asymmetrical frontal brain activity and the processing of emotion. Furthermore, another body of literature suggests that individual differences in the pattern of resting frontal brain electrical activity (EEG) may reflect a predisposition (i.e., trait) to experience/express positive and negative emotion in infants (see, e.g., Fox, 1991, 1994) and adults (see, e.g., Davidson, 1993). For example, Fox and his colleagues have noted a relation between individual differences in resting frontal EEG activity and affective/temperamental style. Infants who displayed greater relative resting right frontal EEG activity were more likely to cry and exhibit distress to an approaching stranger during the second half of the first year of life compared with infants who exhibit greater relative resting left frontal EEG activity (Davidson & Fox, 1989; Fox, Bell, & Jones, 1992). A similar relation between the pattern of resting frontal EEG asymmetry and affective style has been noted in adults.

In a series of studies with adults, Davidson and his colleagues have noted a relation between the pattern of resting frontal EEG activity and affective style. Adults who exhibit a pattern of greater relative resting right frontal EEG activity are known to rate affective film clips more negatively (Tomarken, Davidson, & Henriques, 1990) and likely to be more depressed (Henriques & Davidson, 1990, 1991) compared to adults who exhibit greater relative resting left frontal EEG activity. In addition, adults who exhibited a stable pattern of right frontal asymmetry across a three-week time period reported more intense negative emotion in response to negative affective film clips, whereas individuals who displayed a stable pattern of left frontal EEG asymmetry reported more intense positive affect in response to positive affective film clips (Wheeler, Davidson, & Tomarken, 1993).

The startle response is a brainstem- and forebrain-mediated behavioral affect that occurs in response to the presentation of a sudden and intense stimulus, and its neural circuitry is well mapped (Davis, Hitchcock, & Rosen, 1987). While the startle paradigm has been used extensively in studies of conditioned fear in animals, this paradigm has been adapted for studies concerning the etiology of anxiety in humans. For example, a number of studies have noted relations between startle amplitude and the processing of emotion and individual differences in personality. Adults exhibit exaggerated startle responses during the processing of highly arousing negatively valenced stimuli and attenuated startle responses during the processing of highly arousing positively valenced stimuli (see Lang, Bradley, & Cuthbert, 1990). Furthermore, there are known to be individual differences in the startle response. Adults who score high on trait measures of anxiety (Grillon, Ameli, Foot, & Davis, 1993) and children who are behaviorally inhibited (Snidman & Kagan, 1994) are known to exhibit a heightened baseline startle response.

Using a design identical to that reported by Kagan and Snidman (1991b), Fox and his colleagues (Calkins, Fox, & Marshall, 1996) examined the behavioral and psychophysiological antecedents of shyness in a group of infants selected at age 4 months for temperamental constellations thought to predict behavioral inhibition and shyness in early childhood. Eighty-one healthy infants were selected at age 4 months from a larger sample of 207 infants. The infants were observed in their homes at age 4 months and videotaped as they responded to novel auditory and visual stimuli. The 81 infants were selected by their frequency of motor activity and the degree of positive and negative affect displayed in response to these novel stimuli, and three reactivity groups were formed: a *negative reactive* ($n = 31$) group, which comprised infants who displayed both high amounts of motor activity and negative affect and low amounts of positive affect; a *positive reactive* ($n = 19$) group, which comprised infants who displayed both high amounts of motor activity and positive affect and low amounts of negative affect; and a *low reactive* ($n = 31$) group, which comprised infants who displayed low amounts of motor activity and low amounts of both positive affect and negative affect. The infants were then seen in the laboratory at 9, 14, and 24 months, at which time regional brain electrical activity (EEG) was recorded using a lycra stretch cap while the infant was seated, alert, and attentive. EEG was recorded from the left and right anterior and posterior brain regions and the startle eye-blink response was recorded during a stranger approach situation. In addition, behavioral responses to the presentation of unfamiliar social and nonsocial stimuli were indexed at 14 and 24 months. We noted that the infants described above who were classified as *negative reactive* at 4 months exhibited greater fear-potentiated startle (Schmidt & Fox, 1998) and greater relative right frontal EEG activation asymmetry at ages 9 (Calkins et al., 1996) and 24 months (Fox, Calkins, & Bell, 1994), and more behavioral inhibition at age 14 months (Calkins et al., 1996) compared to infants in the other two temperamentally reactive groups. It is seems plausible then to speculate that the frontal EEG and startle measures may be indexing individual differences in forebrain sensitivity given the dense connections between the frontal cortex and forebrain limbic areas.

The pattern of frontal EEG activity and heightened startle response suggests that the highly negative reactive infants may have a lower threshold for arousal in forebrain limbic areas involved in regulating stress. Overall, these sets of behavioral and physiological data suggest that some infants may have a tem-peramental bias towards shyness in early childhood. These features appear early in the first year of life, remain stable during the first two years of life, are the same types of behaviors and physiological patterns observed in some inbred strains of highly reactive animals, and appear to have a genetic etiology.

Childhood Behavioral and Physiological Correlates

The pattern of physiological and behavioral responses seen in temperamentally reactive infants appears to be preserved into the preschool and early school age years and is predictive of shyness. In a series of studies of preschoolers and early school age children, Schmidt and Fox and their colleagues have noted that preschoolers who displayed a high proportion of shy behavior during peer play groups at age 4 exhibited significantly greater relative resting right frontal EEG asymmetry (Fox et al., 1995, 1996) and higher morning basal salivary cortisol levels (Schmidt et al., 1997) compared to children displaying relatively less shy behavior at age 4. Also, children displaying a high degree of observed shy behavior were rated as contemporaneously shy at age 4 by their mothers and a significant proportion of them were likely to have been in the *negative reactive* temperamental group at age 4 months. Kagan and his colleagues (Kagan, Reznick, & Snidman, 1987, 1988; Snidman & Kagan, 1994) had also noted earlier that temperamentally shy children were characterized by elevated morning basal cortisol levels, a high and stable heart rate, and exaggerated startle responses compared to their non-shy counterparts. More recently, Schmidt, Fox, Schulkin, and Gold (1999a) found that temperamentally shy children exhibit a distinct pattern of physiological responses across different physiological measures in response to stress. Schmidt et al. (1999a) noted that, compared with their non-shy counterparts, temperamentally shy 7-year-olds exhibited a significantly greater increase in right, but not left, frontal EEG activity and a significantly greater increase in heart rate during a self-presentation task as the task became more demanding. These physiological responses were paralleled by an increase in overt signs of behavioral anxiety. We also noted that children who were classified as low in social competence (a feature of shyness) exhibited a significantly greater change in salivary cortisol reactivity in response to the self-presentation task compared to socially competent children (Schmidt et al., 1999b). These data suggest that children who are classified as temperamentally shy during the preschool and early school age years exhibit a distinct pattern of frontal brain activity, heart rate, salivary cortisol levels during baseline conditions and in response to stress and are likely to have been highly reactive infants.

Adult Behavioral and Physiological Correlates and Outcomes

One of the goals of our research program on shyness has been to examine the developmental course and outcomes of temperamental shyness beyond the early childhood years given that temperamental shyness appears to remain stable and predictive of developmental outcomes (Caspi, Elder, & Bem, 1988). In the main, the behavioral and physiological correlates and outcomes associated with temperamentally shy children are comparable to those seen in adults who score high on trait measures of shyness. For example, adults reporting a high degree of trait shyness are likely to report concurrent feelings of negative self-worth and problems with depression in both the elderly (Bell et al., 1993) and young (Schmidt & Fox, 1995) adult populations and display a distinct pattern of central and autonomic activity during resting conditions and in response to social stressors (see Schmidt & Fox, 1999, for a review).

In two separate studies (Schmidt, 1999; Schmidt & Fox, 1994), we have examined the behavioral and physiological correlates of shyness in a group of young adults who scored high on self-report measures of trait shyness (Cheek & Buss, 1981). We recorded regional brain electrical activity (EEG) and heart rate during baseline conditions and during a socially challenging situation. We found that, compared to their nonshy counterparts, adults reporting a high degree of trait shyness exhibited greater relative baseline right frontal EEG activity and a higher and more stable heart rate in anticipation of a social encounter with an unfamiliar same-sex peer. The adult findings extended our prior work with temperamentally shy children; that is, a similar pattern of physiological activity was observed during baseline and socially challenging situations on frontal brain activity and heart rate in adults who scored high on a self-report measure of trait shyness that was noted in temperamentally shy children and high reactive infants. Regardless of age, temperamental shyness was related to greater relative right frontal EEG activity during baseline conditions and an increase in autonomic activity during social stress. Given the similarities in physiological activity between temperamentally shy children and young adults during baseline and emotionally challenging conditions, these data, taken together, raise the possibility that the origins of shyness for some people may be rooted in early temperamental constellations which may be inherited and preserved over the lifespan.

Summary

The animal and human evidence reviewed in this section suggest that the origins of human shyness may be linked to dysregulation of some components of the fear system. There may be individual variation in this dysregulation which may have a genetic basis. This individual variation in dysregulation of fear responses may appear early in life, and its behavioral and physiological expression may remain modestly preserved during development for some people. Although the evidence reviewed in this section provides a strong case for the notion of a biological predisposition to shyness in some people, there is, however, equally compelling evidence of significant environmental contributions to shyness (see, e.g., Fox, Henderson, Rubin, Chalkins & Schmidt, 2001). It is to a discussion of these influences that we now turn.

ENVIRONMENTAL CONTRIBUTIONS

Parental and Familial Relationships

Mother–Child Attachment

The idea that early mother–infant interaction is a significant determinant of social and emotional development has a long history that can be traced not only to the work of Freud and psychoanalytic thinkers but also to more recent ideas proffered by John Bowlby and his seminal work on attachment theory (e.g., Bowlby, 1969). According to Bowlby and his disciples (e.g., Ainsworth, Blehar, Waters, & Wall, 1978) social competence is developed through a secure mother–infant attachment. A secure attachment allows the infant to develop a sense of trust in the caregiver. The establishment of trust allows the child to explore his or her social world, to develop social skills, and to develop a sense of efficacy in succeeding in a complex social world and foster the development of social competence. The child who is socially competent looks forward to engaging in social situations rather than avoiding them. On the other hand, the child who is characterized by an insecure attachment may not develop the same degree of trust with his or her caregiver. The mother of the child who is insecurely attached may not be sensitive, nor rewarding of the child's cues that will allow her child to develop a sense of efficacy. The inability to develop a secure attachment and sense of trust with the primary caregiver may delay or compromise the development of appropriate social skills and social competence. Thus, the insecurely attached child lacking social skills and social competence is likely to feel awkward in social situations and may eventually begin to avoid them entirely. A number of studies have indeed corroborated these theoretical notions. For example, several studies have noted relations between patterns of attachment and differences in social competence during the early and middle school age years (Cohn, 1990; Jacobson & Wille, 1986; Sroufe & Fleeson, 1986). Overall, insecure attachment status was predictive of and concurrently related to low social competence.

Parental Sensitivity

A second area of inquiry that demonstrates the contribution of familial influences on early childhood social development concerns the work on parental sensitivity. There are a number of studies which have shown that variations in parental sensitivity are predictive of social withdrawal in children (Hetherington & Martin, 1986; Maccoby & Martin, 1983; Martin, 1975). Overall, these sets of studies demonstrate that parents who provide warmth and support and set clear expectations have socially competent and sociable children; parents who are distant and rejecting, on the other hand, tend to have children who are characterized as shy and socially withdrawn.

Maternal Beliefs

A third line of research on familial influences has noted important relations between maternal beliefs about parenting and child-rearing and children's social development. For example, a number of studies have noted that maternal beliefs about modes of learning social skills, reactive strategies, attributions, and emotions contribute to social development (see Burgess, Rubin, Cheah, & Nelson, this volume, *Chapter 7*; Mills & Rubin, 1993, for extensive reviews). Rubin and his colleagues (Mills & Rubin, 1993) have noted that, among other things, mothers of socially withdrawn children were less tolerant of unskilled social behavior than other mothers, were more angry, disappointed, guilty, and embarrassed when asked about these behaviors and were more inclined to blame them on traits residing within their children (see also Evans, *Chapter 8*).

Maternal Personality

A final area of study concerning familial relationships and its relation to shyness is that of maternal personality and emotional well-being. There is well-documented evidence that the mother's personality influences the child's social development. Mothers who are depressed are known to display less positive affect and reduced levels of stimulation when interacting with their infants (Cohn, Matias, Tronick, Connell, & Lyons-Ruth, 1986; Cohn & Tronick, 1989; Field, 1986; Field et al., 1988). These behavioral symptoms are apparently transmitted to the infant. For example, infants of depressed mothers are known to display less positive affect and increased irritability (Cohn et al., 1986; Cohn & Tronick, 1989; Field, 1986; Field et al., 1985), and greater relative right frontal EEG activity (a marker of stress) (Dawson, Grofer Klinger, Panagiotides, Hill, & Spieker, 1992; Field, Fox, Pickens, & Nawrocki, 1995) compared to infants of non-depressed mothers. Maternal personality also appears to play an important role in childhood shyness.

In an extensive study, Engfer (1993) noted consistent relations between maternal personality and childhood shyness during the first six years of life, particularly for girls. Maternal self-report of degree of nervousness, depressiveness, irritability, neuroticism, and shy inhibition measured at four months after delivery were highly predictive of observed shy behavior at age 6 years for girls. A similar relation was also noted between maternal personality measures of nervousness, depression, and shy inhibition collected at 18 months after delivery and observed shy behavior at age 6 for girls. In addition, contemporaneous measures of maternal depression were highly correlated with observed shy behavior at age 6.

Summary

The extant literature reviewed above provides compelling evidence for the role of parental, familial, and extra-familial relationships on influencing early childhood social and emotional development (Hartup, 1983; Rubin, Hymel, Mills, & Rose-Krasnor, 1991; Rubin & Mills, 1988). In light of the evidence reviewed above one question then becomes: Is biology or environment in and of themselves sufficient to account for the development of shyness in some people? While the case has been made that it appears that each seems to contribute to the origins of shyness, it is possible that considering both in concert may help to explain additional variance that neither one in isolation can explain. We now turn to an example of how one's biology and environment may interact to account for the development of shyness, at least in some people.

A DIATHESIS–STRESS MODEL OF SHYNESS

The comparative and human evidence reviewed above raise the possibility that there are both genetic/biological and environmental contributions to shyness. We believe that these independent literatures speak to the importance of considering the interplay of biology and environment in understanding the development of shyness. This is further underscored by the findings that not all temperamentally reactive infants, nor all insecurely attached infants, develop shyness, suggesting that it is most likely produced by an interplay of both biology and environment. Accordingly, we propose a diathesis–stress model that might be helpful in attempting to understand the origins of shyness in some people. This model is presented in Figure 2.1.

Along with Kagan (1994), we speculate that there may be a subset of infants who are born with a biological push towards shyness. This biological predisposition is linked to genetic variation in neurochemical and physiological systems involved in the regulation of fear and the fear system. There is a large and growing literature that there are genetic contributions to complex human traits such as shyness.

We speculate that genes that code for the regulation of serotonin may play an important role in the regulation and dysregulation of some components of the

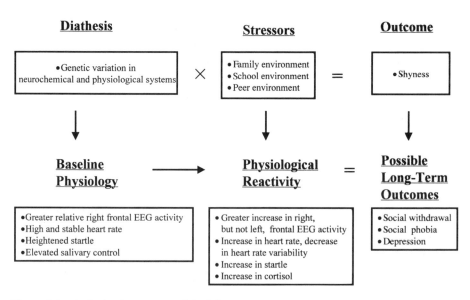

Figure 2.1 A diathesis–stress model of shyness

fear system. We base this claim on recent studies that have noted an allelic association of a short allele of the serotonin transporter gene with adults' neuroticism (Lesch et al., 1996) and the determination of neonatal temperament (Ebstein et al., 1998). The presence of this genetic polymorphism may contribute to a reduced efficiency of serotonin promotion and a reduced serotonin expression. Serotonin has been implicated as a major neurotransmitter involved in anxiety and withdrawal because of its effects on regulating mood and emotional states (Westenberg et al., 1996).

We speculate that the action of this reduced serotonin expression may be particularly evident in the forebrain limbic and frontal cortex where there are dense concentrations of serotonin receptors. The reduction of serotonin may play an important role in regulating the amygdala and HPA system; that is, serotonin may serve to inhibit (or regulate) the action of amygdaloid firing and activation of the hypothalamic system. Without the regulating effects of serotonin, the amygdala and the HPA system become overactive in some individuals with this serotonin genetic polymorphism. The overactive amygdala stimulates the HPA system and the release of increase cortisol. Cortisol (corticosterone in animals) is known to facilitate fear-related behaviors and responses in animals and humans, including heightened CRH startle responses (Lee, Schulkin, & Davis, 1994) and freezing behavior (Takahashi & Rubin, 1994) in rats. Moreover, exogenous administration of synthetic cortisol is known to increase in right frontal EEG activity (a marker of stress) and anxious mood in healthy human adults (Schmidt, Fox, Goldberg, Smith, & Schulkin, 1999) and adults with agitated depression (i.e., comorbidity of depression and anxiety) are known to exhibit elevated endo-genous cortisol levels (Gold, Goodwin, & Chrousos, 1988). The overactive amygdala and dysregulated HPA system perhaps leads to the increase activity noted on resting psychophysiological and neuroen-docrine measures that index forebrain and frontal cortical functioning, compo-nents of the fear system. As noted above, the startle response, autonomic, and frontal EEG measures are all known to be sensitive to the manipulation of cor-tisol. Thus, it may not be a coincidence that temperamentally shy children are characterized by elevated basal cortisol levels, high and stable resting heart rate, exaggerated baseline startle, and greater relative resting right frontal EEG activ-ity. It is possible that dysregulation of the HPA system triggered by an overac-tive amygdala serves to maintain the pattern of resting physiological activity in temperamentally shy children. This scenario is illustrated in Figure 2.1 in which genetic variation of neurochemical and physiological systems, in this case, the reg-ulation of serotonin may contribute to greater relative resting right frontal EEG activity, a high and stable resting heart rate, exaggerated baseline startle responses, and elevated morning basal cortisol levels. In short, these baseline measures may be indexing different components (levels) of a dysregulated fear system at rest.

It is also possible that increased cortisol due to dysregulation of the HPA system brought about by a genetic vulnerability in the serotonergic system con-tinues to "prime" the amygdala and its related components of the fear system. The amygdala is known to be involved in the appraisal of emotional valence and intensity (e.g., Gallagher & Holland, 1994). Now that it is dysregulated and main-tained by cortisol, the temperamentally shy child becomes hypervigilant and appraises all environmental stimuli as threatening. The continual priming of the fear system serves to "kindle" the brain circuits regulating normal fear responses, reducing its sensitivity and lowering its threshold for stimulation in response to environmental stimuli (Rosen & Schulkin, 1998).

We further speculate that it may, however, not be enough to have a genetic/bio-logical bias towards shyness. Environmental stressors are also needed (see also Nachmias, Gunnar, Mangelsdorpf, Parritz, & Buss, 1996), which might include familial and extra-familial relationships. For example, maternal insensitivity or rejection by peers may be significant environmental influences that contribute to the development of shyness in some children who already have a biological push towards it. As can be seen in Figure 2.1, when the person with a genetic diathe-sis towards a dysregulated fear system meets social stress, the diathesis is mani-fested on multiple behavioral and physiological levels. For example, there may be an increase in focus on the self, increase in behavioral anxiety, increase in right, but not left, frontal brain activity, increase in heart rate, and an increase in adrenocortical activity. Frontal lobe functioning may become dysregulated and perhaps the person has less cognitive control over regulating his or her emotions and behavior in response to stress. The inability to regulate the experience of negative emotion reflected in an increase in right frontal EEG and heart rate, and adrenocortical reactivity during stress may then lead to an increased expres-sion of anxious behavior and social withdrawal. It is possible that exposure to social situations may be too stressful for people with this genetic diathesis, and their only coping strategies may involve avoiding social interactions altogether. We know, however, that engaging in social interactions is imperative to the development of early social skills and social competence. Now the person's adaptive coping strategies soon become maladaptive, possibly leading him or her down a path towards social withdrawal, social isolation, and perhaps even depression.

It is important to point out that we do not view this model as strictly uni-directional, as there is a complex relation between biology and environment. For example, children's temperament influences maternal practices and attitudes; children seek out environments that are compatible with their temperaments. There are many children who present with features that would be describe as "biological predispositions" but who do not develop shyness. These children may be protected by environmental factors such as warm and sensitive caregiving. There are, in addition, many instances where children without biological corre-lates predictive of shyness develop shyness.

CONCLUSIONS

The origins of shyness are complex and undoubtedly multiply determined through an interaction of genes, biology, and environment. We believe that the etiology of shyness is probably linked to dysregulation of some components of the fear system, and that there appears to be considerable variation in fear responses in humans, possibly due to genetic variation. We reviewed evidence from several disparate sources that are beginning to converge in a systematic way to suggest that there may be a possible genetic/biological contribution to shyness, at least in some people. We also believe, as do others (e.g., Kagan, 1991), that genetic and biological factors are neither necessary nor sufficient to cause shyness. There are many significant environmental influences such as mother–infant attachment status and parental sensitivity which, by themselves, or in concert with biological predispositions, may contribute to shyness. We con-cluded by describing a diathesis-stress model of shyness which may facilitate our understanding of the complex interplay between biology and context in shyness. Future research would be wise to consider the stability of biological and environmental measures used in the study of shyness. Change appears to be the rule rather than the exception. Many children who exhibit particular patterns of early infant temperament which are predictive of shyness never develop shyness. Furthermore, there are many children whose infant temperament was highly predictive of shyness during the preschool years but who are no longer contemporaneously shy during the early school age years even though their physiological patterning may remain stable. It would be prudent for researchers working in the area of human shyness to identify mechanisms that determine or contribute to stability and change in temperamental shyness over development. It is also important to consider how these mechanisms may influence individual differences in shyness, since there are theoretical (Asendorpf, 1989; Buss, 1986) and empirical (Asendorpf, 1990; Crozier, 1999) reasons to believe that there are different types of shyness in children.

ACKNOWLEDGEMENTS

This chapter was written with the support of grants from the Social Sciences and Humanities Research Council of Canada (SSHRC410-99-1206) and the Natural Sciences and Engineering Research Council of Canada (NSERC203710-1999) awarded to the first author.

REFERENCES

Adamec, R. E. (1991). Individual differences in temporal lobe sensory processing of threatening stimuli in the cat. *Physiology and Behavior, 49*, 445–464.

Ainsworth, M. D. S., Blehar, M., Waters, E., & Wall, S. (1978). *Patterns of attachment.* Hillsdale, NJ: Erlbaum.

Asendorpf, J. B. (1989). Shyness as a final common pathway for two different kinds of inhibition. *Journal of Personality and Social Psychology, 57*, 481–492.

Asendorpf, J. B. (1990). Beyond social withdrawal: Shyness, unsociability, and peer avoidance. *Human Development, 33*, 250–259.

Auerbach, J. G., Benjamin, J., Faroy, M., Geller, V., & Ebstein, R. (2001). DRD4 related to infant attention and information processing: A developmental link to ADHD? *Psychiatric Genetics, 11*, 31–35.

Ball, D., Hill, L., Freeman, B., Eley, T. C., Strelau, J., Riemann, R., Spinath, F. M., Angleitner, A., & Plomin, R. (1997). The serotonin transporter gene and peer-related neuroticism. *NeuroReport, 8*, 1301–1304.

Bell, I. R., Martino, G. M., Meredith, K. E., Schwartz, G. E., Siani, M. W., & Morrow, F. D. (1993). Vascular disease risk factors, urinary free cortisol, and health histories in older adults: Shyness and gender interactions. *Biological Psychology, 35*, 37–49.

Benjamin, J., Li, L., Patterson, C., Greenberg, B. D., Murphy, D. L., & Hamer, D. H. (1996). Population and familial association between D4 dopamine receptor gene and measures of novelty seeking. *Nature Genetics, 12*, 81–84.

Blizard, D. A. (1989). Analysis of stress susceptibility using the Maudsley Reactive and Non-reactive strains. In D. S. Palermo (Ed.), *Coping with uncertainty: Behavioral and developmental perspectives* (pp. 75–99). Hillsdale, NJ: Erlbaum.

Blizard, D. A. & Welty, R. (1971). Cardiac activity in the mouse: Strain differences. *Journal of Comparative and Physiological Psychology, 77*, 337–344.

Boissy, A. (1995). Fear and fearfulness in animals. *Quarterly Review of Biology, 70*, 165–191.

Bowlby, J. (1969). *Attachment and loss. Vol. 1.* New York: Basic Books.

Buss, A. H. (1986). A theory of shyness. In W. H. Jones, J. M. Cheek, & S. R. Briggs (Eds.), *Shyness: Perspectives on research and treatment* (pp. 39–46). New York: Plenum.

Buss, A. H. & Plomin, R. (1984). *Temperament: Early developing personality traits.* Hillsdale, NJ: Erlbaum.

Calkins, S. D., Fox, N. A., & Marshall, T. R. (1996). Behavioral and physiological antecedents of inhibited and uninhibited behavior. *Child Development, 67*, 523–540.

Carroll, D., Hewitt, J. K., Last, K. A., Turner, J. R., & Sims, J. (1985). A twin study of cardiac reactivity and its relationship to parental blood pressure. *Physiology and Behavior, 14,* 103–106.

Caspi, A., Elder, G. H., & Bem, D. J. (1988). Moving away from the world: Life-course patterns of shy children. *Developmental Psychology, 24,* 824–831.

Cheek, J. M. & Buss, A. H. (1981). Shyness and sociability. *Journal of Personality and Social Psychology, 41,* 330–339.

Cheek, J. M. & Krasnoperova, E. N. (1999). Varieties of shyness in adolescence and adulthood. In L. A. Schmidt & J. Schulkin (Eds.), *Extreme fear, shyness, and social phobia: Origins, biological mechanisms, and clinical outcomes* (pp. 224–250). New York: Oxford University Press.

Cloninger, C. R. (1987). A systematic method for clinical description and classification of personality variants. *Archives of General Psychiatry, 44,* 573–588.

Cloninger, C. R., Adolfsson, R., & Svrakic, N. M. (1996). Mapping genes for human personality. *Nature Genetics, 12,* 3–4.

Cohen, D. J., Dibble, E., & Grawe, J. M. (1977). Fathers' and mothers' perceptions of children's personality. *Archives of General Psychiatry, 34,* 480–487.

Cohn, D. A. (1990). Child–mother attachment of six-year-olds and social competence at school. *Child Development, 61,* 152–162.

Cohn, J. F., Matias, R., Tronick, E. Z., Connell, D., & Lyons-Ruth, D. (1986). Face-to-face interactions of depressed mothers and their infants. In E. Z. Tronick & T. Field (Eds.), *Maternal depression and infant disturbance* (pp. 31–45). San Francisco, CA: Jossey-Bass.

Cohn, J. F. & Tronick, E. Z. (1989). Specificity of infant's response to mothers' affective behavior. *Journal of the American Academy of Child and Adolescent Psychiatry, 28,* 242–248.

Collins, R. L. (1964). Inheritance of avoidance conditioning in mice: A diallel study. *Science, 103,* 1188–1190.

Crozier, W. R. (1981). Shyness and self-esteem. *British Journal of Social Psychology, 20,* 220–222.

Crozier, W. R. (1999). Individual differences in childhood shyness: Distinguishing fearful and self-conscious forms of shyness. In L. A. Schmidt & J. Schulkin (Eds.), *Extreme fear, shyness, and social phobia: Origins, biological mechanisms, and clinical outcomes* (pp. 14–29). New York: Oxford University Press.

Davidson, R. J. (1993). The neuropsychology of emotion and affective style. In M. Lewis & J. M. Haviland (Eds.), *Handbook of emotion* (pp. 143–154). New York: Guilford.

Davidson, R. J. & Fox, N. A. (1989). The relation between tonic EEG asymmetry and ten-month-old emotional response to separation. *Journal of Abnormal Psychology, 98,* 127–131.

Davidson, R. J. & Rickman, M. (1999). Behavioral inhibition and the emotional circuitry of the brain: Stability and plasticity during the early childhood years. In L. A. Schmidt & J. Schulkin (Eds.), *Extreme fear, shyness, and social phobia: Origins, biological mechanisms, and clinical outcomes* (pp. 67–87). New York: Oxford University Press.

Davis, M., Hitchcock, J. M., & Rosen, J. B. (1987). Anxiety and the amygdala: Pharmacological and anatomical analysis of the fear-potentiated startle paradigm. In G. Bower (Ed.), *The psychology of learning and motivation* (Vol. 21, pp. 263–305). San Diego, CA: Academic Press.

Dawson, G., Grofer Klinger, L., Panagiotides, H., Hill, D., & Spieker, S. (1992). Frontal lobe activity and affective behavior in infants of mothers with depressive symptoms. *Child Development, 63,* 725–737.

Deary, I. J., Battersby, S., Whiteman, M. C., Connor, J. M., Fowkes, F. G., & Harmar, A. (1999). Neuroticism and polymorphisms in the serotonin transporter gene. *Psychological Medicine, 29,* 735–739.

DiLalla, L. F., Kagan, J., & Reznick, J. S. (1994). Genetic etiology of behavioral inhibition among 2-year-old children. *Infant Behavior and Development, 17,* 405–412.

Ebstein, R. P., Levine, J., Geller, V., Auerbach, J., Gritsenko, I., & Belmaker, R. H. (1998). Dopamine D4 receptor and serotonin transporter promoter in the determination of neonatal temperament. *Molecular Psychiatry, 3,* 238–246.

Ebstein, R. P., Novick, O., Umansky, R., Priel, B., Osher, Y, Blaine, D., Bennett, E. R., Nemanov, L., Katz, M., & Belmaker, R. H. (1996). Dopamine D4 receptor (D4DR) exon III polymorphism associated with the human personality trait of novelty seeking. *Nature Genetics, 12,* 78–80.

Eley, T. C. & Plomin, R. (1997). Genetic analyses of emotionality. *Current Opinion in Neurobiology, 7,* 279–284.

Engfer, A. (1993). Antecedents and consequences of shyness in boys and girls: A 6-year longitudinal study. In K. H. Rubin & J. Asendorpf (Eds.), *Social withdrawal, inhibition, and shyness in childhood* (pp. 49–79). New Jersey: Erlbaum.

Field, T. (1986). Models of reactive and chronic depression in infancy. In E. Z. Tronick & T. Field (Eds.), *Maternal depression and infant disturbance* (pp. 47–60). San Francisco, CA: Jossey-Bass.

Field, T., Fox, N. A., Pickens, J., & Nawrocki, T. (1995). Relative right frontal EEG activation in 3- to 6-month-old infants of depressed mothers. *Developmental Psychology, 31,* 358–363.

Field, T., Healy, B., Goldstein, S., Perry, S., Bendall, D., Schanberg, S., Zimmerman, E., & Kuhn, C. (1988). Infants of depressed mothers show "depressed" behavior even with nondepressed adults. *Child Development, 59,* 1569–1579.

Field, T., Sandberg, D., Garcia, R., Vega-Lahr, N., Goldstein, S., & Guy, L. (1985). Prenatal problems, post-partum depression, and early mother-infant interaction. *Developmental Psychology, 12,* 1152–1156.

Flint, J., Corley, R., DeFries, J. C., Fulker, D. W., Gray, J. A., Miller, S., & Collins, A. C. (1995). A simple genetic basis for a complex psychological trait in laboratory mice. *Science, 269,* 1432–1435.

Fox, N. A. (1991). If it's not left, it's right: Electroencephalogram asymmetry and the development of emotion. *American Psychologist, 46,* 863–887.

Fox, N. A. (1994). Dynamic cerebral processes underlying emotion regulation. In N. A. Fox (Ed.), The development of emotion regulation: Behavioral and biological considerations. *Monographs of the Society for Research in Child Development* (pp. 152–166), *59* (2–3, Serial No. 240).

Fox, N. A., Bell, M. A., & Jones, N. A. (1992). Individual differences in response to stress and cerebral asymmetry. *Developmental Neuropsychology, 8,* 161–184.

Fox, N. A., Calkins, S. D., & Bell, M. A. (1994). Neural plasticity and development in the first two years of life: Evidence from cognitive and socioemotional domains of research. *Development and Psychopathology, 6,* 677–696.

Fox, N. A., Henderson, H. A., Rubin, K. H., Calkins, S. D., & Schmidt, L. A. (2001). Continuity and discontinuity of behavioral inhibition and exuberance: Psychophysiological and behavioral influences across the first four years of life. *Child Development, 72,* 1–21.

Fox, N. A., Rubin, K. H., Calkins, S. D., Marshall, T. R., Coplan, R. J., Porges, S. W., Long, J. M., & Stewart, S. (1995). Frontal activation asymmetry and social competence at four years of age. *Child Development, 66,* 1770–1784.

Fox, N. A., Schmidt, L. A., Calkins, S. D., Rubin, K. H., & Coplan, R. J. (1996). The role of frontal activation in the regulation and dysregulation of social behavior during the preschool years. *Development and Psychopathology, 8,* 89–102.

Gallagher, M., Graham, P. W. A., & Holland, P. C. (1990). The amygdala central nucleus and appetitive Pavlovian conditioning: Lesions impair one class of conditioned behavior. *Journal of Neuroscience, 10,* 1906–1911.

Gallagher, M. & Holland, P. C. (1994). The amygdala complex: Multiple roles in associative learning and attention. *Proceedings of the National Academy of Sciences, 91,* 11771–11776.

Glowa, J. R., Geyer, M. A., Gold, P. W., & Sternberg, E. M. (1992). Differential startle amplitude and corticosterone response in rats. *Neuroendocrinology, 56,* 719–723.

Gold, P. W., Goodwin, F. K., & Chrousos, G. P. (1988). Clinical and biochemical manifestations of depression (two parts). *New England Journal of Medicine, 319,* 348–353; 413–420.

Goldman, D., Malhotra, A., Urbanek, M., Guenther, D., Robin, R., Virkkunen, M., Linnoila, M., & Long, J. (1996). The dopamine DRD2 and DRD4 receptors: Lack of association to alcoholism, substance abuse and novelty seeking in Finnish Caucasians and Southwestern American Indians. *Psychiatric Genetics Abstracts, 6,* 162.

Grillon, C., Ameli, R., Foot, M., & Davis, M. (1993). Fear-potentiated startle: Relationship to state/trait anxiety in healthy subjects. *Biological Psychiatry, 33,* 566–574.

Hamer, D. & Copeland, P. (1998). *Living with our genes.* New York: Doubleday.

Harrington, G. M. (1981). The Har strains of rats: Origins and characteristics. *Behavior Genetics, 11,* 445–468.

Hartup, W. W. (1983). The peer system. In E. M. Hetherington (Vol. Ed.), *Handbook of Child Psychology, Vol. 4, Socialization, personality, and social development* (pp. 103–196). New York: Wiley.

Henriques, J. B. & Davidson, R. J. (1990). Regional brain electrical asymmetries discriminate between previously depressed subjects and healthy controls. *Journal of Abnormal Psychology, 99,* 22–31.

Henriques, J. B. & Davidson, R. J. (1991). Left frontal hypoactivation in depression. *Journal of Abnormal Psychology, 100,* 535–545.

Hetherington, E. M. & Martin, B. (1986). Family factors and psychopathology in children. In H. C. Quay & J. S. Werry (Eds.), *Psychopathological disorders of childhood* (3rd edn., pp. 332–390). New York: Wiley.

Hirshfeld, D. R., Rosenbaum, J. F., Biederman, J., Bolduc, E. A., Faraone, S. V., Snidman, N., Reznick, J. S., & Kagan, J. (1992). Stable behavioral inhibition and its association with anxiety disorder. *Journal of the American Academy of Child and Adolescent Psychiatry, 31,* 103–111.

Hitchcock, J. & Davis, M. (1986). Lesion of the amygdala, but not the cerebellum or the red nucleus, block conditioned fear as measured with potentiated startle paradigm. *Behavioral Neuroscience, 100,* 11–22.

Jacobson, J. L. & Wille, D. E. (1986). The influence of attachment pattern on developmental changes in peer interaction from the toddler to the preschool period. *Child Development, 57,* 338–347.

Jang, K. L., Livesley, W. J., & Vernon, P. A. (1996). The genetic basis of personality at different ages: A cross-sectional twin study. *Personality and Individual Differences, 21,* 299–301.

Jones, W. H., Briggs, S. R., & Cheek, J. M. (Eds.) (1986). *Shyness: Perspectives on research and treatment.* New York: Plenum.

Jonsson, E. G., Nothen, M. M., Gustavsson, J. P., Neidt, H., Brene, S., Tylec, A., Propping, P., & Sedvall, G. C. (1997). Lack of evidence for allelic association between personality traits and the dopamine D4 receptor gene polymorphisms. *American Journal of Psychiatry, 154,* 697–699.

Kagan, J. (1991). Continuity and discontinuity in development. In S. E. Brauth, W. S. Hall, & R. J. Dooling (Eds.), *Plasticity of development* (pp. 11–26). Cambridge, MA: MIT Press.

Kagan, J. (1994). *Galen's prophecy: Temperament in human nature.* New York: Basic Books.

Kagan, J. (1999). The concept of behavioral inhibition. In L. A. Schmidt & J. Schulkin (Eds.), *Extreme fear, shyness, and social phobia: Origins, biological mechanisms, and clinical outcomes* (pp. 3–13). New York: Oxford University Press.

Kagan, J., Reznick, J. S., & Snidman, N. (1987). The physiology and psychology of behavioral inhibition in children. *Child Development, 58*, 1459–1473.

Kagan, J., Reznick, J. S., & Snidman, N. (1988). Biological basis of childhood shyness. *Science, 240*, 167–171.

Kagan, J. & Snidman, N. (1991a). Temperamental factors in human development. *American Psychologist, 46*, 856–862.

Kagan, J. & Snidman, N. (1991b). Infant predictors of inhibited and uninhibited profiles. *Psychological Science, 2*, 40–44.

Kapp, B. S., Frysinger, R. C., Gallagher, M., & Haselton, J. R. (1979). Amygdala central nucleus lesions: Effects on heart rate conditioning in the rabbit. *Physiology and Behavior, 23*, 1109–1117.

Kumakiri, C., Kodama, K., Shimizu, E., Yamanouchi, N., Okada, S., Noda, S., Okamoto, H., Sato, T., & Shirasawa, H. (1999). Study of the association between the serotonin transporter gene regulatory region polymorphism and personality traits in a Japanese population. *Neuroscience Letters, 263*, 205–207.

LaHoste, G. J., Swanson, J. M., Wigal, S. B., Glabe, C., Wigal, T., King, N., & Kennedy, J. L. (1996). Dopamine D4 receptor gene polymorphism is associated with attention deficit hyperactivity disorder. *Molecular Psychiatry, 1*, 121–124.

Lang, P. J., Bradley, M. M., & Cuthbert, B. N. (1990). Emotion, attention, and the startle reflex. *Psychological Review, 97*, 377–395.

LeDoux, J. E. (1996). *The emotional brain.* New York: Simon and Schuster.

LeDoux, J. E., Iwata, J., Cicchetti, P., & Reis, D. J. (1988). Different projections of the central amygdaloid nucleus mediate autonomic and behavioral correlates of conditioned fear. *Journal of Neuroscience, 8*, 2517–2519.

LeDoux, J. E., Sakaguchi, A., Iwata, J., & Reis, D. J. (1986). Interruption of projections from the medial geniculate body to an archi-neo-striatal field disrupts the classical conditioning of emotional responses to acoustic stimuli in the rat. *Neuroscience, 17*, 615–627.

Lee, Y., Schulkin, J., & Davis, M. (1994). Effect of corticosterone on the enhancement of the acoustic startle reflex by corticotropin releasing factor (CRF). *Brain Research, 666*, 93–98.

Lesch, K. P., Bengel, D., Heils, A., Sabol, S. Z., Greenberg, B. D., Petri, S., Benjamin, J., Muller, C. R., Hamer, D. H., & Murphy, D. L. (1996). Association of anxiety-related traits with a polymorphism in the serotonin transporter gene regulatory region. *Science, 274*, 1527–1531.

Maccoby, E. E. & Martin, J. A. (1983). Socialization in the context of the family: Parent-child interaction. In E. M. Hertherington (Vol. Ed.), *Handbook of child psychology, Vol. 4. Socialization, personality, and social development* (pp. 1–102). New York: Wiley.

Martin, B. (1975). Parent-child relations. In F. Horowitz (Ed.), *Review of child development research* (pp. 463–540). Chicago: University of Chicago Press.

Matheny, A. (1989). Children's behavioral inhibition over age and across situations: Genetic similarity for a trait during change. *Journal of Personality, 57*, 215–235.

Mills, R. S. L. & Rubin, K. H. (1993). Socialization factors in the development of social withdrawal. In K. H. Rubin & J. Asendorpf (Eds.), *Social withdrawal, inhibition, and shyness in childhood* (pp. 117–148). New Jersey: Erlbaum.

Nachmias, M., Gunnar, M., Mangelsdorf, S., Parritz, R., & Buss, K. (1996). Behavioral inhibition and stress reactivity: Moderating role of attachment. *Child Development, 67*, 508–522.

Nader, K. & LeDoux, J. (1999). The neural circuits that underlie fear. In L. A. Schmidt & J. Schulkin (Eds.), *Extreme fear, shyness, and social phobia: Origins, biological mechanisms, and clinical outcomes* (pp. 119–139). New York: Oxford University Press.

Plomin, R. (1986). *Development, genetics, and psychology.* Hillsdale, NJ: Erlbaum.

Plomin, R. (1989). Environment and genes: Determinants of behavior. *American Psychologist, 44*, 105–111.

Plomin, R. DeFries, J. C., McClearn, G. E., & Rutter, M. (1997). *Behavioral Genetics* (3rd edn.) New York: W. H. Freeman.

Plomin, R. & Rowe, D. C. (1979). Genetic and environmental etiology of social behavior in infancy. *Developmental Psychology*, *15*, 62–72.

Plomin, R. & Rutter, M. (1998). Child development, molecular genetics, and what to do with genes once they are found. *Child Development*, *69*, 1223–1242.

Rosen, J. B. & Davis, M. (1988). Enhancement of acoustic startle by electrical stimulation of the amygdala. *Behavioral Neuroscience*, *102*, 195–202.

Rosen, J. B., Hamerman, E., Sitcoske, M., Glowa, J. R., & Schulkin, J. (1996). Hyperexcitability: Exaggerated fear-potentiated startle produced by partial amygdala kindling. *Behavioral Neuroscience*, *110*, 43–50.

Rosen, J. B. & Schulkin, J. (1998). From normal fear to pathological anxiety. *Psychological Review*, *105*, 325–350.

Rubin, K. H., Hymel, S., Mills, R. S. L., & Rose-Krasnor, L. (1991). Conceptualizing different pathways to and from social isolation in childhood. In D. Cicchetti & S. Toth (Eds.), *Internalizing and externalizing expressions of dysfunction: Rochester Symposium on Developmental Psychopathology* (Vol. 2, pp. 91–122). Hillsdale, NJ: Erlbaum.

Rubin, K. H. & Mills, R. S. L. (1988). The many faces of social isolation in childhood. *Journal of Clinical and Consulting Psychology*, *56*, 916–924.

Rubin, K. H., Stewart, S. L., & Coplan, R. J. (1995). Social withdrawal in childhood: Conceptual and empirical perspectives. In T. Ollendick & R. Prinz (Eds.), *Advances in clinical child psychology* (Vol. 17, pp. 157–196). New York: Plenum Press.

Schmidt, L. A. (1999). Frontal brain electrical activity in shyness and sociability. *Psychological Science*, *10*, 316–320.

Schmidt, L. A. & Fox, N. A. (1994). Patterns of cortical electrophysiology and autonomic activity in adults' shyness and sociability. *Biological Psychology*, *38*, 183–198.

Schmidt, L. A. & Fox, N. A. (1995). Individual differences in young adults' shyness and sociability: Personality and health correlates. *Personality and Individual Differences*, *19*, 455–462.

Schmidt, L. A. & Fox, N. A. (1998). Fear-potentiated startle responses in temperamentally different human infants. *Developmental Psychobiology*, *32*, 113–120.

Schmidt, L. A. & Fox, N. A. (1999). Conceptual, biological, and behavioral distinctions among different categories of shy children. In L. A. Schmidt & J. Schulkin (Eds.), *Extreme fear, shyness, and social phobia: Origins, biological mechanisms, and clinical outcomes* (pp. 47–66). New York: Oxford University Press.

Schmidt, L. A., Fox, N. A., Goldberg, M. C., Smith, C. C., & Schulkin, J. (1999). Effects of acute prednisone administration on memory, attention, and emotion in healthy human adults. *Psychoneuroendocrinology*, *24*, 461–483.

Schmidt, L. A., Fox, N. A., Perez-Edgar, K., Lu, S., & Hamer, D. H. (2001). Association of dopamine receptor (DRD4) gene with attention problems in normal childhood development. *Psychiatric Genetics*, *11*, 25–29.

Schmidt, L. A., Fox, N. A., Rubin, K. H., Sternberg, E. M., Gold, P. W., Smith, C., & Schulkin, J. (1997). Behavioral and neuroendocrine responses in shy children. *Developmental Psychobiology*, *30*, 127–140.

Schmidt, L. A., Fox, N. A., Schulkin, J., & Gold, P. W. (1999a). Behavioral and psychophysiological correlates of self-presentation in temperamentally shy children. *Developmental Psychobiology*, *35*, 119–135.

Schmidt, L. A., Fox, N. A., Sternberg, E. M., Gold, P. W., Smith, C., & Schulkin, J. (1999b). Adrenocortical reactivity and social competence in seven year olds. *Personality and Individual Differences*, *26*, 977–985.

Schmidt, L. A. & Schulkin, J. (Eds.) (1999). *Extreme fear, shyness, and social phobia: Origins, biological mechanisms, and clinical outcomes*. New York: Oxford University Press.

Schmidt, L. A., & Trainor, L. J. (2001). Frontal brain electrical activity (EEG) distinguishes *valence* and *intensity* of musical emotions. *Cognition and Emotion, 15*, 487–500.

Schulkin, J., McEwen, B. S., & Gold, P. W. (1994). Allostasis, amygdala, and anticipatory angst. *Neuroscience and Biobehavioral Reviews, 18*, 385–396.

Snidman, N. & Kagan, J. (1994). The contribution of infant temperamental differences to acoustic startle response. [Abstract.] *Psychophysiology, 31*, S92.

Sroufe, L. A. & Fleeson, J. (1986). Attachment and the construction of relationships. In W. Hartup & Z. Rubin (Eds.), *The nature and development of relationships.* Hillsdale, NJ: Erlbaum.

Suomi, S. J. (1991). Uptight and laid-back monkeys: Individual differences in response to social challenge. In S. E. Brauth, W. S. Hall, & R. J. Dooling (Eds.), *Plasticity of development* (pp. 27–56). Cambridge, MA: MIT Press.

Swanson, J. M., Sunohara, G. A., Kennedy, J. L., Regino, R., Fineberg, E., Wigal, T., Lerner, M., Williams, L., LaHoste, G. J., & Wigal, S. (1998). Association of the dopamine receptor D4 (DRD4) gene with a refined phenotype of attention deficit hyperactivity disorder (ADHD): A family-based approach. *Molecular Psychiatry, 3*, 38–41.

Takahashi, L. K. & Rubin, W. W. (1994). Corticosteroid induction of threat-induced behavioral inhibition in preweanling rats. *Behavioral Neuroscience, 107*, 860–868.

Tomarken, A. J., Davidson, R. J., & Henriques, J. B. (1990). Resting frontal brain asymmetry predicts affective responses to films. *Journal of Personality and Social Psychology, 59*, 791–801.

Westenberg, H. G., Murphy, D. L., & den Boer, J. A. (Eds.) (1996). *Advances in the neurobiology of anxiety disorders.* New York: Wiley.

Wheeler, R. W., Davidson, R. J., & Tomarken, A. J. (1993). Frontal brain asymmetry and emotional reactivity: A biological substrate of affective style. *Psychophysiology, 30*, 82–89.

Zimbardo, P. G. (1977). *Shyness: What is it and what to do about it.* New York: Symphony Press.

Chapter 3

Behavioral Inhibition: Physiological Correlates

Peter J. Marshall *and* **Joan Stevenson-Hinde**

FUNCTIONAL CONSIDERATIONS
TOWARDS A NEUROBIOLOGICAL MODEL OF BI
Physiological Measures That Have Been Related to BI
    EEG
    Cortisol
    Heart period
    Heart period variability
EVALUATING THE MODEL
THE WAY FORWARD
Selecting Individuals Who Are Extreme
Integration with Measures from Other Domains
New Directions
ACKNOWLEDGEMENTS
REFERENCES

Behavioral inhibition to the unfamiliar (BI) refers to "the child's initial behavioral reactions to unfamiliar people, objects, and contexts, or challenging situations" (Kagan, Reznick, & Snidman, 1985, p. 53). Behaviorally inhibited children are characteristically watchful, wary, and quiet in new situations, including social interactions with unfamiliar people. BI may be viewed as a temperamental construct reflecting relatively stable individual differences in behavioral style (e.g., Goldsmith et al., 1987). Longitudinal studies have demonstrated BI to be at least moderately stable throughout childhood (e.g., Kagan, Reznick, Snidman, Gibbons, & Johnson, 1988; Scarpa, Raine, Venables, & Mednick, 1995; Stevenson-Hinde & Shouldice, 1995, 1996), and twin studies have indicated a significant heritable component (e.g., DiLalla, Kagan, & Reznick, 1994; see also Schmidt, Polak,

International Handbook of Social Anxiety: Concepts, Research and Interventions Relating to the Self and Shyness. Edited by W. Ray Crozier and Lynn E. Alden.
© 2001 John Wiley & Sons Ltd.

& Spooner, this volume, *Chapter 2*). Given this heritability and stability, Kagan and others have gone on to identify physiological correlates of BI, with neurobiological models focused on the amygdala (e.g., Kagan, 1994). The aim of our chapter is to consider such a model, with a view to encompassing various correlates of BI—particularly EEG data, cortisol levels, and cardiac functioning (i.e., heart period and respiratory sinus arrhythmia).

FUNCTIONAL CONSIDERATIONS

Ethological considerations suggest that the study of causal mechanisms may be facilitated by considerations of function and evolution (e.g., Hinde, 1987; Tinbergen, 1963). Regarding BI, one may postulate an underlying "fear behavior system", which like other motivational systems involves a variety of responses "distinguished on the basis of common causation . . . [and] . . . usually found to subserve a particular biological function" (Baerends, 1976, pp. 731–733). A behavior systems approach stresses organization within any particular system as well as between different systems: "In the study of behavior as well as neuroscience the investigator must typically deal with interlocking *networks* of organizational processes, rather than being satisfied with simple linear conceptualisations" (Fentress, 1991, p. 78). Such non-linear organization will be reflected in the neurobiological model of BI that follows. Furthermore, a behavior systems approach may be used to conceptualize *individual differences* in BI. That is, one may postulate a unique threshold of arousal of a fear behavior system within each individual, which nevertheless may be amenable to change during the course of development (Stevenson-Hinde & Shouldice, 1996, Fig. 11.1, p. 242).

We may go on to ask how such a fear behavior system, which is both characteristic of our species and yet shows individual differences, may have evolved. Fear of the unfamiliar is a *ubiquitous* characteristic, not only within our own species, but also over a broad range of species, ranging from pumpkinseed sunfish to other primates (e.g., Gosling & John, 1999; Stevenson-Hinde, Stillwell-Barnes, & Zunz, 1980; Wilson, Coleman, Clark, & Biederman, 1993). It is usually potent, interrupting ongoing behavior, and finely tuned to the situation. Such a characteristic, found within and across species, suggests that fearful behavior may have been selected for during the course of evolution. That is, individuals who exhibited wariness of the unfamiliar would have been more apt to survive and leave offspring—or to have increased their inclusive fitness—compared to those who did not. Thus, our propensity to show BI may have been guided by natural selection, with the function being protection from harm (Stevenson-Hinde & Shouldice, 1996). As Bowlby (1969/1982, p. 64) argued,

> It is against this picture of man's environment of evolutionary adaptedness that the environmentally stable behavioral equipment of man is considered. Much of this equipment, it is held, is so structured that it enables individuals of each sex and each age-group to take their places in the organized social group characteristic of the

species . . . not a single feature of a species' morphology, physiology, or behavior can be understood or even discussed intelligently except in relation to that species' environment of evolutionary adaptedness.

Thus, rather than being "irrational" or "abnormal", wariness of the unfamiliar should be viewed as an adaptive consequence of our evolutionary past, which we all share.

Furthermore, and while not denying the role of experience in development, we may apply a functional argument to the consistent *individual differences* in BI. It is now recognized that natural selection is likely to produce not rigid behavior but behavior adapted to particular circumstances, so that some genetic variability would exist. In addition to the twin studies referred to in this volume (*Chapter 2*), Stevenson, Batten, and Cherner (1992) have shown that with 8- to 18-year-olds, fears concerning harm possibly relevant during the course of evolution (e.g., fear of the unknown, fear of animals, fear of danger) do have significant heritability estimates, while modern-day fears not involving risk of life (e.g., fear of criticism, fear of medical procedures) do not. Wilson, Clark, Coleman, and Dearstyne (1994) have speculated how natural selection may have produced "phenotypically inflexible genotypes", as well as "phenotypically plastic genotypes". Referring to "shyness" and "boldness"—characteristics found in a wide range of species and not unlike "high BI" and "low BI"—they argue that in a *constant* environment the inflexible shy or bold individuals should replace the plastic form. Wilson et al. then extend their argument to *heterogeneous* environments, as follows: "If the opportunities for risk-prone and risk-averse individuals are temporally variable, however, natural selection will promote a mixture of innate and facultative forms, whose relative proportions will depend on the magnitude of temporal variation" (p. 445). Other evolutionary processes such as frequency-dependent selection and habitat choice could also maintain genetic variability (Maynard Smith, 1989).

This emphasis on selection for different types of individuals is compatible with Kagan's approach to BI—namely that children who are extreme, with either high or low BI, are qualitatively different from children in the mid-range. In a chapter devoted to extremes, Kagan concludes "The reluctance to acknowledge that, on some occasions, it is useful to examine extreme groups that may be qualitatively different from the rest of the sample has been slowing theoretical progress in psychology" (Kagan, Snidman, & Arcus, 1998, p. 80). Thus, although many of the following results treat BI as a continuum, we should bear in mind that it is also meaningful to create categories of BI (e.g., Stevenson-Hinde & Glover, 1996).

TOWARDS A NEUROBIOLOGICAL MODEL OF BI

Neurobiological models of BI have arisen from the literature concerning the neural basis of fear and anxiety in both animals and humans. Charney and Deutch

(1996) summarized three necessary features of neural fear systems in the brain. First, afferent sensory input is needed to capture the salient physical characteristics of a potentially threatening stimulus. Second, the capability for affective assessment of stimuli, including the comparison with past experience, is crucial. Third, efferent projections mediate the endocrine, autonomic and motor responses to the threat (see Figure 3.1). We may add another aspect, namely that responses may feed back to the brain to provide information relevant to the regulation of further behavioral and physiological responses.

A neurobiological model of BI posits that inhibited children may differ from uninhibited children at various levels—in peripheral sensory receptor systems, in the early relaying of sensory information through the thalamus, in the process-

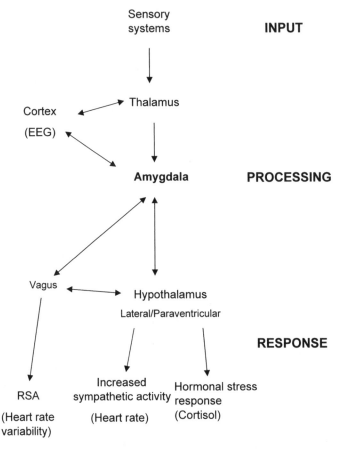

Figure 3.1   A neurobiological model of behavioral inhibition. Schematic representation of some of the pathways which might be activated in novel or challenging situations, with the amygdala playing a central role. (Parentheses indicate the physiological measures central to the present chapter)

ing of sensory data in the cortex or in subcortical structures such as the amygdala, in the efferent autonomic, neuroendocrine, and motor responses, or in the feedback from these responses.

Of these possibilities, the dominant theme in current models of BI concerns differences between inhibited and uninhibited children at the level of subcortical processing. Kagan and co-workers have proposed that the contrast in reactions to novelty of inhibited and uninhibited children arises from variation in the excitability of neural circuits of the limbic system (Kagan & Snidman, 1991). In particular, this model focuses on the central nucleus of the amygdala, which has been extensively implicated in the generation of fear (Davis, 1992). As reviewed by Schulkin and Rosen (1999), damage to the amygdala interferes with fear-related behavior, stimulation of the central nucleus of the amygdala activates neural circuitry underlying startle responses, stimulation heightens attention toward fearful events, and neurons within the amygdala are reactive to fearful signals. "Thus data from many avenues strongly suggest that the amygdala and its associated neural circuitry appraise fearful signals and orchestrate behavioral and autonomic responses to these events" (Schulkin & Rosen, 1999, p. 144).

The amygdaloid fear circuit can be activated by partially processed sensory information from the thalamus, by more complex sensory and associative information from the cortex, or by general situational information delivered from the hippocampus (LeDoux, 1995). The central nucleus of the amygdala is the primary source of amygdaloid projections to subcortical sites that modulate responses to a threatening stimulus. These sites include the lateral hypothalamus, which is particularly important in mediating autonomic responses, and the paraventricular hypothalamus, which plays a key role in regulating the hypothalamic–pituitary–adrenal (HPA) endocrine response.

The model of increased subcortical activation in inhibited children allows predictions to be made about the central and peripheral manifestations of this limbic excitability in relation to BI. More specifically, increased activity of the central nucleus of the amygdala would be expected to result in increased activity at sites that have extensive connections with the central nucleus. As suggested by Figure 3.1, increased amygdaloid activation may be associated with changes in cortical (e.g., EEG), autonomic (e.g., cardiac), or endocrine (e.g., cortisol) functioning. The following section provides a review of studies that have examined these possibilities.

Physiological Measures That Have Been Related to BI

Four physiological measures, all of which may be monitored non-invasively, arise from the neurobiological model of BI presented in Figure 3.1; EEG measures from the frontal cortex, cortisol levels, heart period, and heart period variability. Each will be considered in turn, in relation to the model on the one hand and to BI on the other.

EEG

The amygdala receives input from diverse areas of the cortex, which suggests a role for the amygdala in the integration and association of sensory and affective information (LeDoux, 1995). Of particular significance for the BI model is the suggested association within the amygdala of stimulus representations with their affective attributes, or their appetitive or aversive significance (Davidson & Irwin, 1998). One source of neural information about the affective value of a stimulus is the frontal cortex, which has been associated with the regulation of motivational responses to appetitive or aversive stimuli (Fox, 1991). Reciprocal communication between the frontal cortex and the amygdala is therefore likely to be important for the expression and regulation of responses to potentially aversive or rewarding stimuli (McDonald, 1998). Within the BI model, several studies have related individual differences in approach or withdrawal behaviors in infancy and childhood to patterns of activation in the frontal region of the brain. The specific focus of this work has primarily been the use of hemispheric asymmetry in frontal brain activation as an index of motivational tendencies related to BI (see below). Such hemispheric asymmetries are often examined by recording electrical activity from left and right frontal scalp sites using electroencephalographic (EEG) techniques. The component of the EEG signal that is usually of interest in this respect is alpha wave activity, which occurs in the frequency range of 8–13 Hz in adults and at lower frequencies in children. EEG alpha wave activity is commonly used as a measure of regional brain activity, with decreased alpha power corresponding to increased neuronal activity (for review, see Davidson, Jackson, & Larson, 2000). A difference in EEG alpha power between the left and right frontal EEG electrodes is therefore assumed to reflect relative differences in neuronal activity between the left and right regions of the frontal cortex. Because the relation is inverse, decreased alpha power in the EEG from the left frontal electrode relative to alpha power from the right frontal electrode is taken as indicating increased neuronal activity in the left frontal region of the cortex compared with the right frontal region. Such a pattern may be referred to as "left frontal asymmetry" as it reflects greater activation of the left compared with the right frontal region. In contrast, "right frontal asymmetry" refers to the reverse.

Fox (1991, 1994) and Davidson (1992) have argued that the functional significance of frontal EEG asymmetry may be conceptualized in terms of motivational systems of approach and withdrawal. In this perspective, the left frontal region promotes appetitive, approach-directed emotional responses, while the right frontal region promotes withdrawal-directed responses to perceived aversive stimuli. Individual differences in frontal asymmetry may therefore serve as an index of relative approach and withdrawal motivations. Evidence for this comes from studies of adults, children, and infants. In adults, left frontal asymmetry has been associated with higher scores on a self-report scale assessing motivational sensitivity to incentive or reward, while right frontal asymmetry has been associated with self-reported withdrawal tendencies (Harmon-Jones & Allen,

1997; Sutton & Davidson, 1997). With infants and young children, a number of studies of frontal EEG asymmetry have worked within the BI paradigm, focusing on the tendency to approach or withdraw from novel situations or stimuli. Fox, Calkins, and Bell (1994) found that infants who displayed a pattern of stable right frontal EEG asymmetry across the first two years of life tended to be more inhibited at both 14 and 24 months of age compared with infants who exhibited a pattern of stable left frontal EEG. Fox, Henderson, Rubin, Calkins, and Schmidt (2001), working with a selected sample, found that infants who went on to be consistently inhibited up to 4 years of age exhibited stronger right frontal EEG asymmetry at 9 and 14 months of age than infants who were to become less inhibited. The latter group of infants exhibited weak right frontal EEG at 9 months of age and left frontal EEG asymmetry at 14 months of age. Davidson and colleagues screened a large sample ($N = 386$) of 31-month-old toddlers in order to select groups of high, middle, and low BI based on each child's behavior in a series of laboratory episodes (see Davidson, 1994). The selected children were followed up and seen at 38 months in a laboratory session during which EEG was recorded. The high BI group showed right frontal asymmetry, while the low BI group showed left frontal asymmetry. The middle BI group showed an asymmetry level that was intermediate between the two extreme groups.

In the early months of life, fear-eliciting stimuli include loud noises or loss of support, but fear of strangers does not appear until around 6 to 9 months of age (e.g., Bronson, 1972). Using longitudinal samples, researchers such as Kagan and Fox have examined infant characteristics in the first half-year of life in order to elucidate possible temperamental precursors of inhibition to novelty in late infancy and toddlerhood. The main finding from this work is that infants who display a high degree of irritability and negative affect during the early months of life are more likely to exhibit inhibited social behavior as toddlers than infants who display high levels of positive affect. Kagan and Snidman (1991) reported that 4-month-old infants selected for high motor activity and high frequency of crying were more likely than other less reactive infants to exhibit behavioral inhibition as toddlers. Similarly, Calkins and Fox (1992) found that, in an unselected sample, infants displaying high levels of negative reactivity at 5 months of age were more likely to be behaviorally inhibited at 24 months of age. Since this original work, further studies have examined whether infants who are active and irritable in the first few months of life also display a unique EEG activation pattern in infancy that may be related to later BI. These studies have generally shown relations between high negative reactivity in early infancy, right frontal EEG asymmetry, and BI in later infancy. Calkins, Fox, and Marshall (1996) found that infants who were selected at 4 months of age for high frequencies of motor behavior and negative affect tended to show right frontal EEG asymmetry at 9 months of age, and were more behaviorally inhibited at 14 months of age compared with infants who showed either high positive affect or low general levels of positive and negative reactivity at 4 months of age. However, it is notable that across the whole sample, frontal EEG asymmetry at 9 months of age was not related to BI at 14 months. This suggests a more complex interplay between infant reactivity,

EEG asymmetry and later BI, a point that is further elaborated by Fox et al. (2001).

A recent report has extended the examination of EEG–BI relations into middle childhood. Earlier in this section we referred to the study described by Davidson (1994), in which right frontal EEG asymmetry was associated with high levels of BI in the third year of life. Davidson and Rickman (1999) followed up this sample, with assessments of BI at 9 years of age and an EEG evaluation one year later. Based on BI at 9 years, the sample was divided into groups of high, middle, and low BI children. The relation between BI at age 9 years and brain activity at age 10 was similar to the relation that had been observed at age 3 years. The high BI group showed relative right frontal activation at 10 years of age, whereas the low BI group showed relative left frontal activation. The pattern of EEG asymmetry for the middle group was intermediate between the patterns of the two extreme groups.

Although similar contemporaneous relations were found at both ages, Davidson and Rickman found no significant stability in either BI or the EEG asymmetry index between the assessments in the third year of life and the corresponding assessments in middle childhood. They provide a number of possible explanations of this instability, including the difficulty of creating analogous yet age-appropriate scenarios for BI, and the considerable plasticity that is occurring in both behavioral and brain development over the relatively long time period that was used.

Despite the instability in EEG asymmetry between 3 and 10 years of age, Davidson and Rickman hypothesized that the small number of children showing right frontal activation *at both ages* would be more likely to be inhibited than children showing stable left frontal activation. Although hindered by low group sizes, these analyses indicate that children showing stable right frontal activation were indeed more likely to have been inhibited at 3 years of age.

In summary, EEG studies indicate a relation between right frontal activation and BI, from infancy to middle childhood. It is likely that the frontal cortex plays an important role in the regulation of responses to novelty, and the extensive connections between the frontal cortex and the amygdala lend weight to the utility of EEG measures in developing a neurobiological model of BI. The examination of EEG alpha asymmetry in relation to individual differences in approach and withdrawal tendencies remains a fertile area of study and debate in both adults and children. For further discussion of this area, the interested reader is referred to Davidson (1998).

Cortisol

Response to a threat may involve activation of the hypothalamic–pituitary–adrenal (HPA) system, with the secretion of cortisol from the adrenal gland as "the final step in a series of complex events" (Takahashi & Kalin, 1999, p. 100). The production of cortisol is principally regulated by the paraventricular region of the hypothalamus, which produces cortisol-releasing hormone (CRH). CRH stimulates the cells in the anterior pituitary that produce adrenocorticotrophic hormone (ACTH), which is released into general circulation and in turn stimulates the cortex of the adrenal glands to produce cortisol and release it into the bloodstream.

Cortisol levels in children can be noninvasively assessed from saliva samples collected in the home, laboratory or school environments. Salivary cortisol levels have been studied in relation to various aspects of child temperament, including BI (for review, see Stansbury & Gunnar, 1994). There is a theoretical rationale for relations between BI and cortisol levels, since subcortical structures such as the amygdala have important regulatory effects on the HPA axis via the paraventricular hypothalamus (de Kloet, 1991). In the neurobiological model presented here, BI is associated with a more reactive amygdala, which in turn may be expected to be accompanied by a more reactive HPA axis. Support for this aspect of the BI model has been mixed, despite the suggestion of early work that high baseline cortisol levels are associated with high BI. Kagan, Reznick, and Snidman (1987) found elevated cortisol levels in 5.5-year-olds who had been classified as behaviorally inhibited at 21 months of age, compared with those who had been classified as uninhibited at 21 months. Inhibited behavior at 5.5 years of age was also associated with high levels of cortisol measured at the same age. One other recent study of young children is that of Schmidt et al. (1997), who found that 4-year-olds who showed high levels of anxious and unoccupied behavior in laboratory play sessions with unfamiliar peers showed significantly higher morning salivary cortisol levels compared with less wary children.

While the above studies considered baseline levels of cortisol, studies from Megan Gunnar's laboratory have also examined the relations between inhibited behavior in childhood and dynamic changes in adrenocortical activity over periods of social transition (e.g., de Haan, Gunnar, Tout, Hart, & Stansbury, 1998; Gunnar, Tout, de Haan, Pierce, & Stansbury, 1997; Tout, de Haan, Campbell, & Gunnar, 1998). These studies have suggested that the relation between socially inhibited behavior and cortisol levels may be more complex than was suggested by the previous work. For instance, de Haan et al. (1998) found home cortisol levels to be associated with more anxious, internalizing behavior in 2-year-olds, but also found that the cortisol response to starting preschool was correlated with more assertive, angry, and aggressive behavior rather than with socially inhibited or anxious behavior. Gunnar (1994) suggests one reason why inhibited children may not show elevated cortisol reactivity during such transitions. Unlike less fearful children, inhibited children tend to avoid the kinds of social and physical activities that would elicit elevations in cortisol. Another interesting suggestion raised by Gunnar is that adrenocortical activity may not map neatly onto fear- or stress-related constructs, but rather that cortisol levels may be related to the maintenance or failure of coping strategies.

A complement to this suggestion is the study of Nachmias et al. (1996), who examined cortisol responses of 18-month-olds to the Ainsworth Strange Situation and a challenging coping episode. Analyses also included attachment classification and an index of BI for each child. Infants who were highly inhibited and insecurely attached showed greater cortisol responses to the Strange Situation and the challenging coping episode, compared with children who were highly inhibited but securely attached. The cortisol increase for inhibited-insecure infants was also greater than that for the uninhibited infants, whether securely or insecurely attached. The authors suggest that mothers in insecure dyads who have inhibited children may interfere with their children's strategies for coping with an unfamiliar and/or stressful situation. This disruption of an inhibited child's coping strategy is then reflected in a greater increase in cortisol compared with an inhibited and secure child whose coping strategy is not disrupted. Indeed from an attachment theory perspective, direct interference from mothers need not be implicated. That is, a securely attached child would be expected to have a more adequate coping strategy than an insecurely attached child.

Recent ideas concerning the central action of corticosteroids have raised further interesting suggestions about the HPA system and fear-related behaviors. As discussed above, hypothalamic production of cortisol-releasing hormone (CRH) regulates the production of circulating cortisol. In turn, the levels of peripheral cortisol feed back to control further CRH production. In all the above studies, peripheral cortisol levels were assessed using salivary assay techniques. However, CRH itself may have central effects that can produce fear states, and there have been recent suggestions that central CRH levels can dissociate from peripheral cortisol levels. Schulkin (1994; also Schulkin & Rosen, 1999) hypothesizes that there is a second CRH system in extrahypothalamic sites (e.g., the central nucleus of the amygdala) that is regulated in a different way to the HPA system, and that the effects of this central CRH may in fact underlie a central state of fear. The resulting prediction is that excessively fearful children would have greater central levels of CRH than less fearful children, although this will practically and ethically remain an untestable hypothesis given that central measurement would involve the collection of cerebrospinal fluid.

Heart Period

Autonomic activity is regulated by a set of hypothalamic and brainstem nuclei which establish patterns of sympathetic and parasympathetic activation across the various bodily systems. Given a motivationally significant event, these brainstem mechanisms are themselves adjusted by descending connections from higher structures such as the amygdala. For instance, outputs from the central nucleus of the amygdala include neural pathways to the lateral hypothalamus, which controls sympathetic nervous system responses via brainstem centers (Spyer, 1989). Sympathetic responses to a stressor would include increased adrenergic activity at the sinoatrial cardiac pacemaker, which would cause the heart to beat faster. This sequence provides a rationale for the use of heart period (HP) in the BI model as a noninvasive peripheral marker of limbic activity. The supposition is that inhibited children should show consistently lower HP (higher heart rate) and larger decreases in HP in response to unfamiliarity, compared to uninhibited children (Kagan, 1994). Although the autonomic emphasis in Kagan's model is on sympathetic activation, there may be other modes of cardiac auto-nomic control under stress (Cacioppo, Uchino, & Berntson, 1994). Indeed, the existence of efferent pathways from subcortical structures such as the amygdala to the vagus, which controls parasympathetic activity in the viscera, suggests that parasympathetic involvement in the behavioral modulation of HP is also likely (Porges, 1995).

The main source of information about relations between HP and BI in child-hood comes from the longitudinal study by Kagan and his associates (e.g., Kagan et al., 1988). Children in this sample had been classified as inhibited or uninhib-ited at 21 months, based on a BI assessment during a laboratory visit. At 21 months, 4 years, and 5.5 years, children who were classed as inhibited at 21 months had significantly lower HP than uninhibited children across a range of labora-tory tasks (Kagan et al., 1984; Reznick et al., 1986). However, at 7.5 years, HP in such episodes no longer differentiated the two original behavioral groups (Kagan et al., 1988).

In addition to tonic between-group differences in HP, Kagan also found that inhibited children tended to show larger decreases in HP to stressors compared to uninhibited children. At every age of assessment (from 21 months to 7.5 years of age), children who were classed as inhibited at 21 months were more likely than uninhibited children to show a decrease in HP across the trials of a test or across a battery of cognitive tests. In addition, inhibited children attained their lowest HP earlier in the course of the assessment than did uninhibited children (Kagan et al., 1988).

At 7.5 years of age, children who were inhibited at 21 months showed larger decreases in HP than uninhibited children in response to a change in posture from sitting to standing. Such a postural change is accompanied by a reflexive increase in sympathetic influence on the heart, and Kagan regards a larger decrease in HP upon standing as being indicative of a more reactive sympathetic nervous system (Kagan, 1994).

As well as relating HP at each age to the initial 21-month behavioral assess-ment, Kagan also examined the concurrent relations of HP and BI. At each age of assessment (21 months, 4, 5.5, and 7.5 years), HP during quiet or active tasks was significantly negatively correlated with BI as assessed at that age (Kagan et al., 1984, 1988; Reznick et al., 1986). Furthermore, children who were inhibited at all four assessment ages had the lowest levels of mean HP at each age, while consistently uninhibited children had the highest levels of mean HP at each assessment (Kagan, Reznick, & Snidman, 1988).

Outside the Harvard work, only a few studies have examined HP in relation to BI. In an unselected sample of 2-year-olds, Calkins and Fox (1992) found that BI was unrelated to baseline levels of HP. Studies that have found significant BI–HP relations have utilized either large sample sizes or a selection procedure to focus on extremes. Scarpa, Raine, Venables, and Mednick (1997) explored HP–BI relations in a large, unselected sample ($N = 1,793$) of 3-year-old Maurit-ian children. The sample was divided up into high, medium, and low BI groups based on observer ratings of BI. The high BI group showed significantly higher baseline heart rate (lower HP) than the low BI group, an effect which remained significant after covarying ethnicity, gender, physical size, and crying behavior.

Marshall and Stevenson-Hinde (1998) examined relations between BI and HP in a sample of children who were selected at 4 years according to criteria for high or low BI on the basis of both a maternal questionnaire and interviewer ratings at home. Subsequent laboratory assessments at 4.5 and 7 years involved further BI ratings as well as the measurement of HP over a series of episodes. No significant relations emerged between BI and HP over the whole sample. However, HP predicted which of the children in the high inhibition group would remain inhibited at 7 years: HP at 4.5 years was significantly lower for children with high BI ratings at 4.5 who remained highly inhibited at 7 years compared to children with high BI at 4.5 years who were less inhibited at 7 years. Contemporaneous relations between inhibition and HP at 4.5 years were found only when attachment security was considered in combination with inhibition grouping (Stevenson-Hinde & Marshall, 1999), as discussed at the end of this chapter.

After reviewing the use of various psychophysiological measures in the assessment of childhood anxiety, Beidel (1989) concluded that HP is a useful variable in this respect and that researchers in the field would be well advised to include it in their assessment battery. This conclusion was based mainly on the evidence from Kagan's longitudinal study, in which HP was among the strongest physiological correlates of BI. In the decade since Beidel's review, HP has remained a useful variable in BI research, especially when methods permit extreme children to be examined. HP is easily measured in the laboratory, and further analyses can provide measures of heart period variability.

Heart Period Variability

The time interval between heartbeats shows distinct variability (Appel, Berger, Saul, Smith, & Cohen, 1989). Heart period variability (HPV), which is correlated with HP, is primarily a result of fluctuations in nerve traffic at the sinoatrial (SA) pacemaker node of the heart, which receives input from both the sympathetic and parasympathetic branches of the autonomic nervous system. Challenging situations would be expected to elicit a decrease in HPV, a change which could be mediated by sympathetic cardiac activation, withdrawal of parasympathetic cardiac influence, or a combination of the two (Cacioppo et al., 1994). These autonomic changes are primarily mediated via the hypothalamus and associated brainstem centers, which share connections to the amygdala (McDonald, 1998). In the context of the BI model, it may be expected that inhibited children would display lower HPV than uninhibited children, an expectation that was supported by Kagan's initial study. Kagan and colleagues employed heart period standard deviation (HPSD) as a measure of total HPV in their longitudinal study of BI. In the first assessment of Kagan's longitudinal sample at 21 months, behaviorally inhibited children had significantly lower HPSD than uninhibited children (Kagan et al., 1984). When assessed at 4 years and 5.5 years, children classed as inhibited at 21 months had significantly lower HPSD compared with children who had been originally classed as uninhibited. Furthermore, at both 4 and 5.5 years, HPSD was also significantly negatively correlated with inhibition as assessed at those ages (Reznick et al., 1986). However, at 7.5 years, HPSD was not significantly correlated with BI as rated at that age, and it no longer differentiated the groups that were based on the 21-month assessment (Kagan et al., 1988).

Since the original findings concerning HPSD, other studies of BI–HPV relations have employed cardiac measures that are designed to index aspects of HPV that have been related to specific neural processes. The global HPV signal may be thought of as a composite of several periodic oscillations plus an element of aperiodic noise. Parsing the HPV signal into its component oscillations can potentially yield information about the autonomic mediation of cardiac activity: parasympathetic influences on the SA node are manifested in relatively high-frequency oscillations in HP, while sympathetic influences produce lower frequency oscillations in HP (Akselrod et al., 1981; Saul, 1990). Many studies utilizing measures of HPV in the child development literature have been concerned with the high-frequency oscillations in HP that are associated with the breathing cycle. During inspiration, HP transiently decreases, while during expiration, HP increases (Hirsch & Bishop, 1981). These oscillations constitute the reflexive phenomenon of respiratory sinus arrhythmia (RSA), which primarily reflects the influence of the vagus nerve, a primary component of the parasympathetic nervous system, on the heart (see Berntson, Cacioppo, & Quigley, 1993). Porges (1995) has presented RSA as an index of the primary vagal cardiorespiratory center in the brainstem, the nucleus ambiguus (NA). Behavioral influences on RSA are likely to be mediated by descending projections to the NA from higher structures such as the amygdala, which could direct a reduction in baroreflex gain under conditions of stress or effort. This would effectively diminish the basal level of vagal activity that is subject to phasic inhibitory modulation, leading to a decrease in RSA magnitude (Berntson et al., 1993). Placing this in the context of a neurobiological model of BI leads to the hypothesis that high BI would be associated with low RSA. However, as the following studies show, support for this hypothesis is mixed.

Early studies of RSA and social behavior in infants found an association between RSA and approach or withdrawal tendencies. Richards and Cameron (1989) found that baseline RSA was positively correlated with parent-reported tendency to approach at 6 months of age. Fox and Stifter (1989; see also Fox, 1989) found that infants with high baseline RSA at 14 months of age exhibited shorter latencies to approach a stranger and a novel object compared to infants with low RSA. Similar associations were found between 5-month RSA and 14-month behavioral measures: infants with high RSA at 5 months of age displayed a shorter latency to approach a stranger 9 months later.

Despite the promising findings of the above studies, BI–RSA associations have not been forthcoming from the literature. There was no relation between a measure of RSA and fearful behavior in infancy (Snidman, Kagan, Riordan, & Shannon, 1995), and BI and RSA were unrelated at 24 months (Calkins & Fox,

1992). Rubin, Hastings, Stewart, Henderson, and Chen (1997) found that RSA "did not clearly distinguish consistently inhibited toddlers from the other groups" (p. 480). In early childhood, Marshall and Stevenson-Hinde (1998) found no significant relations between RSA and BI in a longitudinal study at 4.5 and 7 years of age. Thus, despite promising early findings relating RSA to approach behaviors in infancy, studies with toddlers and children have failed to find similar relations at later ages. This is somewhat surprising, given Kagan's original finding of lower total HPV being associated with higher BI through early childhood and the high correlation of total HPV measures with measures of RSA (Marshall, 1997). Further work is addressing this issue, including the examination in BI studies of dynamic changes in RSA with changes in behavioral tasks, which has proved to be a valuable technique in research in other domains of early regulatory behaviors (e.g., Calkins, 1997).

Since RSA primarily indexes parasympathetic cardiac influences, and given the focus of Kagan's BI model on sympathetic arousal, some researchers have felt that a measure of cardiac sympathetic activation may be more appropriate for use within the BI framework. Low-frequency (LF) variability in HP (around 0.1 Hz) has been proposed as a marker of cardiac sympathetic modulation (e.g., Pagani, Rimoldi, & Malliani, 1992). However, although the evidence for a substantial sympathetic contribution to LF oscillations is strong, any attempt to quantify this contribution is hindered by the added presence in this frequency range of variability that is parasympathetically mediated (Malik & Camm, 1993). In an attempt to overcome this problem, Snidman (1989) proposed a novel method for interpreting the LF component by making the extreme assumption that parasympathetic influences are evenly distributed across the entire HPV power spectrum. Using this rationale, Snidman demonstrated that changes in HPV over several cognitive tasks in inhibited preschoolers were more likely to be the result of sympathetic influences than were HPV changes in uninhibited children. However, controversy still surrounds the precise interpretation of LF variability, although Mezzacappa, Kindlon, Earls, and Saul (1994) suggest that changes in LF power with postural manipulations may be a useful indicator of sympathetic influences on HP. One study of BI to utilize this technique is that of Snidman et al. (1995), who examined LF variability during supine and erect sleep in early infancy in relation to later measures of BI. LF variability during erect sleep at 2 weeks and 4 months of age was related to BI scores at 14 and 21 months. Furthermore, changes in LF variability between the supine and erect postural states at 2 weeks predicted BI at 14 and 21 months. These results were interpreted as indicating that LF power, and the change in LF power with postural manipulations at 2 weeks of age, were early markers of sympathetically-biased cardiac autonomic regulation that predicted later behavioral regulation.

In summary, measures of heart period variability have promoted an active area of investigation in BI research. Kagan's initial findings of lower HPV in inhibited children compared with uninhibited children sparked further inquiry using more specific indices of HPV. Future studies may further benefit from a more integrated approach to indexing cardiac autonomic influences (e.g., Cacioppo et al., 1994). More specific measures of cardiac sympathetic influence (e.g., preejection period; PEP) are currently being used in some developmental labs, which may lead to new insights into the autonomic dynamics of BI.

EVALUATING THE MODEL

Over the course of this chapter, we have reviewed the evidence for physiological correlates of BI as predicted by the neurobiological model of increased amygdaloid excitability to novelty in inhibited children. Although each physiological measure has contributed to our understanding of BI, it is also evident that BI–physiology associations may be modest, possibly hiding underlying complexity. This issue is of fundamental relevance to the entire BI construct (e.g., Kagan, 1998).

Testing the hypotheses generated by the neurobiological model of BI involves monitoring peripheral response systems that are some way downstream of the brain structure of interest—namely, the amygdala. The multiply-determined nature of peripheral physiological responses immediately introduces noise into physiological data that may be unrelated to the activity of the subcortical site of interest. In addition, the developmental plasticity of both behavior and physiology adds further complexity. However, patterns of change as well as stability have always been of inherent interest to BI researchers (e.g., Kagan et al., 1988), and recent BI work has focused on related issues including the dynamic relations of behavioral change with changes in physiological measures (e.g., Fox et al., 2001).

Although the amygdala-based neurobiological model of BI makes certain physiological predictions, the above complications raise many issues for researchers interested in the physiological correlates of BI. For instance, Kagan (1998) notes that "a particular cortisol level has no universal meaning across a large sample of infants and young children" (p. 193). Despite such reservations, work stemming from the neurobiological model of BI has contributed much to our understanding of inhibited behavior in young children (Kagan, 1994). Indeed, the inclusion of the physiological level of analysis in the BI paradigm has provided a focus on neurobehavioral regulation that has stimulated a plethora of research and debate. In addition, with the realization of the complexities, there has also been an increased understanding of how BI–physiology relations may be clarified by particular conceptual, methodological, and analytical strategies. We will now illustrate two such strategies, with examples from our own work.

THE WAY FORWARD

Selecting Individuals Who Are Extreme

BI is usually treated as a dimension, reflecting *quantitative* differences between individuals. However, to return the point made in the first section, any dimension of BI may also reflect *qualitative* differences between individuals, and natural selection may even have fostered "phenotypically inflexible genotypes" in certain environments (e.g., Wilson et al., 1994). Thus, as Kagan has argued over the years, a focus on extremes may promote both theoretical and empirical progress. The identification of extreme groups can be strengthened by the use of longitudinal samples to enable the identification of children who are consistently inhibited or uninhibited. In turn, such an approach may aid the investigation of the physio- logical correlates of BI. For example, Marshall and Stevenson-Hinde (1998) found that although BI was moderately stable between 4.5 and 7 years, predicted relations between BI and cardiac measures did not occur at either age. However, children who were highly inhibited at both ages had lower HP at 4.5 years than children who were uninhibited at both ages. Furthermore, these consistently inhibited children had significantly lower HP at 4.5 years than children who were highly inhibited at 4.5 years but who became less inhibited at 7 years (Marshall & Stevenson-Hinde, 1998).

Integration with Measures from Other Domains

As we have already seen with BI and cortisol (Nachmias et al., 1996), another domain that might inform relations between BI and physiology is the child's quality of attachment to mother. Whereas BI assessments involve behavior in unfamiliar situations such as meeting a stranger, attachment assessments involve behavior on reunion with a well-known caregiver, usually mother. The attach- ment focus is on how a child uses mother as a "secure base" when distressed, typically observed in reunion episodes within the Ainsworth strange situation. Thus, a behaviorally inhibited child—who would withdraw when a stranger entered and, after being left alone, would not be comforted by the stranger— might nevertheless be relatively easily soothed by the mother upon reunion with her and hence judged securely attached. A characteristic of secure children is that, through interactions with a sensitively responsive caregiver, they are able to express their emotions in a relaxed and open manner. With such "emotional coherence" (Grossmann & Grossmann, 1991, p. 108) secure children would be expected to show a direct relation between autonomic functioning and behavior to strangers.

Relations between cardiac functioning and BI were indeed clarified by taking attachment status into account (Stevenson-Hinde & Marshall, 1999). Analyses of HP were carried out using three BI groups (low, medium, and high) and two attachment groups (secure and insecure). Only the secure children showed the predicted relation between cardiac functioning and BI—with HP highest for the low BI group, next highest for the medium BI group, and lowest for the high BI group. In other words, secure children were enabled to express their own tem- peramental style in a coherent way, permitting physiology and behavior to be in tune with each other.

Thus, according to attachment theory, secure children feel free to express their emotions in the knowledge that they will be supported, whereas insecure children have developed behavioral "strategies" for dealing with emotions. These involve closing down for the avoidant (A) pattern, over-reacting for the ambivalent (C) pattern, or taking charge for the controlling (CN) pattern. Such strategies may interfere with or even over-ride the predicted relation between behavioral style and indices of autonomic functioning. It is therefore possible that the significant relations that have been found between BI and HP (and BI and cortisol, as shown above) may reflect only secure children, who in fact comprise about two-third of most samples.

New Directions

New directions to enhance our understanding of the biology of BI concern the development of new tasks and methodologies to test facets of the amygdala model, as well as refinements of the model itself.

The current neurobiological model of BI proposes that the main difference between inhibited and uninhibited children lies in the sensitivity of subcortical limbic structures such as the amygdala. However, as outlined earlier in this chapter, such a difference could also arise at other points in the sequence of physiological events associated with the processing of novel stimuli. One possible refinement of the model involves differences between inhibited and uninhibited children in very early processing of sensory stimuli. Some BI studies are now including the assessment of early- and mid-latency auditory evoked responses in order to investigate this possibility.

Another current direction is the use of eyeblink startle paradigms, which are providing insights into the dynamics of emotion and motivation (see Lang, 1995). The eyeblink startle response is of greater amplitude when an acoustic startle probe is presented during the presentation of negatively-valenced visual stimuli compared with the presentation of positively-valenced stimuli. A related methodology is the use of startle probes in classical conditioning paradigms. The magnitude of the startle response is potentiated when it is elicited in the presence of a stimulus that signals an impending aversive event (Brown, Kalish, & Farber, 1951). Michael Davis and colleagues mapped the neural circuitry of acoustic startle in the rat, and found that projections from the central nucleus of the amygdala to a specific area of the brainstem modulate the fear-potentiated startle response (Davis, 1986; Davis, Falls, Campeau, & Kim, 1993). This led to the proposal that the magnitude of startle potentiation in a fear state may index the sensitivity of the amygdala to fear-related stimuli. Individual differences in eyeblink startle response under a fear state would therefore be expected to relate to individual differences in the susceptibility to fear or anxiety, including BI. In adults, high trait anxiety has been associated with augmented fear-potentiated startle responses (Grillon, Ameli, Foot, & Davis, 1993). In the BI literature, very few studies have used any kind of startle paradigm, and findings have been mixed (Snidman & Kagan, 1994; Schmidt et al., 1997; Schmidt & Fox, 1998). Although theoretically a promising area, very little work has examined potentiated startle in the context of fear conditioning in children, although some current work with adolescents is addressing this issue (Grillon et al., 1999).

Obviously, any BI model should keep abreast of developments in the neurobiological literature concerning the neural bases of fear and anxiety. For instance, it has been emphasized that the amygdala is not a homogeneous structure—neither structurally nor functionally (e.g., Swanson & Petrovich, 1998). Other related structures nearby include the bed nucleus of the stria terminalis, which has a similar morphology to the central nucleus of the amygdala. Like the central nucleus, the bed nucleus activates hypothalamic and brainstem targets involved in behavioral and physiological signs of fear and anxiety. As outlined above, much of the literature relating the amygdala to fear responses is based on animal models of startle responses during classical conditioning. In these models, fear responses to a benign cue (the conditioned stimulus, e.g., a tone or a light) are potentiated by repeated presentation of an aversive stimulus (the unconditioned stimulus, e.g., a shock) in the presence of the cue. Damage to the central nucleus of the amygdala reduces the magnitude of the fear potentiation effect of the conditioned stimulus (Davis et al., 1993). Although this literature is the basis for the amygdala-centered neurobiological model of BI, it is important to note that BI is not usually viewed in the context of classical fear conditioning: there are no obvious analogues for conditioned and unconditioned stimuli in the BI model. Recent work from the animal literature may provide new insights into this problem. Davis and colleagues have suggested that the bed nucleus plays a role in the potentiation of fear responses in situations which do not involve classical conditioning, such as prolonged exposure to a threatening, unfamiliar ambient environmental stimulus (e.g., a bright light). Davis (1998) suggests that the amygdala might be linked to more stimulus-specific fear, while the bed nucleus might be involved in a form of longer-latency anxiety. Further research may clarify the relation of the amygdala to the bed nucleus, as well as the role of the bed nucleus in the behavioral manifestation of anxiety. Such investigations should be monitored, as they have implications for neurobiological models of BI.

One other point concerns the heavy reliance of the BI model on data from non-primate animal studies. Inferences from such animal models are most likely well-founded, but the BI model needs to keep abreast of developments in the primate/human literature. Models of affective neuroscience in humans are utilizing various sources of data, including functional neuroimaging techniques and patients with amygdala damage, to provide new insights on the role of the amygdala in humans (Davidson & Irwin, 1998). It is vitally important that the model of BI keeps apace of these developments.

Another implication of the reliance of the BI model on non-primate animal data is the neglect of the influence of the frontal cortex, especially the prefrontal region. Primates and non-primates do differ in the convergence of projections from cortical areas to the amygdala (McDonald, 1998). In addition to these between-species differences in mature individuals, developmental change occurs within a species. In humans, the prefrontal area of the cortex shows a prolonged functional maturation over childhood (Goldman-Rakic, Bourgeois, & Rakic,

1997) and is thought to play a crucial role in the development of behavioral control and self-regulation (Diamond, 1990; Kopp, 1982). The prefrontal cortex has regulatory control over subcortical structures, including the capability to inhibit amygdaloid responses (Morgan, Romanski, & Ledoux, 1993). This implies that models of BI should make some reference to this developmental increase in cortical regulatory capability. For example, over time, children form cognitive representations of the world that are assumed to have cortical substrates. For some behaviorally inhibited children, continued pairing of novel situations and the subjective experience of fear in infancy and early childhood may result in representations of the world as a fear-provoking and uncertain place (Derryberry & Reed, 1994). By middle childhood, these representations may start to regulate and guide behavior, with a decreasing dependence on the physiological states originally associated with BI (Marshall & Stevenson-Hinde, 1998). The understanding of BI in infancy through middle childhood and its dynamic relations to physiological variables may therefore have consequences for understanding the development of representations of the self in relation to the world. In turn, this knowledge may aid the understanding of the manifestation of social anxiety as discussed in many of the diverse chapters in the current volume.

ACKNOWLEDGEMENTS

We thank R. A. Hinde and E. B. Keverne for their constructive comments throughout the preparation of this chapter.

REFERENCES

Appel, M. L., Berger, R. D., Saul, J. P., Smith, J. M., & Cohen, R. J. (1989). Beat-to-beat variability in cardiovascular variables: Noise or music? *Journal of the American College of Cardiology, 14,* 1139–1148.

Akselrod, S., Gordon, D., Ubel, F. A., Shannon, D. C., Barger, A. C., & Cohen, R. J. (1981). Power spectrum analysis of heart rate fluctuation: A quantitative probe of beat-to-beat cardiovascular control. *Science, 213,* 220–213.

Baerends, G. P. (1976). The functional organization of behaviour. *Animal Behaviour, 24,* 726–738.

Beidel, D. C. (1989). Assessing anxious emotion: A review of psychophysiological assessment in children. *Clinical Psychology Review, 9,* 717–736.

Berntson, G. G., Cacioppo, J. T., & Quigley, K. S. (1993). Respiratory sinus arrhythmia: Autonomic origins, physiological mechanisms, and psychophysiological implications. *Psychophysiology, 30,* 183–196.

Bowlby (1969/1982). *Attachment and Loss, Volume 1: Attachment.* London: Hogarth.

Bronson, G. W. (1972). Infants' reactions to unfamiliar persons and novel objects. *Monographs of the Society for Research in Child Development, 37* (3; Serial No. 148).

Brown, J. S., Kalish, H. I., & Farber, I. E. (1951). Conditioned fear as revealed by magnitude of startle response to an auditory stimulus. *Journal of Experimental Psychology, 41,* 317–328.

Cacioppo, J. T., Uchino, B. N., & Berntson, G. G. (1994). Individual differences in the autonomic origins of heart rate reactivity: The psychometrics of respiratory sinus arrhythmia and preejection period. *Psychophysiology, 31,* 412–419.

Calkins, S. D. (1997). Cardiac vagal tone indices of temperamental reactivity and behavioral regulation in young children. *Developmental Psychobiology, 31,* 125–135.

Calkins, S. D. & Fox, N. A. (1992). The relations among infant temperament, security of attachment, and behavioral inhibition at twenty-four months. *Child Development, 63,* 1456–1472.

Calkins, S. D., Fox, N. A., & Marshall, T. R. (1996). Behavioral and physiological antecedents of inhibited and uninhibited behavior. *Child Development, 67,* 523–540.

Charney, D. S. & Deutch, A. (1996). A functional neuroanatomy of fear and anxiety: Implications for the pathophysiology and treatment of anxiety disorders. *Critical Reviews in Neurobiology, 10,* 419–446.

Davidson, R. J. (1992). Anterior cerebral asymmetry and the nature of emotion. *Brain and Cognition, 20,* 125–151.

Davidson, R. J. (1994). Temperament, affective style, and frontal lobe asymmetry. In G. Dawson & K. W. Fischer (Eds.), *Human behavior and the developing brain* (pp. 518–536). New York: Guilford.

Davidson, R. J. (1998). Anterior electrophysiological asymmetries, emotion, and depression: Conceptual and methodological conundrums. *Psychophysiology, 35,* 607–614.

Davidson, R. J. & Irwin, W. (1998). The functional neuroanatomy of emotion and affective style. *Trends in Cognitive Sciences, 3,* 11–21.

Davidson, R. J., Jackson, D., & Larson, C. (2000). Human electroencephalography. In J. T. Cacioppo, L. G. Tassinary, & G. G. Berntson (Eds.), *Principles of psychophysiology* (2nd edn.) (pp. 27–52). New York: Cambridge University Press.

Davidson, R. J. & Rickman, M. (1999). Behavioral inhibition and the emotional circuitry of the brain. In L. A. Schmidt & J. Schulkin (Eds.), *Extreme fear, shyness, and social phobia* (pp. 67–87). Oxford: Oxford University Press.

Davis, M. (1986). Pharmacological and anatomical analysis of fear conditioning using the fear-potentiated startle paradigm. *Behavioral Neuroscience, 100,* 814–824.

Davis, M. (1992). The role of the amygdala in fear and anxiety. *Annual Review of Neuroscience, 15,* 353–375.

Davis, M. (1998). Are different parts of the extended amygdala involved in fear versus anxiety? *Biological Psychiatry, 44,* 1239–1247.

Davis, M., Falls, W. A., Campeau, S., & Kim, M. (1993). Fear-potentiated startle: A neural and pharmacological analysis. *Behavior Brain Research, 58,* 175–198.

de Kloet, E. R. (1991). Brain corticosteroid receptor balance and homeostatic control. *Frontiers in Neuroendocrinology, 12* (2), 95–164.

de Haan, M., Gunnar, M. R., Tout, K., Hart, J., & Stansbury, K. (1998). Familiar and novel contexts yield different associations between cortisol and behavior among 2-year-old children. *Developmental Psychobiology, 33,* 93–101.

Derryberry, D. & Reed, M. A. (1994). Regulatory processes and the development of cognitive representations. *Development and Psychopathology, 8,* 215–234.

Diamond, A. (1990). Developmental time course in human infants and infant monkeys, and the neural bases of inhibitory control in reaching. In A. Diamond (Ed.), *The development and neural bases of higher cognitive functions* (pp. 637–676). New York: New York Academy of Sciences Press.

DiLalla, L. F., Kagan, J., & Reznick, J. S. (1994). Genetic etiology of behavioral inhibition among 2-year-old children. *Infant Behavior and Development, 17,* 405–412.

Fentress, J. C. (1991). Analytical ethology and synthetic neuroscience. In P. Bateson (Ed.), *Development and integration of behavior* (pp. 7–120). Cambridge: Cambridge University Press.

Fox, N. A. (1989). Psychophysiological correlates of emotional reactivity during the first year of life. *Developmental Psychology, 25,* 364–372.

Fox, N. A. (1991). If it's not left, it's right. Electroencephalograph asymmetry and the development of emotion. *American Psychologist, 46*, 863–872.

Fox, N. A. (1994). Dynamic cerebral processes underlying emotion regulation. In N. A. Fox (Ed.), The development of emotion regulation: Biological and behavioral considerations (pp. 152–166). *Monographs of the Society for Research in Child Development, 59* (2–3, Serial No. 240).

Fox, N. A., Calkins, S. D., & Bell, M. A. (1994). Neural plasticity and development in the first two years of life: Evidence from cognitive and socioemotional domains of research. *Development and Psychopathology, 6*, 677–696.

Fox, N. A., Henderson, H. A., Rubin, K., Calkins, S. D., & Schmidt, L. A. (2001). Continuity and discontinuity of behavioral inhibition and exuberance: Psychophysiological and behavioral influences across the first 4 years of life. *Child Development, 72*, 1–21.

Fox, N. A. & Stifter, C. A. (1989). Biological and behavioral differences in infant reactivity and regulation. In G. A. Kohnstamm, J. E. Bates, & M. K. Rothbart (Eds.), *Temperament in childhood* (pp. 169–183). Chichester: John Wiley.

Goldman-Rakic, P. S., Bourgeois, J. P., & Rakic, P. (1997). Synaptic substrates of cognitive development: Life-span analysis of synaptogenesis in the prefrontal cortex of the nonhuman primate. In N. A. Krasnegor, G. Reid Lyon, & P. S. Goldman-Rakic (Eds.), *Development of the prefrontal cortex: Evolution, neurobiology, and behavior* (pp. 27–48). Baltimore: Paul H. Brookes.

Goldsmith, H. H., Buss, A. H., Plomin, R., Rothbart, M. K., Thomas, A., Chess, S., Hinde, R. A., & McCall, R. B. (1987). Roundtable: What is temperament? *Child Development, 58*, 505–529.

Gosling, S. D. & John, O. P. (1999). Personality dimensions in nonhuman animals: A cross-species review. *Current Directions in Psychological Science, 8*, 69–75.

Grillon, C., Ameli, R., Foot, M., & Davis, M. (1993). Fear-potentiated startle: Relationship to the level of the state/trait anxiety in healthy subjects. *Biological Psychiatry, 33*, 566–574.

Grillon, C., Merikangas, K. R., Dierker, L., Snidman, N., Arriaga, R. I., Kagan, J., Donzella, B., Dikel, T., & Nelson, C. (1999). Startle potentiation by threat of aversive stimuli and darkness in adolescents: A multi-site study. *International Journal of Psychophysiology, 32*, 63–73.

Grossmann, K. E. & Grossmann, K. (1991). Attachment quality as an organizer of emotional and behavioral responses in a longitudinal perspective. In C. M. Parkes, J. Stevenson-Hinde, & P. Marris (Eds.), *Attachment across the life cycle* (pp. 93–114). London: Routledge.

Gunnar, M. R. (1994). Psychoendocrine studies of temperament and stress in early childhood: Expanding current models. In J. E. Bates & T. D. Wachs (Eds.), *Temperament: Individual differences at the interface of biology and behavior* (pp. 175–198). Washington, DC: American Psychological Association.

Gunnar, M. R., Tout, K., de Haan, M., Pierce, S., & Stansbury, K. (1997). Temperament, social competence, and adrenocortical activity in preschoolers. *Developmental Psychobiology, 31*, 65–85.

Harmon-Jones, E. & Allen, J. J. (1997). Behavioral activation sensitivity and resting frontal EEG asymmetry: Covariation of putative indicators related to risk for mood disorders. *Journal of Abnormal Psychology, 106*, 159–163.

Hinde, R. A. (1987). *Individuals, relationships, and culture*. Cambridge: Cambridge University Press.

Hirsch, J. A. & Bishop, B. (1981). Respiratory sinus arrhythmia: How breathing pattern modulates heart rate. *American Journal of Physiology, 241*, H620–H629.

Kagan, J. (1994). *Galen's prophecy*. New York: Basic Books.

Kagan, J. (1998). The biology of the child. In N. Eisenberg (Ed.), W. Damon (Series Ed.), *Handbook of child psychology. Vol. 3: Social, emotional, and personality development* (pp. 177–235). New York: Wiley.

Kagan, J., Reznick, J. S., Clarke, C., Snidman, N., & Garcia-Coll, C. (1984). Behavioral inhibition to the unfamiliar. *Child Development, 55*, 2212–2225.

Kagan, J., Reznick, J. S., & Snidman, N. (1985). Temperamental inhibition in early childhood. In R. Plomin & J. Dunn (Eds.), *The study of temperament: Changes, continuities, and challenges* (pp. 53–65). Hillsdale, NJ: Erlbaum.

Kagan, J., Reznick, J. S., & Snidman, N. (1987). The physiology and psychology of behavioral inhibition in children. *Child Development, 58*, 1459–1473.

Kagan, J., Reznick, J. S., & Snidman, N. (1988). Biological bases of childhood shyness. *Science, 240*, 167–171.

Kagan, J., Reznick, J. S., Snidman, N., Gibbons, J., & Johnson, M. O. (1988). Childhood derivatives of inhibition and lack of inhibition to the unfamiliar. *Child Development, 59*, 1580–1589.

Kagan, J. & Snidman, N. (1991). Temperamental factors in human development. *American Psychologist, 46*, 856–862.

Kagan, J., Snidman, N., & Arcus, D. (1998). The value of extreme groups. In R. B. Cairns, L. R. Bergman, & J. Kagan (Eds.), *Methods and models for studying the individual: Essays in honor of Marian Radke-Yarrow* (pp. 65–80). Thousand Oaks, CA: Sage.

Kopp, C. B. (1982). Antecedents of self-regulation: A developmental perspective. *Developmental Psychology, 18*, 199–214.

Lang, P. J. (1995). The emotion probe: Studies of motivation and attention. *American Psychologist, 50* (5), 372–385.

LeDoux, J. E. (1995). Emotion: Clues from the brain. *Annual Reviews of Psychology, 46*, 209–235.

Malik, M. & Camm, A. J. (1993). Components of heart rate variability: What they really mean and what we really measure. *American Journal of Cardiology, 72*, 821–822.

McDonald, A. J. (1998). Cortical pathways to the mammalian amygdala. *Progress in Neurobiology, 55*, 257–332.

Marshall, P. J. (1997). *Behavioral inhibition, heart period, and heart period variability in young children and their mothers.* Unpublished doctoral dissertation. University of Cambridge, Cambridge, UK.

Marshall, P. J. & Stevenson-Hinde, J. (1998). Behavioral inhibition, heart period, and respiratory sinus arrhythmia in young children. *Developmental Psychobiology, 33*, 283–292.

Maynard Smith, J. (1989). *Evolutionary genetics.* Oxford: Oxford University Press.

Mezzacappa, E., Kindlon, D., Earls, F., & Saul, J. P. (1994). The utility of spectral analytic techniques in the study of beat-to-beat heart rate variability. *International Journal of Methods in Psychiatric Research, 4*, 29–44.

Morgan, M. A., Romanski, L. M., & LeDoux, J. E. (1993). Extinction of emotional learning: Contribution of medial prefrontal cortex. *Neuroscience Letters, 163*, 109–113.

Nachmias, M., Gunnar, M., Mangelsdorf, S., Parritz, R. H., & Buss, K. (1996). Behavioral inhibition and stress reactivity: The moderating role of attachment security. *Child Development, 67*, 508–522.

Pagani, M., Rimoldi, O., & Malliani, A. (1992). Low-frequency components of cardiovascular variabilities as markers of sympathetic modulation. *Trends in Pharmacological Sciences, 13*, 50–54.

Porges, S. W. (1995). Orienting in a defensive world: Mammalian modifications of our evolutionary heritage. A Polyvagal Theory. *Psychophysiology, 32*, 301–318.

Reznick, J. S., Kagan, J., Snidman, N., Gersten, M., Baak, K., & Rosenberg, A. (1986). Inhibited and uninhibited children: A follow-up study. *Child Development, 57*, 660–680.

Richards, J. E. & Cameron, D. (1989). Infant heart-rate variability and behavioral developmental status. *Infant Behavior and Development, 12*, 45–58.

Rubin, K. H., Hastings, P. D., Stewart, S. L., Henderson, H. A., & Chen, X. (1997). The consistency and concomitants of inhibition: Some of the children, all of the time. *Child Development, 68*, 467–483.

Saul, J. P. (1990). Beat-to-beat variations of heart rate reflect modulation of cardiac auto-nomic outflow. *News in Physiological Sciences, 5,* 32–37.

Scarpa, A., Raine, A., Venables, P. H., & Mednick, S. A. (1995). The stability of inhib-ited/uninhibited temperament from ages 3–11 years in Mauritian children. *Journal of Abnormal Child Psychology, 23,* 607–618.

Scarpa, A., Raine, A., Venables, P. H., & Mednick, S. A. (1997). Heart rate and skin con-ductance in behaviorally inhibited Mauritian children. *Journal of Abnormal Psychol-ogy, 106,* 182–190.

Schulkin, J. (1994). Melancholic depression and the hormones of adversity. *Current Direc-tions in Psychology, 3,* 41–44.

Schulkin, J. & Rosen, J. B. (1999). Neuroendocrine regulation of fear and anxiety. In L. A. Schmidt & J. Schulkin (Eds.), *Extreme fear, shyness, and social phobia* (pp. 140–172). Oxford: Oxford University Press.

Schmidt, L. A. & Fox, N. A. (1998). Fear-potentiated startle responses in temperamentally different human infants. *Developmental Psychobiology, 32,* 113–120.

Schmidt, L. A., Fox, N. A., Rubin, K. H., Sternberg, E., Gold, P. W., Smith, C., & Schulkin, J. (1997). Behavioral and neuroendocrine responses in shy children. *Developmental Psychobiology, 30,* 127–140.

Snidman, N. (1989). Behavioral inhibition and sympathetic influence on the cardiovascu-lar system. In J. S. Reznick (Ed.), *Perspectives on behavioral inhibition* (pp. 125–138). Chicago: University of Chicago Press.

Snidman, N. & Kagan, J. (1994). The contribution of infant temperamental differences to acoustic startle response. [Abstract.] *Psychophysiology, 31,* S92.

Snidman, N., Kagan, J., Riordan, L., & Shannon, D. (1995). Cardiac function and behav-ioral reactivity during infancy. *Psychophysiology, 32,* 199–207.

Spyer, K. M. (1989). Neural mechanisms involved in cardiovascular control during affec-tive behaviour. *Trends in Neurosciences, 12,* 506–513.

Stansbury, K. & Gunnar, M. R. (1994). Adrenocortical activity and emotion regulation. In N. A. Fox (Ed.), The development of emotion regulation: Biological and behavioral considerations (pp. 108–134). *Monographs of the Society for Research in Child Devel-opment, 59* (2–3, Serial No. 240).

Stevenson, J., Batten, N., & Cherner, M. (1992). Fears and fearfulness in children and ado-lescents: A genetic analysis of twin data. *Journal of Child Psychology and Psychiatry, 33,* 977–985.

Stevenson-Hinde, J. & Glover, A. (1996). Shy girls and boys: A new look. *Journal of Child Psychology and Psychiatry, 37,* 181–187.

Stevenson-Hinde, J. & Marshall, P. J. (1999). Behavioral inhibition, heart period, and res-piratory sinus arrhythmia: An attachment perspective. *Child Development, 70,* 805–816.

Stevenson-Hinde, J. & Shouldice, A. (1995). 4.5 to 7 years: Fearful behavior, fears and worries. *Journal of Child Psychology and Psychiatry, 36,* 1027–1038.

Stevenson-Hinde, J. & Shouldice, A. (1996). Fearfulness: Developmental consistency. In A. J. Sameroff & M. M. Haith (Eds.), *The five to seven year shift: The age of reason and responsibility* (pp. 237–252). Chicago: University of Chicago Press.

Stevenson-Hinde, J., Stillwell-Barnes, R., & Zunz, M. (1980). Subjective assessment of rhesus monkeys over four successive years. *Primates, 21,* 66–82.

Sutton, S. K. & Davidson, R. J. (1997). Prefrontal brain asymmetry: A biological substrate of the behavioral approach and inhibition systems. *Psychological Science, 8,* 204–210.

Swanson, L. W. & Petrovich, G. D. (1998). What is the amygdala? *Trends in Neuroscience, 21,* 323–331.

Takahashi, L. K. & Kalin, N. H. (1999). Neural mechanisms and the development of indi-vidual differences in behavioral inhibition. In L. A. Schmidt & J. Schulkin (Eds.), *Extreme fear, shyness, and social phobia* (pp. 97–118). Oxford: Oxford University Press.

Tinbergen, N. (1963). On the aims and methods of ethology. *Zeitschrift für Tierpsychologie, 20,* 410–433.

Tout, K., de Haan, M., Campbell, E. K., & Gunnar, M. R. (1998). Social behavior correlates of cortisol activity in child care: Gender differences and time-of-day effects. *Child Development, 69,* 1247–1262.

Wilson, D. S., Clark, A. B., Coleman, K., & Dearstyne, T. (1994). Shyness and boldness in humans and other animals. *Trends in Ecology & Evolution, 9,* 442–446.

Wilson, D. S., Coleman, K., Clark, A. B., & Biederman, L. (1993). Shy-bold continuum in pumpkinseed fish (*Leponis gibbosus*)—an ecological study of a psychological trait. *Journal of Comparative Psychology, 107,* 250–260.

Chapter 4

Positively Shy! Developmental Continuities in the Expression of Shyness, Coyness, and Embarrassment

Vasudevi Reddy

SHYNESS AS A POSITIVE EXPERIENCE
Issues of Definition
BEHAVIOURAL EXPRESSIONS OF SHYNESS, COYNESS, AND EMBARRASSMENT:
    THE CENTRALITY OF AMBIVALENCE
Gaze Aversion: Ambivalent Combinations and Timing
Smiles and Smile Controls
Movements of the Head and Hands, Speech Disturbances and Blushing
DEVELOPMENTS IN THE EXPRESSION OF POSITIVE SHYNESS AND COYNESS
Empirical Assumptions and Theoretical Confusions
Shy/Coy Expressions in Early Infancy
Continuities and Developments in Positive Shyness and Coyness
CONCLUSION
REFERENCES

SHYNESS AS A POSITIVE EXPERIENCE

Interpersonal shyness can be a positive experience. The majority of studies of shyness in infancy and childhood, however, have viewed it as a factor that detracts from early interpersonal and object-related engagements, and deprives the child of exploratory and playful experiences. The general focus, in effect, has been on

International Handbook of Social Anxiety: Concepts, Research and Interventions Relating to the Self and Shyness. Edited by W. Ray Crozier and Lynn E. Alden.
© 2001 John Wiley & Sons Ltd.

fearful shyness (Kagan, Reznick, & Snidman, 1988; Kaplan, 1972). However, shyness can result from, and lead to, positive interpersonal experience. We sometimes turn our eyes away from others not just in fear or anxiety but even in desired intimacy—a sentiment neatly expressed by Solomon to his beloved a few thousand years ago,[1] and still experienced today.

Shyness and related emotions can cause, and be caused by, positive feelings in others as well as in the self. For example, praise, especially excessive praise, has been identified as an elicitor of embarrassment in adults (Buss, 1978, cited in Buss, 1980) and even in toddlers (Lewis, Sullivan, Stanger, & Weiss, 1989). Adult embarrassment in certain situations has been shown to lead to an increase in observers' positive feelings towards the embarrassed person (Edelmann, 1982; Miller, 1996; Semin & Manstead, 1982). Bartlett and Izard (1972) showed that shyness has significantly higher self-rated reports of experienced pleasantness than any other "negative" emotion. These data support the findings of Izard (1972) and Mosher and White (1981) which suggest that although it has a strong negative component as well, shyness is not experienced as completely negative and has both a pleasantness dimension and a high level of social interest and attraction (Izard & Hyson, 1986). Many have drawn a distinction between dispositional or trait shyness on the one hand, and situational or state shyness on the other—a distinction which may affect just how positively shyness is experienced. Asendorpf (1985, cited in Asendorpf, 1990) found that shyness and happy mood correlated significantly positively when looking at state shyness within individuals, but correlated significantly negatively when comparing individuals on trait shyness in all situations.

Although William James (1890, p. 432) saw shyness and related states as "incidental emotions" and "pure hindrances" despite which we get along, others have argued that moderate amounts of shyness serve a positive adaptive function in enabling the handling of novel and unpredictable situations and persons (Izard & Hyson, 1986) and in inhibiting socially unacceptable behaviour and thus facilitating co-operation in groups (Ford, 1987, cited by Cheek & Briggs, 1990). The complete absence of shyness may in fact be argued to be an antisocial characteristic (Cheek & Briggs, 1990). Some expressions of shyness and embarrassment, such as blushing, may serve an appeasing function (Castelfranchi & Poggi, 1990). Miller argues that they are perceived as involuntary (and therefore genuine) acknowledgements of social transgressions, thus functioning to appease and smooth possibly difficult interactions (Miller, 1996, p. 145). Further, interpersonal shyness may be attractive because it functions as a comment on an interpersonal act by the other. It may be a fundamental marker for a psychologically significant event and reaction, thus both signalling and inviting interest from the other. However, we know little as yet about how such expressions are perceived and responded to in interaction, or how attractive they are found.

---

[1] "Turn away thine eyes from me, For they have overcome me" (*The Song of Songs*, Part IV, 5).

The behavioural expressions of positive and entirely fearful shyness, while showing some overlap, also differ considerably. As will be shown, much theoretical importance has been attached to more positive expressions of shyness, but relatively little direct empirical exploration. This chapter, while acknowledging some of the difficulties in drawing a sharp distinction between different forms of shyness, attempts to describe the expression of positive shyness through infancy and early childhood.

Issues of Definition

Several issues of definition and focus need first to be clarified. After briefly discussing these issues, this chapter describes the behavioural expressions of shyness and related terms reported in the literature, then discusses some of the ambiguities and contradictions in the field between the descriptions on the one hand, and theories of their development on the other. Some recent research on early shyness is presented briefly which addresses some of these problems and suggests a new look at the psychological implications of age-related continuities and changes in the expressions. The chapter concludes with a description of the continuities and changes in the expressions and offers an alternative explanation of the presence of early and continuing positive shyness.

First, *what are we talking about when we talk of shyness?* Shyness refers both to what has been called a trait or predisposition (i.e., individuals who may be characterized as shy or not shy) and to what has been called a state (i.e., a transient reaction of shyness to particular situations). This chapter will only deal with the development of expressions of "state shyness". Even so, the word still covers a multitude of meanings both in its lay and its scientific usage and there are a number of other overlapping words such as embarrassment, coyness, bashfulness, self-consciousness, inhibition and social anxiety that are often used either interchangeably or as closely linked in different contexts and situations. Several of these terms refer to a rather "fuzzy concept of nonengagement in social interaction" (Asendorpf, 1993) and are used differently by different writers. Most writers tend to group sets of terms together. For instance, shyness may be grouped with embarrassment, or with stranger anxiety and differentiated from coyness and embarrassment (Asendorpf, 1990, 1993), or with sheepishness and bashfulness (Izard & Hyson, 1986), or with a form of self-consciousness and embarrassment on the one hand, and fear on the other (Buss, 1980; Lewis, 1995). The groupings are variable even within the same writers, and reflect a genuine fuzziness of the boundaries of the phenomena. Clearly we cannot proceed with a description until we reach some agreement about our terms; but rather than attempt to resolve the overlap in an artificial way (see Cheek & Briggs, 1990, and Harris, 1984, for a discussion of the futility of such an enterprise), this chapter acknowledges the fuzzy boundaries and seeks to describe in behavioural and contextual terms, expressions which belong in a central area of overlap involving the terms shyness, coyness, bashfulness and embarrassment. The use of contextual information in all descriptions should clarify the psychological meaning of the expressions in every instance, regardless of the semantic label attached.

Second, there is a sizeable literature drawing conceptual and developmental *distinctions between different kinds of shyness and different kinds of embarrassment.* These distinctions, not all in agreement with each other, need to be recognised in order for any description of expressions of shyness to be understood, and in order for such descriptions to be relevant to questions of continuity in the phenomenon. There are three relevant theorists who have drawn distinctions between different kinds of shyness and embarrassment. Buss (1980, 1986) distinguishes between early appearing fearful shyness and late appearing self-conscious shyness, the former appearing early in infancy and the latter not until about 5 years. In a related vein, Lewis (1995; see also this volume, *Chapter 5*) distinguishes between shyness which arises in the first year and is entirely avoidant and negative, and two forms of embarrassment which arise later—one born of self-exposure, arising at around 18 months to 2 years, and one born of self-evaluation, arising at around 3 years. Similarly, Asendorpf (1993), basing his distinctions on Gray's physiological analysis of the causes of inhibition (Gray, 1980, cited by Asendorpf, 1993), separates inhibition to adult strangers which arises early in development, from inhibition to reinforcement arising later in development, painting a developmental picture very similar to Lewis's distinction between exposure and evaluation, and in essence similar to Buss's distinction between fearful and self-consciousness shyness. All three authors link the later appearing forms of shyness or embarrassment with the development of self-consciousness, although they differ somewhat on the age at which they argue self-consciousness develops and on the behavioural criteria they use to describe and detect these various forms of shyness and self-consciousness. As Table 4.1 shows, all three authors suggest that late in the first year of life there is present a form of shyness, and all three agree that this form of shyness is fearful rather than positive, and is elicited by novel situations and persons, while the later appearing forms of shyness, akin to embarrassment, can contain more positive elements. Izard, however, suggests that even the more ambivalent and positive form of shyness may be present very early in infancy, and may be independent of the development of self-conscious cognitions (Izard & Hyson, 1986). As the present chapter shows, even early in the first year there may be expressions of *non*-fearful shyness elicited by familiar and intimate as well as novel persons and interactions and these expressions need to be recognized and built into existing models of the development of shyness, coyness, and embarrassment.

A third issue that must be dealt with before any description of expressions can be accomplished is: *what we wish to mean by the term "expression".* We could refer simply to the facial and bodily configuration over time that is typical (customarily defined as occurring in at least 50% of cases) of a particular emotion word such as shyness. However, there are two reasons why such an

Table 4.1 Theories of shyness and related phenomena in infancy and childhood

Theories	Forms of the phenomena	Predicted age of onset in development	Eliciting contexts	Expressive behaviour
Buss (1980, 1986)	Two forms of shyness: — Early fearful shyness	7 to 9 months (primitive, sensory self)	Novelty, strangers (increased by high tendency to wariness and distress and low sociability)	*Shyness*: Diminution of social behaviour; gaze avoidance; shrinking back or keeping distance; reduced speech; distress, wariness
	— Late (self-conscious) shyness (public self-awareness, embarrassment)	From 5 years of age (advanced, cognitive self-awareness of self as social object)	Novel contexts; conspicuousness; social roles; overpraise; breaches of privacy; exposure of wrongdoing; ridicule	*Embarrassment*: Tentativeness; blushing; giggling; silly smiles; gaze avoidance
Lewis (1995)	Shyness	Middle of first year	Strangers, fear	*Shyness*: Reduced sociability: reductions in gaze, vocalizations, smiles and contact
	Two forms of embarrassment: — Exposure	18 months	Being observed by others	*Embarrassment*: Smiling, gaze aversion, and face/body touching; coy or silly behaviour
	— Self-evaluation	3 years	Potential evaluations of performance by others	
Asendorpf (1990, 1993)	Two forms of social inhibition — Inhibition towards strangers (wariness)	From approximately 8 months, reactions more extended with age, continues to adulthood	Meeting unfamiliar adults (with peers peak at 20 months)	*In infancy*: Clear-cut *wariness*: wary brow with gaze, wary averted gaze, avoidance, cry face or crying. *In early childhood*: mixture of wariness and sociability; lengthy coy expressions of smiling with gaze aversion—peaks at 3 to 4 years
	— Social-evaluative inhibition (evaluative fear)	From 20 months or later; continues into adulthood; strong at adolescence	Anticipation of negative or insufficiently positive evaluation by others (involves perspective taking); Embarrassment is a reactive form of the same emotion	*Embarrassment*: Blushing, smiles with gaze aversion before the apex of the smile ends
Izard & Hyson (1986)	Shyness (a discrete, fundamental emotion)	8 months, or earlier	Novel social situations, attraction, interest and fear on meeting strangers	Avoidance of communicative contact, gaze and head aversion, alternating with smiles, coy/sheepish appearance

interpretation of expression is inadequate. First, the typical configuration may in fact be both hard to find and rather misleading as a criterion. Not all individuals show all expressive components and no one shows any of them all the time. Ellgring (1986) showed that most depressive patients display only one or two of the repertoire of the classical indicators of depression. Similarly Asendorpf (1988) found substantial individual differences in the externalization of dispositional shyness in adults, with cross-situational stability *within* individuals, but low mean intercorrelations of 0.23 between five different indicators of shyness *across* individuals. The cross-individual stability of expressions may also be related to the strength of an emotion—weak expressions of state embarrassment show more idiosyncratic variations and also tend to be less clearly perceivable (Miller, 1996). Further, expressions are not static phenomena—the expression of shyness has a short-term course which must be taken into account—the expression appears to consist of a process of change rather than a peak display (Ricard & Decarie, 1993; Waters, Matas, & Sroufe, 1975). This process of expression may also have a changing pattern even within one incident; based on descriptions of pathological shyness in adults, Kaplan (1972) offers a fascinating description of shyness as occurring in two phases, the first involving the actual social trauma with imminent or manifest anxiety, and the second involving an attempt to regain poise through a variety of means including reticence or playing a role. Such dynamic change in the expression must concern us in trying to understand the expression of shyness in children as well.

Further, *expressions are relational rather than individual events.* How an expression manifests itself may depend very much on who is there to perceive it, and the form of the specific relationship and context (Fridlund, 1994). The effect on observers of embarrassment, for example, can vary depending on their own embarrassability (Miller, 1996), on their own self-esteem (Helmreich, Aronson, & LeFan, 1970) and on their perception of other characteristics (such as competence) of the embarrassed person (Aronson, Willerman, & Floyd, 1966). Cultural differences in the expression of emotional reactions emphasize this point. In some cultures—such as Javanese (Schouten, 1935, cited by van der Molen, 1990), Indian, and Japanese—the expression of shyness, far from being considered problematic, is actually encouraged and is often considered a virtue, quite different from the assertiveness and frankness apparently valued, e.g., in American and Israeli cultures (Zimbardo, 1977). To the extent that interpersonal expressions are open from early in development to the social responses they obtain, expressions of shyness and related emotions must develop differently in contexts where they are viewed with approval and indulgence from contexts where they are considered a problem. Not only are they likely to differ in the intensity and frequency with which they are expressed, but specific configurations and aspects of expression may be differentially present. Nonetheless, the evidence suggests that there may well be universals at the simplest level of something that is recognized as, and functions as, shyness, coyness, bashfulness, or embarrassment (Eibl-Eibesfeldt, 1989).

BEHAVIOURAL EXPRESSIONS OF SHYNESS, COYNESS, AND EMBARRASSMENT: THE CENTRALITY OF AMBIVALENCE

So what do shyness, coyness and embarrassment look like? Several authors have argued that embarrassment and shyness are discrete emotions with a distinctive display even though there are no special facial muscle movements identified with them (e.g., Izard & Hyson, 1986; Keltner, 1995). The single identifying feature common to them is the ambivalent avoidance of communicative contact in some form, for however short a length of time. Izard and Hyson (1986) suggest that the absence of unique facial movement is itself significant—the particular motivational function of shyness is to *avoid* rather than signal emotional communication; thus shyness functions to decrease affective interchange. The behavioural signs of ambivalent avoidance described in the literature centre on combinations of, on the one hand, affiliative or interested behaviours such as gaze and smiling with, on the other, gaze aversion, head aversion, hand movements which either obscure key communicative parts of the self, or nervously explore the self, and loss of or disturbances in speech and vocal contact. In the more negative forms of these emotional reactions, such as in shame or painful self-consciousness, these avoidant behaviours are not combined with evident affiliation and interest. In addition to these forms of ambivalent avoidance, there is blushing, which is arguably the most intense expression of ambivalence, but which may paradoxically serve to increase communicative contact.

Gaze Aversion: Ambivalent Combinations and Timing

Gaze aversion appears to be a critical feature of shyness (and also of coyness, bashfulness and embarrassment) mainly when it is in ambivalent combination with gaze and affiliation. In infancy, "shy" behaviours observed in stranger approach situations often consist of an alternation between, or combination of, avoidance and affiliative behaviour, giving the appearance of coyness or bashfulness (Izard & Hyson, 1986). Gaze aversion without such ambivalence has been seen as more indicative of shame (Izard & Hyson, 1986), or of simple avoidance or regulation of unpleasant arousal. Asendorpf emphasizes that in order for behaviour to be considered as social inhibition (whether of the stranger wariness or the social evaluative kind), there must be evidence of social approach motivation in the first place (whether affiliative, attached, or sexual), rather than a simple absence of motivation to engage (Asendorpf, 1993).

The timing of the gaze aversion in relation to specific events—i.e., to the approach rather than mere presence of a stranger—can also be used to establish the distinction between avoidance and mere disinterest (Sroufe, 1977; Waters, Matas, & Sroufe, 1975). In behavioural terms, ambivalence can be identified in a number of ways: there can be a combination of avoidant and affiliative behaviour, or there can be a rapid alternation between them. The combination of gaze or head aversion with smiling has been emphasized by many observers as the single most important behavioural criterion for identifying shyness, coyness or embarrassment (Amsterdam, 1972; Asendorpf, 1990; Bretherton & Ainsworth, 1974; Greenberg & Marvin, 1982; Izard & Hyson, 1986; Keltner, 1995; Lewis et al., 1989; Young & Decarie, 1977). Similarly, the combination of smiling while maintaining physical distance has been carefully described and argued by Ricard and Decarie (1993) to be an appropriate and positive, rather than a fearful and negative, strategy for becoming familiar with strangers.

Asendorpf (1990) showed that the relative timing of the various components of the expression is critical for its perception by others as a shy or embarrassed smile. Smiles in which the gaze aversion began at least half a second before the beginning of the decline of the peak of the smile (the peak offset) were significantly more often perceived by judges as shy or embarrassed smiles than those in which the gaze aversion began even about half a second after the peak offset. Asendorpf suggests that the aversion of gaze at the most communicative point of the smile (i.e., at its peak intensity) strongly conveys the flavour of ambivalence to observers and may in fact, in an embarrassing situation, be a response to the smile itself—i.e., an attempt to reduce the level of intimacy at the peak of the smile (Asendorpf, 1990).

Lewis (1995) emphasizes that it is active gaze *aversion* rather than gaze *avoidance* that characterizes embarrassment, the former typically involving an immediate return of gaze after the aversion. In shyness or shame (or even fear), on the other hand, Lewis suggests that gaze aversion is typically not followed by an immediate gaze-return motion (Lewis, 1995). Most studies of coyness, stranger wariness, shyness and embarrassment, however, have not described patterns of gaze return (Kaltenbach, Weinraub, & Fullard, 1980; Waters et al., 1975; Ricard & Decarie, 1993) although this may be implied in descriptions of long-drawn-out coy episodes in preschoolers involving a mixture of smiling and gaze aversion and lasting from 15 to 30 seconds (Greenberg & Marvin, 1982).

Ambivalence involving a mixture of smiling and gaze aversion has also been noted in adults as being typical of coyness, shyness and embarrassment. Such expressions have been reported in adults in experimental situations by Asendorpf, as mentioned above (Asendorpf, 1990), and by Keltner (1995). Eibl-Eibesfeldt (1989) presents photographic evidence from a range of cultures—including many less industrialised societies—showing adults, particularly women and girls, engaging in sequences of intense smiles with eye contact accompanied by gaze aversion and then gaze return, often with the smile still continuing.

Smiles and Smile Controls

Several authors note that sheepish smiles and sheepish grins (Miller, 1996) are common in shyness, coyness, bashfulness or embarrassment, although precise descriptions of sheepishness are not common!

Amsterdam (1972; Amsterdam & Greenberg, 1977) described coyness to self in the mirror as involving slight rather than broad smiles. In an unusual description of expressive behaviour in 9- and 12-month-old infants, Young and Decarie catalogued a variety of facial behaviours and differentiated between coy smiles and shy smiles (Young & Decarie, 1977). Coy smiles are described as slight open-mouthed smiles with the upper teeth visible, with the lips retracted fully outward and upward in a crescent shape but not rolled in or everted out. They involve sparkling eyes with narrowing of the eyelids and a pouch under each eye. Shy smiles on the other hand are close-mouthed smiles, with only moderate lip retraction outward and upward, and no narrowing of eyelids or sparkling of the eyes. These authors also differentiate the positive "shy smile" and "coy smile" from an undifferentiated "shy face" (involving no smile), and the negative "fear face" and "sad face".

Keltner (1995) has shown a distinct pattern of muscular smile controls with which many of us will be familiar. They are muscular actions of the lower part of the face, consisting of movements such as pressing the lips together, or puckering, stretching, funnelling, biting, wiping, or sucking them, or raising the chin, dropping the jaw, puffing the cheeks, or bulging the tongue; all of these serve to counteract the upward pull of the smile, or obscure the smile, or both. Although all participants showed such controls, those who reported being embarrassed showed them more frequently, for longer and in greater number than those who reported merely being amused.

This attempted control of smiles, often unsuccessful, is an interesting phenomenon in itself. In Keltner's study, the participants displayed the smile controls in a rest period following an embarrassment-inducing session in which their posed facial expressions were videotaped. In this situation the embarrassment appeared to concern participants' consciousness of their ridiculousness (in making and holding posed facial expressions) and appearance. We do not know, however, whether smile controls also occur in other embarrassment-inducing situations, such as anticipation of evaluation, being exposed to an unexpected audience, seeing yourself in a mirror, being over-complimented, etc.

Smile controls may be due to an attempt not to show one's feelings to an unfamiliar or unknown audience—either because it is potentially rude to be caught smiling in some situations (in which case unsuccessful smile controls could lead in a circular way to further embarrassment), or because it may be too intimate to smile in certain interpersonal situations (Argyle & Dean, 1965). In two incidents involving embarrassment of two different kinds, I observed one 20-month-old with a contorted mouth in attempts to suppress a smile, in which his lips were pressed together and puckered, with the smile still visible. In one incident, the child called out for the mother from another part of the house; the mother answered from a room in which she was sitting with a number of visitors. Hearing the mother's response (and not knowing about the arrival of the visitors) the child came into the room and headed towards the mother with a big smile, saw the visitors, was slightly taken aback, didn't stop smiling but puckered and pressed his lips together and, moving more quickly towards his mother, buried his face in her lap (with his back to the visitors); the mother could then see a broader, unsuppressed smile on his face when he lifted his head slightly. In a second incident a month later, a similar puckered smile (although less broad) was observed, when the child was asked to sing in front of a visitor. The embarrassed smile controls in these two incidents could be explained as an attempt by the child to restore his dignity following an unexpected violation of intimacy (i.e., he was unexpectedly observed calling affectionately to his mother and smiling) or following a situation of conspicuousness. Interestingly, smile controls of this very obvious kind were not observed as a part of the child's repertoire after this period. Smiles often signify a loss of dignity; photographing traditional non-Westernized adults in India, for example, often leads to severe attempts to suppress smiles and look serious, with chastisement directed to the (Westernized) photographer who tricks them into smiling, and particularly into "showing the teeth" (personal observation).

Movements of the Head and Hands, Speech Disturbances and Blushing

There are several studies that have described head movements as a characterizing feature of shyness, coyness or embarrassment. Keltner (1995) showed that embarrassed adult participants more frequently turned their heads away from directly facing the camera and were more likely than amused participants to move their heads downward and to the left. Lewis (1995) noted that embarrassment displays more often involve a tilting of the head and upward gaze aversion rather than downward, which is more characteristic of shyness, shame or fear. Bretherton and Ainsworth (1974), similarly, observed that coy expressions in 12-month-olds involved smiling gaze aversion while cocking or ducking the head to the side. Young and Decarie (1977) describe downward and possibly sideways holding of the head in shy smiles and in shy face (without smiles) by 9- and 12-month-old infants, but do not describe any movements of the head in coy smiles. Although Amsterdam (1972; Amsterdam & Greenberg, 1977) did not describe head movements in coy looks, it is implied in her description of the glances rather than direct looks of toddlers. It is possible that head *tilting* movements are more typical of infants than of adults. In Eibl-Eibesfeldt's photographic records, there are instances of adults tilting as well as turning their heads away while smiling. To some extent the tilting of the head may be a direct effect of the contradictory influences of wanting to look and wanting to turn away. It is unclear whether this is an aspect of the expression which may be controlled by cultural norms about adult behaviour—e.g., about not being too childish by showing obvious coyness/shyness.

Edelmann and Hampson (1979) found that embarrassed adults showed higher amounts of body motion during an embarrassing question than unembarrassed adults. The measure of body motion in this study combined both manipulative gestures (consisting of hand movements while not communicating anything) and the percentage of time spent in other movements (moving the legs and feet or shifting posture during each response). Keltner (1995) found that embarrassed adults tended to touch their faces more frequently than amused adults do.

There may be two different patterns of arm movements in shyness, coyness, bashfulness or embarrassment described in the child and adult literature. One is a pattern shown in photographic records from different cultures by Eibl-Eibesfeldt (1989), of hands flying up to cover the smiling mouth. This seems to occur in very positive situations appearing to result from intimacy and exposure to attention—e.g., compliments, or being suddenly at the centre of attention. Similarly in Japanese culture it is customarily believed that the wide kimono sleeve developed precisely to serve such a function—i.e., to cover the impolite or too revealing smile, while allowing communicative contact with the eyes to continue.

The other is a pattern described in adult embarrassment by Keltner (1995) and in toddlers by Lewis (Lewis et al., 1989); in this pattern the hand movements are described as small and discrete, showing nervous touching of parts of the face, body, hair or clothing. Lewis (1995) suggests that such hand movements occur in embarrassment but not in shame, shyness or fear. Nervous touching of the body, hair, face and clothing, he argues, reflects the person's active focus on the self as a social object in embarrassment, while in shyness, shame or fear the person is likely to be immobile rather than self-exploratory (Lewis, 1995). Izard and Hyson (1986) note automanipulation as one of the characteristics of shy behaviour.

Edelmann and Hampson (1979) found that adults who later reported embarrassment during an experimental procedure showed significantly more frequent speech disturbances during the critical time. Ricard and Decarie (1993) found that in a comparison of overall smiling, looking at and vocalizing behaviour of 9-month-old infants to an adult stranger, only vocalizing (frequency and duration) showed any significant differences between infants who eventually approached the stranger and those who did not. Similarly, Buss (1980) reports reduced speech in shyness, with longer pauses between utterances and lowered volume. In general, speech disturbances have been studied as indicative of dispositional rather than state shyness (Asendorpf, 1990).

Blushing (see Edelmann, this volume, *Chapter 14*) is one of those classic indicators of shyness, coyness, bashfulness and embarrassment which everyone agrees is an important criterion, but about which we know remarkably little. We know that it occurs earlier than the 5 years suggested by Buss (1980; see Darwin, 1872/1998), but it clearly occurs later than the other signs of embarrassment (Lewis, 1995). Future research needs to resolve questions of individual and contextual differences in the origins and development of blushing in early childhood.

DEVELOPMENTS IN THE EXPRESSION OF POSITIVE SHYNESS AND COYNESS

Empirical Assumptions and Theoretical Confusions

We have so far briefly mentioned some theories and predictions concerning different forms of shyness and embarrassment and their development, and we have considered at length the behavioural expression of shyness, coyness and embarrassment in infancy and childhood. Several of the theories about the development of shyness and embarrassment described below are premised upon the *apparent absence* of positive shy, coy, bashful or ambivalent behaviour early in development. However, this is problematic, for the evidence for its absence is neither clear nor convincing.

Buss (1980), for example, sees early or fearful shyness which arises in the first year as consisting entirely of apprehensive, anxious or fearful reactions. Indeed, this form of shyness continues into childhood and adulthood with the same reactions. The signs of such shyness are gaze aversion, shrinking, speech disturbances and an absence of smiling, except for the "occasional sickly smile". That is, the smile in this case appears to be a concession to the social occasion, serving to reflect misery or anxiety rather than any happiness at all. The immediate causes of such shyness may be novelty, the presence of others, or the attention-giving actions of others. On the other hand, the later developing self-conscious shyness or embarrassment which arises from the development of a "social self" and a "cognitive self" after 5 years, is revealed in blushing, gaze aversion, silliness, funny smiles, a nervous laugh, giggling and hands covering the mouth or entire face. This form of shyness or embarrassment can be caused by overpraise, impropriety, breaches of privacy, incompetence and also conspicuousness. Although Buss does not use the label "coy", his description of the kinds of reactions likely in the two forms clearly divides the two on a polarity of negative versus positive/ ambivalent reactions; the presumed absence in the early years of ambivalent smiling, giggling and covering of the mouth or face, and particularly blushing, provide important data for his theory about the late development of self-conscious shyness and embarrassment.

Coyness or ambivalence is also important in Michael Lewis's theory of the development of embarrassment, serving as evidence which separates early shyness in the first year from the two forms of embarrassment which appear at 18 months and 3 years. Coyness *can* indicate embarrassment, and can be identified by the several behavioural features mentioned earlier. The two forms of embarrassment, according to Lewis, both arise from the development of objective self-awareness—the first as a response to an awareness of exposure, and the second as a response to an awareness of evaluation (or potential evaluation). This model is congruent with Darwin's suggestion that while blushing is always caused by observing the attention of other people and thus turning one's own attention to oneself, it is only sometimes (and later in development) related to performing in front of others (Darwin, 1872/1998). Thus being observed, being complimented, and observing oneself in the mirror can, in the 18-month-old infant, all lead to the embarrassment of exposure, although in the older child (after 3 years) or adult, the same situations can lead to consciousness of evaluation.

On the other hand, an early form of shyness (dispositional or trait shyness in the form of fearfulness of others) may be observable from as early as 3 months of age, and is "more likely to be a biological than a psychological variable", showing continuities in personality over development. Such shyness in early infancy is characterized by lower frequencies of gaze, of vocalizations and of smiles to their mothers, and higher preference for solitary play (Lewis & Feiring, 1989, cited in Lewis, 1995). Lewis is very specific in what he refers to as "shy" here, not referring to those aspects of shyness called sheepishness, bashfulness or coyness, but focusing on what may be called inhibition and what he calls "asocial" characteristics (Lewis, 1995).

Miller (1996), supporting Buss (1980), doubts that even the 18-month-old could be said to show embarrassment, or that the mirror image can be said to provoke embarrassment at all. Coy, bashful or sheepish behaviour, according to him, may be a learned response to "better treatment" (i.e., more positive responses) from others in social predicaments, and "may result from the combined influences of the inborn temperaments that make some children shy" (Kagan et al., 1992, cited by Miller, 1996), "and the sheer marvellous novelty of self-recognition" (Miller, 1996, pp. 77–78). Nonetheless, he concludes that even these signs of apparent embarrassment are not present in young children *before* they become self-conscious, i.e., before 18 months or 2 years of age.

However, there *is* convincing evidence that expressions of coyness and ambivalent or positive shyness are displayed in appropriate contexts before 18 months—and at least by the end of the first year, if not earlier. Amsterdam (1972), for instance, noted "coy smiles" in 14-month-olds looking at themselves in a mirror; Lewis and Brooks-Gunn (1979) noted "coyness or silly behaviour which might be taken to indicate embarrassment" in the mirror in 20% of 15-month-olds; Bretherton and Ainsworth (1974) noted that a small proportion of 12-month-olds showed "coy smiles" to the stranger in an experimental situation; and Ricard and Decarie (1993) found ambivalence and alternations of smiling and gaze aversion in 9-month-olds in interactions with strangers.

Asendorpf (1990, 1993) too sees ambivalent shyness as a developmental index, noting that in contrast to the low frequencies reported in studies of toddlers, coy or ambivalent reactions are reported to increase with age both in length and in likelihood of occurrence, reaching a peak at 3 to 4 years (Greenberg & Marvin, 1982). Amsterdam (1972) also found that even though coy looks were first observed at 14 months, only after 20 months did two-thirds of the infants show it. Noting the evidence of coyness at the end of the first year, Asendorpf sees ambivalent reactions—i.e., combination of smiles and gaze aversion—as a key component of wariness towards strangers, whether in infants or in adults (by implication from the data of Kaltenbach et al., 1980), but argues that the late onset of ambivalence (after 12 months) is significant—earlier in infancy the reactions vary between sociable-positive and negative-avoidant, but with age clear-cut negative responses become less likely. Although Asendorpf cautions that similarities in felt uneasiness and inhibited behaviour—reflected in lay psychological terms such as coy, shy or inhibited—may arise from different psychological processes, he leaves open the question of whether the coy smile of young children when they meet a stranger is identical to the embarrassed smile of the adult (Asendorpf, 1990), and presumes that the coy smile does not occur earlier than at the end of the first year.

Thus, the key empirical question seems to centre around displays of ambivalent shyness, coyness, bashfulness or sheepishness in the appropriate contexts, which are most likely to be contexts of exposure rather than of evaluation. The evidence so far is clear that these can be elicited in at least some children even in laboratory situations by 9 months of age at the earliest (Ricard & Decarie, 1993). However, there is reason to doubt the completeness of this evidence. As Asendorpf (1990) noted, there is a peculiar asymmetry in research on shyness. Studies of early shyness have focused on certain kinds of eliciting contexts—i.e., novelty and strangeness. Given that stranger anxiety is known to begin towards the end of the first year, studies have not sought such displays in these contexts before about 9 months of age, and have ignored other contexts in which shyness might be elicited. Studies of shyness at older ages, however, have ignored stranger anxiety and have focused on other contexts. Theories of shyness have naturally focused more broadly on attentional exposure and conspicuousness and violations of intimacy or positive social comments even from familiar persons but have relied on the asymmetrical empirical evidence available (only stranger anxiety situations in infancy) to draw their developmental models. Attentional exposure and conspicuousness can also occur in situations of intimacy—a situation that is much more common in early infancy than is stranger wariness. It is thus possible that this expressive pattern may be displayed in certain intimate contexts in which the infant receives focused attention from others, even earlier than 9 months. There are also positive reasons to believe that this may be the case. There have been reports of smiling with simultaneous gaze aversion at 2 and 3 months of age (Brazelton, Koslowski, & Main, 1974; Stern, 1974), although these reports provide no detailed description of the expressive configuration or its contexts. In the only systematic study of its kind, Stifter and Moyer (1991) report positive gaze aversions in 5-month-olds during peekaboo games with their mothers. These expressions occurring within a high arousal game have been necessarily interpreted primarily as a self-regulation of arousal rather than as indicative of any interpersonal emotion.

Shy/Coy Expressions in Early Infancy

Shy/coy smiles have recently been reported even in 2-month-olds in a longitudinal study of five infants from 7 to 20 weeks of age (Reddy, 2000). All infants showed smiles with simultaneous gaze and/or head aversion (i.e., with the aversion beginning at least 0.5 second before the peak offset of the smile, following Asendorpf, 1990) by at least 11 weeks of age. The smiles were closer to Young and Decarie's (1977) description of coy smiles (with narrowed eyelids and open-mouthed smiles) than shy smiles (with normal eyes and close-mouthed smiles).

The majority (58.7%) of smiles with gaze aversion were followed by an immediate return of gaze to the interactant with gaze return occurring either by the end of the smile or directly after, a pattern noted by Lewis (1995) as a significant indicator of ambivalence rather than avoidance. With age there were higher frequencies of delayed gaze return, consistent with findings regarding increasing control of attention to targets between 1 and 5 months of age (Lamb, Morrison, & Malkin, 1987, cited by Ruff & Rothbart, 1996) and suggesting that control of the components of the expression may increase with age. Head aversion may be more common in infants (accompanying 85% of gaze aversions in this study) than in adults (accompanying 57% of embarrassed reactions, Keltner, 1995). One distinctive feature of these expressions in the infants was the rising and curving movements of the arms (usually of both arms) which more frequently accompanied smiles with gaze and/or head aversion (25%) than ordinary smiles (6%). These movements appeared like rudimentary versions of impulsive covering of the face in adult shyness, and were noticed and remarked on by parents. In further contrast to embarrassed smiles in adults (Keltner, 1995), the infant smiling gaze and/or head aversions were not accompanied by any attempts to suppress the smile through the use of smile controls. The findings suggest that these infant smiles are structurally similar to, but not identical to, the coy smiles described at the end of the first year or later in other studies (Amsterdam & Greenberg, 1977; Bretherton & Ainsworth, 1974; Young & Decarie, 1977). Parents reported that after 15 weeks of age these coy expressions were increasingly directed to strangers and appeared more deliberate and game-like.

Coy smiles were not only responses to strangers and did not appear to reflect wariness as they may do at older ages; they were elicited by familiar adults as well and by themselves in a mirror. The eliciting events for coy smiles were "greetings" (always involving mutual gaze and generally a vocalisation from the other), usually following a short break in interaction. In all infants the first smile following renewal of interaction was more likely to be a coy smile than were second or later smiles, and the mean latencies of coy smiles (time since renewal of interaction) were lower than those of ordinary smiles. These findings suggest both an important similarity and an important difference from the contexts of coy smiles in older children, as at older ages the onset of attention (albeit of familiar persons) was a significant elicitor of coyness. However, unlike in older children, they were not elicited in relation to the infant's performance in any way. In other words, exposure to attention alone, and not evaluation, was a relevant eliciting condition for these smiles.

The parents had spontaneously noticed the more intense smiling gaze aversions in the infants, and had commented that they found the expressions "charming" and "appealing". In a further study we investigated the extent to which naive adults perceived these expressions as shy or coy (Draghi-Lorenz, Reddy, & Morris, in preparation). Naive judges were asked first to label the emotion being experienced by the infant in each of a series of video clips (including examples of this expression as well as other control expressions) and then to rate the emotion in each clip along five different emotion dimensions (happy, shy, interested, surprised, upset). The labels "shy", "coy", "bashful" and "embarrassed" were spontaneously used almost exclusively to describe smiling with simultaneous gaze aversions, although some of the clips showing this expression were more often labelled happy or interested. Across the clips "shy" and related labels were not associated with labels such as "happy" or "interested" (showing high negative correlations), nor with labels describing negative or fearful emotions (no association at all). These labels appeared to be used to describe emotional states orthogonal to the hedonic dimension and different from apprehension and fear. Similarly, on the rating task smiling gaze aversions received higher "shy" ratings than other expressions, particularly when the expression was in a mirror.

The finding that coy smiles are present between 2 and 4 months, which show structural and functional/contextual similarities to those in older children, and which are also spontaneously labelled and rated by naive adults as shy, coy, bashful or embarrassed, suggests strongly that these expressions may not only be present earlier than expected, but that their perceivability and impact on others may contribute to their further development.

Continuities and Developments in Positive Shyness and Coyness

As discussed earlier, most theorists have loaded a heavy psychological responsibility on to the apparent shift from a primarily negative or fearful shyness to ambivalent or positive shyness or coyness. The apparent lateness of this shift (although exactly how late has been a matter of some confusion) has been used as an important datum in several models of shyness and embarrassment. However, the theoretical speculations and the empirical research are not always symmetrical, and we still know relatively little about this phenomenon in infancy.

The data reviewed and presented in this chapter and summarized in Table 4.2 suggest that coy expressions can apparently be found earlier than classic signs of self-consciousness and mirror self-recognition, and are evident at 14 months, 12 months, 9 months, 5 months and even 2 months. These expressions in early infancy are sufficiently structurally and functionally similar to those reported in older infants, to warrant consideration as belonging to the same family of emotional expressions. However, there appear to be important changes with development in various aspects of the expressions and their eliciting contexts. As is the case with many other emotional reactions (Oster, 1997), while an emotional reaction may be present in similar form from early infancy, its affective-contextual meaning (as well as its morphological features) inevitably expands and changes with age.

Table 4.2 Shy, coy and embarrassed reactions at different ages: Expressive patterns and eliciting contexts

Age	Expressive pattern	Interactants	Eliciting contexts
2 months	Coy smiles: smiling with gaze and/or head aversion before peak offset, often with gross curving arm movements (Reddy, 2000), spontaneously labelled and rated by naive adults as shy, coy, bashful or embarrassed (Draghi-Lorenz, Reddy & Morris, under review)	Self in mirror, familiar adults, friendly adult strangers	Onset of attention from others, or from self in mirror, in renewed interaction
4–5 months	Coy smiles becoming games involving several alternations (personal observation)	Friendly adult strangers	While adult stranger and familiar partner not attending to infant
5 months	Smiles followed within 1 second by brief gaze aversion (Stifter & Moyer, 1991)	Mothers	During peekaboo games, mutual smiling
9–12 months	Stranger wariness and ambivalence including wary brow and gaze aversion, coy looks, alternation of smiling and gaze aversion (Bretherton & Ainsworth, 1974; Ricard & Decarie, 1993; Waters et al., 1975)	Adult strangers	Onset of first meeting with strangers
14–15 months	Coy expressions, "silly" behaviour, involving "cute" looks (Amsterdam, 1972; Lewis et al., 1989)	Self in mirror	Presented with a live image of self in mirror
18 months	Shy/coy/embarrassed expressions involving: smiling gaze aversions, hand movements towards the face (Lewis et al., 1989), possibly smile controls (personal observation)	Adult strangers, mother self in mirror	Being exposed to unexpected attention, seeing oneself in a mirror, being over-complimented, being asked to perform
20 months	Wariness towards unfamiliar peers (Brooks & Lewis, 1976; Asendorpf, 1993)	Unfamiliar peers	Meeting unfamiliar peers
3 years	Extended coy smiles involving lengthier expressions (Greenberg & Marvin, 1982)	Adult strangers	Meeting adult strangers
Adults	Shy/coy/embarrassed expressions involving: smiling with gaze aversion before peak offset (Asendorpf, 1990), with face touching and smile controls (Keltner, 1995), hands covering the face (Eibl-Eibesfeldt, 1989), with speech disturbances (Edelmann & Hampson, 1979)	Familiar partners, strangers	Being asked an embarrassing question

The structural similarities in this expression throughout infancy lie in the presence of the ambivalence of smiling with gaze or head aversion, the temporal sequencing of the expression—i.e., with the gaze aversion occurring within the smile (before the end of the peak of the smile), the confirmation of ambivalence with the presence of a majority of gaze-avert-gaze-return-motions rather than gaze aversions which remain away and with the involvement of arm movements rising up over the chest or face in some of these incidents. Structural changes with age in these expressions centre around two aspects of the expression: the development of smile controls and the nature of the arm movements.

Smile controls are completely absent at 2 months, and are clearly evident in adults. There is anecdotal evidence of smile controls at 20 months, but this needs further exploration and confirmation. The absence of early smile controls suggests that the early forms of the expression are uncontrolled reactions to an eliciting context rather than "self-conscious" in the classic sense. However, from the middle of the first year, there is anecdotal evidence that infants begin to play with and use aspects of the expression in games with strangers. This suggests that control over the expression develops gradually, initially in the form of playful or exploratory repetitions of the pattern and eventually in the form of the deliberate inhibition of smiles, probably for simple reasons of attention exposure in the 20-month-old instead of the complex reflections on evaluation in the adult.

The arm movements described in early infancy appear to be gross, uncontrolled reactions in which the arms curve and rise up high over the midline. Clearly, the infant arm movements are nothing like the nervous self-explorations or small face-touching movements described in toddlers and adults (Keltner, 1995; Lewis et al., 1989). They are more likely to be rudimentary forms of the impulsive hand over the mouth shown photographically by Eibl-Eibesfeldt (1989), although evidently lacking in control of the movement. They do not reveal the focus on the self that Lewis (1995) notes as significant in self-exploration, but merely an awareness of the other.

There are contextual similarities and differences in the expressions as well. Shyness, coyness and embarrassment in adults can occur in relation to a stranger or to the remarks of friends and intimates, but rarely in relation to watching the self in a mirror while alone (Miller, 1996). In toddlers, these expressions have been reported in relation to the self in a mirror, to strangers and to the mother and other familiar persons. In the very young infants, only relatively familiar interpersonal partners appear to elicit these expressions; the stranger only elicited them if she first elicited positive interaction rather than just blank looks or avoidance, and the self in a mirror only worked to elicit interaction after previous exposure to the self in the mirror (there is no assumption here that the self in a mirror is seen as anything more than another familiar person). By the end of the fourth month, parental reports suggest that the expression is increasingly elicited by complete strangers. So, early in infancy, these expressions appear to occur in intimate interactions rather than as a response to novelty or ambivalence towards strangers. It makes psychological sense that familiar contexts reveal such ambivalent expressions earlier in infancy than do strange or novel contexts—confident responsiveness to familiar persons and styles of interaction may be more likely to yield a greater variety of emotional expressions.

The function of coy smiles (as judged by a comparison of eliciting events), also shows important continuity and change. Exposure to attention seems to be the key eliciting event leading to these expressions in the first two years. This eliciting event is an important factor even in adult expressions of shyness, coyness and embarrassment, although from the middle of the second year evidence suggests that the individual's own performance becomes relevant to the expression (e.g., being asked to perform, Lewis et al., 1989). The earlier salience of simple exposure to attention as an eliciting context supports the distinction hinted at by Darwin (1872/1998) and theorised by Lewis (1995), between exposure and evaluation as two different elicitors of embarrassment reactions. However, these reactions before 15 months of age are clearly occurring before the development of objective self-awareness and therefore require an alternative explanation to that offered by Lewis (1995). They cannot be explained as simply involving a fearfulness of strangers or as lack of sociability (Lewis, 1995). The ambivalence involved here appears to involve pleasure rather than mere curiosity (Buss, 1980) and a reaction to being positively overwhelmed rather than fear and wariness. They are also unlikely to be simple reflexes, given the specific features of the reactions and their similarity to those appearing later. Mutual gaze, smiling and being smiled at can be arousing at any age (Gale, Spratt, Chapman, & Smallbone, 1975; Martin & Gardner, 1979; Brazelton et al., 1974; Stern, 1974; Field, 1981; Stifter & Moyer, 1991), and gaze aversions can serve to regulate arousal in response to such situations. Asendorpf (1990) suggests that even in adults the gaze aversion during smiling may be a response *to* the smile, reducing the level of intimacy it achieves (Argyle & Dean, 1965). In early infancy smiling gaze aversions are more likely to be responses to the consciousness of the smiling attention of others than consciousness of and reactions to their own smiles. One explanation could be that whereas late occurring coyness and shyness (after 15 or 18 months) may involve a focus of attention on the *self*, earlier coy/shy expressions reveal a focus of attention on the *other*. This explanation is supported also by the differences in the morphology of the expression, viz., the nature of the arm movements and the lack of smile controls.

This interpretation offers support to several important developments in the study of the self. Taken together with findings about early evidence for the self (Bahrick, 1995), and arguments about the interlinked understanding of self and other (Butterworth, 1995; Neisser, 1997; Stern, 1985; Trevarthen, 1993), this evidence of continuities in expression suggests a gradual development from early infancy rather than emergence from a late developing "idea of me" (Lewis, 1994). Further, and intriguingly, these findings suggest that, as William James (1890) argued, in order to look for the self (often implied as a necessary condition for shyness and coyness), we need to look not with*in*, but with*out*, the self. In other words, these early reactions (and their similarities and differences) may initially originate not in an understanding of the *self as an object* of attention, but of the *other as a giver* of attention. The development of such emotional expressions and therefore of the focus on self appears to emerge from an earlier other awareness (Trevarthen, 1993). Further, as Izard suggests (Izard & Hyson, 1986), the occurrence and meaningfulness of these expressions is itself likely to be crucial in shaping the continuing development of this family of emotions.

CONCLUSION

The expression of positive shyness, coyness, bashfulness and embarrassment have been taken as developmental indices by a number of theorists. Its apparent late emergence (in contrast to the early emergence of fearful expressions of shyness) has been used as important evidence in theories of shyness and embarrassment, to indicate the late development of a different class of emotion. However, this expression shows continuities in structure and function from early infancy to adulthood. The particular emotional tone of the expression appears to relate more to intimacy and the stretching of its boundaries than to wariness, whether in infants or in adults. With age, the expression appears to become more controlled and may be increasingly used as a deliberate game or even as a cultural gesture. Also with age, the expression may be elicited by anticipated positive evaluation rather than merely by exposure to attention. This pattern of continuity and change also suggests support for theories arguing for the originally interpersonal bases of self-consciousness.

REFERENCES

Amsterdam, B. (1972). Mirror self-image reactions before age two. *Developmental Psychobiology, 5*, 297–305.

Amsterdam, B. & Greenberg, L. M. (1977). Self-conscious behavior of infants. *Developmental Psychobiology, 10*, 1–6.

Argyle, M. & Dean, J. (1965). Eye-contact, distance and affiliation. *Sociometry, 28*, 289–304.

Aronson, E., Willerman, B., & Floyd, J. (1966). The effect of a pratfall on increasing interpersonal attractiveness. *Psychonomic Science, 4*, 227–228.

Asendorpf, J. B. (1988). Individual response profiles in the behavioral assessment of personality. *European Journal of Personality, 2*, 155–167.

Asendorpf, J. B. (1990). The expression of shyness and embarrassment. In W. R. Crozier (Ed.), *Shyness and embarrassment: Perspectives from social psychology* (pp. 87–118). Cambridge: Cambridge University Press.

Asendorpf, J. B. (1993). Social inhibition: A general-developmental perspective. In H. C. Traue & J. W. Pennebaker (Eds.), *Emotion, inhibition and health* (pp. 81–99). Seattle: Hogrefe and Huber Publishers.

Bahrick, L. E. (1995). Intermodal origins of self-perception. In P. Rochat (Ed.), *The self in infancy: Theory and research* (pp. 349–373). North-Holland: Elsevier.

Bartlett, E. S. & Izard, C. E. (1972). A dimensional and discrete emotions investigation of the subjective experience of emotion. In C. E. Izard (Ed.), *Patterns of emotions: A new analysis of anxiety and depression* (pp. 129–173). New York : Academic Press.

Brazelton, T. B., Koslowski, B., & Main, M. (1974). The origins of reciprocity: The early mother–infant interaction. In M. Lewis & L. A. Rosenblum (Eds.), *The effects of the infant on its caregiver* (pp. 49–76). New York: Wiley.

Bretherton, I. & Ainsworth, M. (1974). Responses of one-year-olds to a stranger in a strange situation. In M. Lewis & L. A. Rosenblum (Eds.), *The origins of fear* (pp. 131–164). New York: Wiley.

Brooks, J. & Lewis, M. (1976). Infants' responses to strangers: Midget, adult and child. *Child Development, 47*, 323–332.

Buss, A. H. (1980). *Self-consciousness and social anxiety.* San Francisco: Freeman.

Buss, A. H. (1986). A theory of shyness. In W. H. Jones, J. M. Cheek, & S. R. Briggs (Eds.), *Shyness: Perspectives on research and treatment* (pp. 39–46). New York: Plenum Press.

Butterworth, G. (1995). The self as an object of consciousness in infancy. In P. Rochat (Ed.), *The self in infancy: Theory and research* (pp. 35–51). North-Holland: Elsevier.

Castelfranchi, C. & Poggi, I. (1990). Blushing as a discourse: Was Darwin wrong? In W. R. Crozier (Ed.), *Shyness and embarrassment: Perspectives from social psychology* (pp. 230–251). Cambridge: Cambridge University Press.

Cheek, J. & Briggs, S. R. (1990). Shyness as a personality trait. In W. R. Crozier (Ed.), *Shyness and embarrassment: Perspectives from social psychology* (pp. 315–337). Cambridge: Cambridge University Press.

Cherny, S. S., Fulker, D. W., Corley, R. P., Plomin, R., & DeFries, J. C. (1994). Continuity and change in infant shyness from 14 to 20 months. *Behavior Genetics, 24*, 365–379.

Darwin, C. (1872/1998). *The expression of the emotions in man and animals* (3rd edn). London: Harper Collins.

Draghi-Lorenz, R., Reddy, V., & Morris, P. (in preparation). Adult perceptions of infant shyness.

Edelmann, R. J. (1982). The effect of embarrassed reactions upon others. *Australian Journal of Psychology, 34*, 359–367.

Edelmann, R. J. & Hampson, S. E. (1979). Changes in non-verbal behaviour during embarrassment. *British Journal of Social and Clinical Psychology, 18*, 385–390.

Eibl-Eibesfeldt, I. (1989). *Human ethology.* New York: Aldine de Gruyter.

Ellgring, H. (1986). Non-verbal expression of psychological states in psychiatric patients. *European Archives of Psychiatry and Neurological Sciences, 236*, 31–34.

Field, T. M. (1981). Infant arousal and affect during early interactions. *Advances in Infancy Research, 1*, 57–100.

Fridlund, A. J. (1994). *Human facial expression: An evolutionary view.* San Diego, CA: Academic Press.

Gale, A., Spratt, G., Chapman, A. J., & Smallbone, A. (1975). EEG correlates of eye contact and interpersonal distance. *Biological Psychology, 3*, 237–245.

Greenberg, M. T. & Marvin, R. S. (1982). Reactions of pre-school children to an adult stranger: A behavioral systems approach. *Child Development, 53*, 481–490.

Harris, P. R. (1984). Shyness and psychological imperialism: On the dangers of ignoring the ordinary language roots of the terms we deal with. *European Journal of Social Psychology, 14*, 169–181.

Helmreich, R., Aronson, E., & LeFan, J. (1970). To err is humanising—sometimes: Effects of self-esteem, competence and a pratfall on interpersonal attraction. *Journal of Personality and Social Psychology, 16*, 259–264.

Izard, C. E. (1972). *Patterns of emotions: A new analysis of anxiety and depression.* New York: Academic Press.

Izard, C. E. & Hyson, M. C. (1986). Shyness as a discrete emotion. In W. H. Jones, J. M. Cheek, & S. R. Briggs (Eds.), *Shyness: Perspectives on research and treatment* (pp. 147–160). New York: Plenum Press.

James, W. (1890). *The principles of psychology* (Vol. 2). New York: Holt.

Kagan, J., Reznick, J. S., & Snidman, N. (1988). Biological bases of childhood shyness. *Science*, *240*, 167–171.

Kaltenbach, K., Weinraub, M., & Fullard, W. (1980). Infant wariness toward strangers reconsidered: Infants' and mothers' reactions to unfamiliar persons. *Child Development*, *51*, 1197–1202.

Kaplan, D. A. (1972). On shyness. *International Journal of Psychoanalysis*, *53*, 439–453.

Keltner, D. (1995). Signs of appeasement: Evidence for the distinct displays of embarrassment, amusement and shame. *Journal of Personality and Social Psychology*, *68*, 441–454.

Lewis, M. (1994). Myself and me. In S. T. Parker, R. W. Mitchell, & M. Boccia (Eds.), *Self-awareness in animals and humans* (pp. 20–34). New York: Cambridge University Press.

Lewis, M. (1995). Embarrassment: The emotion of self-exposure and evaluation. In J. P. Tangney & K. W. Fischer (Eds.), *Self-conscious emotions: The psychology of shame, guilt, pride and embarrassment* (pp. 199–218). New York: Guilford Press.

Lewis, M. & Brooks-Gunn, J. (1979). *Social cognition and the acquisition of self.* New York: Plenum.

Lewis, M., Sullivan, M. W., Stanger, C., & Weiss, M. (1989). Self development and self-conscious emotions *Child Development*, *60*, 146–156.

Martin, W. W. & Gardner, S. N. (1979). The relative effects of eye-gaze and smiling on arousal in asocial situations. *Journal of Psychology*, *102*, 253–259.

Miller, R. S. (1996). *Embarrassment: Poise and peril in everyday life.* New York: Guilford Press.

Mosher, D. L. & White, B. B. (1981). On differentiating shame and shyness. *Motivation and Emotion*, *5*, 61–74.

Neisser, U. (1995). Criteria for an ecological self. In P. Rochat (Ed.), *The self in infancy: Theory and research* (pp. 17–34). North-Holland: Elsevier.

Neisser, U. (1997). The roots of self-knowledge: perceiving Self, It and Thou. In J. G. Snodgrass & R. L. Thompson (Eds.), *The self across psychology: Self-recognition, self-awareness and the self-concept* (pp. 18–33). New York: Annals of the New York Academy of Sciences, Vol. 818.

Oster, H. (1997). Facial expression as a window on sensory experience and affect in newborn infants. In P. Ekman & E. L. Rosenberg (Eds.), *What the face reveals: Basic and applied studies of spontaneous expression using the Facial Action Coding System* (pp. 320–327). New York: Oxford University Press.

Reddy, V. (2000). Coyness in early infancy. *Developmental Science*, *3*, 186–192.

Reddy, V. (1999). Prelinguistic communication. In M. Barrett (Ed.), *The development of language* (pp. 25–50). Hove, Sussex: Psychology Press.

Ricard, M. & Decarie, T. G. (1993). Distance maintaining in infants' reaction to an adult stranger. *Social Development*, *2*, 145–164.

Ruff, H. A. & Rothbart, M. K. (1996). *Attention in early development.* New York: Oxford University Press.

Semin, G. R. & Manstead, A. S. R. (1982). The social implications of embarrassment displays and restitution behaviour. *European Journal of Social Psychology*, *12*, 367–377.

Sroufe, L. A. (1977). Wariness of strangers and the study of infant development. *Child Development*, *48*, 731–746.

Stern, D. N. (1974). Mother and infant at play: The dyadic interaction involving facial, vocal and gaze behaviors. In M. Lewis & L. A. Rosenblum (Eds.), *The effects of the infant on its caregiver.* New York: Wiley.

Stern, D. N. (1985). *The interpersonal world of the infant.* New York: Basic Books, Inc.

Stifter, C. A. & Moyer, D. (1991). The regulation of positive affect: Gaze aversion during mother–infant interaction. *Infant Behavior and Development*, *14*, 111–123.

Trevarthen, C. (1993). The self born in intersubjectivity. In U. Neisser (Ed.), *The perceived self: Ecological and interpersonal sources of self-knowledge* (pp. 121–173). New York: Cambridge University Press.

van der Molen, H. T. (1990). A definition of shyness and its implications for clinical practice. In W. R. Crozier (Ed.), *Shyness and embarrassment: Perspectives from social psychology* (pp. 255–285). Cambridge: Cambridge University Press.

Waters, E., Matas, L., & Sroufe, L. A. (1975). Infants' reactions to an approaching stranger: Description, validation and functional significance of wariness. *Child Development, 46,* 348–356.

Young, G. & Decarie, T. G. (1977). An ethology-based catalogue of facial/vocal behaviour in infancy. *Animal Behaviour, 25,* 95–107.

Zimbardo, P. G. (1977). *Shyness.* Reading, MA: Addison-Wesley.

Chapter 5

Origins of the Self-conscious Child

Michael Lewis

A DEVELOPMENTAL MODEL OF EMOTIONS
THE TWO TYPES OF EMBARRASSMENT: EXPOSURE VS. EVALUATION
Exposure
Evaluation
INDIVIDUAL DIFFERENCES IN EXPOSURE-EMBARRASSMENT
SUMMARY
REFERENCES

To understand what follows, two case studies are briefly presented:

> Victoria is a pretty 3-year-old. When she enters the laboratory she clings to her mother, hiding her head in her skirt when she is spoken to. When asked her name, she does not reply. She readily finishes a puzzle given to her by a research assistant and when complimented about how well she did, Victoria smiles, turns her head, blushes, and moves toward her mother to hold her hand.

> Natasha is also a pretty 3-year-old. She comes into the laboratory without her mother, looks around the room and starts to play. She, too, finishes the puzzle and when complimented, shows a big smile. However, when she gets up from the table, she knocks over a glass and it breaks as it falls to the ground. She sees what she has done, smiles sheepishly, turns away, blushes, and touches her dress nervously.

Both children have shown signs of embarrassment; that is, they blushed, smiled, turned away, and engaged in self-stimulation (Lewis, 1989). Somehow, though, these examples seem different. In this chapter, we will explore this difference, but before doing so we will need to outline a developmental model in regard to emotional development, showing the development of a sense of self, a meta-

International Handbook of Social Anxiety: Concepts, Research and Interventions Relating to the Self and Shyness. Edited by W. Ray Crozier and Lynn E. Alden.
© 2001 John Wiley & Sons Ltd.

representation—or what I have called the *idea of me* (Lewis, 1995). Having done this, we next focus on the development of the earliest self-conscious emotion—embarrassment—and show its earliest manifestation and its subsequent development. Finally, we explore individual differences in this emergent emotion.

A DEVELOPMENTAL MODEL OF EMOTIONS

The model to be presented rests on the proposition that embarrassment belongs to the general class of self-conscious emotions and that these self-conscious emotions require specific cognitions for their emergence. Most of the literature on emotional development focuses on the appearance of what have been called the "primary" or "basic" emotions. These emotions are characterized both by their early appearance and by having universal facial expressions. Beyond the appearance of these early emotions, the emergence of the other emotions remains relatively uncharted. Although some empirical work has appeared on pride, guilt, and shame, especially within an achievement situation (Geppert & Kuster, 1983; Heckhausen, 1984; Lewis, Alessandri, & Sullivan, 1990; Stipek, Recchia, & McClintic, 1992), theories regarding the origin of the later appearing emotions, often called "secondary" or "self-conscious" emotions, are largely unexplored. Operational definitions and the need for a good measurement system are parts of the problem.

The appearance of these emotions, after emergence of the earlier ones, has led to their classification as secondary or derived emotions (see Plutchik, 1980). Another model considers that these emotions follow the primary ones but are not constructed from them (Izard, 1977). The model argued for here proposes that emotions are tied to cognitive processes, those needing the least cognitive support emerging first, and those needing more emerging later (Lewis, 1992; Lewis & Michalson, 1983). Although the sequence of the emergence of these earlier emotions has yet to be fully articulated, it seems that by 6 to 8 months of age they all have appeared (Lewis, 1993). Even so, it is not until the middle of the second year that the secondary or self-conscious emotions are observed (Borke, 1971; Lewis & Brooks-Gunn, 1979; Stipek, 1983).

The model articulated elsewhere (Lewis, 1992; Lewis, Sullivan, Stanger, & Weiss, 1989) can be found in Figure 5.1. In the first months, the "primary" emotions appear. The time of emergence of these emotions is variable and depends upon situation and context. It is reasonably safe to say that they appear either shortly after birth or are seen within the first 6 to 8 months of life (Lewis, 1993). In the second stage, self-referential behavior emerges, which is indicative of the development of a meta-representation. The emergence of this capacity has been associated with such other cognitive features as the use of "me" or "mine" (Lewis & Brooks-Gunn, 1979). Moreover, as proposed by Leslie (1987), we have recently been able to show that self-recognition and/or personal pronoun usage tends to precede pretend play (Lewis & Ramsay, in review). Thus, there is sufficient evidence to suggest that an active meta-representation exists and is used by the middle of the second year of life. In particular, the emergence of this capacity

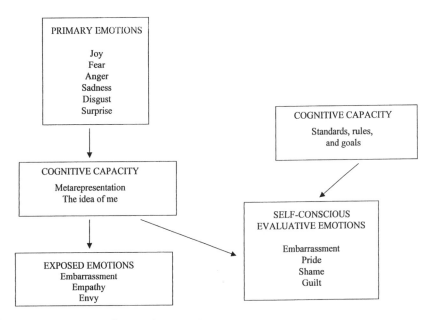

Figure 5.1 Primary and secondary emotions

occurs between 15 and 24 months in normally developing children and requires a mental age of 15 to 18 months to be displayed (Lewis & Brooks-Gunn, 1979; Loveland, 1987a, b).[1]

As can be seen in Figure 5.1, the emergence of self-recognition marks the maturing of the meta-representation. At the same time as this meta-representation can be said to exist, we are able to observe the emergence of what we will call "exposure-embarrassment."

Exposure-embarrassment seems to be related to the emergence of self-referential behavior. Amsterdam (1972), Dickson (1957), and Schulman and Kaplowitz (1977) report instances of self-conscious behavior in children older than 15 months when viewing themselves in mirrors. In our studies (Lewis & Brooks-Gunn, 1979), 20% of the children over 15 months of age who observed themselves in a mirror *without* rouge on their noses, showed coy or silly behavior, which could be taken to reflect embarrassment. Thus, there is reason to believe that the emergence of self-referential behavior is related to embarrassment.

This was tested in a series of studies by Lewis et al. (1989), and we were able to demonstrate that embarrassment did not occur in children who did not show self-recognition in the mirror. In these studies, the self-recognition mirror task was used and embarrassment was observed under four different conditions. The embarrassment-eliciting situations included children looking at themselves in the mirror with other people observing them looking at themselves (mirror condi-

---

[1] The technique of self-recognition is well known; we have called it the mirror rouge test so we will not go into details in regard to the procedure.

tion). A "complimenting condition" involved an experimenter initiating interactions with a child during which the child was given four or five compliments. For example, children were told that they were smart, had beautiful hair, and had lovely clothes. Two other conditions included a request for the child to perform a dance. In one, the experimenter handed the mother a small tambourine and asked the mother to coax the child to dance. In the second, the experimenter herself coaxed the child to dance. They each said, "Let's see you dance. Dance for me, I'll sing 'Old MacDonald'" [or a song familiar to the child]. The dance situation was utilized since conspicuousness is thought to be an elicitor of embarrassment (Buss, 1980). The results of these studies (reported in Lewis et al., 1989), showed a direct relation between embarrassment in these situations and self-referential behavior as measured in a previous rouge/mirror situation. Embarrassment was seen almost only for children who showed self-consciousness (touched their noses). Such findings indicate that embarrassment is related to the emergence of this meta-representation of self.

Observation of Figure 5.1 also indicates that *self-conscious evaluative* emotions do not emerge at this time but appear somewhat later, toward the third year of life. While embarrassment requires only self-consciousness, pride, shame, and guilt appear to require additional cognitive capacities. These include the acquisition of standards as well as the ability to evaluate one's behavior *vis-à-vis* these standards. Present work indicates that the emergence of self-conscious evaluative emotions occurs at about 3 years of age (see Heckhausen, 1984; Kagan, 1981; Lewis, 1992; Lewis, Alessandri, & Sullivan, 1992; Stipek et al., 1992).

The emergence of shame, pride, and guilt almost one and a half to two years after that of exposure-embarrassment suggests several important points:

1. The emergence of embarrassment and shame are not coincidental, thus supporting the premise that embarrassment is not the same as shame.
2. The emergence of embarrassment prior to a self-evaluative capacity suggests that exposure-embarrassment does not require evaluation of the self, either in terms of potential failure or of failure itself. Although embarrassment may require a social audience, it does not appear to need a self-evaluative component.
3. Embarrassment seems to occur under situations in which failure is not likely to be a sufficient explanatory device. For example, in the Lewis et al. (1989) study, embarrassment was most elicited by praise and by observing children looking in the mirror at themselves.

Some have argued that compliments to an adult may have a negative component since they are taught to be modest. It is possible then to argue that for older children and adults, being complimented may have some negative feature. However, to argue that children 15 to 24 months of age have been taught and have learned the issue of modesty is hard to accept. Rather, embarrassment seen in this situation is related more to exposure or attention being paid to the self than to the violation of social mores and values. Thus, this model suggests that there may be two types of embarrassment, each having different developmental timing and being supported by different cognitive processes.

THE TWO TYPES OF EMBARRASSMENT: EXPOSURE VS. EVALUATION

Exposure

Embarrassment elicited by exposure appears to be more similar to shyness than to shame. In certain situations of exposure, people become embarrassed. This type of embarrassment is not related to negative evaluation as in shame. Perhaps the best example is being complimented. The phenomenological experience of embarrassment when complimented is well known. The speaker, introduced with praise, is embarrassed. Buss (1980) has suggested that complimenting elicits social rules for modesty. While this may be the case for adults, it is hard to reconcile learning the rules of modesty in infants as young as 15 to 18 months of age.

Another example of this type of embarrassment can be seen in people's reaction to their public display (Goffman, 1956). When people observe someone looking at them, they are apt to become self-conscious, to look away, and to touch or adjust their bodies. When the observed person is a woman, she will often adjust or touch her hair. An observed man is less likely to touch his hair, but may adjust his clothes or change his body posture. Observed people look either pleased or frightened, rarely sad.

Still another example of exposure-embarrassment comes from a series of experiments I have conducted. In lecturing both to students in my classes as well as other audiences, I often wish to demonstrate that embarrassment can be elicited just by exposure. To demonstrate this point, I inform the audience that I am going to randomly point to someone. I further inform the audience that my pointing has no evaluative component, that it will be random, and not related to anything about the person. Moreover, I inform them that I will close my eyes when pointing. Following these instructions, I point to someone in the room. From the reports of those who are targets of the point, the pointing invariably elicits embarrassment.

The final example comes from a personal observation. I have gone to a dental hygienist to have my teeth cleaned for the past few years. As I sat there with my mouth open, it occurred to me that if I were a dental hygienist I would have a favorite tooth, one which gave me particular pleasure to clean, in part, perhaps because it was easy to clean. With this idea in mind, I asked Barbara, the hygienist, "Which is your favorite tooth?" She stopped her work, looked embarrassed, blushed, and finally said, "How did you know?" Quite by accident I had uncovered her secret. She told me she was not ashamed at having a favorite tooth; just at being "uncovered". This example of embarrassment at being exposed or uncovered has made me realize that the exposure does not have to be about the physical presence but can extend to the secret part of the self (Meares, 1992).

There are many examples of embarrassment in which there is an evaluative component, yet it may be that self-exposure is in reality the elicitor. Take the simple act of walking into a lecture hall a few minutes *before* the speaker is scheduled to talk. A person who arrives on time or even early may attract attention. On such an occasion, one is likely to experience embarrassment. This situation can promote a negative self-evaluation—"I should have been here earlier; I should have stayed at the back of the hall." I believe, however, that the experience of embarrassment may not be caused by negative self-evaluation, but by simple public exposure. However, rather than believe that it is the exposure alone which produces the embarrassment, people choose to look for a negative evaluation. In other words, the negative evaluation follows embarrassment due-to-exposure as people attempt to explain to themselves why they are embarrassed. *That is, once evaluation of the self skills develop (at around 3 years), it is used as a cognitive device since it becomes a prepotent response.*

Evaluation

The second type of embarrassment is related to negative self-evaluation and to shame. The difference in intensity between embarrassment and shame may be due to the nature of the failed standard. People have different standards, some of which are more important than others to their identity. Violation of these less important standards is likely to elicit a less intense form of shame. For example, failure at driving a car may be embarrassing rather than shaming, if driving is less related to the core self. On the other hand, failure at driving a car may be shaming, if it is a core capacity. In these examples, there appear to be some association between embarrassment and shame. Perhaps there is another and important differentiating cause for embarrassment versus shame. Evaluative embarrassment (as exposure-embarrassment) always needs a socially present audience. Shame does not. Thus, evaluative embarrassment would not only be a milder form of shame, but may need to take place in public.

This distinction allows us to return to the two examples given at the beginning of the chapter. Victoria, as you remember, showed embarrassment in a new situation when she became the object of the researcher's attention—when she was complimented. Because of these circumstances, we would conclude that Victoria has exhibited exposure-embarrassment. Natasha, on the other hand, exhibited embarrassment, not when she was the object of attention (complimented), but when she broke the glass. Her embarrassment was caused by evaluation and is an example of evaluative embarrassment. Exposure-embarrassment occurs at the point when the idea of me exists and is utilized in social exchanges. For some children, social exchanges, where they become the center of another's attention and they are aware of the others' attention toward them, produces embarrassment. This capacity, unlike evaluative embarrassment, emerges in the second year of life.

INDIVIDUAL DIFFERENCES IN EXPOSURE-EMBARRASSMENT

Exposure-embarrassment is a normal emotion which requires the cognitive capacities to (1) represent the self to oneself, and (2) notice the attention of others toward the self. These cognitive capacities emerge in the middle of the second year of life. While embarrassment is a normal emotion which we all have, observation of toddlers and young children reveals that some children show more embarrassment than others when they become the object of others' attention. This individual difference is interesting to observe, is probably related to what others have called shy or inhibited, and may have, as I believe, its roots in individual differences in self-attention and in temperament.

Embarrassment has been related to shyness. Izard and Tyson (1986) consider shyness to be sheepishness, bashfulness, and/or a feeling of uneasy or psychological discomfort in social situations. They suggest that shyness results from a vacillation between fear and interest or between avoidance and approach. They relate shyness to fear, not to evaluation. Individuals who are considered shy are not too much concerned with the evaluation of their performance *vis-à-vis* their standards, as they are with being observed. Buss (1980) sees shyness as an emotional response which is elicited by experiences of novelty or conspicuousness. Buss believes shyness and fear are closely related and represent a general fearfulness toward others—again not an evaluative process, except in the cause of fearfulness, such as fear of a stranger.

In a series of studies, we observed 3-month-old children interacting with their mothers (Lewis & Feiring, 1989), and two different types of children were distinguished. The first group of children appear to be socially oriented even by 12 weeks of age. These children looked at, smiled at, and vocalized in interactive sequences with their mothers and preferred to play with their mothers rather than by themselves. We characterized these children as sociable. Unlike the first group, about 20% of the children preferred not to look at, smile at, or vocalize toward their mothers and they also preferred to play by themselves and with toys more than with their mothers (Lewis & Feiring, 1989). These children were called asocial. The children were observed again at 12 months of age and these differences in sociability were maintained. These differences in sociability appear to be similar to what has been called differences in shy or inhibited children (Kagan, Reznick, & Snidman, 1988). These findings suggest that shyness may be similar to embarrassment since it appears early and does not need an evaluative component. Shyness, like fearfulness, is more likely to be biological rather than a psychological variable. Such an approach to shyness seems reasonable in that it fits with a social self view. For example, Kagan et al. (1988) have pointed out that children whom they called inhibited, also appeared shy, withdrawn, uncomfortable in social situations, and fearful. Thus, our own observations, as well as those of others, indicate that shyness related to a constellation of factors is not related to self-evaluation. Moreover, there is some reason to believe that these individual differences have a dispositional or constitutional basis (Eysenck, 1956).

Our interest in individual differences in exposure-embarrassment has led to a series of studies. To begin with, we were interested in the relation between temperament and embarrassment since there is general agreement that temperament, however defined, serves to organize or regulate emotional states and expressions (Allport, 1965; Buss & Plomin, 1984; Goldsmith & Campos, 1982; Lewis, 1989; Thomas, Chess, Birch, Hertzig, & Korn, 1963). Rothbart (Rothbart & Derryberry, 1981; Rothbart & Goldsmith, 1985) and Lewis (1989) have suggested that temperament regulates the latency, duration, and intensity of emotional responses. Using parental reports of infant temperament, a modest relation between emotional expression and temperament has been found (Goldsmith & Campos, 1982). Although these studies were primarily concerned with the relation between temperament and the emotions that appear during the first year of life, the role of temperament in the expression of the more complex, self-conscious emotions is relatively rare (Kochanska, 1993; Lewis, 1992; Rothbart, Ahadi, & Hershey, 1994). For example, several studies have examined the role of temperament in the development of the specific emotions of shame, guilt, and empathy as well as the more broad construct of conscience (see Kochanska, 1993, for a review of this literature). In a series of studies, Kochanska and associates have examined the role of temperament in the development of conscience (Kochanska, 1993; Kochanska, DeVet, Goldman, Murray, & Putman, 1994). Findings suggest that the temperament dimensions of low impulsivity and high effortful control (e.g., the ability to focus and to control inappropriate behavior) are moderating factors in the amount of affective distress that young children, particularly girls, show in response to their moral transgressions. Similarly, Rothbart et al. (1994) found that school-aged children who are high on the temperament dimensions of negative affectivity and effortful control show greater amounts of guilt and shame than children low on these dimensions. In a small subsample looking at predictions from infancy to school age, Rothbart et al. (1994) found high anger/frustration and fearfulness to be positively related to later guilt.

The question addressed in the DiBiase and Lewis (1997) study concerned the relation between temperament and embarrassment. There are several possible ways in which temperament differences may affect embarrassment differences. First, temperament differences may affect embarrassment by affecting the timing of the emergence of self-awareness. We have proposed that children who are easily overstimulated and highly reactive may develop self-awareness sooner than children with more "easygoing" temperaments (see Lewis & Ramsay, 1997). Second, temperament may affect individual differences in embarrassment independent of its effect on self-awareness. Although self-awareness may be necessary for embarrassment, temperament differences may affect embarrassment in those children who already show self-awareness (Edelmann, 1987; Jones, Briggs, & Smith, 1986). Third, temperament may affect the onset of both self-awareness and embarrassment.

Embarrassment was elicited through the use of four distinct situations. First, the experimenter was overly complimentary toward the children, commenting effusively about their clothes, hair, and personal attributes. This situation has been shown to elicit blushing and giggling (Buss, 1980). In the second situation, the mother was instructed to ask her child to dance. She was handed a tambourine and told to use any method that she thought would work. In the third episode, the experimenter asked the child to dance. Here the experimenter played a tambourine and sang "Old MacDonald" while encouraging the child to dance. Finally, children were asked to look at themselves in a mirror. These situations were designed to make the child feel conspicuous and the center of attention, which is thought to elicit embarrassment (Buss, 1980). Embarrassment, measured using Geppert's (1986) coding scheme, was effectively elicited with these situations (see Lewis et al., 1989). Blushing and smiling, followed by gaze aversion and/or self-touching, indicated embarrassment (see also Buss, 1980; Edelmann & Hampson, 1981; Lewis et al., 1989; Modigliani, 1971). Also obtained were measures of self-recognition using the mirror-rouge test. Temperament measures were obtained using the Revised Infant Temperament Questionnaire (RITQ) and the Toddler Temperament Scale (TTS). Each of these questionnaires was designed to rate children on the nine dimensions of temperament proposed by Thomas et al. (1963). The TTS is comparable to the RITQ, but designed for older children.

Infants were classified by temperament using a principal–components analysis with varimax rotation. At 5 months, four factors, accounting for 71% of the variance, had eigenvalues of 1 or greater. The first rotated factor, accounting for 29% of the variance, consisted of negative mood, approach/withdrawal (fearfulness), adaptability, and distractibility. This factor consisted of three of the five dimensions that differentiate infants into the easy–difficult temperament categories described by Thomas et al. (1963), and is consistent with the results of Matheny, Wilson, and Nuss (1984). It also contains the aspects of temperament that Rothbart et al. (1994) and Kochanska et al. (1994) found to be related to self-conscious emotions. The higher the score, the more children were fearful, negative in mood, unadaptable, and distractible. At 13 months, the principal–components analysis with varimax rotation yielded three factors with eigenvalues greater than 1, accounting for 56% of the variance. The first factor accounted for 27% of the variance and was defined by the dimensions of fearfulness, negative mood, nonadaptability, and rhythmicity. As with the 5-month analysis, the higher the score, the more children were fearful, negative in mood, unadaptable, and arrhythmic. The relation between 5- and 13-month temperament factor scores was significant. A score for embarrassment was determined by counting the number of times embarrassment occurred over the four situations used to elicit it. Parental report of temperament is positively related to embarrassment, such that infants who were more fearful, negative in mood, and unadaptable were more likely to show embarrassment than infants who were less fearful, negative in mood, and unadaptable.

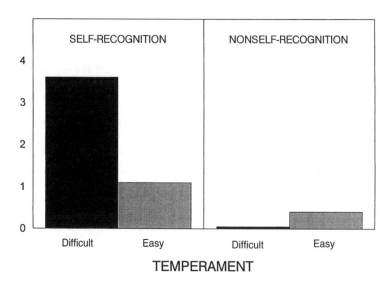

Figure 5.2 Level of embarrassment by self-recognition and easy versus difficult temperament

To assess the interaction between temperament and self-recognition, and embarrassment, four groups were formed at each age: (1) those who showed self-recognition and had temperament scores above the median; (2) those who showed recognition and had temperament scores below the median; (3) those who did not show recognition, but had temperament scores above the median; and (4) those who did not show recognition and had scores below the median on temperament.

Infants who showed self-recognition were more fearful and negative in mood, exhibited significantly more embarrassment than infants who showed self-recognition, and had less of these negative temperament characteristics. Infants who showed no self-recognition, regardless of temperament characteristics, also exhibited little or no embarrassment (see Figure 5.2).

The relation between self-awareness, as measured by self-referential behaviour and embarrassment, has already been demonstrated (Amsterdam & Levitt, 1981; Lewis et al., 1989), and was not, therefore, the focus of this study.

Individual differences in temperament are related to the expression of embarrassment when children show self-recognition. Temperament differences are of no consequence for those children who do not show self-recognition. From these analyses it appears that once infants have the cognitive capacity necessary for the emergence of embarrassment, individual differences in temperament play an important role in its expression. Thus, although embarrassment is dependent on the cognitive capacities associated with self-recognition, individual differences in embarrassment expression are dependent on individual differences in temperament.

In this study, we were able to show a direct interaction between difficult temperament, self-recognition, and embarrassment. In particular, embarrassment was related to temperament once self-recognition appeared. The relationship between temperament and self-recognition was present, but not as strong. We raised the issue that temperament may affect the age of onset of self-recognition and therefore embarrassment. However, temperament may affect both the age of onset of self-recognition and temperament through another mechanism, namely, temperament may make children more prone to focus on themselves. This may give rise to both *earlier* self-recognition and to *more* embarrassment when one becomes the focus of others' attention.

In adults, as described by others (e.g., Duval & Wickland, 1972; Ingram, 1990; Pyszczynski & Greenberg, 1992), attention can be focused externally on the environment or internally on the self. Self-focused attention (or an equivalent construct) has a central role in various theories of attention (Mandler, 1975), attribution (Dweck, 1991; Dweck, Chiu, & Hong, 1995; Weiner, 1986), introspection (Buss, 1980; Hansell & Mechanic, 1991; Mechanic, 1983), and consciousness (Csikszentmihalyi, 1975, 1990; Csikszentmihalyi & Csikszentmihalyi, 1988). To varying degrees, each theory emphasizes the importance of individual differences in the likelihood that attention is focused on the self. Csikszentmihalyi's theory also acknowledges a role for differences in temperament in self-focused attention and self-consciousness. In Csikszentmihalyi's theory, "flow" is defined by intense involvement, deep concentration, loss of a sense of time, and lack of self-consciousness. Individuals differ in the extent to which flow is disrupted by various events, including perceived disparate levels of task challenge and personal skill as well as by internal physiological information associated with such states as hunger or pain. With the disruption of flow, attention becomes focused on the self, and self-consciousness can occur only with this self-focus in attention. Imagine two individuals engrossed in work, one of whom is distracted by hunger pains with the arrival of lunch time, while the other works through the lunch hour without realizing that it has passed. Whereas for one colleague flow was interrupted by internal information, for the other colleague internal information did not intrude on the experience. Thus, the disruption of flow by internal physiological information points to temperament as an important individual difference in self-focused attention and self-consciousness.

In his work on the role of culture, history, and individual consciousness in the perception of pain, Morris (1991) has suggested that individuals' responses to pain may represent how they cope with internal information, information emanating from their own bodies. Extending this view, we propose that individual differences in the onset of objective self-awareness are based, at least in part, on differences in the ability to gate or block internal stimuli as reflected in reactivity to stressful events, including physically and/or emotionally painful ones. The findings by DiBiase and Lewis (1997) on self-recognition and embarrassment led us to consider high reactivity to stress as the aspect of a difficult or negative temperament most closely related to self-awareness. The findings by Kochanska (1995) and Rothbart et al. (1994) are consistent with the view that a lower threshold for stress leads to greater internalization of conscience. Csikszentmihalyi's theory of flow indicates individual differences in the capacity to gate or block from consciousness physiological information associated with stressful events, with a lower threshold for stress likely leading to greater use of regulatory or coping strategies (see Eisenberg & Fabes, 1992; Fox, 1994; Kopp, 1989) to deal with the internal information. Early self-awareness may be one manifestation of the increased use of coping strategies to deal with the information brought on by a low threshold for stress.

In a study by Lewis and Ramsay (1997), self-recognition was assessed at 18 months in a longitudinal sample of infants whose adrenocortical and behavioral responses to inoculation had been observed at 2, 4, 6, and 18 months of age. Because the follow-up age is transitional for the onset of self-recognition, we expected that there would be a comparable number of self-recognizers and non-self-recognizers in the sample. Differences in the stress responses between the self-recognizers and non-self-recognizers were examined before and after the developmental shift in adrenocortical functioning, that is, at 2 to 4 and 6 to 18 months of age. We expected that the self-recognizers would show a greater cortisol response than the non-self-recognizers at the older age level, but that the self-recognizers would not differ in cortisol response at the younger age level.

Finally, given the possibility that experiential factors play a role in self-recognition onset (e.g., Lewis, Brooks-Gunn, & Jaskir, 1985; Schneider-Rosen & Cicchetti, 1984; Tajima, 1982), it seemed important to assess experiential factors to see whether these covaried with the stress response and whether the relation between stress reactivity and self-recognition held after controlling for them. One experiential factor of some interest is life stress events in the family because of the potential impact of life stress on infant stress reactivity and given the possibility that both life stress and infant stress reactivity could affect self-recognition. We predicted that the relation between individual differences in stress reactivity and self-recognition would remain after controlling for life stress. Such a finding would indicate that the reactivity of the infant affects self-recognition onset over and above any effect of the stressfulness of the environment. Self-recognition was observed using the mirror procedure while cortisol and behavioral stress was measured in a way reported in detail elsewhere (see Lewis & Ramsay, 1995a, b).

Our work on stress reactivity found a developmental shift in adrenocortical functioning (Lewis & Ramsay, 1995a, b). Findings for this developmental shift included a decline in magnitude of cortisol response between 2 and 6 months, with no further age change in cortisol response between 6 and 18 months of age. Moreover, there was stability of individual differences in cortisol response between 6 and 18 months, but no stability in cortisol response between 2 or 4 and 18 months of age. This developmental shift and our view on the relation between stress reactivity and objective self-awareness suggest that a high cortisol response from, but not before, 6 months would be associated with an earlier onset of self-recognition.

Table 5.1 Cortisol response and behavioral quieting by self-recognition and age level

	2–4 months	6–18 months
Cortisol response:		
Self-recognizers	0.60 (0.31)	0.35 (0.18)
Non-self-recognizers	0.61 (0.24)	0.15 (0.09)
Behavioral quieting:		
Self-recognizers	0.30 (0.22)	0.38 (0.29)
Non-self-recognizers	0.30 (0.19)	0.67 (0.40)

Note: Standard deviations are in parentheses. N = 19 self-recognizers and 10 non-self-recognizers for cortisol response; N = 20 self-recognizers and 11 non-self-recognizers for behavioral quieting.

Our behavioral measures of stress reactivity included infants' quieting following the inoculation (Lewis & Ramsay, 1995a, b). Consistent with the cortisol results, there was a developmental change toward more rapid quieting between 2 and 6 months, with no further age change in quieting between 6 and 18 months of age. There was no stability of individual differences in quieting between 2 or 4 and 18 months, with a trend for stability in quieting between 6 and 18 months of age. These results led us to examine whether the relation between stress reactivity and self-recognition was comparable for behavioral quieting and cortisol response.

Table 5.1 shows the cortisol response and behavioral quieting measures by self-recognition and age level. The results indicated that high stress reactivity from early infancy is associated with an earlier onset of self-recognition even when life stress events in the family were controlled. High stress reactivity reflects less capacity to gate or regulate internal information stemming from stressful events. The intensity of the internal stimuli, as well as the need to organize the physiological information, appear to facilitate or accelerate the emergence of self-recognition. Csikszentmihalyi (1975, 1990) suggested that the intensity of internal stimuli is related to intersubject differences in adults' self-consciousness. The present findings were consistent with this view and with available evidence that temperament factors play a role in self-recognition and embarrassment (DiBiase & Lewis, 1997) as well as in the internalization of conscience (Kochanska, 1993, 1995; Rothbart et al., 1994). Maturational factors are important in the timing of self-recognition onset. They serve to limit the age that self-recognition first appears. Given this constraint, stress reactivity and temperament factors also affect when self-recognition emerges.

The findings from these studies in our laboratory suggest that individual differences in embarrassment may be a function of both individual processes, such as how the child attends to its bodily sensations, as well as how others respond to them. These processes in turn may be linked to individual differences in physiological processing of information.

Whatever their cause, there is reason to believe that these individual differences are somewhat stable over time. Lewis, Stanger, Sullivan, and Barone (1991) looked at children's responses to similar embarrassment-provoking situations between the second and third years of life. They found that while embarrassment increased with age, those children who showed more embarrassment earlier were also showing more embarrassment later. The emergence of this type of embarrassment—exposure-embarrassment—in the second year of life may be related to other types of individual differences including the shy or inhibited child. It is important to look at this earlier form of embarrassment for it is our belief that individual differences in the second year of life may be important indications of individual differences in self-consciousness in social situations. Thus, while exposure-embarrassment emerges as a function of the cognitive development of the meta-representation of self, individual differences may be an important marker of how early differences in temperament may express themselves in the toddler.

SUMMARY

We began this chapter by describing two children who showed a set of behaviors we have labelled embarrassment. The embarrassment that Victoria exhibited is related to being the object of others' attention; thus, we have called it exposure embarrassment. The elicitor of this type of embarrassment does not require much cognition. It does not require evaluation of the self against standards of behavior, either one's own or others. It does require the cognitions necessary to know that there is an object called "me", what I have called a self-concept, and that others are attending to that object. It is a basic process, which emerges somewhere between 15 to 24 months of age.

Children differ in the degree of "exposure-embarrassment" that they exhibit, some showing extreme forms while others hardly showing any. Those showing extreme forms have been called shy or inhibited. We have argued that individual differences in this form of embarrassment are less likely to be a function of the types of child-rearing they have experienced. Rather, we see individual differences to be related to temperament-like variables. They are more like biological than learning differences and may be related to how well children can regulate their emotional arousal.

Natasha, on the other hand, shows the other type of embarrassment. It is embarrassment which emerges later in life, after 24 months and is most likely seen from 30 months onward. This form of embarrassment requires considerable cognition since it is based on an evaluation ability of the child in regard to how he or she behaves relative to a standard. The cognitions involved here require that the child has a standard and can apply that standard to his or her own behavior. Such cognitions are seen only after 24–30 months of age.

Individual differences in "evaluative embarrassment" are dependent first and foremost on child-rearing practices. These include the type of standards, how they are taught and enforced by the parents. They also include the same simple cognitions seen in the other type of embarrassment, that is a self-concept. It also requires cognitions about others' awareness of ourself. While it is similar to shame in many regards it differs in that it is less intense a negative emotion since it does not involve the attribution of a damaged self and takes place in a social context, something that the emotion of shame does not require.

The data we have gathered on children's emotional development in the first three years allow us to postulate these two different types of embarrassment. Their relation to shyness, fear, and shame, something others have postulated at this time, can only be speculation. Nevertheless, it is clear from our data as well as those who have studied children's attributions—see, for example, Stipek et al. (1992)—that exposure-type embarrassment emerges almost one year prior to the ability to form standards regarding behavior that are independent of the presence of an adult. These data provide evidence for the existence of these two types of embarrassment and their emergence over time.

REFERENCES

Allport, G. (1965). *Pattern and growth in personality*. New York: Holt, Rinehart & Winston.

Amsterdam, B. K. (1972). Mirror self-image reactions before age two. *Developmental Psychology, 5*, 297–305.

Amsterdam, B. K. & Levitt, M. (1981). Consciousness of self and painful self-consciousness. *The Psychoanalytic Study of the Child, 36*, 45–70.

Borke, J. (1971). Interpersonal perception of young children: Egocentrism or empathy. *Developmental Psychology, 7*, 207–217.

Buss, A. H. (1980). *Self consciousness and social anxiety* (pp. 221–247). San Francisco, CA: Freeman.

Buss, A. H. & Plomin, R. (1984). *Temperament: Early developing personality traits*. Hillsdale, NJ: Lawrence Erlbaum Associates Inc.

Csikszentmihalyi, M. (1975). *Beyond boredom and anxiety: The experience of play in work and games*. San Francisco: Jossey-Bass.

Csikszentmihalyi, M. (1990). *Flow: The psychology of optimal experience*. New York: Harper & Row.

Csikszentmihalyi, M. & Csikszentmihalyi, I. S. (1988). *Optimal experience: Psychological studies of flow in consciousness*. Cambridge: Cambridge University Press.

DiBiase, R. & Lewis, M. (1997). The relation between temperament and embarrassment. *Cognition and Emotion, 11*, 259–271.

Dickson, J. C. (1957). The development of self-recognition. *Journal of Genetic Psychology, 91*, 251–256.

Duval, S. & Wickland, R. A. (1972). *A theory of objective self-awareness*. New York: Academic Press.

Dweck, C. S. (1991). Self-theories and goals: Their role in motivation, personality, and development. In R. A. Dienstbier (Ed.), *Nebraska Symposia on Motivation* (pp. 199–235). Lincoln, NE: University of Nebraska Press.

Dweck, C. S., Chiu, C., & Hong, Y. (1995). Implicit theories and their role in judgments and reactions: A world from two perspectives. *Psychological Inquiry, 6*, 267–285.

Edelmann, R. J. (1987). *The psychology of embarrassment*. Chichester, UK: Wiley.

Edelmann, R. J. & Hampson, S. E. (1981). The recognition of embarrassment. *Personality and Social Psychology Bulletin, 7*, 109–116.

Eisenberg, N. & Fabes, R. A. (Eds.) (1992). *New directions for child development: Vol. 55. Emotion and its regulation in early development*. San Francisco: Jossey-Bass.

Eysenck, H. J. (1956). The questionnaire measurement of neuroticism and extraversion. *Revista Psicologia, 50*, 113–140.

Fox, N. A. (Ed.) (1994). The development of emotion regulation: Biological and behavioral considerations. *Monographs of Society for Research in Child Development, 59* (2–3, Serial No. 240).

Geppert, U. (1986). *A coding system for analyzing behavioral expressions of self-evaluative emotions*. Munich, Germany: Max Planck Institute for Psychological Research.

Geppert, U. & Kuster, U. (1983). The emergence of "wanting to do it oneself": A precursor of achievement motivation. *International Journal of Behavioral Development, 6*, 355–370.

Goffman, E. (1956). Embarrassment and social organization. *American Journal of Sociology, 62*, 264–271.

Goldsmith, H. H. & Campos, J. J. (1982). Toward a theory of infant temperament. In R. N. Emde & R. J. Harmon (Eds.), *The development of attachment and affiliative systems* (pp. 161–193). New York: Plenum.

Hansell, S. & Mechanic, D. (1991). Introspectiveness and adolescence. In R. M. Lerner, A. C. Petersen, & J. Brooks-Gunn (Eds.), *Encyclopedia of adolescence* (pp. 560–564). New York: Garland.

Heckhausen, H. (1984). Emergent achievement behavior: Some early developments. In J. Nicholls (Ed.), *The development of achievement motivation* (pp. 1–32). Greenwich, CT: JAI Press.

Ingram, R. E. (1990). Self-focused attention in clinical disorders: Review and a conceptual model. *Psychological Bulletin, 107*, 156–176.

Izard, C. E. (1977). *Human emotions*. New York: Plenum Press.

Izard, C. E. & Tyson, M. C. (1986). Shyness as a discrete emotion. In W. H. Jones, J. M. Cheek, & S. R. Briggs (Eds.), *Shyness: Perspectives on research and treatment* (pp. 147–160). New York: Plenum Press.

Jones, W. H., Briggs, S. R., & Smith, T. G. (1986). Shyness: Conceptualization and measurement. *Journal of Personality and Social Psychology, 5*, 629–639.

Kagan, J. (1981). *The second year: The emergence of self-awareness*. Cambridge, MA: Harvard University Press.

Kagan, J., Reznick, J. S., & Snidman, N. (1988). Biological bases of childhood shyness. *Science, 240*, 167–171.

Kochanska, G. (1993). Towards a synthesis of parental socialization and child temperament in early development of conscience. *Child Development, 64*, 325–347.

Kochanska, G. (1995). Children's temperament, mothers' discipline, and security of attachment: Multiple pathways to emerging internalization. *Child Development, 66*, 597–615.

Kochanska, G., DeVet, K., Goldman, M., Murray, K., & Putman, S. P. (1994). Maternal reports of conscience development and temperament in young children. *Child Development, 65*, 852–868.

Kopp, C. (1989). Regulation of distress and negative emotions: A developmental perspective. *Developmental Psychology, 25*, 343–354.

Leslie, A. M. (1987). Pretense and representation: The origin of "Theory of Mind". *Psychological Review, 94*, 412–426.

Lewis, M. (1989). Culture and biology: The role of temperament. In P. Zelazo & R. Barr (Eds.), *Challenges to developmental paradigms* (pp. 203–226). Hillsdale, NJ: Lawrence Erlbaum Associates, Inc.

Lewis, M. (1992). *Shame: The exposed self*. New York: Free Press.

Lewis, M. (1993). The emergence of emotions. In M. Lewis & J. Haviland (Eds.), *Handbook of emotions* (pp. 223–235). New York: Guilford Press.

Lewis, M. (1995). Aspects of self: From systems to ideas. In P. Rochat (Ed.), *The self in early infancy: Theory and research. Advances in Psychology Series* (pp. 95–115). North Holland: Elsevier Science Publishers.

Lewis, M., Alessandri, S., & Sullivan, M. W. (1990). Violation of expectancy, loss of control, and anger in young infants. *Developmental Psychology, 26* (5), 745–751.

Lewis, M., Alessandri, S., & Sullivan, M. W. (1992). Differences in shame and pride as a function of children's gender and task difficulty. *Child Development, 63,* 630–638.

Lewis, M. & Brooks-Gunn, J. (1979). *Social cognition and the acquisition of self.* New York: Plenum Press.

Lewis, M., Brooks-Gunn, J., & Jaskir, J. (1985). Individual differences in visual self-recognition as a function of mother–infant relationship. *Developmental Psychology, 21,* 1181–1187.

Lewis, M. & Feiring, C. (1989). Infant, mother and mother–infant interaction behavior and subsequent attachment. *Child Development, 60,* 831–837.

Lewis, M. & Michalson, L. (1983). From emotional state to emotional expression: Emotional development from a person–environment interaction perspective. In D. Magnusson & V. L. Allen (Eds.), *Human development: An interactional perspective* (pp. 261–275). New York: Academic Press.

Lewis, M. & Ramsay, D. (1995a). Developmental change in infants' responses to stress. *Child Development, 66,* 657–670.

Lewis, M. & Ramsay, D. (1995b). Stability and change in cortisol and behavioral responses to stress during the first 18 months of life. *Developmental Psychobiology, 28,* 419–428.

Lewis, M. & Ramsay, D. S. (1997). Stress reactivity and self-recognition. *Child Development, 68,* 621–629.

Lewis, M. & Ramsay, D. S. (1999). Effect of maternal soothing on infant stress reactivity. *Child Development, 70* (1), 11–20.

Lewis, M. & Ramsay, D. S. (In review). Self-awareness and pretend play in the second year of life. *Journal of Cognitive Development.*

Lewis, M., Stanger, C., Sullivan, M. W., & Barone, P. (1991). Changes in embarrassment as a function of age, sex and situation. *British Journal of Developmental Psychology, 9,* 485–492.

Lewis, M., Sullivan, M. W., Stanger, C., & Weiss, M. (1989). Self-development and self-conscious emotions. *Child Development, 60,* 146–156.

Loveland, K. A. (1987a). Behavior of young children with Down syndrome before the mirror: Exploration. *Child Development, 58,* 768–778.

Loveland, K. A. (1987b). Behavior of young children with Down syndrome before the mirror: Finding things reflected. *Child Development, 58,* 928–936.

Mandler, G. (1975). *Mind and emotion.* New York: Wiley.

Matheny, A. P., Wilson, R. S., & Nuss, S. M. (1984). Toddler temperament: Stability across settings and over ages. *Child Development, 55,* 1200–1211.

Meares, R. (1992). *The metaphor of play on self: The secret and borderline experience.* Melbourne: Hill of Content Publishing Co.

Mechanic, D. (1983). Adolescent health and illness behavior: Review of the literature and a new hypothesis for the study of stress. *Journal of Human Stress, 9,* 4–13.

Modigliani, A. (1971). Embarrassment, facework, and eye contact: Testing a theory of embarrassment. *Journal of Personality and Social Psychology, 17,* 15–24.

Morris, D. B. (1991). *The culture of pain.* Berkeley: University of California Press.

Plutchik, R. (1980). A general psychoevolutionary theory of emotion. In R. Plutchik & H. Kellerman (Eds.), *Emotion: Theory, research, and experience* (Vol. 1, pp. 3–33). New York: Academic Press.

Pyszczynski, T. & Greenberg, J. (1992). *Hanging on and letting go: Understanding the onset, progression, and remission of depression.* New York: Springer-Verlag.

Rothbart, M. K., Ahadi, S. A., & Hershey, K. L. (1994). Temperament and social behavior in childhood. *Merrill-Palmer Quarterly, 40,* 21–39.

Rothbart, M. K. & Derryberry, D. (1981). Development of individual differences in temperament. In M. Lamb & A. Brown (Eds.), *Advances in developmental psychology* (Vol. 1, pp. 37–77). Hillsdale, NJ: Lawrence Erlbaum Associates, Inc.

Rothbart, M. K. & Goldsmith, H. H. (1985). Three approaches to the study of infant temperament. *Developmental Review*, *5*, 237–260.

Schneider-Rosen, K. & Cicchetti, D. (1984). The relationship between affect and cognition in maltreated infants: Quality of attachment and the development of visual self-recognition. *Child Development*, *55*, 648–658.

Schulman, A. H. & Kaplowitz, C. (1977). Mirror-image response during the first two years of life. *Developmental Psychology*, *10*, 133–142.

Stipek, D. J. (1983). A developmental analysis of pride and shame. *Human Development*, *26*, 42–54.

Stipek, D., Recchia, S., & McClintic, S. (1992). Self-evaluation in young children. *Monographs of the Society for Research in Child Development*, *57* (1, Serial No. 226).

Tajima, N. (1982). *Self-awareness and attachment at 12 months*. Paper presented at Tune Conference, Hokkaido, Japan.

Thomas, A., Chess, S., Birch, H., Hertzig, M. E., & Korn, S. (1963). *Behavioral individuality in early childhood*. New York: New York University Press.

Weiner, B. (1986). *An attributional theory of motivation and emotion*. New York: Springer-Verlag.

Chapter 6

Children's Conceptions of Shyness

Nicola Yuill *and* Robin Banerjee

FORMS OF SHYNESS
OBJECTIVE AND SUBJECTIVE DEFINITIONS OF SHYNESS
DEVELOPMENTAL SEQUENCE OF FORMS OF SHYNESS
EARLIER SELF-CONSCIOUSNESS
SOCIAL ANXIETY AND SELF-PRESENTATION
Cognitive Factors
Social-motivational Factors
SHYNESS ACROSS THE LIFESPAN
CONCLUSIONS
REFERENCES

> *"if they meet a stranger they hide behind their mum's back"*
> *"if someone asks them a question their face disappears"*
> *"at playtime they sit on their own"*
> *"they're a bit scared of people"*
> *"they go bright red when they want to say something in class"*
> *"if they're on stage and there's loads of people watching, they don't want to go on"*

Stage fright, social phobia and fear of strangers: all symptoms that these 6- to 9-year-olds recognize in their descriptions of what it means to be shy. Children as young as 45 months of age have been reported as understanding and using the word "shy" (Ridgeway, Waters, & Kuczaj, 1985), and in her study Yuill (1992a) found that a majority of children from the age of 5 could provide a recognisable definition of shyness. Despite the fact that we all use this word in our everyday

International Handbook of Social Anxiety: Concepts, Research and Interventions Relating to the Self and Shyness. Edited by W. Ray Crozier and Lynn E. Alden.
© 2001 John Wiley & Sons Ltd.

life (or perhaps because of that: see Harris, 1984), its technical use has been inconsistent. In this chapter, we are concerned with what shyness means to children, and the implications of that understanding for their social behaviour. However, in studying this, we need to consider analyses of the technical meaning of the term, and in particular, the seminal work by Buss, also referred to elsewhere in this volume. In particular, we focus on the distinction between fearful and self-conscious shyness.

There is little research directly addressing children's understanding of shyness, but several studies cover the issue tangentially. In this chapter, we first review some analyses of different forms of shyness, together with speculations that have been made about the development of these forms. We then describe some work on developmental changes in children's understanding of shyness. Our next aim is to set this work within the broader context of social anxiety and social cognitive development. What cognitive and motivational changes shape the changes we find in children's understanding of shyness, and what implications do these changes have for children's social behaviour? We focus in particular on age-related changes in the understanding of mental states and on individual differences in concern about social evaluation.

FORMS OF SHYNESS

Two influential theorists draw a similar distinction between types of shyness, and both speculate about the developmental changes in these forms. Baldwin (1894) made a distinction between primary, or "organic" bashfulness, seen in infants, young children and animals, and "true bashfulness", which appears in humans only after the age of 3. This type of shyness involves "reflection . . . upon the self and the actions of self [and] represents the child's direct application of what he knows of persons to his own inner life" (p. 439). This kind of distinction between an early form of shyness and a more mature self-conscious shyness was also articulated by Buss (1986). He described a related model of the development of shyness, which has been very influential in subsequent research. He argued that there are two types of shyness: a fearfulness present from infancy and an independent type of self-conscious shyness which emerges in early childhood. This distinction is important to the work we will discuss later, so we describe it in some detail here.

Buss's two forms of shyness are conceived as different in nature, age of onset and eliciting conditions. The prototypical case of fearful shyness is the stranger wariness that develops from the age of about 7 months, which plays a crucial part in the developmental process of attachment to caregivers (see, e.g., Schaffer & Emerson, 1964). Such shyness is elicited by social novelty. This form of shyness can persist through life, although we can expect older children and adults to become more skilled at masking such fear and putting on appropriate social performances. Evans (this volume, *Chapter 8*) gives examples of behaviour in preschool shy children that suggest what forms this fear may take after the fear displays of infancy. Parents of shy children report their children's dislike of novelty, such as changing from winter to summer clothing or trying new foods.

Such shyness is underpinned by the basic emotion of fear and, like fear, is associated with autonomic signs such as increased heart rate and higher blood pressure (Buss, 1986). Kagan and his colleagues have focused on the physiological basis of such shyness, and see "inhibition" as a temperamental characteristic with a relatively stable course through early childhood (see, e.g., Kagan, 1998; Marshall & Stevenson-Hinde, this volume, *Chapter 3*). It is important to note, however, that fearful shyness is not simply fear. It is associated with motivation to approach (Crozier, 1986), and Mosher and White (1981) see shyness as an oscillation between interest and fear.

Self-conscious shyness, in contrast to fearful shyness, has the distinguishing feature of involving the self as a social object. Such shyness is elicited by feeling conspicuous and exposed to the scrutiny of other people. As with fearful shyness, self-conscious shyness involves concern with a social motivation, in this case, a concern with others' opinions of the self. This concern is one shared by most people to some extent, and has been studied in social psychology under the aegis of "self-presentation": "the process by which individuals attempt to establish an identity by controlling the images of self available to others" (Arkin, Lake, & Baumgardner, 1986, p. 190). As we will see, social psychological models of shyness have focused on the self-conscious concerns that arise from strong self-presentational motivations that are coupled with low confidence in their ability to create a favourable impression (Schlenker & Leary, 1982; Leary, this volume, *Chapter 10*).

Just as the development of fearful shyness is tied in to the normal development of stranger wariness, so self-conscious shyness has a crucial role to play in development, since many authors see it as marking the development of a new consciousness of the self. Buss (1986) points out that blushing in embarrassment is confined to humans, who have the capacity for self-consciousness, and he argues that "public self-awareness is a universal feature of socialisation training" (ibid., p. 41). The cognitive ability to appreciate oneself as a social object is taken as a prerequisite for experiencing this form of shyness. In our view, the development of such shyness marks an important connection with the development of self-presentational concerns, and we develop this idea in the second part of our chapter.

The main claim in Buss's theory of shyness is that fearful shyness appears as stranger wariness in infancy, but that self-conscious shyness does not appear until public self-awareness develops, apparently at the age of about 4–5 years. The two forms of shyness are independent and can co-exist. When Buss's paper appeared, there was very little empirical evidence addressing this developmental question. Buss, Iscoe, and Buss (1979) interviewed parents with children of different ages about when the children displayed embarrassment, and found that there was a peak in first reports of such displays for children of 4 to 5 years of age. Since then, Ridgeway et al. (1985) have shown that a majority of children understand two fear-related terms early on ("afraid" at 27 months, and "frightened" at 33 months), but that children tend not to understand the self-conscious term "embarrassed" until 51 months. According to Buss (1986), the public self-awareness that underlies feelings of embarrassment is not present in infants because they lack both appropriate socialization and cognitive prerequisites.

Specifically, a child must have a cognitive appreciation of the "social self", as well as socialization experiences, such as a parent's comments that other people are observing and judging the child.

OBJECTIVE AND SUBJECTIVE DEFINITIONS OF SHYNESS

We have taken some space to describe the possible developmental pattern of the two forms of shyness, but our concern in this chapter is with children's understanding of shyness. We need first to make explicit the distinction between children's understanding of shyness, their reported experience of shyness and their shy behaviour, as reported by an observer. In many fields of psychology, it is relatively simple to keep these different aspects separate, but this issue is particularly complex in the case of shyness. Fearful shyness could be detected by an observer even if the subject was not aware of feeling shy, and did not have a conception of fearful shyness. On the other hand, turning to self-conscious shyness, we have already suggested that a child cannot be said to be experiencing self-conscious shyness unless that child has a cognitive appreciation that others are viewing and evaluating the self. Furthermore, self-conscious shyness is defined primarily by subjective experience rather than by behaviour, so it would be debatable whether an observer could claim that someone was feeling self-conscious when the subject denied such a feeling. Asendorpf (1986) also points out that shyness is harder to detect from mid-childhood because of children's increasing skill in self-presentation. It is easier to assess such shyness experimentally, for example, by looking at the influence of an audience on both observable behaviour and self-reported cognitions and emotions.

Thus, experiential aspects of self-conscious shyness have a closer relation to cognitive demands than those of fearful shyness. We next examine circumstantial evidence from the cognitive developmental literature to assess whether Buss's claim about the capacity for public self-awareness is supported. We then report some more direct evidence of shifts in conceptions of shyness.

DEVELOPMENTAL SEQUENCE OF FORMS OF SHYNESS

The main developmental thrust of Buss's work is the claim that self-conscious shyness begins at 4–5 years. Although the theory was specifically directed at the development of shy behaviour, self-conscious behaviour is an indication of a cognitive appreciation of the self as observed by others. Thus, Buss's theory should apply to children's *conceptions* of shyness as well as to their expression of shyness. If this is the case, recent work in children's cognitive development should provide a useful guide in predicting when children first think of shyness as involving self-consciousness.

A traditional Piagetian perspective would predict that the ability to see oneself from different points of view would only emerge in the concrete operational stage. Indeed, social-cognitive theorists who work in a Piagetian framework argue that coordinating social perspectives has a prolonged development throughout this stage. Selman in particular (e.g., Selman & Byrne, 1974) proposed several stages of social role-taking. Within his framework, the ability to reflect on the self from others' points of view emerges from around age 8 (Selman, 1980).

Using more recent theoretical perspectives on social cognition, we would expect children to be capable of concern about social evaluation when they become able to understand how one is represented by others—that is, when they develop a theory of mind. Using the traditional false-belief paradigm as an assessment of understanding other minds, it seems that children develop such an explicit awareness of others' beliefs by the age of 4 (e.g., Perner, 1991). Given the theory of mind framework, we would therefore predict that children are capable of understanding self-conscious shyness from this age. This prediction is compatible with Buss's claim that children should develop self-conscious shyness at about 4 to 5 years of age, although his claim was based on data from parental reports rather than theory.

What direct evidence is there for age-changes in conceptions of shyness? Crozier and Burnham (1990) addressed children's understanding of shyness empirically, taking a Piagetian line in arguing that self-conscious shyness requires the cognitive ability to reflect on the self as others see you. In particular, they adopted Selman and Byrne's (1974) work on social role-taking. As we mentioned above, this view predicts that children do not show "self-reflective role-taking" until the age of about 8. This position was supported by Crozier and Burnham's data on shyness. They interviewed children of 5 to 11 years of age about their experience and understanding of shyness. Using both open-ended and forced-choice questions, they found that children tended not to identify self-conscious concerns as giving rise to shyness before the age of 7 to 8.

Using a modified methodology, studies we have conducted on this topic give a picture of shyness conceptions more consistent with Buss's theory (Yuill & Banerjee, 1997). We made two main alterations to the earlier study. First, we addressed only children's understanding of shyness in others. Crozier and Burnham had asked children about their own feelings of shyness, as well as others' shyness, so it is possible that they were reporting their own experiences of shyness. If some children understood self-conscious shyness but did not perceive themselves as shy, this method would have underestimated children's understanding. Second, we simplified the method of assessing understanding of shyness. Children were given a simple forced-choice measure, asking which of two situations would make a hypothetical child feel shy—meeting a stranger or singing alone in front of the class. In two separate samples, there was a significant increase in choice of the self-conscious option between the ages of 4 and 6. Between 80% and 90% of 4-year-olds chose the fearful option, while the majority of 5- and 6-year-olds chose the self-conscious option.

These data support Buss's contention that children begin to show self-conscious shyness from about the age of 5. Furthermore, our findings reflect children's conceptions of shyness, and thus provide convergent evidence to bolster the parental reports of embarrassment reported by Buss and the observations by Ridgeway et al. regarding the use of the emotion term "embarrassed". We argue that this change is a consequence of children's growing understanding of mind at the age of around 4. There is other evidence to support this link. In our study, children who chose the self-conscious option were more likely to understand self-presentational displays of emotion (e.g., putting on a smile after getting hurt to avoid being seen as a cry-baby) than children who chose the fearful option. That is, the children who conceived of shyness in terms of self-conscious concerns were better able to understand how self-presentational motivations can give rise to particular behavioural displays. We explore this association between self-conscious shyness and the understanding of self-presentational motivations in some depth later in this chapter.

EARLIER SELF-CONSCIOUSNESS

The above discussion of self-conscious shyness assumes that the capacity for self-consciousness is primarily a matter of cognitive development. Some authors would vehemently deny such a view, and this is reflected in the lively debate about the nature of children's developing sense of the self. The traditional cognitive viewpoint is that the ability to appreciate differences in perspectives requires a concept of oneself, and this understanding is particularly important for the self-conscious understanding of others' perspectives on the self. However, the 4- to 5-year-old shift is not supported by data from other areas of research. For example, recent research on the development of self-concept has promoted the view that rather than the infantile sensory self being "primitive", it may in fact be a sophisticated achievement that is an important precursor to more "cognitive" views of the self (Butterworth, 1998).

Furthermore, evidence of self-conscious emotions is evident in young children. Lewis and his colleagues (e.g., Lewis, Sullivan, Stanger, & Weiss, 1989; Lewis, this volume, *Chapter 5*) found that toddlers can show "embarrassment behaviours" (smile and gaze aversion) in appropriate circumstances, such as being over-complimented, or being asked to dance in front of an experimenter. Furthermore, Reddy (1997) has observed that this kind of "coy" behaviour can be seen in 3-month-old infants when intimately engaged with an overly-responsive adult. Draghi-Lorenz and Reddy (1997) filmed young infants being subjected to intense regard by an adult observer, and found that the infants showed smiling followed by gaze aversion, in a display that was very reliably labelled by adults as "coy" or "shy". According to Reddy (this volume, *Chapter 4*), we do not need to attribute specific cognitive capacities such as perspective-taking, or theory of mind, to account for such displays.

These observations show that even young children have some kind of affective responsiveness to the *attention* of others, which is qualitatively distinct from a fear reaction. However, self-conscious shyness involves anxiety about *evaluation*, and these coy displays clearly do not demonstrate that infants are experiencing such feelings. We can therefore maintain that self-conscious shyness undergoes a strong shift at 4 to 5 years of age, underpinned by a cognitive appreciation of others' perspectives on the self, but we must modify the claim that self-consciousness does not exist in any form before that. Correspondingly, we are also able to conceive of the idea that self-consciousness develops beyond the age of 4 to 5. For example, Bennett, Yuill, Banerjee, and Thomson (1998) show that it is not until the age of about 7 that children understand embarrassment on the behalf of others. From this age onwards, children could understand feelings of self-consciousness following a faux pas committed by a younger sibling. Furthermore, the often-noted surge of self-conscious feelings in adolescence marks a further development, prompted perhaps by increased bodily consciousness as a result of the physiological changes of puberty, and by changes in the nature of social motivation, such as the increased importance of evaluation by the peer groups.

In summary, children's understanding of shyness does appear to shift from a primarily fear-based conception to a focus on self-consciousness. This is likely to evolve from an early affective sense of self-consciousness through to a cognitive appreciation of the "social self" at around 4 to 5 years. We will see in the following discussion of social anxiety and self-presentation that there are further cognitive and motivational variables that can be used to explain this and other differences in conceptions of shyness, both between and within age groups.

SOCIAL ANXIETY AND SELF-PRESENTATION

As discussed earlier in this chapter, social anxiety is a core feature of "self-conscious shyness", and children's understanding of the processes that give rise to social anxiety is therefore relevant to their conceptions of shyness. This section addresses the factors that influence children's changing understanding of social anxiety, with particular reference to self-presentational processes.

Social anxiety has been characterized by many in terms of concerns about the way one is evaluated by others. In Schlenker and Leary's (1982) formulation mentioned earlier in this chapter, social anxiety results from a high motivation to make a desired (or avoid an undesired) impression on others coupled with doubt that this outcome can be achieved. For example, individuals going to a party may experience social anxiety because they desperately wish to avoid being seen as boring but fear that they inevitably will be judged in this way. Children's appreciation of this concept was explored by Darby and Schlenker (1986). The researchers asked children in the second, fourth, and seventh grades to judge the feelings and behaviours of story characters known to have either high or low motivations to impress an audience and either high or low expectations that they would succeed in this goal. The second-graders appreciated the link between low expectations of success and feelings of anxiety, but predicted that children who were more highly motivated would feel less anxious. The older children, on the other hand, understood that a high motivation to impress could lead to more anxiety. This provides support for the notion that while children in primary school do understand self-conscious feelings in social situations (particularly when expectations for success are low), children in the pre-adolescent period increasingly become aware of the processes by which self-presentational motivations can give rise to social anxiety.

Darby and Schlenker's study does not directly tap children's understanding of the specific self-presentational processes involved. Indeed, there is very little evidence on how children's understanding of self-presentation develops in general. Our own research has shown that children have the cognitive capability for understanding self-presentational motives for behaviour as young as age 5 (Banerjee & Yuill, 1999a). In particular, children of this age are capable of understanding how one person may change his or her behaviour in order to create a particular impression on another person. As expected, this understanding was associated with an appreciation of second-order mental representations (i.e., "thinking about what someone else is thinking"). However, we found in a subsequent study that children's *spontaneous* recognition of self-presentational motives in everyday social situations is limited until around age 8 (Banerjee & Yuill, 1999b). It is interesting to note that this transition occurs roughly between the second and fourth grades, the period when Darby and Schlenker observed a change in understanding how a high motivation to impress can lead to anxiety.

There is further evidence which suggests that children begin to appreciate the link between self-presentation and emotion at around this time. Critically, a conception of shyness as self-consciousness requires an appreciation not just of the "social self" but also of the emotional consequences of social evaluation. Bennett's work on children's understanding of embarrassment (Bennett, 1989; Bennett & Gillingham, 1990; Bennett, Yuill, Banerjee, & Thomson, 1998) demonstrates that children between 7 and 9 years will report social emotions in situations where they or someone for whom they are responsible commits an embarrassing action. Moreover, it is clear from the most recent of these three studies that the reported embarrassment is associated with expectations of negative evaluation by the audience. This provides tentative support for the idea that children in the middle of primary school acquire an understanding of the possible emotional consequences of self-presentational motivations.

Children's understanding of the self-presentational motives that can give rise to social anxiety is likely to be associated not just with age-related transitions but also with individual differences. Indeed, children's own level of social anxiety appears to be linked to their understanding of self-presentational motives in social situations. On the one hand, socially anxious individuals are clearly very sensitive to self-presentational concerns. Research has made it clear that socially anxious individuals are well aware of the causes of their anxiety—so much so that they tend to pay less attention than non-anxious individuals to external cues in the situation (Hope, Heimberg, & Klein, 1990). Clark and Wells (1995; see Clark, this volume, *Chapter 18*), for example, provide examples of the preoccupations of people with social phobia. Quoted remarks from patients include: "They'll think I'm stupid", "They don't like the way I look", "They think I'm boring". Indeed, social anxiety scales for children contain items reflecting such concerns, and in our most recent research (Banerjee & Henderson, in press) we observed that responses to these items are strongly correlated with overall social anxiety.

On the other hand, ongoing research (Banerjee & Henderson, in press) has suggested that socially anxious children find it difficult to understand how successful behavioural strategies can result from these self-presentational concerns. In this study, children were presented with stories in which a character behaves strategically with the implied goal of making a particular impression on an audience (e.g., putting on a show of bravado after getting hurt). Those children who reported high social anxiety (using the "Social Phobia and Anxiety Inventory for Children"; Beidel, Turner, & Morris, 1995) found it more difficult than less anxious children to explain the self-presentational motives underlying the story character's behaviour. We suggest that what remains opaque to these anxious children is not the self-presentational concern *per se*, but rather the process by which the concern gives rise to an effective behavioural display.

Overall, the above material is consistent with Schlenker and Leary's (1982) argument that social anxiety involves a high motivation to impress along with a low perceived ability to succeed in pursuit of that goal (see also Leary, this volume, *Chapter 10*). That is, those who are highly anxious will understand very well the motivation to impress but will have little understanding of how that motivation can be translated into successful action.

This line of argument brings us to the notion that a child's own level of social anxiety is associated with his or her conception of social anxiety. Put briefly, if a child's level of social anxiety is predictive of differences in understanding self-presentational processes, and self-presentational processes are involved in social anxiety, then the child's level of social anxiety should be related to his or her conception of social anxiety. We have some limited evidence in support of this hypothesis. In a recent study by Blackburn (1999), 8- to 9-year-olds were asked to imagine being at a party with unfamiliar children. Children were asked to decide which of two concerns would worry them more: "I don't know anyone" (fearful) or "What will they think of me?" (self-conscious). Interestingly, children who reported higher levels of social anxiety—as measured using the "Social Anxiety Scale for Children—Revised" (La Greca & Stone, 1993)—tended to select the second option as the more worrying. This could reflect a greater sensitivity among socially anxious children to the way in which self-presentational concerns give rise to anxiety.

Further evidence for the idea that children's own level of self-conscious concern is associated with their conceptions of social anxiety was found in another recent study (Banerjee & Smith, 1999). In this study, 6- to 11-year-old children completed newly-constructed public and private self-consciousness scales (derived from Fenigstein, Scheier, & Buss, 1975), and also responded to a story where the protagonist, after breaking a school road safety rule, is given the choice of either seeing the headmaster about the infraction or being singled out in assembly as a reminder to the other children of the importance of road safety. Although most children selected the first option, their justifications for their choice varied systematically. In particular, children who scored high on public self-consciousness were far more likely to refer to negative reactions or evaluations by peers—reflecting self-presentational concerns—when explaining their choice. Furthermore, as one would expect, these children tended to refer to social emotions (e.g., embarrassment) in their justifications more than other children do. Thus, we see again that individual differences in self-consciousness are associated with differences in the understanding of self-presentational processes related to social anxiety.

What kinds of factors are likely to be responsible for these differences in children's conceptions of social anxiety? Theoretically, there is reason to suspect that both cognitive and social-motivational variables are involved. The possible roles of a number of these variables are considered below.

Cognitive Factors

We have already seen evidence earlier in this chapter that aspects of mental-state understanding are related to shyness. For example, we have suggested that an understanding of first-order mental representations (e.g., others' evaluations of the self) is a prerequisite for self-conscious shyness. These kinds of associations should be particularly important in the context of the self-presentational processes discussed above. As briefly alluded to earlier, self-presentation involves second-order mental representations (the actor is thinking about others' representations of him or her), and indeed we found that 4- to 6-year-old children's understanding of self-presentational emotional displays was associated with their performance on a second-order false-belief task (Banerjee & Yuill, 1999a).

However, changes in understanding the anxiety-producing elements of self-presentational concerns may take place some years after the basic understanding of second-order mental representations has been acquired. Interestingly, Selman's (1980) model of social role-taking suggests that there are significant transitions in perspective-taking during pre-adolescence. For example, the ability to see oneself from another person's perspective is said to develop at around age 8 to 9, while the ability to coordinate the perspective-taking of multiple third parties is said to emerge at age 10 to 11. Clearly, a satisfactory conception of the self-presentational processes involved in social anxiety requires these abilities. Admittedly, the evidence on children's appreciation of second-order mental representations has demonstrated that Selman's model considerably underestimates younger children's mental-state understanding. However, it is possible that other important cognitive transitions later in childhood could explain changes in the understanding of social anxiety.

With regard to cognitive prerequisites for understanding social anxiety, we know already that children from age 5 should not have difficulty with understanding the motivation to impress in itself. However, a critical element in understanding social anxiety is the recognition of the potential emotional consequences of that motivation. As discussed below, it is reasonable to expect that the cognitive capabilities necessary for this recognition are not present until later in childhood.

First, we might argue that particular information-processing characteristics of younger children will hamper an accurate prediction of the emotional consequences of self-presentational motivations. At the most basic level, one might argue that understanding how one mental state is linked to another (e.g., seeing how self-presentational motivations may be linked to anxiety) makes more information-processing demands than understanding either mental state on its own. Also, overly simplistic schemas of cause–effect relationships may result in a failure to predict social anxiety on the basis of self-presentational motivations. For example, Darby and Schlenker (1986), in explaining the tendency for young children to associate high levels of self-presentational motivation with low levels of anxiety, cite the argument that young children are less capable than older children of perceiving that a cause may have multiple, differentiated effects. Thus, because they believe that a high self-presentational motivation will generally lead to positive characteristics, they do not admit the possibility of negative consequences like anxiety.

The above explanations focus on global cognitive characteristics, and thus do not help us to formulate hypotheses that are specifically concerned with the emotional domain. Existing research, however, does provide us with this opportunity. Of particular interest here is the work on how children come to understand emotions that arise from idiosyncratic appraisals of an event. Gnepp (1989, p. 158) notes that "When a situation is emotionally equivocal (associated with more than one emotion), it is inappropriate to judge another person's feelings from the situational context alone. Instead . . . personal information is needed before we can predict the person's feelings with any confidence."

At a basic level, even young children are able to see the path from personal information to idiosyncratic appraisal to emotional outcome. For example, 4-year-olds are able to predict happiness and sadness on the basis of a person's idiosyncratic desire (e.g., Mark likes eating grass so he is happy when he gets grass for dinner; see Gnepp, Klayman, & Trabasso, 1982). However, this is a far cry from seeing how an individual's self-presentational concerns can give rise to feelings of anxiety. Indeed, evidence suggests that this kind of understanding is likely to be a comparatively late development. For example, children from age 8 are better than younger children at seeing how one's personality traits can affect one's emotional reaction to a given situation (Gnepp & Chilamkurti, 1988; Yuill & Pearson, 1998). Also, recent evidence on children's understanding of surprise suggests that understanding how surprise emanates from the discovery that one's idiosyncratic beliefs are in fact false does not fully develop until ages 7 to 9 (Ruffman & Keenan, 1996).

In summary, it seems reasonable to argue that cognitive factors must be relevant to an appreciation of the self-presentational processes involved in social anxiety. Specifically, although children from age 5 may be able to understand self-presentational concerns, they may have difficulty in seeing exactly how such concerns can give rise to feelings of anxiety. It is not yet clear whether the specific cognitive factors involved are related to domain-general information-processing or to domain-specific concepts of emotion, but future researchers may justifiably explore both possibilities.

Social-motivational Factors

Although it seems likely that cognitive factors are of importance in children's changing understanding of social anxiety, of at least equal significance are social-motivational factors. Indeed, just because children have the cognitive capability for understanding some phenomenon in a particular way does not mean that they will conceive of the phenomenon in that way. In the present context, the cognitive ability to recognize how self-presentational processes can give rise to social anxiety is not the sole determinant of how social anxiety is conceived. Socialization experiences, which in turn affect children's own motivational orientation, are likely to be relevant not just to age-related transitions, but also to within-age group individual differences in understanding social anxiety.

Let us first examine children's basic appreciation of self-presentational motives in social life. In recent research, mentioned earlier in this chapter (Banerjee & Yuill, 1999b), we demonstrated that children tended not to attribute behaviour to self-presentational motives until around age 8 despite the fact that they regularly ascribed prosocial and other motives to characters at age 6. A cognitive explanation for this is unlikely, since we had already established that children from age 5 were capable of understanding self-presentational motives (Banerjee & Yuill, 1999a). In contrast, social-motivational factors are likely to be responsible for these findings. Children between the ages of 7 and 9 are becoming more worried about social evaluation (Vasey, Crnic, & Carter, 1994), and are beginning to see evaluation as a major function performed by friends (Bigelow & La Gaipa, 1975). It is intuitively appealing to assume that having experience with a concern about social evaluation oneself is a primary antecedent to recognizing the role of such concerns in social anxiety. Using an ecological approach (e.g., Bronfenbrenner, 1979), we may pinpoint changes in social experience which are responsible for the child's initiation into social evaluation concerns.

We argue that the social developments which are most pertinent to the understanding of the role of self-presentational motivations in social anxiety are those that concern the child's peer relations. There is strong evidence that children's peer relations become increasingly important as they progress through primary school (e.g., Ellis, Rogoff, & Cromer, 1981). As peers become a more salient part of children's lives, adherence to peer group norms starts to be the basis for popularity and social acceptance (see Erwin, 1993). If children fail to match the norms of their classmates—or, more importantly, if their classmates *think* that they have failed to match the norms—their social life is likely to suffer. Parker and Gottman (1989) have explicitly recognized this change in motivation. In their model of friendship formation, they argue that while 3- to 7-year-olds have the goal of playful interaction with peers, 8- to 12-year-olds seek peer acceptance by conforming to group norms. The increased importance of group norms at this time is reflected in the "negative gossip" and teasing that is so evident at this age: children are able to establish what the group norms are by seeing what behaviours lead to teasing and gossip (e.g., see Gottman, 1986). Given this state of affairs, it seems to be in the interest of the 8-year-old to be concerned about social evaluation. Moreover, it predisposes the 8-year-old to understand how those concerns can lead to feelings of anxiety.

Earlier in this chapter we showed that the understanding of social anxiety varies not just between age groups but also between individuals within an age group. It is clear that the age-related transitions in social experience discussed above mask many individual differences. The extent to which changes in peer relations take place, and the extent to which any such changes influence concerns about social evaluation, clearly must differ from one child to the next. Similarly, parental and cultural expectations regarding the importance of self-presentational concerns may be expected to vary considerably within any given age group. These differences, coupled with individual predispositions, are likely to cause varying motivational orientations, with some children more likely than others to appreciate how self-presentational motivations lead to social anxiety.

As noted on several occasions above, those who themselves experience social anxiety as a result of self-presentational concerns are likely to understand this process very well. If we accept that socially anxious individuals are sensitive, even oversensitive, to the self-presentational processes involved in anxiety, then we must also agree that the antecedents of social anxiety are relevant to conceptions of social anxiety. Although the aetiology of social anxiety is dealt with elsewhere in this volume, it is important to note here that family factors (e.g., parents who are directive with regard to social behaviour; Mills & Rubin, 1993) and peer factors (e.g., peer rejection experience; Vernberg, Abwender, Ewell, & Beery, 1992) must be considered when looking at individual differences in the actual experience of social anxiety and in the conception of social anxiety.

It seems likely that there are additional individual differences in social-motivational variables which do not necessarily have a bearing on the experience of social anxiety but which do influence conceptions of social anxiety. Although there is little specific evidence, there are some promising lines of research. In particular, differences in mental-state understanding may reflect not simply cognitive characteristics but also motivational variables: some children may be more sensitive than others to the dynamic flow of mental states in social situations. Intriguing evidence for this notion is provided by O'Riordan, Baron-Cohen, Jones, Stone, and Plaisted (1996). Their "faux pas" test assesses second-order mental-state reasoning but is often failed by children who pass standard tests of second-order reasoning. The task requires children to answer questions about the feelings, intentions and attitudes of characters in a story where one character unintentionally insults another. There are clear cognitive prerequisites for passing this task, but additionally we suggest that there are important motivational prerequisites: children must be "tuned in" to the interpersonal processes involved in real-life social situations. Banerjee (2000) observed that children who passed this task tended to be high self-monitors—children who are sensitive to the demands of social situations and change their behaviour to meet those demands (see Snyder, 1974, 1987). Moreover, these children tended to better understand self-presentational strategies such as modesty. It seems reasonable to expect that children who have this broad interpersonal sensitivity will be more likely to understand the self-presentational processes involved in social anxiety. Of course, at the moment this is all rather speculative: we must first break down this rather vague notion of "interpersonal sensitivity" into more clearly definable terms and then explore the contribution of both dispositional and social-experiential factors to the development of this sensitivity.

In summary, we may conclude that children's understanding of how self-presentational concerns can give rise to feelings of social anxiety increases with age as a result of both cognitive and social-motivational factors, and that there are individual differences in the extent to which children within an age group will conceive of these processes.

SHYNESS ACROSS THE LIFESPAN

We have seen that children's appreciation of social aspects of the self changes throughout childhood. A final issue is one that is very rarely addressed: What do children understand about the developmental course of shyness as a trait? As part of a study of children's understanding of the origin and development of individual differences, Yuill (1992b) asked 4- to 10-year-old children a series of questions about shyness. An initial set of questions addressed children's views about whether shyness was under the individual's control. It emerged that the youngest group, 4-year-olds, did not differentiate between traits in this aspect, and were equally divided, perhaps reflecting a random response pattern, while children of 6 to 10 years were almost unanimous in seeing shyness as involuntary. Relating to this, almost all children saw shyness as declining with age, most denying firmly that adults could be shy. The explanation offered by some children was situational: adults were viewed as having more control over social situations and therefore able to avoid situations that could cause embarrassment. For example, Charles (6) said that an individual would tend to become less shy with age "because he'll be bigger and like he could do whatever he likes, couldn't just go to different places if he doesn't want to. If they're too young, they have to go to school." Similarly, Sean (10) noted, "When you're grown up, there's no-one telling you what to do, so you can do what you want, there's no teachers."

Some of the age changes observed in the children's conceptions of shyness are consistent with the theoretical claims discussed earlier in this chapter. For example, some of the 4-year-olds expressed the view that shyness was most intense at birth, because at that stage, every face is unfamiliar. This seems to reflect a conception of fearful shyness. The oldest group more often attributed an inverted-U shape for shyness, suggesting that babies lack the cognitive abilities required to feel shy, and that shyness emerges on starting school, before declining later in life. Some of these children explicitly referred to self-consciousness, noting that youngsters would be made shy when "shown off" by proud parents. However, consistent with the predominant view of shyness as an involuntary reaction, there was just one child in the sample, a 10-year-old, who spontaneously mentioned the possibility of self-presentational control of shyness.

CONCLUSIONS

We have examined a diverse range of evidence in this chapter. Although there has been relatively little research directly targeting children's conceptions of shyness, there are several indications about the kinds of developmental changes that occur and the kinds of mechanisms that are responsible for those changes.

First, school-aged children tend to differ from younger children in the extent to which they characterize shyness as a self-conscious emotion. In line with Buss's theory, children below the age of 4 or 5 tend to associate shy feelings with stranger wariness and fear of novelty. Older children increasingly focus on social evaluation concerns as leading to self-conscious shyness. Furthermore, as we have just seen, children do seem to tie shyness to particular situations: adults are seen as not experiencing much shyness because they are perceived as being able to avoid shyness-eliciting situations. On the other hand, children towards the end of primary school begin to have a clearer insight into how feelings of low self-efficacy combine with self-presentational motivations (e.g., concerns about impression management) to give rise to feelings of anxiety in social situations.

What is responsible for these developmental shifts? We started with Buss's idea that self-conscious shyness requires a cognitive appreciation of the self as a social object. This requires a certain degree of mental-state understanding, not only in terms of understanding others' perspectives on the self but also in terms of how these evaluations by other people can influence one's feelings. This can be thought of in representational terms: an audience forms a representation about an actor, and concern about this representation evokes feelings of self-conscious shyness. As we have seen, this understanding makes considerable information-processing demands, but perhaps more importantly also requires situation-specific knowledge about beliefs and emotions. At the same time, it seems very likely that these cognitive factors are changing in tandem with motivational factors. The self-presentational concerns about social evaluation that underpin feelings of self-conscious shyness are likely to become more salient to children towards the end of primary school, when positive evaluation by peers and perceived adherence to group norms become primary bases for social acceptance.

Notwithstanding the fact that children in primary school tend to focus on shyness as a self-conscious emotion more than younger children, there are also important within-age group differences in children's understanding of the self-presentational processes that give rise to self-conscious shyness. These individual differences are likely to arise from the cognitive and motivational mechanisms that we already believe to be involved in the developmental shifts discussed above: mental-state understanding and concern about social evaluation. Thus, just as children differ from each other in the extent to which they experience social anxiety, there is corresponding variability in their understanding of the processes that give rise to self-conscious emotions. We suggest that there are multidirectional causal links between cognition, motivation and emotion. Specifically, models of self-consciousness in childhood must consider not only the cognitive foundation for self-conscious emotions, but also the possible influence of affective and motivational processes on cognition about the self.

REFERENCES

Arkin, R. M., Lake, E. A., & Baumgardner, A. B. (1986). Shyness and self-presentation. In W. H. Jones, J. M. Cheek, & S. R. Briggs (Eds.), *Shyness: Perspectives on research and treatment* (pp. 189–203). New York: Plenum Press.

Asendorpf, J. (1986). Shyness in middle and late childhood. In W. H. Jones, J. M. Cheek, & S. R. Briggs (Eds.), *Shyness: Perspectives on research and treatment* (pp. 91–103). New York: Plenum.

Baldwin, J. M. (1894). Bashfulness in children. *Educational Review, 8*, 434–441.

Banerjee, R. (2000). The development of an understanding of modesty. *British Journal of Developmental Psychology, 18*, 499–517.

Banerjee, R. & Henderson, L. (in preparation). Social-cognitive factors in childhood social anxiety: A preliminary investigation. *Social Cognition*.

Banerjee, R. & Smith, B. (1999). [Self-reported self-consciousness and concern about social evaluation.] Unpublished data, University of Sussex.

Banerjee, R. & Yuill, N. (1999a). Children's understanding of self-presentational display rules: Associations with mental-state understanding. *British Journal of Developmental Psychology, 17*, 111–124.

Banerjee, R. & Yuill, N. (1999b). Children's explanations for self-presentational behaviour. *European Journal of Social Psychology, 29*, 105–111.

Beidel, D. C., Turner, S. M., & Morris, T. L. (1995). A new inventory to assess childhood social anxiety and phobia: The Social Phobia and Anxiety Inventory for Children. *Psychological Assessment, 7*, 73–79.

Bennett, M. (1989). Children's self-attribution of embarrassment. *British Journal of Developmental Psychology, 7*, 207–217.

Bennett, M. & Gillingham, K. (1990). The role of self-focused attention in children's attributions of social emotions to the self. *Journal of Genetic Psychology, 152*, 303–309.

Bennett, M., Yuill, N., Banerjee, R., & Thomson, S. (1998). Children's understanding of extended identity. *Developmental Psychology, 34*, 322–331.

Bigelow, B. J. & La Gaipa, J. J. (1975). Children's written descriptions of friendship: A multidimensional analysis. *Developmental Psychology, 11*, 857–858.

Blackburn, T. (1999). *Social anxiety, self-consciousness and loneliness in 8–9 year olds: A "Circle Time" initiative.* Unpublished master's thesis, University of Sussex, Brighton, England.

Bronfenbrenner, U. (1979). *The ecology of human development: Experiments by nature and design.* Cambridge, MA: Harvard University Press.

Buss, A. H. (1986). A theory of shyness. In W. H. Jones, J. M. Cheek, & S. R. Briggs (Eds.), *Shyness: Perspectives on research and treatment* (pp. 39–46). New York: Plenum.

Buss, A. H., Iscoe, I., & Buss, E. H. (1979). The development of embarrassment. *Journal of Psychology, 103,* 227–230.

Butterworth, G. (1998). A developmental-ecological perspective on Strawson's "The self". *Journal of Consciousness Studies, 5,* 132–140.

Clark, D. M. & Wells, A. (1995). A cognitive model of social phobia. In R. G. Heimberg, M. R. Leibowitz, D. A. Hope, & F. R. Schneier (Eds.), *Social phobia: Diagnosis, assessment, and treatment* (pp. 69–93) New York: Guilford.

Crozier, W. R. (1986). Individual differences in shyness. In W. H. Jones, J. M. Cheek, & S. R. Briggs (Eds.), *Shyness: Perspectives on research and treatment* (pp. 133–145). New York: Plenum Press.

Crozier, W. R. & Burnham, M. (1990). Age-related differences in children's understanding of shyness. *British Journal of Developmental Psychology, 8,* 179–185.

Darby, B. W. & Schlenker, B. R. (1986). Children's understanding of social anxiety. *Developmental Psychology, 22,* 633–639.

Draghi-Lorenz, R. & Reddy, V. (1997). *Adult recognition of shyness, coyness and embarrassment in young infants.* Paper presented at the British Psychological Society International Conference on Shyness and Self-consciousness. University of Wales, Cardiff.

Ellis, S., Rogoff, B., & Cromer, C. C. (1981). Age segregation in children's social interactions. *Developmental Psychology, 17,* 399–407.

Erwin, P. G. (1993). *Friendship and peer relations in children.* Chichester, Sussex: Wiley.

Fenigstein, A., Scheier, M. F., & Buss, A. H. (1975). Public and private self-consciousness: Assessment and theory. *Journal of Consulting and Clinical Psychology, 43,* 522–527.

Gnepp, J. (1989). Children's use of personal information to understand other people's feelings. In C. Saarni & P. L. Harris (Eds.), *Children's understanding of emotion* (pp. 151–77). New York: Cambridge University Press.

Gnepp, J. & Chilamkurti, C. (1988). Children's use of personality attributions to predict other people's emotional and behavioural reactions. *Child Development, 59,* 743–754.

Gnepp, J., Klayman, J., & Trabasso, T. (1982). A hierarchy of information sources for inferring emotional reactions. *Journal of Experimental Child Psychology, 33,* 111–123.

Gottman, J. M. (1986). The world of coordinated play: Same and cross-sex friendship in young children. In J. M. Gottman & J. G. Parker (Eds.), *The conversations of friends* (pp. 139–191). New York: Cambridge University Press.

Harris, P. R. (1984). Shyness and psychological imperialism: On the dangers of ignoring the ordinary language roots of the terms we deal with. *European Journal of Social Psychology, 14,* 169–181.

Hope, D. A., Heimberg, R. G., & Klein, J. F. (1990). Social anxiety and the recall of interpersonal information. *Journal of Cognitive Psychotherapy, 4,* 185–195.

Kagan, J. (1998) Biology and the child. In Eisenberg, N. (Ed.), *Handbook of child psychology (5th edition) Vol. 3: Social, emotional and personality development* (pp. 177–235). New York: Wiley.

LaGreca, A. M. & Stone, W. L. (1993). Social Anxiety Scale for Children—Revised: Factor structure and concurrent validity. *Journal of Clinical Child Psychology, 22,* 17–27.

Lewis, M., Sullivan, M. W., Stanger, C., & Weiss, M. (1989). Self development and self-conscious emotions. *Child Development, 60,* 146–156.

Mills, R. S. L. & Rubin, K. H. (1993). Socialization factors in the development of social withdrawal. In K. H. Rubin & J. B. Asendorpf (Eds.), *Social withdrawal, inhibition, and shyness in childhood* (pp. 117–148). Hillsdale, NJ: Erlbaum.

Mosher, D. L. & White, B. B. (1981). On differentiating shame and shyness. *Motivation and Emotion, 5,* 61–74.

O'Riordan, M. A., Baron-Cohen, S., Jones, R., Stone, V., & Plaisted, K. (1996). *A new test of social sensitivity: Detection of faux pas in normal development and autism.* Paper presented at the British Psychological Society Developmental Section Annual Conference, Oxford.

Parker, J. G. & Gottman, J. M. (1989). Social and emotional development in a relational context. In J. T. Berndt & G. W. Ladd (Eds.), *Peer relationships in child development* (pp. 95–131). New York: Wiley.

Perner, J. (1991). *Understanding the representational mind.* Cambridge, MA: MIT Press.

Reddy, V. (1997). *The origins of self-conscious affects: Shy/coyness in 2–3 month-olds.* Paper presented at the British Psychological Society International Conference on Shyness and Self-consciousness. University of Wales, Cardiff.

Ridgeway, D., Waters, E., & Kuczaj, S. A. (1985). Acquisition of emotion-descriptive language: Receptive and productive vocabulary norms for ages 18 months to 6 years. *Developmental Psychology, 21,* 901–908.

Ruffman, T. & Keenan, T. R. (1996). The belief-based emotion of surprise: The case for a lag in understanding relative to false belief. *Developmental Psychology, 32,* 40–49.

Schaffer, H. R. & Emerson, P. E. (1964). The development of social attachments in infancy. *Monographs of the Society for Research on Child Development, 29.*

Schlenker, B. R. & Leary, M. R. (1982). Social anxiety and self-presentation: A conceptualization and model. *Psychological Bulletin, 92,* 641–669.

Selman, R. L. (1980). *The growth of interpersonal understanding.* New York: Academic Press.

Selman, R. S. & Byrne, D. F. (1974). A structural-developmental analysis of levels of role-taking in middle childhood. *Child Development, 45,* 803–806.

Snyder, M. (1974). The self-monitoring of expressive behavior. *Journal of Personality and Social Psychology, 30,* 526–537.

Snyder, M. (1987). *Public appearances/private realities: The psychology of self-monitoring.* New York: Freeman.

Vasey, M. W., Crnic, K. A., & Carter, W. G. (1994). Worry in childhood: A developmental perspective. *Cognitive Therapy and Research, 18,* 529–549.

Vernberg, E. M., Abwender, D. A., Ewell, K. K., & Beery, S. H. (1992). Social anxiety and peer relationships in early adolescence: A prospective analysis. *Journal of Clinical Child Psychology, 21,* 189–196.

Yuill, N. (1992a). Children's production and comprehension of trait terms. *British Journal of Developmental Psychology, 10,* 131–142.

Yuill, N. (1992b). Children's conception of personality traits. *Human Development, 35,* 265–279.

Yuill, N. & Banerjee, R. (1997). *Fear or self-consciousness: Children's developing conceptions of shyness.* Paper presented at the British Psychological Society International Conference on Shyness and Self-consciousness. University of Wales, Cardiff.

Yuill, N. & Pearson, A. (1998). The development of bases for trait attribution: Children's understanding of causal mechanisms based on desire. *Developmental Psychology, 34,* 574–586.

Chapter 7

Behavioral Inhibition, Social Withdrawal, and Parenting

Kim B. Burgess, Kenneth H. Rubin, Charissa S. L. Cheah, *and* Larry J. Nelson

DEFINING INHIBITION, SHYNESS, AND SOCIAL WITHDRAWAL
ATTACHMENT, BEHAVIORAL INHIBITION, AND SOCIAL WITHDRAWAL
PARENTING BELIEFS, INHIBITION, AND SOCIAL WITHDRAWAL
PARENTING BEHAVIORS, INHIBITION, AND SOCIAL WITHDRAWAL
GENDER DIFFERENCES, SHYNESS, AND PARENTING
PARENTING AND CULTURE
CONCLUSION
REFERENCES

The study of children's social and emotional development requires that attention be paid to dispositional/biological factors (e.g., temperament), familial interactions and relationships, social contexts (e.g., school, neighborhood), and culture. For example, Hinde (1995) has advanced the notion that development be considered from a multi-level perspective beginning with individual characteristics and progressing to the interaction, relationship, and group levels of analysis and conjecture. At the level of the individual child, developmental scientists have studied such constructs as temperament that might lead to problematic social or behavioral outcomes. One such intrapersonal characteristic is that of "difficult" temperament—a phenomenon typically comprising high activity level and anger proneness, or high emotional reactivity combined with poor regulatory control. Difficult temperament has been thought, by some, to be an early developmental precursor of an externalizing/under-controlled behavior pattern (e.g., Bates, Bayles, Bennett, Ridge, & Brown, 1991; Rubin, Hastings, Chen, Stewart, & McNichol, 1998; Sanson, Oberklaid, Pedlow,

International Handbook of Social Anxiety: Concepts, Research and Interventions Relating to the Self and Shyness. Edited by W. Ray Crozier and Lynn E. Alden.

& Prior, 1991). Another dispositional characteristic, behavioral inhibition, has been regarded as a precursor of an internalizing/overcontrolled behavior pattern (e.g., Fox et al., 1995). The focus of this chapter is on behavioral inhibition and its conceptually related constructs and variants; most notably, social wariness, shyness, and social withdrawal.

For the most part, the study of behavioral inhibition, shyness, and social withdrawal has been dominated by literatures pertaining to putative biological origins. Somewhat in support of this biological perspective has been the consistent report that these phenomena are stable (Caspi & Silva, 1995; Kagan, Reznick, & Snidman, 1987, 1989; Rubin, Coplan, Fox, & Calkins, 1995b; Rubin, Booth, Rose-Krasnor, & Mills, 1995a)—inhibited, shy or withdrawn children appear to remain so from one year to the next. In truth, the stability data reported thus far are rather imperfect. Children do change, and some change more than others. A significant question to ask, therefore, is "What are the factors that predict, or are associated with, both stability and change?"

It bears noting that little is known about the extent to which children's interactions and relationships with others, especially parents, serve as causal or moderating agents in the development of behavioral inhibition, shyness and social withdrawal, and their collective correlates and consequences. The primary purpose of this chapter is to examine the ways in which parent–child relationships and parenting beliefs and behaviors may serve in the development, exacerbation or amelioration of inhibition, shyness, and withdrawal. A secondary purpose of this chapter is to explore child gender differences and cultural differences insofar as the relations between parenting and inhibition, shyness, and withdrawal are concerned. Before proceeding, however, it is necessary to address relevant definitional issues.

DEFINING INHIBITION, SHYNESS, AND SOCIAL WITHDRAWAL

Defining the constructs of behavioral inhibition, shyness, and social withdrawal is an issue of significance because researchers and clinicians have often used these (and other) terms interchangeably (e.g., social isolation, peer neglect), and thus inappropriately. Further, researchers have operationalized each of these constructs in different ways. For a thorough discussion of terminology, we refer the reader to Rubin and Asendorpf (1993). Briefly, in their attempt to bring clarity to this area of study, these authors referred to *inhibition* as the disposition to be wary and fearful when encountering novel (that is, unfamiliar) situations. More specifically, behavioral inhibition was regarded as a pattern of responding or behaving, possibly biologically based, such that when unfamiliar or challenging situations were encountered, the child showed signs of anxiety, distress, or disorganization (e.g., Rubin, Hastings, Stewart, Henderson, & Chen, 1997). *Shyness* was referred to as inhibition in response to novel *social* situations. The consistent display of inhibited or shy behaviors and wary emotions in unfamiliar social or nonsocial situations has been viewed as a precursor to an overcontrolled behavior pattern. *Social withdrawal* referred to the consistent (across situations and over time) display of solitary behavior when encountering both familiar and/or unfamiliar *peers*. *Social isolation* had little to do with the behavioral expression of wariness; rather the term reflected the expression of solitary behavior that results from peer rejection. Simply put, social withdrawal was construed as isolating oneself *from* the peer group, whereas social isolation indicated rejection *by* the peer group.

With regard to social withdrawal in *early* childhood, several different forms of solitary behavior have been described, each of which may have unique psychological properties and meanings. These forms of socially withdrawn behaviors include solitary-passive, solitary-active, and reticent behaviors (Coplan, Rubin, Fox, Calkins, & Stewart, 1994; Rubin, 1982). The common denominator among these different types of solitude is that they occur when the child is among a group of children. *Solitary-passive* behavior involves object exploration and constructive activity while playing at a distance from others. Such behaviors appear to indicate a lack of motivation to either approach or avoid others, and seem not to be associated with psychological maladjustment in early childhood (Coplan & Rubin, 1998; Rubin et al., 1995b). Second, *solitary-active* behavior involves repeated sensorimotor actions with or without objects, and solitary dramatizing. Although infrequent, this behavior has been associated with impulsivity and aggression (Coplan et al., 1994). Third, *reticence* is characterized by the frequent production of onlooking and unoccupied behaviors. While reticent preschoolers may desire peer interaction, thoughts of social approach elicit anxiety/fear and cause the avoidance of interaction. Reticence has been related to overt indicators of anxiety (e.g., crying, automanipulatives), poor performance on cooperative group tasks, and an inability to regulate negative emotions (Coplan et al., 1994; Rubin et al., 1995b). In summary, each of these types of solitude represents independent constellations of behaviors with different psychological meanings.

Importantly, the "meanings" of these forms of solitude change with age. Solitary-passive behavior, for instance, takes on an increasingly negative flavor. For example, Kennedy, Cheah, Rubin, and Fox (1999) recently reported that unsociable 7-year-old children tend to display both reticent *and* solitary-passive behaviors among peers. This finding is consonant with Asendorpf's (1991, 1993) conjecture that, by middle childhood, categories of solitude in the peer group tend to come together to form a single cluster—social withdrawal. It is also the case that solitary-active behavior continues to decrease with age beyond the preschool years, becoming practically non-existent among normally functioning elementary school children (e.g., Rubin, Watson, & Jambor, 1978).

ATTACHMENT, BEHAVIORAL INHIBITION, AND SOCIAL WITHDRAWAL

In examining the etiology of children's behaviors and emotions, it has been common for researchers and clinicians to focus not only on temperament, but also on the quality of the child's relationships with primary caregivers as possible explanatory starting points. Because of the centrality of the parent–child relationship in infancy and early childhood, numerous studies have been conducted on the quality of this relationship, and researchers have often relied on attachment theory as their underlying, conceptual guiding light.

Attachment theorists maintain that the primary relationship develops during the first year of life, usually between the mother and the infant. Maternal sensitivity and responsiveness influence whether the relationship will be secure or insecure (Ainsworth, Blehar, Waters, & Wall, 1978). Researchers have shown that securely attached infants are likely to be well adjusted, socially competent, and successful at forming peer relationships in early and middle childhood (e.g., Egeland, Carlson, & Sroufe, 1993; Shulman, Elicker, & Sroufe, 1994; Sroufe, 1983), whereas insecurely attached children may be less successful at social developmental tasks (Booth, Rose-Krasnor, McKinnon, & Rubin, 1994; Booth, Rose-Krasnor, & Rubin, 1991; Renken, Egeland, Marvinney, Sroufe, & Mangelsdorf, 1989; Rose-Krasnor, Rubin, Booth & Coplan, 1996).

Rubin and colleagues (e.g., Rubin, LeMare, & Lollis, 1990; Rubin & Mills, 1991) have proposed a developmental pathway in which those infants who are temperamentally reactive and who receive insensitive, unresponsive parenting (Kagan, Reznick, Clarke, Snidman, & Garcia-Coll, 1984) come to develop an insecure-ambivalent (C-type) attachment relationship with their primary caregivers (Goldberg, 1990). In novel settings these C babies maintain close proximity to the attachment figure (usually the mother). When the mother leaves the Strange Situation briefly, these infants become quite unsettled. Upon reunion with the mother, these infants show angry, resistant behaviors interspersed with proximity- or contact-seeking behaviors (e.g., Greenspan & Lieberman, 1988). It is argued that this constellation of infant emotional hyperarousability and insecure attachment may lead the child to display inhibited/wary behaviors as a toddler. Further, insecure inhibited toddlers have been posited to be at risk for the development of social withdrawal in childhood (Rubin et al., 1990).

There is now emerging support for linkages between temperament C attachment status, inhibition and social withdrawal. For example, Thompson, Connell, and Bridges (1988) reported that infant proneness to fear predicted distress following maternal separation. Further, infants who are dispositionally reactive to mildly stressful, novel social events are more likely to be classified as insecurely attached C (anxious-resistant) babies than are their less reactive counterparts (Calkins & Fox, 1992; Fox & Calkins, 1993). Studies indicate that anxious-resistant (C) infants are more whiny, easily frustrated, and socially inhibited at age 2 than their secure (B) counterparts (Fox & Calkins, 1993; Matas, Arend, & Sroufe, 1978).

Support for both concurrent and predictive associations between insecure attachment, behavioral inhibition, and social withdrawal comes from more recent studies (e.g., Booth et al., 1994; Rubin et al., 1995a). Further, among clinical samples of mothers with anxiety disorders, Manassis and colleagues reported that 65% of children aged 18 to 59 months were behaviorally inhibited (using Kagan's measures) and that 80% were insecurely attached (Strange Situation), although the authors did not distinguish between A (avoidant) babies and C babies (Manassis, Bradley, Goldberg, Hood, & Swinson, 1995).

The reluctance to explore and socially interact with others impedes the development of social competence (Rubin, Bukowski, & Parker, 1998a). This appears to be a cost of a C-type attachment history (Renken, Egeland, Marvinney, Mangelsdorf, & Sroufe, 1989). Given that the social behaviors of preschoolers and toddlers who have an insecure C-type attachment history are thought to be guided largely by fear of rejection, it is unsurprising to find that when these insecurely attached children are observed in peer group settings, they appear to avoid rejection by demonstrating passive, adult-dependent behavior and withdrawal from social interaction (Renken et al., 1989). Indeed, anxious-resistant C babies tend to be less socially skilled as toddlers and rated by their teachers as more dependent, helpless, tense, and fearful than their secure counterparts (Pastor, 1981). Lastly, C babies lack confidence and assertiveness at age four years (Erickson, Sroufe, & Egeland, 1985); then, at age seven years they are seen as passively withdrawn (Renken et al., 1989).

It bears noting that insecure attachment relationships are also predicted by *maternal* behavior. For example, mothers of insecurely attached C babies are overinvolved and overcontrolling compared to mothers of securely attached babies (Erickson et al., 1985). This finding represents a natural segue to the extant literature on the associations between parenting and behavioral inhibition and social withdrawal.

PARENTING BELIEFS, INHIBITION, AND SOCIAL WITHDRAWAL

Thus far, we have suggested that inhibition and social withdrawal may be a function of both dispositional and attachment relationship characteristics. It is also the case that these phenomena are associated with particular parenting styles (e.g., Hetherington & Martin, 1986; Parker, 1983). To begin with, parents' behaviors may be influenced by their beliefs about when it is that children typically come to demonstrate particular behaviors or ways of thinking; why children behave in the ways they do; and how they can influence growth or discourage maladaptive behavior (Bugental & Goodnow, 1998). In their developmental model, Rubin and colleagues suggest that parents' beliefs about how to socialize their children are determined partly by their children's dispositional characteristics (e.g., Rubin, Nelson, Hastings, & Asendorpf, 1999). Specifically, infant/toddler inhibition is cited as representing a determinant of parenting beliefs and behaviors that, in turn, come to reinforce the development of socially withdrawn behaviors in children (e.g., Mills & Rubin, 1993; Rubin, Hymel, Mills, & Rose-Krasnor, 1991b). Further, these authors proposed that early social fearfulness and inhibition would elicit parenting responses of an overprotective, overcontrolling nature (e.g., Rubin, Stewart, & Chen, 1995c). Such parenting beliefs and behaviors would serve to reinforce social fearfulness.

In a recent longitudinal study, Rubin et al. (1999) explored the relations between children's social fearfulness/shyness at ages 2 and 4 years, and parents' beliefs in preferred rearing styles at these same two time points. Parental perceptions of child shyness/social wariness at age 2 predicted both mothers' and fathers' expressed lack of encouragement of independence. Relatedly, toddlers observed to be inhibited at age 2 years have mothers who endorsed parenting styles pertaining to protection, a punishment orientation, and a lack of emphasis on independence training (Chen et al., 1998). Thus, at an early developmental stage, inhibited/shy children are exposed to attitudes or beliefs about parenting that may foster dependency.

In earlier work, Rubin and colleagues assessed the relations between maternal beliefs about children's development of social skills and their preschoolers' observed social behaviors among familiar others. Those preschoolers whose mothers indicated that the attainment of social skills was relatively unimportant were observed to cry more often when attempting to meet their social goals and to experience less success in their interpersonal negotiations (Rubin, Mills, & Rose-Krasnor, 1989). Further, the children of those mothers who believed that social skills emanated primarily from child temperament factors were less socially assertive and successful during their peer exchanges. Finally, mothers who indicated that they would use highly controlling strategies to socialize social skills (e.g., using coercion and strong commands) had children who were more likely to seek help from others and to use non-assertive social strategies to meet their own social goals. Teachers also rated the children of these mothers as anxious, fearful, and withdrawn.

To gain a more precise picture of withdrawal, Rubin and Mills (1990) presented the mothers of extremely anxious-withdrawn children (as identified by teacher and classmate ratings) with stories describing hypothetical incidents in which their own child consistently behaved in a socially withdrawn fashion among familiar others. Compared to mothers of non-anxious ("normal") children, mothers of anxious-withdrawn children were more likely to suggest that they would use high control strategies (e.g., directives) and would be less likely to display low-power strategies (e.g., redirecting the child) and indirect–no response strategies (e.g., seeking information from others, arranging opportunities for peer interaction, not responding) in reaction to their children's demonstration of socially withdrawn behavior. Also, these mothers were more likely to attribute the consistent display of social withdrawal to dispositional sources; and they expressed more anger, disappointment, embarrassment, and guilt about their children's withdrawn behaviors than did mothers of "normal" children.

The findings described above suggest that children who are socially anxious and withdrawn have mothers who may be overinvolved with, and overcontrolling of them. This pattern of parenting has previously been linked to internalizing difficulties in children (Parker, 1983). Indeed, preschool-age children of depressed mothers exhibit significantly more inhibited and anxious-withdrawn forms of play with both familiar and unfamiliar playmates than do children of non-depressed mothers (Kochanska, 1991; Rubin, Booth, Zahn-Waxler,

Cummings, & Wilkinson, 1991a). Consequently, it may be that mothers of socially withdrawn preschoolers transmit their own internalizing problems to their children through overinvolved parenting. Such a parenting style may exacerbate a child's sense of felt insecurity. Further, it may be that mothers of socially withdrawn children are highly sensitized to their children's social and emotional characteristics; such sensitivity may provoke well-intended overcontrol and overinvolvement. This reaction to their child's social behaviors may produce a mixture of defensive reactions (e.g., downplaying the importance of social skills) and negative emotions.

PARENTING BEHAVIORS, INHIBITION, AND SOCIAL WITHDRAWAL

Given that parental beliefs and cognitions influence parents' behaviors (Bugental & Goodnow, 1998), it may be that the socialization practices of parents whose children are inhibited or withdrawn differ from those of parents whose children are "normal" and socially competent. Parents of socially wary/fearful children may sense their children's difficulties and perceived helplessness; and then might try to support their children directly either by manipulating their child's behaviors in a power assertive, highly directive fashion (e.g., telling the child how to act or what to do) or by actually intervening and taking over for the child (e.g., intervening during peer disputes; inviting a potential playmate to the home). As noted above, the mothers of anxious-withdrawn children endorse the use of highly controlling behaviors to handle their children's social withdrawal in the peer group.

Recently, researchers have shown that parental influence and control do maintain and exacerbate child inhibition and social withdrawal. For example, Rubin et al. (1997) observed toddlers interacting with unfamiliar peers and adults in a variety of novel situations in a laboratory; and they found that the toddlers who were the most inhibited across contexts were rated by their mothers as being of wary/shy temperament. Further, these mothers were observed to display overly solicitous behaviors (i.e., intrusively controlling, unresponsive, physically affectionate) during free play, snack time, and clean-up sessions. When interacting with their inhibited toddlers, then, mothers were highly affectionate and shielding of them when it was neither appropriate nor sensitive to be this way.

In a related longitudinal study, Park, Belsky, Putnam, and Crnic (1997) conducted naturalistic home observations of parents with their *male* infants and toddlers, and later assessed boys' inhibition at age 3. They found that the parents of inhibited boys were high on sensitivity and positive affect but low on intrusiveness; moreover, parents were actually accepting of their child's inhibition or trouble coping with anxiety. It is difficult to compare these findings with those of the Rubin et al. (1997) study. The one constant is that inhibited children do not benefit from a high amount of affection under certain conditions; and it is argued that this particular mode of parenting may reinforce fearful, wary behavior, especially if provided during situations when the demonstration of warmth is inappropriate. The contradictory finding of Park et al. (1997) that parents were *not* intrusive could be explained in light of three factors. First, parenting behaviors were assessed prior to the observation of child inhibition, as opposed to concurrently; this may suggest that parents of inhibited children are actually not overcontrolling in the earliest stage of development, and it is only when they recognize their child's wariness/fearfulness (or it becomes more obvious as their child approaches the toddler and preschool years) that they try to "fix" or change it. Second, Park et al. assessed parents' behaviors in a natural setting with familiar people (i.e., home environment), whereas Rubin et al. assessed parent–child interactions in an unfamiliar laboratory setting with unfamiliar people. Third, Park et al. did not analyze whether parents behaved differently under free-play versus demand situations.

Exploring parental behaviors with respect to the related construct of social reticence, Rubin, Cheah, and Fox (2001) reported that mothers whose preschoolers frequently displayed reticent behavior among unfamiliar peers were more likely than mothers whose children rarely displayed social reticence to use control statements and highly controlling behaviors during a mother–child free-play session. This finding strengthens the contention that children who tend to avoid social interaction have mothers who provide guidance and directives in an otherwise relaxing situation. Directiveness during goal-oriented tasks may be expected of parents (e.g., Kuczynski & Kochanska, 1995), but controlling the child's behavior in a pleasant, non-stressful free-play environment is unnecessary; at the very least, such maternal behavior precludes the child from freely exploring the environment. The use of a highly directive parenting style during free play could suggest that the parent attempts to protect the child from stress or harm when neither is objectively present.

In a related study, Henderson and Rubin (1997) explored whether emotion regulatory processes, as measured physiologically, interacted with parental behavior to predict preschoolers' socially reticent behavior among peers. These researchers began with the premise that vagal tone, a marker of the tonic level of functioning of the parasympathetic nervous system (Porges, 1991), should be associated with the display of social behavior in the peer group. Specifically, children with low vagal tone have been found to be more inhibited in the presence of an adult stranger at age 2 years (Fox, 1989; Rubin et al., 1997), and more reticent among peers at age 4 years (Fox & Field, 1989). Having examined a possible connection between child physiology, child behaviors, and particular parenting styles, Henderson and Rubin (1997) reported that, for preschoolers who showed low resting vagal tone, observed *and* reported maternal directive and critical behaviors were associated with child reticent, wary and anxious behaviors among peers. For children with high resting vagal tone, such maternal direction and criticism were not associated with behavioral reticence.

Examining parents' behaviors toward anxious-withdrawn children (ages $2^1/_2$ to 6 years), LaFreniere and Dumas (1992) found that mothers were poor reciprocators of their own child's displays of positive behavior and positive affect. In addition, these mothers responded aversively to their child's negative behavior and negative affect. Such non-contingent responding to their children's positive behavior accompanied by punishment of negative behavior could hinder a child's development of self-worth and felt security.

Bolstering these results in an older age group, Mills and Rubin (1998) observed that, relative to mothers of normal children, mothers of extremely anxious-withdrawn children (aged 5 to 9 years) directed significantly more behavior control statements to their children. Further, mothers of anxious-withdrawn children used more psychological control statements, defined as devaluation statements or non-responsiveness to the child. Such parenting practices may also be accompanied by expressions of criticism and disapproval, and this negativity may attack the child's sense of self-worth.

In summary, the studies reviewed above provide support for our contention that once an inhibited behavioral style is established, parents may sense the child's anxieties and insecurities, and seek to help the child's mastery of the environment through authoritarian direction, protection, and oversolicitousness (e.g., solving the child's interpersonal and intrapersonal problems for him or her). These findings support the notion that inhibited/wary or shy children have parents who are reluctant to let them explore novel situations. Importantly, parental overcontrol may be a response to children's early displays of behavioral inhibition. Thus, parents may sense their children's anxiety/distress and choose to constrain independent action rather than subjecting their children to possible psychological or physical risk. An unfortunate consequence of constraining children and providing unnecessary assistance is that their opportunities to develop self-regulatory abilities, learn social skills, and build self-confidence are also limited.

The literature on childhood social withdrawal has focused primarily on its "main effects"—those dispositional and parenting characteristics that uniquely explain significant percentages of variance. There have been few studies in which are examined the independent and interactive contributions of temperament and parenting in predicting withdrawn behavior. Cheah, Rubin, and Fox (1999) recently explored the influence of parenting and temperament at preschool age on the display of social solitude in middle childhood. Also considered in this longitudinal study was the notion that the context in which parenting behaviors occur has a direct bearing on "outcomes". For example, the appropriateness of highly controlling parental behavior, whether positive or negative, may depend on the task environment. Therefore, in this study the researchers examined the display of parenting behaviors during both an *un*structured activity (free play) and a structured situation that required parental control (a teaching task).

Among Cheah et al.'s findings was that reticence at age 4 years significantly predicted reticent, socially anxious behaviors at age 7 years. Thus, it seems that the phenomenon of social reticence is a stable characteristic. Further, mothers' displays of highly controlling and oversolicitous behaviors during a free-play session with children age 4 years uniquely predicted behavioral reticence at age 7 years over and above the initial level of reticence at age 4 years. Again, it appears as if those mothers of reticent children who are overcontrolling and over-involved (when it is unnecessary) exacerbate child reticence. Notably, this study reveals that such parenting behaviors make a "contribution" to reticence beyond the contribution of child temperament.

GENDER DIFFERENCES, SHYNESS, AND PARENTING

Researchers have indicated that the long-term outcomes of shyness or socially withdrawn behavior may differ for boys and girls. Specifically, it has been argued that boys' shyness and social withdrawal may be accompanied by greater psychological "costs" than those of girls (Caspi, Elder, & Bem, 1988; Engfer, 1993; Rubin, Chen, & Hymel, 1993). This being the case, it seems appropriate to examine the parenting characteristics associated with shyness and withdrawal in boys versus girls.

To begin with, the quality of the parent–child attachment relationship has been associated with the display of shyness for *boys* but not girls. Insecurely attached (C status) boys, but not girls, are more likely than their secure counterparts to display passive-withdrawn behaviors in early and mid-childhood (Renken et al., 1989). Among toddler and preschool-age children, Stevenson-Hinde (1989) and Engfer (1993) reported that the parents of inhibited and shy girls (but not boys) were warm, responsive, and sensitive. A subsequent study found a higher pro-portion of positive mother–child interactions for moderately shy girls compared to moderately shy boys (Stevenson-Hinde & Glover, 1996). In contrast, Stevenson-Hinde and Glover (1996) also found that mothers interacted more positively with extremely shy boys than they did with extremely shy girls. Thus, any sex differences obtained seemed to depend on the level of shyness or inhi-bition among girls and boys. Whether the authors' index of "positive interaction" could reflect aspects of oversolicitous parenting is a consideration given the Rubin et al. (1997) report that inappropriate and intrusive displays of warmth are associated with socially wary, inhibited behaviors.

MacDonald and Parke (1984) reported that the parents of socially withdrawn preschoolers were less spontaneous, playful, and affectively positive during parent–child play than were the parents of more sociable children. During father–son interactions, they found that *boys* perceived by teachers as socially withdrawn, hesitant with peers, and as spectators during social activities had fathers who were highly directive and less engaging and physically playful. The findings were less clear-cut for socially withdrawn daughters.

In summary, the empirical literature suggests that inhibited/withdrawn boys might experience different socialization histories than girls. Not only is it impor-tant to examine whether parents treat shy/withdrawn boys differently than girls, but also whether boys respond differently than girls to parental behaviors. Noteworthy are the above-described studies suggesting that mothers' and fathers' behaviors are differentially associated with *boys'*, but not girls', displays of social reticence. The one constant among boys and girls, however, is that highly controlling parenting during situations where such control is unnecessary is associated with the display of social reticence.

PARENTING AND CULTURE

The studies described thus far were completed in North America and Northwestern Europe. Yet, there are reasons to believe that the psychological "meanings" of inhibited/shy behavior varies from culture-to-culture (e.g., Chen, Rubin, & Li, 1995). This being the case, it would seem important to study whether the parenting correlates and associations found with inhibition/shyness/withdrawal in North American and Northwest European cultures are different when studied in other venues. On a broader scale, it would also make a good deal of sense to study whether the etiologies of behavioral problems are similar from one culture to another.

Cultural values play an enormous role in determining the meanings of behavioral adaptation and normalcy. For example, the relative adaptive nature of shyness and social withdrawal appears to vary between Western individualistic cultures and Eastern collectivistic cultures. In the former, shy and withdrawn behavior is regarded as maladaptive, reflecting social incompetence, wariness, and anxiety. Thus, it is unsurprising that some North American and Northwestern European parents encourage their children to be assertive and independent in challenging situations. Children are generally socialized to be increasingly assertive and self-reliant rather than reserved and inhibited.

In contrast, achieving and maintaining social order and interpersonal harmony are the primary concerns of both traditional and contemporary collectivistic Chinese societies. Shyness and behavioral inhibition are *positively* evaluated in Chinese culture because these behaviors are considered to reflect social maturity and understanding (e.g., Chen et al., 1995; Ho, 1987; King & Bond, 1985). Consequently, it has been found that shy and inhibited behaviors are valued and encouraged by teachers and peers in Chinese cultures (Chen, Rubin, & Sun, 1992; Chen et al., 1995).

As one might expect, parental beliefs and behaviors are guided by general cultural norms and value systems (Bornstein, 1991). Thus, in a recent study by Chen et al. (1998), information on child-rearing attitudes and beliefs was obtained from Chinese and Canadian mothers. Consistent with previous reports (e.g., Kagan, Kearsley, & Zelazo, 1978), Chinese toddlers were observed to be significantly more inhibited than their Canadian counterparts. Given the Western notion that inhibition/shyness reflects incompetence, wariness and immaturity, North American mothers reported being more protective, controlling, less encouraging of achievement, and less accepting of their inhibited toddlers. Conversely, the direction of the associations between toddler inhibition and parental attitudes was opposite in the Chinese sample: child inhibition was positively associated with acceptance and encouragement of achievement, and negatively associated with parental control. These results illustrate the notion that behavioral inhibition is a culturally bound construct.

In addition to studying East–West similarities or differences in parenting and inhibition, a few researchers have compared Northern and Southern cultures. Schneider, Attili, Vermigly, and Younger (1997) presented middle-class mothers of 7-year-olds in Canada and Italy with hypothetical scenarios depicting children being socially withdrawn. The mothers were asked to indicate why they thought children might act in a withdrawn manner, how they would feel if their child displayed this behavior, and what socialization strategies they would use. The researchers hypothesized that Italian families' strong connection with the extended family would reduce the need for emotional investment in relationships outside the family; hence, these parents would regard peer relationships for their children as unnecessary, or as less important, compared to North Americans (Young & Ferguson, 1981). The authors therefore predicted that Italian parents would regard social withdrawal as less bothersome than would parents in the North American culture. Indeed, Schneider et al. (1997) found that English-Canadian mothers indicated stronger negative reactions to withdrawal than did Italian mothers.

Furthermore, the Italian data showed gender differences with mothers indicating less power assertion in response to girls' withdrawal compared with boys' withdrawal; but there was no similar gender difference in the Canadian sample. These results support the authors' hypothesis that gender roles are likely more distinct in the Italian sample than in the Canadian sample. Italian mothers might find social withdrawal by girls (who are expected to assume domestic roles that require less assertiveness with peers) to be less troublesome than parents in the English-Canadian culture with less defined gender roles. It is difficult to interpret the lack of child gender differences with respect to Canadian parents in this study. But, it is important to note that the sample of parents was a normative one; thus, it was unlike prior research (Rubin & Mills, 1990) in which parents of inhibited or withdrawn children were studied. Moreover, where gender differences have been reported, the dependent measure was derived from observations of parental behaviors and not from questionnaires about parental beliefs.

The cross-cultural studies presented raise questions about the universality and generalizability of the findings reported by the predominantly North American studies on the relations between parenting and inhibition or social withdrawal. It seems important to be aware that, across different cultures, parental beliefs and behaviors are likely to be associated with child behaviors and outcomes in uniquely meaningful ways. Finally, we require longitudinal designs with interactional models concerning parenting and child inhibition or social withdrawal within the context of culture.

CONCLUSION

In conclusion, factors such as child temperament, the parent–child attachment relationship, and parenting beliefs and behaviors play a significant role in the development, maintenance, and amelioration of socially reticent or withdrawn behavior in children. While some infants and toddlers may be physiologically prone to display socially fearful behavior, parents do have a role to play in the development of childhood inhibition and withdrawal and their associated liabilities. It is the case, however, that parental beliefs and behaviors may vary depending on child gender, situational demands/conditions, and culture. North American parents who perceive their infants/toddlers to be socially wary lean toward an overcontrolling, overprotective parenting style when their children reach preschool age. This tendency may serve to maintain or exacerbate the inherent wariness in their children. In turn, the maintenance of a withdrawn profile may lead to negative outcomes such as peer rejection, loneliness, and negative self-regard during the mid-to-late childhood and early adolescent years (Boivin, Hymel, & Bukowski, 1995; Ollendick, Greene, Weist, & Oswald, 1990; Rubin, 1993). In other cultures, however, the continuing developmental associations between parent and child behaviors may yield different adjustment profiles.

Given that *both* inhibited child temperament and particular parenting beliefs and behaviors predict the display of reticent, socially withdrawn behaviors in childhood, it would appear appropriate to question whether the conspiracy between inhibited, shy temperament and oversolicitous/overcontrolling parenting collectively predict later social and psychological difficulty (e.g., internalizing problems). With context and culture in mind, more prospective longitudinal studies and innovative methodologies are required to answer important questions about predictions from inhibited temperament and parent–child relationship variables to specific psychosocial and behavioral outcomes. It is evident from Table 7.1 that few data exist on these fronts.

Table 7.1 Parenting, inhibition, and social withdrawal

Authors	Construct	Age	Parenting measure	Sex differences reported	Cross-cultural differences
Cheah et al. (1999)	Reticence (observed) + Shyness (questionnaire)	4 and 7 years	Observed maternal warmth and control	None	NA
Chen et al. (1998)	Inhibition (observed)	2 years	Parental ratings of parenting styles (protection, punishment, independence training, rejection, encouragement of achievement)	None	Inhibition in Chinese toddlers was correlated positively with maternal acceptance and encouragement of independence but negatively with punishment and rejection. In Canadian toddlers, inhibition was negatively correlated with acceptance and encouragement of achievement, but positively with punishment and protection
Engfer (1993)	Shyness (observed and maternal ratings)	3.3 months and 6.3 years	Observed maternal sensitivity, rated maternal and emotional stability	Whereas at 33 months girls' shyness was negatively related to maternal depression, at 6.3 years maternal depression, insensitivity and anxious overprotection predicted girls' shyness. At 33 months maternal shyness predicted boys' shyness	NA

continued overleaf

Study	Construct	Age	Parenting measure	Findings	
Mills & Rubin (1993)	Withdrawn-internalizing Passive-isolation (peer rating) + internalizing (teacher rating)	5 to 9 years	Ratings of maternal beliefs about proactive teaching strategies, reactive feelings, attributions, and strategies for modifying behavior	None	NA
Mills & Rubin (1998)	Withdrawn-internalizing (teacher and peer ratings)	Kindergarten, Grades 2 & 4	Observed behavioral and psychological control in different behavior contexts (e.g., free play, compliance task)	None	NA
Kochanska (1991)	Social and non-social inhibition (observed)	2–3½ years	Observed maternal encouragement to explore the environment and/or stranger; maternal anger and criticism	Boys were more inhibited to a new environment (nonsocial inhibition), and girls showed more inhibition towards the stranger (social inhibition). Girls received more maternal fostering of interaction with strangers than did boys	NA
Park et al. (1997)	Inhibition (observed)	10–37 months	Observed parental positive and negative affect, sensitivity, intrusiveness, and detachment	Sample consisted of boys only	NA

Table 7.1 (continued)

Authors	Construct	Age	Parenting measure	Sex differences reported	Cross-cultural differences
Rubin et al. (2001)	Reticence (observed) Shyness (questionnaire)	4 years	Observed maternal warmth and control	None	NA
Rubin et al. (1997)	Inhibition (observed) Shyness (observed)	2 years	Observed maternal warmth and control	None	NA
Rubin & Mills (1990)	Social withdrawal withdrawal (observed) + internalizing difficulties (teacher questionnaire)	4 years	Ratings of maternal beliefs about proactive teaching strategies, reactive feelings, attributions, and strategies for modifying behavior	None	NA
Rubin et al. (1999)	Shyness/social fear (questionnaire) + inhibition (observed)	2 and 4 years	Parental ratings of parenting styles (encouragement of independence, protection, rejection, acceptance)	None	NA

Schneider et al. (1997)	Social withdrawal (peer nomination)	7 years	Ratings of maternal beliefs about proactive teaching strategies, reactive feelings attributions, and strategies	Italian mothers indicated lower emotional intensity in response to girls' withdrawal than boys'.	Canadian mothers reported stronger emotional responses to withdrawal, were less likely to see it as an internal/stable factor, and more likely to believe that withdrawal was changeable. Italian mothers were less puzzled about social withdrawal, although more surprised
Stevenson-Hinde & Glover (1996)	Shyness (teacher and parent ratings, observations)		Observed positive mood, gentleness, sensitivity, meshing, enjoyment of child	Mothers of moderately inhibited girls were more warm, responsive, and sensitive than mothers of extremely inhibited girls; but withdrawn boys had parents who were cold, less affectionate and responsive than average boys. However, mothers interacted more positively with high shy boys than girls	NA

REFERENCES

Ainsworth, M. S., Blehar, M. C., Waters, E., & Wall, S. (1978). *Patterns of attachment: A psychological study of the strange situation.* Hillsdale, NJ: Erlbaum.

Asendorpf, J. B. (1991). Development of inhibited children's coping with unfamiliarity. *Child Development, 62,* 1460–1474.

Asendorpf, J. B. (1993). Beyond temperament: A two-factor coping model of the development of inhibition during childhood. In K. H. Rubin & J. B. Asendorpf (Eds.), *Social withdrawal, inhibition, and shyness in childhood* (pp. 265–290). Hillsdale, NJ: Erlbaum.

Bates, J. E., Bayles, K., Bennett, D. S., Ridge, B., & Brown, M. (1991). Origins of externalizing behavior problems at eight years of age. In D. J. Pepler & K. H. Rubin (Eds.), *The development and treatment of childhood aggression.* Hillsdale, NJ: Erlbaum.

Boivin, M., Hymel, S., & Bukowski, W. M. (1995). The roles of social withdrawal, peer rejection, and victimization by peers in predicting loneliness and depressed mood in childhood. *Development and Psychopathology, 7,* 765–785.

Booth, C. L., Rose-Krasnor, L., McKinnon, J., & Rubin, K. H. (1994). Predicting social adjustment in middle childhood: The role of preschool attachment security and maternal style. *Social Development, 3,* 189–204.

Booth, C. L., Rose-Krasnor, L., & Rubin, K. H. (1991). Predicting social adjustment in middle childhood: The role of preschool attachment security and maternal style. *Social Development, 3,* 189–204.

Bornstein, M. H. (1991). Approaches to parenting in culture. In M. H. Bornstein (Ed.), *Cultural approaches to parenting* (pp. 3–19). Hillsdale, NJ: Erlbaum.

Bugental, D. & Goodnow, J. J. (1998). Socialization processes. In N. Eisenberg (Ed.), *Handbook of child psychology* (5th edition): *Social, emotional, and personality development* (pp. 389–462). New York: Wiley.

Calkins, S. D. & Fox, N. A. (1992). The relations among infant temperament, security of attachment, and behavioral inhibition at 24 months. *Child Development, 63,* 1456–1472.

Caspi, A., Elder, G. H., & Bem, D. J. (1988). Moving away from the world: Life-course patterns of shy children. *Developmental Psychology, 24,* 824–831.

Caspi, A. & Silva, P. A. (1995). Temperamental qualities at age three predict personality traits in young adulthood: Longitudinal evidence from a birth cohort. *Child Development, 66,* 486–498.

Cheah, C. S. L., Rubin, K. H., & Fox, N. A. (1999). *Predicting reticence at seven years: The influence of temperament and overprotective parenting at four years.* Poster presentation at the biennial meeting of the Society for Research in Child Development, Albuquerque, NM.

Chen, X., Hastings, P. D., Rubin, K. H., Chen, H., Cen, G., & Stewart, S. L. (1998). Child rearing practices and behavioral inhibition in Chinese and Canadian toddlers: A cross-cultural study. *Developmental Psychology, 34,* 677–686.

Chen, X., Rubin, K. H., & Li, B. (1995). Social and school adjustment of shy and aggressive children in China. *Development and Psychopathology, 7,* 337–349.

Chen, X., Rubin, K. H., & Sun, Y. (1992). Social reputation and peer relationships in Chinese and Canadian children: A cross-cultural study. *Child Development, 63,* 1336–1343.

Coplan, R. J. & Rubin, K. H. (1998). Exploring and assessing non-social play in the preschool: The development and validation of the Preschool Play Behavior Scale. *Social Development, 7,* 72–91.

Coplan, R. J., Rubin, K. H., Fox, N. A., Calkins, S. D., & Stewart, S. L. (1994). Being alone, playing alone, and acting alone: Distinguishing among reticence and passive and active solitude in young children. *Child Development, 65,* 129–137.

Egeland, B., Carlson, E., & Sroufe, L. A. (1993). Resilience as process. *Development and Psychopathology, 5,* 517–528.

Engfer, A. (1993). Antecedents and consequences of shyness in boys and girls: A 6-year longitudinal study. In K. H. Rubin & J. B. Asendorpf (Eds.), *Social withdrawal, inhibition, and shyness* (pp. 49–79). Hillsdale, NJ: Erlbaum.

Erikson, M. F., Sroufe, L. A., & Egeland, B. (1985). The relationship between quality of attachment and behavior problems in preschool in a high risk sample. In I. Bretherton & E. Waters (Eds.), *Growing points of attachment theory and research. Monographs of the Society for Research in Child Development, 50* (Nos. 1–2, Serial No. 209).

Fox, N. (1989). Psychophysiological correlates of emotional reactivity during the first year of life. *Developmental Psychology, 25*, 364–372.

Fox, N. A. & Calkins, S. D. (1993). Pathways to aggression and social withdrawal: Interactions among temperament, attachment, and regulation. In K. H. Rubin & J. B. Asendorpf (Eds.), *Social withdrawal, inhibition, and shyness in childhood* (pp. 81–100). Hillsdale, NJ: Lawrence Erlbaum Associates.

Fox, N. A. & Field, T. (1989). Young children's responses to entry into preschool: Psychophysical and behavioral findings. *Journal of Applied Developmental Psychology, 10*, 527–540.

Fox, N. A., Rubin, K. H., Calkins, S. D., Marshall, T. R., Coplan, R. J., Porges, S. W., Long, J. M., & Stewart, S. (1995). Frontal activation asymmetry and social competence at four years of age. *Child Development, 66*, 1770–1784.

Goldberg, S. (1990). Attachment in infants at risk: Theory, research, and practice. *Infants and Young Children, 2*, 11–20.

Greenspan, S. I. & Lieberman, A. F. (1988). A clinical approach to attachment. In J. Belsky & T. Nezworski (Eds.), *Clinical implications of attachment* (pp. 387–424). Hillsdale, NJ: Erlbaum.

Henderson, H. A. & Rubin, K. H. (1997, April). *Internal and external correlates of self-regulation in preschool aged children.* Poster presented at the Biennial Meeting of the Society for Research in Child Development, Washington, DC.

Hetherington, E. M. & Martin, B. (1986). Family factors and psychopathology in children. In H. C. Quay & J. S. Werry (Eds.), *Psychopathological disorders of childhood* (3rd edn.) (pp. 332–390). New York: John Wiley & Sons.

Hinde, R. A. (1995). A suggested structure for a science of relationships. *Personal Relationships, 2*, 1–15.

Ho, M. K. (1987). *Family therapy with minorities.* Newbury Park, CA: Sage.

Kagan, J., Kearsley, R. B., & Zelazo, P. R. (1978). *Infancy: Its place in human development.* Cambridge, MA: Harvard University Press.

Kagan, J., Reznick, J. S., Clarke, C., Snidman, N., & Garcia-Coll, C. (1984). Behavioral inhibition to the unfamiliar. *Child Development, 55*, 2212–2225.

Kagan, J., Reznick, J. S., & Snidman, N. (1987). The physiology and psychology of behavioral inhibition in children. *Child Development, 58*, 1459–1473.

Kagan, J., Reznick, J. S., & Snidman, N. (1989). Issues in the study of temperament. In G. A. Kohnstamm, J. E. Bates, & M. K. Rothbart (Eds.), *Temperament in childhood* (pp. 133–144). London: Wiley.

Kennedy, A., Cheah, C. S. L., Rubin, K. H., & Fox, N. A. (1999). *Emotion regulation and dysregulation at 7 years of age.* Poster presentation at the biennial meeting of the Society for Research in Child Development, Albuquerque, NM.

King, A. Y. C. & Bond, M. H. (1985). The Confucian paradigm of man: A sociological view. In W. S. Tseng & D. Y. H. Wu (Eds.), *Chinese culture and mental health* (pp. 29–46). Orlando, FL: Academic Press.

Kochanska, G. (1991). Patterns of inhibition to the unfamiliar in children of normal and affectively ill mothers. *Child Development, 62*, 250–263.

Kuczynski, L. & Kochanska, G. (1995). Function and content of maternal demands: Developmental significance of early demands for competent action. *Child Development, 66*, 616–628.

LaFreniere, P. J. & Dumas, J. E. (1992). A transactional analysis of early childhood anxiety and social withdrawal. *Development and Psychopathology*, *4*, 385–402.

MacDonald, K. & Parke, R. D. (1984). Bridging the gap: Parent–child play interaction and peer interactive competence. *Child Development*, *55*, 1265–1277.

Manassis, K., Bradley, S., Goldberg, S., Hood, J., & Swinson, R. P. (1995). Behavioural inhibition, attachment, and anxiety in children of mothers with anxiety disorders. *Canadian Journal of Psychiatry*, *40*, 87–92.

Matas, L. Arend, R. A., & Sroufe, L. A. (1978). Continuity and adaptation in the second year: The relationship between quality of attachment and later competence. *Child Development*, *49*, 549–561.

Mills, R. S. L. & Rubin, K. H. (1993). Socialization factors in the development of social withdrawal. In K. H. Rubin & J. B. Asendorpf (Eds.), *Social withdrawal, inhibition, and shyness in childhood* (pp. 117–148). Hillsdale, NJ: Lawrence Erlbaum.

Mills, R. S. L. & Rubin, K. H. (1998). Are behavioral and psychological control *both* differentially associated with childhood aggression and social withdrawal? *Canadian Journal of Behavioral Science*, *30*, 132–136.

Ollendick, T. H., Greene, R. W., Weist, M. D., & Oswald, D. P. (1990). The predictive validity of teacher nominations: A five-year follow-up of at-risk youth. *Journal of Abnormal Child Psychology*, *18*, 699–713.

Park, S., Belsky, J., Putnam, S., & Crnic, K. (1997). Infant emotionality, parenting, and 3-year inhibition: Exploring stability and lawful discontinuity in a male sample. *Developmental Psychology*, *33*, 218–227.

Parker, G. (1983). *Parental overprotection: A risk factor in psychosocial development*. New York: Grune & Stratton, Inc.

Pastor, D. (1981). The quality of mother–infant attachment and its relationship to toddler's initial sociability with peers. *Developmental Psychology*, *17*, 326–335.

Porges, S. W. (1991). Autonomic regulation and attention. In B. A. Campbell, H. Hayne, & R. Richardson (Eds.), *Attention and information processing in infants and adults*. Hillsdale, NJ: Erlbaum.

Renken, B., Egeland, B., Marvinney, D., Sroufe, L. A., & Mangelsdorf, S. (1989). Early childhood antecedents of aggression and passive-withdrawal in early elementary school. *Journal of Personality*, *57*, 257–281.

Rose-Krasnor, L., Rubin, K. H., Booth, C. L., & Coplan, R. (1996). The relation of maternal directiveness and child attachment security to social competence in preschoolers. *International Journal of Behavioral Development*, *19*, 309–325.

Rubin, K. H. (1982). Nonsocial play in preschoolers: Necessarily evil? *Child Development*, *53*, 651–657.

Rubin, K. H. (1993). The Waterloo longitudinal project: Correlates and consequences of social withdrawal from childhood to adolescence. In K. H. Rubin & J. B. Asendorpf (Eds.), *Social withdrawal, inhibition and shyness in children* (pp. 291–314). Hillsdale, NJ: Erlbaum.

Rubin, K. H. & Asendorpf, J. B. (1993). Social withdrawal, inhibition, and shyness in childhood: Conceptual and definitional issues. In K. H. Rubin & J. B. Asendorpf (Eds.), *Social withdrawal, inhibition and shyness in children* (pp. 3–17). Hillsdale, NJ: Erlbaum.

Rubin, K. H., Booth, C. L., Rose-Krasnor, L., & Mills, R. S. L. (1995a). Social relationships and social skills: A conceptual and empirical analysis. In S. Shulman (Ed.), *Close relationships and socioemotional development* (pp. 63–94). Norwood, NJ: Ablex.

Rubin, K. H., Booth, L., Zahn-Waxler, C., Cummings, M., & Wilkinson, M. (1991a). The dyadic play behaviors of children of well and depressed mothers. *Development and Psychopathology*, *3*, 243–251.

Rubin, K. H., Bukowski, W., & Parker, J. (1998a). Peer interactions, relationships, and groups. In N. Eisenberg (Ed.), *Handbook of child psychology* (5th edition): *Social, emotional, and personality development* (pp. 619–700). New York: Wiley.

Rubin, K. H., Cheah, C. S. L., & Fox, N. A. (2001). Emotion regulation, parenting, and the display of social reticence in preschoolers. *Early Education and Development, 12,* 97–115.

Rubin, K. H., Chen, X., & Hymel, S. (1993). Socioemotional characteristics of withdrawn and aggressive children. *Merrill–Palmer Quarterly, 39,* 518–534.

Rubin, K. H., Coplan, R. J., Fox, N. A., & Calkins, S. D. (1995b). Emotionality, emotion regulation, and preschoolers' social adaptation. *Development and Psychopathology, 7,* 49–62.

Rubin, K. H., Hastings, P. D., Chen, X., Stewart, S. L., & McNichol, K. (1998b). Intrapersonal and maternal correlates of aggression, conflict, and externalizing problems in toddlers. *Child Development, 69,* 1614–1629.

Rubin, K. H., Hastings, P. D., Stewart, S. L., Henderson, H. A., & Chen, X. (1997). The consistency and concomitants of inhibition: Some of the children, all of the time. *Child Development, 68,* 467–483.

Rubin, K. H., Hymel, S., Mills, R. S. L., & Rose-Krasnor, L. (1991b). Conceptualizing different developmental pathways to and from social isolation in childhood. In D. Cicchetti & S. Toth (Eds.), *Rochester symposium on developmental psychopathology,* Vol. 2. (pp. 91–122). Hillsdale, NJ: Erlbaum.

Rubin, K. H., LeMare, L. J., & Lollis, S. (1990). Social withdrawal in childhood: Developmental pathways to peer rejection. In S. R. Asher & J. D. Coie (Eds.), *Peer rejection in childhood* (pp. 217–249). New York: Cambridge University Press.

Rubin, K. H. & Mills, R. S. L. (1990). Maternal beliefs about adaptive and maladaptive social behaviors in normal, aggressive, and withdrawn preschoolers. *Journal of Abnormal Child Psychology, 18,* 419–435.

Rubin, K. H. & Mills, R. S. L. (1991). Conceptualizing developmental pathways to internalizing disorders in childhood. *Canadian Journal of Behavioral Science, 19,* 86–100.

Rubin, K. H., Mills, R. S. L., & Rose-Krasnor, L. (1989). Maternal beliefs and children's competence. In B. H. Schneider, G. Attili, J. Nadel, & R. P. Weissberg (Eds.), *Social competence in developmental perspective* (pp. 313–331). Dordrecht, The Netherlands: Kluwer Academic Publishers.

Rubin, K. H., Nelson, L. J., Hastings, P., & Asendorpf, J. (1999). Transaction between parents' perceptions of their children's shyness and their parenting styles. *International Journal of Behavioral Development, 23,* 937–957.

Rubin, K. H., Stewart, S., & Chen, X. (1995c). Parents of aggressive and withdrawn children. In M. H. Bornstein (Ed.), *Handbook of parenting: Vol. 1. Children and parenting* (pp. 225–284). Mahwah, NJ: Lawrence Erlbaum.

Rubin, K. H., Watson, K., & Jambor, T. (1978). Free play behaviors in preschool and kindergarten children. *Child Development, 49,* 534–536.

Sanson, A., Oberklaid, F., Pedlow, R., & Prior, M. (1991). Risk indicators: Assessments of infancy predictors of preschool behavioral maladjustment. *Journal of Child Psychology and Psychiatry, 32,* 609–626.

Schneider, B. H., Attili, G., Vermigly, P. & Younger, A. (1997). A comparison of middle class English-Canadian and Italian mothers' beliefs about children's peer directed aggression and social withdrawal. *International Journal of Behavioral Development, 21,* 133–154.

Shulman, S., Elicker, J., & Sroufe, L. A. (1994). Stages of friendship growth in preadolescence as related to attachment history. *Journal of Social and Personal Relationships, 11,* 341–361.

Sroufe, L. A. (1983). Infant-caregiver attachment and patterns of adaptation in preschool: The roots of maladaptation and competence. In M. Perlmutter (Ed.), *The Minnesota symposia on child psychology* (Vol. 16, pp. 41–83). Hillsdale, NJ: Lawrence Erlbaum.

Stevenson-Hinde, J. (1989). Behavioral inhibition: Issues of context. In J. S. Reznick (Ed.), *Perspectives on behavioral inhibition* (pp. 125–138). Chicago: University of Chicago Press.

Stevenson-Hinde, J. & Glover, A. (1996). Shy girls and boys: A new look. *Journal of Child Psychology and Psychiatry, 37,* 181–187.

Thompson, R. A., Connell, J., & Bridges, L. J. (1988). Temperament, emotional and social interactive behavior in the strange situation: An analysis of attachment functioning. *Child Development, 59,* 1102–1110.

Young, J. W. & Ferguson, L. R. (1981). *Puberty to manhood in Italy and America.* New York: Academic Press.

Chapter 8

Shyness in the Classroom and Home

Mary Ann Evans

STABILITY OF SHYNESS ACROSS HOME AND SCHOOL

VERBAL PERFORMANCE

ACADEMIC ACHIEVEMENT

HELPING SHY CHILDREN IN THE CLASSROOM

SHYNESS AND ILLNESS

HOME BEHAVIOURS ASSOCIATED WITH SHYNESS

PARENTING SHY CHILDREN

CONCLUDING REMARKS

ACKNOWLEDGEMENT

REFERENCES

Shyness is both a very private and a very public thing—private in that it entails self-evaluations which may or may not be overtly expressed and public because it is most frequently revealed in interactions with unfamiliar others, unfamiliar settings, and uncertain situations. Because of the latter, researchers often study shy children in contexts such as play groups with new peers, novel toys and unfamiliar adults, and problem-solving tasks in research laboratories. However much of the child's life is experienced at home in interaction with parents and at school in classroom discourse. While classrooms may easily be construed as settings which may elicit shyness, we less often think of shyness as being an issue within the familiar and secure context of the home. Yet there are reasons why we should consider the behaviour of shy children in the latter setting. First, to the extent that shyness reflects a behavioural and biological predisposition to be wary, we can anticipate that some continuity will be expressed across home and school, and that there will be situations within the home that will elicit inhibition. Second, to the extent that shyness in children presents a challenge to care-

International Handbook of Social Anxiety: Concepts, Research and Interventions Relating to the Self and Shyness. Edited by W. Ray Crozier and Lynn E. Alden.

givers, we need to understand the manifestations of shyness that both parents and teachers perceive and the ways they respond to them. The purpose of this chapter is to highlight some dimensions of shyness and their manifestations at home and in the classroom, and to bring together suggestions from various sources on teaching and parenting shy children. As chapters in this volume by Reddy (*Chapter 4*) and Burgess, Rubin, Chea, and Nelson (*Chapter 7*) deal substantially with social withdrawal in peer interactions, this topic will be dealt with only peripherally here. In addition, the review is limited to research carried out within Western cultures.

The chapter begins with a consideration of the stability of shyness across these two contexts and then considers verbal behaviour—a major dimension of shyness. The next sections consider academic achievement and how to work with shy children in the classroom. A summary of research concerning the health status of shy children follows, this being a relatively neglected topic in understanding the overall presentation of the shy child at home and at school. The chapter closes with a consideration of shyness on the homefront and parenting shy children. It should be noted that the intent of this chapter is to draw on a diversity of research which has used a variety of terminology and methods for denoting and targeting samples who may loosely be referred to as shy children. This approach is adopted as there is likely substantial overlap in the profiles of the groups sampled despite the conceptual distinctions researchers might hope to denote by different terms. In citing this research within the chapter, the terms used by the authors are usually used, but when generalizing across research, the term "shy" is used.

STABILITY OF SHYNESS ACROSS HOME AND SCHOOL

A number of researchers have demonstrated that shyness in childhood shows substantial stability across time, with correlations ranging from 0.36 to 0.77 across as much as a ten-year period (e.g., Guerin & Gottfried, 1994; Hegvik, McDevitt, & Carey, 1982; Kagan, Reznick, & Snidman, 1989; Pedlow, Sanson, Prior, & Oberklaid, 1993). However correlations between parent and teacher reports are low to modest (Asendorpf, 1990; Hinshaw, Han, Erhardt, & Huber, 1992; Northman, Prior, Sanson, & Oberklaid, 1987; Wang & Kemple, 1993). As an illustration of this point, Eisenberg, Shepard, Fabes, Murpy, and Guthrie (1998) found that mother and teacher ratings of shyness correlated 0.26 at about age 7, 0.38 at about age 9 and not at all at about age 11, and that correlations were higher across time periods as rated by teachers or parents than they were within a time period across informants, even though teachers differed from one period to another. Through doing a cross-tabulation analysis of children whom teachers and parents regarded as high in shyness, Wang and Kemple (1993) observed that there was only a 50% overlap in the individuals.

Through a meta-analysis, Achenbach, McConaughy, and Howell (1987) found that the weighted mean correlation between teacher and parent ratings of over-controlled problems or inhibition was just 0.21 and lower than that for aggression or undercontrolled problems, which was 0.32. Their interpretation of these modest associations was not that raters are unreliable but rather that different informants are in different settings and experience children differently with different perspectives. Children's behaviour undoubtedly is to some extent context specific and shy children are undoubtedly more outgoing at home than at school. However, it also appears that parents and teachers view shyness somewhat differently. According to teacher and parent reports, meeting strangers and being the focus of attention are the most powerful elicitors of shyness. However teachers, but not parents add "being with peers" to this list (Zimbardo & Radl, 1981). In accordance with these reports, Wang and Kemple (1993) found that teachers' ratings of shyness were more highly correlated with activity and sociability than were mothers' ratings. Similarly Hinshaw et al. (1992) found that teacher but not parent ratings of internalizing behaviour correlated strongly with play group observations. Thus, teachers appear to place more emphasis in rating shyness on the quality of the child's peer relationships than do mothers. Mothers, on the other hand, appear to focus on the child's wariness to the unfamiliar, particularly in their daughters. Eisenberg et al. (1998) found that parents' ratings of shyness tended to be negatively correlated with their ratings of the child's popularity but only for boys. For girls, parent ratings of shyness were more related to unoccupied/onlooker behaviour, low social interaction and solitary activity in preschool and to low levels of spontaneous verbalizations to a stranger at ages 9 and 11, all of which were uncorrelated with teacher ratings of shyness. In addition, while parent ratings of behavioural control and attention focusing were positively correlated with their ratings of shyness, these dimensions of behaviour, as rated by teachers, were uncorrelated or negatively correlated with teacher ratings of shyness. As will be noted later in this chapter, some parents studied by Warnke and Evans (1996) see their child's shy behaviour in the home as including being able to concentrate for lengthy periods of time.

Despite these differences there also appear to be some similarities in teacher and parent perceptions. In the study by Eisenberg et al. (1998), among both teachers and parents, ratings of shyness were positively correlated with doing nothing in a potential conflict situation, and negatively with support-seeking at school and instrumental coping at home and school. Thus both parties view the constellation of shyness as including weak support-seeking, self-advocacy and social problem-solving.

VERBAL PERFORMANCE

Many of the behavioural dimensions noted above—such as instrumental coping, seeking support, and interactions with strangers and peers—entail discourse. In addition to physically remaining distant through failure to approach, turning away, and averting gaze, verbal behaviour is the most distinguishing aspect of shyness and of what may be its most extreme manifestation—elective mutism (see Ford, Sladeczek, & Carlson, 1998, and Leonard & Topol, 1993, for a discussion of selective mutism and temperament). As the topic of communicative competence as a dimension of shyness was previously extensively reviewed in a chapter by Evans (1993), it will be given briefer treatment here.

Although shyness is a vague concept, it is commonly accepted that shy individuals are timid, reserved and talk less (McCroskey & Richmond, 1982). Accordingly, researchers (e.g., Asendorpf, 1992, 1994; Coplan, Rubin, Fox, Calkins, & Stewart, 1994; Kagan, Reznick, Snidman, Gibbons, & Johnson, 1988) have used the length of time it takes individuals to make a first remark and total amount of time spent talking as an index of inhibition. They have found that inhibited children take longer to make their first remark, make fewer spontaneous comments and spend less time talking to adults and other children during free play. These observations were made in single sessions. However this verbal reticence appears quite entrenched across time in given situations. Evans (1987) observed fifteen sessions of "Show and Tell" or sharing time in a single kindergarten classroom over the course of the school year. One child in the classroom never took a speaking turn during this activity and seven took an average of just seven speaking turns compared to 20 in their classmates. Reticent children spoke an average of just 12 words per topic versus 38 in their peers, had a shorter mean length of utterance, and volunteered 75% fewer utterances. In addition they rarely told narratives or described absent objects, giving instead simple reports or commenting on an object they were holding.

The reticence of shy individuals is also well known to children themselves. In a study of 227 children in grades, 1, 3, 5, and 7, 84% of children said that they could tell that a peer is shy because he or she doesn't talk (Younger, Schneider, & Pelley, 1993). The salience of lower verbal participation extends to still younger respondents, as even 4-year olds identified the shy puppet as the one who doesn't like to talk to others and doesn't perform at Show and Tell time (Zimbardo & Radl, 1981). Finally, unlike the characteristics of hiding, crying, staying near familiar people, and running away from others which decreased in order of mention across grades one to seven, "doesn't talk," and "gets mixed up while taking" increased in frequency of mention across the grade groups (Younger, Schneider, & Pelley, 1993).

These observations of children parallel the conceptions of senior scholars in the field of shyness. For example, for Buss (1984) shyness is identified by the observable absence of the instrumental activity of social interaction such that shy individuals remain on the fringe of social groups, do not speak up, mumble minimal replies if addressed, and fail to hold up their end of the interaction.

The verbal "style" presented above is hypothesized to stem from two non-mutually exclusive attributes—the individuals' reaction to or appraisal of the interactional situation, and the individual's language competence. Situations which are seen as novel, unfamiliar or formal; in which one sees oneself as having subordinate status or being dissimilar; and in which one feels conspicuous and the focus of attention or evaluation, are situations which elicit shyness, inhibition and communication anxiety and reduce speech (Asendorpf, 1989; Ayers, 1990). School is a prime candidate for many of the aforementioned characteristics and talk among shy children has been demonstrated to differ accordingly in that shy children speak less than non-shys when arriving at school, in classroom discussion time, at school recess, and when leaving for the day (Asendorpf & Meier, 1993; Evans, 1987). It is not surprising that school entry is a main releasing factor in selective mutism (Hesselman, 1983; Halpern, Hammon, & Cohen, 1971; Tancer, 1992) and that shy children are more outgoing and talkative at home than at school (Asendorpf & Meier, 1993; Evans, 1996).

In support of the second hypothesis, there are several research studies to suggest that, on average, shy children are not as verbally competent as their non-shy peers. Masten, Morison, and Pellegrini (1985) found that among children in grades 3 to 6, higher nominations on the sensitive-isolated dimension of a class play sociometric were associated with lower vocabulary subtest scores on the Wechsler Intelligence Scale—Revised, a subtest which requires children to explain the meaning of words. Asendorpf (1994) found a negative correlation between a German version of this same test and classroom inhibition at ages 7 and 10, although not at ages 4, 5, and 6. In addition, he found that those with lower verbal IQ were over-represented among children whose inhibition decreased the least across time. Similarly Engfer (1993) found that children who moved from being low in shyness at age 3 to high in shyness at age 6 obtained lower vocabulary scores. As these results might be due to performance anxiety on the test, perhaps more convincing are studies by Rubin (1982) and Evans (1996). Rubin (1982) found that children who engaged in higher rates of isolate play had lower receptive vocabulary scores on the Peabody Picture Vocabulary Test which requires the respondent pick which of four pictures best illustrates a picture without any verbal response. Similarly Evans (1996) found lower vocabulary scores on the Expressive One Word Picture Vocabulary Test which requires the child to simply name pictured objects with a single word.

Differences in verbal competence are not limited to the areas of semantics. In a study of loquacious versus taciturn children aged 36–74 months, taciturn children obtained lower scores than loquacious children on tests of morphology, syntax, articulation and sentence repetition (Landon & Sommers, 1979). The reticent kindergarten children studied by Evans (1996) also had lower scores on both the Production and Processing components of the Clinical Evaluation of Language Functioning. In particular, a greater proportion of reticent children obtained scores which fell below the 20th percentile in matching a spoken sentence to a picture, recalling information from a spoken paragraph, repeating spoken sentences, and creating sentences using a specified word such as "until" or "after". Semel and Wiig (1980) suggested that scoring below the 20th percentile on three or more subtests indicates possible language deficits. If one uses a more stringent rule of five or more subtests, 27% of the reticent children would have been suspected of language deficits, versus only 14% of their classmates who became more verbal across the year or were more verbal from the outset.

ACADEMIC ACHIEVEMENT

Given the positive correlation between verbal ability and achievement, the information about verbal performance presented in the previous section, and the view that student participation, talkativeness and social interaction are important for the attainment of learning objectives (Daly & Korinek, 1980), shy individuals may be at risk for lower academic achievement. Research following a variety of methodologies supports this speculation. Lower standardized achievement tests scores in elementary school were associated with high scores on the sensitive-isolated dimension of the revised class play sociometric (Masten et al., 1985), with low participation (Finn & Cox, 1992), and with high communication anxiety (Comadena & Prusank, 1988). Similarly, among secondary school students, lower school grades were related to being quiet-withdrawn (Swift & Spivack, 1969). Finally among college students those high in communication apprehension scored lower on portions of the American College Test and had lower grade point averages than those low in communication apprehension (McCroskey & Anderson, 1976).

Even when IQ, a potential mediating factor was partialled out, Masten et al. (1985) found that the sensitive-isolated dimension of the revised class play sociometric was still associated with lower teacher ratings of comprehension and attention on the Devereux Elementary School Behaviour Rating Scale. In contrast, among secondary school students, Davis and Scott (1978) found no difference in reading skill or grade point average between students high versus low in communication apprehension once the lower verbal ability associated with higher communication anxiety was partialled out. This suggests that lower verbal ability associated with communication apprehension may mediate lower academic achievement.

Data collected from teacher ratings also indicate that teachers view the academic performance of shy children less favorably. Teachers rated both withdrawn and aggressive grade 5 children as having more learning problems (Rubin, Hymel, & Chen, 1994). Similarly teachers gave lower ratings to third graders whom they viewed as very quiet in class in the areas of mathematics computations, oral reading, reading comprehension, written expression, group oral expression, one-to-one oral expression, decision-making, problem-solving, and work habits (Evans, Fitzsimmons, & McDermid, 1995). In a study of the perceptions of 462 teachers, McCroskey and Daly (1976) constructed two student profiles which were identical save for one being a verbal student and the other a quiet one who sits in the back of room and seldom participates in class discussions. Teachers rated the latter student as likely to do more poorly in areas of reading, arithmetic, social studies, science, and art. Gordon and Thomas (1967) reported that teachers estimated higher IQ scores among children whom teachers described as ones who plunge into new situations quickly, positively and unhesitantly versus those who stand on the sidelines waiting before gradually getting involved in a new activity, even though the two groups of children were of the same measured intelligence. This bias also appears to extend to children's perceptions in that talkative peers were rated as more approachable and intelligent by students in grades 3–12 in a study by Richmond, Beatty, and Dyba (1985).

While there may be a cluster of shyness "symptoms" that bias adults towards the less favorable judgements noted above, a chief factor is probably verbal performance. In a study by Seligman, Tucker, and Lambert (1972) in which third grade teachers evaluated speech samples of boys, those with "good" voices were perceived as more intelligent than those with "poor" voices. In a later study by Rice, Hadley, and Alexander (1993) adults listened to speech samples of 4–5-year-old children who were speech impaired, speech and language impaired or normally developing, but who all fell within the average range of intelligence on standardized tests. For intelligence, social maturity, leadership qualities, peer relationships and kindergarten success, both speech impaired and speech and language impaired children received lower ratings than normally developing children. Most importantly, these ratings correlated an average of 0.77 with mean length of utterance and intelligibility, characteristics which, according to Evans (1987), distinguished reticent from verbal kindergarten children during classroom Show and Tell. Similarly, Burroughs and Tomblin (1990) found that adult ratings of "maturity", which included intelligence and independence, were predicted by the number of words in speaking turns of children ages 3 to 6.

All of the above supports the unfortunate generalization that preschool, school, and college age individuals who talk less are viewed as less competent, even when there is objective evidence to the contrary, and that shy children are at higher risk for lower academic achievement. Whether teacher expectancy and the behaviours associated with expectancies play a role in this lower academic achievement of shy individuals is unknown.

HELPING SHY CHILDREN IN THE CLASSROOM

Zimbardo (1977, p. 66) provided the following quote from Marilynne Robinson, a second grade teacher.

> Children who are shy in the classroom fear running and dancing to rhythm records. Their voices can barely be heard when asked a question, and will frequently answer "I don't know". They are afraid to sing out, speak out, and in general, afraid to make mistakes. They sit back and wait for someone to ask them to play. If this doesn't happen, they may wander around the playground sometimes finding a "sore finger" so that they may see the nurse.

Her quote nicely summarizes the overall "face" that shy children present as a result of their reluctance to take initiative both verbally and non-verbally in structuring situation, in conversation, in elaborating ideas, in asking questions, and in seeking assistance. Shy children are unlikely to interrupt others or create disturbances in the classroom, but they are quite likely to be inadvertently cut off by their more outgoing peers and to engage their teachers and classmates less on a personal level, thereby becoming less visible. A chief concern, then, is to find ways of helping these children to become more visible participants in classroom activities and discourse. As Honig (1987) has advised, one needs to lure, not force, these children into social interaction. With this in mind, suggestions from various authors are presented below. However it is important to note that there are very few direct tests of the effectiveness of these suggested "interventions".

Observational studies of classrooms have shown that certain activities are more likely than others to be associated with verbal interaction among children. For example, Pellegrini (1984) observed that even when children were situated together, little verbal communication occurred around activities involving paper and pencils, crayons, art, puzzles, and water/sand tables in contrast to block building and housekeeping centres. There is also evidence that smaller groupings with an inconspicuous teacher result in more varied and spontaneous dialogue than larger groups with a teacher leader (Harrod, 1975), and that shy children respond more positively to the advancements of other children than to those of the teacher (Koplow, 1983). Thus it would appear wise for teachers to set up specifically small groups of 2–5 children for activities in curricular areas such as language arts, mathematics, and environmental studies, to pair shy children with a buddy or peer helper, and to provide young children with opportunities for large block, lego, puppet, and fantasy play. Pairing children up in such a way that they alternate speaking and listening roles, such as playing the card game "Fish" in which the players alternately question each other, gives all children the opportunity to speak, not just the more verbal ones. Furman, Rahe, and Hartup (1979) have also suggested that shy children can play more easily with a younger child. Thus making a shy child the older "buddy" may be a way of providing a leadership role in a non-threatening way.

With respect to group instruction and more general classroom discourse, researchers have identified a central action zone consisting of the first row, seats down the middle, and a few seats on either side from which most student discourse emanates, and have found that there are personality differences between students who choose to be within this area and those who do not, the latter being less assertive, less competitive, and less confident (Totusek & Staton-Spicer, 1982). While placing children who are high or moderate in verbalization within this zone increases their verbal participation, this has no effect on children who are low verbalizers (Kenoya, 1976; Mehrabian & Diamond, 1971). Thus methods of increasing verbal participation may have more to do with the interaction style of the teacher than the physical layout of the classroom. A traditional behaviourist approach would be to reinforce or praise shy children for their verbal contributions. Comadena and Prusank (1988) urge teachers to reward these children's speaking attempts, but this runs the risk of drawing attention to the child, making him or her more self-conscious, and resulting in a negative effect. In fact Paget, Nagle, and Martin (1984) found that reticent children responded to praise more than their average counterparts but praise was only effective when given inconspicuously. Thus teachers should be low key in the methods they use.

Nonverbal communication is one way of giving praise in a group situation without drawing undue attention to the child (Richey & Richey, 1978).

In preparation for this chapter, the author drew on interviews with five grade 1 teachers which tapped their experience on encouraging the verbal participation of shy children. Their suggestions, many of which are not covered above, include having a quiet and orderly class, talking to shy children when no one else is around, such as after school, talking to them about family and non-academic issues to establish a personal relationship and trust, providing a chance for one-to-one work with the teacher, and gradually easing them into speaking experiences such as saying their name and then standing up and saying their name in a game-like atmosphere. During group lessons they noted that classmates often talk for the quieter children, take away their thinking time by answering before them, and interrupt their attempts. Thus it was suggested that quieter children be asked for their responses first and that they be asked closed questions that the teacher is sure that they will be able to answer successfully, or open-ended questions to which they could respond appropriately in a wide variety of ways.

Teachers also must be prepared to modify their usual conversational pace and questioning style to give shy children more space within a conversation. Evans (1987) and Evans and Bienert (1992) showed that shy children are the recipients of many questions—between 42 and 55% of teachers' remarks—which are frequently unanswered and in the course of a conversation increasingly require only a single word or yes/no response. When children do reply teachers keenly respond, as shown by Evans, Hauer, and Bienert (1991). They examined conversational response latencies of 19 kindergarten children whose teachers nominated them as "shy" and ranked them at the bottom of lists of verbal participation in class, and 19 controls. "Think-time", or the time between the teacher's remark and the child's response to it, did not differ between the two groups but teachers' "wait-time", or the time between a child's remarks and the teacher's response, was briefer when interacting with the reticent children. In a second study (Evans & Bienert, 1992) teachers implemented a "low control" intervention in which they reduced the number of questions they asked in favour of personal contributions and phatics remarks (e.g., "Oh really!"). This resulted in the children speaking more words, volunteering more content, and taking longer speaking turns, even though they were less obligated to respond to these remarks than to questions. Thus it appears that teachers need to listen with patient and gentle attentiveness, and to pull back from attempting to lead the conversation by questioning in favour of offering comments. Van Kleeck and Street (1982) have also noted that teachers should speak with as rich a language style as they do with other classmates. They may also need to modify their evaluation methods, particularly in the later grades, so that children are not punished for their reluctance or fear of speaking (Comadena & Prusank, 1988), and to establish an atmosphere in which in is clearly acceptable to make mistakes.

Last but not least, as Zimbardo (1977) has noted, "inability to ask for help is one of the most serious by-products of shyness" (p. 70). While all of the above may assist children in trying out their voices, specific and direct coaching in social skills, conversational techniques, and role-playing practice may be needed to help these children to be more assertive and advocate for themselves. This would appear to be especially critical for shy children with language and/or learning disabilities who, in being shy as reviewed above, are already at risk for less engagement in the classroom and lower academic achievement. Shy children are rarely a behaviour problem, and in the list of referrals for enhanced education services, those with learning difficulties are less likely to rise to the top of the referral list than aggressive or inattentive children. These children may also be particularly prone to exam anxiety. Finally, specific assertiveness coaching and strong social networks also appear critical for the child's self-esteem and safety, given the association between victimization and sensitive, anxious, withdrawn and passive characteristics in children (Olweus, 1978, 1991).

SHYNESS AND ILLNESS

As reviewed by Marshall and Stevenson-Hinde (this volume, *Chapter 3*), there is substantial evidence indicating biological differences associated with behavioural inhibition. Shy individuals have a lower threshold for arousal than their non-shy counterparts and thus more frequently experience a state of physiologic hyper-reactivity (Kagan, Reznick, & Snidman, 1987, 1988). This entails a hypersecretion of cortisol which suppresses the immune system and reduces the effectiveness of lymphocytes to combat infection. In addition, stress-induced activation of the sympathetic-adrenomedullary, hypothalamic-pituitary-adrenocortical, and endogenous opiate systems precedes the onset of symptoms related to infection (Buescher, Belfer, Artenstein, & Mougey, 1979; Gruchow, 1979). As a result, behaviourally inhibited or shy individuals may be expected to experience more ill health. In support of this notion, some studies have shown a relationship between shyness and allergies. With respect to adults, as early as 1940, Sheldon, Stevens and Tucker noted a higher incidence of allergies, skin trouble, chronic fatigue, insomnia, and sensitivity to noise and distractions in ectomorphic introverts than in mesomorphic extroverts. More recently, one third of shy college students compared to none of their outgoing counterparts reported hayfever, and participants with professionally diagnosed hayfever had higher self-reported shyness scores than those without (Bell, Jasnoski, Kagan, & King, 1990). With respect to infants and toddlers, mothers of children who were behaviourally inhibited at 21 months retrospectively reported more colic, chronic constipation, and allergies during the first year of life than mothers of comparison children (Rosenberg & Kagan, 1987) and a higher prevalence of atopic allergies, especially hayfever and eczema when the children were between ages 1 and 3 (Kagan, Snidman, Julia-Sellers, & Johnson, 1991).

Two studies (Boyce et al., 1995, and Chung & Evans, 2000) have investigated the relationship between shyness and illness in school-age children. Boyce et al. (1995) hypothesized that environmental stress and individual reactivity would interact in the prediction of respiratory illness. In their first study of 140 children of 3 to 5 years of age, the children were examined for respiratory illness weekly from January through June at their daycare centres. These centres were also characterized as high or low stress settings depending on the frequency of upsetting events such as rejection by peers, change in pick-up or drop-off routine, problems with toileting and quality of the child care environment. Reactivity in children was indexed through cardiovascular reactivity to a series of 20-minute laboratory tasks. While neither stress nor individual reactivity predicted illness in themselves, high reactivity children who were in high-stress settings experienced higher rates of respiratory infection than those in low-stress settings. Children with low reactivity showed no higher incidence of illness in high-stress settings. In a second study of 95 5-year-old children, parents completed diary recordings of the frequency of upper and lower respiratory symptoms in the weeks surrounding their child's entry to kindergarten. Stress was assessed via family report of stressful events and family conflict in previous months. Children experienced an average of three respiratory illnesses in the three months following kindergarten entry, but those with high immune reactivity to school entry who experienced a large number of stressful life events had the highest rates of respiratory illness. An unexpected finding in both studies was that respiratory illness was least frequent in highly reactive children in low-stress environments. In both studies no attempt was made to differentiate between allergies and infectious respiratory problems.

In the study by Chung and Evans (2000) the health of 16 shy and 16 non-shy children from grades 1 and 2 who were matched for age, sex, parental education, family stress, and height/weight ratio was monitored for a period of four weeks in February and March. Parents recorded in daily diaries their child's health complaints, their observations of the child's health and any actions taken. Shy children were drawn from teacher nominations of children whom they considered to be shy and to verbally participate the least in class discussions. On twice as many days in the four weeks (4.69 versus 2.31), shy children versus non-shy children both complained of feeling unwell and their parents observed symptoms of illness in them. In addition there was no difference between shy and non-shy children in the number of days children complained of feeling unwell but parents did not observe symptoms of illnesses, suggesting that shy children were not more prone to somatization or to complaining of ill health to avoid anxiety-provoking situations. An examination of the individual categories of child complaints and parent observations of ill health revealed statistically significant differences in gastrointestinal illness (nausea, vomiting, diarrhoea, cramps) and fatigue as observed by parents, and in gastrointestinal illness and feeling "off" (loss of appetite, irritable, miserable, trouble sleeping) in the complaints of shy children themselves. In addition, all means were higher in the various categories of ill health with the exception of eye and ear infections observed by parents which were virtually the same, and headaches as reported by children which were higher in the non-shy group.

The frequency of migraine is also associated with characteristics that distinguish shy or inhibited children. In a study by Bille (1962), migrainous children, especially girls, rated themselves as more anxious, fearful, tense, and nervous than non-headache children, and parents tended to rate the former group as more anxious, sensitive, apprehensive, tidy, and vulnerable to frustration. Similarly, Kowal and Pritchard (1990) found that children in grades 4–7 who had at least two troublesome headaches a month were rated as more shy-sensitive by their parents but did not rate themselves as more anxious than non-headache controls.

In the above studies there is little consistency in the types of illness more frequently displayed by shy children. This is probably a function of the range of illnesses documented in a particular study, the age of the child, and the time period over which recording or retrospective accounts were collected. For example, respiratory illnesses due to allergies are less frequent in the winter months of February and March tracked by Chung and Evans (2000) than in the spring and fall periods examined by Boyce et al. (1995), or across the entire year as in the study by Bell et al. (1990). In addition, how "shyness" was defined or measured varied between studies. Nonetheless there is apt to be substantial overlap between the target groups above, and thus these studies collectively show that shy children are likely to be sick more often. This entails missing more school, having to make more transitions back to school, feeling less than optimal when performing tasks, and requiring more of their caregivers at home. When at school, feeling unwell on top of their shyness may exacerbate a child's apparent social withdrawal with peers and verbal reticence in the classroom. With respect to the home, the more frequent illnesses of shy children may create some parenting stress or make parents feel that their children are more vulnerable.

HOME BEHAVIOURS ASSOCIATED WITH SHYNESS

In many studies of shyness, researchers ask mothers to rate their children's behaviour on a series of items tapping characteristics of shyness to gain a numerical index of the degree of shyness displayed (see section on stability above). Warnke and Evans (1996) adopted a different qualitative approach and asked parents about their everyday experience of shyness in their 4- and 5-year-old children who were rated by teachers as being in the bottom third of verbal participation in their junior kindergarten and nursery school settings. Families were primarily middle class and 91% of the mothers had some form of post-secondary education, ranging from vocational college to graduate school. Mothers were asked, "Tell me about instances in the past six months in which your child exhibited shy or anxious behaviour." In response, mothers volunteered an average of seven different behaviours.

Two categories were most frequently mentioned. Forty-nine per cent of parents reported sleep disturbances comprising nightmares, difficulty sleeping through the night, teeth grinding, somnambulance, bed-wetting and having to sleep with parents. These reports align with the report by Reznick et al. (1986) that 20–50% of inhibited children had nightmares and fears during their second and third years. The second major difficulty (45%) was that of separating—be it at daycare/nursery schools or to stay with a babysitter or even a grandparent. This problem persisted from two weeks to eight months and in several cases was still unresolved among these 4- and 5-year-old children. Many of these mothers expressed difficulty finding caregivers for their children. Next in frequency was wariness towards strangers (37%) which is reflected in items on the shyness questionnaire used by Asendorpf (1990), but reported equally frequently (37%) was a preference to play with children who were less boisterous or noisy. Several mothers indicated that their sons or daughters complained that loud children hurt their ears or that their sons preferred to play with girls whose play was quieter and gentler. Several mothers also noted that their children did not like loud noises such as a school bell or sound of popping balloons. This is consistent with previous reports that introverted adults prefer less intense visual and auditory stimuli (Eysenck, 1983; Smith, 1968; Stelmack & Campbell, 1974). Equally prominent was difficulty coping with changes in routine (35%) which frequently sparked temper tantrums, and the category "picky eating" (33%). Mothers reported refusals to try new foods, sensitivity to different colours and textures in food, and a very restricted set of foods that their child would eat. Struggles at mealtime were commonplace and some mothers worried about the adequacy of their children's diet. Czeschlik (1997) also noted that shy adults reported being more bothered by noises and bright lights that others do not seem to notice, and having lower gustatory and smell thresholds.

All of the above were spontaneously noted by at least a third of these parents. About a fifth of parents commented on their child's reluctance to try new things and activities (24%), the clinginess of their children at home (20%) as though their children followed them around on a short rope, their rejection of caregiving from fathers (18%), and signs of anxiety such as teeth grinding, thumb sucking, and chewing on clothing (18%). An orderliness and adherence to rules was also noted in 24% of the children including a strong sense of justice/morality (see also Kochanska, DeVet, Goldman, Murray, & Putman, 1994) and tidiness.

Although not an issue at home, a problem that was brought to their attention was the child's reticence at school or preschool (27%). For example, mothers reported that their children had been very slow to warm up, or were still not talking after seven months, or could not ask the teacher for help, or spoke barely in a whisper. Similarly with respect to peer interaction which spans both home and school, 18% of mothers noted that their children were unassertive with peers, were unable to stand up for themselves when taken advantage of by other children, or had a difficult time making friends. These reports are in accordance with observational studies of socially withdrawn children in play groups in which withdrawn children direct fewer requests to their play partners (Rubin & Borwick, 1984) and whose requests are more often of a low cost nature and less sophisticated form (Evans & Ellis, 1992; Rubin & Borwick, 1984). By way of contrast, when some parents (12%) reported that their shy child tended to play alone, mothers noted that their children could be very focused, playing with the same toy or engaging in pretend play for extended periods of time.

Finally, 14% of mothers mentioned struggles around dressing such as unwillingness to wear new clothing or clothes that are difficult to get off, or insistence that clothes be put on in a certain order. The same percentage reported that their child loathed being the centre of attention. While this was mentioned most with respect to performing in front of others or an audience, some mothers indicated that their children were even uncomfortable thinking about being at their own birthday parties.

In considering all of these reports together, one notes that many of the reports reflect negative reactions to what many children would construe as fun, "neat" or exciting, and also that the reports largely map onto the major dimensions of shyness—social withdrawal, inhibition to the unfamiliar, reticence, and anxiety. Noteworthy also are child characteristics reported by mothers which fit under the categories of what researchers would call onlooker behaviour and long solitary play episodes. Mothers phrased these things in a positive way, reporting that their children were reflective, showed strong observation skills, had rich fantasy lives, and were able to entertain themselves for hours. In summary mothers are well aware of the different interactional style of these children, they experience substantial psychological dependence from them, they struggle with daily hassles in dressing, eating, sleeping, and going places, but they also appreciate positively what they characterize as a reflective, self-entertaining, and quiet play style.

Lastly, it must be noted that the advantage of asking mothers an open-ended question is that it allowed parents to report a broader range of behaviours associated with shyness than what would have been afforded by predetermined items to be rated on Likert-type scales. This is at the expense of having all parents report on the same items. Nonetheless, some of the problems spontaneously cited by parents are in accordance with findings of Engfer (1993) who asked mothers to rate various items for 25 boys and 14 girls. In particular, among her many correlations she found that mothers concurrently perceived their shy 6-year-olds as more moody/oversensitive and less socially competent, and had given them higher ratings on sleeping problems at 18 months.

Together with findings from the previous sections, a composite picture emerges of shyness at home and what parents have to cope with. Their mothers perceive them as less verbally competent than do mothers of other children, as less assertive with peers, and as untalkative at school. They deal daily with resistance and wariness to newness and change whether in people, food, clothing, routines, or activities. They cope more often with suboptimal health in their children and sleep disruptions. They are sought out frequently by their children for caregiving and comfort. In sum, these children present with a number of needs beyond our traditional conceptions of wariness to the unfamiliar.

PARENTING SHY CHILDREN

What parents do in response to their child's shyness, and whether parental behaviour might contribute to or ameliorate it, has received increasing attention.

Many children who are shy as toddlers become substantially more outgoing while others do not, leading to the speculation that parenting may be at least partly responsible for these differences and the course of shyness beyond toddlerhood.

In a 1990 study of mothers of 4-year-olds, Rubin and Mills found that mothers of the six withdrawn-internalizing children they studied responded to two hypothetical scenarios of social isolation by saying that they would use more "high power" strategies (punishments, commands, threats) than did mothers of average children. Thus it appeared to the authors that mothers of shy children were overly directive—a style which would be detrimental to healthy development. However the concurrent assessment of social withdrawal and parenting behaviours makes it difficult to infer causal direction. In fact Engfer (1993) found that children who remained shy from 3 to 6 years were both observed by the researchers and rated by their parents as more difficult, noncompliant, and moody, leading Engfer to acknowledge that these children may have been more difficult to care for and elicited the more power-assertive parenting strategies that she too observed. Similarly, Henderson and Rubin (1997) concluded that children with low vagal tone, reticent behaviour and difficulty regulating their behavior may be more challenging and thus elicit more, the more directive socialization strategies that they observed in mothers.

A second study by Mills and Rubin (1993a) included mothers of 11 withdrawn-internalizing children at each of kindergarten and grade 4. In contrast to their 1990 study, there were no differences between parents of withdrawn-internalizing, aggressive and average children in their reported use of power-assertive strategies. Similarly, parents did not differ in their use of high-power strategies when observed alone with their children, and parents of withdrawn-internalizing children were *less* likely to use high-power strategies when another child joined the mother–child dyad.

Mothers of elementary school age were also studied by Mills and Rubin (1998). Children were classified according to peer nominations and a teacher rating scale resulting in the identification of 7, 4, and 12 withdrawn children in kindergarten grades 2 and 4 respectively. Analyses of variance revealed that mothers of withdrawn children did not differ from those of aggressive or average children in observed behavioural control, which included imperative compliance commands, punishment or threat of punishment, criticism of behaviour, play directives, rewards, and monitoring. Similarly there was no difference in the percentage of mothers of withdrawn versus average children above the median in the use moderate control requests, play directives, rewards, or monitoring. More mothers of withdrawn children were above the 67th percentile in their use of compliance commands, but only in what Mills and Rubin refer to as "stressful" situations requiring cooperation—tidy up, share toy and joint construction of lego house with a peer. This was not the case in dyadic or triadic free play. In addition a disproportionate number of mothers of withdrawn children (5 of 13) ignored their child's bid for attention at least once. The authors again concluded that mothers of withdrawn children are overcontrolling both behaviourally and psychologically but acknowledge the small sample size and low frequency of control as serious limitations to the study.

More recently (Rubin, Hastings, Stewart, Henderson, & Chen, 1997; see also Burgess et al., this volume, *Chapter 7*) observations and coding of mothers' behaviour in laboratory settings have shifted from maternal "control" to maternal "oversolicitousness", operationalized through a composite of tidying up more than 50% of the toys in a clean-up task (intrusive control), interrupting the child more than once at snack time with the apparent goal of assisting the child (unsolicited intervention), high positive affect such as saying "You're great! Mommy loves you!", physical affection, and low responsiveness to the child's bids for attention. The notion here, somewhat reminiscent of that of Bugental (1992), is that oversolicitous parents, while highly affectionate, may be overprotective and prevent their children from engaging in necessary self-coping strategies to overcoming their shyness. In support of this Rubin et al. (1994) found that maternal oversolicitousness was higher for mothers of the 11 consistently inhibited toddlers, who showed inhibition in both a traditional laboratory context and in peer play, than for mothers of children who were inhibited in only one of those two contexts, or who were consistently uninhibited. Surprisingly there were no differences in comparison with mothers of average children. Rubin et al. (1994, p. 480) wrote:

> A mother who is warm and very highly involved in her temperamentally fearful child's activities, while at the same time failing to demonstrate responsivity to her child's cues or sensitivity to her child's needs, in effect may keep her child from having the opportunity to practise his/her coping skills, overcome the dispositional wariness, and develop a sense of self-efficacy. By inappropriately employing the behaviors typically regarded by parenting researchers as positive or authoritative ... this style of parenting may "smother" any nascent self-confidence or independence in the dispositionally fearful toddler and may suggest that it is appropriate to be fearful in novel situations.

This conclusion requires more investigation before it can be translated into parenting advice because it is based on a composite index tapping affection, responsivity, and unsolicited helping. It would be valuable in the future to disentangle these different behaviours within the oversolicitousness index to know whether particular parts of this constellation of behaviour are more highly associated with inhibition than others. In addition, because the assessment of inhibition and maternal oversolicitiness was contemporaneous and interaction is bidirectional in nature, the direction of causality cannot be determined. Rubin et al. (1997) reported that consistently inhibited children were the group most upset in response to separation and reunion. This laboratory task preceded most of the tasks in which the maternal behaviour was coded. Thus it is possible that mothers of consistently inhibited children may have offered more affection and positive affect in response to the greater distress earlier displayed, again speaking to the need to separate the behaviours within the oversolicitousness composite. Finally it would be valuable to have some sense of parents' own disposition. Mothers who are shy themselves may be more uncomfortable when observed, which might contribute to the behaviours recorded. Nonetheless this is clearly valuable research and positive refinement over previous conceptions which focused only on "power" and "assertion" for which inconsistent findings were obtained.

In the aforementioned study by Warnke and Evans (1996), mothers were asked about what they would say or do in the situations of shy behaviour they reported experiencing with their children and in two hypothetical scenarios. In one (taken from Rubin & Mills, 1990) the child plays alone at a birthday party and in the other cries at being picked up by the mother's visiting friend. Their responses were coded into seven levels of directiveness. Mothers frequently indicated that they responded with verbal and physical reassurance and comfort, encouragement and suggestions to redirect behaviour and conversation to gather information and try to reason with their child. Only rarely did they mention anything beyond level 4, a category which entailed bribery and joining in the activity themselves, and they did so only after listing other strategies. Their responses were most directive in the hypothetical birthday party scenario where they indicated that they would encourage their child to play with the other children, and if unsuccessful, would invite another child to join their child. Only a handful of mothers said that, as a last resort, they would bribe their child to join in with the other children, believing that once involved she or he would have a good time.

In describing the challenging behaviours presented by their child at home, parents also described proactive strategies on their part to reduce anticipated upsets, such as telling children in advance about changes in routine, the arrival of unfamiliar visitors, or impending parent departures; joining in with their children at new activities; and laying new clothes out in advance of asking their child to wear them. In situations evoking anxiety and wariness, these were noted along with offering encouragement, comfort, and reassurances. Thus there was little indication in these data that these mothers were particularly "high power".

Rubin and Mills (1990) also examined parents' emotional response to withdrawal by asking parents to rate how they would feel in the hypothetical situations of social-withdrawal presented according to nine emotions—angry, embarrassed, amused, disappointed, concerned, pleased, surprised, puzzled, and guilty and concluded from the ratings that mothers of anxious-withdrawn children are more angry and disappointed in their children, and feel more guilt and embarrassment. The study by Warnke and Evans (1996) sheds a different light on these ratings. Rather than asking parents to rate a list of emotions, parents were asked to first rate the intensity of their affective reaction from very weak to very strong, and then to label it and elaborate on this.

Mothers did indicate disappointment and sadness but it is important to note that they elaborated this as being over the fact that the child would be missing out on the fun to be experienced at a birthday party. It was not disappointment *in* their child as phrased by Rubin and Mills (1990). Guilt and sadness were expressed over situations of having to leave their child in a state of distress when separating. Frustration was tied to the wish that the child would have outgrown separation distress and stranger anxiety by age 4. Anger did emerge, but only in the hypothetical scenario in which the child cries at being picked up by a visiting strange adult. That anger was directed at the adult, not the child, for assuming the child to be outgoing, and if embarrassment was mentioned, it was for the adult friend, not the parent herself. The other emotional responses which mothers frequently volunteered to the birthday party scenario and stranger wariness situations were acceptance and empathy, emotions which were not in the list of emotions provided by Rubin and Mills (1990) for parental rating. Mothers often noted that they had been shy themselves and could relate to what their children were going through. The elaborative comments of these mothers about their emotions suggests that previous characterizations of mothers of withdrawn children as having "pronounced anger, disappointment, guilt and embarrassment" (Mills & Rubin, 1993b, p. 112) may be unwarranted. In fact in a second study reported in Mills and Rubin (1993a), mothers of withdrawn-internalizing children gave lower ratings to feelings of disappointment, guilt, sadness, surprise, and puzzlement than mothers of average children, findings that were opposite to their 1990 study.

In summary, researchers have studied different dimensions of parental behaviour in different combinations, often studying small numbers of target parents, using different methodologies, and with inconsistent findings. In addition to the influence on the findings of varying socio-economic status in samples and open-ended interviews versus constrained written questionnaires and checklists, there are also ambiguities in how parental behaviour might be coded. For example, the response "Don't cry" might be coded according to its surface structure or locutionary form as "command" or according to its illocutionary intent and prosody as "comfort". Nonetheless it does appear that parents of shy children may be somewhat frustrated with their child's continued shyness, and are fairly directive but affectionate in parenting them. As Bugental (1992) earlier suggested, mothers react to shy children with concern, sympathy and in some case frustration, especially if the child is older, and adopt quick-fix strategies to ease their child's discomfort such as telling their child what to do and how to do it, or speaking for the child.

Whether such behaviours constitute "over"directiveness/protection/affection or a level of directiveness/protection/control different but appropriate for shy children remains to be addressed by longitudinal and intervention research in which shyness at time 1 is partialled out before predicting the contribution of parenting to shyness at time 2. Until then, any conclusions are speculative and perhaps influenced by our cultural value judgements. Is a bribe necessarily negative? Does a difference in control between mothers of shy and non-shy children's behaviour translate into "overcontrol"? "Over" for whom?—the child who might "need" the strategy at the time or the parent, perhaps shy herself, who might have her own concerns? Might a lack of differences between parenting in shy and non-shy children be equally interpreted as insensitivity to their needs? In short, we need to consider the transactional nature of parenting and the meaning that behaviours have within the interactants' history and predispositions in order to understand the parenting of shy children

Noticeably absent in this section thus far is mention of fathers. Unfortunately fathers less often volunteer to participate in research and it is questionable whether those who do are representative of those who do not. However, mothers are only part of the parenting equation. Mothers interviewed in the study by Warnke and Evans (1996) sometimes said that their husbands would respond quite differently, being less patient than they themselves. This perception is in accord with findings by Bacon and Ashmore (1985) that fathers are more accepting of shy behaviours in their daughters, considering it to be cute, than in their sons, where it is regarded as sissy, and with observations of Stevenson-Hinde, Hinde, and Simpson (1986) and Simpson and Stevenson-Hinde (1985) that fathers are annoyed with shyness in their sons. As there also appear to be differences in the sensitivity of fathers to shyness depending on their own temperament (Zimbardo, 1977) there is also a need to incorporate individual differences among parents in considering the responses of mothers versus fathers to their children's shyness. Nonetheless, as researchers we should have no apologies for focusing on mothers who carry the majority of the caregiving role.

Our understanding of parenting shy children is clearly only in its infancy and one hesitates to make suggestions in this domain. However, it makes intuitive sense, and there is some research to support this, that protecting shy children from all anticipated anxiety and frustration and always acting for them is not likely to desensitize them to anxiety-provoking situations or encourage self-reliance and self-regulation. As Goleman (1994) has put it: "parents who engineer gradual emboldening exercises for their children offer them what may be a lifelong corrective to their fearfulness" (p. 213). For example, parents should make a point of enrolling their shy children in nursery school because this experience can prepare children for the demands of kindergarten. In fact Ladd and Price (1987) have shown that children with greater preschool experience exhibited fewer anxious behaviours in the first few months of school and became less anxious over the course of the year. Exposure to a broader range of peer contexts prior to kindergarten was also associated with lower anxiety scores at the end of kindergarten and fewer absences and nurse visits. Gersten (1989) also noted that children who showed a shift from high behavioural inhibition at 21 months to less inhibition in kindergarten had mothers who reported enrolling them in daycare and introducing peers into the home in an effort to reduce their shyness.

With the same "desensitization" principle in mind, it also appears that parents, while not being harsh, should set firm limits and not pick up and comfort their child at every whimper. In a study by Arcus and Gardner (1993), highly reactive infants whose reactivity scores decreased from 5 months to 14 months had mothers who had issued more firm and direct commands to stop their children from approaching dangerous or forbidden objects in the home than had mothers of infants whose reactivity scores remained high. The former mothers also held their fretting infants less. These findings were especially true for boys. Kagan's (1994) interpretation was that these mothers did not reward excessive crying and that their sharp reprimands create "a punctuous, temporary state of uncertainty" which, in being repeated over the course of toddlerhood, helps the child to habituate to feelings of uncertainty.

Finally as with teachers, parents should be attentive and patient listeners to shy children, refrain from answering for them, give them conversational space, and provide conversational models and contexts to help them practise participating in a variety of discourse with adults and children.

CONCLUDING REMARKS

In summary, shyness presents as a constellation of behaviours. How parents and teachers respond to these children may be an important mediator in their development. The quiet style, more frequent displays of anxiety and upset, and more frequent illnesses of these children are natural elicitors of protectiveness in parents, especially for daughters, as well as a degree of impatience, especially for sons, both of which probably need to be modulated. Parents and teachers may also need to discretely explain to other adults who interact with these children that what is fun and thrilling for many children is downright unpleasant and stressful for the shy child. Finally, they should consciously seek to design gradually more challenging settings and experiences which these children can enjoy with others. At the same time, we as researchers can perhaps learn from the parents and teachers who see positive qualities in the children's shyness, and question a culture valuing extroversion to the potential detriment of those on the other end of the continuum.

ACKNOWLEDGEMENT

Grateful acknowledgement is extended to the Social Sciences and Humanities Research Council of Canada for their financial support toward the collection of data in the studies by Evans and colleagues reported within this chapter.

REFERENCES

Achenbach, T. M., McConaughy, S. H., & Howell, C. T. (1987). Implications of cross-informant correlations. *Psychological Bulletin, 101,* 213–232.

Arcus, D. & Gardner, S. (March, 1993). *When biology is not destiny.* Poster presented at the Biennial Meeting of the Society for Research in Child Development, New Orleans.

Asendorpf, J. B. (1989). Shyness as a final common pathway for two kinds of inhibition. *Journal of Personality and Social Psychology, 53,* 542–549.

Asendorpf, J. B. (1990). The development of inhibition during childhood: Evidence for situational specificity and a two-factor model. *Developmental Psychology, 26,* 721–730.

Asendorpf, J. B. (1992). A Brunswikean approach to trait continuity. *Journal of Personality, 60,* 53–77.

Asendorpf, J. B. (1994). The malleability of behavioural inhibition: A study of individual developmental functions. *Developmental Psychology, 30,* 912–919.

Asendorpf, J. H. & Meier, G. (1993). Personality effects on children's speech in everyday life: sociability-mediated exposure and shyness-mediated reactivity to social situations. *Journal of Personality and Social Psychology, 64,* 1072–1083.

Ayers, J. (1990). Situational factors and audience anxiety. *Communication Education, 39,* 283–291.

Bacon, M. K. & Ashmore, R. D. (1985). How mothers and fathers categorize descriptions of social behavior attributed to daughters and sons. *Social Cognition, 3,* 193–217.

Bell, I. R., Jasnoski, M. L., Kagan, J., & King, D. S. (1990). Is allergenic rhinitis more frequent in young adults with extreme shyness? A preliminary survey. *Psychosomatic Medicine, 52,* 517–525.

Bille, B. (1962). Migraine in school children. *Acta Paediatrica, 51* (supplement 136), 14–151.

Boyce, W., Chesney, M., Alkon, A., Tschann. J. M., Adams, S., Chesterman, B., Cohen, F., Kaiser, P., Folkna, S., & Wara, D. (1995). Psychobiologic reactivity to stress and childhood respiratory illnesses. *Psychosomatic Medicine, 57,* 411–422.

Buescher, E. L., Belfer, M. L., Artenstein, M. S., & Mougey, E. H. (1979). A prospective study of corticosteroid and catecholamine levels in relation to viral respiratory illness. *Journal of Human Stress* (September), 18–28.

Bugental, D. B. (1992). Affective and cognitive processes within threat-oriented family systems. In I. Sigel, A. McGillicuddy-DeLisi, & J. Goodnow (Eds.), *Parental belief systems: The psychological consequences for children* (pp. 219–248). Hillsdale, NJ: Lawrence Erlbaum.

Burroughs, E. I. & Tomblin, J. B. (1990). Speech and language correlates of adults' judgements of children. *Journal of Speech and Hearing Disorders, 55,* 485–494.

Buss, A. H. (1984). A conception of shyness. In J. A. Daly & J. C. McCroskey (Eds.), *Avoiding communication: Shyness, reticence and communication apprehension* (pp. 39–50). Beverly Hills: Sage.

Chung, J. & Evans, M. A. (2000). Shyness and symptoms of illness in young children. *Canadian Journal of Behavioural Science, 32,* 49–57.

Comadena, M. E. & Prusank, D. T. (1988). Communication apprehension and academic achievement among elementary and secondary school students. *Communication Education, 37,* 270–277.

Coplan, R. J., Rubin, K. H., Fox, N. A., Calkins, S., & Stewart, S. (1994). Being alone, playing alone and acting alone: Distinguishing among reticence and passive and active solitude in young children. *Child Development, 65,* 129–137.

Czeschlik, T. (July, 1997). *Shyness and reactivity.* Paper presented at the International Conference on Shyness and Self-consciousness. Cardiff, Wales.

Daly, A. & Korinek, J. (1980). Interaction in the classroom: An overview. In D. Nimmo (Ed.), *Communication yearbook, 4* (pp. 515–532). New Brunswick, NJ: Transaction Books.

Davis, G. F. & Scott, M. D. (1978). Communication apprehension, intelligence and achievement among secondary school students. In B. R. Ruben (Ed.), *Communication yearbook* (pp. 458–472). New Brunswick, NJ: Transaction Books.

Eisenberg, N., Shepard, S. A., Fabes, R. A., Murphy, B., & Guthrie, I. K. (1998). Shyness and children's emotionality, regulation and coping: Contemporaneous, longitudinal, and across-context relations. *Child Development, 69,* 767–790.

Engfer, A. (1993). Antecedents and consequences of shyness in boys and girls; A six year longitudinal study. In K. H. Rubin & J. B. Asendorpf (Eds.), *Social withdrawal, inhibition and shyness* (pp. 49–80). Hillsdale, NJ: Erlbaum.

Evans, M. A. (1987). Discourse characteristics of reticent children. *Applied Psycholinguistics, 8,* 171–184.

Evans, M. A. (1993). Communicative competence as a dimension of shyness. In K. H. Rubin & J. B. Asendorpf (Eds.), *Social withdrawal, inhibition and shyness in children* (pp. 189–212). Hillsdale, NJ: Erlbaum.

Evans, M. A. (1996). Reticent primary grade children and their more talkative peers: Verbal, nonverbal and self-concept characteristics. *Journal of Educational Psychology, 88,* 739–749.

Evans, M. A. & Bienert, H. (1992). Control and paradox in teacher conversations with shy children. *Canadian Journal of Behavioural Science, 24,* 502–516.

Evans, M. A. & Ellis, P. (May, 1992). *Requestive strategies of reticent and verbal children at play.* Paper presented at University of Waterloo Biennial Conference on Child Development, Waterloo, Ontario.

Evans, M. A., Fitzsimmons, M., & McDermid, B. (April, 1995). *A longitudinal study of reticence: Kindergarten through grade three.* Poster presented at the Biennial Meeting of the Society for Research in Child Development, Indianapolis.

Evans, M. A., Hauer, R., & Bienert, H. (April, 1991). *Conversational response latencies of teachers and reticent children.* Poster presented at the Biennial meeting of the Society for Research in Child Development, Seattle.

Eysenck, H. J. (1983). The social application of Pavlovian theories. *Pavlovian Journal of Biological Science, 18,* 117–125.

Finn, J. D. & Cox, D. (1992). Participation and withdrawal among fourth-grade pupils. *American Educational Research Journal, 29,* 141–162.

Ford, M. A., Sladeczek, I. E., & Carlson, J. (1998). Selective mutism: Phenomenological characteristics. *School Psychology Quarterly, 13,* 192–227.

Furman, W., Rahe, D., & Hartup, W. W. (1979). Rehabilitation of socially withdrawn preschool children through mixed-age and same-sex socialization. *Child Development, 50,* 915–922.

Gersten, M. (1989). Behavioural inhibition in the classroom. In J. S. Reznick (Ed.), *Perspectives in behavioural inhibition* (pp. 71–91). Chicago: University of Chicago Press.

Goleman, D. (1994). *Emotional intelligence.* New York: Bantam Books.

Gordon, E. & Thomas, A. (1967). Children's behavioral style and the teacher's appraisal of their intelligence. *Journal of School Psychology, V,* 292–300.

Gruchow, H. A. (1979). Catecholamine activity and infection disease episodes. *Journal of Human Stress* (September), 11–17.

Guerin, D. W. & Gottfried, A. W. (1994). Developmental stability and change in parental reports of temperament: A ten-year longitudinal investigation from infancy through preadolescence. *Merill–Palmer Quarterly, 40,* 334–355.

Halpern, W. L., Hammond, J., & Cohen, R. (1971). A therapeutic approach to speech phobia: Elective mutism revisited. *Journal of the Academy of Child Psychiatry, 10,* 94–107.

Harrod, P. M. F. (1975). Talk in junior and middle school classroom: An exploratory investigation. *Educational Review, 29,* 97–106.

Hegvik, R. L., McDevitt, S. C., & Carey, W. B. (1982). The Middle Childhood Temperament Questionnaire. *Developmental and Behavioural Pediatrics, 3,* 197–200.

Henderson, H. & Rubin, K. H. (April, 1997). *Internal and external correlates of self-regulation in preschool-aged children.* Poster presented at the Society for Research in Child Development, Washington, DC.

Hesselman, S. (1983). Elective mutism in children. *Acta Paedopsychiatrica, 49,* 297–310.

Hinshaw, S. P., Han, S., Erhardt, D., & Huber, A. (1992). Internalizing and externalizing behavior problems in preschool children: Correspondence among parent and teacher ratings and behavior observations. *Journal of Clinical Child Psychology, 21,* 143–150.

Honig, A. S. (1987). The shy child. *Young Children, 42,* 54–64.

Kagan, J. (1994). *Galen's prophecy.* New York: Basic Books.

Kagan, J., Reznick, J. S., & Snidman, N. (1987). The physiology and psychology of behavioral inhibition in young children. *Child Development, 58,* 1459–1473.

Kagan, J., Reznick, J. S., & Snidman, N. (1988). Biological bases of childhood shyness. *Science, 240,* 167–171.

Kagan, J., Reznick, J. S., & Snidman, N. (1989). Issues in the study of temperament. In G. A. Kohnstamm, J. E. Bates, & M. K. Rothbart (Eds.), *Temperament in childhood* (pp. 133–152). New York: Wiley.

Kagan, J., Snidman, N., Julia-Sellers, M., & Johnson, M. O. (1991). Temperament and allergic symptoms. *Psychosomatic Medicine, 53,* 332–340.

Kenoya, M. (1976). Location and interaction in row and column seating arrangements. *Environment and Behaviour, 8,* 265–282.

Kochanska, G., DeVet, K., Goldman, M., Murray, P., & Putman, S. (1994). Maternal reports of conscience development and temperament in young children. *Child Development, 65,* 852–868.

Koplow, L. (1983). Feeding the "turtle": Helping the withdrawn child to emerge in the classroom. *Exceptional Child, 30,* 127–132.

Kowal, A. & Pritchard, D. (1990). Psychological characteristics of children who suffer from headache: A research note. *Journal of Child Psychology and Psychiatry, 4,* 637–649.

Landon, S. J. & Sommers, R. K. (1979). Talkativeness and children's linguistic abilities. *Language and Speech, 2,* 269–275.

Ladd, G. W. & Price, J. M. (1987). Predicting children's social and school adjustment following the transition from preschool to kindergarten. *Child Development, 58,* 1168–1189.

Leonard, H. L. & Topol, D. A. (1993). Elective mutism. *Child and Adolescent Psychiatric Clinics of North America, 2,* 695–707.

Masten, A., Morison, P., & Pellegrini, D. (1985). A revised class play method of peer assessment. *Developmental Psychology, 21,* 523–533.

McCroskey, J. C. & Anderson, J. F. (1976). The relationship between communication apprehension and academic achievement among college students. *Human Communication Research, 3,* 73–81.

McCroskey, J. C. & Daly, J. A. (1976). Teacher expectations of the communication apprehensive child in the elementary school. *Human Communication Research, 3,* 67–72.

McCroskey, J. C. & Richmond, V. P. (1982). Communication apprehension and shyness: Conceptual and operational distinctions. *Central States Speech Journal, 33,* 458–468.

Mehrabian, A. & Diamond, S. (1971). Effects of furniture arrangements, props and personality interactions. *Journal of Personality and Social Psychology, 20,* 18–30.

Mills, R. S. L. & Rubin, K. H. (1993a). Socialization factors in the development of social withdrawal. In K. H. Rubin & J. B. Asendorpf (Eds.), *Social withdrawal, inhibition and shyness in childhood* (pp. 117–148.) Hillsdale, NJ: Erlbaum.

Mills, R. S. L. & Rubin, K. H. (1993b). Parental ideas as influences on children's social competence. In S. Duck (Ed.), *Understanding relationship processes* (pp. 98–117). Newbury Park, CA: Sage Publications.

Mills, R. S. L. & Rubin, K. H. (1998). Are behavioural and psychological control both differentially associated with childhood aggression and social withdrawal? *Canadian Journal of Behavioural Science, 30,* 132–136.

Northman, E., Prior, M., Sanson, A., & Oberklaid, F. (1987). Toddler temperament as perceived by mothers versus day caregivers. *Merill–Palmer Quarterly, 33,* 213–229.

Olweus, D. (1978). *Aggression in the schools: Bullies and whipping boys.* Washington, DC: Hemisphere (Wiley).

Olweus, D. (1991). Bully/victim problems among school children: Basic facts and effects of a school based intervention program. In D. Pepler & K. H. Rubin (Eds.), *The development and treatment of childhood aggression* (pp. 411–448). Hillsdale, NJ: Erlbaum.

Paget, K., Nagle, R., & Martin, R. (1984). Interrelationships between temperament characteristics and first grade teacher–student interactions. *Journal of Abnormal Child Psychology, 12,* 547–560.

Pedlow, R., Sanson, A., Prior, M., & Oberklaid, F. (1993). Stability of maternally reported temperament from infancy to 8 years. *Developmental Psychology, 29*, 998–1007.

Pellegrini, A. (1984). The effects of classroom ecology of preschoolers' functional uses of language. In A. Pellegrini & T. Yawkey (Eds.), *The development of oral and written language in social contexts* (pp. 129–141). Norwood, NJ: Ablex.

Reznick, J., Kagan, J., Snidman, N., Gersten, M., Baak, K., & Rosenberg, A. (1986). Inhibited and uninhibited children; A follow-up study. *Child Development, 57*, 660–680.

Rice, M., Hadley, P., & Alexander, A. (1993). Social biases toward children with speech and language impairments: A correlative causal model of language limitations. *Applied Psycholinguistics, 14*, 445–471.

Richey, H. & Richey, M. (1978). Nonverbal behavior in the classroom. *Psychology in the Schools, 15*, 571–576.

Richmond, V. P., Beatty, M. J., & Dyba, P. (1985). Shyness and popularity: Children's views. *Western Journal of Speech Communication, 49*, 116–125.

Rosenberg, A. & Kagan, J. (1987). Iris pigmentation and behavioral inhibition. *Developmental Psychobiology, 20*, 377–392.

Rubin, K. H. (1982). Social and social-cognitive characteristics of young isolate, normal, and sociable children. In K. H. Rubin & S. H. Ross (Eds.), *Peer relationships and social skills in childhood* (pp. 353–374). New York: Springer-Verlag.

Rubin, K. H. & Borwick, D. (1984). Communication skills and sociability. In H. Sypher and J. Applegate (Eds.), *Communication by children and adults* (pp. 152–170). Beverly Hills: Sage.

Rubin, K. H., Hastings, P. D., Stewart, S. L., Henderson, H. A., & Chen, X. (1997). The consistency and concomitants of inhibition: Some of the children, all of the time. *Child Development, 68*, 467–483.

Rubin, K. H., Hymel, S., & Chen, X. (1994). The social-emotional characteristics of extremely aggressive and extremely withdrawn children. *Merill–Palmer Quarterly, 39*, 518–534.

Rubin, K. H. & Mills, R. S. L. (1990). Maternal beliefs about adaptive and maladaptive social behaviors in normal, aggressive, and withdrawn preschoolers. *Journal of Abnormal Child Psychology, 18*, 419–435.

Seligman, C. R., Tucker, G. R., & Lambert, W. E. (1972). The effects of speech style and other attributes on teachers' attitudes toward pupils. *Language in Society, 1*, 131–142.

Semel, E. M. & Wiig, L. (1980). *Clinical evaluation of language function*. Columbus, OH: Merrill.

Sheldon, W. H., Stevens, S. S., & Tucker, W. B. (1940). *The varieties of human physique: An introduction to constitutional psychology*. New York: Harper.

Smith, S. L. (1968). Extroversion and sensory threshold. *Psychophysiology, 5*, 293–299.

Simpson, A. E. & Stevenson-Hinde, J. (1985). Temperamental characteristics of three- to four-year-old boys and girls and child–family interactions. *Journal of Child Psychology and Psychiatry, 26*, 43–53.

Stelmack, R. M. & Campbell, K. B. (1974). Extroversion and auditory sensitivity to high and low frequency. *Perceptual and Motor Skills, 38*, 875–879.

Stevenson-Hinde, J., Hinde, R., & Simpson, A. E. (1986). Behavior at home and friendly or hostile behavior in preschool. In D. Olweus, J. Block, & M. R. Yarrow (Eds.), *Development of antisocial and prosocial behavior* (pp. 127–145). New York: Academic Press.

Swift, M. S. & Spivack, G. (1969). Achievement related classroom behavior of secondary school normal and disturbed students. *Exceptional Children, 35*, 677–684.

Tancer, N. K. (1992). Elective mutism: A review of the literature. In B. Lahey & A. E. Costean (Eds.), *Advances in clinical psychology* (Vol. 14, pp. 265–288). New York: Plenum.

Totusek, P. & Staton-Spicer, A. (1982). Classroom seating preferences as a function of student personality. *Journal of Experimental Education, 50*, 159–163.

Van Kleek, A. & Street, R. (1982). Does reticence just mean talking less? Qualitative differences in the language of talkative and reticent preschoolers. *Journal of Psycholinguistic Research, 11,* 609–629.

Wang, Y. & Kemple, K. (March, 1993). *Congruence in mother and teacher ratings of early shyness.* Paper presented at the Society for Research in Child Development. New Orleans.

Warnke, S. & Evans, M. A. (August, 1996). *Don't blame mother: Parenting styles associated with childhood shyness.* Paper presented at the International Society for the Study of Behavioural Development, Quebec City.

Younger, A., Schneider, B., & Pelley, G. (March, 1993). *Children's behavioural descriptions of their shy, withdrawn peers.* Paper presented at the Biennial meeting of the Society for Research in Child Development, New Orleans.

Zimbardo, P. G. (1977). *Shyness: What it is. What to do about it.* Reading, MA: Addison Wesley.

Zimbardo, P. G. & Radl, S. L. (1981). *The shy child: A parent's guide to preventing and overcoming shyness from infancy to adulthood.* New York: McGraw-Hill.

Section Two

Social and Personality Factors

Introduction

Social and Personality Factors

W. Ray Crozier *and* **Lynn E. Alden**

THE SELF IN SOCIAL ANXIETY
The Roots of Social Anxiety
Shyness, Embarrassment, and the Self
INDIVIDUAL DIFFERENCES
CONCLUDING REMARKS
REFERENCES

The chapters in Section Two of the *Handbook* are concerned with the impact of social anxiety on processes of social interaction. In Chapter 1, we pointed out that social discomfort is commonplace in routine or mundane social encounters, whether these are with neighbours, acquaintances, or work colleagues, or transactions in shops, offices, restaurants, and so on. A considerable body of research shows that individual differences in shyness and social anxiety impact on both transitory encounters and longer-term relationships. The chapters in this section examine these issues. Inevitably they refer back to the preceding section on the development of inhibition and shyness, as chapters on self-consciousness, embarrassment, and blushing consider the emergence of these or their antecedents in childhood. They also anticipate the third section, on Clinical Perspectives and Interventions, since no hard and fast line can be drawn between shyness or social anxiety on the one hand, and the clinical condition of social phobia on the other. Also, fear of embarrassment forms part of the DSM-IV criteria for social phobia (see Widiger, this volume, *Chapter 15*, Table 15.1), and fear of blushing is frequently a presenting problem in social phobia (Edelmann, *Chapter 14*).

THE SELF IN SOCIAL ANXIETY

If one were to identify a theme that runs through this set of chapters, it would surely be *the self*. There seems to be too much of the self in shyness. There is a

International Handbook of Social Anxiety: Concepts, Research and Interventions Relating to the Self and Shyness. Edited by W. Ray Crozier and Lynn E. Alden.

contrast between the poised, engrossed behaviour of the person who is at ease in social interaction and the person who is preoccupied with the self and with the impression being made, and whose uncertainties about what to say or do are related to the fluster associated with such preoccupation. Of course, this contrast may be in the eye of the shy individual and may not be warranted by the facts, but it is no less real for that. As responses to the Stanford Shyness Survey indicate (Zimbardo et al., 1975), shy people can appear to others as self-centred, conceited, or arrogant. For example, one person said to one of us about shy people, "What makes them think people are so interested in them?" On a recent train journey, a woman was overheard to say of another, whom she alleged was reluctant to go out to meet people, "She's obsessed about people looking at her". Why is shyness (and social anxieties more generally) associated with self-preoccupation? How are self-processes related to the cognitions, affect and behaviours characteristic of social anxiety?

The Roots of Social Anxiety

These questions are the focus of Leary's chapter (*Chapter 10*). Leary is well known for his advocacy of the self-presentation model of social anxiety (he regards shyness as the combination of social anxiety with inhibited behaviour). Here he suggests that the unique human ability to reflect upon the self and to consider how one appears to others may have evolved to facilitate interpersonal understanding, with the benefits this brings to social living. This capacity has implications for emotions in general and social anxiety in particular. It widens the range of emotions that can be experienced, makes a psychological reality of symbolic threats to well-being as well as physical threats, and permits awareness of how one's conduct might be viewed by others. In short, it produces the conditions for a social anxiety that is more than a simple fear of the unfamiliar which, as we have seen, does not require a sophisticated level of self-consciousness.

Gilbert and Trower (*Chapter 12*) also consider the advantages of an evolved self-consciousness in terms of the acquisition of a "theory of mind" that enables the theorist to gain insight into the intentions of other people and to predict their actions. A theory of mind also assists in the development of socially important relationships. As their model has evolved, Gilbert and Trower have placed greater emphasis on the individual's beliefs about his or her attractiveness to others, since friendships and sexual partners are important for successful group living. They regard the individual's attribution (or projection) of negative attitudes towards himself or herself as central to social anxiety. Their biological model, with its emphasis on the struggle for rank and status (which is ultimately in the service of reproductive success), shares with Leary's account a debt to Mead's conception of the self. Leary also places fear of social rejection at the core of social anxiety suggesting, in an elaboration of self-presentation theory, that impression management concerns are potent to the extent that they increase the risk of rejection. However, whereas Gilbert and Trower argue that self-awareness can produce the conditions for social anxiety to occur, they claim that it is not necessary for this experience—for example, many other species also show social anxiety. This contrasts with Leary' s position that self-awareness *is* necessary, but is not sufficient for social anxiety; a motivation to create a desired impression is also required. The resolution of this difference presumably relates to the distinction—noted above and evident throughout Section One—between fear of unfamiliar others and fear of what others will think.

Leary's chapter explores the thesis that "the content of a person's self-thoughts helps to determine whether a particular interpersonal context causes shy anxiety and inhibition or confident poise and sociability". He examines this in terms of the literature on the relationship between shyness and self-esteem and attributions for performance. Bruch (*Chapter 9*) also examines the role of negative self-statements and attribution style in social interaction processes. The emphasis in Baldwin and Fergusson's account of self-knowledge (*Chapter 11*) is on thinking processes rather than the contents of thoughts. They examine this in terms of *relational schemas*, which are defined as cognitive representations of self and other that have been abstracted from regularities in social experience. They comprise a self-schema ("I can never think what to say") and an other-schema ("people will find me boring"). These schemas have important consequences for information processing, including heightened vigilance to cues for criticism or rejection. Baldwin and Fergusson review an impressive body of research that demonstrates how such schemas can be activated in the laboratory, for example, by using subtle priming methods. These methods can be used to address questions about the implications of these schemas for, say, evaluation of the self in terms of others' standards. More importantly, perhaps, their chapter draws out the implications of this empirical work for clinical intervention. As they argue, "When we frame the negative expectancies of socially insecure individuals as elements of an activated relational schema, we broaden our therapeutic options in a number of ways". Thus, effort can be directed to make more accessible by repeated activation and consolidation alternative and more positive schemas.

Shyness, Embarrassment, and the Self

An alternative conception of shyness has regarded it as an emotion related to shame, guilt, and embarrassment (Izard & Hyson, 1986). Recent years have seen a surge of interest in the "self-conscious emotions" (Tangney & Fischer, 1995), particularly embarrassment (Miller, 1996) and shame (Gilbert & Andrews, 1998). This research has thrown up several questions for researchers into shyness and social anxiety. What is the relationship between these emotions and anxiety? When people are shy are they experiencing anxiety or some other emotion, like shame or embarrassment? Blushing is commonly associated with embarrassment, but do people also blush when they are shy or ashamed? How is blushing related to the heightened sympathetic nervous system arousal characteristic of anxiety states? Buss (1980) offered an ambitious attempt to answer these questions, regarding shame, shyness, and embarrassment (and audience anxiety) as different aspects of social anxiety, all of which shared self-attention as its core property.

Miller (*Chapter 13*) returns to these issues in considering the relationship between shyness and embarrassment. He regards these as "siblings" who share a common parent—they are both aversive states that reflect concerns about what others think of us. He argues that embarrassment is a reaction to a sudden and unexpected predicament that is usually advantageous and serves valuable social functions—embarrassment frequently elicits positive responses from others. Shyness, however, is more pervasive and longer lasting, is an anticipation of what might go wrong in routine situations and, far from having positive functions, it impairs social life. Shy people tend to be viewed negatively (Lord & Zimbardo, 1985; Paulhus & Morgan, 1997; Yost & Loiacono, 1997). Miller suggests that embarrassment finds expression in blushing and a distinct sequence of facial movements whereas shyness has no unique response pattern (gaze and head aversion, anxious hand movements, etc. are not unique to shyness). He reviews research that distinguishes shyness and embarrassment. It is of interest that students of embarrassment have paid considerable attention to how people cope with their predicament, attention that can be traced back to Goffman's writings on facework practices (Goffman, 1972). Furthermore, others present will try to help the embarrassed person recover poise, as they too recognize their responsibility for the success of the interaction. Attention to coping in shyness emphasizes social withdrawal, and also the isolation of the shy individual, perhaps reflecting an assumption that shy people escape the situation or else passively (and helplessly) endure their difficulties. Are shy people too ashamed of their condition to involve others, or is shyness seldom noticed unless the individual's abrupt departure or interaction style brings an encounter to an end (creates embarrassment)?

Blushing is a puzzling phenomenon that is as yet little understood in psychological or physiological terms. It can serve as a useful social signal yet it is uncontrollable. It leaves the person conspicuous when he or she typically least wants to be seen. Although it is regarded as the "hallmark" of embarrassment (Buss, 1980), it does not always occur in this state, while other psychologists argue that it is a characteristic response of shame and shyness, too. Edelmann (*Chapter 14*) provides a detailed review of what is known about blushing. Advances in the measurement of skin colour, facial blood flow and skin temperature are currently facilitating research into the psychophysiology of blushing. A recurrent theme in research is that the blush is a response to self-attention. This attention is often unwanted, and occurs when the person has committed a faux pas or is embarrassed in some way. However, people do blush simply when they are conspicuous and also when they are publicly praised, complimented, or thanked. Like other signs of embarrassment, the blush serves useful affiliation functions and people tend to be viewed in a more positive light after they have created a faux pas when they blush. The notion that the blush functions as a signal of appease-ment has attracted empirical inquiry as well as speculation about the evolution-ary origins of the blush in animal displays of submission.

INDIVIDUAL DIFFERENCES

Research into individual differences in social anxiety as a trait has been stimu-lated by a trait conception of shyness. Studies have shown that the various scales that have been produced to measure shyness are intercorrelated to a substantial degree and seem to be measuring a common factor. Thus, Briggs and Smith (1986) carried out an analysis of five scales and reported correlations between them that ranged from 0.70 to 0.86, with a mean correlation of 0.77. Shyness is correlated with but separate from the "Big Five" traits of extraversion and neu-roticism (Briggs, 1988). Notwithstanding this unidimensional structure, Jonathan Cheek and his colleagues (Cheek & Briggs, 1990; Cheek & Krasnoperova, 1999) have set out a model of shyness that postulates three components, somatic anxiety, cognitive, and social competence components. All three are regarded as important elements of shyness but all need not be present in any one individual and there is variation in the emphasis assigned to each in any one person's shyness. These components have been the focus of research reviewed in this section, although the emphasis has been on cognitive and behavioural components.

The involvement of the self in social anxiety implies that variation in self-related processes is a factor in individual differences in shyness and social anxiety. There is considerable evidence to support this thesis. Leary (*Chapter 10*) predicts that if self-awareness is necessary for social anxiety then a predisposi-tion towards this would be associated with individual differences in anxiety, a prediction that is supported for trait measures like Public Self-consciousness (Fenigstein, Scheier, & Buss, 1975; see also Miller, *Chapter 13*). Bruch (*Chapter 9*) reviews evidence for individual differences in self-efficacy beliefs and attribu-tions. Shy individuals perceive they have less ability than do the less shy and there is a larger discrepancy between their perceptions of their capabilities and their perceptions of others' expectations for their performance. These beliefs are resis-tant to feedback indicating successful performance; indeed, success may only raise the expectations of others, as these are perceived by shy people, and serve to make the shy person even more pessimistic. Baldwin and Fergusson (*Chapter 11*) explain individual differences in terms of the relational schemas that have been built up through the individual's experience of social relationships and the attitudes to them of significant others such as their primary caregivers. They consider that anxious individuals may have experienced a history within the family of "interactions that foster an exaggerated sense of self as a social object being evaluated against high standards for acceptance, coupled with few opportunities for expressive communication and the kind of social inter- actions that might hone social skills, modify misconceptions and temper social pressures".

This research has focused on cognitions and affect. Individual differences in behaviour may also reflect self-processes. There has been a line of argument that socially anxious people lack the social skills needed for effective social interac- tion (for example, the social skills therapy movement associated with Argyle's theorizing; Trower, Bryant, & Argyle, 1978) with the implication that reticence and keeping in the background are produced by skills deficits. Clearly there is uncertainty about what is meant by social skills, and it is important to maintain a distinction between deficits in competence and in performance. Bruch (*Chapter 9*) reviews research into social skills deficits. Shy people speak for less of the time and make shorter utterances. They also interject more agreements and acknowl- edgements of what the other has said and exhibit fewer dominant and assertive speech acts. Shyness is correlated with less accuracy at decoding nonverbal cues. They tend to be less skilful in turn-taking in conversation, verbal fluency, intro- ducing topics for conversation, and in expressiveness. Miller (*Chapter 13*) sug- gests that differences in skill serve to distinguish shyness from embarrassability; whereas people with good social skills are unlikely to be shy, they are not immune from embarrassment; on the other hand, those prone to embarrassment are more sensitive to social norms and values.

Notwithstanding these findings, the current emphasis among theorists is on the shy person's underestimation of his or her skills and on the deployment of coping strategies. Leary argues that the inhibited behaviour of the shy person is not a product of anxiety but represents strategies designed to minimize threat, akin to a protective self-presentation style (Arkin, 1981). This explanation contrasts not just with skills accounts but also with accounts of inhibition in terms of attention processes (for example, insufficient attention being paid to the task due to anxious self-preoccupation or to the recruitment of working memory capacity by worrisome thinking). The question of whether the characteristic behaviours of shy people are strategic, or reflect the inhibition of performance by anxiety, the activation of pessimistic schemas, or low efficacy expectations, or represent a diminished repertoire is an important one that has attracted some empiri- cal studies, but the issues are not resolved and more research needs to be undertaken.

CONCLUDING REMARKS

The chapters in this section take different approaches to the social discomfort that can be experienced in routine social situations. Taken together, they provide a valuable picture of contemporary research. Compared to the previous section there is a shift away from fear of the unfamiliar person or situation to a preoccupation with what other people think. Theoretical approaches to this preoccupation are influenced by conceptualizations of the self that can be traced to Mead and Goffman. Schlenker and Leary's influential self-presentation model of social anxiety features strongly in all chapters. Despite its antecedents in philosophical and sociological discourse, the research is based on a strong empirical foundation. Indeed, it draws upon much novel and ingenious experimentation, whether in priming and activating schemas, analysing social skills, or measuring colouring of the face. Nevertheless, this scientific rigour is not seen as an end in itself, all the chapters return to one of the central preoccupations of the *Handbook*, how to help people to overcome their social anxieties.

REFERENCES

Arkin, R. M. (1981). Self-presentation styles. In J. T. Tedeschi (Ed.), *Impression management theory and social psychological research* (pp. 311–333). New York: Academic Press.

Briggs, S. R. (1988). Shyness: Introversion or neuroticism? *Journal of Research in Personality, 22*, 290–307.

Briggs, S. R. & Smith, T. G. (1986). The measurement of shyness. In W. H. Jones, J. M. Cheek, & S. R. Briggs (Eds.), *Shyness: Perspectives on research and treatment* (pp. 47–60). New York: Plenum Press.

Buss, A. H. (1980). *Self-consciousness and social anxiety.* San Francisco: Freeman.

Cheek, J. M. & Briggs, S. R. (1990). Shyness as a personality trait. In W. R. Crozier (Ed.), *Shyness and embarrassment: Perspectives from social psychology* (pp. 315–337). Cambridge: Cambridge University Press.

Cheek, J. M. & Krasnoperova, E. N. (1999). Varieties of shyness in adolescence and adulthood. In L. A. Schmidt & J. Schulkin (Eds.), *Extreme fear, shyness, and social phobia: Origins, biological mechanisms, and clinical outcomes* (pp. 224–250). New York: Oxford University Press.

Fenigstein, A., Scheier, M. F., & Buss, A. H. (1975). Public and private self-consciousness: Assessment and theory. *Journal of Consulting and Clinical Psychology, 43*, 522–527.

Gilbert, P. & Andrews, B. (Eds.) (1998). *Shame: Interpersonal behavior, psychopathology, and culture.* New York: Oxford University Press.

Goffman, E. (1972). *Interaction ritual.* Harmondsworth, England: Penguin.

Izard, C. E. & Hyson, M. C. (1986). Shyness as a discrete emotion. In W. H. Jones, J. M. Cheek, & S. R. Briggs (Eds.), *Shyness: Perspectives on research and treatment* (pp. 147–160). New York: Plenum Press.

Lord, C. G. & Zimbardo, P. G. (1985). Actor-observer differences in the perceived stability of shyness. *Social Cognition, 3*, 250–265.

Paulhus, D. L. & Morgan, K. L. (1997). Perceptions of intelligence in leaderless groups: The dynamic effects of shyness and acquaintance. *Journal of Personality and Social Psychology, 72*, 581–591.

Schlenker, B. R. & Leary, M. R. (1982). Social anxiety and self-presentation: A conceptualization and model. *Psychological Bulletin, 92*, 641–669.

Tangney, J. P. & Fischer, K. W. (Eds.) (1995). *Self-conscious emotions: The psychology of shame, guilt, embarrassment and pride.* New York: Guilford Press.

Trower, P., Bryant, B., & Argyle, M. (1978). *Social skills and mental health.* London: Methuen.

Yost, J. H. & Loiacono, D. M. (1997). *Struggling in social quicksand: Does shyness lead to negative first impressions?* Paper presented at the Welsh Branch of the British Psychological Society International Conference on Shyness and Self-consciousness. Cardiff.

Zimbardo, P. G., Pilkonis, P. A., & Norwood, R. (1975). Shackles of shyness. *Psychology Today, UK Edition, 1*, No. 6, 24–27.

Chapter 9

Shyness and Social Interaction

Monroe A. Bruch

INTERNAL COGNITIVE-PERCEPTUAL RESPONSES
Negative Self-statements
Attributional Responses
Self-appraisal Processes
Self-protective vs Acquisitive Interaction Goals
EXTERNAL VERBAL–NONVERBAL BEHAVIORS
Self-protective Function of Verbal Content
Implications of Trower and Gilbert's Model for Verbal Content
Application of Ickes' Dyadic Interaction Paradigm
SOCIAL SKILLS DEFICITS
Decoding Skills Deficits
Conversational Skills Deficits
Social Skill Deficits in Childhood and as a Vulnerability Factor
NEW DIRECTIONS
CONCLUSIONS
REFERENCES

The objective of this chapter is to examine the relationship between shyness and problems in social interaction. Although there is very little longitudinal research on the reciprocal nature of how shyness impacts one's partners in an interaction and in turn how the shy person is affected by the behavior of these partners, there is substantial interest in how personality processes relate to interpersonal behavior. Recently, Asendorpf and Wilpers (1998) showed that components of the Five-Factor model of personality accounted for significant variance in a number of aspects of college students' interpersonal behavior over an 18-month period. In

International Handbook of Social Anxiety: Concepts, Research and Interventions Relating to the Self and Shyness. Edited by W. Ray Crozier and Lynn E. Alden.

addition to the five factors, these investigators also studied the reciprocal relationship between trait shyness and quality of interpersonal behaviors. Over the study's time period, shy in contrast to non-shy participants were much slower in developing friendships, had fewer friends, were less likely to fall in love, and reported less social support from existing friends. Interestingly, Asendorpf and Wilper's findings also showed that while personality was related to differences in relationship qualities over time, the opposite was not true. That is, changes in level of shyness showed no relation to the degree that the network of friends of participants grew quickly or slowly, whether they fell in love or not, or whether they felt significant support or little support. Such unidirectional results suggest that not only may personality characteristics (including shyness) be crystalized by early adulthood but that, contrary to expectations, later personality is unlikely to be shaped by the nature of one's present social interaction.

Although Asendorpf and Wilper's findings are but one study, the fact that shyness is related to change in social interaction, but that the opposite was not true, suggests that this personality characteristic plays a significant role in creating discomfort in and difficulties with social interaction. Therefore, study of the relationship between shyness and maladaptive social interaction is important for several reasons. First, the effectiveness of an individual's everyday social interaction plays a crucial role in the development and maintenance of satisfying interpersonal relationships. For instance, it is recognized that self-disclosure of one's thoughts and feelings is essential for moving a mere acquaintanceship to a personal friendship (Taylor & Altman, 1987). However, the natural progression of building relationships from a series of social interactions seems less likely to occur for shy, in contrast to non-shy, people. The shy person's tendency to disaffiliate by avoiding eye contact is just one example of an interactive behavior that is likely to impede the development of relationships with others.

Second, effectiveness in one's social interaction is not only important for the domain of social relationships but is also important for successful adjustment in other life domains. In the educational domain, effectiveness in social interaction can facilitate the learning process in that it provides greater access to instructors' perspectives for their course subject matter, it enables one to negotiate classroom learning tasks, and it increases opportunities for learning more effective study and test-taking skills. In the career domain, effective social interaction is necessary for gathering vocational information, exploring interests, engaging in job interviews, and communicating with supervisors and co-workers (e.g., Phillips & Bruch, 1988).

Finally, a third reason for studying the relationship between shyness and social interaction is the fact that stress can result from cultural expectations regarding the importance of gregarious behavior. In work and leisure situations, Western European and North American cultural expectations are typically that people should be friendly, outgoing, and sociable. For example, children who appear nonsociable are likely to be ridiculed and bullied (Rubin, 1993), while adults who appear nonsociable are perceived as being less successful in their careers and social lives. Thus, from a diathesis–stress perspective (see Monroe & Simons, 1991), being shy may create a greater vulnerability to experiencing negative emotions (e.g., depression) when such a person encounters situations where the expectancy is that participants will be highly gregarious.

In this chapter, I will focus on dispositional or trait shyness which is defined as anxious self-preoccupation and behavioral inhibition in various social contexts due to the prospect of interpersonal evaluation (Buss, 1980). Although situational shyness as a transitory state is common, dispositional shyness, which has both inherited and learned origins (see Schmidt, Polak, & Spooner, this volume, *Chapter 2*), is more likely to create significant and lasting problems in social interaction. Also, it is important to recognize that shyness can be distinguished from several related constructs. First, Cheek and Buss (1981) indicate that shyness can be distinguished from low-sociability which entails a nonfearful preference for not desiring to affiliate with others. Likewise, Asendorpf (1990) differentiates between unsociable children (i.e, those who have less contact with peers due to a low approach motive rather than a high avoidance motive) and shy children who are high in both tendencies and are, thus, conflicted in social situations. Second, Briggs (1988) indicates that shyness can be distinguished from introversion which entails an inward cognitive focus, a preference for solitude, but an ability to interact comfortably with others when desirable. Thus, an introvert should be relatively low on both sociability and shyness.

Before beginning our discussion of the research literature on shyness and social interaction, a final clarification is necessary. The research that forms the basis of our understanding of the social interaction of shy persons typically stems from one of two theoretical perspectives. First, personality trait approaches that emphasize person–environment transactions (e.g., Caspi, 1998) assume that there are stable individual differences in shyness. In addition, these approaches assume that individual differences in transaction with environmental circumstances serve to organize patterns of behavior over time. This approach to shyness typically involves classification of participants as high or low in shyness based on a self-report measure of shyness or social anxiety. A second perspective stems from social psychological models of social behavior such as Schlenker and Leary's (1982) self-presentational model of social anxiety. Approaches such as this are less interested in individual differences and are more interested in the social cognition or perceptual processes that relate to the experience of shyness. Research from this perspective typically involves laboratory manipulations of perceptions and collection of ratings regarding expectations about oneself and others in social situations. Therefore, as I discuss the research literature, the reader should be mindful of the particular theoretical approach underlying the work in specific studies.

In the sections that follow, I will examine a number of interpersonal response components that appear to be related to difficulties that shy persons experience in their social interactions. These response components include: (a) internal cognitive-perceptual responses, (b) external verbal and nonverbal behavior, and (c) social skills deficits. Following the review of response components, I will discuss several new directions in research on shyness and social interaction and, finally, I will summarize the key conclusions of this chapter.

INTERNAL COGNITIVE-PERCEPTUAL RESPONSES

The most studied aspect of shyness relative to social interaction is the shy person's internal cognitive-perceptual responses prior to, during, and following an interaction. In the section that follows the role of four types of cognitive-perceptual variables are examined. These four variables are: negative self-statements, attributional responses, self-appraisal processes, and self-protective social goals. Of specific interest are the types of social interaction that are found for each of these variables.

Negative Self-statements

Self-statements refer to internal speech that is self-referent and accompanies any social or intellectual task. People who score high on measures of shyness or social anxiety consistently report more negative, self-deprecatory thoughts relative to social interaction (e.g., Bruch, Gorsky, Collins, & Berger, 1989). Shy persons, do not consistently differ, however, from the non-shy in the frequency of their positive self-statements (Glass & Arnkoff, 1994).

Research on the social interaction correlates of negative self-statements has focused on a number of variables that theoretically should be associated with self-deprecatory thoughts. One correlate is the amount of subjective anxiety experienced relative to an interaction. Subjective anxiety is typically assessed following an interaction using a measure such as the Multiple Affect Adjective Checklist (Zuckerman & Lubin, 1965). Studies by Glass, Merluzzi, Biever, and Larsen (1982), Bruch and Pearl (1995), Myszka, Galassi, and Ware (1986) and Sturmer (1999) involved shy participants engaged in conversation with a peer who was a stranger. In these studies both self-statements and subjective anxiety were assessed. Across all four studies, results showed that frequency of negative self-statements was directly correlated with greater amounts of subjective anxiety, suggesting that there is a synchrony between negative cognitive and negative affective responses of shy persons in interactions involving conversation with a stranger.

A second correlate consists of other types of cognitive responses that reflect a shy person's attentional concerns during social interaction. Using a laboratory social interaction, Melchior and Cheek (1990) and Bruch, Hamer, and Heimberg (1993) found that frequency of negative self-statements was associated with greater concern about one's partner's evaluation, rating oneself as performing ineffectively, and spending more time focusing on oneself than on the interaction task and partner. Demonstrating that negative self-statements are correlated with these maladaptive cognitive responses supports the notion that shy persons have a misplaced attentional focus during social interaction, which is likely to interfere with their performance.

A third correlate of a shy person's negative self-statements is behavioral mani-festations of nonverbal anxiety during an interaction. When nonverbal aspects of anxiety are coded from videotaped interactions, Bruch et al. (1989), Glass and Furlong (1990), and Sturmer (1999) found a direct correlation between the fre-quency of negative self-statements and the frequency of gaze aversion, hands constrained, fidgeting and nervous laughter. Also, Bruch et al. (1989) found that negative self-statements were correlated with the size of the discrepancy between participants' report of the visibility of their anxious behaviors (e.g., fidgeting) and coding of the same behaviors based on a videotape of the interaction. That is, the more negative thoughts reported, the greater the tendency of participants to overestimate the amount of anxious behaviors they manifested relative to judges' objective count of anxious behaviors. Furthermore, this discrepancy does not appear to be driven by the participants' experience of internal arousal because heart rate level during the interaction was uncorrelated with participants' esti-mates of anxious behavior or with the degree of discrepancy.

Attributional Responses

A second cognitive-perceptual variable that correlates with social interaction is attributional responses. Most research on shyness and attributional processes has focused on differences in attributional style between shy and non-shy persons. Results show that shy persons attribute negative outcomes in interpersonal situ-ations to internal and uncontrollable causes (Anderson & Arnoult, 1985; Bruch & Pearl, 1995). Very little of this research has focused, however, on the direct relationship between attributional style and the responses of shy persons during social interactions. One exception is the study by Bruch and Pearl (1995) in which attributional style ratings for negative interpersonal events were related to symp-toms of shyness following an interaction in which the participant was required to initiate a conversation with a stranger of the opposite gender. The attributional style dimensions of locus (i.e., internally), stability, and controllability were assessed and related to negative self-statements, subjective report of anxiety, and when participants terminated the conversation (i.e., social withdrawal). Analyses showed that the tendency to attribute negative interpersonal events to uncon-trollable causes (e.g., somatic arousal) was associated with emitting more nega-tive self-statements during the interaction. Attributing negative interpersonal events to uncontrollable and external causes were each uniquely associated with greater subjective anxiety during the interaction. None of the attributional style dimensions was uniquely associated, however, with how quickly participants withdrew from the conversation. Bruch and Pearl's results are consistent with the notion that the maladaptive attributional style of shy persons is related to specific negative cognitive and affective reactions experienced in the context of an interaction.

Taking a different approach, Alden (1987) studied how different types of social feedback to shy and non-shy persons related to their causal attributions about their performance outcomes. Participants engaged in an initial interaction for practice and then a subsequent interaction with a different partner. They received one of four types of feedback pattern: improvement, deterioration, success, or failure. Alden (1987) assessed participants' causal attributions using Weiner's (1986) four-fold model of ability, effort, luck, and task difficulty. She found that shy persons provided with feedback that they were improving attributed this outcome to greater personal effort. Although the improvement condition produced an internal attribution among shy persons, these improvements were attributed to the unstable factor of effort rather than the more stable factor of ability. Non-shy persons, on the other hand, attributed both consistent success and improvement to ability while shy persons attributed consistent success to luck or low task difficulty, both of which are external factors. Although Alden did not expect that a brief exposure to positive feedback would unseat a shy person's maladaptive attributional responses, her findings suggest that positive outcomes in social interactions may lack reinforcement value for the shy person.

Self-appraisal Processes

A third cognitive-perceptual variable that is related with social interaction responses involves self-appraisal processess. Alden and Wallace (1995; Wallace & Alden, 1991, 1995, 1997; see also Alden, this volume, *Chapter 17*) have conducted a series of studies focusing on the content of self-appraisal processes of shy persons prior to an interaction and following the receipt of feedback about the adequacy of their interaction.

Essentially, their research involves three variables: perceived social standards (i.e., the level of interaction effectiveness expected by others and by oneself), perceived personal ability (i.e., level of social self-efficacy), and type of social feedback (i.e., positive or negative). As perceived social standards are complicated by subjective judgements, Wallace and Alden (1991) developed a "visual scale" rating procedure that presented videotaped interactions of people displaying various degrees of social effectiveness to serve as anchors for social skillfulness. Participants are shown the videotapes and encouraged to watch them as often as necessary before making their ratings of perceived social standards.

In an initial study, Wallace and Alden (1991) found that shy and non-shy persons did not differ in their perceptions of the standards other people held for them. This finding is interesting in light of Leary, Kowalski, and Campbell's (1988) conclusion that shy persons believe that others are generally critical of them. In terms of one's own standards, shy persons employed lower personal standards for their performance than did non-shy persons, indicating that they expected less of themself.

With regard to self-perceived ability, Wallace and Alden (1991) found that shy, in contrast to non-shy, individuals perceived themselves as having less ability.

Consequently, shy persons evidenced a larger discrepancy than non-shy persons between their perception of their own performance capabilities and their perception of others' expectations for their performance. The appraisal problem that occurs for shy persons, therefore, is not that they believe that others hold impossible standards, or that shy persons hold perfectionistic self-standards. The problem is that the shy person's low ability perception results in a discrepancy between perceived ability and the perceived standards of others, resulting in low self-efficacy beliefs for social interaction.

Next, Wallace and Alden (1995) tested whether feedback following an interaction would affect the discrepancy between perceived ability and perceptions of others' standards relative to a subsequent interaction. They were interested specifically in positive feedback, because while it is assumed that positive feedback should be beneficial, there is evidence that shy persons ignore or discredit such feedback (Alden, 1987). Social feedback was manipulated by varying the confederate's behavior and by spontaneous comments made by the experimenter following an initial interaction. Next, participants' perceptions and ratings were collected prior to what participants believed would be a second interaction that would take place with a peer. Results indicated that, following positive feedback, shy, in contrast to non-shy, men rated their ability for an upcoming interaction significantly lower than their estimation of the social standards others would hold for them in the upcoming interaction. The same pattern also emerged for shy men who received negative feedback or no feedback. In contrast, non-shy men who received positive feedback or no feedback rated their ability to perform effectively in an upcoming interaction higher than they rated the standards that others would hold for them, while non-shy men who were given negative feedback rated their ability as similar to others' expectations. Finally, the results also showed that shy men rated their ability lower than they rated their own standards for their performance in the interaction regardless of condition, while non-shy men rated their ability similar to their personal standard.

Wallace and Alden (1997) argued that persons with a clinical level of social anxiety (i.e., social phobia) are quite likely to hold inaccurate perceptions of the social standards others hold for them. Thus, Wallace and Alden (1997) compared social phobics with a nonanxious control group on the discrepancy between self-perceived ability and perceptions of the standards others held for them after receiving either positive or negative feedback. Results indicated that social phobics showed a significant discrepancy between perceived ability (lower) and perceptions of others' standards (higher) while controls showed no such discrepancy. However, in contrast to results for shy undergraduates, following positive feedback social phobics showed an increase in the discrepancy between perceived ability and perceived standards of others relative to an upcoming interaction while controls showed no discrepancy. With negative feedback, social phobics showed a decrease between perceived ability and others' standards while controls did not.

Supplementary analyses showed that the increase in discrepancy following positive feedback was due to social phobics raising their perceptions of the standards others held for their behavior rather than lowering their ratings of perceived ability. As Wallace and Alden (1997) suggest, it appears that following positive feedback persons who are highly socially anxious are concerned that others will expect more from them in subsequent interactions. Therefore, positive feedback about one's social interaction may not be perceived in a manner that facilitates the shy person in modifying his or her negative self-perceptions.

Self-protective vs Acquisitive Interaction Goals

As people approach and then engage in social interaction, their behavior presumably is directed by one of two types of interaction goals: gaining approval and avoiding disapproval (Arkin, 1981). In the case of shyness, Arkin, Lake, and Baumgardner (1986) argue that shy persons are primarily motivated to avoid disapproval, and thus adopt self-protective approaches in their interaction. Self-protective approaches are characterized by acting cautiously, attempting to create a "safe" impression, deflecting attention away from oneself, and expressing attitudes and opinions that are non-extreme. Non-shy people, on the other hand, are motivated by the desire to gain positive social outcomes, and thus use acquisitive approaches in their interaction. In an acquisitive approach, people engage in active, direct, and appropriate attention-seeking behaviors designed to lead to rewarding interactions. Consequently, Arkin et al.'s (1986) model hypothesizes that shy persons typically focus on self-protective strategies (to avoid disapproval) and ignore acquisitive strategies while non-shy persons adopt an opposite approach.

Despite this intriguing hypothesis, only recently has a scale been developed to assess this variable relative to actual social interactions. In a study involving shyness and self-disclosure, Meleshko and Alden (1993) developed and used a measure of self-protective vs acquisitive social goals (i.e., Social Self-Presentation Style Scale, S-SPSS). Administered following an actual interaction, the S-SPSS asked participants to rate the approaches they took when interacting with their conversation partner. Using a reciprocal self-disclosure paradigm, Meleshko and Alden (1993) had shy and non-shy participants interact with a confederate such that each took turns to talk about themselves on a list of topics that varied in intimacy level. Confederates self-disclosed at either a high or low level of intimacy as determined by the topic selected. Although it might be expected that shy persons exposed to a confederate who disclosed at a high level of intimacy would be more cautious, results indicated that regardless of disclosure level, shy persons reported engaging in more self-protective and fewer acquisitive response strategies. In contrast, non-shy participants reported just the opposite pattern and this was true regardless of the confederates' degree of intimacy.

Using a conversation with an other-gender stranger, Bruch et al. (1993) had male undergraduates complete the S-SPSS along with other cognitive-affective symptom measures following the conversation. Results showed that the self-rated shyness symptoms of "felt nervous", "acted awkward", and "concerned that my partner would be critical" correlated positively with greater use of self-protective strategies and negatively with use of acquisitive strategies. Negative self-statements also correlated positively with self-protective strategies and negatively with acquisitive strategies. Time spent focusing on self versus partner issues during the conversation was positively correlated with the use of self-protective strategies but uncorrelated with the use of acquisitive strategies.

Finally, in Wallace and Alden's (1997) comparison of social phobics and non-phobics self-appraisal processes following feedback, they also administered the S-SPSS. Results showed that social phobics reported more self-protective than acquisitive strategies during a conversation regardless of whether they received positive or negative feedback. Thus, even in the face of evidence that an interaction is going well, it appears that social phobics will "play it safe" and continue to use more self-protective strategies. Also, a statistical interaction revealed that social phobics reported less use of acquisitive strategies than nonphobics following negative feedback, suggesting that when an interaction goes poorly, non-shy persons will persist in their use of acquisitive strategies. These investigators also found that, regardless of social phobia status, participants with a greater own ability–other standard discrepancy reported greater use of self-protective strategies and less use of acquisitive strategies. Therefore, the results from all three studies are consistent with Arkin's (1981) notion that the basis for a shy person's selection of self-protective over acquisitive strategies is due to his or her preoccupation with avoiding criticism and disapproval because of self-perceived inadequacies.

EXTERNAL VERBAL–NONVERBAL BEHAVIORS

When unable to avoid or leave a situation, it appears that shy people can be differentiated from non-shy people on the basis of observable behavior during social interaction. For instance, shy persons are less likely to initiate conversations and more likely to speak less, to make brief comments, and to take longer to respond (Leary & Kowalski, 1995). However, although a vast array of verbal and nonverbal behaviors are associated with shyness in the context of social interaction, it is essential that some theoretical framework be used to understand the strategic purpose of these behaviors.

Generally, investigators have used one of the following theoretical models in studying the strategic intent of the overt behavior of shy persons. As previously described, Arkin's (1981) self-protection theory proposes that shy persons manifest behaviors in an interaction that are likely to protect them from social disapproval. Similarly, Leary's self-presentational approach (Schlenker & Leary, 1982; Leary & Kowalski, 1995) assumes that because shy people doubt their ability to convey a particular impression to others, they will engage in relatively passive affiliative behaviors during an interaction. Finally, Trower and Gilbert's (1989) ethological/psychobiological model of social anxiety proposes that shyness occurs within the context of the organism's defense system, which includes dominance hierarchies and strategies that handle intraspecies conflict and facilitate functioning in complex social groups. As a result of this defense system, shy persons continuously appraise situations, monitoring their behavior and checking for possible threats. For the shy person, submissive behaviors presumably reduce the chance of disapproval (a form of aggression) from the dominant member and allow the person to remain a part of the group (see Gilbert & Trower, this volume, *Chapter 12*).

In the section that follows, I will examine research that has employed one of these approaches in analyzing the purpose that specific verbal and nonverbal responses play in the social interaction of shy persons. Also, I will discuss research based on the Dyadic Interaction Paradigm of Ickes and Tooke (1988) which assesses verbal and nonverbal behaviors at the dyad level rather than at the individual level.

Self-protective Function of Verbal Content

Although previous shyness research has focused on nonverbal and paralinguistic indicators of anxiety, typically the content of the shy person's conversational speech is not examined. Using Stiles's (1978) scheme for coding the interpersonal intent of conversational speech, Leary, Knight, and Johnson (1987) predicted that shyness would be associated with conveying proportionately less objective information, personal opinions, advice giving, and interpretation of another's behavior. Responses such as these presumably run the risk of displaying one's ignorance, starting an argument, or having one's ideas rejected. In contrast, Leary et al. (1987) predicted that shyness would be associated with conveying proportionately more questions, acknowledging receipt of another's message, conveying more agreements, and reflecting another's experience into words. All of these responses presumably are safe because they convey interest in the other person, prompt one's partner to continue speaking, and generally keep attention focused on the partner rather than on the shy person. Verbal response analysis was based on a laboratory interaction in which shy and non-shy participants engaged in a get-acquainted conversation with a peer who was a stranger. Analyses of verbal content showed that shyness was associated with increased use of agreements and acknowledgements and with a lesser tendency to convey objective information. The other hypotheses, however, were not supported. In addition, and consistent with previous analysis of speech behavior of shy persons (e.g., Natale, Entin, & Jaffe, 1979), the results showed that shy in contrast to non-shy persons spent less time talking and made fewer utterances. These indicators of speech frequency are also consistent with a self-protective response strategy.

Bruch et al. (1989; Study 2) attempted to replicate and extend Leary et al.'s (1987) results by applying Stiles's coding scheme to transcripts of "get-acquainted" conversations between shy undergraduates and an other-gender confederate. Results failed to find any association between shyness and the use of particular verbal content codes as hypothesized by Leary et al. However, shy in contrast to non-shy participants talked less and made fewer utterances, just as Leary et al. found. The lack of strong support for the self-protective function of verbal content in Leary et al. (1987) and Bruch et al. (1989) might be attributed to the use of a "get-acquainted" conversation task. This type of conversation elicits a high proportion of edification codes (i.e., conveying factual information) relative to other codes, perhaps because interactants need to provide basic information about themselves before being able to converse more freely.

Meleshko and Alden (1993) tested the notion that the content of shy persons' self-disclosures would reflect a self-protective strategy, in that such disclosures would be low in intimacy. Consistent with this prediction, results indicated that shy participants disclosed at only a moderate level of intimacy regardless of whether their partner disclosed at a high or low level of intimacy. In addition, shy participants did not reciprocate their partner's disclosures as well as did non-shy participants and the nature of shy, in contrast to non-shy, participants' disclosures were correlated with less liking and more discomfort by their interaction partners. Meleshko and Alden (1993) conclude that the latter findings suggest that adoption of self-protective strategies may elicit negative reactions despite the belief that they will lessen the chances for disapproval.

Implications of Trower and Gilbert's Model for Verbal Content

As indicated previously, Trower and Gilbert (1989) propose that the verbal and nonverbal behaviors of shy persons reflect the operation of a safety system designed to reduce the threat of rejection by other persons who are the dominant members in a social context (e.g., boss at work). Recently, Walters and Hope (1998) tested this approach by comparing social phobics to nonanxious controls in terms of their responses in a "get-acquainted" conversation with a confederate. They hypothesized that social phobics, in contrast to controls, would manifest more verbal and nonverbal responses that reflect submission rather than dominance, and avoidance rather than cooperation (i.e., directly engaging the partner). Results showed that social phobics compared to controls evidenced fewer dominance behaviors such as giving commands, bragging, and interrupting, and fewer cooperative behaviors such as offering praise and directly facing the partner. However, the two groups did not differ on submissive or avoidance behaviors (e.g., gaze aversion). Consequently, although results were limited, they provide some support for the notion that the external, interaction responses of shy persons serve a safety function to reduce the likelihood of rejection by other members of one's social group.

Application of Ickes's Dyadic Interaction Paradigm

Although not a specific theory about the strategic purpose of verbal and non-verbal responses during an interaction, Ickes's approach to assessing social interaction provides an established method for determining the manner in which personality attributes operate in initial interactions by examining how they correlate with dyad level behaviors (e.g., frequency of mutual gazes). The dyadic interaction paradigm (Ickes & Tooke, 1988; Ickes, Bissonnette, Garcia, & Stinson, 1990) involves an unobtrusive videotape recording of spontaneous social interactions recorded in a controlled observational setting. The videotapes yield a wide range of reliably coded verbal and nonverbal responses which can be analyzed at both the individual and dyadic level. When the dyad members' scores on an interaction behavior were correlated at a specific magnitude (i.e., exceeded $r = 0.24$), a dyad level variable was created by aggregating their individual scores.

In a study by Garcia, Stenson, Ickes, Bissonnette, and Briggs (1991) the dyadic interaction paradigm was used to assess the relationship of men's and women's shyness on dyad level verbal and nonverbal behaviors. Mixed-gender dyads were formed by randomly assigning male and female strangers into pairs without regard for their scores on a measure of shyness and ratings of their physical attractiveness. The association of shyness with dyad level behaviors was analyzed while statistically controlling for physical attractiveness.

Results showed that men's shyness was negatively correlated with the frequency and duration of dyad members' speaking turns, the number of questions they asked each other, the amount of positive affect they displayed to each other (i.e., smiles and laughter), the number of direct gazes at one's partner, and the number of mutual gazes. Also, men's shyness was negatively correlated with the dyad members' ratings of the perceived quality of their interaction. In contrast, women's shyness was significantly related with only two dyad-level measures. Women's shyness was negatively correlated with the number of each individual's direct gazes and the number of mutual gazes that the dyad members displayed.

After examining the data pattern for direct and mutual gazes, Garcia et al. (1991) offered an intriguing interpretation of how men's shyness impacts the pattern of interaction in a mixed-gender dyad. They suggest that the greater the men's shyness, the more they managed to keep their female partners from establishing and breaking eye contact by glancing at the women only for brief amounts of time. By their behavior, the shy men could control the onset, offset, and overall amount of mutual gaze activity during the interaction. Therefore, Garcia et al. speculate that eye contact patterns may serve as a marker variable of how shyness affects the behavior of both dyad members. In particular, they conclude that shy men may use this as a strategy to deal with feelings of anxiety in the situation; however, such gaze control tactics may be maladaptive in the long run because they correlated with dyad members' ratings of dissatisfaction with the interaction.

SOCIAL SKILLS DEFICITS

The topic of shyness and social skills deficits is complex and difficult to summarize. From inspection of the research literature one could argue that shy, as compared to non-shy, persons are more likely to have social skills deficits because they perform more poorly in social interactions (e.g., Twentyman & McFall, 1975). Also, given evidence suggesting the inherited as well as learned nature of shyness, such skill deficits are likely to develop due to poor parental modeling of effective social skills (Bruch, 1989). However, from another perspective, it can be argued that the poor performance of shy persons is due to the inhibiting effects of anxiety which may interrupt the execution of otherwise effective responses. For example, Hill (1989) found that shy and non-shy participants were relatively similar in their knowledge of appropriate social behavior, but that shy participants were less likely to employ these responses and did not believe they had the ability to do so effectively.

In addition to differing perspectives, there is also controversy among investigators concerning how to define social skills. Some investigators argue that social skills should be defined at a molar level (e.g., sense of timing) rather than at a molecular level (e.g., eye contact, smile), because the former has a more discernible impact on the satisfaction interactants experience as well as on judges' ratings of effectiveness (Fischetti, Curran, & Weissberg, 1977). Communication researchers also add another perspective to social skills effectiveness not typically addressed by personality and clinical psychologists. These investigators argue that conversational speech skills are an important aspect of one's social skills repetoire and they have identified some critical differences between shy and non-shy persons (e.g., Manning & Ray, 1993; Prisbell, 1991).

In the section that follows, I will examine selected research studies that have addressed the question of whether shy persons possess social skill deficits. While answers to this question are often discussed in relation to comparing the effectiveness of alternative treatment approaches, the interest here is in what types of skill deficits exist, if at all, for shy persons.

Decoding Skills Deficits

One of the critical aspects of social interaction involves the accurate decoding of nonverbal behavioral cues (Costanzo & Archer, 1989). Although Riggio (1986) provided evidence that self-reported shyness is negatively correlated with a self-report measure of decoding skill (i.e., emotional sensitivity), this research did not expose participants to actual social stimuli when assessing decoding skill. Schroeder (1995) administered Costanzo and Archer's (1989) Interpersonal Perception Task (IPT) to undergraduate participants who varied in shyness. The IPT is a videotaped stimulus which depicts brief scenes of social interaction that include six examples of five interaction cue domains: kinship, deception, competition, status, and intimacy. Each scene is accompanied by an objective, multiple-choice question about some aspect of the people in the scene. For example, one of the intimacy scenes shows a man and woman talking to each other about a trip, and participants are asked to indicate the relationship between the people (e.g., acquaintances, brother and sister, just friends). Participants fill out an answer sheet which yields an accuracy score based on the number of questions answered correctly.

Schroeder (1995) found that shyness was negatively correlated with decoding skill accuracy for interpersonal situations involving kinship, competition, intimacy, and status but not for deception, which showed no correlation. Recognizing that inaccuracy in decoding can be a function of the interfering effects of anxiety as well as social skill deficits, Schroeder (1995) also administered a measure of cognitive interference to assess its relation with decoding skill. Results indicated that cognitive interference showed little systematic relationship with IPT domain scores suggesting that a shy person's problem in interpersonal perception may be in part due to inadequate development of certain social information-processing skills.

Conversational Speech Deficits

Although the nature of the relationship between social skills and conversational speech is poorly understood, presumably one's social skills repetoire is in part manifested in speech content (e.g., Conger, Wallander, Mariotto, & Ward, 1980). In a number of scattered studies, communication researchers and social psychologists have analyzed the verbal content and pattern of conversational speech relative to shyness. Prisbell (1991), for instance, compared shy and non-shy undergraduates on two self-report measures of communication skill. Participants were asked to focus on a recent social interaction and then to complete a measure of communication skills (e.g., turn-taking ability) and communicative adaptability (e.g., using humor to reduce tension). Results showed that shy, in contrast to non-shy, individuals perceived themselves as less skillful in turn-taking abilities, verbal fluency, and expressiveness (i.e., facial expressions, vocal variety, appropriate volume, and gesturing skills). In terms of communicative adaptability, shy participants perceived themselves as lacking in the ability to ease tension with humor, to show warmth and empathy, to regain their own composure, and to articulate their thoughts in a conversation.

Manning and Ray (1993) analyzed transcripts from get-acquainted conversations in same gender dyads made up of shy participants and same gender dyads made up of non-shy participants. Their goal was to produce a descriptive comparison of the conversation patterns that characterized these two polarized groups. Results showed that the pairing of shy persons led to the following conversation patterns. Opening sequences were dominated by setting talk (i.e., details of the physical environment) and by cycling through pretopical sequences (i.e., question and answer pairs). Typically, pretopical sequences led to a new pretopical sequence and rarely led to initiation of a topic. In contrast, non-shy dyads minimized setting talk, exchanged their names, and showed a willingness to select a topic.

Another difference found by Manning and Ray (1993) involved how shy versus non-shy dyads managed the transition from one speaker to the next.

Among the different types of speaker transition options, shy dyads favored "leaving the floor open" which essentially signaled the current speaker to continue speaking following the pause that preceded a possible transition. Members of non-shy dyads typically handled transitions by showing greater willingness to speak at these transition points. Finally, transcript analysis revealed that non-shy dyads generated topical talk by drawing on their "situated identities". That is, because participants were all students, non-shy dyads evoked this topic early in the conversation. By contrast, members of shy dyads drew on their identity as students either very late in the conversation or not at all.

Social Skill Deficits in Childhood and as a Vulnerability Factor

In the most comprehensive examination of social skill deficits and shyness, Spence, Donovan and Brechman-Toussaint (1999) compared samples of socially phobic children and non-disordered children ages 7–14 on a variety of social skills indices. Children's social skill performance was assessed in a multifaceted manner. The assessment included parent and child report of social skills, child report of assertive responding, direct observation in a naturalistic setting, and behavior observations of specific social skills during a structured role-play task.

Results showed that socially phobic children were less socially skilled as rated by both themselves and their parents. In addition, they were less assertive on a measure requiring them to select among alternative responses to a social situation. They were also less capable of formulating effective assertive responses in an extended role-play procedure consisting of six rights assertion situations and six positive assertion situations. In terms of social competence ratings based on observation in both classroom and playground settings, results showed that phobic children engaged in fewer peer interactions (based on exchange of verbal, nonverbal, or physical contact responses) and were less likely to initiate interactions. Finally, concerning observations of whether the interaction partner responded positively, negatively or ignored the target child, results showed that phobic children received more negative responses, were ignored more often, and received fewer positive responses than did nonanxious controls. Given the diversity of measurement strategies and the consequently lower scores for socially phobic children across virtually all of the measures, this study provides compelling support that very shy children show social skill deficits.

With evidence that substantial social skill deficits might exist in childhood, it is reasonable to argue that such deficits could act as a vulnerability factor that might exacerbate symptoms of shyness. Borrowing from Leary and Kowalski's (1995) notion that social skill deficits can serve as antecedents to the experience of shyness because poor skills lead to doubts about one's self-presentational competence, Segrin (1996, 1999) tested whether social skill deficits serve as a vulnerability factor in the development of social anxiety. In an initial study (Segrin, 1996), undergraduates were randomly paired into dyads to engage in a discussion about the "events of the day" with someone who was a stranger. Conversations were videotaped and served as the basis for behavioral assessments of social skills. Following the conversation, participants completed a battery of self-report measures and returned in three to four months to complete the self-report measures a second time. Assessment of social skill deficits was based on three measures: a self-report social skills inventory, partner's ratings on a 17-item skill measure (e.g., "s/he was a good listener") by Cupach and Spitzberg (1981) and behavioral response codings (e.g., frequency of gaze averted, silence, etc.). Measures of social anxiety, dysphoria, loneliness, and stress (i.e, negative life events) were also collected. Prediction of social anxiety level at time 2, based on the interaction of stress and social skill deficits, showed that under higher levels of stress, deficits in some social skills appear to create an increased vulnerability to social anxiety. Specifically, the greater the observer-rated social skill deficit for participants reporting greater stress, the more the increase in social anxiety. Segrin (1996) suggests that the types of social behavior that were the focus of observers' ratings are the most consequential for potentially evoking negative evaluation from others.

In a follow-up study, Segrin (1999) found that both self-reported and partner-rated communication skills deficits predicted an increase in social anxiety over a 4-month period. However, unlike the previous study, there was no significant interaction with stress, and over a longer 9-month interval the initial level of social skill deficit was not predictive of any increase in social anxiety over time. Because social anxiety was so stable over time in contrast to dysphoria, Segrin (1999) concludes that the potential role of social skill deficits as an antecedent to shyness may be difficult to evaluate but is likely to occur.

NEW DIRECTIONS

Although our review has identified aspects of shyness that are correlated with maladaptive responses prior to or during social interaction, much of this research has considered shyness in isolation from other personality and contextual factors. Specific personality and contextual factors could serve as moderator or mediator variables that either increase or help to explain the relationship between shyness and social interaction behaviors. Baron and Kenny (1986) define a moderator variable as one that increases the relationship between a predictor (e.g., shyness) and a criterion (e.g., ineffective interaction) for some subset of persons on the predictor (e.g., high shy). In contrast, a mediator is a third variable that accounts for the relationship between a predictor and a criterion. A mediated relationship exists when the significant bivariate correlation between the predictor and criterion is reduced to zero or near zero when both the predictor and mediating variable are regressed on the criterion (see Baron & Kenny, 1986).

One new direction in research on shyness is Cheek and Krasnoperova's (1999) model of shyness subtypes based on the moderator variable of interpersonal orientation. Essentially, interpersonal orientation is the degree to which a person prefers a more independent or autonomous style of dealing with people versus a more dependent and reassuring style. The former is labeled as a withdrawn subtype and the latter as a dependent subtype. According to Cheek and Krasnoperova, these subtypes are expected to differ in the types of social motivation they bring to social interactions. For instance it is likely that dependent, in contrast to withdrawn, shy people are more likely to evidence greater affiliative needs and to report greater negative affect in interactions that have the potential to diminish connectedness with others (e.g., rights assertion situations), although dependent subtypes should report less loneliness than withdrawn subtypes because they want and seek contact with others.

Cheek and Krasnoperova (1999) found that dependent, in contrast to withdrawn, shy persons needed people for emotional support, positive stimulation, and for social comparison purposes. Dependent subtypes were also less lonely than withdrawn subtypes. In a separate study, Cheek, Krasnoperova, and Bruch (1999) replicated the previous differences and also found that dependent subtypes reported more negative self-statements than did withdrawn subtypes relative to day-to-day social interactions over a two-week period. Presumably, dependent subtypes should report a greater frequency of negative self-statements because some items reflect concerns about how one's anxiety and inhibition could impact the status of one's social relationships.

Although not a direct test of Cheek and Krasnoperova's shyness subtypes classification, Bruch, Rivet, Heimberg, Hunt, and McIntosh (1999) tested the notion that persons high in shyness and dependence would be most likely to experience greater negative affect when responding to rights assertion situations. Presumably, such situations are more threatening to this subgroup because they combine concern about making an ineffective response plus alienating one's interaction partner. Results showed that participants high in shyness and in dependence reported the highest level of subjective anxiety when constructing verbal replies to printed rights assertion situations. Given the promising nature of initial tests of this model of shyness subtypes, future research should extend this approach to actual social interaction situations to evaluate the potential moderating role of subtypes on specific interaction behaviors.

A second new direction conceptualizes shyness as only one of several antecedent factors that contribute to ineffectiveness in social interaction. Rather than examining single relationships between trait shyness and specific aspects of social ineffectiveness, this approach focuses on the construction and testing of a conceptual model that offers a theoretical explanation of how ineffectiveness in social interaction develops. Recently, Bruch, Berko, and Haase (1998) tested one such model which attempted to account for men's ineffectiveness in social interaction. Given evidence that men as compared to women are socialized to be less expressive of their thoughts and feelings, emotional inexpressiveness was postulated as a mediator of several exogenous variables which were hypothesized as antecedent to social ineffectiveness. These factors consisted of shyness, holding traditional beliefs about the masculine role, and low physical attractiveness. Based on previous empirical research, a rationale was given as to how all three of these antecedent factors should contribute to emotional inexpressiveness which, in turn, should directly predict social ineffectiveness.

Using a structural equation-modeling approach (Jöreskog & Sörbom, 1993), Bruch et al. (1998) tested the validity of a mediated model of men's ineffectiveness in social interaction. Results confirmed that emotional inexpressiveness mediated the relationship between the three antecedent personality attributes and men's social ineffectiveness. All three of these attributes predicted emotional inexpressiveness, indicating that either some or all of their effect on social ineffectiveness is mediated by men's tendencies to avoid emotional self-expression. In comparing whether the relationship of shyness with social ineffectiveness was fully or only partially mediated by emotional inexpressiveness, path coefficients revealed that shyness has both a direct and an indirect (mediated) relationship with social ineffectiveness. Given the interesting results of Garcia et al. (1991) for dyad level behaviors of shy men, application of this conceptual model to analyses of dyad level patterns of verbal and nonverbal behavior would be quite interesting and may lead to a theoretical basis for explaining possible gender differences in shyness.

CONCLUSIONS

Aspects of shyness that appear to be related to problems of social interaction include internal cognitive-perceptual responses, external verbal and nonverbal behaviors, and deficits in some social skills. Our review showed that much of the research in this area is at the descriptive level; however, in some cases such as Alden and Wallace's social appraisal approach, research involves testing a more sophisticated series of theoretical notions. Arkin's (1981) self-protection model of shyness continues to influence research on both internal and external aspects of shyness that impact social interaction. Garcia et al.'s (1991) application of Ickes's dyadic interaction paradigm is promising, not only for its merits as an unobtrusive method of assessing interaction, but also for its capacity to analyze dyad level response patterns. The selected review of the social skills literature suggests that more attention should be paid to the role of social skill inadequacies in maintaining the shy person's problems in social interaction. Deficits in decoding skills and in conversational communication behaviors might be relevant in fostering interactions that prove less satisfying to both members. Finally, several new directions in shyness research show potential for providing a more complete description of how aspects of shyness may adversely impact the quality of one's social interaction.

REFERENCES

Alden, L. E. (1987). Attributional responses of anxious individuals to different patterns of social feedback: Nothing succeeds like improvement. *Journal of Personality and Social Psychology, 52,* 100–106.

Alden, L. E. & Wallace, S. T. (1995). Social phobia and social appraisal in successful and unsuccessful social interactions. *Behaviour Research and Therapy*, *33*, 497–505.

Anderson, C. A. & Arnoult, L. H. (1985). Attributional style and everyday problems in living: Depression, loneliness, and shyness. *Social Cognition*, *3*, 16–35.

Arkin, R. M. (1981). Self-presentation styles. In J. T. Tedeschi (Ed.), *Impression management in social psychological research* (pp. 311–333). New York: Academic Press.

Arkin R. M., Lake, E. A., & Baumgardner, A. H. (1986). Shyness and self-presentation. In W. H. Jones, J. M. Cheek, & S. R. Briggs (Eds.), *Shyness: Perspectives on research and treatment* (pp. 189–203). New York: Plenum Press.

Asendorpf, J. B. (1990). Beyond social withdrawal: Shyness, unsociability, and peer avoidance. *Human Development*, *33*, 250–259.

Asendorpf, J. B. & Wilpers, S. (1998). Personality effects on social relationships. *Journal of Personality and Social Psychology*, *74*, 1531–1544.

Baron, R. M. & Kenny, D. A. (1986). The moderator–mediator variable distinction in social psychological research: Conceptual, strategic, and statistical considerations. *Journal of Personality and Social Psychology*, *51*, 1173–1182.

Briggs, S. R. (1988). Shyness: Introversion or neuroticism? *Journal of Research in Personality*, *22*, 290–307.

Bruch, M. A. (1989). Familial and developmental antecedents of social phobia: Issues and findings. *Clinical Psychology Review 9*, 34–47.

Bruch, M. A., Berko, E., & Haase, R. F. (1998). Shyness, masculine ideology, physical attractiveness, and emotional inexpressiveness: Testing a mediational model of men's interpersonal competence. *Journal of Counseling Psychology*, *45*, 84–97.

Bruch, M. A., Gorsky, J. M., Collins, T. M., & Berger, P. A. (1989). Shyness and sociability reexamined: A multicomponent analysis. *Journal of Personality and Social Psychology*, *57*, 904–915.

Bruch, M. A., Hamer, R. J., & Heimberg, R. G. (1993). Shyness and public self-consciousness: Additive or interactive relation with social interaction? *Journal of Personality*, *63*, 47–63.

Bruch, M. A. & Pearl, L. (1995). Attributional style and symptoms of shyness in a heterosocial interaction. *Cognitive Therapy and Research*, *19*, 91–107.

Bruch, M. A., Rivet, K. M., Heimberg, R. G., Hunt, A., & McIntosh, B. (1999). Shyness and sociotropy: Additive and interactive relations in predicting interpersonal concerns. *Journal of Personality*, *67*, 373–406.

Buss, A. H. (1980). *Self-consciousness and social anxiety*. San Francisco: W. H. Freeman & Co.

Caspi, A. (1998). Personality development across the life course. In N. Eisenberg (Ed.), *Handbook of child psychology*: Vol 3. *Social, emotional, and personality development* (pp. 311–388). New York: Wiley.

Cheek, J. M. & Buss, A. H. (1981). Shyness and sociability. *Journal of Personality and Social Psychology*, *41*, 330–339.

Cheek, J. M. & Krasnoperova (1999). Varieties of shyness in adolescence and adulthood. In L. A. Schmidt & J. Schulkin (Eds.), *Extreme fear, shyness, and social phobia: Origins, biological mechanisms, and clinical outcomes*. New York: Oxford University Press.

Cheek, J., Krasnoperova, E., & Bruch, M. A. (1999). Withdrawn and dependent subtypes of shyness. In Schmidt, L. A. & Cheek, J. M. (Chairs), *Symposium: Shyness: From temperament to self-concept*. American Psychological Association, Boston, MA.

Conger, A. J., Wallander, J. L., Mariotto, M. J., & Ward, D. (1980). Peer judgements of heterosexual-social anxiety and skill: What do they pay attention to anyhow? *Behavioral Assessment*, *2*, 243–259.

Costanzo, M. & Archer, D. (1989). Interpreting the expressive behavior of others: The Interpersonal Perception Task. *Journal of Nonverbal Behavior*, *13*, 225–245.

Cupach, W. R. & Spitzberg, B. H. (1981). *Relational competence: Measurement and validation.* Unpublished manuscript, Illinois State University, Department of Communication, Normal, IL.

Fischetti, M., Curran, J. P., & Weissberg, H. W. (1977). Sense of timing. *Behavior Modification, 1,* 179–194.

Garcia, S., Stinson, L., Ickes, W., Bissonnette, V., & Briggs, S. (1991). Shyness and physical attractiveness in mixed-sex dyads. *Journal of Personality and Social Psychology, 61,* 35–49.

Glass, C. R. & Arnkoff, D. B. (1994). Validity issues in self-statement measures of social phobia and social anxiety. *Behaviour Research and Therapy, 32,* 255–267.

Glass, C. R. & Furlong, M. (1990). Cognitive assessment of social anxiety: Affective and behavioral correlates. *Cognitive Therapy and Research, 14,* 365–384.

Glass, C. R., Merluzzi, T. B., Biever, J. L., & Larsen, K. H. (1982). Cognitive assessment of social anxiety: Development and validation of a self-statement questionnaire. *Cognitive Therapy and Research, 6,* 37–55.

Hill, G. J. (1989). An unwillingness to act: Behavioral appropriateness, situational constraint, and self-efficacy in shyness. *Journal of Personality, 57,* 871–890.

Ickes, W. & Tooke, W. (1988). The observational method: Studying the interaction of mind and bodies. In S. Duck (Ed.), *The handbook of personal relationships: Theory, research, and interventions* (pp. 79–97). New York: Wiley.

Ickes, W., Bissonnette, V., Garcia, S., & Stinson, L. (1990). Using and implementing the dyadic interaction paradigm. In C. Hendrick & M. Clark (Eds.), *Review of personality and social psychology* (Vol. 11, pp. 16–44). Newbury Park, CA: Sage.

Jöreskog, K. G. & Sörbom, D. (1993). *LISREL 8 user's reference guide.* Chicago: Scientific Software International.

Leary, M. R., Knight, P. D., & Johnson, K. A. (1987). Social anxiety and dyadic conversation: A verbal response analysis. *Journal of Social and Clinical Psychology, 5,* 34–50.

Leary, M. R. & Kowalski, R. M. (1995). *Social anxiety.* New York: Guilford Press.

Leary, M. R., Kowalski, R. M., & Campbell, C. D. (1988). Self-presentational concerns and social anxiety: The role of generalized impression expectancies. *Journal of Research in Personality, 22,* 308–321.

Manning, P. & Ray, G. (1993). Shyness, self-confidence and social interaction. *Social Psychology Quarterly, 56,* 178–192.

Melchior, L. A. & Cheek, J. M. (1990). Shyness and anxious self-preoccupation during a social interaction. *Journal of Social Behavior and Personality, 5,* 117–130.

Meleshko, K. G. A. & Alden, L. E. (1993). Anxiety and self-disclosure: Toward a motivational model. *Journal of Personality and Social Psychology, 64,* 1000–1009.

Monroe, S. M. & Simons, A. D. (1991). Diathesis–stress theories in the context of life stress research: Implications for the depressive disorders. *Psychological Bulletin, 110,* 406–425.

Myszka, M. T., Galassi, J. P., & Ware, W. B. (1986). Comparison of cognitive assessment methods with heterosocially anxious college women. *Journal of Counseling Psychology, 33,* 401–407.

Natale, M., Entin, E., & Jaffe, J. (1979). Vocal interruptions in dyadic communication as a function of speech and social anxiety. *Journal of Personality and Social Psychology, 37,* 865–878.

Phillips, S. D. & Bruch, M. A. (1988). Shyness and dysfunction in career development. *Journal of Counseling Psychology, 35,* 159–165.

Prisbell, M. (1991). Shyness and self-reported competence. *Communications Research Reports, 8,* 141–148.

Riggio, R. E. (1986). Assessment of basic social skills. *Journal of Personality and Social Psychology, 51,* 649–660.

Rubin, K. H. (1993). The Waterloo Longitudinal Project: Correlates and consequences of social withdrawal from childhood to adolescence. In K. H. Rubin & J. B. Asendorpf

(Eds.), *Social withdrawal, inhibition, and shyness in childhood* (pp. 291–314). Hillsdale, NJ: Erlbaum.

Schlenker, B. R. & Leary, M. R. (1982). Social anxiety and self-presentation: A conceptualization and a model. *Psychological Bulletin, 92*, 641–669.

Schroeder, J. E. (1995). Self-concept, social anxiety, and interpersonal perception skills. *Personality and Individual Differences, 19*, 955–958.

Segrin, C. (1996). The relationship between social skills deficits and psychological problems: A test of a vulnerability model. *Communication Research, 23*, 425–450.

Segrin, C. (1999). Social skills, stressful life events, and the development of psychological problems. *Journal of Social and Clinical Psychology, 18*, 14–34.

Spence, S. H., Donovan, C., & Brechman-Toussaint, M. (1999). Social skills, social outcomes, and cognitive features of childhood social phobia. *Journal of Abnormal Psychology, 108*, 211–221.

Stiles, W. B. (1978). Verbal response modes and dimensions of interpersonal roles: A method of discourse analysis. *Journal of Personality and Social Psychology, 36*, 693–703.

Sturmer, P. J. (1999). *A comparison of cognitive assessment methods for deriving states of mind: Structured inventory versus thought listing.* Doctoral dissertation at University at Albany, State University of New York.

Taylor, D. A. & Altman, I. (1987). Communication in interpersonal relationships: Social penetration processes. In M. E. Roloff & G. R. Miller (Eds.), *Interpersonal processes: New directions in communication research* (pp. 257–277). Newbury Park, CA: Sage.

Trower, P. & Gilbert, P. (1989). New theoretical conceptions of social anxiety and social phobia. *Clinical Psychology Review, 9*, 19–35.

Twentyman, C. T. & McFall, R. M. (1975). Behavioral training of social skills in shy males. *Journal of Consulting and Clinical Psychology, 43*, 384–395.

Wallace, S. T. & Alden, L. E. (1991). A comparison of social standards and perceived ability in anxious and nonanxious men. *Cognitive Therapy and Research, 15*, 237–254.

Wallace, S. T. & Alden, L. E. (1995). Social anxiety and standard-setting following social success or failure. *Cognitive Therapy and Research, 19*, 613–631.

Wallace, S. T. & Alden, L. E. (1997). Social phobia and positive social events. The price of success. *Journal of Abnormal Psychology, 106*, 416–424.

Walters, K. S. & Hope, D. A. (1998). Analysis of social behavior in individuals with social phobia and nonanxious participants using a psychobiological model. *Behavior Therapy, 29*, 387–407.

Weiner, B. (1986). *An attributional theory of emotion and motivation.* New York: Springer-Verlag.

Zuckerman, M. & Lubin, B. (1965). Manual for the *Multiple Affect Adjective Checklist.* San Diego, CA: Edits Publishers.

Chapter 10

Shyness and the Self: Attentional, Motivational, and Cognitive Self-processes in Social Anxiety and Inhibition

Mark R. Leary

THE CONSTRUCT OF SHYNESS
SELF AND EMOTION
SELF-ATTENTION
SELF-PRESENTATIONAL MOTIVATION
Self-presentational Antecedents of Social Anxiety
Self-presentation and Shy Behavior
SELF-RELATED COGNITIONS
Self-concept and Self-perceptions
Self-attributions
Relational Schemas
CONCLUSIONS
REFERENCES

The ability to self-reflect—to take oneself as the object of one's own thoughts—is perhaps the most striking psychological difference between human beings and all other animals. A few other species, such as chimpanzees and orangutans, are able to recognize their reflections in mirrors and even to imagine the world from the perspectives of other individuals (Gallup, 1977), but no other animal can

International Handbook of Social Anxiety: Concepts, Research and Interventions Relating to the Self and Shyness. Edited by W. Ray Crozier and Lynn E. Alden.
© 2001 John Wiley & Sons Ltd.

think about itself in the complex ways that are characteristic of human beings or construct and act upon abstract and symbolic mental representations of itself. The fact that only human beings have the ability for sophisticated self-thought suggests that people possess some kind of cognitive apparatus that most other animals do not. This mechanism, which is commonly called the *self*, reflects more than intelligence per se, but rather appears to involve a qualitatively distinct kind of cognitive ability (Gallup & Suarez, 1986).

Having the ability to think consciously about themselves opens human beings up to a great variety of behaviors and experiences that are simply impossible in organisms without a self. For example, possessing a self permits deliberate long-term planning for the future, counterfactual thinking (imagining how events might have turned out differently), the intentional adoption of new symbolic selves (such as identities and roles), introspection, self-evaluation, recognition of one's mortality (and, thus, fear of death), intentional deception of others, and self-directed action (Sedikides & Skowronski, 1997). The self-system also allows people to encode, remember, and retrieve complex self-relevant information in ways that are unavailable to other animals. People have many beliefs, attitudes, and feelings about themselves that, when salient, affect their reactions to specific situations. And, on top of all this, possessing a self allows human beings to be motivated by conscious self-interest and to react to symbolic, ego-relevant events that have no effect whatsoever on self-less animals. As can be seen, by virtue of having a self, people live in a very different psychological world than other animals.

This chapter focuses on some of the ways in which the self—the human capacity for self-attention and its attendant cognitive and motivational processes—is involved in shyness. Many theorists have discussed the relationship between shyness and specific self-related phenomena such as self-awareness, self-esteem, self-presentation, self-efficacy, and self-regulation. The goal of this chapter is to provide a broader, more integrative view, showing how and why various aspects of the self are so strongly implicated in social anxiety and inhibition.

The chapter is organized in the following way. After briefly clarifying my use of the term "shyness", I will explore the relationship between the self and emotion, and consider the implications of their relationship for understanding social anxiety and inhibition. The bulk of the chapter then considers three distinct but overlapping ways in which the self is involved in shyness. First, self-awareness itself is necessary because shyness is a consequence of thinking about oneself, and particularly oneself-in-relation-to-others, in specific ways. Second, shyness involves thinking specifically about how one is perceived and evaluated by other people, and thinking about oneself from others' perspectives is a central feature of the human self. Third, shyness is affected by the self-relevant cognitions that people hold—their self-concepts, self-attributions, relational schemas, and so on. As we will see, the content of a person's self-thoughts helps to determine whether a particular interpersonal context causes shy anxiety and inhibition or confident poise and sociability.

THE CONSTRUCT OF SHYNESS

Shyness has been conceptualized in a number of ways, so I wish to clarify what I mean by shyness in this chapter. As I use the term, shyness is "a psychological syndrome that includes both subjective social anxiety and inhibited social behavior" (Leary, 1986, p. 29). Viewed in this way, shyness involves both affective and behavioral features.

Affectively, shyness involves *social anxiety*—anxiety that is aroused by "the prospect or presence of interpersonal evaluation in real and imagined social settings" (Schlenker & Leary, 1982, p. 642). People experience anxiety about many kinds of events that pose real, anticipated, and imagined threats to their well-being. We use the label social anxiety when the threat involves how one is perceived and evaluated by other people. Because all instances of shyness involve social anxiety, I will rely heavily on theory and research involving social anxiety throughout the chapter.

The behavioral aspects of shyness involve inhibited, reticent, and withdrawn social behaviors. In extreme instances, behavioral withdrawal may be total, as when a person avoids a social event altogether. In other cases, people may withdraw partially by participating only minimally in difficult social encounters. When shy, people talk less than they otherwise do, and they may display other evidence of disaffiliation such as gaze aversion, a closed body position, and other social-distancing behaviors.

Although social anxiety and inhibition often occur together, they must be considered separately. Behavioral inhibition and withdrawal are not automatic consequences of anxiety, and, in fact, anxiety often leads to increased affiliation (Schachter, 1951). Furthermore, people often feel quite socially anxious yet do not display evidence of their subjective distress. These observations suggest that the affective and behavioral aspects of shyness are distinct reactions that require separate consideration.

Like many psychological reactions, shyness (and social anxiety) may be regarded as both a state and a trait. On one hand, the degree to which an individual feels and acts shyly changes as a function of the interpersonal context. Sometimes a person may not be shy at all, whereas at other times he or she may be quite shy. Thus, shyness fluctuates over situations, reflecting its statelike nature. On the other hand, people clearly differ in how shy they generally are. Some people are rarely if ever shy; other individuals are shy much of the time. Looking at these individual differences in shyness, we can regard shyness as a personality trait (Crozier, 1979, 1986). When the distinction between state and trait shyness (or state and trait social anxiety) is important, I will try to make it clear which one I am discussing.

SELF AND EMOTION

Clearly, a self is not needed for emotion. No reasonable person would deny that other animals experience emotions—such as fear, sadness, and rage—despite their inability to self-reflect. However, the human ability for self-reflexive thought expands the range of emotions that human beings can experience and broadens the variety of situations that can evoke emotional reactions, relative to other animals. First, having a self permits an organism to react emotionally to *imagined* stimuli and events. Whereas nonhuman animals typically experience emotions in direct response to stimuli that are immediately present or to cues that are conditioned to an emotionally-charged stimulus, people can experience emotions when they think about events from their pasts and in their futures, as well as self-relevant events that are entirely imaginary. Whereas other animals feel fear, for example, only in response to an immediate fear-producing stimulus, human beings can literally scare themselves through self-focused thinking. Likewise, whereas other animals become angry only when threatened in some way, people can work themselves into a rage from ruminating about real and imagined slights against them. Much human emotion is in response to internal representations of remembered, anticipated, and imagined situations involving oneself.

Second, having a self opens up the possibility of responding not only to events that have implications for one's immediate physical and social well-being, as most animals do, but also to events that symbolically threaten the image that people construct of themselves in their own heads. For example, people react with pride to praise and with anger to insults, although the kudos or disparagement may have implications for nothing other than their mental representations of themselves. Similarly, they react emotionally to suggestions that others do not see them the way they see themselves (Swann, Pelham, & Krull, 1989), and experience strong emotions when their personal self-images are affected by the turn of events (Baumeister, 1991). Because they can self-reflect, people may defend their egos with about as much fervor as other animals defend their lives, offspring, and territories.

Third, having a self allows people to think about themselves from the perspectives of other individuals. An organism that has a self can not only think about itself, but it can think about what other organisms think. Mead (1934) was among the first to suggest that having a self permits people to imagine what others may be thinking and feeling, ponder how other people see them, and foretell others' likely reactions to their behaviors. Recent research on both young children and nonhuman primates supports his reasoning: the capacity for self-reflection is tied closely to the ability to see the world, including oneself, from others' perspectives (Gallup & Suarez, 1986). Thus, another consequence of having a self is that people can experience emotions in response to what they think other people think. Thus, people may worry about what others think of them, try to regulate the kinds of impressions other people form, and become distressed when others do not perceive them as they would like (Leary, 1995; Leary & Kowalski, 1995; Miller, 1996). An animal without a self has no such concerns because it cannot think about itself from others' perspectives.

Clearly, the human capacity for self-thought has important implications for emotional experience and expression, including those associated with social anxiety. Without a self that allows them to imagine potentially problematic social situations in the future, consider abstract threats to symbolic aspects of the self, and see themselves through the eyes of other people, people would be unable to feel socially anxious.

SELF-ATTENTION

Whenever people are awake, their focus of attention changes almost constantly. Even when devoting most of our attention to a particular stimulus or task, our attention nonetheless shifts from thing to thing (Buss, 1980). Sometimes, our attention is directed at the world outside ourselves. When we focus on an engrossing movie or the scenery that passes by as we drive down the highway, we are focused externally. At other times, however, people focus on and think about themselves—either their inner subjective world of thoughts, feelings, and sensations (often called private self-awareness) or their outer appearance and behavior (public self-awareness).

Self-awareness is necessary in order for people to experience social anxiety. A person who was not thinking about him- or herself at all could not feel socially anxious. However, the person must not only be thinking about him- or herself, but also thinking about how he or she is viewed by other people—what Wegner and Giuliano (1982) called "tacit other/focal self awareness" (p. 171). In this state, the focus of the person's attention is ultimately on him- or herself, but the self is tacitly viewed from other people's perspectives. Early symbolic interactionists recognized that the ability to self-reflect was closely tied to the ability to think about oneself from the perspectives of other people, and that adopting the perspectives of other people requires a self (Mead, 1934). In fact, it has been suggested that the cognitive mechanism that allows self-reflection may have evolved precisely because natural selection favored ancestral homonids who could take the perspectives of other members of the group (Crook, 1980; Sedikides & Skowronski, 1997). If true, this speculation suggests that the self evolved because of the advantages of knowing what others were thinking rather than for the purpose of inner self-reflection per se.

Given that self-attention underlies social anxiety (and, thus, shyness), we would expect that people who think about themselves a great deal—and particularly those who think about themselves from others' perspectives—should be more prone to social anxiety and shyness than those who spend less time in self-focused thought. In fact, this is the case. Dozens of studies have documented a moderate correlation between public self-consciousness on the one hand and social anxiety, shyness, and social phobia on the other (e.g., Bruch, Hamer, & Heimberg, 1995; Cheek & Buss, 1981; Hope & Heimberg, 1988; Leary, 1983).

At the bare minimum, then, the self is implicated in the experience of shyness because people who are not self-aware simply will not feel socially anxious. However, as we will see, although self-attention is necessary for social anxiety to occur, it is by no means sufficient.

SELF-PRESENTATIONAL MOTIVATION

The ability to think about oneself from the perspectives of other people was a benchmark in the evolution of the human mind. The ability to consider how one is perceived by other individuals allows people to predict how others are likely to respond to them and to regulate their behavior in ways that will have desired effects on other people. All intentional social influence requires the ability to see the world from the perspective of others. However, whatever the advantages of being able to see oneself through others' eyes, this ability underlies human beings' pervasive and often distressing concern with how they are perceived and evaluated by other people. People appear to be universally concerned with others' impressions of them, and highly motivated to make particular desired impressions on at least certain other people.

This concern with one's public image is not misplaced. To the extent that people's outcomes in life partially depend on how others regard them, effective living requires people to pay some degree of attention to others' impressions of them and adjust their behavior to convey impressions that will facilitate their attainment of desired goals (Leary, 1995; Schlenker, 1980). People can achieve many of their goals in life only if others perceive them in particular ways—as possessing certain attributes or being a certain kind of person. Furthermore, according to Goffman (1959), conveying public images that are appropriate to the immediate situation is essential in order for social interactions to proceed smoothly. Given the importance of people's social images, we should not be surprised that people behave in ways that will make desired impressions on others, whatever those impressions may be in a particular instance. Of course, an excessive concern with others' impressions can lead to maladaptive behaviors and other problems when people take desperate measures to impress others, but the self-presentational motive itself is normal and beneficial.

Many people think of self-presentation as deceitful and manipulative, but it is inherently neither. Although people sometimes convey impressions of themselves that do not jibe with reality or with how they see themselves, more commonly people simply convey those aspects of themselves that are appropriate to the immediate situation and portray them in a favorable but realistic light. Thus, their self-presentations may be auspicious and tactical (and even slightly embellished), but they are not necessarily false (Leary & Kowalski, 1990; Schlenker, 1980).

Self-presentational Antecedents of Social Anxiety

According to the self-presentation theory of social anxiety (Schlenker & Leary, 1982), concerns about one's public impressions lie at the heart of social anxiety and, hence, shyness. As long as people are either oblivious to the impression they are making on others (i.e., they are not self-aware whatsoever) or they are self-aware but believe that they are making the kinds of impressions they desire to make, they should not feel socially anxious. However, when people are motivated to make desired impressions on others but do not think that they will successfully do so, they will feel anxious and likely (but not always) display the behavioral characteristics of shyness, such as inhibition and reticence. According to self-presentation theory, anything that increases the individual's motivation to make a desired impression or lowers the likelihood that the person will expect to make that impression will heighten social anxiety. Because the literature regarding the self-presentational theory of social anxiety has been reviewed extensively elsewhere, I will not do so here. Suffice it to say that, with a few exceptions, the idea that social anxiety (and shyness) arises from self-presentational concerns has received strong empirical support. (For reviews of the relevant evidence, see Leary, 2001; Leary & Kowalski, 1995; Patterson & Ritts, 1997; Schlenker & Leary, 1982; Shepperd & Arkin, 1990.)

In a recent extension of self-presentation theory, I noted that not all failures to make desired impressions result in social anxiety (Leary, 2001). People often realize that they are making an impression on others that differs from how they would like to be seen, yet they do not feel socially anxious. Thus, although all instances of social anxiety arise from self-presentational concerns, not all self-presentational concerns lead to anxiety. Rather, people's concerns about their public impressions appear to cause social anxiety (and shyness) only to the extent that the person believes that the impressions that other people form of him or her have undesired implications for *relational evaluation*—the degree to which other people regard their relationships with the individual as close, important, or valuable. Put differently, people feel socially anxious when they believe that the impressions they make on others will not lead others to value their relationships with the individual as much as they desire, and particularly if those impressions may lead others to actually devalue, avoid, or reject them (Leary, 1990; Leary, Koch, & Hechenbleikner, 2001). At its core, then, social anxiety involves concerns with social rejection, although the proximal cause centers on the impressions that one is making on others because those impressions are primary determinants of social acceptance and rejection (Leary, 1995).

This refinement of the self-presentational theory emerged from the assumption that people possess a strong and pervasive "need to belong" that evolved because social acceptance and group living were advantageous, if not essential, for survival and reproduction in the ancestral environment (Baumeister & Leary, 1995). Social anxiety may be viewed as an "early warning system" that alerts people to potential threats to social acceptance or, more precisely, relational evaluation. People feel socially anxious when they believe they might make an impression that will cause others not to value them as social participants (friends, coalition members, mates, or whatever). Like most aversive emotions, social anxiety alerts the individual to possible threats to his or her social well-being and motivates behaviors designed to correct the situation and eliminate the anxiety (Baumeister & Tice, 1990). Warned that their self-presentations may result in relational devaluation, people can behave in ways that lower the likelihood of rejection. (For a related discussion of the functions of embarrassment, see Miller & Leary, 1992.)

Gilbert and Trower (1990; Trower & Gilbert, 1989; see Gilbert & Trower, this volume, *Chapter 12*) have offered a similar evolutionary argument that traces social anxiety to concerns with one's image. However, their perspective gives precedence to concerns regarding dominance and high status rather than social acceptance. In their view, failing to make impressions that will maintain one's dominance within the group causes social anxiety, and the shy behaviors of socially anxious people in these instances are analogous to the submissive, appeasing reactions of lower-status primates in deference to higher-ranking members of the group. When this happens, people not only feel socially anxious but also switch from an agonic mode of relating to others (based on a dominance hierarchy of power and threat) to a hedonic mode in which they try to create impressions that will promote social acceptance, support, and reassurance. Thus, although Gilbert and Trower acknowledge that concerns with being valued and accepted can precipitate social anxiety, they view agonic motives as primary.

My own sense is that, whenever people feel socially anxious in agonic encounters, their primary concern still involves the degree to which they are accepted (relationally valued) by the more dominant individual. This is not to say that agonic threats cannot cause fear and submissiveness independently of concerns with relational evaluation; they undoubtedly can. However, reactions that arise from agonic encounters involve a distinct set of adaptations that differ from those involved in what we normally think of as social anxiety, which center on concerns with social acceptance and rejection.

Whichever view one takes, the processes by which people assess the kinds of impression they are making on others further involve the self in at least three ways. First, such an assessment inherently requires the person to "get into the heads" of other people to draw inferences about how he or she is being perceived, and, as we have seen, this process of tacit other/focal self-awareness involves the self (Wegner & Giuliano, 1982).

Second, once such an inference is made, the person must determine whether the impression he or she is making is sufficient. This process involves a self-directed comparison of the impression the person thinks he or she is making (or will make in the future) to some standard. These judgments require (and, in fact, are often initiated by) self-focused attention (Carver & Scheier, 1985). People have ideas regarding how they want to be perceived by others, and these ideas serve as standards or reference values against which their public impressions (or, more precisely, their beliefs about the kinds of impressions they are making) are judged. The process of comparing one's own behavior to these internal standards in an inherent part of the self-system; people seem virtually incapable of self-reflecting in any depth without evaluating themselves and their progress toward their goals, including the goal of making particular impressions. Carver and Scheier (1985, 1986) have written extensively about the self-regulatory processes that are involved in shyness.

Third, these self-presentational standards—the kinds of impressions that people want to make—are tied to many other aspects of the self-system. People's self-presentational goals are linked to their perceptions of who they are, who they want to be, who they ought to be, and who they might become—that is, to their real, desired, ought, and possible selves (e.g., Higgins, 1987; Markus & Nurius, 1986). These self-presentational goals are also tied to people's desires to maintain certain images in their own eyes and to feel good about themselves (Baumeister, 1982).

Self-presentation and Shy Behavior

The self-presentational theory of social anxiety helps to explain certain features of shy behavior. Many writers have implicitly assumed that shy people act in an inhibited, reticent, and withdrawn manner *because* they feel socially anxious. However, the assumption that anxiety per se causes inhibition is unfounded. Not only do emotions not directly cause specific behaviors (Frijda, 1986), but in certain circumstances, people who feel anxious are unusually active and sociable rather than passive and withdrawn (Schachter, 1951).

The self-presentational perspective suggests that the behaviors that tend to accompany social anxiety often reflect a general interpersonal strategy that is designed to minimize the threat in difficult social encounters in which the person's public image is at stake. When people do not think that they can make impressions that will maintain their relational value in other people's eyes, they may opt for self-presentations that will avoid making a blatantly unfavorable impression that might lead to social rejection. Arkin (1981) was among the first to propose that shy people prefer a "protective" self-presentational style that is designed to avoid significant losses in social approval over an "acquisitive" style that is focused on obtaining approval. Research regarding the passive, inhibited, and reticent behavior of socially anxious and shy individuals supports this hypothesis (Arkin, 1981; Bruch, Hamer, & Heimberg, 1995; DePaulo, Epstein, & LeMay, 1990; Schlenker & Leary, 1982; Shepperd & Arkin, 1990; see also Bruch, this volume, *Chapter 9*). Although a protective self-presentational style may not result in highly favorable evaluations, it is unlikely to make negative impressions or lead to rejection.

Thus, the construction and assessment of one's public image involve self-processes at many levels. The mere ability to think of oneself from others' perspectives and to regulate one's public impressions requires a self, as does the selection of the particular impressions that one will convey and the assessment of one's self-presentational effectiveness.

SELF-RELATED COGNITIONS

When people think about how they are perceived by others and about the implications of others' perceptions of them for relational evaluation, their assessment is affected not only by the interpersonal context but by their pre-existing beliefs about themselves. Two individuals confronting the same difficult social encounter may react quite differently because they bring to the situation different sets of beliefs about their personal characteristics. In this section, we take a look at three distinct types of self-related cognitions—those involving the person's personal characteristics, attributions, and relationships with other people.

Self-concept and Self-perceptions

Research consistently shows that people who score high on measures of shyness and social anxiety perceive themselves differently than people who score lower. First, shy (and socially anxious) people rate themselves less positively than those who are less shy. Overall, shy and socially anxious people tend to rate themselves as less physically attractive, less socially skilled, and less self-presentationally adept, both in general and within the context of particular social encounters (Alden, 1987; Jackson, Towson, & Narduzzi, 1997; Meleshko & Alden, 1993; Miller, 1995; Montgomery, Haemmerlie, & Edwards, 1991; Riggio, Throckmorton, & DePaola, 1990). Not surprisingly, then, shyness also correlates negatively with measures of self-esteem (Cheek & Buss, 1981; Crozier, 1995; Jones, Briggs, & Smith, 1986; Miller, 1990), and positively with the tendency to self-criticize (Ishiyama & Munson, 1993). Furthermore, shyness is associated with a lower sense of self-efficacy in interpersonal settings (Hill, 1989). Self-efficacy regarding one's ability to make desired impressions on other people appears to be particularly important in social anxiety, as the self-presentation theory suggests (Leary & Atherton, 1986; Maddux, Norton, & Leary, 1988). (For a review of differences in how low and high socially anxious people view themselves, see Patterson & Ritts, 1997.)

Evidence regarding whether these differences in self-beliefs reflect true differences in appearance, personality, behavior, and interpersonal effectiveness is mixed. Taken as a whole, the general conclusion appears to be that although social anxiety and shyness are negatively correlated with the possession of certain positive attributes (such as social skill, physical attractiveness, and conversational ability), the relationships are weak, and socially anxious/shy people tend to perceive themselves less positively than the objective evidence warrants (Alden, 1984; Alden & Cappe, 1981; Curran, Wallander, & Fischetti, 1980; Melchoir & Cheek, 1990; Montgomery et al., 1991; Pilkonis, 1977). Thus, people prone to social anxiety may correctly perceive that they are regarded as less desirable social interactants, but their self-perceptions also appear to be biased in a negative direction.

Even so, whether or not their perceptions are accurate, people who perceive themselves less desirably tend to be more socially anxious and shy because these perceptions lead them to doubt that they will make desired impressions on others (Leary & Kowalski, 1995). Thus, contrary to what has sometimes been assumed, negative self-perceptions do not cause social anxiety directly. Rather, the effects of negative self-perceptions on shyness are mediated by the person's assumptions regarding how he or she is regarded by others. People who perceive themselves less favorably are likely to assume that they will not make as favorable an impression on others and, as a result, they will feel more anxious than people with more favorable self-beliefs.

The relationship between self-esteem and social anxiety requires special attention. Based on the fact that trait self-esteem correlates moderately with social anxiety/shyness, many theorists have implicitly assumed that low self-esteem predisposes people to be socially anxious and shy. However, we have little evidence that self-esteem per se has any effect on social anxiety (or, for that matter, on any other emotion). As we have seen, *beliefs* about one's personal characteristics and abilities may affect social anxiety (because those beliefs have implications for the impressions that one is likely to make on others), but the link between how one *feels* about oneself—self-esteem—and social anxiety is less straightforward. The sociometer theory of self-esteem suggests that self-esteem may be fruitfully conceptualized as a subjective indicator of the degree to which the individual is being valued and accepted versus devalued and rejected by other people (Leary, 1999; Leary & Downs, 1995). To the extent that this is true, low self-esteem and social anxiety are co-effects of real, anticipated, or imagined relational devaluation rather than causally related (Leary et al., 2001). People who have low trait self-esteem are more prone to social anxiety because, by virtue of feeling less valued and accepted by other people (Leary, 1999), they are more commonly worried about the kinds of impressions they are making than people who are high in trait self-esteem.

Self-attributions

People's reactions to difficult interpersonal encounters are also affected by the attributions that they make for their difficulties. The same event may elicit quite different reactions depending on how a person interprets and explains it to him- or herself. For example, an employer's aloofness may evoke anxiety if an employee thinks that the boss is displeased with his or her performance, empathic concern if the reaction is attributed to the fact that the boss is preoccupied with a family member's illness, or no reaction whatsoever if it is attributed to the fact that the boss is simply an aloof person. Although it has rarely been rarely stated explicitly, the process of making attributions—of explaining one's experiences—requires a self. When people try to make sense out of what happens to them, they are necessarily thinking self-relevant thoughts. Presumably, animals without a self do not wonder about why things happen to them or make conscious attributions.

Much research has shown that the attributions of dispositionally shy and socially anxious people differ from those of the less shy and anxious, although it is not always clear whether these differences reflect causes or effects of shyness (or perhaps both). Perhaps the most well-documented finding is that shy (and socially anxious) people do not make the kinds of self-serving attributions that are commonly observed in most people. Considerable research and everyday observation attest that people generally make attributions that put them in the best possible light. For example, most people egotistically believe that they are responsible for good outcomes but minimize their apparent responsibility for bad ones (Blaine & Crocker, 1993). Not only do shy (and socially anxious) people *not* show this typical pattern of self-serving attributions, but they tend to accept negative evaluations as accurate and even reject positive information about themselves (e.g., Alden 1987; Asendorpf, 1987).

Some studies have shown that, unlike most individuals, shy people do not make different kinds of attributions for success and failure, whereas other studies have found that shy people actually display a reversal of the self-serving bias— claiming more personal responsibility for failure than for success (Alden, 1987; Anderson & Arnoult, 1985; Arkin, Appelman, & Burger, 1980; Teglasi & Fagin, 1984; Teglasi & Hoffman, 1982). Along the same lines, Shepperd, Arkin, and Slaughter (1995) found that, unlike participants who scored low in shyness, shy participants did not make excuses when they performed poorly on an intellectual test. In a study of attributions for a group's performance (Bradshaw & Stasson, 1998), shy participants minimized their responsibility for both group success and group failure, and did not make different attributions for successful and failing group outcomes. In contrast, non-shy participants made group-serving attributions, giving the group more responsibility for success than failure. Although socially anxious people will make self-serving attributions in special circumstances (such as when they think that their social performance has improved over time; Alden, 1987), they generally do not do so.

The source of these attributional differences is not completely clear. One possibility is that the motive to maintain self-esteem is weaker for shy individuals than for most other people. As a result, they do not possess "normal" ego-defensive tendencies, and thus lack the desire to claim responsibility for their successes and minimize responsibility for their failures. Although possible, several findings argue against the idea that shy people are simply less motivated to see themselves favorably. For example, people with unfavorable self-concepts affectively prefer positive feedback about themselves (even while acknowledging that negative feedback is more accurate) (Swann, Griffin, Predmore, & Gaines, 1987). Furthermore, some evidence of self-serving biases has been found among shy people. For example, Shepperd et al. (1995) found that shy participants who performed well on a test subsequently rated the test as more valid than those who performed poorly, and, as noted, Alden (1987) found that socially anxious participants claimed credit for a successful performance if they thought they had improved over time.

A second possibility is that, rather than reflecting shy people's true beliefs, these attributional patterns may reflect self-presentational tactics designed to convey an unassuming image. As noted earlier, shy people prefer a protective self-presentational style that is designed to avoid losing social approval (Arkin, 1981). Thus, they may be less concerned with using self-serving attributions to make positive impressions than with making modest attributions that avoid the potential disapproval that self-aggrandizing attributions may bring. The quiet, unassuming, self-effacing interpersonal style of socially anxious and shy people is consistent with this interpretation (Leary & Kowalski, 1995; Shepperd & Arkin, 1990). The self-presentational nature of socially anxious people's attributions is also reflected in the fact that their attributions are affected by the nature of the audience to whom they express their attributions. In particular, shy people's attributions are least self-serving when their concerns with social evaluation are greatest, suggesting that they are making attributions that they think will avoid unfavorable evaluations and disapproval (Arkin et al., 1980). In brief, although it is plausible that certain patterns of self-critical attributions may underlie social anxiety and shyness, the attributions that shy people make to explain themselves to others reflect efforts to convey a particular image as much as their real interpretations of events.

Relational Schemas

People's reactions to interpersonal situations are affected not only by their beliefs about themselves (e.g., their self-concepts), but by their generalized, often implicit beliefs about social interactions and relationships. Baldwin (1992) coined the term *relational schemas* to refer to cognitive structures that represent regularities in patterns of interpersonal interactions and relationships. Relational schemas are networks of beliefs, assumptions, and expectations regarding oneself in relation to others (either particular other people or people in general). For example, after a series of rejecting, humiliating experiences with attractive women, a man may develop a relational schema regarding social encounters with attractive women that then guides his future interactions with them.

For our purposes, relational schemas are important because, once primed by situational events, schemas guide people's interpretations of and reactions to those events. Several studies have shown that priming people's relational schemas, even subliminally, affects their self-evaluations, emotional reactions, and behaviors (see Baldwin & Fergusson, this volume, *Chapter 11*). For example, priming thoughts of particular individuals and previous relationships affects people's responses in the present situation (Baldwin, 1994; Baldwin, Carrell, & Lopez, 1990). Once a particular relational schema has been activated, it affects how people construe the immediate situation, provides a script that guides their behavior, creates expectations regarding likely events, and makes certain self-images salient. For example, when the man's "attractive woman" relational schema is activated by the presence of such a woman, he will be led to interpret her behavior in particular ways (e.g., perhaps seeing her quietness as snobbery rather than shyness), expect certain outcomes of the interaction (e.g., that she will ultimately snub him), have a script for his responses (e.g., expecting rejection, he may be distant or dismissive), and more easily think of himself in particular ways (e.g., socially inept, unattractive). A man with a different relational schema might navigate an encounter with the same woman quite differently. Importantly, either man's relational schema involves neither himself nor the woman in isolation, but rather self-in-relation-to-other.

Evidence suggests that shy people's relational schemas differ from those of the less shy. That is, in addition to perceiving themselves less positively as described above, shy people may be disposed to view interactions and relationships differently than the non-shy. For example, shy people have more negative expectations about social interactions. Specifically, they have higher expectations of making undesired impressions, failing to meet other people's standards, having an unpleasant experience, and being rejected (Bates, Campbell, & Burgess, 1990; Jackson et al., 1997; Lucock & Salkovskis, 1988; Patterson, Churchill, & Powell, 1991; Wallace & Alden, 1991), suggesting that their relational schemas include assumptions regarding how they will be regarded by others and whether others will accept or reject them (Leary, Kowalski, & Campbell, 1988).

Baldwin and Main (in press) demonstrated how relational schemas can develop, then subsequently trigger social anxiety in a laboratory experiment. Participants completed a measure of public self-consciousness, then answered an attitude questionnaire on a computer. Every third trial, approving or disapproving feedback was provided on the screen in the form of pictures of smiling or frowning faces that were accompanied by one of two distinctive tones. After completing the questionnaire, participants interacted with a confederate for five minutes. During the conversation, the computer began emitting one of the two tones. Self-report measures showed that participants who were high in self-consciousness had a more negative mood, felt less poised, and anticipated greater rejection when they had talked to the confederate in the presence of the tone that had been associated with disapproval (the frowning faces) than the tone that had been paired with approval (the smiling faces). In essence, Baldwin and Main had created in their participants a (rather unusual) relational schema of the nature "When that particular sound is present, I will be rejected". Priming the schema during the interaction then increased their social anxiety.

In line with a schematic approach to social anxiety, socially anxious people remember negative social feedback better than low anxious people (O'Banion & Arkowitz, 1977), possibly because it is more consistent with their relational schemas (Kuiper & Rogers, 1979). To make matters worse, Ammerman and Hersen (1986) found that participants who scored high in social anxiety were more affected by negative expectancies (believing that an interaction partner was snobbish and difficult to approach) than participants who were low in social anxiety.

CONCLUSIONS

The self-processes that underlie shyness are an integral part of everyday social life. People are not only regularly aware of themselves, but aware that other people are thinking about them. As a result, they are often motivated to convey impressions of themselves that will help them to obtain their social and personal goals. To convey such impressions successfully, they not only consider how they are regarded in the eyes of other people, but rely on their vast storehouse of knowledge about themselves in order to gauge the accuracy, credibility, and viability of the images they might project. They judge their self-presentational effectiveness on an ongoing basis, explicitly or implicitly comparing the impressions that other people are forming of them to the kinds of impressions they want to make. These judgments are affected both by their inferences about other people's perceptions of them and by their own self-concepts, attributions, and relational schemas. These mundane patterns of thought and behavior require very sophisticated cognitive machinery that permits people to think about themselves as well as to consider what others are thinking (and, in nearly infinite regress, to think about what others are thinking about what they are thinking that others are thinking).

Much of the time, people find social encounters unproblematic, and they are only vaguely aware of the operations of the self. However, when people believe that they will not be perceived as they desire and, thus, may suffer losses in relational evaluation, they become acutely, sometimes painfully self-aware, experience social anxiety, and often show signs of inhibition, reticence, and social withdrawal. The attentional, motivational, and cognitive self-processes that underlie shyness are part and parcel of the human mind, but only in certain circumstances do they alert us that our social images are in jeopardy.

REFERENCES

Alden, L. E. (1984). An attributional analysis of assertiveness. *Cognitive Therapy and Research, 8*, 607–618.

Alden, L. E. (1987). Attributional responses of anxious individuals to different patterns of social feedback: Nothing succeeds like improvement. *Journal of Personality and Social Psychology, 52*, 100–106.

Alden, L. E. & Cappe, R. (1981). Nonassertiveness: Skill deficit or selective self-evaluation. *Behavior Therapy, 12*, 107–114.

Ammerman, R. T. & Hersen, M. (1986). Effects of scene manipulation on role-play test behavior. *Journal of Psychopathology and Behavioral Assessment, 8*, 55–67.

Anderson, C. A. & Arnoult, L. H. (1985). Attributional style and everyday problems in living: Depression, loneliness, and shyness. *Social Cognition, 3*, 16–35.

Arkin, R. M. (1981). Self-presentational styles. In J. T. Tedeschi (Ed.), *Impression management theory and social psychological research* (pp. 311–333). New York: Academic Press.

Arkin, R. M., Appelman, A. J., & Burger, J. M. (1980). Social anxiety, self-presentation, and the self-serving bias in causal attribution. *Journal of Personality and Social Psychology, 38*, 23–35.

Asendorpf, J. B. (1987). Videotape reconstruction of emotions and cognitions related to shyness. *Journal of Personality and Social Psychology, 53*, 542–549.

Baldwin, M. W. (1992). Relational schemas and the processing of social information. *Psychological Bulletin, 112*, 461–484.

Baldwin, M. W. (1994). Primed relational schemas as a source of self-evaluative reactions. *Journal of Social and Clinical Psychology, 13*, 380–403.

Baldwin, M. W., Carrell, S. E., & Lopez, D. F. (1990). Priming relationship schemas: My advisor and the Pope are watching me from the back of my mind. *Journal of Experimental Social Psychology, 26*, 435–454.

Baldwin, M. W. & Main, K. T. (in press). Social anxiety and the cued activation of relational knowledge. *Personality and Social Psychology Bulletin*.

Bates, G. W., Campbell, I. M., & Burgess, P. M. (1990). Assessment of articulated thoughts in social anxiety: Modification of the ATSS procedure. *British Journal of Clinical Psychology, 29*, 91–98.

Baumeister, R. F. (1982). A self-presentational view of social phenomena. *Psychological Bulletin, 91*, 3–26.

Baumeister, R. F. (1991). *Escaping the self*. New York: Basic Books.

Baumeister, R. F. & Leary, M. R. (1995). The need to belong: Desire for interpersonal attachments as a fundamental human motivation. *Psychological Bulletin, 117*, 497–529.

Baumeister, R. F. & Tice, D. M. (1990). Anxiety and social exclusion. *Journal of Social and Clinical Psychology, 9*, 165–195.

Blaine, B. & Crocker, J. (1993). Self-esteem and self-serving biases in reactions to positive and negative events. In R. F. Baumeister (Ed.), *Self-esteem: The puzzle of low self-regard* (pp. 55–85). New York: Plenum.

Bradshaw, S. D. & Stasson, M. F. (1998). Attributions of shy and not-shy group members for collective group performance. *Small Group Research, 29*, 282–307.

Buss, A. H. (1980). *Self-consciousness and social anxiety*. San Francisco: Freeman.

Bruch, M. A., Hamer, R. J., & Heimberg, R. G. (1995). Shyness and public self-consciousness: Interactive relation with social interaction? *Journal of Personality, 63*, 47–63.

Carver, C. S. & Scheier, M. F. (1985). Aspects of self, and the control of behavior. In B. R. Schlenker (Ed.), *The self and social life* (pp. 146–174). New York: McGraw-Hill.

Carver, C. S. & Scheier, M. F. (1986). Analyzing shyness: A specific application of broader self-regulatory principles. In W. H. Jones, J. M. Cheek, & S. R. Briggs (Eds.), *Shyness: Perspectives on research and treatment* (pp. 173–185). New York: Plenum.

Cheek, J. M. & Buss, A. H. (1981). Shyness and sociability. *Journal of Personality and Social Psychology, 41*, 330–339.

Crook, J. H. (1980). *The evolution of human consciousness*. Oxford: Clarendon Press.

Crozier, W. R. (1979). Shyness as a dimension of personality. *British Journal of Social and Clinical Psychology, 18*, 121–128.

Crozier, W. R. (1986). Individual differences in shyness. In W. H. Jones, J. M. Cheek., & S. R. Briggs (Eds.), *Shyness: Perspectives on research and treatment* (pp. 133–145). New York: Plenum.

Crozier, W. R. (1995). Shyness and self-esteem in middle childhood. *British Journal of Educational Psychology, 65*, 85–95.

Curran, J. P., Wallander, J. L., & Fischetti, M. (1980). The importance of behavioral and cognitive factors in heterosexual-social anxiety. *Journal of Personality, 48*, 285–292.

DePaulo, B. M., Epstein, J. A., & LeMay, C. S. (1990). Responses of the socially anxious to the prospect of interpersonal evaluation. *Journal of Personality, 58*, 623–640.

Frijda, N. (1986). *The emotions*. Cambridge: Cambridge University Press.

Gallup, G. G., Jr. (1977). Self-recognition in primates: A comparative approach to the bidirectional properties of consciousness. *American Psychologist, 32*, 329–338.

Gallup, G. G., Jr. & Suarez, S. D. (1986). Self-awareness and the emergence of mind in humans and other primates. In J. Suls & A. G. Greenwald (Eds.), *Psychological perspectives on the self* (Vol. 3, pp. 3–26). Hillsdale, NJ: Erlbaum.

Gilbert, P. & Trower, P. (1990). The evolution and manifestation of social anxiety. In W. R. Crozier (Ed.), *Shyness and embarrassment: Perspectives from social psychology* (pp. 144–177). New York: Cambridge University Press.

Goffman, E. (1959). *The presentation of self in everyday life*. New York: Doubleday.

Higgins, E. T. (1987). Self-discrepancy: A theory relating self and affect. *Psychological Review, 94*, 319–340.

Hill, G. J. (1989). An unwillingness to act: Behavioral appropriateness, situational constraint, and self-efficacy in shyness. *Journal of Personality, 57*, 871–890.

Hope, D. A. & Heimberg, R. G. (1988). Public and private self-consciousness and social phobia. *Journal of Personality Assessment, 52*, 626–639.

Ishiyama, F. I. & Munson, P. A. (1993). Development and validation of a self-critical cognition scale. *Psychological Reports, 72*, 147–154.

Jackson, T., Towson, S., & Narduzzi, K. (1997). Predictors of shyness: A test of variables with self-presentational models. *Social Behavior and Personality, 25*, 149–154.

Jones, W. H., Briggs, S. R., & Smith, T. G. (1986). Shyness: Conceptualization and measurement. *Journal of Personality and Social Psychology, 51*, 629–639.

Kuiper, N. A. & Rogers, T. B. (1979). Encoding of personal information: Self-other differences. *Journal of Personality and Social Psychology, 37*, 499–514.

Leary, M. R. (1983). Social anxiousness: The construct and its measurement. *Journal of Personality Assessment, 47*, 66–75.

Leary, M. R. (1986). Affective and behavioral components of shyness: Implications for theory, measurement, and research. In W. H. Jones, J. M. Cheek, & S. R. Briggs (Eds.), *Shyness: Perspectives on research and treatment* (pp. 27–38). New York: Plenum.

Leary, M. R. (1990). Responses to social exclusion: Social anxiety, jealousy, loneliness, depression, and low self-esteem. *Journal of Social and Clinical Psychology, 9*, 221–229.

Leary, M. R. (1995). *Self-presentation: Impression management and interpersonal behavior*. Boulder, CO: Westview Press.

Leary, M. R. (1999). The social and psychological importance of self-esteem. In R. M. Kowalski & M. R. Leary (Eds.), *The social psychology of emotional and behavioral problems* (pp. 197–221). Washington, DC: American Psychological Association.

Leary, M. R. (2001). Social anxiety as an early warning system: A refinement and extension of the self-presentational theory of social anxiety. In S. G. Hofmann & P. M. DiBartolo (Eds.), *From social anxiety to social phobia: Multiple perspectives* (pp. 321–334). New York: Allyn & Bacon.

Leary, M. R. & Atherton, S. C. (1986). Self-efficacy, social anxiety, and inhibition in interpersonal encounters. *Journal of Social and Clinical Psychology, 4*, 256–267.

Leary, M. R. & Downs, D. L. (1995). Interpersonal functions of the self-esteem motive: The self-esteem system as a sociometer. In M. Kernis (Ed.), *Efficacy, agency, and self-esteem* (pp. 123–144). New York: Plenum.

Leary, M. R., Koch, E., & Hechenbleikner, N. (2001). Emotional responses to interpersonal rejection: A theory of social emotion. In M. R. Leary (Ed.), *Interpersonal rejection* (pp. 145–166). New York: Oxford University Press.

Leary, M. R. & Kowalski, R. M. (1990). Impression management: A literature review and two-component model. *Psychological Bulletin, 107*, 34–47.

Leary, M. R. & Kowalski, R. M. (1995). *Social anxiety*. New York: Guilford.

Leary, M. R., Kowalski, R. M., & Campbell, C. (1988). Self-presentational concerns and social anxiety: The role of generalized impression expectancies. *Journal of Research in Personality, 22*, 308–321.

Lucock, M. P. & Salkovskis, P. M. (1988). Cognitive factors in social anxiety and its treatment. *Behaviour Research and Therapy, 26*, 297–302.

Maddux, J. E., Norton, L. W., & Leary, M. R. (1988). Cognitive components of social anxiety: An investigation of the integration of self-presentation theory and self-efficacy theory. *Journal of Social and Clinical Psychology, 6*, 180–190.

Markus, H. & Nurius, P. (1986). Possible selves. *American Psychologist, 41*, 954–969.

Mead, G. H. (1934). *Mind, self, and society*. Chicago: University of Chicago Press.

Meleshko, K. G. A. & Alden, L. E. (1993). Anxiety and self-disclosure: Toward a motivation model. *Journal of Personality and Social Psychology, 64*, 1000–1009.

Melchior, L. A. & Cheek, J. M. (1990). Shyness and anxious self-preoccupation during a social interaction. *Journal of Social Behavior and Personality, 5*, 117–130.

Miller, R. S. (1995). On the nature of embarrassability: Shyness, social evaluation, and social skill. *Journal of Personality, 63*, 315–339.

Miller, R. S. (1996). *Embarrassment: Poise and peril in everyday life*. New York: Guilford.

Miller, R. S. & Leary, M. R. (1992). Social sources and interactive functions of emotion: The case of embarrassment. In M. Clark (Ed.), *Emotion and social behavior* (pp. 202–221). Beverly Hills: Sage.

Montgomery, R. L., Haemmerlie, F. M., & Edwards, M. (1991). Social, personal, and interpersonal deficits in socially anxious people. *Journal of Social Behavior and Personality*, *6*, 859–872.

O'Banion, K. & Arkowitz, H. (1977). Social anxiety and selective memory for affective information about the self. *Social Behavior and Personality*, *5*, 321–328.

Patterson, M. L., Churchill, M. E., & Powell, J. L. (1991). Interpersonal expectancies and social anxiety in anticipating interaction. *Journal of Social and Clinical Psychology*, *10*, 414–423.

Patterson, M. L. & Ritts, V. (1997). Social and communicative anxiety: A review and meta-analysis. In B. R. Burleson (Ed.), *Communication yearbook 20* (pp. 263–303). Thousand Oaks, CA: Sage.

Pilkonis, P. A. (1977). The behavioral consequences of shyness. *Journal of Personality*, *45*, 596–611.

Riggio, R. E., Throckmorton, B., & DePaola, S. (1990). Social skills and self-esteem. *Personality and Individual Differences*, *11*, 799–804.

Schachter, S. (1951). Deviance, rejection, and communication. *Journal of Abnormal and Social Psychology*, *46*, 190–207.

Schlenker, B. R. (1980). *Impression management: The self-concept, social identity, and interpersonal relations*. Monterey, CA: Brooks/Cole.

Schlenker, B. R. & Leary, M. R. (1982). Social anxiety and self-presentation: A conceptualization and model. *Psychological Bulletin*, *92*, 641–669.

Sedikides, C. & Skowronski, J. J. (1997). The symbolic self in evolutionary context. *Personality and Social Psychology Review*, *1*, 80–102.

Shepperd, J. A. & Arkin, R. M. (1990). Shyness and self-presentation. In W. R. Crozier (Ed.), *Shyness and embarrassment: Perspectives from social psychology* (pp. 286–314). New York: Cambridge University Press.

Shepperd, J. A., Arkin, R. M., & Slaughter, J. (1995). Constraints on excuse-making: The deterring effects of shyness and anticipated retest. *Personality and Social Psychology Bulletin*, *21*, 1061–1072.

Swann, W. B., Jr., Griffin, S., Predmore, S., & Gaines, E. (1987). The cognitive-affective crossfire: When self-consistency confronts self-enhancement. *Journal of Personality and Social Psychology*, *52*, 881–889.

Swann, W. B., Jr., Pelham, B. W., & Krull, D. S. (1989). Agreeable fancy or disagreeable truth? Reconciling self-enhancement and self-verification. *Journal of Personality and Social Psychology*, *57*, 782–791.

Teglasi, H. & Fagin, S. S. (1984). Social anxiety and self-other biases in causal attribution. *Journal of Research in Personality*, *18*, 64–80.

Teglasi, H. & Hoffman, M. A. (1982). Causal attributions of shy subjects. *Journal of Research in Personality*, *16*, 376–385.

Trower, P. & Gilbert, P. (1989). New theoretical conceptions of social anxiety and social phobia. *Clinical Psychology Review*, *9*, 19–35.

Wallace, S. T. & Alden, L. E. (1991). A comparison of social standards and perceived ability in anxious and nonanxious men. *Cognitive Therapy and Research*, *15*, 237–254.

Wegner, D. M. & Giuliano, T. (1982). The forms of social awareness. In W. Ickes & E. S. Knowles (Eds.), *Personality, roles, and social behavior* (pp. 165–198). New York: Springer-Verlag.

Chapter 11

Relational Schemas: The Activation of Interpersonal Knowledge Structures in Social Anxiety

Mark W. Baldwin *and* Patricia Fergusson

THE CONTENT OF RELATIONAL SCHEMAS IN SOCIAL ANXIETY
INFORMATION-PROCESSING EFFECTS
RESEARCH: THE ACTIVATION OF RELATIONAL SCHEMAS
Activation of Attachment Orientations
Activation of Self-evaluative Styles
Schema Application and Self-focus
Associative Networks and Spreading Activation
Cued Activation of Relational Schemas
SUMMARY AND CLINICAL IMPLICATIONS
CONCLUSION
ACKNOWLEDGEMENTS
REFERENCES

The problem of social anxiety is, by definition, both interpersonal and cognitive in nature. At the core of social anxiety is the compelling expectation, and fear, of negative interpersonal evaluation. For individuals with clinically significant social anxiety, this expectation poisons their outlook on relationships, undermines their attempts at smooth social interaction, and clouds their interpretation and memory of social outcomes.

A theme common to many of the classic writings of interpersonal and psychodynamic psychologists is that people's thoughts and feelings about their social

International Handbook of Social Anxiety: Concepts, Research and Interventions Relating to the Self and Shyness. Edited by W. Ray Crozier and Lynn E. Alden.
© 2001 John Wiley & Sons Ltd.

interactions are shaped by cognitive-affective-motivational structures, conceptualized as internal representations of significant relationship experiences. More recently, a number of contemporary theorists (e.g., Andersen & Berk, 1998; Baldwin, 1992; Horowitz, 1988; Safran, 1990; Stern, 1985; Westen, 1991), have advocated the integration of these theoretical insights with the research and methods of social cognitive psychology, to enhance our understanding of how interpersonal knowledge is brought to bear on everyday perceptions and interpretations. In this chapter we review the results of one such research program.

The fear of negative evaluation involves images or representations about how social interactions likely will ensue—images that link apprehension about behaving in an embarrassing or inferior manner with expectations of being rejected, humiliated or otherwise devalued as a consequence. The model presented here is primarily concerned with the cognitive representations that underlie such anxieties. In approaching a new situation, what autobiographical memories resonate with the current context, and trigger negative social expectations? What causes certain images or outcomes (e.g., being teased or mocked) to enter into mind so easily, effortlessly, and automatically that they seem not only plausible but also inevitable? What social categories (e.g., "loser") influence—even implicitly—the interpretation of ongoing experience? How might it be possible to modify the categories that become activated, to replace dysfunctional structures with more functional ones?

Central to the current formulation is the construct of *relational schemas* (Baldwin, 1992). The key premise of this social cognitive model is that, over time, various knowledge structures evolve on the basis of regularities in interpersonal experiences. Relational schemas are hypothesized to comprise a self-schema representing a particular view of oneself (e.g., awkward self) and an other-schema representing a certain type of interaction partner (e.g., critical other). Importantly, just as these views unfold not in isolation, but in a relational context, the cognitive representations of self and other are embedded in interpersonal scripts that represent a typical pattern of interaction. We have found it useful to frame these interpersonal scripts in terms of a collection of *if . . . then* outcome expectancies (e.g., "If I act awkwardly, then they will criticize me"). The intellectual roots of the relational schemas approach in such notions as working models (Bowlby, 1969) and internal objects (Greenberg & Mitchell, 1983) are readily apparent (see Baldwin, 1992, for a review).

THE CONTENT OF RELATIONAL SCHEMAS IN SOCIAL ANXIETY

Over the course of development, what might people learn about their interpersonal interactions that can give rise to social anxiety? "He could never live up to his father's expectations." "She never felt accepted for who she was." "He was always smothered, overprotected." An interpersonal understanding of the developmental antecedents of social anxiety is reflected both in the vernacular of everyday discourse and in the literature. Social apprehension among socially anxious individuals is theorized to emerge from experiences of being dominated, criticized and rejected by others. Psychologists studying the interpersonal memories of socially anxious people have identified early relationships marked by an emphasis on the opinions of others, the use of control and shame in disciplinary interactions, and a less affectionate parental style—factors that perhaps do not encourage, or provide ample opportunities for, expressive and inquisitive communication (see, e.g., Bruch & Cheek, 1995). Such a history may be characterized by interactions that foster an exaggerated sense of self as a social object being evaluated against high standards for acceptance, coupled with few opportunities for expressive communication and the kind of social interactions that might hone social skills, modify misconceptions, and temper social pressures. This emphasis on social approval and high standards is communicated over time through repeated similar experiences, usually under the guidance of a parent or primary caregiver (e.g., "I talked about myself to our guests and my father reprimanded me"; "I said the wrong thing and my mother sternly disapproved").

These overlearned patterns of interactions are the building blocks of relational schemas. Over time, these kinds of repeated social experiences become aggregated and associated in memory with other similar events via their shared features (e.g., "I made a mistake and my teacher mocked me"; "I expressed my feelings toward her and she laughed at me"). Episodic memories of social failures, humiliations, and rejections, coupled with generic knowledge about the social world, become organized and linked together in an associative network to produce a more generic relational schema. Eventually, an individual with such a history may learn to expect that any social imperfection will be met with disapproval in a way that could potentially jeopardize each new or emerging relationship.

Interpersonal expectations are, of course, linked with a range of interpersonal motives and affective reactions. Various researchers, particularly Leary and his colleagues (Schlenker & Leary, 1982; Leary & Kowalski, 1995; see Leary, this volume, *Chapter 10*) emphasize the necessity of two conditions that give rise to social anxiety: a strong concern about the kind of impression one is making coupled with an expectation that one will be unable to make the particular impression sought. Typically, people seek to make a positive impression and to produce positive outcomes such as acceptance and respect. Unfortunately, if they view themselves as inadequate, others as critical, and interactions as following a failure-rejection script, they are left with little hope of eliciting a positive interaction.

Note that, by focusing on cognitive factors in social anxiety, our intent is not to ignore or give short shrift to other factors such as genetic, temperament, or physiological contributions (e.g., Kagan, Reznick, & Snidman, 1987, 1988). There is plenty of evidence supporting such influences, as reviewed in other chapters in this volume. Clearly, however, throughout the lifespan there is a complex and

SELF	INTERPERSONAL SCRIPT	OTHER
Incompetent	If I fail, then others will criticize me	Critical
Boring	If I am not interesting, they will ignore me	Rejecting
Awkward	If I say something foolish, they will disrespect me	Disapproving

Figure 11.1   Sample relational schemas theoretically associated with social anxiety

dynamic interplay between relational experiences and existing vulnerabilities, be they genetic, temperamental, or other. For instance, the classic, early-learning analysis can easily be expanded to be consistent with other approaches that emphasize non-cognitive factors, or experiences occurring in adulthood rather than the childhood family context. For example, people with anxious temperaments may attend to, recall, and elaborate on experiences and situations particularly relevant to social anxiety. Or, a person undergoing a disruptive situation in adulthood such as an evaluative job or a tumultuous relationship might dwell on similar past experiences, integrating them into a generic model of negative interaction sequences. In any case, the result is a cognitive structure—a relational schema—that represents negative interpersonal expectations. Our goal in this particular chapter is to explore the cognitive structures and processes that mediate the influence of past interactions and learning on current experiences of social anxiety.

Figure 11.1 illustrates the three basic elements of relational schemas as they apply to social anxiety. Self-schemas may include an image of oneself as incompetent, boring, or unworthy. The schema representing other people might depict them as critical, disapproving, and rejecting. Going beyond these self and other schemas, we can imagine a number of interpersonal scripts or outcome expectancies that support and consolidate these images of self and others (e.g., If I speak my mind, they might disapprove; If I make a mistake, they will criticize or reject me; If I stumble over my words, they will think I'm stupid).

INFORMATION-PROCESSING EFFECTS

Central to the present model is the notion that while relational schemas may originate from specific interpersonal experiences, over time they become the generic cognitive maps that guide us through our social world and shape our social perceptions, interpretations, and expectations. Drawing from the social cognitive literature (e.g., Fiske & Taylor, 1984), one should predict that relational schemas, like other knowledge structures, would demonstrate information-processing consequences including attention, inference, and memory effects. Indeed, research into the cognitive concomitants of social anxiety fits well with a relational schemas interpretation. For example, schemas are known to direct attention to schema-relevant aspects of interpersonal events. Several authors have documented such biases, including a high level of vigilance to the self (self-consciousness) and one's failures or shortcomings, and to social criticism and rejection (see Wallace & Alden, 1991; Pozo, Carver, Wellens, & Scheier, 1991; Ryan, Plant, & Kuczkowski, 1991; Winton, Clark, & Edelmann, 1995; Hartmann, 1983; Taylor & Arnow, 1988). Similarly, the interpretation of those aspects to which attention is drawn should be biased in predictable ways: research has documented that socially-anxious people interpret ambiguous information as self-relevant and negative (e.g., "Their empty glance must mean they dislike me"; "If they leave early, it's because I'm boring them"; see Clark & Wells, 1995, for overview; also Clark, this volume, *Chapter 18*). Relational schemas also facilitate recall for schema-relevant events. When negative, dysfunctional relational schemas dominate, they can function to organize negative interpersonal experiences (social failures, rejections) so that they are perceived and recalled as more pervasive in one's interpersonal history than is warranted. An important aspect of this process is the "postmortem" processing of events described by Clark and Wells (1995): Following interpersonal events, socially phobic individuals are described as expending considerable cognitive energy elaborating on the negative aspects of social interactions. These negative features may then become deeply encoded in memory and integrated with other similar memories of social failure.

Relational schemas also are closely tied to social behaviour. Negative evaluative expectancies, coupled with motives to avoid rejection, can lead to social awkwardness and the kinds of safety behaviours described in the social anxiety literature (e.g., avoiding self-disclosure; Clark & Wells, 1995). Such behaviours have the potential to elicit the kinds of responses from others that confirm the very expectations from which the behaviours emerged. Social awkwardness and avoidance may evoke negative or somewhat dismissive responses from others—responses that ultimately reinforce the problematic relational schema (Stopa & Clark, 1993). We emphasize, then, that the information-processing effects of relational schemas are integral to the kinds of self-perpetuating cognitive-behavioural cycles that have been articulated by several interpersonal theorists (e.g., Safran, 1990; Strupp & Binder, 1984; Kiesler, 1982).

It follows then, that these information-processing effects are critical for understanding the process by which relational schemas can become dysfunctional over time and resilient to disconfirming interpersonal information. It has been noted that ". . . the more past experience there is, the less relative impact for change any single specific episode will have. History builds up inertia" (Stern, 1985, p. 113). The cumulative interplay between experience, and the development of relational schemas from which expectancies and information-processing effects emanate, are critical for understanding the process by which dysfunctional relational schemas can, over time, become increasingly intransigent. At the same time, this process may give clues as to possible routes to cognitive change.

Thus, many of the well-known characteristics of knowledge structures and schematic processing have been documented in the social anxiety literature. We now turn to research rooted in a specific set of basic principles, from the social cognition literature, involving schema accessibility and activation. Much of the work we present does not target social anxiety per se, but rather addresses the more general issues of insecurity associated with romantic attachments and self-evaluation. Drawing on data demonstrating correlations between social anxiety and both low self-esteem (e.g., Cheek & Buss, 1981) and insecure attachment (Duggan & Brennan, 1994) we use this body of social cognition research to offer a new perspective on the problems of the socially insecure. Our overriding objective then is to enhance our understanding of the negative expectations inherent to social difficulties by going beyond cognition about self or others in isolation to conceptions that link the two in a relational network.

RESEARCH: THE ACTIVATION OF RELATIONAL SCHEMAS

Clark and Wells (1995) describe the self-schema of socially phobic individuals as precarious. These clinicians observe that asking sufferers to imagine a range of different situations—such as picturing themselves on a desert island—can produce shifts in the degree to which their dominant self-conceptions are those focused on concerns about social inadequacies. In our own informal interviews with socially anxious individuals we have also observed comments implying a fundamentally likeable self, but one whose positive aspects could be easily inhibited or disabled by the overwhelming negative contingencies the individual sees as inherent to many, if not most, social interactions.

In these clinical observations are allusions to a number of principles integral to the relational schemas model. First, people have multiple relational schemas available to them. We all develop knowledge structures representing self as, for example, a son or daughter, teacher, patient, etc. Such images are intimately associated with complementary other-schemas (parent, student, doctor) respectively and the interpersonal scripts through which they become defined. Similarly, most of us know what it feels like to be liked and accepted, but also what it feels like to be rejected, dominated, or criticized. We assume that socially anxious people also have available to them schemas that represent a wide range of interpersonal situations, although their rejection scripts are probably more developed and better elaborated than those of other individuals.

A critical factor determining the influence of these different schemas, however, is the extent to which each is *activated* at a particular moment, to shape the processing of information about the current or anticipated interaction (see, e.g., Higgins, 1996, for a detailed discussion of the social cognitive principle of activation). The particular relational schemas of socially anxious individuals, we suggest, cause problems, not because they represent the *only* schemas available to them, but because they are the ones that are chronically accessible—that is, the most easily activated in a variety of interpersonal contexts. If a situation, or, for that matter, an imagination exercise, were to activate a more functional relational schema, we would expect the individual to show no symptoms of social anxiety.

The research presented below draws from the methods of social cognition, incorporating both individual difference and experimentally manipulated variables to understand these processes. Studies confirm that there are notable individual differences in social anxiety, attachment security, self-esteem, and so on, that correspond to individual differences in the chronic accessibility of specific relational schemas. At the same time, studies also show that simple experimental and situational manipulations can increase or decrease feelings of social anxiety, self-criticism, and so on, by modifying the activation of various schemas. Once we adopt a relational schema framework, then, we can begin to hypothesize about different types of relational schemas available to people, their cognitive accessibility, and the conditions under which one or another schema becomes activated and applied to the situation at hand. The relational schemas framework represents a shift in perspective, not only in its emphasis on cognition about relationships but, perhaps more importantly, from a focus on the *content* of cognitions (which leads to treatments marked by attempts to change them) to understanding the *processes* by which they operate.

Consider two studies recently conducted to examine the idea that the information processing tendencies of socially insecure individuals reflect the chronic accessibility of relational schemas that embody expectations of being socially humiliated and rebuffed. In the first study (Baldwin & Regehr, 1998), student participants read a vignette in which they were depicted having an encounter with an unfamiliar classmate before one of their university lectures. Over the course of the conversation, the stimulus person asked to borrow the participant's class notes, made a teasing remark, and offered a supportive comment when the participant spilled a cup of coffee. As predicted, on the basis of previous research into the interpretive biases associated with social anxiety, participants high in social anxiety (established by such measures as the Fears Questionnaire, Marks & Matthews, 1979), tended to interpret such ambiguously friendly behaviour as negative, anticipated that the person would evaluate them negatively, and were less motivated to spend further time with this new acquaintance.

In the second study Baldwin and Regehr (1998) used a cognitive priming technique to examine the role of schema activation in understanding the information-processing biases accompanying social anxiety. If such biases derive from the activation of relational schemas, then it should be possible to prime particular types of relational models and observe corresponding information-processing effects—even in a group of students who were not typically socially anxious. Specifically, in this study, the researchers used a priming technique to activate relational schemas representing either social acceptance or social rejection. Participants first spent a few minutes visualizing a person they knew who was either typically accepting of them, or typically somewhat rejecting and critical. They were instructed to "picture this person's face" and "imagine being with this person". Shortly afterwards, they read the ambiguous vignette described above. Consistent with the activated schema, those primed with a rejecting relationship showed a pattern of construals analogous to those shown by the chronically socially anxious participants in the first study.

This kind of priming study does more than simply demonstrate the role of relationship cognition in shaping self and social-evaluative perceptions. Such findings highlight the important principle of schema activation. Via remarkably subtle priming procedures, we can temporarily activate particular relational schemas that can, in turn, lead people to process information in uncharacteristic ways. Indeed, as the research shows, a random sample of individuals can be induced to construe an interpersonal situation in ways remarkably similar to those who struggle with social anxiety, or insecure attachment, or low self-esteem. In this sense, priming techniques have the potential to serve as an experimental analogue to the processes involved in social anxiety as well as other disorders. More important for present purposes, however, is the notion that information-processing phenomena, including attention, inference and behavioral effects, are guided not solely by the relational schema *available* in memory (a necessary condition), but also by the relational schemas *activated* in a particular context (see Baldwin, Keelan, Fehr, Enns, & Koh-Rangarajoo, 1996; Higgins, 1996). Such an analysis implies of course that people (including those with chronic dispositional tendencies toward social anxiety) have a repertoire of relational schemas available for activation—schemas representing various kinds of interpersonal relationships (e.g., secure, conflictual, accepting, etc.). Chronic tendencies, or stability in personality (Baldwin, 1999), can be understood in terms of the ease or fluency with which one model rather than another becomes activated (Baldwin et al., 1996). The question relevant to the present discussion, then, is whether we can override, via activation manipulations, what might be considered "default models" or chronic information-processing tendencies. The answer to such questions have far-reaching implications because they represent a shift in thinking away from documenting stable, chronic patterns or cognitions to the conditions associated with change and flexibility.

Activation of Attachment Orientations

Adult attachment theory assumes that, on the basis of early, internalized relationships with attachment figures, individuals develop a stable working model that yields an attachment "style" (Hazan & Shaver, 1987). This style is presumably carried forward into adulthood, and applied to romantic and significant relationships. Typically, roughly 55% of adults characterize themselves as "secure", that is, comfortable being close to, and depending on, significant others. Roughly 25% characterize themselves as "avoidant", or uncomfortable with closeness; and roughly 20% characterize themselves as "anxious/ambivalent", desiring more closeness and dependency than is usually available from their relationship partners. The latter, insecure, styles of relating correlate with numerous outcomes, including loneliness, relationship breakup, and so on.

From a perspective emphasizing internally represented relationships, we certainly adhere to the notion that knowledge structures emanating from early attachment figures are fundamentally at the root of later relationship patterns, both secure and insecure. The question we ask is whether there is evidence for multiple relational schemas even among individuals with chronic tendencies, and how malleable might such patterns be. Baldwin et al. (1996) addressed issues of schema availability and accessibility in a series of studies examining attachment-relevant knowledge structures. These researchers first established participants' attachment orientations (i.e., secure, avoidant, or anxious/ambivalent). Participants' portrayals of their ten most significant relationships revealed that, despite having a predominant attachment style, individuals had multiple attachment models available to them: Eighty-eight per cent of participants reported experience with more than one attachment pattern across their ten relationships. A second study showed that even though most people could generate exemplar relationships corresponding to all three styles, the ease with which they could do so depended on their chronic attachment orientation. For example, individuals with avoidant global attachment orientations were able to think of avoidant relationships with greater ease or fluency than were other participants. It appears then that attachment styles, and the relationship patterns associated with them, derive from both the availability of particular kinds of experiences, and the cognitive fluency or accessibility that high exposure to a relational model or interaction pattern produces. Thus, stable or chronic relational orientations reflected the ease with which certain information or interpretations came to mind. Drawing from research on the "availability heuristic" (Tversky & Kahneman, 1973), Baldwin et al. (1996) suggested that social outcomes that come to mind easily (that are chronically accessible) will be judged as "truer" or more likely to occur, despite other possibilities that might be cognitively available. While most individuals can conjure up images of past experiences involving such outcomes as abandonment, social humiliation or rejection, they do not carry these mental representations with them to each new social interaction, nor do they behave as if these outcomes were inevitable.

Again, the notion of multiple models implies individuals should be able to override their chronic tendencies, by accessing other, less fluent relational structures. For example, previous research (Frazier, Byer, Fischer, Wright, & DeBord, 1996) has shown that people's global attachment orientations predict the kind of dating partners to whom they are attracted: avoidantly attached people prefer to date similarly avoidant people, for instance, whereas anxious/ambivalent individuals prefer to date similarly ambivalent partners. Since people have various attachment models available to them, social cognitive theory would predict that it should be possible to temporarily activate a specific model with predictable information-processing and motivational effects. In a third study, Baldwin et al. (1996) asked participants to imagine a relationship in which they felt either secure, avoidant, or anxious-ambivalent. The activation of this kind of relational knowledge influenced participants' subsequent attraction to, and willingness to meet, potential dating partners whose descriptions characterized them as having one of the three attachment styles. For example, participants primed to feel avoidant were indeed most willing to meet an avoidant dating partner. These findings are significant for several reasons. They add to the existing data by demonstrating that activated relational schemas influence not only self- and social-evaluative perceptions, but have behavioural and motivational implications as well in very fundamental relationship domains. They also provide additional evidence for the existence of multiple relational schemas. Finally, they further demonstrate that, despite the fact that people may be classified according to chronic tendencies or styles, we can experimentally activate other relational schemas with predictable information-processing effects. It appears then that what is stable or chronic about our self- and social perceptions is the accessibility or activation potential of the relational schemas from which they derive (Baldwin, 1999).

Activation of Self-evaluative Styles

A key element of social anxiety is sufferers' tendency to evaluate themselves and their behaviour from the perspective of others in the interaction. They see themselves falling short of people's standards, and being criticized and rejected as a result. A number of studies have shown the impact of activated relational schemas on the self-evaluative process. Baldwin and Holmes (1987, Study 1), for instance, assessed the activation of evaluative standards by using two primes that represented different value systems. A sample of undergraduate women underwent a guided visualization technique designed to prime either their parents, or friends from campus. Ten minutes later, they rated their enjoyment of a sexually permissive fictional story. Participants who had visualized their parents rated the passage significantly less exciting and enjoyable than those who had visualized campus friends; thus, it appears they were trying to regulate their behavior in a direction consistent with the values and evaluative standards in the primed relationship. In a follow-up study, Baldwin, Carrell, and Lopez (1990) used a subliminal priming technique to assess a related question. They found that after Catholic women read a sexually permissive story, subliminal exposure to the disapproving face of Pope John Paul II influenced their self-ratings (anxious, competent, moral) in a more self-critical direction. Significantly, however, only the self-ratings of women characterizing themselves as practicing Catholics, and those who were exposed to the disapproving face of the Pope (as opposed to the disapproving face of an unfamiliar figure), were affected in such a manner. Such findings underscore the theoretical importance of activating *pre-existing* cognitive structures representing particular evaluative others (Baldwin et al., 1990).

A number of priming studies have demonstrated effects of activated relational models representing accepting versus critical others on self-evaluations, interpersonal behaviours, as well as the kinds of social-evaluative concerns that are so integral to social insecurities. In a study involving a sample of University of Michigan graduate students, Baldwin et al. (1990) administered subliminal presentations of the scowling, disapproving face of Dr. Robert Zajonc, then director of the department. Students' self-evaluations of their own research work were more negative following this prime than following neutral or accepting primes. To rule out the possibility that the facial expression on the slide was the sole key element in the priming effect, Baldwin (1994, Study 1) conducted a conceptually similar study using names rather than faces as stimuli. Participants were asked to provide the names of people who fit a variety of characteristics, among them someone who was accepting and non-evaluative and someone who was judgemental and critical. One of these names (depending on condition) was then used as a subliminal prime. Following a difficult task, those receiving the *critical* prime reported lower levels of self-esteem than those receiving the *accepting* prime. Interestingly, while the pattern of results on the self-esteem measure demonstrated effects on some purely self-evaluative items (e.g., "I feel displeased with myself") the most prominent effects were observed on items reflecting social-evaluative concerns (e.g., "I'm worried about what other people think of me"). These kinds of effect are consistent with the kinds of imagined reaction that we assume such a relationship would foster and, significantly, also represent the kinds of social evaluative concern that are a signature of socially insecure individuals.

Another study demonstrated that such priming effects are indeed mediated by changes in how self-relevant information is processed. Baldwin and Holmes (1987) investigated the idea that a primed relationship activates a set of inference rules or procedures that influence self-experience (Baldwin, 1999). These researchers employed two priming conditions, both designed to engender feelings of being liked and appreciated by another. In one condition, however, acceptance was *contingent* on satisfying some performance standard (i.e., being liked because of one's abilities). In the other condition, acceptance was noncontingent on any such conditions. Participants later evaluated their performance on a difficult task designed to create a failure experience. As expected, those primed with a contingent relationship evaluated themselves more negatively and, interestingly, demonstrated a pattern of self-construals consistent with a depressive cognitive style (Beck & Emery, 1985): internal attributions for poor performance and an increased likelihood of overgeneralizing by attributing specific outcomes to global, stable characteristics about oneself. The effects of these priming studies, then, go beyond the induction of globally positive or negative emotions. Embodied in these internalized relationships are a set of inference rules that then guide self-construals and social perceptions (Baldwin, 1999).

Schema Application and Self-focus

Are we at the mercy of any relational model that is momentarily activated? Will relational schemas, once activated, inevitably produce effects consistent with the expectations and rules inherent in the primed structures? These are important questions as they speak to the potential for change by addressing the mechanisms underlying cognitive flexibility versus rigidity. In a number of studies, subtle manipulations have revealed important parameters regarding the conditions under which the prime is indeed most likely to produce an assimilation effect in which information is processed according to the cognitive structures of the activated schema. In most priming research, including the studies described above, the experimental primes are designed to function implicitly by presenting them either subliminally or unobtrusively. On the other hand, when the prime is obvious enough that people are aware of its influence they can adjust their judgements, and the effects either disappear or move in the direction opposite to that indicated by the prime (e.g., Baldwin, 1994, Study 2). The extent to which the activated schema is applied to the situation-at-hand, then, is strongly influenced by people's attention to the prime and assumptions about the source of their interpretations (Baldwin, 1999). In the absence of information disconfirming a given interpretation, it is logically assumed to arise from aspects or features of the situation-at-hand and therefore be experienced as a more apt or "true" interpretation. In such circumstances, the primed relational schema becomes, or is more likely to become, the lens through which information is processed (Baldwin, 1994). Alternatively, when individuals can focus on the primed schema as a potential determinant or influence in their judgements, they can then marshal defenses or coping resources to actively refute the activated perceptions.

This analysis can be applied to the finding that there is a correlation between social anxiety and public self-consciousness, or a concern about making an impression on others (Hope & Heimberg, 1988; Leary & Kowalski, 1993). Basic research has shown that when people are highly focused on themselves, either as an individual difference tendency (self-consciousness) or as a result of experimental manipulation (self-focus, induced by having participants see their reflection in a mirror), they are particularly likely to adopt the evaluative styles and standards of an activated relational schema. In a number of the self-evaluation priming studies reported above (Baldwin, 1994; Baldwin & Holmes, 1987) more explicit primes designed to activate accepting and critical or rejecting relational schemas did indeed produce corresponding self-evaluative reactions, but only under conditions of experimentally induced self-awareness (Baldwin, 1994; Baldwin & Holmes, 1987). In studies of social anxiety, manipulated self-focus, when combined with individual tendencies toward negative social expectations, produce heightened distress about social interactions and poorer social skills (Alden, Teschuk, & Tee, 1992; Burgio, Merluzzi, & Pryor, 1986). Thus, social anxiety arises from the joint influence of negative interpersonal expectations and a focus on the self and the impression one is making (Leary & Kowalski, 1995).

Associative Networks and Spreading Activation

Before applying these research findings to issues of change, it is important to understand more fully how activated schemas operate to produce the various effects we have discussed. When we present participants with a relational prime, what exactly are we activating? We have emphasized that relational schemas, when activated, resonate with those past experiences that are the foundation of internalized relationships. Embedded in these relational knowledge structures is a set of "if–then" interaction expectancies from which views about the self and others are inferred. For example, an activated judgemental relationship may lead to the expectation, "If I stumble, I will be rejected", followed by information-processing biases through which a sense of self as a social loser is, at least momentarily, deduced. Is there any more direct evidence for this process? Arguably, some of the effects we have described could still be interpreted in terms of affective priming whereby self- and interpersonal evaluations are simply congruent with the positive or negative mood that one or another relational prime induces.

Effective therapeutic interventions are dependent on understanding the mechanisms that dictate how past experiences function to fill in gaps in perception, such as when particular meanings or interpretations are ascribed to ambiguous circumstances. A primary theoretical premise of the relational schemas model is that these social-cognitive effects emanate from the associative structure among its elements. We noted earlier that a relational schema comprises a schema for self, other, and the if–then links of an interpersonal script. Through repeated experiences, these elements form an interconnected associative network that functions as a modular unit. Activation of only one element is required to automatically activate, through associative links, the entire schema (Baldwin, 1992). We suggest that it is through this process that relational schemas acquire their automatic nature and become so fluent or accessible.

A procedure borrowed from cognitive psychology, the lexical-decision task, has been useful for testing such hypotheses and revealing the way activation spreads across associative links among elements of a relational schema. In this reaction time task, subjects are presented with letter-strings on a computer screen and asked to identify, as quickly as possible, whether each string is a word or nonword. Previous research has demonstrated that word identification is quicker in the context of an associated word (Meyer & Schvaneveldt, 1971): for example, reading the prime word *doctor* leads to quicker identification of the target word *nurse* than unrelated words such as *bread*. Baldwin and Sinclair (1996) adapted the lexical decision task to examine spreading activation among elements of if–then cognitive structures reflecting the links between self-views and social acceptance—contingencies that are assumed to underlie various self-esteem disturbances. If such interpersonal expectations function through spreading activation, then activating the IF element (If I fail) should, through associative links, activate the expected THEN interpersonal outcome (people will reject me). As hypothesized on the basis of this reasoning, individuals with low self-esteem were quicker than those with high self-esteem both at identifying rejection-related words following a prime word representing failure (versus success), and at identifying acceptance-related words following a prime word representing success (versus failure). The inclusion of positive and negative, but noninterpersonal, target words ruled out a simple valence-congruency explanation of the results. Baldwin and Sinclair (1996, Study 3) took this phenomenon further by then experimentally activating a contingent versus noncontingent relationship, using the kind of visualization techniques described earlier. Results once again confirmed the parallel between chronically accessible and temporarily activated structures. Participants primed with a highly contingent accepting relationship showed the "if–then" pattern of effects consistent with the contingency scripts utilized by individuals with low self-esteem.

Extending this research to social anxiety, we begin to understand how a variety of seemingly innocuous cues (e.g., a slight, virtually unobservable hesitation in one's own speech) can activate a schema of self as socially inept, schemas of others as critical and judgemental, and expectations of absolute social rejection, perhaps with little or no awareness regarding the source of such predictions. The process of spreading activation helps us to gain insights as to how particular social outcomes are brought so easily to mind, and how they come to be experienced as almost inevitable at the earliest stages of an interaction.

In addition to revealing automatic spreading across elements of relational schemas, reaction-time tasks represent useful tools for uncovering the implicit expectancies underlying various traits or dysfunctional conditions (Baldwin, 1999). If, as the data suggest, interpersonal scripts operate at least to some degree according to automatic processes via spreading activation, self-report methods that reflect deliberate processing may tell only part of the story. Individuals may not always report the beliefs that guide their behaviour either because such beliefs are not consciously accessible to them or because they are disinclined to report concerns that are so obviously irrational (e.g., If I am warm and friendly, people will ridicule me). Assessment methods involving split-second reactions may circumvent these or other defensive tendencies, and in some instances may show a better correspondence with actual behaviour than self-reports (see Dovidio, Kawakami, Johnson, Johnson, & Howard, 1997, for an example from the prejudice literature). As most clinicians know, clients, in the context of the therapy session, can be quite adept at reporting the rational response or belief, and "correcting" cognitions according to therapeutic teachings. The rational expectation, however, may not "pop" into mind in vivo, at the critical moment, at which time more tacit beliefs may dictate how the interaction will be played out.

Cued Activation of Relational Schemas

The research reviewed thus far points to the influence of activated relational schemas in producing the kinds of insecurities that are characteristic of socially anxious individuals. Structures representing rejecting, or conditionally accepting, others can lead people to be self-critical, anxious, and less motivated toward developing close relationships. As outlined in Leary's (Schlenker & Leary, 1982) two-factor formulation of social anxiety, some research has shown that these effects are especially pronounced when negative interpersonal expectancies are coupled with a heightened concern about the self and the impression one is making.

In normal daily life, relational schemas can become activated in a manner similar to the priming manipulations we have used: A person might have a conversation with a critical, rejecting person, for example, and this might leave them in an insecure state of mind for the rest of the day. Recent work by Andersen and colleagues (e.g., Andersen & Berk, 1998) has shown that this can occur even as a result of meeting someone who *reminds* one of a particular significant other. Often, though, activation occurs via cues or triggers that have been associated in the past with negative social experiences. Certain situations, such as a cocktail party, certain types of people, such as tall people with beards, or even certain seemingly neutral stimuli, such as a specific song on the radio, can serve to activate a network of negative memories, thoughts, and emotions. Some (e.g., Bouton, 1991) have argued that such cued activation poses a challenge to exposure therapies. It is not always enough for a client to learn a new way of seeing things (e.g., that social interactions sometimes can be positive); it is also necessary to ensure that the newly learned structure successfully generalizes across situations. The important factor is that the positive relational schema must be the one that is activated in the stressful social situation, rather than the old, dysfunctional structure. The successful therapy client may report, then, that "I started to feel anxious, and then I thought of you and what you would say to me in this situation".

In our final study (Baldwin & Main, in press) we examined this phenomenon of cued activation by asking whether a conditioning paradigm could be used to create an association between a neutral cue and a specific relational schema. This cue was again presented later in the session, during a stressful social interaction, to see if it would trigger schema-consistent responses to the potentially anxiety-provoking situation. Fifty-six undergraduate women first completed a bogus questionnaire on a computer. They were asked a number of multiple-choice questions about mundane topics, such as their favourite flavour of ice cream or their preference for movie genres. They were told that the questions had been pretested with a sample of their peers, who had indicated which answer was the most socially desirable; the participant was now to answer honestly so we could "see if people's opinions and attitudes line up" with the ideals of their peers. They were given periodic feedback, consisting of a row of smiling faces (indicating desirability and acceptance) or frowning, disgusted faces (indicating undesirability and rejection) to tell them whether their answers were consistent with the standards. This bogus feedback was given every few questions in a fixed random order, unrelated to the participant's actual answers. The conditioning procedure involved pairing these interpersonal stimuli with distinctive tone sequences, generated by the computer 0.5 seconds before the faces were displayed. One tone sequence (which we will call the *CS-acceptance*) was paired 10 times with the acceptance feedback, while another (the *CS-rejection*) was paired 10 times with the rejection feedback. The tones were counterbalanced across subjects.

Adapting a procedure described by Stopa and Clark (1993) to create a stressful social situation, we then told participants that they would participate in a 5-minute conversation with a male experimenter, who was in fact a well-dressed experimental confederate. He interacted in a reserved manner, allowing uncomfortable pauses to occur, and initiating conversation only after a pause of 30 seconds. During this conversation a computer on the other side of the room, which the experimenter ostensibly had been working on periodically to develop new programs, repeatedly emitted one of three tone sequences. Some participants were exposed to their CS-acceptance tones, some to their CS-rejection tones, and some heard Control tones they had not heard before. The confederate was blind to condition.

Various measures taken after the interaction showed a clear impact of the cues. Self-reported mood, specifically anxiety, was more negative in the CS-rejection condition and more positive in the CS-acceptance condition. Participants' ratings of how they thought their interaction partner saw them were more positive in the CS-acceptance condition. Thus, the cues successfully triggered positive or negative social expectations.

We also tested the two-factor formulation of social anxiety (Schlenker & Leary, 1982) by splitting the sample into groups of participants who were high versus low in public self-consciousness (Fenigstein, Scheier, & Buss, 1975). As the model would predict, women low in self-focus reported little anxiousness across the board (see Figure 11.2). Those high in self-consciousness reported higher levels of anxiety in the Control, and especially in the CS-rejection, conditions.

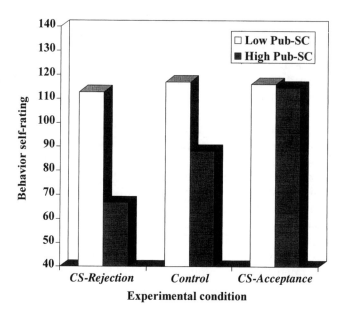

Figure 11.2   Self-reported anxiety as a function of cue condition and level of public self-consciousness (Baldwin & Main, 1999)

Self-conscious people, concerned with the impressions they are making, are more prone to social anxiety, then, especially when they also have an activated expectancy of negative social outcomes. In the condition where the background tones cued a relational schema representing acceptance, however, highly self-conscious participants were no more anxious than their low self-conscious counterparts. A parallel statistical interaction was observed on a measure filled out by the confederate. Thus, the activation manipulation affected not only subjects' feelings and perceptions, but also their actual conversational behaviour.

This study confirms that it is possible, using simple conditioning procedures, to create a cue that can trigger positive or negative relational schemas. Once activated, these schemas can shape perceptions of, and reactions to, a stressful social situation. As a result, people—particularly self-conscious people—can become more socially anxious with the activation of a rejecting schema, but less socially anxious with the activation of an acceptance schema.

SUMMARY AND CLINICAL IMPLICATIONS

We have reviewed a number of experimental studies that lend empirical support to many of the basic tenets of the relational schemas model. We now turn to things practical, and outline how these findings might be applied to the dysfunctional and chronic relational structures that guide, or misguide, the social perceptions and interactions of the socially insecure.

We have argued that while it is fruitful to study socially anxious individuals' cognitions about self and about others, further insights may be gained by linking these two components together and examining interpersonal script cognition and the process by which these scripts operate. When we frame the negative expectancies of socially insecure individuals as elements of an activated relational schema, we broaden our therapeutic options in a number of ways. As we have seen, self-evaluations, social perceptions, and interpersonal behaviour shift in predictable ways according to the nature of the person's relational schemas. What is most promising for change, however, is the finding that people have varied relational models from which to draw in interpreting current experience. The sense of self and others, including interpersonal expectations and behaviours, can be as multifaceted as the relational network that makes up a person's developmental history and current interpersonal milieu. As a result, even a simple or innocuous activation procedure can substitute positive for negative social expectancies, thereby momentarily reducing the tendency to make negative interpretations of interpersonal situations and to behave in a socially anxious manner.

Since fairly brief activation techniques, even among the chronically self-conscious or insecure, can be effective in helping individuals draw from memories that afford an alternative, more positive or charitable, self-experience, the challenge is to extend this principle beyond the laboratory. Therapeutically, we need to identify and understand those qualities and conditions that foster this process—that enable people to access such memories and bring them to the foreground in interpreting their social milieu. Indeed, the ability to take advantage of positive relational schemas, even when such experiences are few in one's relational history, may be pivotal for determining adaptive versus dysfunctional oucomes. For example, children from very aberrant, high-risk backgrounds (e.g., those characterized by poverty, parental psychopathology and conflict) may be able to overcome adversity and avoid later dysfunctional lifestyles if they can draw on a single relational model that represents an alternative to their more typical poor quality environment (Werner & Smith, 1992).

For the socially insecure, whose life story is dominated by well-elaborated and consolidated rejection scripts, the key to change may well be to increase the accessibility of other relational schemas that afford an adaptive view on one's interpersonal world and functioning. We can borrow in part from narrative approaches such as those outlined by White and Epston (1990) where clients are encouraged to "re-author" their lives. Part of this process involves transforming previously nondescript, inchoate experiences into more consolidated models that afford a more adaptive perspective on one's social world. From our perspective, the goal for the therapist is to increase the accessibility or fluency of the client's previously dormant or latent relational schemas, through repeated activation and the consolidation of positive memories. As a result, the positive schema's associated outcomes or expectancies may come to represent events that clients can "easily imagine happening," and increase the likelihood that they will become the window through which current experience is viewed.

Techniques that foster this process might not require excessively long-term treatment, but rather a better understanding of the mechanisms that dictate how the activation of one relational schema comes to supersede another. Such approaches go beyond simply identifying the negative thought processes of socially anxious individuals to asking what other cognitive maps these individuals have available to them, and exploring how we can increase the chronic accessibility of these alternative interpersonal schemas to improve social functioning. The techniques we are suggesting would represent a shift from many early cognitive models that emphasize confronting irrational beliefs (Ellis, 1977) or challenging automatic thoughts (Beck & Emery, 1985). Clinicians' attempts to challenge, or restructure irrational or skewed cognitions may lead to resistance by clients: For example, providing clients with positive self-statements may be met with skepticism or such responses as "it's your job to say that". For the client, various reconceptions or "rational" alternatives do not always fit with their inner experience, and even if they are accepted within the safety of the therapeutic relationship, they may not always "ring true" at the critical moment. Indeed, it is worth considering that the cognitions and negative expectancies of socially anxious individuals may, in a sense, be quite rational when placed in the context of the relational model or schema from which they arose. Rather, the problem is one of misapplication. When we shift our thinking away from changing conscious thoughts, to activating different relational models, we can perhaps undermine resistance or the kinds of feelings that lead clients to question the veracity of their "new" thoughts. Ultimately, cognitions based on *existing* relational schemas may flow more easily than the restructured or corrected cognitions generated by a therapist.

While one goal of therapy, from the perspective presented here, could centre around techniques for increasing the degree of *chronic* accessibility or fluency of particular relational schemas, the second task would involve methods for ensuring that the positive or more desirable relational schema is *activated* at the right time, or applied to the appropriate situation. While it is possible to activate more positive, secure models in the lab, through direct primes, outside the research context we obviously do not have this level of control. The process by which relational schemas are normally activated in day-to-day interactions, or how memories of secure, or rejecting and conflictual, attachments are reinstated through various cues, is one that we understand imperfectly. It appears, however, that a variety of cues, including contexts, motives, subtle characteristics of an interaction partner (see, e.g., Andersen & Berk, 1998), certain foods, or perhaps a song on the radio are potential triggers of an element of a relational schema that can then activate, via spreading activation, the entire knowledge structure. An encounter with a "popular" high school acquaintance can transform a secure, accomplished adult, at least momentarily, into an insecure teenager, with behaviours or self-experiences that reflect many of the IF . . . THEN concerns associated with that developmental period. Alternatively, other cues may trigger memories of secure relationships that foster a sense of acceptance and very positive self-regard. For many children, a teddy bear, blanket, or other seemingly meaningless item from home, can help them smoothly negotiate a variety of novel or anxiety-provoking situations. These kinds of "transitional" objects can be strong triggers of the type of safety and security schemas embodied in parental relationships and the home environment (cf. Winnicott, 1953; Stern, 1985). Similarly, panic attacks can be allayed, and individuals with agoraphobia can venture to otherwise feared and avoided situations, when accompanied by a "safe" companion or object (Taylor & Arnow, 1988). Indeed some programs, such as The Stanford Agoraphobia Exposure Protocol (Brouillard & Telch, 1988) encourage the use of "response aids" (objects or people) to allay anxiety to a level that permits entry to a feared situation. Finally, as we have seen, a very brief conditioning process can successfully establish links between neutral cues and specific relational schemas (Baldwin & Main, 1999). The challenge, then, is to identify procedures for establishing and modifying socially anxious individuals' access to security feelings and positive expectancies.

Clearly, to the extent that cues in the therapeutic context resemble those from the eventual social interactions, we might expect therapeutic shifts to more readily occur. Group therapy settings may be particularly facilitative of these goals precisely because they provide a format for activating various scripts in an interpersonal context. Just as primes can be used experimentally to understand activation effects of particular models, group members can be used as natural primes to explore interpersonal scripts, their activation, and as a vehicle for change. Potentially, like the therapeutic alliance, aspects of the group situation can come to represent cues that trigger the kinds of knowledge structures that help socially insecure individuals safely and confidently navigate their social environment. Such settings can advance our understanding of the kinds of triggers to which individual group members are responding, as well as the nature of the knowledge structures activated.

Studies examining the structure of relational schemas and some of the conditions under which schemas, once activated, will be *applied* to self and social perceptions inform us as to some potentially important mechanisms for change. As we have seen, a variety of cues can come to trigger virtually any component of a relational schema that in turn can activate, through spreading activation, a complete set of interconnected conceptions about oneself and others, including images about social outcomes. To the extent that these processes function *automatically*, without awareness, people are particularly vulnerable to potentially undesirable social and behavioural consequences. As we have seen, when people are not aware of the factors directing their perceptions—when they are not tracking the source of their self-evaluations or interpersonal interpretations—either because the source is not salient or because their attention is focused elsewhere (on themselves), they are most susceptible to influence (see also Bowers, 1984). Consistent with some psychodynamic formulations, then, therapeutic change, and the application of more adaptive relational schemas, may first require an approach that enables clients to refute or defend against the inappropriate or negative schemas with an understanding of their source and the triggers that bring them to mind so easily. Recall that experimentally, subjects are able to override or counteract the negative effects of activated relational schemas representing criticism and rejection simply by attending to them as a possible influence. Interventions that activate problematic structures, such as priming procedures or guided imagery (e.g., Horowitz, 1988) may help facilitate awareness of biased perceptions and the internalized relationships from which such views emanate.

CONCLUSION

While the interpersonal underpinnings of social anxiety have not been neglected in the literature, they have perhaps not been fleshed out or emphasized in a way that optimizes their conceptual and therapeutic utility. The present formulation is fundamentally a dynamic one that integrates a number of research findings by casting the self-statements, expectancies, behaviours and information-processing effects as outcomes of a comprehensive and tightly integrated relational schema representing patterns of interpersonal experience. The present view is not at odds with other cognitive or cognitive-behavioural models that have contributed greatly to our understanding of social anxiety and that are certainly forefront in the development of effective therapeutic techniques. Rather, the current perspective places greater emphasis on understanding interpersonal components and, additionally, shifts emphasis from "content" to "process" by mapping out the mechanisms by which interpersonal expectations operate and are maintained via the activation and application of relational schemas. More significantly, we have presented a research program that, we hope, could move clinical research forward by applying some of the methods and theoretical perspectives of social cognition to the problems of the socially insecure.

ACKNOWLEDGEMENT

Preparation of this chapter was supported by a grant from the Social Sciences and Humanities Research Council of Canada to the first author. We thank John Walker for his helpful comments on an earlier draft of this chapter.

REFERENCES

Alden, L. E., Teschuk, M., & Tee, K. (1992). Public self-awareness and withdrawal from social interactions. *Cognitive Therapy and Research, 16,* 249–267.

Andersen, S. M. & Berk, M. S. (1998). Transference in everyday experience: Implications of experimental research for relevant clinical phenomena. *Review of General Psychology, 2,* 81–120.

Baldwin, M. W. (1992). Relational schemas and the processing of social information. *Psychological Bulletin, 112,* 461–484.

Baldwin, M. W. (1994). Primed relational schemas as a source of self-evaluative reactions. *Journal of Social and Clinical Psychology, 13,* 380–403.

Baldwin, M. W. (1999). Activation and accessibility paradigms in relational schemas research. In D. Cervone & Y. Shoda (Eds.), *Coherence in personality* (pp. 127–154). New York: Guilford.

Baldwin, M. W., Carrell, S. E., & Lopez, D. F. (1990). Priming relationship schemas: My advisor and the Pope are watching me from the back of my mind. *Journal of Experimental Social Psychology, 26,* 435–454.

Baldwin, M. W. & Holmes, J. G. (1987). Salient private audiences and awareness of the self. *Journal of Personality and Social Psychology, 52,* 1087–1098.

Baldwin, M. W., Keelan, J. P. R., Fehr, B., Enns, V., & Koh-Rangarajoo, E. (1996). Social cognitive conceptualization of attachment working models: Availability and accessibility effects. *Journal of Personality and Social Psychology, 71,* 94–104.

Baldwin, M. W. & Main, K. T. (in press). Social anxiety and the cued activation of relational knowledge. *Personality and Social Psychology Bulletin.*

Baldwin, M. W. & Regehr, C. (1998). *Assimilation/contrast effects in priming of evaluative expectations.* Unpublished raw data, University of Winnipeg.

Baldwin, M. W. & Sinclair, L. (1996). Self-esteem and "if . . . then" contingencies of interpersonal acceptance. *Journal of Personality and Social Psychology, 71,* 1130–1141.

Beck, A. T. & Emery, G. (1985). *Anxiety disorders and phobias: A cognitive perspective.* New York: Basic Books.

Bouton, M. E. (1991). A contextual analysis of fear extinction. In P. R. Martin (Ed.), *Handbook of behavior therapy and psychological science* (pp. 435–453). New York: Pergamon Press.

Bowers, K. S. (1984). On being unconsciously influenced and informed. In K. S. Bowers & D. Meichenbaum (Eds.), *The unconscious reconsidered* (pp. 227–272). New York: Wiley.

Bowlby, J. (1969). *Attachment and loss: Vol. 1. Attachment.* New York: Basic Books.

Brouillard, M. & Telch, M., (1988). The Stanford Agoraphobia Exposure Protocol. In C. B. Taylor & B. Arnow, *The nature and treatment of anxiety disorders* (Appendix 3, pp. 342–368). New York: The Free Press.

Bruch, M. A. & Cheek, J. M. (1995). Developmental factors in childhood and adolescent shyness. In R. G. Heimberg, M. R. Liebowitz, D. A. Hope, & F. R. Schneier (Eds.), *Social phobia: Diagnosis, assessment, and treatment* (pp. 163–182). New York: Guilford Press.

Burgio, K. L., Merluzzi, T. V., & Pryor, J. B. (1986). Effects of performance expectancy and self-focused attention on social interaction. *Journal of Personality and Social Psychology, 50*, 1216–1221.

Cheek, J. M. & Buss, A. H. (1981). Shyness and sociability. *Journal of Personality and Social Psychology, 41*, 330–339.

Clark, D. M. & Wells, A. (1995). A cognitive model of social phobia. In R. G. Heimberg, M. R. Liebowitz, D. A. Hope, & F. R. Schneier (Eds.), *Social phobia: Diagnosis, assessment, and treatment* (pp. 69–93). New York: Guilford Press.

Dovidio, J. F., Kawakami, K., Johnson, C., Johnson, B., & Howard, A. (1997). On the nature of prejudice: Automatic and controlled processes. *Journal of Experimental Social Psychology, 33*, 510–540.

Duggan, E. S. & Brennan, K. A. (1994). Social avoidance and its relation to Bartholomew's adult attachment typology. *Journal of Social and Personal Relationships, 11* (1), 147–153.

Ellis, A. (1977). The basic clinical theory of rational emotive therapy. In A. Ellis & R. Grieger (Eds.), *Handbook of rational-emotive therapy*. New York: Springer.

Fenigstein, A., Scheier, M. F., & Buss, A. H. (1975). Public and private self-consciousness: Assessment and theory. *Journal of Consulting and Clinical Psychology, 43*, 522–527.

Fiske, S. T. & Taylor, S. E. (1984). *Social cognition*. New York: Random House.

Frazier, P., Byer, A. L., Fischer, A. R., Wright, D. M., & DeBord, K. A. (1996). Adult attachment style and partner choice: Correlational and experimental findings. *Personal Relationships, 3*, 117–136.

Greenberg, J. R. & Mitchell, S. A. (1983). *Object relations in psychoanalytic theory*. Cambridge, MA: Harvard University Press.

Hazan, C. & Shaver, P. R. (1987). Romantic love conceptualized as an attachment process. *Journal of Personality and Social Psychology, 52*, 511–524.

Hartmann, L. M. (1983). A metacognitive model of social anxiety: Implications for treatment. *Clinical Psychological Review, 3*, 435–456.

Higgins, E. T. (1996). Knowledge activation: Accessibility, applicability, and salience. In E. T. Higgins & A. W. Kruglanski (Eds.), *Social psychology: Handbook of basic principles* (pp. 133–168). New York: Guilford.

Hope, D. A. & Heimberg, R. G. (1988). Public and private self-consciousness and social phobia. *Journal of Personality Assessment, 52*, 626–639.

Horowitz, M. J. (1988). *Introduction to psychodynamics*. New York: Basic Books.

Kagan, J., Reznick, J. S., & Snidman, N. (1987). The physiology and psychology of behavioral inhibition in children. *Child Development, 58*, 1459–1473.

Kagan, J., Reznick, J. S., & Snidman, N. (1988). Biological basis of childhood shyness. *Science, 240*, 167–171.

Kiesler, D. J. (1982). Interpersonal theory for personality and psychotherapy. In J. C. Anchin & D. J. Kiesler (Eds.), *Handbook of interpersonal psychotherapy* (pp. 3–24). New York: Pergamon Press.

Leary, M. R. & Kowalski, R. M. (1993). The Interaction Anxiousness Scale: Construct and criterion-related validity. *Journal of Personality Assessment, 61*, 136–146.

Leary, M. R. & Kowalski, R. M. (1995). The self-presentation model of social phobia. In R. G. Heimberg, M. R. Liebowitz, D. A. Hope, & F. R. Schneier (Eds.), *Social phobia: Diagnosis, assessment, and treatment* (pp. 94–112). New York: Guilford Press.

Leary, M. R. & Kowalski, R. M. (1995). *Social anxiety*. New York: Guilford.

Marks, I. M. & Mathews, A. M. (1979). Brief standard self-rating for phobic patients. *Behaviour Research and Therapy, 17*, 263–267.

Meyer, D. & Schvaneveldt, R. W. (1971). Facilitation in recognizing pairs of words:

Evidence of a dependence between retrieval operations. *Journal of Experimental Psychology*, *90*, 227–234.

Pozo, C., Carver, C. S., Wellens, A. R., & Scheier, M. F. (1991). Social anxiety and social perception: Construing others' reactions to the self. *Personality and Social Psychology Bulletin*, *17*, 355–362.

Ryan, R. M., Plant, R. W., & Kuczkowski, R. J. (1991). Relation of self-projection processes to performance, emotion, and memory in a controlled interaction setting. *Personality and Social Psychology Bulletin*, *17*, 427–434.

Safran, J. D. (1990). Towards a refinement of cognitive therapy in light of interpersonal theory: I. Theory. *Clinical Psychology Review*, *10*, 87–103.

Schlenker, B. R. & Leary. M. R. (1982). Social anxiety and self-presentation: A conceptualization and model. *Psychological Bulletin*, *92*, 641–669.

Stern, D. N. (1985). *The interpersonal world of the infant.* New York: Basic Books.

Stopa, L. & Clark, D. N. (1993) Cognitive processes in social phobia. *Behaviour Research and Therapy*, *31*, 255–267.

Strupp, H. H. & Binder, J. L. (1984). *Psychotherapy in a new key: A guide to time-limited dynamic psychotherapy.* New York: Basic Books

Taylor, C. B. & Arnow, B. (1988). *The nature and treatment of anxiety disorders.* New York: The Free Press.

Tversky, A. & Kahneman, D. (1973). Availability: A heuristic for judging frequency and probability. *Cognitive Psychology*, *4*, 207–232.

Wallace, S. T. & Alden, L. E. (1991). A comparison of social standards and perceived ability in anxious and nonanxious men. *Cognitive Therapy and Research*, *15*, 237–254.

Werner, E. E. & Smith, R. S. (1992). *Overcoming the odds: High risk children from birth to adulthood.* Ithaca, NY: Cornell University Press.

Westen, D. (1991). Social cognition and object relations. *Psychological Bulletin*, *109*, 429–455.

White, M. & Epston, D. (1990). *Narrative means to therapeutic ends.* New York: W. W. Norton & Company.

Winnicott, D. W. (1953). Transitional objects and transitional phenomena. *International Journal of Psycho-Analysis*, *34*, 1–9.

Winton, E. C., Clark, D., & Edelmann, R. J. (1995). Social anxiety, fear of negative evaluation and the detection of negative emotion in others. *Behaviour Research and Therapy*, *33*, 193–196.

Chapter 12

Evolution and Process in Social Anxiety

Paul Gilbert *and* **Peter Trower**

SOCIAL ANXIETY, RANK, AND SUBMISSIVE BEHAVIOUR
Is Fearful Submissive Behaviour Adaptive for Humans?
Competition for Attractiveness and the Manipulation of Affect
Theory of Mind
Social Anxiety and Competition
Submissive Defensive Behaviours are Unattractive
AN EVOLUTIONARY PROCESS MODEL
Process 1: Relationship Classification
Process 2: The Dilemma
Process 3: The Anxious Self as Unattractive
Process 4: Damage Limitation
Process 5: Internal Attentiveness
Process 6: Cognitive Overload
Process 7: Cognitive Distortions
Process 8: Feedback
WHAT DOES AN EVOLUTIONARY APPROACH ADD?
THERAPY IMPLICATIONS
CONCLUSION
REFERENCES

Most contemporary theories of social anxiety recognise that humans are innately capable of feeling socially anxious in certain contexts. Social anxiety, with its key features of social wariness, submissive behaviour and social avoidance has clear evolved functions in group living species. These behaviours evolved to defend the individual in contexts where competing for resources was primarily via aggres-

International Handbook of Social Anxiety: Concepts, Research and Interventions Relating to the Self and Shyness. Edited by W. Ray Crozier and Lynn E. Alden.
© 2001 John Wiley & Sons Ltd.

sive strategies. They are not well suited to contexts where competition is for attractiveness, competence and social desirability. However, it is the attracting-displays that are essential to many types of human relationships such as coopera-tion, friendship formation, group belonging, and sexual relating. In this chapter we argue that social anxiety relates to the degree to which anxious people see relationships as hierarchically competitive, and see others as evaluators ready to notice and discriminate against those who are seen as socially incompetent, unattractive, or anxious in some way. Socially anxious people would very much like to be seen as desirable and competent but see themselves as relatively low in status (or ability to defend their status) and with few allies. This position was proposed by Trower and Gilbert (1989), and has empirical support. We explore a process model of social anxiety based on evolutionary ideas (including theory of mind) and suggest how this model may be useful in guiding therapy.

SOCIAL ANXIETY, RANK, AND SUBMISSIVE BEHAVIOUR

There is growing recognition that various emotions (Nesse, 1990, 1998), cognitive abilities (Cosmides & Tooby, 1992), and behaviours have been shaped by the chal-lenges of the social ecologies that animals have been faced with during their evolution (Buss, 1999; Gilbert, 1989; Simpson & Kenrick, 1997). Dominance hier-archies have been the social context for the evolution of mental mechanisms of most mammals, including humans, for millions of years. As a result, important reasoning (Cummins, 1999), motivational (Gilbert, 1989, 1997a), and behavioural repertoires (e.g., submissive behaviour; Allan & Gilbert, 1997; Gilbert, 2000a; Harper, 1985) have been shaped by the need to operate within hierarchically organised social groups and relationships. In most primate social groups, social anxiety and submissive behaviour play key roles in the social cohesiveness of the group and aggression control (Burnstein, 1980). For example, an animal has to be able to evaluate the chances of success (or possible injury) of any competi-tive encounter over resources. The judgement of superior–inferior is therefore crucial to the behaviour that follows (Gilbert & McGuire, 1998). While those who see themselves as more powerful or dominant are able to escalate a challenge, it is the ability of a subordinate to "predict" the outcome of an encounter and behave defensively by refraining from challenging, backing down if challenged, and displaying submissive signals, that curtails and limits fighting, allows a rank order to be established, and facilitates social cohesion (Burnstein, 1980).

The purpose of a submissive display is to signal to the dominant recognition of subordinate status by displays of fear, flight motivation, and submissive pos-tures (Harper, 1985). These are good defences for dealing with aggressive con-flict for they may well succeed in convincing a dominant that the individual sees him/herself as subordinate and therefore not a threat. Such signals also seem to affect various physiological processes in the dominant (Gilbert & McGuire, 1998). Moreover, subordinate animals who do not obey "the social rules" of deference to the more powerful are at risk of serious injury and mortality (Higley et al., 1996).

How an animal behaves in relationship to another depends in part on its evaluation of its estimated relative rank (Sapolsky, 1990a, b). In humans this is related (among other things) to social comparison evaluations (Allan & Gilbert, 1995; Gilbert, Price, & Allan, 1995) and self-esteem. In general, socially anxious people have low self-esteem (see themselves as inferior; Leary & Kowalski, 1995). Trower et al. (1998) found that in an experimentally controlled conversation, where a confederate (lecturer) broke certain social conversational rules (e.g., interrupting the flow of conversation), socially anxious but not non-anxious students rated themselves as inferior and felt responsible for the cause of the difficulties in the conversation. Gilbert (2000b) found that in both a student and a depressed group, social anxiety (as measured by the Fear of Negative Evaluation Scale (FNE; Leary, 1983) and the Social Interaction Anxiety Scale (SIAS; Cox & Swinson, 1995)) were highly correlated with negative and unfavourable social comparisons.

Some submissive behaviours in humans can be used affiliatively or to ingratiate oneself with higher ranking others (Scott, 1990). But in regard to social anxiety the essence of a submissive strategy is *damage limitation* (Gilbert, 2000a). There is now much evidence that the socially anxious person is focused on (submissive) damage-limiting self-presentations rather than acquisitive ones (Leary & Kowalski, 1995; Wells et al., 1995). In social interactions socially anxious people avoid or reduce eye contact, make few initiations in conversations and use a whole variety of what have been called safety behaviours (Wells et al., 1995) including avoidance. Gilbert, Pehl, and Allan (1994) found a variety of such submissive behaviours to be highly correlated with social anxiety in students as measured by the FNE. A recent study found that social anxiety (as measured by the FNE and the SIAS) was highly correlated with submissive behaviour in both students and a severely depressed group (Gilbert, 2000b). Arrindell et al. (1990) has also shown that distress at having to act assertively is highly associated with social anxiety.

Is Fearful Submissive Behaviour Adaptive for Humans?

Elements of fearful subordinate defences designed for dealing with potential aggression (e.g., appearing timid, eye contact avoidance, or inhibition of challenge) can still be adaptive in some contexts (e.g., meeting an aggressive drunk young male on a train, one avoids eye contact and probably would not initiate a conversation!). A degree of social anxiety in new social situations gives us time to test things out and helps us to learn and respect social rules and hierarchical relationships via deference. For example, it would be rare for a first-year student to challenge a professor, but the reverse is relatively common—with differences in manner between them (Scott, 1990). Keltner and Harker (1998) have also reviewed the evidence for the value of fearful submissive display in shame. In a potential shame situation (e.g., a child told off by a parent, or being found to have broken social rules) a shame display (gaze averted, slumped posture and inhibited) rather than defiance is likely to reduce rather than escalate aggression. Even this display, however, may be less useful if it is believed to be faked. Hence the value of a human submissive display depends on the context and meaning that both the actor and the audience give to it.

However, as we will argue below, there are also contexts where submissive displays seem non-adaptive, "unskilful", or unattractive. In fact, it is not even clear how effective fearful submissive strategies are for deterring human aggression in some contexts. For example, it is often the submissive, anxious child who is most vulnerable to being picked on and bullied (Schuster, 1996). Depending on the group (Wright, Giammarino, & Parad, 1986) it may be the "affiliative", "fun" and "popular" child who is best at deterring or deflecting aggression.

There is in fact much debate on how mechanisms that evolved in one context can become maladaptive in another (Buss, 1999). Space does not allow us to pursue this area, nor explore the potential reproductive payoffs of adopting submissive strategies, but the interested reader is referred to Nesse and Williams (1995) and Wakefield (1999). The remainder of this chapter will focus on how the socially anxious activate submissive behaviours (e.g., appearing timid, eye contact avoidance, impoverished speech, shaky voice, body language that communicates lack of confidence) and how these can be maladaptive in many affiliative and relationship-building contexts and contribute to an escalating anxiety cycle.

Competition for Attractiveness and the Manipulation of Affect

There is of course much more to social relating than simply defending against threats. All animals are confronted by the need to compete for resources such as food, sexual partners, social positions, and even friends (Buss, 1999; Tooby & Cosmides, 1996). The strategies for such competition vary greatly between different primate species. While some use high rates of intimidation and aggression and maintain strict hierarchies (with subordinates submitting readily and keeping a watchful distance from the more dominant), others, including humans, rely more on cooperative alliances, and where they will compete to have (relatively) high attractiveness or desirability ratings. In other words, humans often compete *to be chosen* (for example) as a valued mate, friend, group member, or even leader (Gilbert, 1989, 1997a; Tooby & Cosmides, 1996). To be approved of, liked, valued, or esteemed by others is probably one of the most powerful of human social motives.

Aggressive tactics rely on the ability of the aggressor to overpower or frighten the other into submission. Submissive strategies work when they turn off or inhibit the aggression of a more powerful other. To a significant extent hierarchies form from the preparedness of subordinates to submit, back down, or space themselves and not elicit aggression (Burnstein, 1980). The strategies for attrac-

Table 12.1 Variation of status-enhancing and maintaining strategies

Strategy	Aggression	Attractiveness
Tactics used	Coercive Threatening Authoritarian	Showing talent Show competence Affiliative
Outcome desired	To be obeyed To be reckoned with To be submitted to	To be valued To be chosen To be freely given to
Purpose of strategy	To inhibit others To stimulate fear in others	To inspire, attract others To stimulate positive affect in others

Adapted from Gilbert and McGuire (1998).

tiveness enhancement, however, are the opposite. To be attractive to other individuals one must manipulate their *positive emotions* and feelings (not their fear). Generally this requires positive engagement. The manipulation of the positive emotions of others, so that they like, value, or desire one's company, is key to many prosocial relationships such as developing cooperative alliances, friendship, sexual relationships, and even be accepted in the group (Barkow, 1989; Gilbert, 1989, 1997a). These two strategies are presented in Table 12.1.

What is at stake here, from an evolutionary point of view, is the ability to create relationships where others will invest in one's own self-interests—your friends support and defend you and share resources with you; your sexual partner(s) fall in love with you and are faithful; the dominate (boss) values your work and promotes your career. In most aspects of life the manipulation of positive emotions in others towards the self—they see you as able, desirable, or useful in some respect—is key to social success.

If one is successful in appearing attractive, then one elicits positive signals from others, such as liking, affection, support, and approval. These are reassuring, create a sense of safeness (Gilbert, 1993), are status-enhancing, soothing, physiologically regulating (McGuire & Troisi, 1998) boosting of immune functioning (Uchino, Cacioppo, & Kiecolt-Glaser, 1996) and strengthen positive self-schema (Gilbert, 1992). And, of course, the value of social support to health and prosperity is well known. Eliciting approval and liking, however, means that we will, at times, need to make some sort of "status bid" or displays to be recognized as having desirable qualities. This is the basis of impression management (Leary, 1995) which Barkow (1989) has referred to as "competing for prestige" and Gilbert (1989, 1997a) as "competing for positive social attention".

Theory of Mind

One way to work out how to be attractive to others, and to whom to target one's efforts, is by having insight into other people's desires and motives. To do this we use what has been called the *theory of mind* (Bryne, 1995). Theory of mind abilities are believed to have evolved during recent primate evolution (Baron-Cohen, 1997; Bryne, 1995; O'Connell, 1998), and represent cognitive abilities to understand how others think and make predictions of their behaviour (also called mind reading). It is the "I think that you think" basis of metacognition. Evolutionists believe that we gain insights into how others think and feel from having insight into our own minds—a form of self-consciousness with a (limited) capacity to reflect on one's own feelings and motives. However, we should underline the distinction between empathy and projection (Gilbert, 1989). Empathic abilities means, for example, "I buy my wife the present she would like" (e.g., a new dress). Projection is "I buy the present I would like if I were her" (new guitar!). Using our own feelings and thoughts to judge what is in the minds of others is projection. Understanding that others *may not* think or feel as we do is related to the higher forms of empathy. For the most part it is projection (not empathy) that social anxiety research has focused on.

Although not formulated in evolutionary terms, mind-reading (projection) abilities have been seen as central to the development of social anxiety (e.g., Wells, Clark, & Ahmad, 1998). The focus is on a form of self-consciousness of "how I think I look in the eye of others". Socially anxious people construct negative images of themselves to themselves and (project) assume that others will have the same view about them (Bates & Clark, 1998; Wells et al., 1998). Goss, Gilbert, and Allan (1994) found that for negative traits people use projection. In students, there was a high correlation ($r > 0.8$) between scores on a questionnaire that measured self-evaluation (e.g., "I see myself as inadequate") and beliefs about evaluation by others (e.g., "I think others see me as inadequate"). We do not know if the same is true for positive traits.

As theory of mind abilities develop, children show self-conscious affects of shame and embarrassment associated with growing awareness of, and beliefs about, their relative attractiveness in the minds of others (Lewis, 1992, 1993; see also this volume, *Chapter 5*). That is, they have awareness of themselves as "an object for others" and whether they can create positive or negative experiences in others. Many evolutionary important relationships (friendships and sexual partners) will be influenced by how skilfully we operate "as an object for others"—what value we have to others. From here on the competition for attractiveness increasingly comes to be a key mediator of social anxiety. Gilbert (2000b) found that social anxiety (in a student and a depressed group) was highly associated with "thinking that others look down on the self and see the self as inferior".

One cannot have an identity as a desirable object (friend, lover, academic, interesting person, etc.) unless others (at some point) are also prepared to define and respond to the self in this way. It follows then that a person can experience disapproval (or failing to elicit positive emotions in others about the self) as profoundly threatening because it can undermine the creation of a desired identity and sense of self, with serious implications for being able to make or retain important relationships. These insights are not new; the notion of awareness of self-as-an-object-in-the-eyes-of-the-other was a concept developed by Mead (1934) and Sartre (1957/1943), who called it Being-for-Others. And before them, Cooley (1964/1902) had referred to the looking-glass self. The looking-glass self has three cognitive aspects: "The imagination of our appearance to the other person; the imagination of his judgement of that appearance; and some sort of self feeling, such as pride or mortification" (as quoted by Scheff, 1988, p. 398). In fact individuals can switch focus back and forth from self-focus to other-focus (Duval & Wicklund, 1972).

Theory of mind abilities seem particularly useful to envisage how to impress others and be attractive; to understand what others will feel about one's self-presentation. This capacity to switch focus and utilize theory of mind abilities can be used not only in moment-to-moment interactions but also to predict the outcome of interactions in the future. In this way one can set about winning those valued special places in the hearts of friends, allies, and sexual partners by trying to appear special to them. Social anxiety, like shame, however, is often about believing that one is or will be seen as unattractive in some way (Gilbert, 1998a, b; Hope, Sigler, Penn, & Meier, 1998).

It is worth recalling that theory of mind abilities are linked into more primitive defence systems. Theory of mind is not necessary for social anxiety; many species of animal (mice and rats) without theory of mind show obvious social anxiety in appropriate contexts. Fear of strangers in humans (an early forerunner of social anxiety) develops around 9 months, before theory of mind abilities develop.

Social Anxiety and Competition

For much of the time we engage in impression management (Leary, 1995) and attractiveness enhancement (Barkow, 1989; Etcoff, 1999)—for example, in our choice of clothes, make up, or studying hard to make us more desirable to an employer. Not only are these behaviours used as markers of belonging to certain groups (Baumeister & Leary, 1995) and provide a focus for self-identity, they are also, to some degree, competitive (Barkow, 1975, 1989; Wolfe, Lennox, & Cutler, 1986). It is easy to lose in such competitions and be seen as relatively unattractive. For example, people choose in favour of another; the person you want to be your lover prefers someone else; at the party people prefer to talk with others rather than you; at the conference your work does not generate much interest and people walk out to hear another paper when you appear!

Unfortunately, the socially anxious person is caught in a dilemma between going for attractiveness enhancement (which, if successful, could bring those various benefits noted above) or going for damage limitation (like those with low self-esteem; Wood et al., 1994). Consider the difference between those who go to a party to meet with friends, share jokes and stories and have a good time, and those who go to the party fearful of whether they will be accepted and able to hold their own in conversations. The first group see the party as a relatively safe opportunity to develop friendships and possible sexual relationships (e.g., gains), while the latter start from a defensive position (e.g., of potential losses). In fact, as noted above, there is now much evidence that socially anxious people focus on damage-limiting self-presentations rather than acquisitive ones (Leary & Kowalski, 1995). This is not because they do not want to make bids on raising their attractiveness ratings in the eyes of others (they would like to be seen as competent, able, and attractive) but that these efforts cue anxiety because they are, at one level, rank-improving or status bids. We might consider this analogous to a non-human low-ranking primate who would like to engage in sex or feed at the best food sites, but these "claims" are associated with anxiety over possible attacks from above. Such a primate's approach behaviour in these contexts is tense, vigilant, and often inhibited.

Hope et al. (1998) had socially anxious and non-anxious students participate in a conversation with a confederate under the observation of another subject. As predicted by Trower and Gilbert (1989) it was found that the anxious students perceived relationships as more competitive (rank related) than the non-anxious, but they did *not* attempt to compete, and believed they came across as inferior, inadequate, and as needing help and reassurance. Moreover, they believed that this was not attractive to their targets but that the other participants found them annoying and desired to get away from them. The authors concluded that the anxious subjects sought to avoid rejection by emphasizing their subordinate status, but believed they had been unsuccessful in this.

As suggested elsewhere (Trower & Gilbert, 1989; Gilbert & Trower, 1990), the socially anxious can find it very difficult *not to* operate in a competitive frame of mind or mentality (Gilbert, 1989). They *would* like to raise their status and be seen as able, talented and desirable (thus giving access to the benefits of being attractive). However, once the person has constructed the social situation as a competition for attractiveness, with an audience of potential rejecting, critical evaluators (Beck, Emery, & Greenberg, 1985) and doubt their ability to manipulate the positive emotions in the other(s). With a risk of being seen as relatively unattractive, incompetent or undesirable (especially if they get anxious), they are forced into damage limitation (submissive strategies).

There are, of course, many situations where it may be desirable to be of a lesser rank, and even occupying an "inferior" position is preferable. This is partly because one can exist in a low rank position without feeling "personally" inferior, or one is able to admire the talents of others. One feels under no pressure to make a bid for raising status because one's present status is acceptable. Think about your first conference. If you are happy to let everyone else ask the questions and to sit happily at the back, then anxiety will be low. But if you feel under some pressure to ask a question, then anxiety might increase. Socially anxious people are either not happy with their attractiveness ratings and would like to make "bids" to be seen as (more) attractive and accepted, or they think that they have to impress others in some way. In an earlier paper (Trower & Gilbert, 1989) we argued that they wish to dominate others, but to state this more accurately, they want to raise their status and be seen as competent, fun, strong and/or able-attractive, but in so doing avoid being seen as inferior and unattractive actors.

Submissive Defensive Behaviours are Unattractive

Humans have limited resources for investing in friendships and sexual partners, and therefore those in whom we do invest have to be able to repay that investment (Tooby & Cosmides, 1996). Thus we are attracted to those who in some way will support our own self-interests. Individuals who appear too anxious may not be confident enough to defend us if that becomes necessary. They may not initiate new ventures or contribute new resources, etc.—in other words they may be poor bets for investment. The signals of (social) anxiety are probably only attractive to the extent that they signal safeness and lack of aggressiveness but become unattractive when they signal a lack of confidence to engage in certain roles.

This chapter has suggested that social defensive behaviours (which evolved over millions of years for dealing with aggression) can be maladaptive for dealing with threats in prosocial contexts. Prosocial, friendly and cooperative behaviour does require a minimum of confident assertive display in the normal reciprocation process of interaction (Argyle, 1991; Baumeister, 1982) which socially anxious people find very difficult (e.g., Alden & Bieling, 1998; Clark & Wells, 1995). Warding off potential damage to social presentations by over-practising what to say, talking only briefly, not interrupting others or not creating "verbal space" to participate in conversations, eye contact avoidance, or leaving long pauses, makes socially anxious people unattractive to others. Moreover, as Clark and Wells (1995) note, behaviours like eye contact avoidance cut the person off from potentially corrective information, for example, that the other person is not rejecting them.

Eye-to-eye and face-to-face contact are other areas where socially anxious people struggle. When shy and anxious people try to meet the eye gaze of the other they can feel greatly *impelled* not to do so but turn away. Eye contact avoidance seems to have at least two functions. Dixon (1998) has argued that in humans and animals the use of cut-off (turning away from threatening or arousing stimuli) is an automatic effort to control arousal; that is, by not looking at the other person (or feared object) one reduces the input of signals that increase arousal and activates flight. Second, eye contact avoidance is also a signal to the other of "no-threat" or deference. Unfortunately, others do see such behaviours as eye contact avoidance as unattractive, suggesting lack of confidence, insincerity and deceptiveness (Larsen & Shackelford, 1996).

AN EVOLUTIONARY PROCESS MODEL

Many people feel uneasy about possible social rejection (e.g., asking someone out), going to a new place (school, workplace) or so forth. For many, these are normal anxiety experiences to be coped with. For some, though, anxiety will become intolerable; too easily triggered, too intense, or of too long duration. The analysis in this chapter leads to a model of social anxiety where social anxiety emerges from particular sequences in defensive processing of interactions and

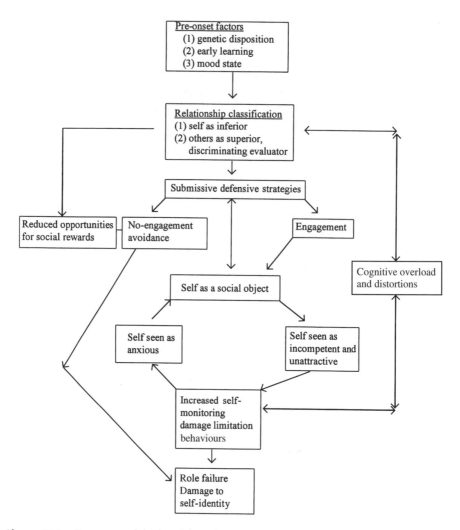

Figure 12.1 Process model of social anxiety

coping which utilizes evolved mental mechanisms. This model is given in Figure 12.1.

Process 1: Relationship Classification

People enter the relationship in which social anxiety will occur having already classified the relationship as being ranked and hierarchical, with "inferior and superior" actors, and where status can easily be lost. It is unknown how far they view the social world in general this way and much may depend on the type of social anxiety. Evidence suggests that socially anxious people automatically place themselves in an inferior position in relation to others (Leary & Kowalski, 1995; Trower et al., 1998). Moreover, what theory of mind data exist would seem to indicate that the socially anxious believe others do see them negatively—of relatively low rank in regard to attractiveness, confidence, and competence (Gilbert, 2000b; Wells et al., 1998). There are various factors that may predispose individuals to enter relationships with this cognitive set (or relational schema; see Baldwin & Fergusson, this volume, *Chapter 11*), e.g., of self as inferior and others as superior or powerful. These include:

- *Genetic factors*   There may be genetic dispositions for traits such as behavioural inhibition, fearfulness or shyness. These incline individuals to adopt submissive strategies in various social contexts.
- *Early learning*   These can be various, such as having parents who stress the danger of others in the social world, or early experiences of bullying where they were victims of hostility or rejection at home or school.
- *Background state*   Low moods and various physiological states may increase the tendency to see social relationships as threats. For example, a person may be relatively extrovert and enjoy parties but when depressed she or he shuns parties and becomes socially anxious. On the other hand social anxiety may precede depression and is frequently co-morbid with depression (Alpert et al., 1997; Davidson et al., 1994; Schneier et al., 1992). Social anxiety might reduce the ability to develop supportive, valuing relationships and thus lose out on all the benefits (including physiological) that go with them.

Process 2: The Dilemma

Having classified the relationship as ranked, with self as "having inferior qualities" and others as "having superior qualities or power", socially anxious people are now on the horns of a dilemma—to engage or not engage. If they engage in (say) conversation, telling a joke, or inviting out a possible sexual partner, they may do it badly and be vulnerable to put-down, rejection, and shame (Beck et al., 1985). If they do not engage in some kind of status bid for attractiveness (e.g., stay quiet) they are still social objects in the social arena, aware that others may evaluate them as non-engagers or as shy and uninteresting. Moreover, they will lose whatever potential benefits were available from engaging (e.g., if you don't ask the potential sexual partner out you will never know if it could have worked out). And if they avoid altogether (e.g., do not enter the social arena at all) then they will forgo any benefits of entering.

A number of researchers have drawn attention to the fact that one problem for the socially anxious is that they feel they *must* impress others, but have unrealistic ideas on what this implies they must do and must avoid doing (Leary & Kowalski, 1995). That is why they rehearse and try to predict what will impress others. But, as we argued earlier (Trower & Gilbert, 1989; Trower, Gilbert, &

Sherling, 1990), their up-rank bids may be quickly abandoned in social situations because they cue anxiety (and defensive processing). The socially anxious then become more focused on what not to do, i.e., damage limitation (e.g., don't be foolish, don't show, or hide, symptoms of anxiety).

Process 3: The Anxious Self as Unattractive

Many animals display clear social anxiety and submissive behaviours but this does not mean they have much in the way of self-consciousness of their self-presentations or theory of mind. However, as we outlined earlier, humans are able to be aware of their self-presentations and their likely impact on others (theory of mind), and have developed a sense of self as a social object (Lewis, 1992; see Lewis, this volume, *Chapter 5*) which can become a focus of vulnerability in social anxiety. This process operates to greatly magnify social anxiety. One reason for this is because, in the context of competing for attractiveness, the signals of social anxiety and submissive behaviour are (the anxious person believes) unattractive to others. Through self-consciousness and associated attributions for such negative qualities of self, the risk may now become enlarged to the whole of the self being judged as unattractive, odd, or too anxious (Trower & Chadwick, 1995; Wells, 1998).

Process 4: Damage Limitation

Information processing from Processes 1 and 2 automatically primes submissive defences (that are highly conserved and originally evolved for dealing with potential social aggression). This raises arousal and further engagement of submissive behaviours of eye contact avoidance, inhibitions of thought and behaviour, and desires to escape. Such behaviours are part of an evolved, damage-limitation (submissive) strategy, experienced as automatic and can be extremely difficult to control. The person is (increasingly) aware they he or she is (for example) telling a joke badly, making a conversational interjection poorly, or lacking confidence in asking for a date. He or she may be aware of bodily symptoms such as shaky voice or hands, sweating, stuttering, blushing. In one sense self-monitoring fuels feelings of shame at their own poor performance (Gilbert, 1998b). Theory of mind abilities (projection of negative view of oneself) indicate that others will view their (anxious) behaviours negatively. This now increases anxiety as well as instigating what Clark and Wells (1995) call safety behaviours (in evolutionary and behavioural terms these are defensive behaviours—seen as "safe" by the anxious individual, but in fact often serve to exacerbate the symptoms and/or maintain the anxiety). Because socially anxious people become increasingly attuned to how (badly) they are doing in manipulating the positive emotions of others, anxiety builds further, accentuating submissive strategies. Now they find it increasingly difficult to override submissive defences of high anxiety, inhibition of outputs, and eye contact avoidance.

Process 5: Internal Attentiveness

At this stage there is feedback from the "symptoms" of the submissive defence (anxiety) onto the damage they are doing to efforts at a positive self-presentation and the creation of a positive image of self in the eyes of others (and to oneself; see, Ingram, 1990; Clark & Wells, 1995). Many socially anxious people are disappointed in themselves partly because of their anxiety and can take it as further evidence that they are weak, incompetent, and unattractive. The greater the damage to this social self-identity the greater the risk of depression, as it may be associated with such beliefs as "I will never be able to get people to like, value or choose me" (Gilbert, 1997b).

Process 6: Cognitive Overload

As anxiety spins out of control cognitive systems are reaching overload. One the one hand the person is seeking to appear attractive, competent and able. However, at the same time, he or she is engaged in (unattractive) damage limitation having to control or mask anxiety, be attentive to the audience but also cutting off from it (e.g., eye contact avoidance) and monitoring outputs (e.g., "how do I sound, what do I look like?"; Wells et al., 1998). Such individuals become engaged in excessive projection and mind-reading operations, anticipating what others think about them, trying to identify threats, preparing to back off quickly if necessary, and searching for deception even if others are acting friendly. As a number of models of social anxiety have suggested (e.g., Rapee & Heimberg, 1997) this is just too many "balls in the air" with not enough cognitive capacity to actually perform the task at hand (e.g., tell the joke, make a smooth conversational interjection). In addition, as attention is turned inward (self-focus) there is less capacity to attend outward to true evidence about others' reactions, thus reducing the opportunity for obtaining information that disconfirms their negative attributions.

Process 7: Cognitive Distortions

Much human thinking has built-in distortive mechanisms. Humans have a variety of specific (positive) self-distortions (warm glow illusions) that help them to cope in a variety of situations (Krebs & Denton, 1997). However, as stress increases, different types of distortion occur. When under threat there can be an inflated estimation of danger and "better safe than sorry thinking" (Gilbert, 1998c). Thus socially anxious people often overestimate the danger and damage they are doing to their social efforts. Typical domains of distortion include:

- *Being rejected* The socially anxious may believe others are more rejecting and contemptuous of their efforts than in fact they are (Wells et al., 1998). As Clark and Wells (1995) point out, they may think they are the centre of attention when they are not; they may think others pay more (negative) attention to them than they do. We suspect that at one level they *would like* others to pay attention to them if they could perform well and that would raise their attractiveness ratings—in other words, the socially anxious may actually have a heightened need for attention and approval.
- *Being deceived and disqualifying the positive* Even when people appear friendly they may assume that this is deceptive and are thus not reassured (people are only being nice to me to be kind; my husband only says I look nice because he wants sex with me).
- *Being unable to deceive* They may feel they cannot deceive others of their inner feelings. Space does not allow us to explore this here but the ability to deceive others is an important social skill (O'Connell, 1998). One reason why people may cope with their social anxiety is because they believe they can hide it (deceive others—"people don't know what I am feeling inside"). This stops the spiral of anxiety. Once they think they can not hide "it", self-conscious mechanisms may take over and become more disabling.

It is of course important to recognize that in some contexts the socially anxious person may not be so distorted. For example, in going for job interviews (other things being equal) the confident individual is more likely to get the job than the very unconfident. There is now much evidence that attractive and confident individuals do better in many arenas of life (i.e., are more sexually desirable, get better jobs, have more friends; Etcoff, 1999). Further, in many contexts social anxiety is not attractive to others (e.g., Larsen & Shackelford, 1996).

Process 8: Feedback

Repeated experiences of symptoms of social anxiety feed back into beliefs that others are threats and that self is inferior, which strengthens and maintains the social anxiety cycle. Increasingly the person predicts (in advance) that he or she will feel anxious and perform poorly. This accentuates shame affect and unattractive self-identity.

This process model attempts to outline the interactions between innate defensive processes and various affect, cognitive, and behavioural operations that are involved in social anxiety. It is difficult to outline them in clear stages or sequences because they operate as fast integrated processes. Nonetheless, as we will note below, they suggest points for intervention in the therapy of social anxiety.

WHAT DOES AN EVOLUTIONARY APPROACH ADD?

The evolutionary approach helps to clarify why "relationship classification" is key to the process of social anxiety (Trower & Gilbert, 1989). If people see themselves as being with friends and people who care about them, then these submissive defences may be rarely activated; that is, they feel relatively safe and information processing is primarily via safety systems (Gilbert, 1993). Indeed, many of our everyday social anxieties are reduced when we are with caring others or friends. In going to the dance as an adolescent we usually like to go with friends rather than alone. And one element of social anxiety that we sometimes find in the more severe cases is that the person did not have many close or reliable friends in childhood (perhaps as a result of being too anxious to make them). This means there is an interaction between cooperative (alliance formation skills) and rank-orientated dispositions. As will be noted below, treating social anxiety may therefore require work on the nature and skills of friendship (alliance) formation.

Second, even though people may consciously or rationally know that the situation they are going into is unlikely to be very hostile, there can still be a triggering of automatic defences at an "emotional" or "gut" level, suggesting that some brain processes have analysed it that way. This is why people feel a situation to be threatening even when rationally they can see that it probably is not. People may even become angry with themselves for being anxious when they consciously see there is no real need. Rational and conscious beliefs are not necessarily accurate indicators of activated evolved strategies. There is in fact considerable work to suggest that sometimes we do not have access to some of the strategic decisions our brain makes about situations (LeDoux, 1998). This means that some of the decision-making processes above may not be made consciously. Moreover, the brain may make other rapid decisions that do not reach consciousness and are not available for self-report. Theories that rely only on conscious report may be limited.

Third, because evolution theory is rooted in evolved mental mechanisms it can include biological (as opposed to purely psychological) sensitivities. For example, there is good evidence that social signals have fairly direct impacts on physiology, and this has been shown in the role of supportive relationships on immune functions and stress hormones (Uchino et al., 1996) and social threats on 5-HT and cortisol (see Gilbert & McGuire, 1998, for a review; Sapolsky, 1994). Also, mood shifts are associated with physiological changes and can change dispositions for defensive processing of many types. For example, as people become depressed they may also become more socially anxious, more fearful of separation from loved others, and more fearful of dying. In addition, as people become more socially anxious they may become more vulnerable to depression. This evolutionary approach can bridge the psychology/biology divide and help in the recognition that various pathological related "schema" and coping processes are not just from "learning" but are basic to human nature (Gilbert, Bailey & McGuire, 2000).

THERAPY IMPLICATIONS

The therapy implications do not contradict other models (e.g., Bates & Clark, 1998; Clark & Wells, 1995; Rapee & Heimberg, 1997) but extend them by introducing a number of additional elements.

1. It is important to explore how people classify relationships and their position within those that are seen as hierarchical. Various alternative ways of classifying relationships can be explored. When low status or low self-esteem is prominent, it needs to be addressed (Fennell, 1998). If people also feel defeated and unable to reach desired goals they are at risk of depression (Gilbert & Allan, 1998).
2. Discussion of the evolutionary model helps people to understand both the reason for their symptoms and why they are so powerful; it also helps them to depersonalize these symptoms and recognize the intrusion of basic submissive defences into potentially affiliative contexts (e.g., social gatherings). Their social anxiety makes sense and is not just "pathology".
3. When social anxiety revolves around an ability to defend status or to cope with conflicts, then assertive behaviour training may be helpful; but when it concerns the development of friendships then other types of social skills training may be more appropriate. This may involve how to show an interest in others (listening skills) rather than be self-focused or overly trying to impress, and in dating situations it will involve positive assertion rather than submissive behaviour, which may be perceived as unattractive, as discussed earlier. There may also be gender differences, and it is helpful to discuss the issue of competing for attractiveness as this is part of normal social intercourse. For both interventions, exposure and practice may be crucial.
4. As in standard cognitive therapy (Beck et al., 1985; Clark & Wells, 1995; Wells, 1998) the typical negative thoughts about self and others elicited in social situations can be ascertained and challenged. Various techniques such as attention redirection or defocusing (not assuming everyone is focused on the self) can also be helpful.
5. Patients can experience both the fear of the consequences of social interactions (damage to self-presentation, reputation, perceived attractiveness to others) and fear of the emotions elicited in social situations. For some patients the focus is on the damage to a reputation rather than the "fear of fear". If fear of fear dominates the picture then cognitive methods for tolerating negative affect (Dryden, 1995) in social situations may be useful.
6. When the strength of the activation of defensive, submissive strategies increases, social avoidance and concealing (or what cognitive therapists call safety behaviours) also increase. The underlying beliefs can be challenged. There is good evidence that simply helping people to change their cognitive set and reduce or interrupt submissive defence (safety behaviours) can help to produce different, anxiety-disconfirming outcomes (Wells, 1998).

7. Although we have not had space to explore it here, fear of deception is a key issue in some cases. Some very disabled people might find it difficult to trust others even when they are acting in friendly and accepting ways. This "more paranoid" dimension to social anxiety requires separate consideration. Indeed, exploring the fear of deception in getting close to people can be central to severe social anxiety. Some patients are very fearful that getting close to others will expose them to exploitation/rejection.

The evolutionary approach works with each dimension of our defensive strategies: the cognitive elements (e.g., relationship classification, self-other evaluations, issues of deception); the emotion elements (e.g., affect toleration, affect control); and behavioural elements (social avoidance, concealment, assertiveness training and friendship developing skills). If social anxiety is co-morbid with other disorders (such as depression) then these may need to be addressed—and at times a social anxiety will remit as a depression remits. Patients may have social skills but not be able to use them when high defensiveness dominates (Trower et al., 1990).

CONCLUSION

This chapter has suggested that social anxiety originally evolved in contexts where aggression and physical harm were possible (and common) outcomes in social interactions. However, this defensive system (with its effects on arousal, inhibition of outputs and acquisitive behaviour, social communication controls) has been recruited to cope with other sources of social threat, where some kind of evaluation is occurring. This does not mean that all who feel that their status is under threat will become anxious. For example, those with antisocial personalities may be equally sensitive to status threats but usually automatically select aggressive defences. And there is no reason to believe that some people who are socially anxious in one context (e.g., at work) can not be aggressive in another (e.g., to their children). Nor does it mean that those who have felt anxious in social contexts and felt humiliated do not harbour desires for revenge.

The disorder of social anxiety, however, is defined by its behavioural defence. Those who are aggressive to status threats are rarely called socially anxious and are far less likely to engage in avoidance behaviour or other safety behaviours. Clearly for them issues of attractiveness work in different ways. Most socially anxious and phobic people, however, are not only sensitive to social threat in the form of loss of attractiveness (being seen as dull, boring, stupid, timid, or outright odd) but the automatic defences to such threats are submissive strategies. However, these exacerbate the problem, making such people feel even more unattractive, both to themselves and to others. Projection and "mind reading" arise when anxious individuals think that others see (and judge) them in the same negative light as they see themselves. This further drives the anxiety cycle.

Evolutionary theory will only be one approach to the understanding of social anxiety, but it is likely that adequate theories of this potentially debilitating and relatively common problem can be aided with an evolutionary dimension. In this chapter we have tried to illuminate how the issues of evolved natural defences to social threats, the shift to ranking via attractiveness rather than aggression, and the roles of self-consciousness and mind reading contribute to the complex of processes that occur in social anxiety.

REFERENCES

Alden, L. E. & Bieling, P. (1998). Interpersonal consequences of the pursuit of safety. *Behaviour Research & Therapy, 36,* 53–64.

Allan, S. & Gilbert, P. (1995). A social comparison scale: Psychometric properties and relationship to psychopathology. *Personality and Individual Differences, 19,* 293–299.

Allan, S. & Gilbert, P. (1997). Psychopathology and submissive behaviour. *British Journal of Clinical Psychology, 36,* 467–488.

Alpert, J. E., Uebelacker, L. A., McLean, N. E., Nierenberg, A. A., Pava, J. A., Worthington III, J. J., Tedlow, J. R., Rosenbaum, J. F., & Fava, M. (1997). Social phobia, avoidant personality disorder and atypical depression: Co-occurrence and clinical implications. *Psychological Medicine, 27,* 627–633.

Argyle, M. (1991). *Cooperation: The basis of sociability.* London: Routledge.

Arrindell, W. A., Sanderman, R., Hageman, W. J. J. M., Pickersgill, M. J., Kwee, M. G. T., Van der Molen, H. T., & Lingsma, M. M. (1990). Correlates of assertiveness in normal and clinical samples: A multidimensional approach. *Advances in Behaviour Theory and Research, 12,* 153–282.

Barkow, J. H. (1975). Prestige and culture: A biosocial interpretation (with peer review). *Current Anthropology, 16,* 533–572.

Barkow, J. H. (1989). *Darwin, sex and status: Biological approaches to mind and culture.* Toronto: University of Toronto Press.

Baron-Cohen, S. (1997). How to build a baby who can read minds: Cognitive mechanism in mindreading. In S. Baron-Cohen (Ed.), *The maladapted mind: Classic readings in evolutionary psychopathology* (pp. 207–239). Hove, Sussex: Psychology Press.

Bates, A. & Clark, D. M. (1998). A new cognitive treatment for social phobia: A single-case study. *Journal of Cognitive Psychotherapy, 12,* 289–322.

Baumeister, R. F. (1982). A self-presentational view of social phenomena. *Psychological Bulletin, 91,* 3–26.

Baumeister, R. F. & Leary, M. R. (1995). The need to belong: Desire for interpersonal attachments as a fundamental human motivation. *Psychological Bulletin, 117,* 497–529.

Beck, A. T., Emery, G., & Greenberg, R. L. (1985). *Anxiety disorders and phobias: A cognitive approach.* New York: Basic Books.

Burnstein, I. S. (1980). Dominance: A theoretical perspective for ethologists. In D. R. Omark, F. F. Strayer, & D. G. Freedman (Eds.), *Dominance relations: An ethological view of conflict and social interaction* (pp. 71–84). New York: Garland Press.

Buss, D. M. (1999). *Evolutionary psychology: The new science of mind.* Boston, MA: Allyn & Bacon.

Byrne, R. (1995). *The thinking ape: Evolutionary origins of intelligence.* Oxford: Oxford University Press.

Clark, D. M. & Wells, A. (1995). A cognitive model of social phobia. In R. G. Heimberg, M. R. Liebowitz, D. A. Hope, & F. R. Schneier (Eds.), *Social phobia: Diagnosis, assessment and treatment* (pp. 69–93). New York: Guilford Press.

Cooley, C. H. (1964). *Human nature and the social order*. New York: Schocken Books (First published 1902).

Cosmides, L. & Tooby, J. (1992). Cognitive adaptations for social exchange. In J. H. Barkow, L. Cosmides, & J. Tooby (Eds.), *The adapted mind: Evolutionary psychology and the generation of culture* (pp. 193–228). New York: Oxford University Press.

Cox, B. J. & Swinson, R. J. (1995). Assessment and measurement of social phobia. In M. B. Stein (Ed.), *Social phobia: Clinical and research perspectives* (pp. 261–269). Washington, DC: American Psychiatric Press.

cummins, d. d. (1999). Cheater detection is modified by social rank: The impact of dominance on the evolution of cognitive functions. *Evolution and Human Behavior*, *20*, 229–248.

Davidson, J., Turnball, C., Strickland, R., & Belyea, M. (1994). Comparative diagnostic criteria for melancholia and endogenous depression. *Archives of General Psychiatry*, *41*, 506–511.

Dixon, A. K. (1998). Ethological strategies for defence in animal and humans: Their role in some psychiatric disorders. *British Journal of Medical Psychology*, *71*, 417–446.

Dryden, W. (1995). *Brief rational emotive behaviour therapy*. Chichester, Sussex: Wiley.

Duval, S. & Wicklund, R. A. (1972). *A theory of objective self-awareness*. San Diego, CA: Academic Press.

Etcoff, N. (1999). *Survival of the prettiest: The science of beauty*. New York: Doubleday.

Fennell, M. J. V. (1998). Low self-esteem. In N. Tarrier, A. Wells, & G. Haddock (Eds.), *Treating complex cases: The cognitive behavioural approach* (pp. 217–240). Chichester, Sussex: Wiley.

Gilbert, P. (1989). *Human nature and suffering*. Hove, Sussex: Erlbaum.

Gilbert, P. (1992). *Depression: The evolution of powerlessness*. Hove, Sussex: Erlbaum.

Gilbert, P. (1993). Defence and safety: Their function in social behaviour and psychopathology. *British Journal of Clinical Psychology*, *32*, 131–154.

Gilbert, P. (1997a). The evolution of social attractiveness and its role in shame, humiliation, guilt and therapy. *British Journal of Medical Psychology*, *70*, 113–147.

Gilbert, P. (1997b). *Overcoming depression: A self-help guide using cognitive behavioral techniques*. London: Robinsons.

Gilbert, P. (1998a). What is shame? Some core issues and controversies. In P. Gilbert & B. Andrews (Eds.), *Shame: Interpersonal behavior, psychopathology and culture* (pp. 3–38). New York: Oxford University Press.

Gilbert, P. (1998b). Shame and humiliation in the treatment of complex cases. In N. Tarrier, G. Haddock, & A. Wells (Eds.), *Complex cases: The cognitive behavioural approach* (pp. 241–271). Chichester, Sussex: Wiley.

Gilbert, P. (1998c). The evolved basis and adaptive functions of cognitive distortions. *British Journal of Medical Psychology*, *71*, 447–464.

Gilbert, P. (2000a). Varieties of submissive behavior as forms of social defence: Evolution and psychopathology. In L. Sloman & P. Gilbert (Eds.), *Subordination: Evolution and mood disorders*. New York: Erlbaum.

Gilbert, P. (2000b). The relationship of shame, social anxiety and depression: An evolutionary exploration. *Clinical Psychology and Psychotherapy*, *7*, 174–189.

Gilbert, P. & Allan, S. (1998). The role of defeat and entrapment (arrested flight) in depression: An exploration of an evolutionary view. *Psychological Medicine*, *28*, 584–597.

Gilbert, P., Bailey, K., & McGuire, M. (2000). Evolutionary psychotherapy: Principles and outline. In P. Gilbert & K. Bailey (Eds.), *Genes on the couch: Explorations in evolutionary psychotherapy* (pp. 3–27). Hove, Sussex: Psychology Press.

Gilbert, P. & McGuire, M. (1998). Shame, social roles and status: The psychobiological continuum from monkey to human. In P. Gilbert & B. Andrews (Eds.), *Shame: Interpersonal behavior, psychopathology and culture* (pp. 99–125). New York: Oxford University Press.

Gilbert, P., Pehl, J., & Allan, S. (1994). The phenomenology of shame and guilt: An empirical investigation. *British Journal of Medical Psychology*, *67*, 23–36.

Gilbert, P., Price, J. S., & Allan, S. (1995). Social comparison, social attractiveness and evolution: How might they be related? *New Ideas In Psychology*, *13*, 149–165.

Gilbert, P. & Trower, P. (1990). The evolution and manifestation of social anxiety. In W. R. Crozier (Ed.), *Shyness and embarrassment: Perspectives from social psychology* (pp. 144–177). Cambridge: Cambridge University Press.

Goss, K., Gilbert, P., & Allan, S. (1994). An exploration of shame measures: I: The "other as shamer scale". *Personality and Individual Differences*, *17*, 713–717.

Harper, R. C. (1985). Power, dominance and nonverbal behavior: An overview. In S. L. Ellyson & J. F. Dovidio (Eds.), *Power, dominance and nonverbal behavior*. New York: Springer-Verlag.

Higley, J. D., Mehlman, P. T., Higley, S., Fremald, B., Vickers, J., Lindell, S. G., Taub, D. M., Suomi, S. J., & Linnoila, M. (1996). Excessive mortality in young free-ranging male nonhuman primates with low cerebrospinal fluid 5-hydroxyindoleacetic acid concentrations. *Archives of General Psychiatry*, *53*, 537–543.

Hope, D. A., Sigler, K. D., Penn, D. L., & Meier, V. (1998). Social anxiety, recall of interpersonal information and social impact on others. *Journal of Cognitive Psychotherapy*, *12*, 303–322.

Ingram, R. E. (1990). Self–focused attention in clinical disorders: Review and a conceptual model. *Psychological Bulletin*, *107*, 156–176.

Keltner, D. & Harker, L. A. (1998). The forms and functions of the nonverbal signal of shame. In P. Gilbert & B. Andrews (Eds.), *Shame: Interpersonal behavior, psychopathology and culture* (pp. 78–98). New York: Oxford University Press.

Krebs, D. L. & Denton, K. (1997). Social illusions and self-deception: The evolution of biases in person perception. In J. A. Simpson & D. T. Kendrick (Eds.), *Evolutionary social psychology* (pp. 21–47). Mahwah, NJ: Erlbaum.

Larsen, R. J. & Shackelford, T. K. (1996). Gaze avoidance: Personality and social judgments of people who avoid direct face-to-face contact. *Personality and Individual Differences*, *21*, 907–917.

Leary, M. R. (1983). A brief version of the fear of negative evaluation scale. *Personality and Social Psychology Bulletin*, *9*, 371–375.

Leary, M. R. (1995). *Self-presentation: Impression management and interpersonal behavior*. Boulder, CO: Westview Press.

Leary, M. R. & Kowalski, R. M. (1995). *Social anxiety*. New York: Guilford Press.

LeDoux, J. (1998). *The emotional brain*. London: Weidenfeld & Nicolson.

Lewis, M. (1992). *Shame: The exposed self*. New York: The Free Press.

Lewis, M. (1993). The emergence of human emotions. In M. Lewis & J. M. Haviland (Eds.), *Handbook of emotions* (pp. 223–235). New York: Guilford Press.

Mead, G. H. (1934). *Mind, self and society*. Chicago: University of Chicago Press.

McGuire, M. T. & Troisi, A. (1998). *Darwinian psychiatry*. New York: Oxford University Press.

Nesse, R. M. (1990). Evolutionary explanations of emotions. *Human Nature*, *1*, 261–289.

Nesse, R. (1998). Emotional disorders in evolutionary perspective. *British Journal of Medical Psychology*, *71*, 397–416.

Nesse, R. M. & Williams, G. C. (1995). *Evolution and healing: The new science of Darwinian medicine*. London: Weidenfeld & Nicolson.

O'Connell, S. (1998). *Mindreading: How we learn to love and lie*. London: Arrow.

Rapee, R. M. & Heimberg, R. G. (1997). A cognitive behavioral model of anxiety in social phobia. *Behaviour Research and Therapy*, *35*, 741–756.

Sapolsky, R. M. (1990a). Adrenocortical function, social rank and personality among wild baboons. *Biological Psychiatry*, *28*, 862–878.

Sapolsky, R. M. (1990b). Stress in the wild. *Scientific American*, January, 106–113.

Sapolsky, R. M. (1994). Individual differences and the stress response. *Seminars in the Neurosciences, 6*, 261–269.

Sartre, J.-P. (1957). *Being and nothingness.* London: Methuen. (Original work published 1943.)

Scheff, T. J. (1988). Shame and conformity. The deference-emotion system. *American Review of Sociology, 53*, 395–406.

Schuster, B. (1996). Rejection, exclusion, and harassment at work and in schools: An integration of results from research on mobbing, bullying and peer rejection. *European Psychologist, 1*, 293–317.

Schneier, F., Johnson, J., Hornig, C. D., Liebowitz, M. R., & Weissman, M. M. (1992). Social phobia: Comorbidity and morbidity in an epidemiologic sample. *Archives of General Psychiatry, 49*, 282–288.

Scott, J. C. (1990). *Domination and the arts of resistance.* New Haven: Yale University Press.

Simpson, J. A. & Kenrick, D. T. (1997). *Evolutionary social psychology.* Mahwah, NJ: Lawrence Erlbaum.

Tooby, J. & Cosmides, L. (1996). Friendship and the banker's paradox: Other pathways to the evolution of adaptations for altruism. *Proceedings of the British Academy, 88*, 119–143.

Trower, P. & Chadwick, P. (1995). Pathways to defence of the self: A theory of two types of paranoia. *Clinical Psychology: Science and Practice, 2*, 264–278.

Trower, P. & Gilbert, P. (1989). New theoretical conceptions of social anxiety and social phobia. *Clinical Psychology Review, 9*, 19–35.

Trower, P., Gilbert, P., & Sherling, G. (1990). Social anxiety, evolution and self-presentation. An inter-disciplinary perspective. In H. Leitenberg (Ed.), *Handbook of social anxiety* (pp. 11–45). New York: Plenum Press.

Trower, P., Sherling, G., Beech, J., Harrop, C., & Gilbert, P. (1998). The socially anxious perspective in face to face interaction: An experimental comparison. *Clinical Psychology and Psychotherapy: An International Journal of Theory and Practice, 5*, 155–166.

Uchino, B. N., Cacioppo, J. T., & Kiecolt-Glaser, J. K. (1996). The relationship between social support and physiological processes: A review with emphasis on underlying mechanisms and implications for health. *Psychological Bulletin, 119*, 488–531.

Wakefield, J. C. (1999). Evolutionary versus prototype analysis of the concept of disorder. *Journal of Abnormal Psychology, 108*, 374–399 (with commentary, pp. 400–472).

Wells, A. (1998). Cognitive therapy for social phobia. In N. Tarrier, A. Wells, & G. Haddock (Eds.), *Treating complex cases: The cognitive behavioural approach* (pp. 1–26). Chichester, Sussex: Wiley.

Wells, A., Clark, D. M., & Ahmad, S. (1998). How do I look with my mind's eye? Perspective taking in social phobic imagery. *Behaviour Research and Therapy, 36*, 631–634.

Wells, A., Clark, D. M., Salkovskis, P., Ludgate, J., Hackman, A., & Gelder, M. (1995). Social phobia: The role of in-situation safety behaviours in maintaining anxiety and negative beliefs. *Behaviour Therapy, 26*, 153–161.

Wood, J. V., Giordano-Beech, M., Taylor, K. L., Michela, J. L., & Gaus, V. (1994). Strategies of social comparison among people with low self esteem: Self-protection and self-enhancement. *Journal of Personality and Social Psychology, 67*, 713–731.

Wolfe, R. N., Lennox, R. D., & Cutler, B. L. (1986). Getting along and getting ahead: Empirical support for a theory of protective and acquisitive self-presentation. *Journal of Social and Personality Psychology, 50*, 356–361.

Wright, J. C., Giammarino, M., & Parad, H. W. (1986). Social status in small groups: Individual-group similarity and social "misfit". *Journal of Personality and Social Psychology, 50*, 523–536.

Chapter 13

Shyness and Embarrassment Compared: Siblings in the Service of Social Evaluation

Rowland S. Miller

COMPARING EMBARRASSMENT AND SHYNESS
Antecedents
Phenomenology
Physiology
Nonverbal Behavior
Development
Individual Differences
Interactive Effects
SIMILARITIES OF THE STATES
CONCLUSIONS
REFERENCES

Almost anyone reading this chapter has been embarrassed (Miller, 1992, 1996), and most of us have been shy (Carducci, 1999). Indeed, the prevalence of embarrassment and shyness in human social life suggests that central aspects of our dealings with others may be involved in the two states. In fact, embarrassment and shyness may share the same origins, at least in part. Both of them may emerge from the same primal social motive: arguably, neither embarrassment nor self-conscious shyness would exist if people did not care what others thought of them.

On the other hand, one of the two states may generally be adaptive whereas the other is detrimental, and one may be a short-lived emotion whereas the other is a longer-lasting mood. Thus, although they are close relations with much in

International Handbook of Social Anxiety: Concepts, Research and Interventions Relating to the Self and Shyness. Edited by W. Ray Crozier and Lynn E. Alden.
© 2001 John Wiley & Sons Ltd.

common, embarrassment and shyness also seem to be even more distinct than ordinary siblings typically are. They share a parent but little else. Consider them step-siblings—with the same mother but different fathers—who were raised in different homes.

In what follows, I address these assertions and explore the similarities and differences embarrassment and shyness present to an empirically-minded genealogist. Daringly, I will suggest that—unlike shyness—embarrassment is usually advantageous and beneficial, typically serving valuable interactive functions: People who are appropriately embarrassed in the face of adverse circumstances make *better* impressions on others than do those who remain unperturbed (Semin & Manstead, 1982). In contrast, shyness more often impairs social life, interfering with interactions that would be more rewarding if shyness did not intrude. Regrettably, however, shyness is probably the more pervasive state, occurring more often and lasting longer.

To develop these arguments, I compare and contrast the antecedents, feelings, physiology, behavior, developmental origins, dispositional correlates, and interactive effects of embarrassment and shyness. Although the two states spring from the same fundamental sources, they are nevertheless quite different, as we will see.

COMPARING EMBARRASSMENT AND SHYNESS

Embarrassment is an acute state of surprised, awkward abashment and chagrin that results from events that confound our expectations and increase the threat of unwanted evaluations from real or imagined audiences (Miller, 1996). Embarrassed people tend to feel exposed and conspicuous, befuddled and bewildered, and inept and maladroit (Parrott & Smith, 1991; Tangney, Miller, Flicker, & Barlow, 1996). Shy people also feel awkward and ill-at-ease, but are typically anxious and tense instead of flustered and foolish; they also experience worry and dread that does not fit their circumstances (Bruch & Cheek, 1995; van der Molen, 1990). Obviously, both states are uncomfortable, aversive experiences. Why are they so common? What events bring them on?

Antecedents

Both embarrassment and shyness are, first and foremost, *social* experiences that rarely occur when people are completely alone. This aspect of shyness is widely known; indeed, it is always an important component of researchers' conceptualizations of shyness, which usually include both the anxiety shy people feel at the prospect of evaluation from others and the inhibited interactive behavior that shy people display in their dealings with others (Bruch & Cheek, 1995; Leary & Kowalski, 1995). There is more uncertainty about the role of social evaluation in producing embarrassment, but surveys of embarrassing incidents (e.g., Miller,

1992; Stonehouse & Miller, 1994) demonstrate that embarrassment also requires some form of (real or imagined) unwanted attention from others. On occasion, in 2% of their embarrassing experiences (Tangney et al., 1996), people do report becoming embarrassed when no one else is present. However, such episodes always involve either conscious contemplation of what others would think if they were present or an actual threat of imminent discovery (like that felt by a person who realizes, having entered the wrong restroom, that someone else could walk in at any moment). Even when rare "solitary" embarrassments occur, they entail imaginary audiences in which people envision evaluation from others (see Schlenker, 1980).

However, the social events that cause embarrassment are different from those that cause shyness. Embarrassment typically follows *unanticipated*, startling events that threaten to convey some unwanted, usually undesirable, image of oneself to others. More often than not, these are mishaps or misbehavior in which an individual violates a norm of deportment, civility, self-control, or grace (Miller, 1992). In such instances, people may trip and fall, spill their drinks, rip their pants, stall their cars, fart inadvertently, and forget others' names; episodes like these account for almost two-thirds of all embarrassing events (Miller, 1996).

However, not all embarrassed people have misbehaved. Embarrassment can also result when interactions go awry through no fault of one's own, or when innocent targets are made the butt of practical jokes by playful (or malicious) others. More subtly, embarrassment may occur when one is merely associated in others' eyes with someone else who does something embarrassing. In such situations, which I describe as "team embarrassments" (Miller, 1996), people may be abashed by the misbehavior of their partners even when they have personally done nothing wrong. Embarrassment can clearly be thrust upon us by the actions of others and may even occur when we are simply hapless bystanders to others' misdeeds.

Still, in all of these situations, unexpected, surprising events communicate an unwanted, usually unappealing, image of the embarrassed person to others. Whether or not the adverse image is appropriate or justified, embarrassed people typically labor under the reasonable concern that others have suddenly received undesired information about them.

No such damage has been done when shyness occurs. Indeed, the situations that engender shyness are rarely surprising accidents. Instead, they are usually encounters in which people dread unwanted evaluations from others *before anything has happened* to cause such adverse judgements. Moreover, such encounters may be quite ordinary interactive events. Shyness is more common among people who are in unfamiliar settings meeting desirable or high-status others for the first time than it is among people on familiar turf who are interacting with old friends (Leary & Kowalski, 1995); nevertheless, the situations that engender shyness are still commonplace and customary as opposed to notable and extraordinary. Thus, whereas embarrassment is ordinarily a *reaction* to remarkable, atypical events that have done unwanted harm to a person's desired social image, shyness usually results from the *anticipation* of unwanted evaluations that have yet to occur in situations that are more mundane (Asendorpf, 1990; Harris, 1990).

This divergence is a key distinction between embarrassment and shyness in my view, but I should note that a few antecedents of embarrassment do not tidily fit this pattern. For one thing, excessive public attention can cause embarrassment when one's behavior is entirely reputable or, more remarkably, when one is obviously being approved and accepted by one's peers. For instance, people sometimes become embarrassed when they receive excessive public praise (Miller, 1996); too many compliments and too much acclaim can be disconcerting. Simple conspicuousness can be embarrassing, too; people invariably suffer some chagrin when they are picked at random from a crowd and everyone else is asked to stare at them (Lewis, 1995). Relatively few embarrassments—only 3% of our embarrassing episodes—result from such conspicuousness or "overpraise" (Miller, 1996). Nevertheless, such events resemble those that engender shyness in producing aversive arousal in advance of any certain indication of impending disapproval from others.

On the other hand, conspicuousness and overpraise differ from most shyness-evoking events in suddenly making their targets the obvious focus of pronounced, singular inspection from others. Like other embarrassing circumstances, they are startling changes in the course of interaction that make the specter of social evaluation more salient. Conceivably, they have come to evoke embarrassment because, for most people, any sort of conspicuousness has so often been paired with derision and disapproval, especially during adolescence (Miller, 1996).[1] In this sense, then, conspicuousness and overpraise resemble other embarrassing circumstances in being surprising unwanted events.

Thus, the boundaries of the categories of the events that produce embarrassment and shyness may be a bit fuzzy, but the prototypical antecedents of the two states are quite distinct. Both are social phenomena that require the real or imagined presence of others, but embarrassment follows events that portend real damage to a person's image in the eyes of others, whereas shyness precedes and anticipates such events. In keeping with these discrete origins, the two states feel somewhat different as well.

Phenomenology

Embarrassment is characterized by feelings of surprise, exposure, fluster, and chagrin (Miller & Tangney, 1994; Parrott & Smith, 1991). Most embarrassments

---

[1] It is very likely that embarrassment can generalize from one situation to another in such a manner. For instance, people can be embarrassed by merely witnessing someone else's humiliating predicament even when the person is a stranger with no connection to them. Such "empathic embarrassment" tends to be mild but it is recognizably real embarrassment that probably stems from observers' learned aversion to embarrassing circumstances of any sort (Miller, 1987). This generalizability of embarrassment may be another intriguing difference between it and shyness: empathic embarrassment exists, but vicarious shyness does not (Harré, 1990).

are startling. When they occur, people feel unhappily exposed and conspicuous, often expressing the wish that they could escape or hide. They also feel awkward, ungainly, and clumsy, and are suffused with sheepish regret and chagrin. They dread others' judgements, are usually abashed, and are sometimes mortified. The prototype of embarrassment, then, involves startled, awkward sheepishness.

Importantly, these feelings typically strike without warning, washing over people suddenly, but tend to be short-lived; embarrassment lasts for only minutes at a time (Miller & Tangney, 1994). In these and all other respects (as we will see), embarrassment is unquestionably an *emotion*, rather than a mood. Emotions evidence (a) quick onset, (b) brief duration, and (c) unbidden occurrence, and appear to be the result of (d) relatively nonconscious, automatic appraisal (Ekman, 1992); thus, they occur suddenly and spontaneously, without conscious consideration, but last only minutes, not hours or days. Embarrassment displays all of these characteristics and thus is not simply a more diffuse and lasting mood.[2]

In contrast, shyness *is* a *mood* that comprises a discernibly different mix of affects. Shyness often lasts for long periods of time, waxing and waning gradually; it is also mediated by controlled (as opposed to automatic) cognitions and depends on one's conscious construction of a situation as an intimidating environment (Leary & Kowalski, 1990; Schlenker & Leary, 1982). Indeed, to the extent shy people are provided a rationale or interpretation for an interaction that reduces its inherent threat of social evaluation, their shyness is substantially reduced. When Mark Leary (1986b) gave dispositionally shy college students a plausible but groundless external excuse for a conversation to go badly (background noise that was said to be impossibly "loud", but actually was not), they evidenced less arousal and less reticence and behaved in an affable, relaxed style that was no different from that of people who were not shy at all. In short, when they were given a non-threatening way to think about an upcoming interaction, their shyness disappeared. A similar intervention would presumably influence a rush of embarrassment less effectively—"Remember, you will have a good reason for walking in on your mother-in-law in her toilet"—because embarrassment emerges from less conscious, more automatic appraisals of the environment. As an anxious "*future-oriented* mood state" in which one prepares to deal with imminent danger, shyness may be based in part in a perceived lack of control that increases one's seeming peril (Barlow, Chorpita, & Turovsky, 1996, p. 253); thus, any point of view that increases a person's conscious self-presentational efficacy before a threatening interaction begins is likely to ameliorate shyness (Leary & Kowalski, 1995).

Further, whereas embarrassment is a mix of surprise and chagrin, shyness is a blend of fear and excitement that is usually less intense and less negative than embarrassment (Izard & Youngstrom, 1996; Mosher & White, 1981). Shy people are cowed by the dreadful prospect that they will be rejected by others, so they

---

[2] Emotions can also be distinguished by distinctive physiological reactions and characteristic expressive behaviors (Ekman, 1992). As the upcoming discussions of physiology and nonverbal behavior will suggest, embarrassment possesses these emotional markers as well.

are worried and apprehensive. They also tend to be preoccupied with their own imagined inadequacies so that they ruminate about their self-perceived short-comings (van der Molen, 1990; Leary & Kowalski, 1995). Still, as painful as these thoughts and feelings may be, they are ordinarily less keen than the rush of emotion that may overwhelm people when embarrassment strikes. Shyness and embarrassment feel different, and, in keeping with their distinct phenome-nal characters, they may have recognizably different physiological substrates as well.

Physiology

Shyness seems to be a "fight-or-flight" response that activates the sympathetic nervous system (Borkovec, Stone, O'Brien, & Kaloupek, 1974). Autonomic arousal occurs as people become tense and anxious; their heart rates increase, digestion slows, and their hands cool as blood is diverted from their skins to their muscles. There is also greater activity in the right frontal lobe of the brain (Schmidt & Fox, 1998).

Less is known about the physiology of embarrassment, but the existing data suggest that embarrassment evokes similar responses and adds a few more, typically activating both sympathetic and parasympathetic responses (Leary, Rejeski, Britt, & Smith, 1998). Like shyness, embarrassment causes sym-pathetic arousal, alerting and energizing people, and activating the frontal lobes (Devinsky, Hafler, & Victor, 1982); unlike shyness, embarrassment also subse-quently elicits heart rate deceleration, an apparent parasympathetic response (Buck & Parke, 1972). Conceivably, ordinary embarrassment is a two-step pro-cess in which realization of one's predicament causes an initial rush of surprised arousal that is followed by parasympathetic withdrawal as, stupefied and abashed, we try to shrink and hide from our mortifying plights (Frijda, 1986; Leary et al., 1998).

Tentatively, then, shyness and embarrassment may engender distinguishable patterns of physiological activity. Certainly, embarrassment is often accompanied by a remarkable physical signature that shyness does not share: a *blush*. The visible reddening of the cheeks that typifies embarrassment is due to vasodila-tion of facial veins that are equipped with beta-adrenergic receptors that are not commonly found in venous tissue (Mellander, Andersson, Afzelius, & Hellstrand, 1982). As a result, these veins behave differently than other epidermal capil-laries; while other peripheral blood vessels are constricting, facial veins may be dilating, bringing more blood near the surface of the cheeks (Drummond, 1989). People cannot control this reaction, which can be distinguished from the flush-ing that follows exercise or intoxication and is limited to the upper chest, neck, and face—the areas of the body that are most likely to be visible to others (Leary, Britt, Cutlip, & Templeton, 1992).

Why should we be endowed with such a distinctive involuntary capacity? One provocative possibility is that blushing evolved as a reliable communication to others that embarrassment has occurred (Castelfranchi & Poggi, 1990). As an unmistakable signal of a person's chagrin, blushing presumably reassures observers that an embarrassed person recognizes and regrets his or her misbehavior; this helps audiences to distinguish those who are genuinely contrite and worthy of forgiveness from those who are remorseless and who may transgress again.

Thus, arguably, there is a distinctive interpersonal signal of embarrassment because embarrassment is adaptive, and there is no unique signal of shyness because shyness is not. This assertion—that embarrassment is desirable and beneficial but shyness is maladaptive and disadvantageous—is one to which I will return later in the chapter. For now, let me demonstrate that, in keeping with this argument, embarrassment (but not shyness) is easily detectable even in the absence of a blush.

Nonverbal Behavior

There is no particular facial expression that denotes embarrassment, but there is a coherent *sequence* of nonverbal behaviors that distinguishes it from other states. When they become embarrassed, people typically avert their gazes, avoiding eye contact with others (Keltner, 1995), and then try not to smile by biting their lips or pulling down the corners of their mouths. They usually fail, and break into ambivalent, sheepish grins that differ from those of genuine amusement (Asendorpf, 1990). They also bow their heads, cover their faces with a hand (Keltner, 1995), make exaggerated body movements (Edelmann & Hampson, 1981), and make more speech errors (e.g., stammering and stuttering) than they do when they are poised and calm (Edelmann & Hampson, 1979).

This all takes about five seconds (Keltner, 1995), and the pattern makes a person's embarrassment plain to any observer. Indeed, observers can usually tell just how embarrassed someone else is (Marcus & Miller, 1999). In addition, when all of these cues—gaze aversion, smile controls, face touches, and head movements—are present, audiences can reliably distinguish embarrassment from related states such as amusement, shame, and guilt (Keltner, 1995; Keltner & Buswell, 1996).

Shyness does not present such a coherent portrait. When they are shy, people exhibit disaffiliative, avoidant behavior that reduces the immediacy of their contact with others, but they do not consistently display a specific pattern of nonverbal behavior that reliably notifies others that they are shy. They look at others less, smile less, speak less often and converse less responsively, and may even stand further away (Asendorpf, 1990; Leary & Kowalski, 1995), but these are actions that characterize disinterest or dullness, too.

Notably, then, embarrassment has distinctive physical and behavioral concomitants that distinguish it from other states, but shyness does not. Embarrassment appears to be a discrete emotion (Keltner & Buswell, 1997), but shyness is not. (Indeed, some theorists—e.g., Leary, 1986a, and this volume, *Chapter 10*— think that shyness is best considered a *syndrome* that pairs an anxious mood with behavioral avoidance and inhibition.) Still, despite these and the other differences we have noted thus far, embarrassment and shyness are members of the same affective family; thus, they appear to be subject to similar developmental influences.

Development

Shyness is clearly heritable (see Schmidt, Polak, & Spooner, this volume, *Chapter 2*), but it may come in two forms (Buss, 1986; Crozier, 1999): early-developing *fearful shyness*, which underlies the stranger anxiety displayed by very young children (Kagan & Resnick, 1986), and later-developing *self-conscious shyness*, which emerges as children begin to appreciate what others are thinking of them. Toddlers become self-conscious around $1\frac{1}{2}$ or 2 years of age when they are able to recognize themselves in a mirror; at that age, children display their first signs that they are aware of social evaluation (DiBiase & Lewis, 1997). Thereafter, self-conscious shyness continues to develop (see Reddy, this volume, *Chapter 4*, and Lewis, this volume, *Chapter 5*) until it reaches a peak in adolescence.

Embarrassment follows a similar trajectory. Children exhibit no signs of embarrassment before the onset of self-recognition, but behavior that resembles embarrassed sheepishness and abashment can be elicited from them once self-consciousness begins (Lewis, Stanger, Sullivan, & Barone, 1991). However, a mature capacity for embarrassment appears to take years to develop. For instance, 5-year-olds do not become embarrassed (as adults may) by the simple realization that others are aware of their misbehavior; only when they are actually chastized by a critical audience do they show any signs of chagrin (Bennett & Gillingham, 1991). Embarrassment resulting from the mere presence of witnesses in an awkward situation does not begin until youngsters are around 11 years of age (Bennett, 1989), when they finally possess the cognitive maturity and perspective-taking skills to appreciate fully what others may be thinking of them (e.g., Selman, 1976). Susceptibility to indirect predicaments such as "team" embarrassment and empathic embarrassment begins at the same age (Bennett & Cormack, 1996; Bennett, Yuill, Banerjee, & Thomson, 1998). Evidently, children do not experience some of the subtle chagrin that adults do until they are capable of sophisticated perspective-taking and can appreciate what others may be thinking even when those others are merely watching them but saying nothing; only then are they embarrassed by the *assumed* evaluations of others in the fashion of adults.

Thus, like self-conscious shyness, embarrassment seems to emerge from the self-conscious ability to hold oneself as the object of one's attention. Cognitive development also shapes embarrassment, and it may meaningfully influence shyness as well (although few studies have addressed this point). Regardless, embarrassment and shyness are also similar in being molded by socialization and family and peer relations (see Saarni, 1993). Certainly, the interactions of children with their parents and their peers play an important role in determining whether a child's shy behavior gradually fades or is reinforced (Bruch & Cheek, 1995).

In a similar manner, youngsters learn that certain public actions will be met with teasing and ridicule, and they come to dread such transgressions and to be embarrassed by them. Children are tough audiences; whereas adult observers are usually sympathetic and supportive to embarrassed people in their midst (Metts & Cupach, 1989), fifth-graders are much more likely to deride and laugh at another person's embarrassing predicament, doing so more than half the time (Stonehouse & Miller, 1994). Such harsh treatment may be one reason that people come to dread excessive attention from others; among children, becoming the conspicuous object of others' interest may more often lead to disapproval and reproach than to acceptance and approbation. Mere conspicuousness may then become embarrassing: "After hundreds of repetitions, conspicuousness becomes so closely associated with embarrassment that close scrutiny by others can cause embarrassment" all by itself (Buss, 1980, p. 233).

Then, with all of these influences in place, youngsters enter adolescence, an age of dramatic physical and interactive changes that presents challenging new roles and social dilemmas (Buss, 1980). Many teenagers find themselves in strange, ungainly new bodies just as they become keenly concerned with the images they present to the other sex. It may be no surprise, then, that teenagers experience more intense embarrassments than adults do (Miller, 1992), and shyness reaches its peak (Buss, 1980). Certainly, "if God wanted to create a perfect recipe for embarrassment, the teen years might be it" (Miller, 1996, p. 87). Most cases of extreme social anxiety, or social phobia, begin then, too (Stein, Walker, & Forde, 1996), but, fortunately, they occur in many fewer people than do shyness and embarrassment.

Individual Differences

Because shyness and embarrassment are shaped by similar developmental influences, it is not surprising that they share some dispositional roots. Individual differences in susceptibility to embarrassment (or "embarrassability") and shyness are both related to public self-consciousness, so that people who routinely envision what others are thinking of them experience more embarrassment and shyness than do people who are heedless of their public images (Miller, 1995). Importantly, however, both embarrassability and shyness are even more closely related to fear of negative evaluation (Miller, 1995). Shy and embarrassable people worry about rejection from others; they fret about potential social disapproval, and worriedly anticipate unfavorable judgements when they come to others' attention. Thus, they can be said colloquially to be between a rock and a hard place: they are attentive to others' judgements of them, but they dread such evaluations and fear that they are more negative than they really are.

Beyond this common core, however, the individual differences that underlie the two states provide another way to differentiate them. For instance, a person's global level of social skill and communicative competence has much to do with whether or not he or she is shy (Evans, 1993; Jackson, Towson, & Narduzzi, 1997). Compared to those who are not shy, shy people feel more awkward and less proficient in ordinary interactions with others, and they do a poorer job of managing their small talk; in general, they are less adept at rewarding, responsive conversation (Asendorpf, 1990; Manning & Ray, 1993). However, global social skill is unrelated to embarrassability (Miller, 1995); although people who are maladroit tend to be shy and apprehensive before anything goes wrong in social life, they do not manifest more embarrassment after some predicament occurs. Conversely, whereas people who have excellent social skills are unlikely to be shy, they are not immune to embarrassment; the various personal pitfalls and provocations from others that can cause embarrassment often befall them, too.

If instead of treating social skill as a global construct we consider its constituent components (see Riggio, 1986; Spitzberg & Cupach, 1989), there *are* significant relations between embarrassability and certain specific skills (Miller, 1995). People who can flexibly adjust their behavior to fit different situations— who are high in "social control" (Riggio, 1986)—are somewhat less prone to embarrassment than those who are less adept and dexterous. Interactive agility may help people to extricate themselves from embarrassing predicaments with a minimum of distress. Social control accounts for four times more variance in dispositional shyness than in embarrassability, however, and a better predictor of embarrassability is a person's sensitivity to social norms (Miller, 1995). Highly embarrassable people are especially aware of and concerned about the normative appropriateness of their behavior They attend to social rules and dread violations of them, expecting more severe consequences when any transgression occurs. By comparison, people who are less susceptible to embarrassment take a more relaxed view; they are less alert to norms and less apprehensive if any are breached.

Altogether, highly embarrassable people do not seem to stumble and blunder into different types of embarrassing predicaments than the rest of us, but they do react more intensely to those they encounter (Miller, 1992). Their heightened sensitivity to the appropriateness of their behavior, coupled with their chronic dread of what others may be thinking of them, probably leads them to hold themselves to stricter, less forgiving codes of conduct than other people face.

At least they do not dislike themselves as much as shy people tend to do. Poor self-regard is a notable correlate of dispositional shyness; in general, "shy people tend to have fairly extensive problems with low self-esteem" (Cheek & Melchior, 1990, p. 59). Highly embarrassable people also tend to have low self-esteem, but the link is more modest. In fact, the correlation between embarrassability and self-worth disappears completely when fear of negative evaluation—which is also higher among people of low self-esteem—is taken into account (Miller, 1995). This is not true of shyness, which is uniquely related to self-regard above and beyond the influence of fear of negative evaluation (Miller, 1995).

Overall, then, self-conscious shyness and embarrassability seem to share a parent in their self-conscious dread of disregard from others. Both are states born of concern over social evaluation. They have different fathers, however. Shyness emerges from poor interpersonal competence and low self-regard, whereas embarrassment stems from attentiveness to and respect for social norms. Although related, the two states are step-siblings with a shared theme and quite different facets.

Their differences are also evident in the interventions practitioners recommend for those who are extremely shy or unduly embarrassable. Social skills training is ordinarily a centerpiece of efforts to ameliorate shyness (see Henderson & Zimbardo, this volume, *Chapter 19*; van der Molen, 1990), but it is rarely included in therapies for excessive embarrassment. Instead, embarrassment interventions usually focus on the cognitive restructuring of exaggerated fears of social disapproval (e.g., Edelmann, 1990). Cognitive therapies are often recommended for shy people as well, but with a different emphasis; their targets are typically the irrational self-doubt (Glass & Shea, 1986) and anxious self-preoccupation (Alden & Cappe, 1986) that accompany shyness.

Embarrassability and dispositional shyness clearly have much in common, but they can also be distinguished from one another in an intelligible manner: whereas embarrassability hinges on sensitivity to social norms, shyness depends on perceptions of low self-worth and deficient social skills. Of course, respect for a culture's norms is probably adaptive most of the time, whereas nervous self-doubt is not. Perhaps we should not be surprised, then, that—to the extent that states of embarrassment and shyness resemble the traits that influence them—embarrassment is usually adaptive in social life and shyness is not.

Interactive Effects

As we have seen, when people become embarrassed by startling, unwanted events that portray them to others in undesirable ways, they typically blush and/or display a patterned sequence of nonverbal behavior that makes their embarrassment plain to others. Moreover, if they believe that an observer has not noticed their embarrassment, they are more likely to mention it aloud than they would have been had the observer acknowledged their chagrin (Leary, Landel, & Patton, 1996). Thus, either because people's embarrassment is unmistakable (see Marcus & Miller, 1999) or because they actually inform others of their distress, observers usually know when someone becomes embarrassed.

Thereafter, though they may seem to be in disarray, embarrassed people usually manage to respond to their predicaments in ways that are reassuring to others. Disconcerted and flustered, embarrassed people occasionally just leave without explanation. More rarely (and almost always when they believe that others have intentionally created their difficulties), they angrily counterattack. Most of the time, however, embarrassed people behave in humble, conciliatory, or playful manners that are comforting and pleasing to their audiences (Cupach & Metts, 1990, 1992; Miller, 1996).

For instance, the two most frequent responses to embarrassing circumstances are (a) efforts to repair any damage or inconvenience that was caused and (b) outright apologies in which people express regret for their misbehavior and offer assurances of better conduct in the future (Miller, 1996). Another frequent response is humor, which is especially likely after physical pratfalls or failures of self-control such as inadvertent belches (Cupach & Metts, 1992); people may acknowledge their transgressions—and perhaps show that they are uninjured—by lightheartedly making jokes at their own expense.

Moreover, while they are trying to regain others' approval, embarrassed people are especially friendly, helpful, and eager to please (see Apsler, 1975). In general, embarrassment usually motivates polite, accommodating, and amicable behavior.

Importantly, this style of behavior usually succeeds in impressing others favorably. Displays of appropriate embarrassment do not rouse rejection and make matters worse; instead, they ordinarily elicit acceptance and support from others (Edelmann, 1982). After some misbehavior occurs, observers actually view those who respond with flustered chagrin more favorably than they view those who somehow remain implacable and unperturbed (Semin & Manstead, 1982). If their children seem embarrassed after some misbehavior, for instance, parents levy less punishment than the children get when they do not seem abashed by their actions (Semin & Papadopoulou, 1990). Remarkably, when we are in embarrassing situations, *"others will like us and treat us better if we do become embarrassed* than they will if we remain unruffled, cool, and calm" (Miller, 1996, p. 152).

This result is consistent with the possibility that embarrassment functions in social life as a reliable gesture of appeasement—a nonverbal apology—that helps to forestall disapproval and rejection from others (Keltner & Buswell, 1997). By communicating that a transgressor is aware of—and regrets—his or her misbehavior, visible embarrassment may reassure audiences of the person's good intentions. As a result, audiences can afford to remain tolerant of, and dismiss as aberrant, behavior that would otherwise be worrisome.

So it is that adults who witness someone's embarrassment usually react in *supportive, kindly* ways to the abashed person (Metts & Cupach, 1989). Adolescent audiences are less compassionate, as I noted earlier, but adult observers usually respond to others' embarrassments with empathy, explicit reassurance, or friendly humor (Metts & Cupach, 1989). Only rarely do adults respond to a person's obvious embarrassment with criticism, rebuke, or malicious laughter, and even when they do say something that increases a hapless person's embarrassment, they usually have friendly intentions (Sharkey, 1993).

The same cannot be said of shyness and the reactions it engenders from others. Shy people interact with others in an impoverished manner (Asendorpf, 1990); they either avoid others altogether or behave in an inhibited, guarded fashion that is likely to seem either aloof or timid. Instead of eliciting sympathy, this unfriendly, unrewarding behavior is more likely to elicit "neglect, rejection, or victimization (e.g., bullying)" (Bruch & Cheek, 1995, p. 174). Indeed, over time, shy people make new friends much more slowly and fall in love much less often than those who are not shy (Asendorpf & Wilpers, 1998). They also tend to be more lonely (Dill & Anderson, 1999). Ironically, then, in doubting themselves and acting on their fears of social disapproval before anything has gone wrong, shy people sometimes elicit from others the very disapproval they dreaded in the first place.

In contrast, by communicating concerned chagrin *after* surprising miscues have occurred, embarrassed people reassure others and avoid rejection. Embarrassment is a desirable, useful response to real threats, whereas shyness is an undesirable response to imagined potential threats. Thus, embarrassment is usually adaptive, but shyness is usually not.

SIMILARITIES OF THE STATES

Embarrassment and shyness are obviously quite distinct. They emerge from recognizably different social antecedents, create different feelings, engender divergent reactions, and elicit dissimilar responses from others, as Table 13.1 shows.

Nonetheless, embarrassment deserves mention in this *Handbook* because it shares a familial bond with shyness. Embarrassment develops hand-in-hand with children's understanding of others' evaluations of them, and embarrassability covaries with fear of negative evaluation and a concern for the appropriateness of one's behavior. The events that cause embarrassment entail actual or imminent damage to one's desired image in the eyes of others. There is little doubt (for these and additional reasons; see Miller, 1996) that embarrassment is a social-evaluative emotion that exists because people care what others think of them.

Shyness, of course, is also a social-evaluative state (Schlenker & Leary, 1982). Neither self-conscious shyness nor embarrassment would occur if people were

Table 13.1 Distinguishing embarrassment and shyness

Characteristic	Embarrassment	Shyness
Antecedent	Disrupted interaction	Normal interaction
Phenomenology	Startled chagrin	Nervous trepidation
Nature of state	Emotion	Mood
Cognitive source	Automatic appraisal	Controlled cognition
Timing	Abrupt and reactive: after predicaments occur	Gradual and anticipatory: before predicaments occur
Duration	Short-lived	Long-lived
Onset of mature form	Early adolescence	Infancy (fearful shyness) or early adolescence (self-conscious shyness)
Behavioral sequelae	Apologetic conciliation	Inhibited disaffiliation
Interactive result (in moderation)	Sympathy and acceptance	Mild disapproval
Proximal cause	Social-evaluative concern	Social-evaluative concern
Evolutionary verdict	Adaptive	Maladaptive

genuinely heedless of the judgements of others, and it is this core characteristic that links the two states.

Why should the stray opinions of strangers have such power to affect our moods and emotions? A plausible evolutionary explanation suggests that social concerns such as these emerged in an era in which survival depended on one's ability to maintain satisfactory relations with one's fellows (see Baumeister & Tice, 1990; and Gilbert & Trower, this volume, *Chapter 12*). When early humans lived in small tribal groups, social rejection was a fearsome prospect. Those who were forced to live alone were much less likely to survive and reproduce. Selective pressures would have favored psychological mechanisms that (a) alerted people to worrisome events that could lead to abandonment by others, and (b) provided helpful means to forestall or prevent such ostracism or exclusion. Social anxieties such as shyness that fostered a cautious approach to important interactions, and emotions such as embarrassment that alerted people to miscues and motivated reparative responses, may have been such mechanisms. Both were aversive, but both were evolutionarily advantageous.

But why, then, do I and others now suggest that "whereas embarrassment is a proper emotion and indeed a mark of certain virtue, shyness is verging on the pathological" (Harré, 1990, p. 198)? The answer lies in the ranges of situations in which the two states occur. Reasonable concern over social evaluation is still a useful commodity in social life. Even social anxiety (in low, manageable doses) is desirable in many situations; after all, anxiety is a normal response to intimidating challenges (Izard & Youngstrom, 1996). As Leary suggests in this volume (*Chapter 10*), innocuous caution in social situations can ward off potential disapproval. However, the fear, worry, and awkwardness of shyness are usually exaggerated responses to the unfamiliar but benign situations in which they occur. By definition, shyness is wariness and dread that is disproportional to the actual magnitude of the threat one faces. Further, because it occurs in ordinary, unremarkable situations, shyness is probably much more prevalent in social life than embarrassment.

Embarrassment can be blown out of proportion, too, but it is probably adaptive over a wider range of intensity. Even high embarrassability that exaggerates one's reactions to a given predicament does not inhibit or impair normal behavior to the same extent as high shyness in advance of any evaluation. However, excessive embarrassability *is* costly. Those who are very susceptible to embarrassment probably overreact to trivial events, becoming disconcerted by situations that would not faze the rest of us. This is problematic because, in contrast to appropriate, measured embarrassment in response to a predicament (which makes good impressions on observers), excessive fluster and agitation (such as running away in panic) make bad impressions (Levin & Arluke, 1982).

Excessive embarrassability is also associated with *chronic blushing* that occurs in public settings in the absence of any overt predicament (Leary & Meadows, 1991). Chronic blushers frequently find themselves blushing in ordinary situations that involve innocent contact with others, and they may come to dread their blushing episodes so much, and avoid interaction with others so thoroughly, that they meet the diagnostic criteria for social phobia (Edelmann, 1990). Of course, they are almost always shy.

Exaggerated fear of embarrassment, which is one of the defining characteristics of social phobia (American Psychiatric Association, 1994), can also be troublesome. Almost everybody avoids embarrassment when possible, but some people go to extraordinary lengths to steer clear of situations that hold any potential for embarrassment (Miller, 1996). This sometimes entails personal risk, as people avoid using condoms, avoid pelvic or prostate examinations, or even forgo psychotherapy in order to avoid embarrassment.

Still, chronic blushing and immoderate fear of embarrassment are not really examples of embarrassment run amok. Chronic blushers are typically socially anxious but *not* embarrassed until their blushing starts; only after their public loss of control makes them feel conspicuous do they ordinarily begin to feel abashed (Edelmann, 1990). Similarly, those who fear embarrassment in advance of any predicament are manifesting anticipatory anxiety and not embarrassment at all. Like those who are shy, they are using anxious, avoidant coping to deal with threats that have not occurred and possibly never will.

Indeed, in order to properly distinguish shyness and other social anxieties from embarrassment, we should remember that any event that causes embarrassment will also arouse social anxiety if it can be foreseen. (The converse is not true: many circumstances that cause shyness are not embarrassing at all.) Although embarrassment occasionally ensues, the difficulties faced by chronic blushers and those who fear embarrassment are rooted in anticipatory social anxiety, not embarrassment. Still, the very existence of these problems is another reminder that, despite their differences, shyness and embarrassment are members of the same affective family. They serve the same social-evaluative master.

We should also not forget that *too little* shyness or embarrassment may also be dysfunctional. People who are without shyness or who cannot be embarrassed—who are either always certain that they are being judged in a desired fashion or who care not at all what others think (Leary & Kowalski, 1995)—have a disability that is relatively unlikely to come to the notice of clinicians and researchers, but they are handicapped, nonetheless. They lack a feedback mechanism that would help them to avoid needless social disapproval, and they may seem narcissistic, ruthless, or arrogant to others. In particular, people who cannot be embarrassed may seem to lack a conscience; emerging evidence suggests that they are more likely than others to be antisocial psychopaths (Miller, 1999).

In short, there is probably a curvilinear, inverted "U" relation between both social anxiety and embarrassability and personal adjustment, and this is an important similarity underlying the two dispositions. Low-to-moderate levels of both are normal and adaptive, but as one's worries about others' judgements either become excessive or vanish completely, difficulty follows. The social anxiety manifested as shyness is usually undesirable, and it has a longer reach than embarrassment, occurring much more often. Still, the motive from which it springs is beneficial, and we would be much worse off without it.

CONCLUSIONS

Humans are clearly equipped with psychological mechanisms that prepare us to monitor and react to social evaluation. Shyness and embarrassment are two such states, and they are recognizably kin to one another, born of the same fundamental human motivation to be accepted by others (see Baumeister & Leary, 1995). In moderation, neither is necessarily problematic, and both may be dysfunctional when they are extremely low or excessively high.

However, even when it is moderate, shyness differs from embarrassment, which is desirable over a wider range. Embarrassment is typically a profitable, adaptive reaction to the inevitable predicaments of social life, whereas shyness interferes with fulfilling interaction. Shyness is an anticipatory mood state, whereas embarrassment is an emotion elicited by events that have already occurred. The two states feel different and engender different types of behavior; shyness is characterized by inhibition and avoidance whereas embarrassment is typified by conciliation and remediation. The two are undoubtedly members of the same extended family, but students of social life will do well to distinguish them clearly: someone who is rarely shy may be admirable but someone who is never embarrassed "is lacking some important human quality, is insensitive, thoughtless, or uncaring, a 'brazen hussy' or an 'arrogant son of a bitch' " (Crozier, 1990, p. 7).

REFERENCES

Alden, L. E. & Cappe, R. (1986). Interpersonal process training for shy clients. In W. H. Jones, J. M. Cheek, & S. R. Briggs (Eds.), *Shyness: Perspectives on research and treatment* (pp. 343–355). New York: Plenum.

American Psychiatric Association (1994). *Diagnostic and statistical manual of mental disorders* (4th edn.). Washington, DC: Author.

Apsler, R. (1975). Effects of embarrassment on behavior toward others. *Journal of Personality and Social Psychology, 32*, 145–153.

Asendorpf, J. B. (1990). The expression of shyness and embarrassment. In W. R. Crozier (Ed.), *Shyness and embarrassment: Perspectives from social psychology* (pp. 87–118). Cambridge: Cambridge University Press.

Asendorpf, J. B. & Wilpers, S. (1998). Personality effects on social relationships. *Journal of Personality and Social Psychology, 74*, 1531–1544.

Barlow, D. H., Chorpita, B. F., & Turovsky, J. (1996). Fear, panic, anxiety, and disorders of emotion. In D. A. Hope (Ed.), *Perspectives on anxiety, panic, and fear* (pp. 251–328). Lincoln, NE: University of Nebraska Press.

Baumeister, R. F. & Leary, M. R. (1995). The need to belong: Desire for interpersonal attachments as a fundamental human motivation. *Psychological Bulletin, 117*, 497–529.

Baumeister, R. F. & Tice, D. M. (1990). Anxiety and social exclusion. *Journal of Social and Clinical Psychology, 9*, 165–195.

Bennett, M. (1989). Children's self-attribution of embarrassment. *British Journal of Developmental Psychology, 7*, 207–217.

Bennett, M. & Cormack, C. (1996). Age and embarrassment at others' gaffes. *Journal of Social Psychology, 136*, 113–115.

Bennett, M. & Gillingham, K. (1991). The role of self-focused attention in children's attributions of social emotions to the self. *Journal of Genetic Psychology, 152,* 303–309.

Bennett, M., Yuill, N., Banerjee, R., & Thomson, S. (1998). Children's understanding of extended identity. *Developmental Psychology, 34,* 322–331.

Borkovec, T. D., Stone, N., O'Brien, G., & Kaloupek, D. (1974). Identification and measurement of anxiety in an analogue social situation. *Journal of Consulting and Clinical Psychology, 44,* 157–161.

Bruch, M. A. & Cheek, J. M. (1995). Developmental factors in childhood and adolescent shyness. In R. G. Heimberg, M. R. Liebowitz, D. A. Hope, & F. R. Schneier (Eds.), *Social phobia: Diagnosis, assessment, and treatment* (pp. 163–182). New York: Guilford Press.

Buck, R. W. & Parke, R. D. (1972). Behavioral and physiological response to the presence of a friendly or neutral person in two types of stressful situations. *Journal of Personality and Social Psychology, 24,* 143–153.

Buss, A. H. (1980). *Self-consciousness and social anxiety.* San Francisco: W. H. Freeman.

Buss, A. H. (1986). A theory of shyness. In W. H. Jones, J. M. Cheek, & S. R. Briggs (Eds.), *Shyness: Perspectives on research and treatment* (pp. 39–46). New York: Plenum.

Carducci, B. J. (1999). *Shyness: A bold new approach: The latest scientific findings, plus practical steps for finding your comfort zone.* New York: HarperCollins.

Castelfranchi, C. & Poggi, I. (1990). Blushing as a discourse: Was Darwin wrong? In W. R. Crozier (Ed.), *Shyness and embarrassment: Perspectives from social psychology* (pp. 230–251). Cambridge: Cambridge University Press.

Cheek, J. M. & Buss, A. H. (1981). Shyness and sociability. *Journal of Personality and Social Psychology, 41,* 330–339.

Cheek, J. M. & Melchior, L. A. (1990). Shyness, self-esteem, and self-consciousness. In H. Leitenberg (Ed.), *Handbook of social and evaluation anxiety* (pp. 47–82). New York: Plenum.

Crozier, W. R. (1990). Introduction. In W. R. Crozier (Ed.), *Shyness and embarrassment: Perspectives from social psychology* (pp. 1–15). Cambridge: Cambridge University Press.

Crozier, W. R. (1999). Individual differences in childhood shyness: Distinguishing fearful and self-conscious shyness. In L. A. Schmidt & J. Schulkin (Eds.), *Extreme fear, shyness, and social phobia: Origins, biological mechanisms, and clinical outcomes* (pp. 14–29). New York: Oxford University Press.

Cupach, W. R. & Metts, S. (1990). Remedial processes in embarrassing predicaments. In J. Anderson (Ed.), *Communication yearbook 13* (pp. 323–352). Newbury Park, CA: Sage.

Cupach, W. R. & Metts, S. (1992). The effects of type of predicament and embarrassability on remedial responses to embarrassing situations. *Communication Quarterly, 40,* 149–161.

Devinsky, O., Hafler, D. A., & Victor, J. (1982). Embarrassment as the aura of a complex partial seizure. *Neurology, 32,* 1284–1285.

DiBiase, R. & Lewis, M. (1997). The relation between temperament and embarrassment. *Cognition and Emotion, 11,* 259–271.

Dill, J. C. & Anderson, C. A. (1999). Loneliness, shyness, and depression: The etiology and interrelationships of everyday problems in living. In T. Joiner & J. C. Coyne (Eds.), *The interactional nature of depression* (pp. 93–125). Washington, DC: American Psychological Association Press.

Drummond, P. D. (1989). Mechanism of social blushing. In N. W. Bond & D. A. T. Siddle (Eds.), *Psychobiology: Issues and applications* (pp. 363–370). Amsterdam: Elsevier Science.

Edelmann, R. J. (1982). The effect of embarrassed reactions upon others. *Australian Journal of Psychology, 34,* 359–367.

Edelmann, R. J. (1990). *Coping with blushing.* London: Sheldon Press.

Edelmann, R. J. & Hampson, R. J. (1979). Changes in non-verbal behaviour during embarrassment. *British Journal of Social and Clinical Psychology, 18,* 385–390.

Edelmann, R. J. & Hampson, R. J. (1981). The recognition of embarrassment. *Personality and Social Psychology Bulletin, 7,* 109–116.

Ekman, P. (1992). An argument for basic emotions. *Cognition and Emotion, 6,* 169–200.

Evans, M. A. (1993). Communicative competence as a dimension of shyness. In K. H. Rubin & J. B. Asendorpf (Eds.), *Social withdrawal, inhibition, and shyness in childhood* (pp. 189–212). Hillsdale, NJ: Erlbaum.

Frijda, N. H. (1986). *The emotions.* New York: Cambridge University Press.

Glass, C. R. & Shea, C. A. (1986). Cognitive therapy for shyness and social anxiety. In W. H. Jones, J. M. Cheek, & S. R. Briggs (Eds.), *Shyness: Perspectives on research and treatment* (pp. 315–327). New York: Plenum.

Harré, R. (1990). Embarrassment: A conceptual analysis. In W. R. Crozier (Ed.), *Shyness and embarrassment: Perspectives from social psychology* (pp. 181–204). Cambridge: Cambridge University Press.

Harris, P. R. (1990). Shyness and embarrassment in psychological theory and ordinary language. In W. R. Crozier (Ed.), *Shyness and embarrassment: Perspectives from social psychology* (pp. 59–86). Cambridge: Cambridge University Press.

Izard, C. E. & Youngstrom, E. A. (1996). The activation and regulation of fear and anxiety. In D. A. Hope (Ed.), *Perspectives on anxiety, panic, and fear* (pp. 1–59). Lincoln, NE: University of Nebraska Press.

Jackson, T., Towson, S., & Narduzzi, K. (1997). Predictors of shyness: A test of variables associated with self-presentational models. *Social Behavior and Personality, 25,* 149–154.

Kagan, J. & Reznick, J. S. (1986). Shyness and temperament. In W. H. Jones, J. M. Cheek, & S. R. Briggs (Eds.), *Shyness: Perspectives on research and treatment* (pp. 81–90). New York: Plenum.

Keltner, D. (1995). Signs of appeasement: Evidence for the distinct displays of embarrassment, amusement, and shame. *Journal of Personality and Social Psychology, 68,* 441–454.

Keltner, D. & Buswell, B. N. (1996). Evidence for the distinctness of embarrassment, shame, and guilt: A study of recalled antecedents and facial expressions of emotion. *Cognition and Emotion, 10,* 155–171.

Keltner, D. & Buswell, B. N. (1997). Embarrassment: Its distinct form and appeasement functions. *Psychological Bulletin, 122,* 250–270.

Leary, M. R. (1986a). Affective and behavioral components of shyness: Implications for theory, measurement, and research. In W. H. Jones, J. M. Cheek, & S. R. Briggs (Eds.), *Shyness: Perspectives on research and treatment* (pp. 27–38). New York: Plenum.

Leary, M. R. (1986b). The impact of interactional impediments on social anxiety and self-presentation. *Journal of Experimental Social Psychology, 22,* 122–135.

Leary, M. R., Britt, T. W., Cutlip, W. D., II, & Templeton, J. L. (1992). Social blushing. *Psychological Bulletin, 112,* 446–460.

Leary, M. R. & Kowalski, R. M. (1990). Impression management: A literature review and two-component model. *Psychological Bulletin, 107,* 34–47.

Leary, M. R. & Kowalski, R. M. (1995). *Social anxiety.* New York: Guilford Press.

Leary, M. R., Landel, J. L., & Patton, K. M. (1996). The motivated expression of embarrassment following a self-presentational predicament. *Journal of Personality, 64,* 619–636.

Leary, M. R. & Meadows, S. (1991). Predictors, eliciters, and concomitants of social blushing. *Journal of Personality and Social Psychology, 60,* 254–262.

Leary, M. R., Rejeski, W. J., Britt, T., & Smith, G. E. (1998). *Physiological and affective differences between anticipated and unanticipated embarrassment.* Unpublished manuscript.

Levin, J. & Arluke, A. (1982). Embarrassment and helping behavior. *Psychological Reports, 51,* 999–1002.

Lewis, M. (1995). Embarrassment: The emotion of self-exposure and evaluation. In J. P.

Tangney & K. W. Fischer (Eds.), *Self-conscious emotions: The psychology of shame, guilt, embarrassment, and pride* (pp. 198–218). New York: Guilford Press.

Lewis, M., Stanger, C., Sullivan, M. W., & Barone, P. (1991). Changes in embarrassment as a function of age, sex and situation. *British Journal of Developmental Psychology, 9,* 485–492.

Manning, P. & Ray, G. (1993). Shyness, self-confidence, and social interaction. *Social Psychology Quarterly, 56,* 178–192.

Marcus, D. K. & Miller, R. S. (1999). The perception of "live" embarrassment: A social relations analysis of class presentations. *Cognition and Emotion, 13,* 105–117.

Mellander, S., Andersson, P., Afzelius, L., & Hellstrand, P. (1982). Neural beta-adrenergic dilatation of the facial vein in man: Possible mechanism in emotional blushing. *Acta Physiologica Scandinavica, 114,* 393–399.

Metts, S. & Cupach, W. R. (1989). Situational influence on the use of remedial strategies in embarrassing predicaments. *Communication Monographs, 56,* 151–162.

Miller, R. S. (1987). Empathic embarrassment: Situational and personal determinants of reactions to the embarrassment of another. *Journal of Personality and Social Psychology, 53,* 1061–1069.

Miller, R. S. (1992). The nature and severity of self-reported embarrassing circumstances. *Personality and Social Psychology Bulletin, 18,* 190–198.

Miller, R. S. (1995). On the nature of embarrassability: Shyness, social evaluation, and social skill. *Journal of Personality, 63,* 315–339.

Miller, R. S. (1996). *Embarrassment: Poise and peril in everyday life.* New York: Guilford Press.

Miller, R. S. (1999, August). *Embarrassment, shame, and misbehavior.* Paper presented at the meeting of the American Psychological Association, Boston.

Miller, R. S. & Tangney, J. P. (1994). Differentiating embarrassment and shame. *Journal of Social and Clinical Psychology, 13,* 273–287.

Mosher, D. L. & White, B. B. (1981). On differentiating shame and shyness. *Motivation and Emotion, 5,* 61–74.

Parrott, W. G. & Smith, S. F. (1991). Embarrassment: Actual vs. typical cases, classical vs. prototypical representations. *Cognition and Emotion, 5,* 467–488.

Riggio, R. E. (1986). Assessment of basic social skills. *Journal of Personality and Social Psychology, 51,* 649–660.

Saarni, C. (1993). Socialization of emotion. In M. Lewis & J. Haviland (Eds.), *Handbook of emotions* (pp. 435–446). New York: Guilford Press.

Schlenker, B. R. (1980). *Impression management: The self-concept, social identity, and interpersonal relations.* Monterey, CA: Brooks/Cole.

Schlenker, B. R. & Leary, M. R. (1982). Social anxiety and self-presentation: A conceptualization and model. *Psychological Bulletin, 92,* 641–669.

Schmidt, L. A. & Fox, N. A. (1998). The development and outcomes of childhood shyness: A multiple psychophysiologic measure approach. In R. Vasta (Ed.), *Annals of child development* (Vol. 13, pp. 1–20). London: Jessica Kingsley.

Selman, R. L. (1976). Social-cognitive understanding: A guide to educational and clinical practice. In T. Lickona (Ed.), *Moral development and behavior* (pp. 299–316). New York: Holt, Rinehart & Winston.

Semin, G. R. & Manstead, A. S. R. (1982). The social implications of embarrassment displays and restitution behavior. *European Journal of Social Psychology, 12,* 367–377.

Semin, G. R. & Papadopoulou, K. (1990). The acquisition of reflexive social emotions: The transmission and reproduction of social control through joint action. In G. Duveen & B. Lloyd (Eds.), *Social representations and the development of knowledge* (pp. 107–125). Cambridge: Cambridge University Press.

Sharkey, W. F. (1993). Who embarrasses whom? Relational and sex differences in the use of intentional embarrassment. In P. J. Kalbfleisch (Ed.), *Interpersonal communication: Evolving interpersonal relationships* (pp. 147–168). Hillsdale, NJ: Erlbaum.

Spitzberg, B. H. & Cupach, W. R. (1989). *Handbook of interpersonal competence research.* New York: Springer-Verlag.

Stein, M. B., Walker, J. R., & Forde, D. R. (1996). Public speaking fears in a community sample: Prevalence, impact on functioning, and diagnostic classification. *Archives of General Psychiatry, 53,* 169–174.

Stonehouse, C. M. & Miller, R. S. (1994, July). *Embarrassing circumstances, week by week.* Paper presented at the meeting of the American Psychological Society, Washington, DC.

Tangney, J. P., Miller, R. S., Flicker, L., & Barlow, D. H. (1996). Are shame, guilt, and embarrassment distinct emotions? *Journal of Personality and Social Psychology, 70,* 1256–1264.

van der Molen, H. T. (1990). A definition of shyness and its implications for clinical practice. In W. R. Crozier (Ed.), *Shyness and embarrassment: Perspectives from social psychology* (pp. 255–285). Cambridge: Cambridge University Press.

Chapter 14

Blushing

Robert J. Edelmann

BLUSHING AND EMBARRASSMENT
Situations Evoking Blushing
THE NATURE OF BLUSHING: PHYSIOLOGICAL ASPECTS
THEORETICAL EXPLANATIONS FOR BLUSHING
Blushing as Appeasement
Blushing as Affiliation
Social Evaluative Account
INDIVIDUAL VARIATION IN BLUSHING
Age and Blushing
Gender and Blushing
Cultural Differences in Blushing
Individual Differences in Blushing Propensity
CHRONIC BLUSHING AND SOCIAL PHOBIA
FUTURE DIRECTIONS
ACKNOWLEDGEMENTS
REFERENCES

Charles Darwin (1872/1998, p. 310), writing more than a century ago, commented:

> Blushing is the most peculiar and most human of human expressions. Monkeys redden from passion but it would take an overwhelming amount of evidence to make us believe that any animal can blush.

Using both his own and the observations of others Darwin noted that:

> The young blush more freely than the old but not during infancy;
> The blind do not escape; The tendency to blush is inherited;
> In most cases the face, ears and neck are the sole parts which redden.

International Handbook of Social Anxiety: Concepts, Research and Interventions Relating to the Self and Shyness. Edited by W. Ray Crozier and Lynn E. Alden.
© 2001 John Wiley & Sons Ltd.

He also concluded (p. 319) that:

> The facts now given are sufficient to show that blushing, whether or not there is any change in colour, is common to most, probably to all, of the races of man.

Given Darwin's eloquent account of blushing and his remarkable insights into such a fascinating human expression, it is perhaps surprising that serious scientific investigations of many of the issues he raised has only occurred within the past two decades. Writing in 1992, Leary, Britt, Cutlip, and Templeton comment that "despite its apparent universality, little scientific attention has been devoted to blushing" (p. 446). Indeed, not only is the physiological mechanism that mediates blushing still poorly understood to date (Drummond, 1997), but many questions remain as to the exact function that blushing might serve. Two recent excellent reviews of the blushing and embarrassment literature (Keltner & Buswell, 1997; Leary et al., 1992) highlight these and other central issues. They also serve to illustrate the fact that mainstream social science research has only recognized within the past 10 to 15 years the importance of blushing and embarrassment to both emotion research and human social functioning.

Leary et al. and Keltner and Buswell focus upon differing issues in their reviews, and these are drawn together in the current chapter. In addition, the chapter incorporates additional material both with regard to physiological aspects of blushing and chronic blushing. The latter is particularly pertinent given both the overall theme of this volume relating as it does to social anxiety and my own recent research interest concerning chronic blushing and the role of skin temperature changes in relation to social phobia.

The chapter is organized into five central sections, discussing the relationship between embarrassment and blushing, physiological aspects of blushing, theoretical accounts of blushing, individual variations in blushing, and blushing in relation to social anxiety/phobia.

BLUSHING AND EMBARRASSMENT

In one study, 95% of respondents indicated that they rarely, if ever, blushed when they were alone (Leary & Meadows, 1991); other studies report similar findings (Tangney, Miller, Flicker, & Barlow, 1996). This highlights the fact that blushing is a social phenomenon. In this context, a number of authors have argued that the blush is the primary nonverbal signal of embarrassment (Buss, 1980; Castelfranchi & Poggi, 1990; Darwin, 1872/1998) and, indeed, blushing has been described as the hallmark of embarrassment (Buss, 1980). Miller (1996, p. 135) contends that:

> There are a variety of expressive signals that may reliably inform bystanders that someone is embarrassed, and foremost among them is the most dramatic, most peculiar, and most uncontrollable of them all: The blush.

A number of experimental studies have also shown blushing to be a core component of embarrassment (Edelmann & Hampson, 1981; Keltner, 1995). However, reports of blushing during embarrassment show considerable variation, ranging from 21% in a sample of Spanish students (Edelmann et al., 1989) to 92% in a sample of US students (Miller & Tangney, 1994).

In this context is it interesting to note that while both experimental and observational studies show that blushing frequently accompanies actually experienced embarrassment, blushing is *assumed* by respondents to be a feature which is typical of embarrassment; that is, it is assumed that blushing is virtually always present in association with embarrassment. Thus, Parrott and Smith (1991) found that while 58% of respondents mentioned blushing as occurring during an actual embarrassing episode, 89% assumed that blushing was typical of embarrassment. It may then be the case that retrospective reports of blushing which are not specifically targeted towards an actual blushing/embarrassing episode may reflect stereotypical culture-specific accounts of blushing rather than providing a true reflection of actual blushing.

In contrast to the assumption that blushing and embarrassment are one and the same, others have argued that blushing accompanies other emotional states, such as shame and anger, and therefore does not uniquely signal embarrassment (Lewis, 1993). In a similar vein, Leary et al. (1992) argue that blushing can accompany a range of different emotions and that it is 'not tied to any emotion or specific set of emotions' (p. 446).

Interestingly, other behaviours which accompany embarrassment, such as gaze aversion and facial and postural movements (Asendorpf, 1990; Edelmann & Hampson, 1979, 1981), signal embarrassment independently of blushing. Indeed, research suggests that the recognition of embarrassment from such cues occurs within five seconds of an embarrassing event (Keltner, 1995). Blushing in contrast seems to reach its peak about 15 to 20 seconds after the triggering episode (Shearn et al., 1990). On this basis it has been argued that blushing becomes most visible after embarrassment can be identified by observers (Keltner & Buswell, 1997).

While the balance of evidence does then point to a great deal of commonality between blushing and embarrassment, embarrassment may occur in the absence of blushing and blushing may occur in the absence of embarrassment. As Miller (1996) points out, "blushing and embarrassment are not synonymous— each may occur without the other—but they overlap considerably . . . blushing is a reliable signal of embarrassment" (p. 137).

Given the close relationship between blushing and embarrassment it is perhaps not surprising that situations typically associated with blushing are those typically described in relation to embarrassment, that is, situations involving unwanted or undesired social attention.

Situations Evoking Blushing

In relation to embarrassment a number of researchers have documented the occurrence of embarrassment following the transgression of conventions governing social interactions (Cupach & Metts, 1990; Edelmann, 1987; Gross &

Stone, 1964; Keltner & Buswell, 1996; Miller, 1992; Sharkey & Stafford, 1990). While most such classification schemes focus upon behavioural elements, Miller's (1992) system emphasises the role played by those present in eliciting the blush.

Interestingly, the one study to date which has sought to classify explicitly blush-eliciting rather than embarrassing circumstances has produced a system combining both the behavioural elements used in such classification schemes with Miller's role-based system. In so doing, Shields, Mallory, and Simon (1990) classified descriptors of blush-eliciting circumstances into three categories: others present saying or doing something accidentally or intentionally to provoke a blush; by one's own faux pas, that is, social lapses, slips of the tongue and clumsiness; by one's own actions other than faux pas, such as speaking before an audience or being introduced by someone. Shields et al. report that 55% of the descriptions they obtained related to others evoking the blush, 24% described instances in which the respondent's own actions or thoughts evoked the blush, while in 15% of cases the respondent's own faux pas accounted for the blushes.

Similar categories are discussed by Leary et al. (1992) in their review. They refer to four categories of situations which elicit blushing: threats to public identity, praise and other forms of positive attention, scrutiny, and accusations of blushing.

A common thread runs through all descriptors, whether it is embarrassment or blushing which acts as the starting point. In relation to the act performed there is a perception on the part of the sufferers that their behaviour is in some way deficient (or in the case of praise, that they may not adequately convey their appreciation or fear they may not be able to sustain their performance in the future) and is subject to public scrutiny which they would prefer to avoid. Of particular interest in relation to blushing is the frequency with which respondents report that others present intentionally or unintentionally provoke a blush and accompanying embarrassment.

Many authors have noted that the mere presence of others can be sufficient to evoke blushing. In Japan, embarrassment which results simply from being exposed to others is referred to as surface *haji* (Lebra, 1983). As Leary and Meadows (1991) note, some people blush when interacting with authorities, when the centre of attention, or simply when they are stared at by another person. Leary et al. (1992) argue that such a response may relate in part to evaluation apprehension and may in part be an automatic response to steady stares. Others have noted that blushing can be induced simply by telling someone they are blushing, even if this is not initially the case and/or the situation is not defined as embarrassing (Edelmann, 1987, 1990c). Blushing itself can then be sufficient to provoke extreme embarrassment (Edelmann, 1987; Timms, 1980). Leary and colleagues suggest that such information-induced blushing may be a special case of scrutiny-induced blushing. Staring and blushing may then be the human equivalent of a dominance-submission display; inducing blushing in others may represent an attempt to assert one's assumed status, making another feel small and inferior. In this context, those who report a chronic fear of blushing frequently refer to feeling inadequate and inferior (Edelmann, 1990c). However, while blushing may make people feel inferior this does not explain why people blush when being told they are doing so, even when not initially blushing. One might assume that people would dismiss such a suggestion in the same way that they might dismiss the suggestion that they are angry, or indeed experiencing any other emotion, if this were not in fact the case.

In short, blushing sends a signal to others about our social discomfort; it is perceived as a sign of social inadequacy or inferiority and hence a "state" to avoid. However, because of its involuntary nature it is impossible to avoid blushing. Given its pervasive nature it is perhaps surprising that the physiological mechanism underlying blushing has yet to be precisely specified.

THE NATURE OF BLUSHING: PHYSIOLOGICAL ASPECTS

Vasodilation of the face which occurs during blushing also occurs as a result of physical exertion, due to alcohol consumption, in relation to sexual arousal and as menopausal "hot flushes". However, it has been argued that blushing is physiologically distinguishable from facial flushing that occurs for non-social reasons (Leary et al., 1992).

Leary et al. (1992) and Leary and Kowalski (1995) distinguish two types of blush which they refer to as the classic/embarrassed blush and the creeping blush. The former appears rapidly on the face, neck, and ears and is relatively uniform over these areas while the latter occurs more slowly, starting with red blotches on the chest, neck, or jaw and then spreading slowly upwards. Leary et al. (1992) suggest that the former is more likely to occur in general social settings while the latter is more likely to be observed in speakers who are giving a prepared talk to an audience. Although these differences in blushing can undoubtedly be observed, the blush region is localised to the face, ears, neck, and upper chest (Leary et al., 1992). This is possibly because the facial cutaneous vasculature is denser and has greater capacitance and is nearer the surface of the skin in the facial region (Cutlip & Leary, 1993). Embarrassed people often blush as the flow of blood to the face increases (Drummond, 1989); this is followed by a slower rise in facial temperature (Drummond & Lance, 1987; Shearn et al., 1990, 1992). However, while the extent and nature of blushing has been documented, the physiological mechanisms that mediate blushing are poorly understood (Drummond, 1997, p. 163).

Parasympathetic influences with regard to blushing seem unlikely (Drummond, 1997). Thus, while parasympathetic vasodilator reflexes have been noted in the forehead and lips in response to noxious stimulation in the mouth and face (Drummond, 1994) such responses do not seem to occur in other facial areas, such as the cheeks, which are associated with blushing (Drummond, 1995).

Warming the skin initiates reflex release of sympathetic vasoconstrictor tone by an α-adrenergic mechanism which regulates blood flow to some extent in various parts of the face (Drummond, 1997). However, while such a mechanism could explain increasing blushing in relation to increasing facial temperature it does not explain the initial onset of blushing. It is also too general a mechanism to explain purely social blushing (Drummond, 1997).

Others have postulated that β-adrenergic receptors, the stimulation of which induces vascular dilation, are associated with blushing (Mellander et al., 1982). These authors have argued that a high density of such receptors in human facial veins might account for the restricted distribution of blushing and that susceptibility to blushing might vary as a function of the density of β-adrenoceptors in the facial vasculature. Indeed, Drummond (1997), in an experimental evaluation of this thesis, found that Beta blockade partially inhibited blood flow (blushing) during singing for both frequent and infrequent blushers (as defined by the Blushing Propensity Scale; Leary & Meadows, 1991), supporting the contention that β-adrenoceptors have some influence on blushing. However, vascular responses were similar for both groups in spite of higher ratings of self-consciousness for the frequent compared with the infrequent blushers. A similar lack of relationship between physiological parameters and blushing propensity has been reported by Mulkens, de Jong, and Bögels (1997) and Mulkens et al. (1999b). Hence psychological discomfort does not appear to influence intensity of blushing as measured by physiological parameters.

One possibility is that concern about or awareness of blushing may not directly reflect the actual amount of blushing. Research with both clinical and non-clinical populations supports such a contention. In this context, Edelmann and Skov (1993) report an association between blushing propensity and measures of anxiety sensitivity and awareness of bodily sensations, suggesting a relationship between reported awareness of blushing and concerns with bodily symptoms.

The possibility that reported blushing frequency relates to anxiety about blushing rather than to actual blushing also receives support from a recent experimental study (Drummond, 2001). True and false feedback about blood flow was given to a group of high and a group of low scorers on the Blushing Propensity Scale during an embarrassing task (singing) and an innocuous task (reading aloud). High scorers were more self-conscious and thought that they blushed more intensely than low scorers during most of the tasks, including the reading tasks when blood flow actually decreased.

Finally, it seems that social phobics, many of whom report a fear of blushing as their prime concern, do not differ physiologically in anxiety-provoking situations from their non-socially anxious counterparts, while reporting more psychological discomfort in such situations (Edelmann & Baker, 1997, in press). In other words, those who describe themselves as being prone to blushing do not seem to blush more intensely than others who think they blush infrequently—fear of blushing does not seem to relate directly to actual amount of blushing. This issue clearly has important clinical implications and is discussed further in relation to chronic blushing and social phobia.

THEORETICAL EXPLANATIONS FOR BLUSHING

In contrast to his theorizing in relation to other emotions Darwin did not attribute an adaptive function to blushing. Darwin considered that blushing and related states, under which rubric he included shame and shyness, were related to the uniquely human capacity to view oneself, and in particular one's public presentation, from someone else's perspective. That is, the causal factor in inducing blushing was thinking about what others think of us.

More recently, theorists have also argued that embarrassment, self-presentational concerns and fear of negative evaluations by others act as triggers for blushing (Edelmann, 1990a, b, c, 1991; Leary & Meadows, 1991; Sattler, 1966). A related view developed by Leary et al. (1992) is that blushing is often a response to unwanted social attention. Leary and his colleagues argued that, because blushing is associated not only with negative affective states such as embarrassment and social anxiety, but also with the receipt of overwhelming praise or even with mere scrutiny, factors other than merely the negative affective state are responsible for evoking blushing. They argued that two factors in particular are of relevance. First, attention from others focuses on qualities intrinsic in the individual's behaviour or person and, second, the attention is not desired. Although these various theories differ in their emphasis they tend to share a common theme—i.e., social attention is central to blushing.

Blushing as Appeasement

An alternative argument is that blushing serves as an appeasement display, the function of which is to placate others (Castelfranchi & Poggi, 1990; Keltner, 1995; Keltner, Young, & Buswell, 1997; Leary & Kowalski, 1995; Leary & Meadows, 1991). Appeasement is the process by which individuals placate or pacify others in situations of potential or actual conflict. For an individual who anticipates aggression from another, displaying apologetic, submissive and affiliative behaviour can prevent or reduce the other person's aggression and re-establish relations (Keltner, Young, & Buswell, 1997). Numerous accounts of appeasement have been documented for non-human primates (Altman, 1967; de Waal & Ren, 1988; Van Hoof, 1972; see Keltner & Buswell, 1997, for a summary). Thus, a typical appeasement action when a lower status primate is threatened by a higher status one is for the lower status primate to avert his or her eyes, looking at the dominant one obliquely. Humans similarly appease others with submissive non-verbal displays such as constricted posture, head downwards movement and gaze aversion (Ellyson & Dovidio, 1985; Keltner, 1995; Keltner et al., 1997).

Interestingly, such behaviours, in addition to face-touching and smiling, are typical of embarrassment (Edelmann & Hampson, 1979; Keltner 1995). Blushing, as noted, is also assumed to be part of an outward display of embarrassment. As Leary and Kowalski (1995) point out, blushing is often accompanied by gaze aversion and a nervous or silly grin. In short, blushing, because of its association with other embarrassed behaviours, has led to the proposition that it has evolved from the appeasement system of other species and serves an appeasement-related function in humans (Keltner et al., 1997). However, in one of the few empirical evaluations of the placation/appeasement theory of blushing, Halberstadt and Green (1993) found only a weak relationship between individuals' tendency to blush and measures of submission/dominance and abasement. As these authors note, though, while this may mean that a predisposition to blush is not associated with a tendency to appeasement it does not exclude the possibility that blushing is associated with appeasement or apology as a response specific to each particular context.

With reference to human beings, Castelfranchi and Poggi (1990, p. 242) argue:

> Appeased by a blush, which means an acknowledgement of a value and, possibly, an apology for its violation, the group is less likely to be aggressive towards or isolate the individual. So the blush is useful to the blusher because it protects the individual from the group's aggression or isolation.

They further contend (p. 240) that blushing serves as an "acknowledgement, a confession, and an apology aimed at inhibiting the others' aggression or avoiding social ostracism".

The appeasement account, in equating human blushing with the behaviour of non-human animals, provides an evolutionary-functional analysis of blushing which relates to physical and social survival (Keltner & Buswell, 1997). Indeed, the appeasement/placation theory of blushing provides an intuitively reasonable explanation for both blushing and behaviours associated with embarrassment. However, it is not without its problems (Halberstadt & Green, 1993; Leary et al., 1992). Issues which are difficult to reconcile with the appeasement theory include questions such as why dark-skinned individuals blush even if the blush cannot be easily seen; why blushes appear to be involuntary so that they cannot be voluntarily exhibited even when it might be desirable to do so; and why people might wish to control their blushes even if they are serving a valuable purpose. In addition, it seems that in many instances, blushing, as with embarrassment, acts to do more than merely placate others. It can also act as a non-verbal apology, evoking shared amusement with others and even sympathy (de Jong, 1999). As Keltner and Buswell (1997) note with regard to embarrassment, the display incorporates an affiliative as well as a submissive response.

Blushing as Affiliation

A number of authors have noted that the very act of being embarrassed can be seen as part of an apology, being used as a way of allowing minor indiscretions to be passed over quickly and forgotten by the interactants (Edelmann, 1987). Observers report high levels of affiliative emotions such as amusement and sympathy or empathy in response to others' embarrassment (Edelmann, 1994; Fink & Walker, 1977; Keltner et al., 1997; Metts & Cupach, 1989; Miller, 1987; Sharkey & Stafford, 1990). In certain contexts non-verbal signs of discomfort or embarrassment tend to be viewed favourably, enhancing the standing of the person performing the embarrassing actions (Edelmann, 1982; Semin & Manstead, 1982). In one particular study, embarrassment when requesting help produced significantly more helping than when no embarrassment was displayed (Levin & Arluke, 1982).

In this context Leary and Meadows (1991) suggest that blushing serves as a "remedial display" serving to mitigate others' negative reactions to behaviours than might otherwise result in public humiliation or loss of social esteem. Interestingly, when participants in a study were told they had not blushed they resorted to other means to restore their identity, that is by rating themselves more favourably on self-relevant questionnaires in comparison with participants who had been informed they had blushed (Leary, Landel, & Patton, 1996). Results confirming the remedial effect of social blushing are reported in a further experimental study (de Jong, 1999). Participants who evaluated scripts describing an actor following a mishap, viewed the actor less negatively, as being less responsible for the incident, and as more trustworthy when the actor was described as blushing than when he or she was described as showing no overt signs of shame or embarrassment.

In Miller's (1996, p. 146) words "blushing communicates bona fide sensitivity, gentility, and apologetic chagrin to observers" (see also this volume, *Chapter 13*). Such actions may also serve to modify the behaviour of observers present. In this context, a number of authors have noted that others present are likely to react to, and become involved in, the actor's embarrassment and will frequently assist the actor with their remedial strategies. An actor trying to ignore or cover his or her blushing and embarrassment may well leave the observers flustered, not knowing whether they too should ignore or play along with the reaction or even terminate the interaction. Contrition on the part of the actor provides the observers with an opportunity to collude with the actor in helping to remedy the situation.

There are then clear indications that blushing can serve an affiliative function. However, as Miller further notes, there are problems with such an explanation for blushing. Blushing can be aversive and serves to make us even more conspicuous when we are already concerned about attention we have drawn to ourselves. In addition, blushing, as noted, is only one of several non-verbal cues to embarrassment and its relationship to other aspects of behaviour needs to be considered.

In short, there is evidence to support the notion that blushing seems to be partly a submissive gesture and partly an affiliative response aiding the restoration of social relations (Keltner & Buswell, 1996). However, while blushing may well have evolutionary significance and serve to aid the restoration of social relations, both theories leave certain aspects of blushing unexplained. One central element in this regard is that the meaning applied to blushing is shaped by the social and cultural context in which the act occurs. This is illustrated by variability in the 'acceptability' of blushing according to age, gender, and culture. Such issues have generally been reviewed in relation to social evaluative aspects of blushing (Keltner & Buswell, 1997) or blushing as a response to social attention (Leary et al., 1992).

Social Evaluative Account

Embarrassment has to do with a failure to present a desired image to others whom we regard as evaluating our performance (Edelmann, 1987; Miller, 1996). In short, embarrassment occurs because we are motivated to behave in a manner which is consistent with social rules and wish to avoid social exclusion. The more prone individuals are to embarrassment, the more concerned they are with other's evaluations, the more concerned they are with gaining approval and the greater their desire to avoid social exclusion (Edelmann, 1985; Edelmann & McCusker, 1986; Halberstadt & Green, 1993; Miller, 1995). The relative absence of embarrassment is associated with antisocial or asocial behaviour (Keltner, Moffitt, & Stouthamer-Loeber, 1995) while an excess of embarrassability relates to excessive and unreasonable social concerns (Edelmann, 1987).

Given the close relationship between blushing and embarrassment it is perhaps not surprising that blushing is seen in a similar light. While a slight blush may well have positive connotations, "remaining cool in the face of untoward events may portray one as crass and unfeeling, but becoming too flustered may portray one as inept" (Miller, 1996, p. 154).

Such display features may relate to the appeasement and affiliation theories. It is inappropriate to be too submissive or to apologize too much. However, the meaning and acceptability of blushing is also shaped by social and cultural factors. As Keltner and Buswell (1997, pp. 264–265) note:

> self-representational capacities allow humans to elaborate the experience of embarrassment and shame into moral concepts involving evaluations of the self in relation to standards and rules. . . . Nonhuman appeasement processes, in contrast, seem to be primarily elicited by concrete, physical events and not elaborated into symbolic concepts that guide social practices and behavior.

The same issues apply to blushing. Such self-evaluative processes are partly shaped by social and cultural expectations. For example, in Victorian England it was seen as acceptable, indeed even desirable, for a bride to blush. Such a blush was seen as a sign of purity. Many women in western societies still apply a cosmetic blush suggesting that a slight colouring for women is still valued by at least some sections of society. It is interesting to observe that, as social values and expectations have changed over time, many women are faced with a conflict—it is both desirable to appear with a cosmetic blush in certain social settings but undesirable to blush in the workplace or other settings where issues of power and dominance are to the fore. At one level this relates to an underlying theme of appeasement but there is clearly a more complex social level to consider.

INDIVIDUAL VARIATION IN BLUSHING

Age and Blushing

Little is known about the development of blushing although a number of studies have evaluated self-conscious behaviours in children and parental and retrospective reports of embarrassment and blushing. In one of the first such studies, Buss, Iscoe, and Buss (1979) sent a questionnaire to the parents of children in three preschool nurseries and four elementary schools. The questionnaires enquired about blushing and other signs of embarrassment that parents had noted in their children during the previous six months. Embarrassment was reported in roughly one in four children in the 3- to 4-year-old group. This proportion jumped to three out of five of the 5-year-olds and stayed at this proportion or more for the remaining age groups. Among those children for whom parents reported episodes of embarrassment, slightly more than half were reported to blush. The possibility that early childhood represents age of onset of blushing is supported by Shields, Mallory and Simon's (1990) findings from a retrospective recall study. When asked the age they first recalled blushing, participants aged from 13 to 55 gave a modal response of 5 with a range from 3 to 25. However, it seems that age of respondent was related to age of recalled first blushing. Thus, of those able to recall, 35% of younger participants reported blushing at the age of 5 or younger and only 6% reported the age of 13 or later. For older participants, only 16% reported blushing at the age of 5 or younger, but 40% reported the age of 13 or later.

These results would seem to correspondent with results obtained in a further study from a group of self-defined adult chronic blushers who were asked their age of recalled onset of blushing (Edelmann, 1990c). The average age reported was 12.6 years. Assuming the parental reports presented by Buss and his colleagues are accurate, then the age of first blushing is clearly discrepant from reported recall of first blushing provided by adults. There are a number of possible explanations for this. It is of course possible that people do not recall their earliest episodes of blushing (Leary et al., 1992) as evidenced by the varying age of recall of first blushing with age reported by Shields et al. (1990). However, it is also possible that blushing changes in significance with age, its perceived negative connotations reaching a peak during early adolescence. Children's concerns about how others evaluate and perceive them increase with age (Elkind, 1980), with self-consciousness peaking in early adolescence (Buss, 1980). Hence, the retrospective recall of adults asked about blushing may reflect their recall of awkward, embarrassing or humiliating experiences associated with the self-consciousness of adolescence. Facial reddening in children, which may be reported as blushing by adult observers, may well occur at a much younger age.

Adolescence is the stage during which strongest fears of blushing are reported (Abe & Masui, 1981) and the tendency to blush may then decline with age. Interestingly in Abe and Masui's study the peak age of fear of blushing in girls at 15 years occurred two years earlier than the peak age of blushing reported for boys, which may reflect general developmental differences between the genders.

Shields et al. (1990) found that while two-thirds of their younger respondents reported blushing frequently, only 28% of those aged 25 or older reported frequent blushing. There is evidence that the neurochemical receptors that control the dilation of the facial veins become less numerous with age (Mellander et al., 1982) and hence one's capacity to blush may decline. Alternatively, people may become less concerned about others' evaluations of them as they get older or they may actually receive less undesired attention from others (Leary et al., 1992). Interestingly, chronic blushers report increased concern about blushing with age, partly because they assume blushing to be an adolescent problem that they will 'grow out of' (Edelmann, 1990b). If one's capacity to blush does indeed decline with age then any increase in concern about blushing with age would clearly be due to cognitive processes involving expectations and assumptions.

Gender and Blushing

Although a few studies suggest that women experience greater fear of blushing, frequency of blushing, and propensity to blush than their male counterparts, the balance of research suggests an absence of gender differences. In one of the earliest studies, Abe and Masui (1981) found a significantly greater prevalence for fear of blushing among females in comparison with males across the age range in a sample of 11- to 23-year-olds. In a further study based upon self-report data, Shields et al. (1990) reported slight gender differences in frequency of blushing. Fifty-two per cent of their female respondents and 44% of their male respondents reported blushing at least once a week. Finally, in an experimental study Shearn et al. (1990) detected greater increases in cheek temperature but not blood volume in females than males when they watched video segments of themselves singing; in addition, females were judged to blush more often than males.

In contrast, a series of studies using the Blushing Propensity Scale report an absence of gender differences in British and American students, the average score on the scale ranging from 35 to 45 for both men and women (Edelmann & Skov, 1993; Halberstadt & Green, 1993; Leary & Meadows, 1991). However, Bögels, Alberts, and de Jong (1996) report significantly higher scores for women in comparison with men in their sample of Dutch students. In addition, they report scores for men (25.4) and women (35.5) which are lower than those reported in these earlier studies. Similarly higher scores for females in comparison with males were reported by Neto (1996) for a sample of Portuguese undergraduates. It is possible that cultural expectations about the desirability or unacceptability of blushing for women and men influence blushing propensity scores.

Cultural Differences in Blushing

A number of studies have evaluated self-reported recall of blushing in different cultures (Edelmann et al., 1989; Edelmann & Iwawaki, 1987; Edelmann & Neto, 1989; Simon & Shields, 1996). With regard to symptoms that respondents recalled in relation to experienced embarrassment, the reported frequency of blushing was, in general, similar in the countries studied: 35% in Japan, 25% in Greece, 29% in Italy, 21% in Spain, and 34% in Germany recalled a blush. The exception was the United Kingdom where 55% of the respondents recalled blushing. It should be kept in mind that these figures are based upon retrospective recall and whether such reported differences correspond to actual physiological differences has not been evaluated. It is possible that blushing is merely a more salient component of an embarrassment prototype to people in the United Kingdom so that they notice and recall it more often, even though it may occur at the same rate across cultures (Miller, 1996). Simon and Shields (1996) report a similar frequency of self-reported blushing among respondents from different ethnic and racial backgrounds. However, blushes were much more visible in people with lighter skins than in those with darker complexions. As Miller (1996) suggests, differences in reported blushing across cultures may then be a reflection of the extent to which they are noticed and remarked upon by others. Interestingly, Drummond and Lim (2000) found that facial blood flow and temperature increased to the same extent in Caucasians and Indians during embarrassing tasks.

Individual Differences in Blushing Propensity

A number of studies suggest that people differ with regard to both their reported propensity to blush and their reported fear of blushing (Bögels, et al., 1996; Mulkens et al., 1997, 1999b; Drummond, 1997; Edelmann, 1991; Edelmann & Skov, 1993; Halberstadt & Green, 1993; Neto, 1996; Leary & Meadows, 1991). With regard to bushing propensity—that is, the extent to which people report that they blush in everyday situations—a specific measure, The Blushing Propensity Scale, was developed by Leary and Meadows in 1991. This is a 14-item scale with each item rated on a five-point scale from never to always blush.

The Blushing Propensity Scale is thus a measure of a person's perception of his or her tendency to blush. A number of studies have found a relationship between reported blushing propensity and a range of self-report measures tapping concerns with the evaluative reactions of others. Leary and Meadows (1991) report that blushing propensity was related to embarrassability, interaction anxiousness, fear of negative evaluation, social physique anxiety, attention to social comparison and self-consciousness. Edelmann and Skov (1993) report a relationship between blushing propensity with anxiety sensitivity, fear of bodily sensations and social anxiety. Finally, Halberstadt and Green (1993) report a relationship between blushing propensity and embarrassability and interaction anxiousness. Similar results have been obtained using single item measures of blushing rather than the Blushing Propensity Scale. Thus, Edelmann (1990c, 1991) found that chronic blushing was associated with social anxiety, state and trait anxiety, and self-consciousness.

In contrast Crozier and Russell (1992) found no relationship between self-reported frequency of blushing and tendency to blush with either public or private self-consciousness. Bögels and colleagues (1996) also report a lack of any significant relationship between private self-consciousness and blushing propensity and a weak relationship between public self-consciousness and blushing propensity. While the differing results between these studies may be due in part to the differing nature of the measures used it does not explain the differences between studies where comparable measures were administered.

Of interest is the generally consistent finding of a relationship between measures of bodily concerns and blushing propensity. In this context the relationship between self-focused attention (specifically directed towards one's own arousal) and blushing propensity reported by Bögels and colleagues is of interest. As the authors note, self-consciousness may not be the appropriate variable to assess in relation to blushing propensity since it fails to assess self-focused attention to arousal, which may be the central component of fear of blushing.

As noted earlier, there does not seem to be a perfect relationship between self-reported blushing, as assessed with the Blushing Propensity Scale, and actual physiological parameters. Thus Mulkens et al. (1997) measured cheek temperature and changes in cheek blood flow while female participants watched a videotape of themselves singing and while watching the shower murder scene from Hitchcock's movie *Psycho*. Increases in cheek temperature and blood flow were greater while watching the videotaped song than while watching the movie segment, irrespective of the person's Blushing Propensity Scale score. However, those who obtained high scores on the Blushing Propensity Scale thought that they blushed more intensely and were more concerned about whether they had blushed than participants with low Blushing Propensity Scale scores. In a more recent study, Mulkens et al. (1999b) investigated whether women who were afraid of blushing would blush more than women who were not afraid of blushing under conditions of high and low social stress. That is, while watching a videotape of themselves singing or watching a test pattern with two male confederates. Increases in facial temperature and skin coloration were similar in both groups in both experimental conditions. However, women who were afraid of blushing thought that they blushed far more intensely that those who were not afraid of blushing.

Similar findings are reported by Drummond (1997) in a study which involved measuring changes in forehead blood flow while participants, who were either high or low scorers on the Blushing Propensity Scale, sang a children's song. Forehead blood flow increased to the same extent during the song in high and low scorers despite higher ratings of self-consciousness in frequent blushers.

Drummond (2001) also reports the lack of a relationship between blushing propensity and physiological indices of blushing.

In other words, differential scores on the Blushing Propensity Scale do not relate to actual differences in the intensity of interoceptive cues related to blushing; that is, to increases in forehead temperature. The ratings are thus likely to reflect individual differences in concern about blushing rather than individual differences in intensity of blushing per se.

CHRONIC BLUSHING AND SOCIAL PHOBIA

As noted, blushing, as with embarrassment, is assumed to be evoked by an external event, whether this involves an actual faux pas or public scrutiny, which results in unwanted or undesired social attention. However, for some people, it appears that fear of blushing evokes considerable discomfiture, without the prerequisite for any external evoking stimulus other than the mere presence of other people (Edelmann 1990a, b, c). I have argued elsewhere (Edelmann, 1987, 1990c) that one possible explanation for this is that people use their own expressive behaviour as cues to interpret their internal states and that this is consistent with the facial feedback hypothesis (Buck, 1980). Hence, a perception that one is blushing may lead to an inference by the person that he or she is embarrassed and will be perceived as being so, which in turn will lead to further blushing. Of course, in line with earlier analyses, it also seems reasonable to assume that people fear blushing because they believe it will be perceived as a sign of ineptness and inadequacy. Given that we are in general motivated to behave in a manner which presents us as competent human beings, it is perhaps not surprising that a chronic fear of blushing can be debilitating. As Mulkens et al. (1997) note, some people find it extremely aversive to blush and even develop a blushing phobia. In a study of self-defined chronic blushers, 62% reported that they had no available strategy to help them cope with blushing while 17% reported that they "coped" by leaving the situation (Edelmann, 1990c). Coping is no doubt made more difficult for some people by their cognitive distortions of the likely cue salience of blushing.

Chronic blushers seem overconcerned with internal cues and thoughts and observers' subsequent reactions to their blushing. This is illustrated by comments from sufferers such as, "I'm going red, why? I wish I could stop"; "When I blush I think what other people must be thinking" and "The fear of blushing is awful. I hate going to places where I am likely to meet other people" (Edelmann, 1990a).

A number of authors have noted that blushing and muscle twitching are common complaints in social phobia (Amies, Gelder, & Shaw, 1983; Cameron et al., 1986; Reich, Noyes, & Yates, 1988; Solyom, Ledwidge, & Solyom, 1986) while for an important subgroup of social phobics their somatic symptoms appear to be the main cause of their social fear.

According to DSM-IV (American Psychiatric Association, 1994, pp. 411–412),

> The essential feature of social phobia is a marked and persistent fear of social or performance situations in which embarrassment may occur ... Individuals with social phobia almost always experience symptoms of anxiety (e.g. palpitations, tremors, sweating ... blushing ...) in the feared social situations ... Blushing may be more typical of social phobia.

Such patients are not so much afraid that others will evaluate them negatively because of their social behaviour, performance, appearance or personality but specifically as a result of their showing somatic symptoms which are not under their voluntary control and which may be noticed by others (Bögels & Reith, 1998). For many social phobics blushing is inherently embarrassing and sufficient to provoke fear of social situations (Bögels et al., 1996).

The notion that certain visible somatic cues characterize social phobia is consistent with general theoretical suppositions (Barlow, 1988; Clark & Wells, 1995; Trower & Gilbert, 1989). While some authors have argued that such somatic symptoms are "further" or "consequential" cues in triggering a cycle of anxiety in social phobics, others have argued that, at least for some social phobics, anticipatory fear of the somatic symptoms acts as the causal agent. Thus Scholing and Emmelkamp (1993) and Mersch et al. (1992) suggest that at least some social phobics focus on, or are particularly sensitive to, bodily cues which may act as causal agents in the generation of social phobia. Indeed, Mersch et al. contend that some social phobics resemble patients with panic disorder in their fear of somatic symptoms.

The issue here is whether social phobics differ with regard to physiological responsiveness—that is, whether they genuinely blush more than their non-socially phobic counterparts or whether it is their (mis)perception and (mis)interpretation of somatic symptoms which is causal with regard to their social fears. Some studies do suggest that social phobics may differ from controls in certain social contexts with regard to specific physiological indices such as heart rate (Hofmann et al., 1995; McNeil et al., 1993) and skin conductance (McNeil et al., 1993). However, the only study to date which has assessed social phobics in relation to both anxious and non-clinical controls and which assessed facial and skin temperature changes in relation to tasks designed to be both demanding and socially relevant report little between group difference on any of the physiological parameters assessed (Edelmann & Baker, 1997, in press). Of interest, however, is the finding from the latter studies that social phobics tended to rate themselves as having higher body heat and heart rate than the other two groups during the first phase of one of the socially relevant tasks (a social conversation). In other words, in line with research findings relating to blushing propensity discussed previously, it is not actual differences in skin temperature which differentiates social phobics from non-social phobics but perceived differences. In this context it is of interest to note that those who fear blushing report more negative learning experiences in relation to blushing than their non-fearful counterparts (Mulkens & Bögels, 1999). Thus, learning plays a large part in the fear of, and negative cognitions associated with, blushing. This no doubt feeds into a general pattern of catastrophic cognitions that social phobics generate in relation to social tasks, as suggested by cognitive models (Barlow, 1988; Clark & Wells, 1995; Trower & Gilbert, 1989). Whether by design or intent intervention studies with social phobics who express a fear blushing have generally been directed towards such processes.

Specific treatments have been developed to overcome fear of blushing in social phobia (Bögels, Mulkens, & de Jong, 1997; Edelmann, 1990b; Mersch et al., 1992; Mulkens et al., 1999a; Scholing & Emmelkamp, 1993). Several case studies report the use of paradoxical interventions in the treatment of blushing (Lamontagne, 1978; Timms, 1980). This is a technique whereby the patient makes a deliberate attempt to bring on symptoms and, if he or she fails to do so, may be told to try harder. Given that blushing is an involuntary response it is perhaps not surprising that people find it difficult to make themselves blush. The mechanism behind this technique is poorly understood but case studies point to a decline in reported blushing. However, as Mersch and colleagues point out, "a disadvantage of paradoxical interventions is that they do not contribute to insight into the processes that lead the change" (p. 200). They further note that "this prevents the acquisition of coping skills" that would enable the client to deal more effectively with future difficulties. These authors present a report of a 30-year-old male, who had a problem of blushing in social situations, and was successfully treated by paradoxical intervention combined with rational emotive therapy. In a further study comparing cognitive and behavioural treatments of fear of blushing, sweating or trembling, Scholing and Emmelkamp (1993) report that both treatments were effective in relation to target behaviours when compared with a waiting list control. Interestingly, after the first four weeks of study the authors found little evidence for improvement. The authors note that, although patients recognized that treatment would centre on their fear of the symptoms, most in fact hoped that, as a result of treatment, they would never blush, sweat, or tremble again. It was only later in therapy that patients began to accept their symptoms and hence were less distressed by them.

An alternative approach is concerned with encouraging patients to direct their attention away from their blushes by focusing on factors outside themselves. This can be the task at hand or specific aspects of the person or people they are interacting with or situational cues (Edelmann, 1990b, Bögels et al. 1997; Mulkens et al., 1999a). Initial results with this approach have been promising. The general consensus then is that at least some social phobics suffer a chronic fear of blushing and that this fear does not relate to actual blushing. Such a contention is in line with research findings relating to individual variation in blushing propensity.

In this context it is of interest to note that endoscopic transthoracic sympathectomy has recently been put forward as a surgical solution for chronic blushing (Telaranta, 1998; Drott et al., 1998). Short-term results from the procedure appear to be positive although this needs to be balanced against the risk of surgical complications and side-effects such as inappropriate bodily or facial sweating and flushing, particularly while eating (Drummond, 2000). Such symptoms are likely to be as distressing as fear of blushing, hence patients opting for surgery may be no better off in the long term. In addition, given that the research evidence to date suggests that anxiety about blushing is the central problem rather than blushing per se, psychological therapy targeting the former problem would appear to be more appropriate than surgery targeting the latter.

FUTURE DIRECTIONS

While the last two decades have witnessed a dramatic increase in our understanding of the physiological mechanisms prompting blushing and psychological processes underlying fear of blushing, many gaps in our knowledge of this fascinating phenomenon remain. Leary et al. (1992) and Keltner and Buswell (1997) raise a number of questions and future research directions with regard to blushing. Further research is required to determine variations across cultures, physiological mechanisms and whether facial reddening differs in association with differing emotional states. The question of the precise function of blushing requires further elaboration. Is it part of a human appeasement display or affiliative response or is it simply the by-product of some other psychological processes? How does visibility of blushing relate to other non-verbal behaviour and social fears? Are there distinct forms of blushing associated with differing social circumstances? Finally a greater understanding is required of individual differences in the variability of actual blushing and how this relates to perception of blushing. This is clearly a central question for clinical research and treatment. At last, a century and a quarter after Darwin's first writings on the subject, research has begun to produce answers to many of the intriguing questions he posed.

ACKNOWLEDGEMENTS

I would like to thank a number of colleagues who were kind enough to update me on their work. I would also like to thank Peter Drummond who was kind enough to comment on an earlier version of this chapter.

REFERENCES

Abe, K. & Masui, T. (1981). Age-sex trends of phobic and anxiety symptoms in adolescents. *British Journal of Psychiatry, 138,* 297–302.
Altman, S. A. (1967). The structure of primate communication. In S. A. Altman (Ed.), *Social communication among primates.* Chicago: University of Chicago Press.

American Psychiatric Association (1994). *Diagnostic and statistical manual of mental disorders* (4th edn.). Washington, DC: American Psychiatric Association.

Amies, P. L., Gelder, M. G., & Shaw, P. M. (1983). Social phobia: A comparative clinical study. *British Journal of Psychiatry, 142*, 174–179.

Asendorpf, J. B. (1990). The expression of shyness and embarrassment. In W. R. Crozier (Ed.), *Shyness and embarrassment: Perspectives from social psychology* (pp. 87–118). Cambridge: Cambridge University Press.

Barlow, D. H. (1988). *Anxiety and its disorders.* New York: Guilford Press.

Buck, R. (1980). Nonverbal behavior and the theory of emotion: The facial feedback hypothesis. *Journal of Personality and Social Psychology, 38*, 81–824.

Bögels, S. M., Alberts, M., & de Jong, P. J. (1996). Self-consciousness, self-focused attention, blushing propensity and fear of blushing. *Personality and Individual Differences, 21*, 573–581.

Bögels, S. M., Mulkens, S., & de Jong, P. J. (1997). Task concentration training and fear of blushing. *Journal of Clinical Psychology and Psychotherapy, 4*, 251–258.

Bögels, S. M. & Reith, W. (1998). Validity of two questionnaires to assess social fears: The Dutch Social Phobia and Anxiety Inventory and the Blushing, trembling and sweating questionnaire. *Journal of Psychopathology and Behavioral Assessment, 21*, 51–66.

Buss, A. H. (1980). *Self-consciousness and social anxiety.* San Francisco: W. H. Freeman.

Buss, A. H., Iscoe, I., & Buss, E. H. (1979). The development of embarrassment. *Journal of Psychology, 103*, 227–230.

Cameron, O., Thyer, B., Nesse, R., & Curtis, G. (1986). Symptom profiles of patients with DSM-III anxiety disorders. *American Journal of Psychiatry*, 143, 1132–1137.

Castelfranchi, C. & Poggi, I. (1990). Blushing as a discourse: Was Darwin wrong? In W. R. Crozier (Ed.), *Shyness and embarrassment: A social psychological perspective* (pp. 230–251). Cambridge: Cambridge University Press.

Clark, D. M. & Wells, A. (1995). A cognitive model of social phobia. In R. G. Heimberg, M. Leibowitz, D. Hope, & F. Schneier (Eds.), *Social phobia: Diagnosis, assessment and treatment* (pp. 69–93). New York: Guilford Press.

Crozier, W. R. & Russell, D. (1992). Blushing, embarrassability and self-consciousness. *British Journal of Social Psychology, 31*, 343–349.

Cupach, W. R. & Metts, S. (1990). Remedial responses to embarrassing predicaments. In J. A. Anderson (Ed.), *Communication yearbook 13.* (pp. 232–352). Newbury Park, CA: Sage.

Cutlip, W. D. II & Leary, M. R. (1993). Anatomic and physiological bases of social blushing: speculations from neurology and psychology. *Behavioural Neurology, 6*, 181–185.

Darwin, C. (1872/1998). *The expression of the emotions in man and animals.* First edition published in 1872 in London by John Murray; the third edition reprinted 1998 in Glasgow by Harper Collins.

de Jong, P. J. (1999). Communicative and remedial aspects of social blushing. *Journal of Nonverbal Behavior, 23*, 197–217.

de Waal, F. B. M. & Ren, R. (1988). Comparison of the reconciliation behavior of sumptail and rhesus macaques. *Ethology, 78*, 129–142.

Drott, C., Cales, G., Olssen-Rex, L., Dalman, P., Faholen, T., & Göthberg, G. (1998). Successful treatment of facial blushing by endoscopic transthoracic sympathicotomy. *British Journal of Dermatology, 138*, 639–643.

Drummond, P. D. (1989). Mechanisms of social blushing. In N. W. Bond & D. A. T. Siddle (Eds.), *Psychobiology: Issues and applications* (pp. 363–370). Amsterdam: Elsevier Science.

Drummond, P. D. (1994). Sweating and vascular responses in the face: normal regulation and dysfunction in migraine, cluster headache and harlequin syndrome. *Clinical Autonomic Research, 6*, 23–27.

Drummond, P. D. (1995). Lacrimation and cutaneous vasoldilation in the face induced by painful stimulation of the nasal ala and upper lip. *Journal of the Autonomic Nervous System, 51*, 109–116.

Drummond, P. D. (1997) The effect of adrenergic blockade on blushing and facial flushing. *Psychophysiology, 34*, 163–168.

Drummond, P. D. (2000). A caution about surgical treatment for facial blushing [letter]. *British Journal of Dermatology, 142*, 194–195.

Drummond, P. D. (2001). The effects of true and false feedback on blushing in women. *Personality and Individual Differences, 30*, 1329–1343.

Drummond, P. D. & Lance, J. W. (1987). Facial flushing and sweating mediated by the sympathetic nervous system. *Brain, 110*, 793–803.

Drummond, P. D. & Lim, H. K. (2000). Blushing for fair and dark skinned people. *Personality and Individual Differences, 29*, 1123–1132.

Edelmann, R. J. (1982). The effect of embarrassed reaction upon others. *Australian Journal of Psychology, 34*, 359–367.

Edelmann, R. J. (1985). Individual differences in embarrassment: Self-consciousness, self-monitoring and embarrassability, *Personality and Individual Differences, 6*, 223–230.

Edelmann, R. J. (1987). *The psychology of embarrassment.* Chichester, Sussex: John Wiley & Sons.

Edelmann, R. J. (1990a). Chronic blushing, self-consciousness and social anxiety. *Journal of Psychopathology and Behavioral Assessment, 12*, 119–127.

Edelmann, R. J. (1990b). *Coping with blushing.* London: Sheldon Press.

Edelmann, R. J. (1990c). Embarrassment and blushing: A component process model, some initial descriptive and cross-cultural data. In W. R. Crozier (Ed.), *Shyness and embarrassment: Perspectives from social psychology* (pp. 205–229). Cambridge: Cambridge University Press.

Edelmann, R. J. (1991). Correlates of chronic blushing. *British Journal of Clinical Psychology, 30*, 177–178.

Edelmann, R. J. (1994). Embarrassment and blushing: Factors influencing face-saving strategies. In S. Ting-Toomey, (Ed.), *The challenge of facework* (pp. 231–267). Albany, NY: State University of New York Press.

Edelmann, R. J., Asendorpf, J., Contarello, A., Zammuner, V., Georgas, J., & Villanueva, C. (1989). Self-reported expression of embarrassment in five European countries. *Journal of Cross-Cultural Psychology, 20*, 357–371.

Edelmann, R. J. & Baker, S. R. (1997). Cognitions and physiological responses in social phobia. *British Psychological Society, 5*, 124.

Edelmann, R. J. & Baker, S. R. (in press). Perception of and actual physiological responses in social phobia. *British Journal of Clinical Psychology.*

Edelmann, R. J. & Hampson, S. E. (1979). Changes in non-verbal behaviour during embarrassment. *British Journal of Social and Clinical Psychology, 18*, 385–390.

Edelmann, R. J. & Hampson, S. E. (1981). The recognition of embarrassment. *Personality and Social Psychology Bulletin, 7*, 109–116.

Edelmann. R. J. & Iwawaki, S. (1987). Self-reported expression and consequences of embarrassment in the United Kingdom and Japan. *Psychologia, 30*, 205–216.

Edelmann, R. J. & McCusker, G. (1986). Introversion, neuroticism, empathy and embarrassability. *Personality and Individual Differences, 7*, 133–140.

Edelmann, R. J. & Neto, F. (1989). Self-reported expression and consequences of embarrassment in Portugal and the U.K. *International Journal of Psychology, 24*, 351–366.

Edelmann, R. J. & Skov, V. (1993). Blushing propensity, social anxiety, anxiety sensitivity and awareness of bodily sensations. *Personality and Individual Differences, 14*, 495–498.

Elkind, D. (1980). Strategic interactions in early adolescence. In J. Adelson (Ed.), *Handbook of adolescent psychology* (pp. 432–444). New York: Wiley.

Ellyson, S. L. & Dovidio, J. F. (1985). *Power, dominance, and nonverbal behavior.* New York: Springer-Verlag.

Fink, E. L. & Walker, B. A. (1977). Humorous responses to embarrassment. *Psychological Reports, 40,* 475–485.

Gross, E. & Stone, G. P. (1964). Embarrassment and the analysis of role requirements. *American Journal of Sociology, 70,* 1–15.

Halberstadt, A. G. & Green, L. R. (1993). Social attention and placation theories of blushing. *Motivation and Emotion, 17,* 53–64.

Hofmann, S. G., Newman, M. G., Ehlers, A., & Roth, W. T. (1995). Psychophysiological differences between subgroups of social phobia. *Journal of Abnormal Psychology, 104,* 224–231.

Keltner, D. (1995). Signs of appeasement: Evidence for the distinct displays of embarrassment, amusement, and shame. *Journal of Personality and Social Psychology, 68,* 441–454.

Keltner, D. & Buswell, B. N. (1996). Evidence for the distinctness of embarrassment, shame, and guilt: A study of recalled antecedents and facial expressions of emotion. *Cognition and Emotion, 10,* 155–171.

Keltner, D. & Buswell, B. N. (1997). Embarrassment: Its distinct form and appeasement function. *Psychological Bulletin, 122,* 250–270.

Keltner, D., Moffitt, T., & Stouthamer-Loeber, M. (1995). Facial expression of emotion and psychopathology in adolescent boys. *Journal of Abnormal Psychology, 104,* 644–652.

Keltner, D., Young R. C., & Buswell, B. N. (1997). Appeasement in human emotion, social practice, and personality. *Aggressive Behavior, 23,* 359–374.

Lamontagne, Y. (1978). Treatment of erythrophobia by paradoxical intention. *Journal of Nervous and Mental Disease, 166,* 304–306.

Leary, M. R., Landel, J. L., & Patton, K. M. (1996). The motivated expression of embarrassment following a self-presentational predicament. *Journal of Personality, 64,* 619–636.

Leary, M. R., Britt, T. W., Cutlip, W. D., II, & Templeton, J. L. (1992). Social blushing. *Psychological Bulletin, 112,* 446–460.

Leary, M. R. & Kowalski, R. M. (1995). *Social anxiety.* New York: Guilford Press.

Leary, M. R. & Meadows, S. (1991). Predictors, elicitors, and concomitants of social blushing. *Journal of Personality and Social Psychology, 60,* 254–262.

Lebra, T. S. (1983). Shame and guilt: A psychocultural view of the Japanese self. *Ethos, 11,* 192–209.

Levin, J. & Arluke, A. (1982). Embarrassment and helping behavior. *Psychological Reports, 51,* 999–1002.

Lewis, M. (1993). Self-conscious emotions: Embarrassment, pride, shame, and guilt. In M. Lewis & J. M. Haviland (Eds.), *Handbook of emotions* (pp. 353–364). New York: Guilford Press.

McNeil, D. W., Vrana, S. R., Melamed, B. G., Cuthbert, B. N., & Lang, P. J. (1993). Emotional imagery in simple and social phobia: Fear vs anxiety. *Journal of Abnormal Psychology, 102,* 212–225.

Mellander, S., Andersson, P., Afzelius, L., & Hellstrand, P. (1982). Neural beta-adrenergic dilation of the facial vein in man: Possible mechanism in emotional blushing. *Acta Physiologica Scandinavica, 114,* 393–399.

Mersch, P. P. A., Hildebrand, M., Lavy, E., & Van Hout, W. J. P. J. (1992). Somatic symptoms in social phobia: A treatment method based upon rational emotive therapy and paradoxical interventions. *Journal of Behavior Therapy and Experimental Psychiatry, 23,* 199–211.

Metts, S. & Cupach, W. R. (1989). Situational influences on the use of remedial strategies in embarrassing predicaments. *Communication Monographs*, *56*, 151–162.

Miller, R. S. (1987). Empathic embarrassment: Situational and personal determinants of reactions to the embarrassment of another. *Journal of Personality and Social Psychology*, *53*, 1061–1069.

Miller, R. S. (1992). The nature and severity of self-reported embarrassing circumstance. *Personality and Social Psychology Bulletin*, *18*, 190–198.

Miller, R. S. (1995). On the nature of embarrassability: Shyness, social evaluation and social skill. *Journal of Personality*, *63*, 315–339.

Miller, R. S. (1996). *Embarrassment. Poise and peril in everyday life.* New York: Guilford Press.

Miller, R. S. & Tangney, J. P. (1994). Differentiating embarrassment from shame. *Journal of Social and Clinical Psychology*, *13*, 273–287.

Mulkens, S. & Bögels, S. M. (1999). Learning history in fear of blushing. *Behaviour Research and Therapy*, *37*, 1159–1167.

Mulkens, S., Bögels, S., & de Jong, P. J. (1999a). Attentional focus and fear of blushing: A case study. *Behavioural and Cognitive Psychotherapy*, *27*, 153–164.

Mulkens, S., de Jong, P. J., & Bögels, S. M. (1997). High blushing propensity: Fearful preoccupation or facial coloration? *Personality and Individual Differences*, *22*, 817–824.

Mulkens, S., de Jong, P. J., Dobbelaar, A., & Bögels, S. (1999b). Fear of blushing irrespective of facial coloration. *Behaviour Research and Therapy*, *37*, 1119–1128.

Neto, F. (1996). Correlates of social blushing. *Personality and Individual Differences*, *20*, 365–373.

Parrott, W. G. & Smith, S. F. (1991). Embarrassment: Actual vs typical cases, classical vs prototypical representations. *Cognition and Emotion*, *5*, 467–488.

Reich, J., Noyes, R., & Yates, W. (1988). Anxiety symptoms distinguishing social phobia from panic and generalized anxiety disorders. *Journal of Nervous and Mental Disease*, *176*, 510–513.

Sattler, J. M. (1966). Embarrassment and blushing: A theoretical review. *Journal of Social Psychology*, *69*, 117–133.

Scholing, A. & Emmelkamp, P. M. G. (1993). Cognitive and behavioural treatments of fear of blushing, sweating or trembling. *Behaviour Research and Therapy*, *31*, 155–170.

Semin, G. & Manstead, A. S. R. (1982). The social implications of embarrassment displays and restitution behaviour. *European Journal of Social Psychology*, *12*, 367–377.

Sharkey, W. F. & Stafford, L. (1990). Responses to embarrassment. *Human Communication Research*, *17*, 315–342.

Shearn, D., Bergman, E., Hill, K., Abel, A., & Hinds, L. (1990). Facial coloration and temperature responses in blushing. *Psychophysiology*, *27*, 687–693.

Shearn, D., Bergman, E., Hill, K., Abel, A., & Hinds, L. (1992). Blushing as a function of audience size, *Psychophysiology*, *29*, 431–436.

Shields, S. A., Mallory, M. E., & Simon, A. (1990). The experience and symptoms of blushing as a function of age and reported frequency of blushing. *Journal of Nonverbal Behavior*, *14*, 171–187.

Simon, A. & Shields, S. A. (1996). Does complexion color affect the experience of blushing? *Journal of Social Behavior and Personality*, *11*, 177–188.

Solyom, L., Ledwidge, B., & Solyom, C. (1986). Delineating social phobia. *British Journal of Psychiatry*, *149*, 464–470.

Tangney, J. P., Miller, R. S., Flicker, L., & Barlow, D. H. (1996). Are shame, guilt, and embarrassment distinct emotions? *Journal of Personality and Social Psychology*, *70*, 1256–1264.

Telaranta, T. (1998). Treatment of social phobia by endoscopic thoracic sympathicotomy. *European Journal of Surgery, Supplement*, *580*, 27–32.

Timms, M. W. H. (1980). Treatment of chronic blushing by paradoxical intention. *Behavioural Psychotherapy*, *8*, 59–61.

Trower, P. & Gilbert, P. (1989). New theoretical conceptions of social anxiety and social phobia. *Clinical Psychology Review, 9*, 19–35.

Van Hoof, J. (1972). A comparative approach to the phylogeny of laughter and smiling. In R. A. Hinde (Ed.), *Non-verbal communication* (pp. 209–237). Cambridge: Cambridge University Press.

Section Three

Clinical Perspectives and Interventions

Introduction

Social Anxiety as a Clinical Condition

Lynn E. Alden *and* **W. Ray Crozier**

CONCEPTUAL ISSUES
Pathological Shyness
Avoidant Personality Disorder
Social Phobia
COMPARISONS
POINTS OF AGREEMENT
DIFFERENCES IN FOCUS
CONCLUSION
REFERENCES

This section of the *Handbook* will consider social anxiety as a clinical disorder. In these chapters, a number of distinguished clinical researchers will present their views on the nature and treatment of severe social anxiety. These introductory comments are intended to provide the background context for the chapters to follow, pointing to some landmarks in the clinical study of social anxiety. They will also highlight some of the major themes that run through the chapters, devoting particular attention to differences in the way that the authors conceptualize and treat disorders caused by severe social anxiety. It is our view that matters of disagreement among experienced researchers point to important areas for future study. As we will see, although writers generally agree on the clinical appearance of social anxiety disorder, there are divergent opinions on the underlying nature of this condition and on which of its various features are key to its understanding and treatment.

International Handbook of Social Anxiety: Concepts, Research and Interventions Relating to the Self and Shyness. Edited by W. Ray Crozier and Lynn E. Alden.
© 2001 John Wiley & Sons Ltd.

CONCEPTUAL ISSUES

Social anxiety has been recognized as a matter of clinical concern within a variety of conceptual frameworks. Three of these are well represented in the scientific literature and in this volume. Specifically, severe social anxiety has been viewed as: an extreme variant of a normal personality trait (pathological shyness), a personality disorder (avoidant personality), and a clinical syndrome (the anxiety disorder, social phobia). Each of these views has a long and distinguished history that goes back to the origins of psychology as a discipline.

Pathological Shyness

The view that severe social anxiety is a manifestation of the personality trait of shyness or timidity underlies the writings of many social and personality psychologists. William James (1890), the father of contemporary research in these areas, viewed shyness as one of the basic human instincts and recognized that this tendency created problems for some people. James is also credited with developing the idea that people have both private and social, or public, selves—a distinction that forms the basis of a number of contemporary social and personality theories of social anxiety (e.g., Schlenker & Leary, 1982). Throughout the first half of the 20th century, shyness was included in multifactorial personality inventories as a basic individual difference (e.g., Guilford & Guilford, 1936; Cattell, 1946). The 1960s and 1970s witnessed efforts by researchers to clarify the domain of shyness and to examine its relationship to other constructs (e.g., Crozier, 1979). These efforts were further advanced by Buss's (1980) writings distinguishing early-developing fearful shyness and later-developing self-conscious shyness, a distinction that led to an explosion of studies on private and public self-consciousness.

The study of shyness as a clinical disorder owes much to the now classic book by Philip Zimbardo, *Shyness, What it is, what to do about it* (Zimbardo, 1977). Zimbardo's writings not only popularized the concept of pathological shyness in the lay public; they led to the development of specialized treatment programs, such as the Stanford Shyness Clinic. In their landmark 1986 volume, *Shyness: Perspectives on research and treatment*, Jones, Cheek and Briggs drew together theoretical research on shyness with descriptions of therapeutic interventions, thereby cementing the notion of shyness as a clinical disorder. Despite recognition that shyness often leads people to seek treatment, most contemporary empirical studies continue to address conceptual rather than clinical issues. One exception to this tendency has been clinical work conducted at the Stanford Shyness Clinic, which is described in detail by Henderson and Zimbardo in *Chapter 19*.

Avoidant Personality Disorder

Within dynamic, interpersonal, and other personological clinical traditions, severe social anxiety has been viewed as a disturbance in personality or character structure. Personality types characterized by social sensitivity and withdrawal appear in early clinical descriptions of personality disorders, most notably in depictions of the schizoid and phobic character styles. For example, Kretschmer (1925) described a hyperaesthetic variant of the schizoid personality that was marked by sensitive susceptibility, shyness, and psychic conflict. Fenichel's (1945) descriptions of the phobic character included such features as the phobic avoidance of desired objects that parallel current descriptions of the avoidant individual. In addition, the early interpersonal writer, Karen Horney, depicted three personality types, which were marked by different interpersonal styles. One of these, the detached personality, displayed an interpersonal style of "moving away from people", which in many ways resembles current views of avoidant personality disorder (Horney, 1945).

Contemporary conceptualizations of avoidant personality disorder have their origins in Theodore Millon's biosocial learning theory. In his books *Modern psychopathology* (1969) and *Disorders of personality* (1981), Millon proposed that the avoidant pattern develops when a child with an anxious temperament is exposed to early social experiences characterized by persistent deprecation, rejection, and humiliation, which results in an *active-detached* coping pattern. Millon's writings led to the inclusion of avoidant personality disorder (APD) in the third edition of the *Diagnostic and Statistical Manual of Mental Disorders* (DSM-III; American Psychiatric Association, 1980). Since then, other models of APD have been developed. For example, A. T. Beck and his colleagues proposed a cognitive model that emphasized the mediating role of cognitive schemas in socially avoidant behaviour (Beck & Freeman, 1990). Various interpersonal writers developed theories that focused on the contribution of core relational schemas to the onset and maintenance of APD (Barber et al., 1997; Benjamin, 1993). According to this view, negative relational schemas colour interpretations of current interactions and lead to a self-perpetuating pattern of re-enacting the early significant relationships that contributed to the individual's social fears. Over the last decade, a number of treatment regimens have been developed and evaluated, including cognitive-behavioural, interpersonal, and pharmacological regimens. All of these have demonstrated some success in lessening symptom severity in individuals with avoidant personality disorder (e.g., Alden, 1989; Barber et al., 1997; Liebowitz et al., 1992; Renneberg, Goldstein, Phillips, & Chambless, 1990).

Social Phobia

Within contemporary biological psychiatry and cognitive-behavioural thinking, severe social anxiety is conceptualized as a clinical syndrome, or constellation of symptoms, that together comprise social phobia. The concept of social phobia was first found in Janet's (1903) descriptions of a condition he termed *phobie des situations sociales*. In the DSM-I and DSM-II, social fears were lumped together with other types of phobias. Following psychodynamic thinking of the time, these phobic conditions were seen to arise from intrapsychic conflicts that had been projected onto situations symbolically related to underlying fears.

Scientific views of the phobias changed with the seminal writings of Isaac Marks, who distinguished social phobia from other types of phobias and presented a behavioural interpretation of these conditions (Marks & Gelder, 1966; Marks, 1969). When the decision was made to move the DSM-III away from its psychodynamic underpinnings toward a more descriptive focus, social phobia was included as a separate disorder (American Psychiatric Association, 1980). The emergence of a distinct diagnostic category led to studies of the epidemiology and clinical presentation of social phobia. Among other advances, this work revealed that many social phobic patients fear multiple social situations (e.g., Liebowitz, Gorman, Fyer, & Klein, 1985). To reflect this, a generalized subtype of social phobia was included in the DSM-III-R along with a non-generalized, or specific, subtype (American Psychiatric Association, 1987). This addition, along with changes in diagnostic procedures to allow simultaneous diagnosis of social phobia and avoidant personality disorder, increased the overlap with APD and led to considerable debate regarding possible distinctions between the two conditions, a debate that continues today. In the 1980s, landmark review articles by Liebowitz et al. (1985) and Heimberg (1989) on what was called the "neglected anxiety disorder" sparked a decade of empirical work on clinical assessment and treatment of social phobia. In particular, the pioneering work of Richard Heimberg on Group Cognitive Behavior Therapy and Michael Liebowitz on pharmacological interventions have pointed to effective interventions for social phobia.

All three clinical perspectives on social anxiety are represented in this section of this *Handbook*. In *Chapter 19*, Henderson and Zimbardo write about treatment of pathological shyness and, in *Chapter 15*, Widiger considers avoidant personality disorder. The remaining chapters consider severe social anxiety in terms of social phobia, which is the conceptual perspective that dominates the clinical literature at present.

COMPARISONS

For many years, research within each framework was conducted more or less independently, although some attempts were made to take advantage of theoretical advances in other areas. As each literature developed, however, there was growing recognition of the need for integration, and, over the last decade, researchers began to compare these three clinical conceptualizations of social anxiety. Although research indicates that there is substantial overlap between the three viewpoints, some differences have been identified.

Severe shyness and social phobia are established through different diagnostic procedures. Shyness is often defined by self-attribution, whereas social phobia is typically determined by clinicians on the basis of DSM criteria assessed through structured interviews. As a result, shyness has been found to be a more hetero-geneous category than social phobia and to include a broader range of negative emotional symptoms (Turner et al., 1990). Shyness also appears to be more preva-lent. Twelve-month prevalence rates for shyness are generally in the range of 20–40% in college students (Spielberger et al., 1984; Zimbardo, 1977), compared with 3–7.9% for social phobia diagnosed according to DSM-III-R criteria. Overall, although individuals who meet diagnostic criteria for social phobia would likely label themselves as severely shy, there appear to be far more self-labelled shy people who would not meet DSM criteria for social phobia.

Like social phobia, avoidant personality disorder (APD) is assessed in refer-ence to DSM diagnostic criteria, typically determined through structured interviews. Because the diagnostic criteria for social phobia and APD are quite similar, the two diagnoses commonly co-occur. Research indicates that the over-whelming majority of individuals with APD also meet diagnostic criteria for Generalized Social Phobia (GSP), and between 50 and 89% of patients with GSP meet criteria for APD (e.g., Fahlen, 1995). Comparative studies indicate that patients with APD report greater social anxiety and depression, lower self-esteem, and display more comorbid diagnoses than do patients with GSP alone, but few other differences emerge (Holt et al., 1992; Turner et al., 1990). The high rate of comorbidity, similarity in diagnostic criteria, and absence of qualitative differences suggest that GSP and APD may represent different points along a continuum of symptom severity. The issue of the distinction between social phobia and APD as well as the cut-off between these two conditions and subclinical social anxiety, continues to be a matter of contention, as is noted by Widiger in *Chapter 15*.

POINTS OF AGREEMENT

However defined, researchers agree that severe social anxiety can create sig-nificant life problems. For example, individuals with social phobia were found to be less likely to marry or to marry later than patients with other anxiety disorders (e.g., Schneier, Johnson, Hornig, Liebowitz, & Weissman, 1992), and socially anxious students were more likely to be lonely and have fewer social interactions than non-anxious students (Dodge, Heimberg, Nyman, & O'Brien, 1987). Both social phobia and shyness have been shown to interfere with aca-demic and occupational functioning (e.g., Phillips & Bruch, 1988). Finally, social phobia has been found to increase the risk for other psychiatric disorders, includ-ing alcohol and drug abuse and comorbid anxiety disorders (e.g., Schneier, Martin, Liebowitz, Gorman, & Fyer, 1989; Schneier et al., 1992). One of the more serious conditions found in conjunction with social anxiety is depression. Between 40 and 50% of patients diagnosed with social phobia or avoidant per-sonality disorder also meet diagnostic criteria for depression. The exact nature of the relationship between social anxiety and depression has been an issue of many empirical studies and is considered in detail by Ingram and his colleagues in *Chapter 16*.

As you will see in the following chapters, clinical writers agree on the developmental course and general appearance of severe social anxiety as described in previous chapters in this volume. Whether conceptualized in terms of pathological shyness, avoidant personality disorder, or social phobia, social anxiety is recognized to have a substantial heritable or biological component that interacts with familial and learning experiences to produce a constellation of physiological, behavioural, and cognitive symptoms. Writers in all three realms recognize that there are individual differences in the extent to which patients display the three sets of symptoms. Finally, clinicians agree that, in the absence of treatment, severe social anxiety is apt to be a longstanding condition that creates ongoing life problems for these patients.

DIFFERENCES IN FOCUS

Despite general agreement on the clinical manifestation of social anxiety, various clinical writers emphasize different features of this condition. As discussed above, some researchers emphasize the enduring nature of social anxiety, a view represented by Widiger (*Chapter 15*) and Henderson and Zimbardo (*Chapter 19*). Other writers place greater emphasis on one or another of the three basic symptom constellations, i.e., behavioural, cognitive, or physiological. Thus, Clark (*Chapter 18*) presents a model of social phobia that emphasizes the role of cognitive processes. Heimberg and his colleagues (*Chapter 20*) examine cognitive-behavioural patterns in this same disorder, as do Sweeney and Rapee (*Chapter 23*). Most contemporary psychiatric researchers emphasize the biological underpinnings of social phobia and avoidant personality disorder, as reflected in the chapter by Hood and Nutt (*Chapter 21*). Finally, some writers underscore the interpersonal nature of social phobia. Alden (*Chapter 17*) discusses the interpersonal processes that contribute to social phobia and Rapee and Sweeney (*Chapter 22*) describe their important recent work on the role of family interaction patterns in childhood social phobia.

As might be expected, these differences in emphasis led to the development of somewhat different clinical interventions, the most prominent of which, cognitive-behavioural therapy and pharmacological treatment, are discussed in this volume. Both approaches are effective, and the relative strengths and limitations of each is a topic of current interest, as noted in chapters by Heimberg and colleagues (*Chapter 20*) and by Hood and Nutt (*Chapter 21*). In addition, Clark (*Chapter 18*) presents preliminary results evaluating a promising new treatment regimen based on his cognitive model of social phobia. Finally, the recognition that social anxiety generally begins early has led to an interest in the development of treatment programs for children, which are described by Sweeney and Rapee (*Chapter 23*).

CONCLUSION

Certainly much remains to be done to further delineate the key features of social anxiety and to develop alternative treatments for patients who fail to respond to existing regimens. Despite this, as you read these chapters, we believe that you will be impressed as we have been by how far we have come in understanding social anxiety as a clinical condition and developing effective interventions to reverse the often devastating effect of social anxiety on the individual's life.

REFERENCES

Alden, L. E. (1989). Short-term structured treatment for avoidant personality disorder. *Journal of Consulting & Clinical Psychology, 57,* 756–764.

American Psychiatric Association (1980). *Diagnostic and statistical manual of mental disorders: 3rd edition.* Washington, DC: Author.

American Psychiatric Association (1987). *Diagnostic and statistical manual of mental disorders: 3rd edition, revised.* Washington, DC: Author.

Barber, J. P., Morse, J. Q., Krakauer, I. D., Chittams, J., & Crits-Christoph, K. (1997). Change in obsessive-compulsive and avoidant personality disorders following Time-limited Supportive-Expressive Therapy. *Psychotherapy, 34,* 133–143.

Beck, A. T. & Freeman, A. (1990). *Cognitive therapy of personality disorders* (pp. 257–282). New York: Guilford.

Benjamin, L. S. (1993). *Interpersonal diagnosis and treatment of personality disorders.* New York: Guilford.

Buss, A. H. (1980). *Self-consciousness and social anxiety.* San Francisco, CA: Freeman.

Cattell, R. B. (1946). *Description and measurement of personality.* New York: World Book.

Crozier, W. R. (1979). Shyness as a dimension of personality. *British Journal of Social and Clinical Psychology, 18,* 121–128.

Dodge, C. S., Heimberg, R. G., Nyman, D., & O'Brien, G. T. (1987). Daily heterosocial interactions of high and low socially anxious college students: A diary study. *Behavior Therapy, 18,* 90–96.

Fahlen, T. (1995). Personality traits in social phobia, I: Comparisons with healthy controls. *Journal of Clinical Psychiatry, 56,* 560–568.

Fenichel, O. (1945). *The psychoanalytic theory of the neurosis.* New York: Norton.

Guilford, J. P. & Guilford, R. B. (1936). Personality factors S, E, and M and their measurement. *Journal of Psychology, 2,* 109–127.

Heimberg, R. G. (Ed.) (1989). Social phobia. *Clinical Psychology Review: Special Issue.*

Holt, C. S., Heimberg, R. G., & Hope, D. A. (1992). Avoidant personality disorder and the generalized subtype of social phobia. *Journal of Abnormal Psychology, 101,* 318–325.

Horney, K. (1945). *Our inner conflicts.* New York: Norton.

James, W. (1890). *The principles of psychology* (Vol. 2). New York: Holt.

Janet, P. (1903). *Les obsessions et la psychasthenie.* Paris: F. Alcan.

Jones, W. H., Cheek, J. M., & Briggs, S. R. (1986). *Shyness: Perspectives on research and treatment.* New York: Plenum Press.

Kretschmer, E. (1925). *Physique and character.* London: Kegan Paul.

Liebowitz, M. R., Gorman, J. M., Fyer, A. J., & Klein, A. F. (1985). Social phobia: Review of a neglected anxiety disorder. *Archives of General Psychiatry, 42,* 729–736.

Liebowitz, M. R., Schneier, F., Campeas, R., Hollander, E., Hatterer, J., Fyer, A., Gorman, J., Papp, L., Davies, S., Gully, R., & Klein, D. F. (1992). Phenelzine vs. atenolol in social phobia: A placebo-controlled comparison. *Archives of General Psychiatry, 52,* 230–237.

Marks, I. M. (1969). *Fears and phobias.* New York: Academic Press.

Marks, I. M. & Gelder, M. G. (1966). Different ages of onset in varieties of phobia. *American Journal of Psychiatry, 123,* 218–221.

Millon, T. (1969). *Modern psychopathology: A biosocial approach to maladaptive learning and functioning.* Philadelphia: W. B. Saunders.

Millon, T. (1981). *Disorders of personality.* New York: Wiley.

Phillips, S. D. & Bruch, M. A. (1988). Shyness and dysfunction in career development. *Journal of Counseling Psychology, 35,* 159–165.

Renneberg, B., Goldstein, A. J., Phillips, D. & Chambless, D. L. (1990). Intensive behavioral group treatment of avoidant personality disorder. *Behavior Therapy, 21,* 363–377.

Schlenker, B. R. & Leary, M. (1982). Social anxiety and self-presentation: A conceptualization and model. *Psychological Bulletin, 92,* 641–669.

Schneier, F. R., Johnson, J., Hornig, C. D., Liebowitz, M. R., & Weissman, M. M. (1992). Social phobia: Comorbidity and morbidity in an epidemiological sample. *Archives of General Psychiatry, 49,* 282–288.

Schneier, F. R., Martin, L. Y., Liebowitz, M. R., Gorman, J. M., & Fyer, A. J. (1989). Alcohol abuse in social phobia. *Journal of Anxiety Disorders, 3,* 15–23.

Spielberger, C. D., Pollans, C. H., & Wordern, T. J. (1984). Anxiety disorders. In S. M. Turner & M. Hersen (Eds.), *Adult psychopathology and diagnosis* (pp. 263–303). New York: Wiley.

Turner, A. M., Beidel, D. & Townsley, R. (1990). Social phobia: A comparison of specific and generalized subtypes and avoidant personality disorder. *Journal of Abnormal Psychology, 101,* 326–331.

Zimbardo, P. G. (1977). *Shyness: What it is, what to do about it.* New York: Addison-Wesley.

Chapter 15

Social Anxiety, Social Phobia, and Avoidant Personality

Thomas A. Widiger

FIVE-FACTOR MODEL OF PERSONALITY
AVOIDANT PERSONALITY DISORDER
BOUNDARIES OF SOCIAL ANXIOUSNESS
Social Phobia versus Avoidant Personality Disorder
    DSM-III
    DSM-III-R
    DSM-IV
    DSM-V
Normal versus Abnormal Social Anxiety
    Responsivity to treatment
    Clinically significant impairment or distress
CONCLUSIONS
REFERENCES

My intention for this chapter is to discuss social anxiousness from the perspective of personality disorder research and theory. I begin with a presentation of the conceptual and empirical support for the general model of personality functioning within which personality disorders will be understood, the Five-Factor Model. I then describe the personality disorder that would be diagnosed in persons with a maladaptive variant of this social anxiousness, the avoidant personality disorder. Following this, I discuss the differentiation of avoidant personality disorder from social phobia, an alternative diagnosis for social anxiousness. Finally, I consider the equally problematic differentiation of normal and abnormal social anxiousness.

International Handbook of Social Anxiety: Concepts, Research and Interventions Relating to the Self and Shyness. Edited by W. Ray Crozier and Lynn E. Alden.
© 2001 John Wiley & Sons Ltd.

FIVE-FACTOR MODEL OF PERSONALITY

Personality is defined traditionally as "the dynamic organization within the individual of those psychophysical systems that determine his characteristic behavior and thought" (Allport, 1961, p. 28). Personality is the way one typically behaves, thinks, and feels. Any particular individual's personality will include a constellation of related and often interacting personality traits. No single term or trait dimension will provide an adequate description of the complex constellation of traits that would fully characterize any particular individual's personality (Widiger, 1993). There are literally thousands of trait terms available within the English language for describing the personalities of oneself and others (Goldberg, 1982).

Faced with this overwhelming complexity, researchers have been devoted to the development of a descriptive taxonomy of personality that would be able to summarize, characterize, and differentiate the most important traits (Digman, 1990). One such model is the Five-Factor Model (FFM) or the Big Five (Costa & McCrae, 1992, 1998; Goldberg, 1990, 1993; Saucier & Goldberg, 1996). The FFM is based on the compelling theory that the most important personality traits will have been encoded within the language (Goldberg, 1982, 1993). Systematic, objective, and comprehensive studies of the encoded language have repeatedly identified five broad domains of personality functioning, identified as neuroticism (ego strength, emotional stability, or negative affectivity), extraversion (surgency or positive affectivity), openness to experience (or unconventionality), agreeableness, and conscientiousness (or constraint) (Digman, 1990). Alternative names for each of these five broad domains are provided parenthetically because, not surprisingly, it is difficult to agree on one word that would adequately represent an entire domain (John & Srivastava, 1999).

Each of the five broad domains can be differentiated into more specific variants or facets. The research of Costa and McCrae (1992, 1995) has been particularly successful in identifying and validating six facets within each domain. For example, the domain of neuroticism can be differentiated into six facets, including anxiousness (e.g., nervous, anxious versus unconcerned, relaxed, cool), angry hostility (e.g., bitter, angry versus even-tempered), depressiveness (e.g., glum, despondent, hopeless, or pessimistic versus optimistic, hopeful), self-consciousness (e.g., timid, embarrassed versus self-assured, glib, shameless), impulsiveness (e.g., tempted, reckless versus controlled, restrained), and vulnerability (e.g., fragile, helpless vs stalwart, brave, fearless).

There is substantial empirical support for the construct validity of the FFM. For example, the five-factor structure has been replicated across a variety of self, peer, and spouse ratings (Costa & McCrae, 1992). Fundamental to the validity of a theory of personality would be a demonstration of temporal stability, and this research has also been compelling (Costa & McCrae, 1994). For example, Costa and McCrae (1988) reported test–retest assessments of the domains of the FFM across a period of years. Six-year test–retest correlations of self-ratings ranged from 0.82 (extraversion) to 0.83 (neuroticism); Seven-year test–retest correlations of peer descriptions ranged from 0.63 to 0.81; and six-year test–retest spouse ratings ranged from 0.77 to 0.80 (Costa & McCrae, 1994). For the individual facets of anxiousness and gregariousness (the facets most relevant to persons described as socially anxious) six-year test–retest correlations of self-ratings were 0.78 and 0.92, respectively, and spouse ratings were 0.75 and 0.73, respectively (Costa & McCrae, 1988). It is also notable that a person's self-rating of anxiousness correlated 0.47 with the spouse's rating of that person's level of anxiousness six years later (0.52 for gregariousness). If one adjusts these correlations for attenuation due to the unreliability of the measure itself (which underestimates the actual temporal stability of anxiousness and gregariousness), stability coefficients usually exceed 0.90 (Costa & McCrae, 1994).

The five fundamental domains of personality have also been identified across the life span, including within children (Halverson, Kohnstamm, & Martin, 1994), adults (Digman, 1990), and the aging (Costa & McCrae, 1994). Fundamental dimensions of personality structure are likely to have a significant degree of heritability, and there has indeed been compelling empirical support for the heritability of the domains and facets of the FFM. The most heavily researched factors have been neuroticism and extraversion (Eaves, Eysenck, & Martin, 1989), the two domains that would be central to an understanding of social anxiety. Using the results of five large twin studies across five different countries (total sample size of 24,000 twin pairs), the average correlations for identical twins and fraternal twins were reported as 0.46 and 0.20 for neuroticism (respectively) and 0.51 and 0.18 for extraversion (respectively) (Loehlin, 1992). The heritability of neuroticism is typically estimated to be approximately 50%; and 60% for extraversion (Plomin & Caspi, 1999). Jang, McCrae, Angleitner, Reimann, and Livesley (1998) examined the heritability of the domains and facets of the FFM using twin data obtained from Germany and Canada. "The results showed that genetic and environmental effects on personality traits were essentially the same in form and magnitude in Germany and Canada" (Jang et al., 1998, p. 1563). Equally important, their findings provided "strong support for hierarchical models of personality that posit a large number of narrow traits as well as a few broader trait factors" (Jang et al., 1998, p. 1563). Anxiousness, as a facet of the broad domain of neuroticism, obtained a correlation between monozygotic twins of 0.32 and 0.46 in the Canadian and German samples, respectively, compared to 0.21 and 0.13 for dizygotic twins. Gregariousness, a facet of extraversion, obtained comparable results of 0.53 and 0.40 for monozygotic twins compared to 0.35 and 0.21 for dizygotic. Heritability estimates for neuroticism and extraversion were 49% and 50%, respectively; for the facets of anxiousness and gregariousness they were 41% and 40%, respectively.

It would not be surprising to find some variation across cultures in the content, emphasis, or structure of trait terms, yet there has been a compelling degree of replication of the FFM across a wide variety of languages, including Dutch, German, Chinese, Czech, Filipino, Hebrew, Hungarian, Italian, Polish, Russian, and Turkish (John & Srivastava, 1999). For example, McCrae and Costa (1997) reported the results of a comparison of the factor structure of the FFM across German, Portuguese, Hebrew, Chinese, Korean, and Japanese languages (N =

7,134). The FFM structure was closely reproduced, even at the level of the facets within each domain. "Because the samples studied represented highly diverse cultures with languages from five distinct language families, these data strongly suggest that personality trait structure is universal" (McCrae & Costa, 1997, p. 509). The domain with the weakest replication has been, not surprisingly, openness to experience, as this was the last and smallest domain to be extracted from the analyses of the English language (Goldberg, 1982, 1990). Based on a review of the extensive cross-cultural research, De Raad, Perugini, Hrebickova, and Szarota (1998) concluded that the findings supported "the general contours of the Big Five model as the best working hypothesis of an omnipresent trait structure" (p. 214).

"One of the apparent strengths of the Big Five taxonomy is that it can capture, at a broad level of abstraction, the commonalities among most of the existing systems of personality traits, thus providing an integrative descriptive model for research" (John & Srivastava, 1999, p. 122). Wiggins (1968) stated in his seminal review of personality research some 30 years ago that "if consensus exists within the realm of temperament structure, it does so with respect to the importance of the large, ubiquitous, and almost unavoidable dimensions of extraversion and anxiety (neuroticism)" (p. 309), the two domains of central importance to an understanding of social anxiousness. He concurred again with this conclusion in his more recent review, although adding to this list the additional three domains of agreeableness, openness, and conscientiousness (Wiggins & Pincus, 1992). Costa, McCrae, and their colleagues have been particularly successful in documenting empirically the predominance of neuroticism, extroversion (versus introversion), agreeableness, openness, and conscientiousness in almost every instrument for the assessment of personality. A detailed summary of this extensive research is provided by Costa and McCrae (1992), Digman (1990), and John and Srivastava (1999).

AVOIDANT PERSONALITY DISORDER

"When personality traits are inflexible and maladaptive and cause significant functional impairment or subjective distress . . . they constitute Personality Disorders" (APA, 1994, p. 630). One of the personality disorders included within the American Psychiatric Association's *Diagnostic and Statistical Manual of Mental Disorders* (DSM-IV; APA, 1994) is the avoidant personality disorder, the diagnostic criteria for which are provided in Table 15.1.

Avoidant personality disorder is defined in DSM-IV as "a pervasive pattern of social inhibition, feelings of inadequacy, and hypersensitivity to negative evaluation, beginning by early adulthood and present in a variety of contexts" (APA, 1994, p. 164). It occurs with equal frequency in males and females (Corbitt & Widiger, 1995) and is one of the more frequently diagnosed personality disorders, occurring in as many as 20–25% of the patients within some clinical settings (Weissman, 1993). Its prevalence is not particularly surprising, as timidity, shyness, and social insecu-

Table 15.1 DSM-IV criteria for avoidant personality disorder

A pervasive pattern of social inhibition, feelings of inadequacy, and hypersensitivity to negative evaluation, beginning by early adulthood and present in a variety of contexts, as indicated by four (or more) of the following:

(1) Avoids occupational activities that involve significant interpersonal contact, because of fears of criticism, disapproval, or rejection
(2) Is unwilling to get involved with people unless certain of being liked
(3) Shows restraint within intimate relationships because of the fear of being shamed or ridiculed
(4) Is preoccupied with being criticized or rejected in social situations
(5) Is inhibited in new interpersonal situations because of feelings of inadequacy
(6) Views self as socially inept, personally unappealing, or inferior to others
(7) Is unusually reluctant to take personal risks or to engage in any new activities because they may prove embarrassing

Source: American Psychiatric Association (1994, pp. 164–165).

rity are not uncommon problems, and are often the basis for persons seeking clinical treatment. Less than 2% of the general population, however, is likely to meet the DSM-IV criteria for its diagnosis (Widiger & Sanderson, 1997).

Persons with avoidant personality disorder will be shy, timid, insecure, and anxious as children (Rothbart & Ahadi, 1994). Adolescence will be a particularly difficult time for persons with this disorder, given the importance during this developmental period of interpersonal popularity, attractiveness, and dating (Bernstein, Cohen, & Velez, 1993). Occupational success as an adult may not be significantly impaired, as long as there is little demand on the job for public performance. Persons with an avoidant personality disorder can in fact find considerable gratification and esteem through a job or career that they are unable to find within their relationships. The job may also serve as a distraction from intense feelings of loneliness (Widiger & Sanderson, 1997).

Their long history of avoiding social situations, however, will have impaired their ability to develop adequate social skills, and will further handicap any eventual efforts to develop relationships (Pilkonis, 1984). They will have a strong desire to develop close personal relationships, but they will feel too insecure to approach others, spending much of their time feeling lonely, isolated, and alone (Millon et al., 1996; Widiger & Sanderson, 1997). They may eventually develop an intimate relationship, to which they will cling with intense dependency. Knowing how difficult it was to obtain this relationship, they may hold onto to it with a desperation and intense fear of being alone once again. As parents, they can be very responsible, empathic, and affectionate toward their children, but they may also impart feelings of social anxiousness and serve as a role model for social awkwardness (along with passing on a genetic disposition toward anxiousness and introversion).

Persons with an avoidant personality disorder are also prone to mood and anxiety disorders, particularly depression and social phobia (Widiger &

Sanderson, 1997). They will often seek treatment for an anxiety disorder but are perhaps prone to developing a psychological (if not physiological) dependence on anxiolytics (Millon et al., 1996). The severity of the avoidant symptomatology will diminish as the person becomes older, due in part to a gradual reduction in peripheral sympathetic activity and adrenocortical responsiveness, as well as the repeated corrective environmental (interpersonal) experiences that will typically occur throughout adulthood.

Widiger, Trull, Clarkin, Sanderson, and Costa (1994) provided a description of each of the DSM-III-R personality disorders from the perspective of the FFM. Avoidant personality disorder was among the most readily understood as a maladaptive variant of the fundamental and common personality traits of neuroticism and introversion. Their description is still applicable:

> From the perspective of the five-factor model, avoidant personality disorder involves (a) introversion, particularly the facets of low gregariousness (no close friends, avoids significant interpersonal contact, and unwilling to get involved with others; APA, 1987); low excitement seeking (exaggerates potential dangers, difficulties, or risks in doing anything outside of normal routine); low activity (avoidance of social and occupational activities, and canceling of social plans); and low assertiveness (not represented within in the DSM-III-R criteria but present within the clinical literature; Millon, 1981; Pilkonis, 1984); and (b) neuroticism, particularly the facets of vulnerability, self-consciousness, and anxiety (e.g., easily hurt by criticism and disapproval, reticent in social situations because of fear of saying something foolish, fears being embarrassed, and afraid of not being liked).
>
> (Widiger et al., 1994, p. 49)

Widiger et al.'s conceptualization of avoidant personality disorder has been examined in 13 independent studies, some of which included multiple tests of the hypotheses. The findings from these studies are summarized in Table 15.2. It is evident from this research that there is compelling empirical support for this personological interpretation of avoidant personality disorder. The research is supportive with respect to both convergent and discriminant validity. Avoidant personality traits, assessed by a variety of methods, are consistently and often highly correlated with the broad domains of personality identified as neuroticism and extraversion, but are rarely correlated with any of the other domains of personality. Similar patterns of findings have been obtained in clinical, community, and college populations, again consistent with the hypothesis that the symptomatology of avoidant personality disorder is a maladaptive variant of common personality traits (Livesley, 1998). There are a few exceptions to the expected findings, but these exceptions are notable precisely because they are so inconsistent with the findings that are usually obtained.

Many of the studies have also conducted multiple regression or canonical variate analyses to assess whether neuroticism and extraversion provide specific contributions to explaining avoidant personality disorder symptomatology, and in each instance the predictions were confirmed (i.e., Coolidge et al., 1994; Ramanaiah & Sharpe, 1998; Trull, Widiger, & Burr, 2001; Wiggins & Pincus, 1989).

Table 15.2 Correlations of avoidant personality disorder with domains of the FFM

Study	Sample	Measures APD	Measures FFM	N	E	O	A	C
Wiggins & Pincus (1989)	550 stdts	MMPI	NEOPI	0.64***	-0.58***	-0.13*	-0.06	-0.13*
Costa & McCrae (1990)	274 comm	MMPI	NEOPI	0.52***	-0.54***	-0.03	-0.02	-0.02
Costa & McCrae (1990)	207 comm	MCMI-I	NEOPI	0.44***	-0.53***	-0.11	0.03	-0.07
Costa & McCrae (1990)	62 comm	MCMI-II	NEOPI	0.36**	-0.32**	-0.11	0.05	0.03
Trull (1992)	54 pts	MMPI	NEOPI	0.55***	-0.63***	-0.27*	-0.16	-0.19
Trull (1992)	54 pts	PDQR	NEOPI	0.36**	-0.39**	-0.20	-0.20	-0.21
Trull (1992)	54 pts	SIDPR	NEOPI	0.25	-0.36**	-0.15	-0.19	0.03
Soldz et al. (1993)	102 pts	MCMI-II	50-BSRS	0.54***	-0.59***	-0.30**	-0.23*	-0.08
Soldz et al. (1993)	102 pts	PDE	50-BSRS	0.23*	-0.57***	-0.39**	-0.17	0.03
West (1993)	457 stdts	MMPI	NEOPI	0.50***	-0.51***	-0.15	-0.12	-0.06
West (1993)	457 stdts	PDQR	NEOPI	0.43***	-0.41***	-0.15	-0.19	0.03
Yeung et al. (1993)	224 comm	SIDP	NEOFFI	0.27***	-0.13	-0.12	0.01	-0.16*
Coolidge et al. (1994)	233 stdts	CATI	NEOPI	0.58***	-0.66***	-0.07	-0.16*	-0.10
Hyer et al. (1994)	80 pts	MCMI-II	NEOPI	0.23*	-0.29**	-0.25*	-0.14	-0.01
Duijsens & Diekstra (1996)	450 comm	VKP	23BB5	0.43***	-0.39***	-0.03	-0.41***	0.02
Duijsens et al. (1995)	210 comm	VKP	5PFT	0.42***	-0.26***	-0.19**	-0.18**	0.03
Ball et al. (1997)	363 pts	SCID-II	NEOFFI	0.45***	-0.33***	0.04	-0.09	-0.20***
Blais (1997)	100 pts	Clinician	Adjectives	0.46***	-0.49***	0.06	0.06	0.13
Dyce & O'Connor (1998)	614 stdts	MCMI-III	NEOPIR	0.63***	-0.48***	-0.12	-0.11	-0.22**
Trull et al. (2001)	232 mixed	PDQR	SIFFM	0.66***	-0.65***	0.14	0.02	-0.26**

*$p < 0.05$; **$p < 0.01$; ***$p < 0.001$.

Notes: APD = avoidant personality disorder; FFM = Five-Factor Model; N = neuroticism; E = extraversion; O = openness; A = agreeableness; C = conscientiousness; stdts = students; comm = community; pts = patients; MMPI = Minnesota Multiphasic Personality Inventory; MCMI = Millon Clinical Multiaxial Inventory; PDQR = Personality Diagnostic Questionnaire-Revised; SIDPR = Structured Interview for Personality Disorders-Revised; PDE = Personality Disorder Examination; CATI = Coolidge Axis II Inventory; VKP = Vragenlijst voor Kenmerken van de Persoonlijkheid; SCID-II = Structured Clinical Interview for DSM-IV Personality Disorders; Clinician = ratings by unstructured clinical interviews; NEOPIR = NEO Five-Factor Inventory Revised; 50-BSRS = 50-Bipolar Self-Rating Scale; NEOFFI = NEO Five-Factor Inventory; 23BB5 = 23 Bipolar Big Five Questionnaire; 5PFT = Five Personality Factor Test; SIFFM = Structured Interview for the Five-Factor Model.

Only a couple of the FFM studies have assessed the relationship of avoidant symptomatology with facets of neuroticism and extraversion, but they have confirmed the expectations. For example, Dyce and O'Connor (1998) reported correlations of 0.49, 0.62, and 0.46 (respectively) with the neuroticism facets of anxiousness, self-consciousness, and vulnerability ($p < 0.001$) and correlations of −0.37, −0.29, and −0.24 with the extraversion facets of gregariousness, activity, and excitement-seeking ($p < 0.01$). Trull et al. (2001) reported correlations of 0.43, 0.70, and 0.56 (respectively) with the neuroticism facets of anxiousness, self-consciousness, and vulnerability ($p < 0.001$) and −0.33, −0.45, and −0.40 with the extraversion facets of gregariousness, activity, and excitement-seeking ($p < 0.001$).

In sum, the research on the association of avoidant personality disorder symptomatology with the domains and facets of the FFM support not only the specific predictions of Widiger et al. (1994) but also provide construct validity for the diagnosis of avoidant personality disorder. Avoidant personality disorder is the presence of extreme elevations on neuroticism and extraversion, two of the most heavily researched and well-established domains of personality functioning. All in all, the personality traits of neuroticism and extraversion have compelling convergent and discriminant validity, temporal stability, heritability, and cross-cultural application (Costa & McCrae, 1998; John & Srivastava, 1999), and persons with the highest elevations on neuroticism and introversion will display the symptomatology of an avoidant personality disorder.

BOUNDARIES OF SOCIAL ANXIOUSNESS

"DSM-IV is a categorical classification that divides mental disorders into types based on criterion sets with defining features" (APA, 1994, p. xxii). The boundaries among these diagnostic categories, however, have been difficult to define and demarcate. Two diagnostic boundaries of particular relevance to social anxiousness are the boundary between social phobia and avoidant personality disorder and the boundary of both of these conditions with normal social anxiousness. Each will be discussed in turn.

Social Phobia versus Avoidant Personality Disorder

Social phobia is an anxiety disorder that involves "a marked and persistent fear of social or performance situations in which embarrassment may occur" (APA, 1994, p. 411). The person fears that he or she will act in a way that will be embarrassing or humiliating. Avoidant personality disorder is a "pervasive pattern of social inhibition, feelings of inadequacy, and hypersensitivity to negative evaluation" (APA, 1994, p. 364). These brief descriptions clearly suggest substantial overlap, and it is indeed the case that persons who meet the diagnostic criteria for one of them will often meet the criteria for the other (Millon et al., 1996; Widiger & Sanderson, 1997).

DSM-III

Avoidant personality disorder and social phobia were both new additions to the third edition of the APA (1980) diagnostic manual. Their original criteria sets were relatively different from one another. For example, consistent with the traditional concept of a phobia (APA, 1994), social phobia was conceptualized as being quite circumscribed in its presentation. Social phobic fears of embarrassment or humiliation arising from interactions with others would be seen in persons with an avoidant personality disorder, but in the case of a social phobia "a specific situation, such as public speaking, is avoided rather than personal relationships" (APA, 1980, p. 324). The four most common situations avoided by persons with a social phobia were specified: "speaking or performing in public, using public lavatories, eating in public, and writing in the presence of others" (APA, 1980, p. 227). In fact, it was noted further that most persons with a social phobia were usually fearful of just one of these four situations: "Generally, an individual has only one Social Phobia" (APA, 1980, p. 227).

DSM-III even excluded the possibility of diagnosing a social phobia if the person met the criteria for an avoidant personality disorder (APA, 1980). This exclusion was consistent with a number of principles guiding the construction of the diagnostic manual (First, Spitzer, & Williams, 1990). "A symptomatically more pervasive disorder preempts the diagnosis of a less pervasive disorder that is based on a symptom that is part of the essential features of the more pervasive disorder" (Spitzer & Williams, 1987, p. 431). In addition, "a diagnosis is not given if its essential features are typically associated features of another disorder whose essential features are also present" (Spitzer & Williams, 1987, p. 431). In the case of social phobia and avoidant personality disorder, it was apparent that avoidant personality disorder is a more pervasive disorder than social phobia and its essential features are readily subsumed by or understood in terms of avoidant personality traits.

DSM-III-R

After the publication of DSM-III, however, it became apparent to anxiety disorder specialists that the phobic behavior of many of their patients failed to be as circumscribed as was required for the diagnosis of social phobia. The statement in DSM-III that "generally an individual has only one Social Phobia" (APA, 1980, p. 227) proved to be quite inaccurate. Many of the persons who sought treatment from anxiety disorder specialists had much more generalized and pervasive patterns of social inhibition (Spitzer & Williams, 1985). Many of them would have met the DSM-III criteria for an avoidant personality disorder, but they would seek treatment from anxiety disorder clinics because their social phobic symptomatology was often their prominent or immediate concern (Frances, 1980).

Anxiety disorder specialists, however, were reluctant to diagnose these patients with an avoidant personality disorder because this diagnosis might imply that they should not be the primary therapists for these patients, and they could provide a treatment that was shown empirically to have a significant effect on the avoidant personality disorder symptomatology (Liebowitz, 1992).

They argued for the inclusion of a new anxiety disorder diagnosis in DSM-III-R that would include the more pervasive symptomatology and would provide a diagnosis consistent with their treatment expertise (Spitzer & Williams, 1985). The authors of DSM-III-R responded to this request by eliminating the avoidant personality disorder exclusion criterion and, more importantly, by including a new subtype to the diagnosis of social phobia, identified as "generalized". Generalized social phobia would be diagnosed "if the phobic situation includes most social situations" (APA, 1987, p. 243).

The inclusion of a generalized subtype, however, complicated the distinction between social phobia and avoidant personality disorder (Widiger, 1992). One potential distinction might have been the age of onset, as personality traits are generally evident since late childhood or early adolescence (APA, 1994; Halverson et al., 1994), but social phobia was also described in DSM-III-R as being chronic and usually beginning "in late childhood or early adolescence" (APA, 1987, p. 242).

As the conceptualization and diagnostic criteria for social phobia were being broadened, the diagnostic criteria for avoidant personality disorder were also being revised in a manner that would effectively subsume more instances of social phobia (Millon, 1996). The DSM-III criteria for avoidant personality disorder were based heavily on the description of the disorder developed by Millon (1981). However, the confinement of the criteria set to Millon's formulation received substantial criticism (e.g., Gunderson, 1983; Kernberg, 1984). Therefore, the DSM-III-R criteria were revised in part to include more of the features of the traditional concept of a "phobic character". "DSM-III-R includes additional features of the psychoanalytic concept of the inhibited phobic character, such as an exaggeration of the risks of everyday life and an inordinate fear of being embarrassed" (Widiger, Frances, Spitzer, & Williams, 1988, p. 790), many of which, however, would be seen in persons diagnosed with a generalized social phobia (Millon, 1996).

DSM-IV

A number of studies were conducted after the publication of DSM-III-R that explored the nature and frequency of the co-occurrence of social phobia with avoidant personality disorder, and the authors of some of these studies attempted to provide a meaningful distinction between these two disorders, such as severity of social skill deficits, level of anxiety, or degree of personal feelings of insecurity (e.g., Herbert, Hope, & Bellack, 1992; Holt, Heimberg, & Hope, 1992; Turner, Beidel, & Townsley, 1992). However, all of these distinctions have been more quantitative than qualitative. If there was any distinction, it appeared to reflect a severity of dysfunction rather than a fundamental difference between an anxiety disorder and a personality disorder (Widiger, 1992).

An effort, however, was made during the process of developing DSM-IV to revise the criteria set for avoidant personality disorder to provide meaningful distinctions. Millon (1996) suggested that "avoidant personality disorder is essentially a problem of relating to persons; social phobia has been formulated largely as a problem of performance situations" (p. 760). More specifically, "persons with social phobia may have a multitude of satisfying social/personal relationships with others; the individual with avoidant personality disorder is socially withdrawn, has few close relationships, and desires close relationships but does not trust others sufficiently to relate closely without assurances of acceptance" (Millon, 1996, p. 760).

Millon's hypotheses, however, do appear to be based largely on expectations that were more appropriate for the description of DSM-III social phobia than for the description of DSM-III-R or DSM-IV generalized social phobia. In addition, there does not appear to be much empirical support for this distinction. Nevertheless, Millon (1991, 1996), as the primary author of the DSM-IV criteria set for avoidant personality disorder, implemented a number of revisions that were intended to facilitate a differentiation from generalized social phobia. For example, the DSM-III-R diagnostic criterion "is reticent in social situations because of a fear of saying something inappropriate or foolish, or of being unable to answer a question" (APA, 1987, p. 353) was revised to "is inhibited in new interpersonal situations because of feelings of inadequacy" (APA, 1994, p. 665). The new DSM-IV criterion is more indicative of a personality trait as it is more general in its description (e.g., inhibited rather than simply reticent; feelings of inadequacy rather than a specific fear of saying something foolish). In addition, many of the revisions emphasized a person's self-image of being inadequate, inept, unappealing, or inferior rather than referring to feelings of anxiety or fear within social situations. For example, the DSM-III-R diagnostic criterion, "fears being embarrassed by blushing, crying, or showing signs of anxiety in front of other people" (APA, 1987, p. 353) was replaced by "views self as socially inept, personally unappealing, or inferior to others" (APA, 1994, p. 665).

It is possible that these revisions will reduce the overlap and diagnostic cooccurrence with generalized social phobia, but the revisions may still fail to identify a distinct diagnostic category (Livesley, 1998). Many of the avoidant diagnostic criteria continue to refer to symptomatology that will be seen in persons with a generalized social phobia (e.g., "avoids occupational activities that involve significant interpersonal contact, because of fears of criticism, disapproval or rejection", APA, 1994, p. 664). In addition, social phobia was revised for DSM-IV in a manner that would contribute to more overlap rather than to improved differentiation. For example, added to the description of its associated features were references to most of the features that have been suggested in prior studies for differentiating avoidant personality disorder from social phobia or had been added to the DSM-IV criteria set for avoidant personality disorder to differentiate it from generalized social phobia, including "low self-esteem or feelings of inferiority" and "poor social skills" (APA, 1994, p. 413). "In more severe cases, individuals may . . . have no friends or cling to unfulfilling relationships [and] completely refrain from dating" (APA, 1994, p. 413). The description of its course is again consistent with the description of a characteristic personality trait: "social phobia typically has an onset in the mid-teens, sometimes emerging out of a childhood history of social inhibition or shyness . . . Duration is frequently lifelong" (APA, 1994, p. 414).

DSM-V

The diagnosis of avoidant personality disorder excluded the diagnosis of social phobia in DSM-III; some now argue that the diagnosis of generalized social phobia should exclude avoidant personality disorder in DSM-V: "We believe that the more extensive evidence for syndromal validity of social phobia, including pharmacological and cognitive-behavioral treatment efficacy, make it the more useful designation in cases of overlap with avoidant personality" (Liebowitz et al., 1998, p. 1060). The primary basis for this argument is the responsivity of persons diagnosed with avoidant personality disorder to pharmacologic treatments. "One may have to rethink what the personality disorder concept means in an instance where 6 weeks of phenelzine therapy begins to reverse longstanding interpersonal hypersensitivity as well as discomfort in socializing" (Liebowitz, 1992, p. 251).

Specific treatment responsivity is a compelling basis for making distinctions among diagnostic categories, but pharmacologic responsivity is not as specific as is suggested by Liebowitz (1992). The benefits of phenelzine are not in fact specific to anxiety disorders, as it is itself a relatively nonspecific antidepressant (Gorman & Kent, 1999; Stahl, 1998). In addition, as Liebowitz acknowledged elsewhere, "all patients with psychiatric illness experience pathologic anxiety" (Gorman, Liebowitz, & Shear, 1992, p. 1) that will often benefit from anxiolytic treatments. It is in particular a false assumption that personality disorders are unresponsive to pharmacologic interventions (Sanislow & McGlashan, 1998). Neurochemical processes are as important in the presence and expression of personality and personality disorders as they are in the presence and expression of anxiety disorders (Siever & Davis, 1991). It is not at all inconsistent with the concept of a personality trait to "begin to reverse" in the presence of sustained alterations to neurochemical functioning. Personality disorders (and, as indicated below, even normal personality traits) can be affected significantly by sustained alterations to neurochemical functioning.

Liebowitz (1992), however, fears that most clinicians do not recognize the lack of specificity of pharmacotherapy, and may in fact have false expectations regarding the treatment of personality disorders that will contribute to inadequate treatment decisions. "The danger . . . is that, in my experience, practitioners tend to regard [personality disorders] as amenable to psychoanalytic psychotherapy rather than pharmacotherapy or behavioral approaches" (Liebowitz, 1992, p. 251). One will indeed observe a mistaken assumption that a personality disorder implies the presence of a psychosocial rather than a biogenetic etiology, and an intervention using an insight-oriented psychotherapy rather than a pharmacotherapy (Gunderson & Pollack, 1985). However, this inaccurate and misbegotten expectation is itself being expressed and endorsed by Liebowitz (1992), rather than by any particular practitioner. False distinctions should be discouraged and corrected, rather than endorsed, encouraged, or reified by revising the nomenclature to be consistent with them.

A more important question is whether the central or fundamental pathology of the patient being diagnosed with a generalized social phobia or an avoidant personality disorder is best understood as a disorder of anxiety or of personality, and the answer to this question is unclear. There is currently no presentation in DSM-IV to indicate what is meant by or would qualify as an anxiety disorder (an extensive discussion of what is meant by a personality disorder is provided: APA, 1994, pp. 629–634). One potential definition or requirement for classification as an anxiety disorder might be that the underlying pathology is confined largely to or is predominated by a dyscontrol or dysregulation of anxiety, the presumptive focus of the pharmacologic treatment for an anxiety disorder. If this is indeed the case, then an argument could be made for focusing or confining treatment largely on improvements in the control, moderation, or regulation of anxiety.

However, the pathology of persons with a generalized social phobia or an avoidant personality disorder might not be confined to a dysregulation in the neurochemical mechanisms of anxiety. Altering this neurochemistry to help control or minimize feelings of anxiety will be helpful to persons with an avoidant personality disorder (as the facet of anxiousness will indeed be an important component; Widiger et al., 1994), but a treatment confined to the symptoms of anxiety may not resolve or even address the full or primary source for a person's shyness, self-consciousness, social isolation, insecurity, and feelings of vulnerability (Millon et al., 1996; Widiger & Sanderson, 1997). This is perhaps why pharmacologic treatment of generalized social phobia is rarely complete or comprehensive in its effects and must often be sustained to maintain its effects (Gorman et al., 1992).

Curing persons of their social behavior after only six weeks of pharmacotherapy might be inconsistent with the concept of a personality disorder, or at least would be consistent with the presence of a specific neurochemical pathology that was treated successfully by the medication, analogous to the treatment of an infection by penicillin or a virus by an antibiotic. Once a curative medication has effectively destroyed, removed, or otherwise treated the pathology, the treatment may no longer be needed. Pharmacotherapies for mental disorders, however, are rarely effective in this manner (Gorman et al., 1992), due perhaps to the presence of a more extensive and pervasive psychopathology. Many of the features of a generalized social phobia and an avoidant personality disorder (e.g., shyness, insecurity, and inhibition) may not even reflect the neurochemical mechanisms of anxiety. Liebowitz (1992) is correct that optimal treatment of an avoidant personality disorder will often include a pharmacologic intervention, but confining the treatment to this approach could be as (if not more) inadequate and ineffective as failing to include any pharmacotherapy.

In sum, the pathology of persons with a generalized social phobia or an avoidant personality disorder is probably more pervasive than simply a dysfunction or dysregulation of anxiety. There are prototypic cases of social phobia and avoidant personality disorder that will be easily distinguished and may even require distinct approaches to treatment. However, the boundary between social phobia and avoidant personality disorder is, at best, diffuse, particularly for the generalized variant. The treatment of generalized social phobia and avoidant personality disorder should then be informed by the models of pathology and treatment developed for both anxiety and personality disorders. Encouraging clinicians to consider a generalized social phobia or an avoidant personality disorder to represent simply a dysregulation in the control or expression of anxiousness will likely fail to give adequate recognition to the contribution of other components of personality functioning, including (but not limited to) self-consciousness, self-image, and feelings of inhibition and vulnerability (Millon et al., 1996; Pilkonis, 1984).

Normal versus Abnormal Social Anxiety

The second boundary controversy is the one with normal social anxiousness. The primary diagnostic label for the anxiety disorder that involves "a marked and persistent fear of social or performance situations in which embarrassment may occur" (APA, 1994, p. 411) is social phobia, but an alternative title is provided parenthetically as "social anxiety disorder" (APA, 1994, p. 411). A rationale for the alternative title is that the broadening of the diagnosis of social phobia into a generalized variant that begins in childhood, is characteristic of everyday functioning, is pervasive in its effects, and continues throughout adulthood, is inconsistent with the concept of a phobia, defined in DSM-IV as an "irrational fear of a *specific* object, activity, or situation" (APA, 1994, p. 770, my emphasis). A phobia is by definition specific, yet it is now also subtyped as generalized. The DSM-IV Anxiety Disorders Work Group therefore proposed changing the name from social phobia disorder to social anxiety disorder (Liebowitz, 1992).

The title change was also encouraged by the pharmaceutical industry in order to facilitate a wider consideration of anxiolytics by the general public. Many persons will experience themselves as having significant feelings of social anxiety, but few of them would go so far as describing themselves as being socially phobic. Altering the name of the disorder from social phobia to social anxiety would facilitate a broader application of the diagnosis, and may indeed be more consistent with how the diagnosis is in fact used in general clinical practice.

On the other hand, broadening the diagnosis of social phobia does underscore the question of how to distinguish the boundary between normal versus abnormal social anxiety. Two issues that have been considered in making this distinction are responsivity to treatment and level of impairment. The merits of using each of these as a criterion of demarcation will be discussed.

Responsivity to Treatment

The apparent responsivity of anxiety symptomatology to pharmacologic treatment does indicate that persons with any level of social anxiousness can benefit from clinical treatment. However, responsivity to treatment does not necessarily indicate the presence of psychopathology. Responsivity to pharmacologic agents has often been used as an indicator for the presence of a neurochemical pathology (e.g., Klein, 1999; Liebowitz, 1992) but this assumption can be mistaken.

As noted earlier, the neurochemical mechanisms of actions of pharmacologic interventions are often diverse and nonspecific (Gorman & Kent, 1999; Stahl, 1998) and are unlikely to be confined to a specific or even identifiable neurochemical pathology. Antidepressants and anxiolytics may at times be effective simply by impairing, inhibiting, blocking, or otherwise altering normal (rather than dysregulated or dyscontrolled) neurochemical mechanisms of anxiousness or sadness (Widiger & Sankis, 2000). They are helpful but they may not be curing, removing, or altering an underlying neurochemical pathology; they may instead be effective by simply diminishing a person's experience of anxiousness.

For example, Knutson et al. (1998) "examined the effects of a serotonergic reuptake blockade on personality and social behavior in a double-blind protocol by randomly assigning 51 medically and psychiatrically healthy volunteers to treatment with a selective serotonin reuptake inhibitor (SSRI), paroxetine ... (N = 25), or placebo (N = 26)" (p. 374). Volunteers were recruited through local newspapers. None of them met currently, or throughout their lifetime, the DSM-IV diagnostic criteria for any mental disorder, as assessed with a semistructured interview. None of them had ever received a psychotropic medication, had ever abused drugs, or had ever been in treatment for a mental disorder, nor were any of them currently seeking or desiring treatment for a mental disorder (including social phobia). They were in many respects above normal in psychological functioning. The paroxetine (and placebo) treatment continued for four weeks. Knutson et al. reported that the SSRI administration (relative to placebo) reduced significantly their scores on a self-report inventory measure of neuroticism (or negative affectivity) and increased scores on a laboratory measure of social affiliation (i.e., a cooperative, dyadic puzzle-solving task that was observed and coded by raters blind to personality measures and treatment condition). The magnitude of changes on the self-report and laboratory measures of negative affectivity and social affiliation were even correlated with plasma levels of SSRI within the SSRI treatment group. As concluded by Knutson et al. (1998), this was a clear "empirical demonstration that chronic administration of a selective serotonin reuptake blockade can have significant personality and behavioral effects in normal humans in the absence of baseline depression or other psychopathology" (p. 378).

Clinically Significant Impairment or Distress

"For most people, some degree of social anxiety is more the rule than the exception" (Frances, First, & Pincus, 1995, p. 246). The average person experiences some degree of anxiousness, self-consciousness, and feelings of vulnerability in response to stress (Costa & McCrae, 1992). As Liebowitz and colleagues have acknowledged, "anxiety reactions are ubiquitous phenomena of normal human life" (Gorman et al., 1992, p. 1). Currently, most theorists, clinicians, and researchers would not classify the level of social anxiousness experienced by the average person in normal life as indicating the presence of a mental illness.

"Very few people are completely free of anxiety when giving a speech or having to mingle with strangers at a party" (Frances et al., 1995, p. 246). This level of social anxiousness is considered to be normal, and may even be helpful and adaptive to functioning (e.g., contributing to a motivation to be appropriately concerned about the acceptance of one's behavior, speech, or appearance by others; Rothbart & Ahadi, 1994). Normal social anxiousness can be painful, bothersome, and even troubling to experience, but it is useful in alerting persons to signs of social (and physical) threat (Buss, 1996).

The absence of normal levels of social anxiousness is in fact considered by some to be central to the pathology of another mental disorder, psychopathy (Patrick, 1994). Lykken (1995) suggests that most persons lack the glib social charm of the psychopath because most persons are by nature "a little shy, a bit self-conscious, afraid to say the wrong thing, afraid to alienate, a little tongue-tied, inclined to get a bit rattled when it is your turn to say something" (p. 136). The prototypic psychopath lacks the capacity to feel this normal level of social anxiety and will be very comfortable, relaxed, and at ease with others. "The psychopath is nearly always free from minor reactions popularly regarded as "neurotic" or as constituting 'nervousness' " (Cleckley, 1941, p. 206). "It is highly typical for him not only to escape the abnormal anxiety and tension . . . but also to show a relative immunity from such anxiety and worry as might be judged normal or appropriate" (Cleckley, 1941, p. 206).

"Social anxiety does not mean that an individual has the clinical diagnosis of social phobia" (Frances et al., 1995, p. 246). The diagnosis should only be given if the social avoidance results in a clinically significant level of impairment or distress (APA, 1994). "In DSM-IV, each of the mental disorders is conceptualized as a clinically significant behavioral or psychological syndrome or pattern that occurs in an individual and is associated with present distress (e.g., a painful symptom) or disability (i.e., impairment in one or more important areas of functioning)" (APA, 1994, p. xxi). "The diagnosis [of social phobia] is reserved for those individuals whose social anxiety is so severe as to be significantly impairing" (Frances et al., 1995, p. 246). The clinically significant impairment criterion "helps establish the threshold for the diagnosis of a disorder in those situations in which the symptomatic presentation by itself (particularly in its milder forms) is not inherently pathological and may be encountered in individuals for whom a diagnosis of 'mental disorder' would be inappropriate" (APA, 1994, p. 7).

The threshold for clinical significance used by most persons is the presence of sufficiently distressing symptomatology (Widiger & Corbitt, 1994). Distress is a fallible but useful indicator for determining clinical significance, as it can indicate the presence of the fundamental components of a mental disorder: the presence of a harmful impairment in psychological functioning and an absence of adequate volitional capacity to simply do (or feel) otherwise (Frances, Widiger, & Sabshin, 1991; Widiger & Sankis, 2000). Mental disorders can be understood as dyscontrolled organismic impairments in psychological functioning (Klein, 1999; Widiger & Trull, 1991). "Involuntary impairment remains the key inference" (Klein, 1999, p. 424). Distress is a fallible but valid indicator because it suggests that the person lacks the ability to simply change (alter, adjust, or remove) the problematic symptom (Frances et al., 1991). Persons seek professional intervention in large part to obtain the insights, techniques, skills, or other tools (e.g., medications) that increase their ability to better control their mood, thoughts, or behavior (Bergner, 1997).

In sum, responsivity to pharmacologic interventions does not itself indicate the presence of psychopathology. Psychopathology is better understood as the presence of a dyscontrolled maladaptivity, or an impairment to psychological functioning that cannot be corrected by simply choosing or deciding to think, feel, or do otherwise (Widiger & Sankis, 2000). Responsivity to or presence within treatment are not adequate operational definitions for psychopathology, as persons without psychopathology can benefit from treatment. Psychopathology, however, will imply a need for treatment, given the presence of dyscontrol and a clinically significant maladaptivity, and this treatment, even for instances of personality disorder, may indeed be highly effective (Perry, Banon, & Ianni, 1999; Sanislow & McGlashan, 1998).

CONCLUSIONS

Social anxiety is a common experience of everyday life. At what point it should be classified as indicating the presence of a mental disorder and, if so, which one, has been and will likely continue to be problematic and controversial. Much of the difficulty in determining the optimal classification is perhaps due in large part to the requirement that mental disorders be classified as distinct diagnostic categories (Widiger, 1997; Widiger & Costa, 1994). If there is no qualitative distinction between normal and abnormal social anxiousness, and no qualitative distinction between an anxiety and a personality disorder, it is not surprising to find that the effort to make a categorical distinction has been highly problematic.

The absence of a discrete point of demarcation among diagnostic categories, however, does not necessarily suggest that no meaningful or valid distinction can be made (Wakefield, 1999; Widiger, 1997). There is perhaps little doubt that persons at the highest levels of neuroticism and introversion would be appropriately and validly diagnosed as having an avoidant personality disorder; there will be many persons who are clearly more appropriately and validly diagnosed with a social phobia rather than an avoidant personality disorder; and there will be many persons with only minor feelings of social anxiousness that do not warrant any diagnosis of a mental disorder. But, when social anxiousness is assessed and distributed across all persons, when the full range of social anxiousness is considered, precise points of demarcation between normal social anxiety, social phobia, and avoidant personality disorder can be difficult to demarcate.

REFERENCES

Allport, G. (1955). *Becoming: Basic considerations for a psychology of personality*. New Haven, CT: Yale University Press.

Allport, G. (1961). *Pattern and growth in personality*. New York: Holt, Reinhart & Winston.

APA (1980). *Diagnostic and statistical manual of mental disorders* (3rd edn.). Washington, DC: American Psychiatric Association.

APA (1987). *Diagnostic and statistical manual of mental disorders* (3rd edn., rev. edn.). Washington, DC: American Psychiatric Association.

APA (1994). *Diagnostic and statistical manual of mental disorders* (4th edn.). Washington, DC: American Psychiatric Association.

Ball, S. A., Tennen, H., Poling, J. C., Kranzler, H. R., & Rounsaville, B. J. (1997). Personality, temperament, and character dimensions and the DSM-IV personality disorders in substance abusers. *Journal of Abnormal Psychology, 106*, 545–553.

Bergner, R. M. (1997). What is psychopathology? And so what? *Clinical Psychology: Science and Practice, 4*, 235–248.

Bernstein, D. P., Cohen, P., & Velez, N. (1993). Prevalence and stability of the DSM-III-R personality disorders in a community-based survey of adolescents. *American Journal of Psychiatry, 150*, 1237–1243.

Blais, M. A. (1997). Clinician ratings of the five-factor model of personality and the DSM-IV personality disorders. *Journal of Nervous and Mental Disease, 185*, 388–393.

Buss, D. M. (1996). Social adaptation and the five major factors of personality. In J. S. Wiggins (Ed.), *The Five-Factor Model of personality. Theoretical perspectives* (pp. 180–207). New York: Guilford.

Cleckley, H. (1941). *The mask of sanity*. St. Louis: Mosby.

Coolidge, F. L., Becker, L. A., Dirito, D. C., Durham, R. L., Kinlaw, M. M., & Philbrick, P. B. (1994). On the relationship of the five-factor personality model to personality disorders: Four reservations. *Psychological Reports, 75*, 11–21.

Corbitt, E. M. & Widiger, T. A. (1995). Sex differences among the personality disorders: An exploration of the data. *Clinical Psychology: Science and Practice, 2*, 225–238.

Costa, P. T. & McCrae, R. R. (1988). Personality in adulthood: A six-year longitudinal study of self-reports and spouse ratings on the NEO Personality Inventory. *Journal of Personality and Social Psychology, 54*, 853–863.

Costa, P. T. & McCrae, R. R. (1990). Personality disorders and the five-factor model of personality. *Journal of Personality Disorders, 4*, 362–371.

Costa, P. T. & McCrae, R. R. (1992). *Revised NEO Personality Inventory (NEO-PI-R) and NEO Five-Factor Inventory (NEO-FFI) professional manual*. Odessa, FL: Psychological Assessment Resources.

Costa, P. T. & McCrae, R. R. (1994). Set like plaster? Evidence for the stability of adult personality. In T. Heatherton & J. L. Weinberger (Eds.), *Can personality change?* (pp. 21–40). Washington, DC: American Psychological Association.

Costa, P. T. & McCrae, R. R. (1995). Domains and facets: Hierarchical personality assessment using the Revised NEO Personality Inventory. *Journal of Personality Assessment*, *64*, 21–50.

Costa, P. T. & McCrae, R. R. (1998). Trait theories of personality. In D. F. Barone, M. Hersen, & V. B. van Hasselt (Eds.), *Advanced personality* (pp. 103–121). New York: Plenum.

De Raad, B., Perugini, M., Hrebickova, M., & Szarota, P. (1998). Lingua franca of personality: Taxonomies and structures based on the psycholexical approach. *Journal of Cross-Cultural Psychology*, *29*, 212–232.

Digman, J. M. (1990). Personality structure: Emergence of the five-factor model. *Annual Review of Psychology*, *41*, 417–440.

Duijsens, I. & Diekstra, R. F. W. (1996). DSM-III-R and ICD-10 personality disorders and their relationship with the big five dimensions of personality. *Personality and Individual Differences*, *21*, 119–133.

Dyce, J. A. & O'Connor, B. P. (1998). Personality disorders and the five-factor model: A test of facet-level predictions. *Journal of Personality Disorders*, *12*, 31–45.

Eaves, L. J., Eysenck, H. J., & Martin, N. G. (1989). *Genes, culture, and personality: An empirical approach*. New York: Academic Press.

First, M. B., Spitzer, R. L., & Williams, J. B. W. (1990). Exclusionary principles and the comorbidity of psychiatric diagnoses: A historical review and implications for the future. In J. D. Maser & C. R. Cloninger (Eds.), *Comorbidity of mood and anxiety disorders* (pp. 83–109). Washington, DC: American Psychiatric Press.

Frances, A. J. (1980). The DSM-III personality disorders section: A commentary. *American Journal of Psychiatry*, *137*, 1050–1054.

Frances, A. J., First, M. B., & Pincus, H. A. (1995). *DSM-IV guidebook*. Washington, DC: American Psychiatric Press.

Frances, A., Widiger, T., & Sabshin, M. (1991). Psychiatric diagnosis and normality. In D. Offer & M. Sabshin (Eds.), *The diversity of normal behavior* (pp. 3–38). New York: Basic Books.

Goldberg, L. R. (1982). From ace to zombie: Some explorations in the language of personality. In C. D. Spielberger & J. N. Butcher (Eds.), *Advances in personality assessment* (Vol. 1, pp. 203–234). Hillsdale, NJ: Lawrence Erlbaum.

Goldberg, L. R. (1990). An alternative "description of personality": The Big-Five factor structure. *Journal of Personality and Social Psychology*, *59*, 1216–1229.

Goldberg, L. R. (1993). The structure of phenotypic personality traits. *American Psychologist*, *48*, 26–34.

Gorman, J. M., Liebowitz, M. R., & Shear, M. K. (1992). Panic and anxiety disorders. In R. Michels (Ed.), *Psychiatry* (chapter 32). Philadelphia, PA: J.B. Lippincott.

Gorman, J. M. & Kent, J. M. (1999). SSRIs and SNRIs: Broad spectrum of efficacy beyond major depression. *Journal of Clinical Psychiatry*, *60* (supplement 4), 33–38.

Gunderson, J. G. (1983). DSM-III diagnoses of personality disorders. In J. Frosch (Ed.), *Current perspectives on personality disorders* (pp. 20–39). Washington, DC: American Psychiatric Press.

Gunderson, J. G. & Pollack, W. S. (1985). Conceptual risks of the Axis I-II division. In H. Klar & L. J. Siever (Eds.), *Biologic response styles: Clinical implications* (pp. 81–95). Washington, DC: American Psychiatric Press.

Halverson, C. F., Kohnstamm, G. A., & Martin, R. P. (Eds.) (1994). *The developing structure of temperament and personality from infancy to adulthood*. Hillsdale, NJ: Erlbaum.

Herbert, J. D., Hope, D. A., & Bellack, A. S. (1992). Validity of the distinction between generalized social phobia and avoidant personality disorder. *Journal of Abnormal Psychology*, *102*, 332–339.

Holt, C. S., Heimberg, R. G., & Hope, D. A. (1992). Avoidant personality disorder and the generalized subtype in social phobia. *Journal of Abnormal Psychology*, *102*, 318–325.

Hyer, L., Brawell, L., Albrecht, B., Boyd, S., Boudewyns, P., & Talbert, S. (1994). Relationship of NEO-PI to personality styles and severity of trauma in chronic PTSD victims. *Journal of Clinical Psychology, 50*, 699–707.

Jang, K. L., McCrae, R. R., Angleitner, A., Riemann, R., & Livesley, W. J. (1998). Heritability of facet-level traits in a cross-cultural twin sample: Support for a hierarchical model. *Journal of Personality and Social Psychology, 74*, 1556–1565.

John, O. P. & Srivastava, S. (1999). The Big Five trait taxonomy: History, measurement, and theoretical perspectives. In L. A. Pervin & O.P. John (Eds.), *Handbook of personality. Theory and research* (pp. 102–138). New York: Guilford.

Kernberg, O. F. (1984). Problems in the classification of personality disorders. *Severe personality disorders* (pp. 77–94). New Haven, CT: Yale University Press.

Klein, D. F. (1999). Harmful dysfunction, disorder, disease, illness, and evolution. *Journal of Abnormal Psychology, 108*, 421–429.

Knutson, B., Wolkowitz, O. M., Cole, S. W., Chan, T., Moore, E. A., et al. (1998). Selective alteration of personality and social behavior by serotonergic intervention. *American Journal of Psychiatry, 155*, 373–379.

Liebowitz, M. R. (1992). Diagnostic issues in anxiety disorders. In A. Tasman & M. B. Riba (Eds.), *Review of psychiatry* (Vol. 11, pp. 247–259). Washington, DC: American Psychiatric Press.

Liebowitz, M. R., Barlow, D. H., Ballenger, J. C., Davidson, J., Foa, E. B., Fyer, A. J., Koopman, C., Kozak, M. J., & Spiegel, D. (1998). DSM-IV anxiety disorders: Final overview. In T. A. Widiger, A. J. Frances, H. A. Pincus, R. Ross, M. B. First, W. Davis, & M. Kline (Eds.), *DSM-IV sourcebook* (Vol. 4, pp. 1047–1076). Washington, DC: American Psychiatric Association.

Livesley, W. J. (1998). Suggestions for a framework for an empirically based classification of personality disorder. *Canadian Journal of Psychiatry, 43*, 137–147.

Loehlin, J. C. (1992). *Genes and environment in personality development.* Newbury Park, CA: Sage.

Lykken, D. T. (1995). *The antisocial personalities.* Hillsdale, NJ: Lawrence Erlbaum.

McCrae, R. R. & Costa, P. T. (1997). Personality trait structure as a human universal. *American Psychologist, 52*, 509–516.

Millon, T. (1981). *Disorders of personality. DSM-III: Axis II.* New York: Wiley.

Millon, T. (1991). Avoidant personality disorder: A brief review of issues and data. *Journal of Personality Disorders, 5*, 353–362.

Millon, T. (1996). Avoidant personality disorder. In T. A. Widiger, A. J. Frances, H. A. Pincus, R. Ross, M. B. First, & W. W. Davis (Eds.), *DSM-IV sourcebook* (Vol. 2, pp. 757–766). Washington, DC: American Psychiatric Association.

Millon, T., Davis, R. D., Millon, C. M., Wenger, A., Van Zullen, M. H., Fuchs, M., & Millon, R. B. (1996). *Disorders of personality. DSM-IV and beyond* (2nd edn.). New York: John Wiley & Sons.

Patrick, C. J. (1994). Emotion and psychopathy: Startling new insights. *Psychophysiology, 31*, 415–428.

Perry, J. C., Banon, E., & Ianni, F. (1999). Effectiveness of psychotherapy for personality disorders. *American Journal of Psychiatry, 156*, 1312–1321.

Pilkonis, P. A. (1984). Avoidant and schizoid personality disorders. In H. E. Adams & P. B. Sutker (Eds.), *Comprehensive handbook of psychopathology* (pp. 479–494). New York: Plenum.

Plomin, R. & Caspi, A. (1999). Behavioral genetics and personality. In L. A. Pervin & O. P. John (Eds.), *Handbook of personality. Theory and research* (2nd edn., pp. 251–276). New York: Guilford Press.

Ramanaiah, N. V. & Sharpe, J. P. (1998). Structure of the Coolidge Axis II Inventory personality disorder scales from the five-factor model perspective. *Psychological Reports, 83*, 947–952.

Rothbart, M. K. & Ahadi, S. A. (1994). Temperament and the development of personality. *Journal of Abnormal Psychology*, *103*, 55–66.

Sanislow, C. A. & McGlashan, T. H. (1998). Treatment outcome of personality disorders. *Canadian Journal of Psychiatry*, *43*, 237–250.

Saucier, G. & Goldberg, L. R. (1996). The language of personality: Lexical perspectives on the Five Factor Model. In J. S. Wiggins (Ed.), *The Five Factor Model of personality: Theoretical perspectives* (pp. 21–50). New York: Guilford.

Siever, L. J. & Davis, K. L. (1991). A psychobiological perspective on the personality disorders. *American Journal of Psychiatry*, *148*, 1647–1658.

Soldz, S., Budman, S., Demby, A., & Merry, J. (1993). Representation of personality disorders in circumplex and five-factor space: Explorations with a clinical sample. *Psychological Assessment*, *5*, 41–52.

Spitzer, R. L. & Williams, J. B. W. (1985). Proposed revisions in the DSM-III classification of anxiety disorders based on research and clinical experience. In A. H. Tuma & J. Maser (Eds.), *Anxiety and the anxiety disorders* (pp. 759–773). Hillsdale, NJ: Lawrence Erlbaum.

Spitzer, R. L. & Williams, J. B. W. (1987). Revising DSM-III: The process and major issues. In G. L. Tischler (Ed.), *Diagnosis and classification in psychiatry. A critical appraisal of DSM-III* (pp. 425–434). New York: Cambridge University Press.

Stahl, S. M. (1998). Basic psychopharmacology of antidepressants, part 1: Antidepressants have seven distinct mechanisms of action. *Journal of Clinical Psychiatry*, *59* (supplement 4), 5–14.

Trull, T. J. (1992). DSM-III-R personality disorders and the five-factor model of personality: An empirical comparison. *Journal of Abnormal Psychology*, *101*, 553–560.

Trull, T. J., Widiger, T. A., & Burr, R. (2001). A structured interview for the assessment of the five-factor model of personality: 2. Facet-level relations to the Axis II personality disorders. *Journal of Personality*, *69*, 175–198.

Turner, S. M., Beidel, D. C., & Townsley, R. M. (1992). Social phobia: A comparison of specific and generalized subtypes and avoidant personality disorder. *Journal of Abnormal Psychology*, *102*, 326–331.

Wakefield, J. C. (1999). Evolutionary versus prototype analyses of the concept of disorder. *Journal of Abnormal Psychology*, *108*, 374–399.

Weissman, M. M. (1993). The epidemiology of personality disorders: A 1990 update. *Journal of Personality Disorders*, *7*, 44–62.

West, K. (1993). *The placement of cognitive and perceptual aberrations within the five-factor model*. Unpublished manuscript. University of Kentucky, Lexington.

Widiger, T. A. (1992). Generalized social phobia versus avoidant personality disorder: A commentary on three studies. *Journal of Abnormal Psychology*, *101*, 340–343.

Widiger, T. A. (1993). The DSM-III-R categorical personality disorder diagnoses: A critique and an alternative. *Psychological Inquiry*, *4*, 75–90.

Widiger, T. A. (1997). Mental disorders as discrete clinical conditions: Dimensional versus categorical classification. In S. M. Turner & M. Hersen (Eds.), *Adult psychopathology and diagnosis* (3rd edn., pp. 3–23). New York: John Wiley & Sons.

Widiger, T. A. & Corbitt, E. (1994). Normal versus abnormal personality from the perspective of the DSM. In S. Strack & M. Lorr (Eds.), *Differentiating normal and abnormal personality* (pp. 158–175). New York: Springer.

Widiger, T. A. & Costa, P. T. (1994). Personality and personality disorders. *Journal of Abnormal Psychology*, *103*, 78–91.

Widiger, T. A., Frances, A. J., Spitzer, R. L., & Williams, J. B. W. (1988). The DSM-III-R personality disorders: An overview. *American Journal of Psychiatry*, *145*, 786–795.

Widiger, T. A. & Sanderson, C. J. (1997). Personality disorders. In A. Tasman, J. Kay, & J. A. Lieberman (Eds.), *Psychiatry* (Vol., 2, pp. 1291–1317). Philadelphia, PA: W.B. Saunders.

Widiger, T. A. & Sankis, L. M. (2000). Adult psychopathology: Issues and controversies. *Annual Review of Psychology, 51,* 377–404.

Widiger, T. A. & Trull, T. J. (1991). Diagnosis and clinical assessment. *Annual Review of Psychology, 42,* 109–133.

Widiger, T. A., Trull, T. J., Clarkin, J. F., Sanderson, C., & Costa, P. T. (1994). A description of the DSM-III-R and DSM-IV personality disorders with the five-factor model of personality. In P. T. Costa & T. A. Widiger (Eds.), *Personality disorders and the five-factor model of personality* (pp. 41–56). Washington, DC: American Psychological Association.

Wiggins, J. S. (1968). Personality structure. *Annual Review of Psychology, 19,* 293–350.

Wiggins, J. S. & Pincus, H. A. (1989). Conceptions of personality disorder and dimensions of personality. *Psychological Assessment, 1,* 305–316.

Wiggins, J. S. & Pincus, H. A. (1992). Personality: Structure and assessment. *Annual Review of Psychology, 43,* 473–504.

Yeung, A. S., Lyons, M. J., Waternaux, C. M., Faraone, S. V., & Tsuang, M. T. (1993). The relationship between DSM-III personality disorders and the five-factor model of personality. *Comprehensive Psychiatry, 34,* 227–234.

Chapter 16

Social Anxiety and Depression

Rick E. Ingram, Wiveka Ramel, Denise Chavira,
and **Christine Scher**

MORBIDITY AND COMORBIDITY: THE EPIDEMIOLOGY OF DEPRESSION AND SOCIAL
    ANXIETY
Epidemiology of Depression and Social Anxiety
  Impairment
Age of onset
Course
Temporal Relationships
CROSS-CULTURAL ISSUES IN DEPRESSION AND SOCIAL ANXIETY
Cultural Issues in Depression
Cultural Issues in Social Anxiety
PSYCHOLOGICAL VARIABLES IN DEPRESSION AND SOCIAL ANXIETY: BEHAVIOR,
    COGNITION, AND AFFECT
Behavioral Characteristics of Social Anxiety and Depression
Cognition in Social Anxiety and Depression
  Thought content
  Attentional processes
  Memory processes
  Judgement processes
  An organizational framework
Affective Processes in Social Anxiety and Depression
  The tripartite model of depression and anxiety
SUMMARY
REFERENCES

*International Handbook of Social Anxiety: Concepts, Research and Interventions Relating to the Self
and Shyness.* Edited by W. Ray Crozier and Lynn E. Alden.
© 2001 John Wiley & Sons Ltd.

Depression is a problem that afflicts millions of individuals. In its clinical forms, depression evidences a diverse range of symptoms and is associated with significant impairment that cuts across all aspects of an individual's functioning. At its most serious level, depression is widely recognized as a precipitant of suicide (Ingram, Miranda, & Segal, 1998). Social anxiety may lack some of the most severe and grave clinical implications of depression, but it is also a widespread and extremely troubling condition. Like depression, social anxiety is linked to a wide variety of behaviors and clinical features that range from "ordinary" shyness to the psychiatric condition of social phobia that significantly impairs people's ability to function effectively.

As common and as troubling as each of these conditions can be, social anxiety and depression frequently overlap. In fact, of all the psychiatric conditions that may be associated with social anxiety, depression is among the most common. This is hardly surprising in that the high incidence of comorbidity between depression and anxiety conditions is generally well known. Such comorbidity presents significant conceptual as well as methodological issues for researchers who attempt to study the causes, correlates, and consequences of these conditions, both in isolation and in combination. As such, one important consideration in understanding social anxiety is to understand how it is related to depression.

In this chapter we examine the relationship between social anxiety and depression. In particular, we address some of the possible reasons for the overlap between these two conditions, and explore some of the distinctions that separate these psychological problems as well as the commonalities that unite them. To set the stage for understanding these issues, we start with an epidemiological exploration of the occurrence, and co-occurrence, of depression and social anxiety that focuses on the prevalence of these problems as well as some of the descriptive features of each disorder. No cultural group is immune from depression or social anxiety, and we thus next address cross-cultural data on these psychological problems. We conclude with an examination of the behavioral, cognitive, and affective similarities and distinctions between depression and social anxiety.

MORBIDITY AND COMORBIDITY: THE EPIDEMIOLOGY OF DEPRESSION AND SOCIAL ANXIETY

As we have noted, although depression and social anxiety can occur in isolation, they also frequently co-occur. We thus turn to an exploration of the comorbidity of these two conditions, and then examine data on age of onset, clinical course, and the temporal relationship between depression and social anxiety. In doing so, we use both the terms *social anxiety* and *social phobia*. Although these terms tend to be used interchangeably, and are frequently used to describe the same condition, we use social phobia when the data pertain to the diagnosable condition of social phobia rather than to the more general condition of anxiety in social situations.

Epidemiology of Depression and Social Anxiety

Two large-scale epidemiological studies addressed comorbidity between social phobia and depression. The first of these, the Epidemiologic Catchment Area study (ECA: see Robins & Regier, 1991), used the third edition of the *Diagnostic and Statistical Manual of Mental Disorders* (DSM-III; American Psychiatric Association, 1980) to assess the prevalence rates of a number of psychiatric conditions in Baltimore, Durham, New Haven, Los Angeles, and St. Louis—cities that were chosen to represent a broad cross-section of American communities. With the exception of New Haven, diagnoses of depression and social phobia were examined in each of these cities, resulting in a sample of 14,263 persons ages 18 and over. Among the 2.4% of persons diagnosed with social phobia at any point during their lives, 16.6% also met criteria for lifetime major depression (see Schneier, Johnson, Hornig, Liebowitz, & Weissman, 1992). Rates of comorbidity between social phobia and major depression were similarly high when one-year prevalence rates were examined; among the 4.2% of persons with a social phobia diagnosis during the course of a year, 23.7% also had a diagnosis of major depression (Regier, Rae, Narrow, Kaelber, & Schatzberg, 1998). Indeed, major depression represented one of the most prevalent comorbid diagnoses among persons with social phobia (Regier et al., 1998; Schneier et al., 1992).

In a follow-up to the ECA study, the National Comorbidity Survey (NCS; Kessler et al., 1994), also employed DSM-defined criteria to derive diagnoses among more than 8,000 persons with ages ranging from 15 to 54. Despite some methodological differences between the NCS and the ECA study, comorbidity rates between social phobia and depression for this survey were again quite high. Among the 13.3% of persons with a lifetime diagnosis of social phobia, 37.2% also had a lifetime diagnosis of major depression. Indeed, in the NCS, major depression represented the second most prevalent diagnosis among persons with social phobia, falling behind only simple phobia (Magee, Eaton, Wittchen, McGonagle, & Kessler, 1996).

Impairment

Although the high rates of comorbidity between social phobia and depression found in the NCS and the ECA studies raise questions about the level of impairment that might be associated with social anxiety that is comorbid with depression, few studies have examined such impairment. However, findings of impairment in persons with social phobia and other comorbid diagnosis might be informative about the added level of impairment that accompanies depression. Compared to those with social phobia alone, both the NCS and ECA samples have revealed increased impairment in persons with comorbid social phobia. For example, individuals whose social phobia is comorbid with other disorders report increased rates of treatment seeking, role impairment (i.e., participants reported that social phobia interfered "a lot" with their lives), and suicidality (including thinking about death and suicide as well as actual suicide attempts).

If prognosis can be defined as one element of impairment, then there is some evidence that comorbidity itself is associated with more impairment. For instance, the presence of psychiatric comorbidity has been found to be associated with a poorer prognosis in social phobia (Davidson, Hughes, George, & Blazer, 1993). Additionally, Keller (1992) found that depressed patients with anxiety disorders had slower recovery time than depressed patients without comorbid anxiety. However, comorbidity does not appear to be related to some other indices of impairment such as rates of financial need as indicated by the receipt of welfare or disability payments (Magee et al., 1996; Schneier et al., 1992).

Age of Onset

Epidemiological and patient sample studies tend to suggest that the mean age of onset for social phobia is in the mid-teens to the early 20s, with onsets after age 25 being relatively uncommon (Magee et al., 1996; Schneier et al., 1992), although at least one study found a mean onset age of as early as 11.5 years (Regier et al., 1998). Age of onset differences among social phobia subtypes have also been suggested. For instance, treatment studies tend to find that patients with the generalized subtype (fear of "most" social situations) have a younger age of onset than those with nongeneralized, or circumscribed, subtypes (Heimberg, Hope, Dodge, & Becker, 1990). Examination of epidemiologically derived rather than treatment subtypes, however, suggests a somewhat different pattern of onset for different social phobia subtypes. For instance, using latent class analyses of the NCS data, Kessler, Stein, and Berglund (1998) found two social phobia groups: individuals *with fears limited to public speaking* and persons with *other social fears*. These groups appear to parallel nongeneralized and generalized social phobia. In contrast to previous findings, Kessler et al. found that the age of onset did not differ between these two subtypes, with both showing the same rise in the mid-teens that has been reported for social phobia in general.

The mean and median ages of onset for depression tend to be much later and more variable than those associated with social phobia. According to ECA findings, the mean age of onset is 27 years old and individuals between the ages of 18 and 44 are at highest risk (Klerman & Weissman, 1989). Although previous data had shown the mean age of onset to be in the mid 30s, throughout the 1970s, studies began to show higher rates of depression at younger ages; more specifically, it appeared that higher lifetime risks for depression were associated with cohorts born after World War II (Klerman & Weissman, 1989). Interestingly, while a similar age of onset decrease has been found in Edmonton, Canada and New Zealand (Bland, Newman, & Orn, 1988; Joyce, Oakley-Browne, Wells, Bushnell, & Hornblow, 1990; Wells, Bushnell, Hornblow, Joyce, & Oakley-Browne, 1989), this finding has not been replicated in Korea, Puerto Rico, or for Mexican Americans living in Los Angeles (Burnam, Hough, Escobar, & Karno, 1987; Karno et al., 1987).

Course

Although social phobia has a relatively unremitting course, in general, according to NCS epidemiological data (Kessler et al., 1998), some social phobia subgroups are distinguishable in terms of their probability of recovery over time. Given sufficient time, most people with *speaking-only* social phobia recover, with a cumulative recovery rate reaching a plateau of about 90%, approximately 30 years after onset. By contrast, the cumulative recovery rate in social phobia that is *not* linked to speaking is about 50 to 55% and takes longer to reach (about 40 years). Thus, this latter form of social phobia is not only more severe in that more social domains are affected, it is also longer-lasting than speaking-only social phobia and in many cases seems to be a lifetime problem.

As with age of onset, the course for major depression is more variable than that for social phobia. According to the NIMH Collaborative Study of the Psychobiology of Depression, major depression is a chronic and recurrent disorder. For example, longitudinal data reported by Keller et al. (1992) found that a significant percentage of patients continued to suffer from depressive symptomatology at each assessment point. More specifically, Keller et al. found that the recovery rate during the first six months of the depressive episode was 54%; thereafter the probability of recovery was 70% within 1 year, 81% within 2 years, 87% within 4 years, and 88% within 5 years. Given its more episodic nature than social anxiety, individuals with depression thus tend to recover more quickly, but they also face a high risk for *relapse* (Keller, Lavori, Lewis, & Klerman, 1983). Comorbidity with anxiety and other disorders also increases the risk for depression relapse (Keller, Lavori, Rice, Coryell, & Hirschfeld, 1986; Keller et al., 1992).

Temporal Relationships

Although studies of the age of onset and course of depression and anxiety typically focus on each of these conditions separately, research on temporal relationships between the two conditions must, by definition, focus simultaneously on depression and social phobia. In general, studies investigating the temporality of comorbid conditions have found that social phobia precedes mood, substance use, and eating disorders (Alpert, Maddocks, Rosenbaum, & Fava, 1994; Brewerton, Lydiard, Ballenger, & Herzog, 1993; Wittchen & Vossen, 1995). For example, the International World Health Organization/U.S. Alcohol, Drug Abuse and Mental Health Administration Composite International Diagnostic Interview Field Trial (Lepine et al., 1993), found that among individuals who had a lifetime comorbid disorder of social phobia and major depression, social phobia preceded depression in 70.8% of the cases. In another study of individuals with primary social phobia and comorbid major depression, 91% experienced social phobia that preceded the onset of major depression by an average of 13.2 years

(Stein, Tancer, Gelernter, Vittone, & Uhde, 1990). Using the ECA data to assess the comorbidity of anxiety and mood disorders, Regier et al. (1998) found that the mean age of onset of anxiety (15 years old) in depressed patients with comorbid simple or social phobia was younger than that of their major depression onset (25 years old). In patients with comorbid major depression and panic disorder, however, the mean age of onset was 20 years old for panic disorder and 21 years old for their major depression. Furthermore, the percentage of patients who had an onset of major depression before age 14 was small (7%) relative to onset of social phobia before age 14 (93%). Particularly striking in this study were the odds ratios for depression and comorbid social phobia; the odds were more than five times greater that anxiety would precede the onset of major depression than depression would precede the onset of anxiety. Specifically, 72% of the patients had social phobia first while 5% had depression first.

It is worth noting that some patients with primary depression develop a true fear of embarrassment in social situations, which occurs only during episodes of major depression and also remits along with the depression (Dilsaver, Qamar, & Del Medico, 1992). In this case social phobia is considered secondary, and a true social phobia diagnosis can only be made if the individuals had social phobia symptoms during a time when he or she was not depressed.

CROSS-CULTURAL ISSUES IN DEPRESSION AND SOCIAL ANXIETY

Empirical findings on cultural differences in psychopathology are often inconsistent, and correspondingly, understanding how specific ethnic variables influence the manifestation of psychological disorders has been a daunting task. In specific regard to affective conditions, research investigating the relationship between ethnicity and depression is abundant in comparison to the published data on ethnicity and social anxiety. Although the focus of earlier studies has been to assess differences in prevalence rates across ethnic groups, more recent studies have begun to examine why such differences between groups exist. Indeed, even though the majority of available research involves comparisons between groups, many researchers contend that the future of ethnic minority mental health lies in the exploration of within group processes. Nevertheless, given the data available, we now turn to an examination of cross-cultural issues in depression and social anxiety, and will comment on the differences and similarities across these two conditions.

Cultural Issues in Depression

According to studies in both the United States and other countries, depressive disorders exist across cultures, although prevalence rates and how these disorders are conceptualized frequently vary. To review, within the United States, the ECA did not find consistent differences between African Americans and Caucasians (Somervell, Leaf, Weissman, Blazer, & Bruce, 1989). In contrast, the National Comorbidity Study (NCS) found lower rates of affective disorders in African Americans when compared to Caucasians that was not explained by controlling income or education. Cross-cultural comparisons between Hispanics and Caucasians have also been inconsistent. According to ECA data from the Los Angeles site, the lifetime prevalence rate of major depression was lower among Hispanics when compared to Caucasians (Burnam et al., 1987), although Hispanics had a higher incidence than Caucasians (Horwath, Johnson, Klerman, & Weissman, 1992). Conflicting findings were also present when the ECA data were compared to the NCS, which found higher prevalence rates of affective disorders in Hispanics when compared to Caucasians (Kessler et al., 1998). Cross-national studies of other Hispanic ethnic groups, namely Puerto Ricans, find prevalence rates that are similar to those of the ECA sites (Canino et al., 1987). An overview of rates among Asian countries find particularly low rates in Taiwan, and, in Korea, similar rates as those presented in the ECA. Despite these variations in prevalence rates, higher rates of major depression in women are fairly consistent across cultures (Paykel, 1992). In most countries, except Taiwan, there is almost a 2:1 ratio of women to men who experience major depression.

Relative to other psychological disorders, a fair amount has been written about the culture specific expression of depression. International studies suggest that depression in non-European cultures (e.g., India, China, Iraq, Indonesia, Nigeria, Philippines) is more likely to be characterized by somatic aspects rather than by psychological features (Bazzoui, 1970; Kleinman, 1982). More specifically, the World Health Organization compared patients from Canada, India, Iran, Japan, and Switzerland (World Health Organization, 1983; Sartorius, Jablensky, Gulbinat, & Ernberg, 1980) and found that cognitive and affective symptoms such as depressed mood, guilt, low-self-esteem, suicidal ideation, and feelings of worthlessness were less frequent among non-European populations (e.g., Iran, Japan, and India) while somatic symptoms were more common. For example, guilt feelings were present in 69% of the Swiss sample but only in 32% of the Iranian sample; and suicidal ideation was present in 70% of the Canadian sample but only in 40% of the Japanese sample. Within the United States, findings are inconsistent regarding differences in levels of depression across cultural groups, however the trend toward greater endorsement of somatic symptoms among Asian Americans has been replicated (Farooq, Gahir, Okyere, Sheikh, & Oyebode, 1995; Kuo, 1984; Ying, 1988).

Cultural beliefs are likely to influence the perception and expression of depression. For example, guilt may not be frequently endorsed in cultures that encourage the externalization of blame (El-Islam, 1969), while low self-esteem may be less likely in cultures that sanction humility and self-debasement (Marsella, Walker, & Johnson, 1973; Yanagida & Marsella, 1978). In addition, in Eastern cultures that adhere to Buddhist beliefs, suffering is seen as a natural state, therefore an individual from this culture is less likely to seek treatment for existential crises or depressed mood. For similar reasons, a clinician from this culture is also likely to minimize the significance of such complaints (Xu, 1987). Furthermore, in countries such as China, depressed emotions are traditionally regarded as shameful to self and family and may therefore not be disclosed outside of the family (Kleinman, 1980). Kleinman (1986) also argues that countries such as China have agrarian roots, and therefore that physical complaints are most important because they may affect an individual's ability to contribute to the group.

Within the United States, the acculturation level of the individual is an important variable to consider when trying to understand depressive symptoms. For at least two reasons, the process of acculturation, where an individual from one culture adopts the beliefs and behaviors of a host culture, is hypothesized to have both a direct and indirect relationship to depression. First, the process in and of itself may cause distress and, second, it is likely to influence the values, beliefs, and world-views of an individual. Presently, however, findings addressing the relationship between depression and acculturation are inconsistent. Low acculturation in some ethnic groups has been seen as a risk factor for depression (Golding & Burnam, 1990; Neff & Hoppe, 1993; Zamanian, Thackrey, Starrett, & Brown, 1992); it may be that those who maintain ties with their culture of origin are at greater risk for feelings of alienation, lack of acceptance, and thwarted aspirations. Opposing studies suggest that higher levels of acculturation negatively impact mental health (Arroyo & Zigler, 1995; Kaplan & Marks, 1990; Nguyen & Peterson, 1993; Sorenson & Golding, 1988). More specifically, it has been argued that behaviors which distance ethnic minorities from their culture of origin may result in the internalization of damaging stereotypes, feelings of worthlessness, and loss of culture. Although data are inconsistent, it is likely that these ethnic-experience variables have a significant influence on various cognitive processes that, in turn, are likely to affect the expression of depressive symptomatology.

Cultural Issues in Social Anxiety

Research on the association between social anxiety, ethnicity, and culture is scarce when compared to the depression literature. According to the NCS, comparable prevalence rates were found among Caucasians, African Americans, and Hispanics (Magee et al., 1996). Cross-national studies find the prevalence rate in Puerto Rico to be similar to that of the five ECA sites while, interestingly, particularly low prevalence rates of social phobia are found in Asian countries. With regard to gender differences, higher prevalence rates of lifetime social phobia have been found among women from the ECA sites, Korea and urban Taiwan; the gender ratio is more skewed in Asian countries where prevalence rates are as low as 0% for Korean males. The predominance of social phobia in women is consistent with other epidemiological findings (Kessler et al., 1994), however it is inconsistent with U.S. treatment studies which frequently find equal or slightly higher rates of social phobia in men (Manuzza, Fyer, Liebowitz, & Klein, 1990).

The low rates of social phobia in East Asian countries are perplexing in light of research that has documented the presence of taijin-kyofu-sho (TKS), a syndrome resembling social phobia, in Japan and Korea (Aune & Aune, 1996; Murphy, 1982). TKS has been described as an East Asian cultural pattern of social anxiety (Chang, 1997) but studies suggest that there is significant overlap with the symptoms and characteristics of both social phobia and avoidant personality disorder (Kleinknecht, Dinnel, Kleinknecht, Hiruma, & Harada, 1997; Ono et al., 1996). Unlike social phobia, which involves the fear of humiliating the self, TKS is the fear of offending others by embarrassing them or by making them uncomfortable by a personal flaw or shortcoming. Manifestations of this condition may involve a fear of blushing, fear of emitting an unpleasant body odor, or a fear of exposing an unsightly body part.

The low rates of social anxiety in Asian countries are also inconsistent with a framework of cultural behavior which proposes that cultures which foster an interdependent sense of self, such as that purported to be present in Asian countries, are more vulnerable to social anxiety. According to this model, cultures with an interdependent self-construal (Asian, Latin American, and some southern European countries) emphasize the importance of relationships, conformity, agreeableness, and modesty; in contrast, cultures with an independent self-construal are governed by autonomy, personal abilities, desires, and attributes. Recent findings tend to support these hypotheses (Kleinknecht et al., 1997; Okazaki, 1997). In a study of college students, Asians scored higher on a measure of interdependent self-construal and lower on independent self-construal than Caucasians. Furthermore, they also scored higher on measures of social anxiety and depression scores than Caucasians. However, when the covariance between depression and social anxiety was controlled in hierarchical regression analyses, ethnicity and self-construal variables were predictors of social anxiety but not depression (Okazaki, 1997). Further analyses suggested that those Asian Americans who were less acculturated to mainstream American culture were more likely to report higher avoidance and distress in social situations.

Other research has also suggested that ethnic-experience variables (e.g., ethnic identity, perceived discrimination, social affiliation) might be important when investigating social anxiety. Stephan and Stephan (1989) found that Asians expressed more social anxiety about interacting with Caucasians than did Hispanics and had fewer positive interactions and attitudes toward Caucasians than did Hispanics. For Asians, negative relations with Caucasians and stronger in-group affiliation was associated with high levels of intergroup anxiety. For Hispanics, lower relative status and perceptions of stereotyping were associated with high levels of intergroup anxiety. Diagnostically, this cultural finding poses a challenge as an individual may not report symptoms of social anxiety when they are among members of their own ethnic group; the current version of the *Diagnostic and Statistical Manual* (DSM-IV) does not present specific guidelines on how to address this issue.

These findings exemplify the importance of considering cultural variables when assessing, treating, or investigating depression and social anxiety. However, for depression it would appear that cultural variables affect how the disorder is expressed whereas for social anxiety/phobia, cultural factors may serve as a vulnerability to distress. It is also important to note that, for depression and social anxiety alike, various methodological explanations can be offered to explain cross-cultural differences or the absence of expected findings. First, the use of interview schedules which were developed in English and translated to other languages may affect the sensitivity of the instrument in non-English-speaking countries. Second, it may be that East Asian cultures are less willing to disclose information in the structured interviews used by epidemiological studies. Also, these instruments, with their Western psychiatric focus, may not be sensitive to patterns of symptomatology found in other countries (Chapman, Mannuzza, & Fyer, 1995; Guarnaccia, Rubio-Stipec, & Canino, 1989). Continued research in the area is necessary to further delineate true cultural variations from methodological flaws.

PSYCHOLOGICAL VARIABLES IN DEPRESSION AND SOCIAL ANXIETY: BEHAVIOR, COGNITION, AND AFFECT

Having described the characteristics of depression and social anxiety as they pertain to epidemiology and culture, we now turn to an examination of psychological variables. Although we discuss these variables as falling into separate categories of behavior, cognition, and affect, we note that these are merely convenient distinctions, and acknowledge that such variables interact in the expression of depression and social anxiety.

Behavioral Characteristics of Social Anxiety and Depression

Depression and social anxiety share several behavioral characteristics, as well as evidence a number of distinctions. For example, avoidance of social situations is a core feature of social anxiety and frequently occurs in depression, yet individuals with social anxiety tend to be characterized by arousal-linked behaviors in social situations (e.g., blushing, fidgeting), while depressed individuals without co-existing anxiety do not typically exhibit evidence of such arousal.

One way to view behavior is through the lens of the current diagnostic system, which attempts as much as possible to promulgate diagnostic criteria that are based on observable behaviors. For the most part, a review of the DSM-IV criteria for social phobia and major depression suggests very little overlap between the behaviors that characterize these two disorders. The cardinal criteria for major depression are sad mood or a lack of interest in activities in which one usually takes pleasure; these symptoms are accompanied by several additional difficulties such as appetite, sleep and libido disturbances, impaired concentration, fatigue, observable slowed or increased movement, feelings of guilt or worthlessness, and suicidal ideation. In contrast, the cardinal feature of social phobia is a persistent fear of situations where one may be scrutinized by others, and thus where one might experience humiliation or embarrassment. Exposure to such situations typically results in anxiety and arousal linked behavior, and sometimes includes panic attacks. As a result, these situations are often avoided. Thus, the criteria for major depression emphasize affective symptoms of sadness and anhedonia while the criteria for social phobia emphasize affective symptoms of fear and anxiety as well as avoidance. Except for behaviors characteristic of social withdrawal, the behavioral features of depression and social phobia appear more characterized by distinctions rather than similarities.

Another aspect of behavioral functioning can be seen in the situational context in which a behavior is exhibited. In particular, situational specificity clearly differentiates depression from social anxiety. Although, given the ubiquity of situations in which people must interact with others, socially anxious individuals might be impaired in a number of situations, by definition, anxiety is only aroused in *social* situations. Depression, on the other hand, is seen as more chronic and is evidenced throughout virtually all situational contexts. Thus, specificity versus chronicity can be characterized as a behavioral variable that differentiates social anxiety from depression.

Cognition in Social Anxiety and Depression

Relative to the paucity of data on the behavioral features of depression and social anxiety, there are a wealth of data on cognitive functioning in depression and social anxiety. From a theoretical perspective, Beck's schema model suggests that anxiety and depression are each characterized by mood-congruent biases that operate throughout all aspects of cognitive processing, such as attention, reasoning, and memory (Beck, 1976; Beck & Clark, 1988). Broadly defined, anxiety is characterized by maladaptive schemas involving threat, whereas depressive schemas involve themes of deprivation and loss. Thus, each disorder is presumed to differ with respect to cognitive content, although potentially similar cognitive processes may operate in both disorders. Even though the model proposed by Beck was the first cognitive model to address both depression and anxiety, as a variety of experimental techniques have been adapted to the investigation of cognition in psychopathology in the last two decades, and data have begun to accumulate, several additional theoretical models on the relationship between depression and anxiety have emerged (e.g., Clark & Watson, 1991; Ingram & Kendall, 1986; MacLeod & Mathews, 1991; Williams & Oaksford, 1992). We will review the empirical findings on cognitive variables in depression and social anxiety and then interpret the conclusions in terms of a conceptual framework developed by Ingram and Kendall (1986). These empirical findings can be organized according to thought content, attentional processes, memory biases, and judgement biases.

Thought Content

The empirical findings from studies on depressive and anxious thought content present a relatively clear picture (see Kendall & Ingram, 1989, for a review). Depressive affect seems most closely associated with self-referent, definite, and past-oriented cognitions of sadness, failure, degradation, and loss. Anxiety, on the other hand, appears most closely associated with future-oriented and "questioning" cognitions of broadly defined danger and harm. In the specific case of social anxiety, individuals with social phobia tend to hold the view that social and performance situations are particularly threatening, and they have an excessive concern about how they are perceived and evaluated by others (Rapee & Heimberg, 1997).

Attentional Processes

Dichotic listening, visual dot-probe detection, lexical decision tasks, and emotionally modified Stroop tasks have been the primary tools used for studying attentional biases. The general conclusion from research in this area is that individuals with social anxiety show an attentional bias for socially menacing information, while the evidence for attentional bias for negative information in depression is more mixed (see Mathews & MacLeod, 1994; Mineka & Sutton, 1992, for reviews). Most of the studies on social anxiety have used the Stroop paradigm, which tests attentional interference by measuring the latencies for naming the color of emotionally valenced versus neutral words (e.g., Holle, Neely, & Heimberg, 1997; Maidenberg, Chen, Craske, Bohn, & Bystritsky, 1996; Mattia, Heimberg, & Hope, 1993; McNeil et al., 1995). The results indicate that individuals with social phobia are slower to name the color of social threat words than non-threat words, suggesting a difficulty in ignoring the content of social threat words. Asmundson and Stein (1994) found that individuals with social phobia devoted disproportional attentional resources to social threat words but not to physical threat or neutral words in a dot-probe task, which has been hypothesized to be a more direct measure of attentional allocation than the Stroop task (MacLeod, Mathews, & Tata, 1986). Many researchers believe that this attentional bias for threat may play a role in the maintenance of anxious states.

The empirical evidence for an attentional bias toward negative stimuli in depressed individuals is somewhat less clear. Although some studies have not been able to detect any differences in depressed individuals' attentional processing of negatively valenced stimuli (Hill & Knowles, 1991; MacLeod et al., 1986; Mogg, Bradley, Williams, & Mathews, 1993), a number of studies have found evidence for attentional interference or vigilance in depressed individuals (e.g., Gotlib & Cane, 1987; Gotlib & McCann, 1984; Lemelin et al., 1996; Mogg, Bradley, & Williams, 1995) or in those vulnerable to depression (e.g., Ingram,

Bernet, & McLaughlin, 1994). The fact that several of these studies did not assess anxious symptoms in the depressed individuals may be part of the reason for these mixed results. However, in a study that did compare depression and anxiety (Mogg et al., 1995), depressed individuals surprisingly showed greater vigilance for supraliminally presented (i.e., words displayed for 1,000 msec) anxiety words than the anxious participants. The authors suggested that other factors, such as age differences and level of severity of psychiatric disorder, may also explain some of the equivocal aspects identified in the empirical literature on attentional biases among depressed individuals. In summary, attentional biases appear to be present in both social phobia and depression, although the evidence is somewhat stronger for attentional interference in individuals with social phobia.

Memory Processes

Most studies on mood-congruency effects in memory have employed either (a) explicit memory tests (i.e., cued recall and recognition) using depth-of-processing tasks like self-referent encoding or incidental recall paradigms, or (b) implicit memory tests in which participants are not explicitly directed to search their memory for previously learned material (e.g., lexical decision and word stem completion tasks). In general, studies on anxiety and depression (e.g., Greenberg & Alloy, 1989; Ingram, Kendall, Smith, Donnell, & Ronan, 1987) support the content-specificity hypothesis proposed by Beck (1976), which argues that individuals with particular disorders are more likely to process information consistent with their disorders, which in turn helps to maintain the disorder. The findings are particularly strong in the area of depression (e.g., Bradley, Mogg, & Millar 1996; Ingram et al., 1987; Matt, Vázquez, & Campbell, 1992; Watkins, Vache, Verney, Muller, & Mathews, 1996) but there are some inconsistencies in terms of memory biases in individuals with social phobia. For example, Cloitre, Cancienne, Heimberg, Holt, and Liebowitz (1995) failed to find differences between social phobic and control participants, as both groups showed greater recall and recognition for threat and positive words than for neutral words. Similarly, a study by Lundh and Öst (1997) failed to find any differences between socially phobic individuals and controls on explicit and implicit memory for positive, neutral, social and physical threat words, but a small subgroup of patients with nongeneralized social phobia showed an implicit bias for threat words. Thus, depressed and anxious individuals generally both evidence memory biases specific to their vulnerabilities, although it should be noted that there are some inconsistencies regarding the extent to which individuals with social phobia share this memory disposition.

Judgement Processes

The majority of studies in this domain has been conducted with subclinical populations and has attempted to assess the influence of affective states on the interpretation of ambiguous information. Moreover, the preponderance of these studies have investigated the effect of anxiety on interpretation and judgement rather than the effect of depression on these variables. Tasks include interpretation of ambiguous situations and sentences, text comprehension studies, categorization, impression formation, and causal attributions. As with memory biases, results from studies on judgemental biases generally demonstrate mood-congruent effects of emotional states on judgement processes, suggesting that negative emotional states increase judgements concerning the probability of negative and threatening events, as well as the likelihood of negative interpretation of ambiguous stimuli. For example, Amir, Foa, and Coles (1998) found that socially phobic individuals interpreted ambiguous social situations as more negative than either non-anxious controls or those with obsessive-compulsive disorder. Moreover, this effect occurred only for self-relevant scenarios. When individuals with social phobia were asked to choose possible interpretations of ambiguous situations from the perspective of a "typical person", the negative interpretation was not seen.

Several studies have found that individuals with social phobia are more critical of their own performance on anxiety-producing tasks than are non-anxious controls (e.g., Alden & Wallace, 1995; Rapee & Lim, 1992; Wallace & Alden, 1997). For example, after giving a brief speech, Rapee and Lim (1992) found that participants with social phobia rated their performance as worse than did observers. Similarly, Wallace and Alden (1997) reported that, for patients with generalized social phobia, social success led to self-protective social goals, negative emotional states and perceptions that others would expect more in future interaction. These results suggest that positive social events may not contribute to a revision of negative self- and social judgements in patients with social phobia.

Some studies have directly compared anxious and depressed individuals on various interpretation and judgement processes. MacLeod and Byrne (1996) compared anxious and depressed individuals on their anticipation of future positive and future negative experiences. They reported that anxious individuals showed greater anticipation of future negative experiences than control participants, whereas depressed individuals, who also had elevated anxiety levels, showed both greater anticipation of negative experiences and reduced anticipation of positive experiences. Ingram et al. (1987) used a measure designed to assess attributions in depression, the Attributional Style Questionnaire (ASQ; Seligman, Abramson, Semmel, & von Baeyer, 1979) in a study with depressed and test anxious individuals and found that only the depressed participants displayed attributional deficits that both minimized positive experiences and maximized negative experiences. These data are consistent with those of Heimberg, Vermilyea, Dodge, Becker, and Barlow (1987), who found a similar pattern of attributional tendencies when comparing dysthymic and anxious patients, particularly for negative outcomes. More specifically, Heimberg et al. found that the dysthymic participants showed a self-debasing attributional pattern for negative outcomes, but participants with anxiety did so only if they were also depressed. Although these latter studies did not assess social anxiety per se, and must therefore be regarded cautiously, they are noted because they did explicitly compare anxious states with depressed states. To the extent that anxiety processes functions similarly in all anxiety states, these results may suggest conclusions about the similarity or distinctiveness of judgement processes in depression and social anxiety; namely that judgement processes appear to be consistent with the affective dimensions of the particular disorder.

An Organizational Framework

Clearly, a number of different cognitive variables have been studied by depression and anxiety researchers. Ingram and Kendall (1986) and Ingram et al. (1998) have described a framework for organizing the variables examined in cognitive psychopathology research. This framework is based on the conceptual and empirical distinctions between cognitive structures and processes that have been proposed by researchers such as Goldfried and Robins (1983), Hollon and Kriss (1984), and Kihlstrom and Nasby (1981).

According to this framework, cognition can be viewed as consisting of conceptually distinct components that include cognitive structures, cognitive propositions, cognitive operations, and cognitive products. Structure is seen as the associations and linkages among internally stored information. Propositions, or cognitive content, constitute the stored information. Together, cognitive structures and propositions are usually defined as schemas. Operations, in the most general sense, are viewed as the processes that encode and manipulate incoming information and assess and retrieve previously stored information, while products are conceptualized as the cognitions, thoughts, decisions, and images that result from the interaction of incoming information with internal structures and propositions.

A second aspect of the conceptual framework proposed by Kendall and Ingram (1989) and Ingram et al. (1998) focuses on partitioning the various components that comprise psychopathological functioning. They argued that a useful conceptual metaphor for understanding the relationship between different variables and different disorders is to employ a model that views the variance in psychopathology analogously to variance in experimental research. Specifically, the variance in psychopathology can be conceptually "partitioned" in much the same way that experimental variance is partitioned by an ANOVA or virtually any other statistical procedure. In any experimental outcome, for example, several presumably identifiable sources of variance converge to contribute to a score on a given measure; variance uniquely due to an experimental manipulation or treatment (main effects) and variance that is common to more than one experimental procedure (an interaction).[1] Similarly, the ultimate symptomatic expression of a particular disorder can be conceptualized as the convergence of what has been referred to as unique or *critical* psychopathological features and *common* psy-

---

[1] This model also incorporates error variance, which is not discussed because it is not directly relevant to this topic.

chopathological features. Critical features thus reflect variance that is uniquely characteristic of a particular disorder and are defined as those features that not only differentiate disorder from nondisorder, but that also differentiate one disorder from another. In contrast to critical psychopathological features, common features are generally characteristic of more than one disorder and are conceptualized as common or shared psychopathological variance. Although these features do not differentiate between particular disorders, they do differentiate disorder from nondisorder. That is, while common features are not unique to a given disorder, they are "unique" to psychopathology in general and thus broadly separate adaptive from maladaptive functioning.

Applying this framework to our review of cognitive variables, we might conclude that depressed and socially anxious individuals seem to differ on some specific components and thus evidence some critical features. Additionally, they may also be similar in other areas and thus evidence some common features. In general, the specific propositions contained in the active structures appear to be different for depressed and socially anxious individuals (e.g., self-schemas related to threatening information for individuals with social phobia versus negative information related to loss, failure, and so forth for depressed individuals). These schemas may, in turn, lead to differential sensitivity to particular kinds of environmental stimuli and potentially produce different attentional and memory tendencies. On the other hand, these cognitive operations may not be dissimilar in their underlying and recurring processing of dysfunctional information per se, but because different information is processed and accessed from memory, their resultant cognitive products seem to be reasonably distinct. For example, although products such as attributions and the nature of thoughts about the self and the situation appear to be different for depressed versus socially anxious individuals, there is not enough information to conclude that the attentional and memory information-processing mechanisms are different between the two disorders. According to the framework we have described, then, schematic structures appear to be critical variables, while the operational variables, which represent common features, may nevertheless result in cognitive products that are different for depression and social anxiety.

Affective Processes in Social Anxiety and Depression

Affective variables are at the core of socially anxious and depressive processes. Aside from the obvious differences in the predominant affect in each of these conditions, questions have arisen as to how similar or distinct such conditions may be. For example, although DSM-IV criteria indicate that persons with social phobia and those with depression differ substantially in their clinical presentations, the epidemiological data we have previously reviewed suggest, at least is some cases, considerable overlap in these states. Research that is not epidemiological in nature also shows significant overlap between depressive and anxious states. For example, in an extensive review of both self- and clinician-rated anxiety and depression, Clark and Watson (1991) found a great deal of overlap between ratings of anxiety and ratings of depression.

Such comorbidity may result from several sources (Ingram et al., 1998). Among these factors are (a) when high prevalence rates for each disorder lead to the co-occurrence of two disorders by chance or sampling bias, (b) when imprecise diagnostic criteria include overlapping symptoms for more than one disorder, (c) when one disorder encompasses or leads to another disorder, (d) when the coexistence of disorders actually represents another discrete disorder or represent different aspects of the same disorder, or (e) when the disorders are a function of correlated causal processes (Klein & Riso, 1993). Apparent comorbidity can also result from assessment artifacts such as overlap in items on measures of "different" disorders (Frances, Widiger, & Fryer, 1990).

The Tripartite Model of Depression and Anxiety

Assuming that at least some of the comorbidity seen in social anxiety and depression stems from causal overlap in the underlying affective states, how can such similarities (and where they exist, differences) be conceptualized? Clark and Watson (1991) and Watson and Clark (1984) have proposed a tripartite model of depression and anxiety that attempts to account for both the similarities and differences among these affective states. They suggest that anxiety and depression can be conceptualized on three dimensions: (1) negative affect (NA), encompassing states such as nervousness, tension, worry, sadness, anger, guilt, and disgust, (2) positive affect (PA), characterized by interest, enthusiasm, and an overall zest for life, and (3) physiological arousal, such as a racing heart, sweating, and trembling.

In terms of similarities or common factors, the tripartite model proposes that both depression and anxiety are characterized by high levels of negative affect. Unlike anxiety, however, depression is also characterized by low levels of positive affect (anxious individuals can, in theory, experience both high negative and positive affect). Another distinguishing or critical feature is that anxiety, but not depression, evidences high physiological arousal (Clark & Watson, 1991). The tripartite model of anxiety and depression provides an interesting and useful framework for investigating affective and symptom specificity, and overlap between social phobia and depression.

Several recent studies have examined the hypothesized structure of the tripartite model (e.g., Joiner, 1996) or combined diagnostic groups (e.g., Watson et al., 1995a, b) and two studies have examined aspects of the tripartite model specifically in persons with social phobia and major depression. In the first of these studies, negative and positive affect were examined in persons with DSM-III diagnoses of several anxious and depressive disorders, including social phobia and major depression. Diagnoses of social phobia and major depression were both related to increased levels of negative affect and decreased levels of positive affect, although these relationships were stronger for major depression diagnoses (Watson, Clark, & Carey, 1988). In the second study, each factor of the tripartite model was examined in persons with DSM-IV diagnoses of anxious and depressive disorders, again including both major depression and social phobia. As in the previous study, diagnoses of major depression and social phobia were both related to increased levels of negative affect and decreased levels of positive affect; moreover, while the relationship between negative affect and depression was again much stronger than the relationship between negative affect and social phobia, these disorders' relationships with positive affect were equally strong. Additionally, both diagnoses were unrelated to the physiological arousal factor of the tripartite model (Brown, Chorpita, & Barlow, 1998).

Although strong conclusions based on these studies with depression and social phobia would be premature, two observations are warranted. First, major depression and social phobia appear to have a number of features in common; both these disorders evidence relationships with positive and negative affect (e.g., nervousness, worry, sadness, anger, anhedonia). Indeed, when examined in the context of the tripartite model, major depression and social phobia appear to have symptoms that are more common than unique. Second, although social phobia was unrelated to physiological arousal in the study by Brown et al. (1998), this factor deserves further investigation as a symptom cluster differentiating social phobia from major depression; certainly, the risk of situationally-induced panic attacks among persons with social phobia suggests that physiological arousal may be an important component of social phobia for many affected persons.

Additionally, it should be noted that the tripartite model was developed to account for unique and common factors in depression and generalized anxious affective states, and may not be as relevant for social anxiety. Moreover, the model may better account for critical and common factors when these affective states are in their milder ranges. Thus, it may be the case that when these affective states reach clinical proportions, the differences that might have existed at more subclinical levels become diminished; for example, when social anxiety reaches the point at which it becomes a diagnosable disorder, positive affect may decrease significantly. Nevertheless, despite the fact that research has not uniformly supported all predictions, the tripartite model remains an important means of providing a structure for conceptualizing and testing the similarities and differences between depressive and anxious states.

SUMMARY

In this chapter we have attempted to examine some of the similarities and distinctions between social anxiety and depression. We started with a discussion of the epidemiology of these problems, both in their independent and their comorbid forms. We then turned to an assessment of the research that has examined the cultural and ethnic variance in depression and social anxiety. We also examined the behavioral, cognitive, and affective features of these two psychological conditions. As is evident from our review, depression and anxiety clearly show some areas of strong overlap, and some areas of clear distinctiveness. Appreciation of these similarities and differences should not only inform efforts to more completely understand the etiology and correlates of depression and social anxiety, but should also serve to advise therapists that these variables may have important implications for the kinds of treatment employed as well as for the efficacy expected from the treatment.

REFERENCES

Alden, L. E. & Wallace, S. (1995). Social phobia and social appraisal in successful and unsuccessful social interactions. *Behaviour Research and Therapy, 33*, 497–505.

Alpert, J. E., Maddocks, A., Rosenbaum, J. F., & Fava, M. (1994). Childhood psychopathology retrospectively assessed among adults with early onset major depression. *Journal of Affective Disorders, 31*, 165–171.

American Psychiatric Association (1980). *Diagnostic and statistical manual of mental disorders* (3rd edn.). Washington, DC: Author.

American Psychiatric Association (1987). *Diagnostic and statistical manual of mental disorders* (revised 3rd edn.). Washington, DC: Author.

American Psychiatric Association (1994). *Diagnostic and statistical manual of mental disorders* (4th edn.). Washington, DC: Author.

Amir, N., Foa, E., & Coles, M. (1998). Negative interpretation bias in social phobia. *Behaviour Research and Therapy, 36*, 945–957.

Arroyo, C. G. & Zigler, E. (1995). Racial identity, academic achievement, and the psychological well-being of economically disadvantaged adolescents. *Journal of Personality and Social Psychology, 69*, 903–914.

Asmundson, G. & Stein, M. (1994). Selective processing of social threat in patients with generalized social phobia: Evaluation using a dot-probe paradigm. *Journal of Anxiety Disorders, 8*, 107–117.

Aune, K. S. & Aune, R. K. (1996). Cultural differences in the self-reported experience and expression of emotions in relationships. *Journal of Cross-Cultural Psychology, 27*, 67–81.

Bazzoui, W. (1970). Affective disorder in Iraq. *British Journal of Psychiatry, 117*, 195–203.

Beck, A. T. (1976). *Cognitive therapy and the emotional disorders*. New York: International Universities Press.

Beck, A. T. & Clark, D. (1988). Anxiety and depression: An information processing perspective. *Anxiety Research, 1*, 23–36.

Bland, R. C., Newman, S. C., & Orn, H. (Eds.) (1988). Epidemiology of psychiatric disorders in Edmonton. *Acta Psychiatrica Scandinavica, 77* (supplement 338).

Bradley, B., Mogg, K., & Millar, N. (1996). Implicit memory bias in clinical and non-clinical depression. *Behaviour Research and Therapy, 34*, 865–879.

Brewerton, T. D., Lydiard, R. B., Ballenger, J. C., & Herzog, D. B. (1993). Eating disorders and social phobia. *Archives of General Psychiatry, 50*, 70.

Brown, T. A., Chorpita, B. F., & Barlow, D. H. (1998). Structural relationships among dimensions of the DSM-IV anxiety and mood disorders and dimensions of negative affect, positive affect, and autonomic arousal. *Journal of Abnormal Psychology, 107*, 179–192.

Burnam, M. A., Hough, R. L., Escobar, J. I., & Karno, M. (1987). Six month prevalence of specific psychiatric disorders among Mexican Americans and non-Hispanic whites in Los Angeles. *Archives of General Psychiatry, 44*, 687–691.

Canino, G. J., Bird, H. R., Shrout, P. E., Rubio-Stipec, M., Bravo, M., Martinez, R., Sesman, M., & Guevara, L. M. (1987). The prevalence of specific psychiatric disorders in Puerto Rico. *Archives of General Psychiatry, 44*, 727–735.

Chang, S. C. (1997). Social anxiety (phobia) and east Asian culture. *Depression and Anxiety, 5*, 115–120.

Chapman, T. F., Mannuzza, S., & Fyer, A. J. (1995). Epidemiology and family studies of social phobia. In R. G. Heimberg, M. R. Liebowitz, D. A. Hope, & F. R. Schneier (Eds.), *Social Phobia: Diagnosis, assessment and treatment* (pp. 21–40). New York: Guilford Press.

Clark, L. A. & Watson, D. (1991). Tripartite model of anxiety and depression: Psychometric evidence and taxonomic implications. *Journal of Abnormal Psychology, 100*, 316–336.

Cloitre, M., Cancienne, J., Heimberg, R., Holt, C., & Liebowitz, M. (1995). Memory bias does not generalize across anxiety disorders. *Behaviour Research and Therapy, 33*, 305–307.

Cross-National Collaborative Group (1992). The changing rates of major depression. Cross national comparison. *Journal of the American Medical Association, 268*, 3098–3105.

Davidson, J. R., Hughes, D. L., George, L. K., & Blazer, D. G. (1993). The epidemiology of social phobia: Findings from the Duke Epidemiological Catchment Area Study. *Psychological Medicine, 23*, 709–718.

Dilsaver, S. C., Qamar, A. B., & Del Medico, V. J. (1992). Secondary social phobia in patients with major depression. *Psychiatry Research, 44*, 33–40.

El-Islam, F. (1969). Depression and guilt: A study at an Arab psychiatric center. *Social Psychiatry, 4*, 56–58.

Farooq, S., Gahir, M. S., Okyere, E., Sheikh, A. J., & Oyebode, F. (1995). Somatization: A transcultural study. *Journal of Psychosomatic Research, 39*, 883–888.

Frances, A. J., Widiger, T., & Fryer, M. R. (1990). The influence of classification methods on comorbidity. In J. D. Maser & C. R. Cloninger (Eds.), *Comorbidity of mood and anxiety disorders* (pp. 41–59). Washington, DC: American Psychiatric Press.

Goldfried, M. R. & Robins, C. (1983). Self-schemas, cognitive bias, and the processing of therapeutic experiences. In P. C. Kendall (Ed.), *Advances in cognitive-behavioral research and therapy*. New York: Academic Press.

Golding, J. M. & Burnam, A. M. (1990). Immigration, stress, and depressive symptoms in a Mexican-American community. *Journal of Nervous and Mental Disease, 178*, 161–171.

Gotlib, I. & McCann, C. (1984). Construct accessibility and depression: An examination of cognitive and affective factors. *Journal of Personality and Social Psychology, 47*, 427–439.

Gotlib, I. & Cane, D. (1987). Construct accessibility and clinical depression: A longitudinal investigation. *Journal of Abnormal Psychology, 96*, 199–204.

Greenberg, M. & Alloy, L. (1989). Depression versus anxiety: Processing of self- and other-referent information. *Cognition and Emotion, 3*, 207–223.

Guarnaccia, P. J., Rubio-Stipec, M., & Canino, G. (1989). Ataques de nervios in the Puerto Rican Diagnostic Interview Schedule: The impact of cultural categories on psychiatric epidemiology. *Culture, Medicine, and Psychiatry, 13*, 275–295.

Heimberg, R. G., Hope, D. A., Dodge, C. S., & Becker, R. E. (1990). DSM-III-R subtypes of social phobia: Comparison of generalized social phobics and public speaking phobics. *Journal of Nervous and Mental Disease, 178*, 172–179.

Heimberg, R. G., Vermilyea, J. A., Dodge, C. S., Becker, R. E., & Barlow, D. (1987). Attributional style, depression, and anxiety: An evaluation of the specificity of depressive attributions. *Cognitive Therapy and Research, 11*, 537–550.

Hill, A. B. & Knowles, T. (1991). Depression and the "emotional" stroop effect. *Personality and Individual Differences, 12*, 481–485.

Holle, C., Neely, J., & Heimberg, R. (1997). The effects of blocked versus random presentation and semantic relatedness of stimulus words on response to a modified stroop task among social phobics. *Cognitive Therapy and Research, 21*, 681–697.

Hollon, S. D. & Kriss, M. (1984). Cognitive factors in clinical research and practice. *Clinical Psychology Review, 4*, 35–76.

Horwath, E., Johnson, J., Klerman, G. L., & Weissman, M. M. (1992). Depressive symptoms as relative and attributable factors for first-onset major depression. *Archives of General Psychiatry, 49*, 817–823.

Ingram, R., Bernet, Z., & McLaughlin, S. (1994). Attentional allocation processes in individuals at risk for depression. *Cognitive Therapy and Research, 18*, 317–332.

Ingram, R. E. & Kendall, P. C. (1986). Cognitive clinical psychology: Implications of an information processing perspective. In R. E. Ingram (Ed.), *Information processing approaches to clinical psychology*. Orlando, FL: Academic Press.

Ingram, R. E., Kendall, P. C., Smith, T. W., Donnell, C., & Ronan, K. (1987). Cognitive specificity in emotional distress. *Journal of Personality and Social Psychology, 53*, 734–742.

Ingram, R. E., Miranda, J., & Segal, Z. V. (1998). *Cognitive vulnerability to depression*. New York: Guilford Press.

Joiner, T. E. (1996). A confirmatory factor-analytic investigation of the tripartite model of depression and anxiety in college students. *Cognitive Therapy and Research, 20*, 521–539.

Joyce, P. R., Oakley-Browne, M. A., Wells, J. E., Bushnell, J. A., & Hornblow, A. R. (1990). Birth cohort trends in major depression: Increasing rates and earlier onset in New Zealand. *Journal of Affective Disorders, 18*, 83–90.

Kaplan, M. S. & Marks, G. (1990). Adverse effects of acculturation: Psychological distress among Mexican American young adults. *Social Science and Medicine, 31*, 1313–1319.

Karno, M., Hough, R. L., Burnam, M. A., Escobar, J. I., Timbers, D. M., Santana, F., & Boyd, J. H. (1987). Lifetime prevalence of specific psychiatric disorders among Mexican Americans and non-Hispanic whites in Los Angeles. *Archives of General Psychiatry, 44*, 695–701.

Keller, M. B. (1992). The naturalistic course of anxiety and depressive disorders. *Clinical Neuropharmacology, 15*, 171–173.

Keller, M. B., Lavori, P. W., Lewis, C. E., & Klerman, G. L. (1983). Predictors of relapse in major depressive disorder. *Journal of the American Medical Association, 250*, 3299–3304.

Keller, M. B., Lavori, P. W., Mueller, T. I., Endicott, J., Coryell, W., Hirschfeld, R. M., & Shea, T. (1992). Time to recovery, chronicity and levels of psychopathology in major depression: A five-year prospective follow-up. *Archives of General Psychiatry, 49*, 809–816.

Keller, M. B., Lavori, P. W., Rice, J., Coryell, W., & Hirschfeld, R. M. (1986). The persistent risk of chronicity in recurrent episodes of nonbipolar major depressive disorder: A prospective follow-up. *American Journal of Psychiatry, 143*, 24–28.

Kendall, P. & Ingram, R. (1989). Cognitive-behavioral perspectives: Theory and research on depression and anxiety. In P. Kendall & D. Watson (Eds.), *Anxiety and depression: Distinctive and overlapping features*. (pp. 27–53). Orlando, FL: Academic Press.

Kessler, R. C., McGonagle, K. A., Zhao, S., Nelson, C. B., Hughes, M., Eshleman, S., Wittchen, H. U., & Kendler, K. S. (1994). Lifetime and 12-month prevalence of DSM-III-R psychiatric disorders in the United States: Results from the National Comorbidity Survey. *Archives of General Psychiatry, 51*, 8–19.

Kessler, R. C., Stein, M. B., & Berglund, P. (1998). Social phobia subtypes in the National Comorbidity Survey. *American Journal of Psychiatry, 155*, 613–619.

Kihlstrom, J. F. & Nasby, W. (1981). Cognitive tasks in clinical assessment: An exercise in applied psychology. In P. C. Kendall & S. D. Hollon (Eds.), *Assessment strategies for cognitive-behavioral interventions*. New York: Academic Press.

Klein, D. & Riso, L. P. (1993). Psychiatric disorders: Problems of boundaries and comorbidity. In C. G. Costello (Ed.), *Basic issues in psychopathology* (pp. 19–66). New York: Guilford Press.

Kleinknecht, R. A., Dinnel, D. L., Kleinknecht, E. E., Hiruma, N., & Harada, N. (1997). Cultural factors in social anxiety: A comparison of social phobia symptoms and Taijin Kyofusho. *Journal of Anxiety Disorders, 11*, 157–177.

Kleinman A. (1980). Major conceptual and research issues for cultural (anthropological) psychiatry. *Culture, Medicine and Psychiatry, 4*, 3–13.

Kleinman, A. (1982). Neurasthenia and depression: A study of somatization and culture. *Culture and Medical Psychiatry, 6*, 117.

Kleinman, A. (1986). *Social origins of distress and disease: Depression, neurasthenia and pain in modern China*. New Haven, CT: Yale University Press.

Klerman, G. L. & Weissman, M. M. (1989). Increasing rates of depression. *Journal of the American Medical Association, 261*, 2229–2235.

Kuo, W. (1984). Prevalence of depression among Asian-Americans. *Journal of Nervous and Mental Disease, 172*, 449–457.

Lemelin, S., Baruch, P., Vincent, A., Laplante, L., Everett, J., & Vincent, P. (1996). Attention disturbance inhibition or processing resource deficit? *The Journal of Nervous and Mental Disease, 184*, 114–121.

Lepine, J. P., Wittchen, H.-U., Essau, C. A., et al. (1993). Lifetime and current comorbidity of anxiety and depressive disorders: Results from the international WHO/ADAMHA CIDI Field Trials. *International Journal of Methods in Psychiatric Research, 3*, 67–77.

Lundh, L. G. & Öst, L. G. (1997). Explicit and implicit memory bias in social phobia. The role of subdiagnostic type. *Behaviour Research and Therapy, 35*, 305–317.

MacLeod, A. & Byrne, A. (1996). Anxiety, depression, and the anticipation of future positive and negative experiences. *Journal of Abnormal Psychology, 105*, 286–289.

MacLeod, C., Mathews, A., & Tata, P. (1986). Attentional bias in emotional disorders. *Journal of Abnormal Psychology, 95*, 15–20.

MacLeod, C. & Mathews, A. (1991). Cognitive-experimental approaches to the emotional disorders. In P. Martin (Ed.), *Handbook of behavior therapy and psychological science: An integrative approach* (pp. 116–150). New York: Pergamon Press.

Magee, W. J., Eaton, W. W., Wittchen, H., McGonagle, K. A., & Kessler, R. C. (1996). Agoraphobia, simple phobia, and social phobia in the National Comorbidity Survey. *Archives of General Psychiatry, 53*, 159–168.

Maidenberg, E., Chen, E., Craske, M., Bohn, P., & Bystritsky, A. (1996). Specificity of attentional bias in panic disorder and social phobia. *Journal of Anxiety Disorders, 10*, 529–541.

Mannuzza, S., Fyer, A. J., Liebowitz, M. R., & Klein, D. F. (1990). Delineating the boundaries of social phobia: Its relationship to panic disorder and agoraphobia. *Journal of Anxiety Disorders, 4*, 41–59.

Marsella, A. J., Walker, E., & Johnson, F. (1973). Personality correlates of depression in college students from different ethnic groups. *International Journal of Social Psychiatry, 19*, 77–81.

Mathews, A. & MacLeod, C. (1994). Cognitive approaches to emotion and emotional disorders. *Annual Review of Psychology, 45*, 26–52.

Matt, G., Vázquez, C., & Campbell, W. (1992). Mood-congruent recall of affectively toned stimuli: A meta-analytic review. *Clinical Psychology Review, 12*, 227–255.

Mattia, J., Heimberg, R., & Hope, D. (1993). The revised stroop color-naming task in social phobics. *Behaviour Research and Therapy, 31*, 305–313.

McNeil, D., Ries, B., Taylor, L., Boone, M., Carter, L., Turk, C., & Lewin, M. (1995). Comparison of social phobia subtypes using stroop tests. *Journal of Anxiety Disorders, 9*, 47–57.

Mineka, S. & Sutton, S. (1992). Cognitive biases and the emotional disorders. *Psychological Science, 3*, 65–69.

Mogg, K., Bradley, B., Williams, R., & Mathews, A. (1993). Subliminal processing of emotional information in anxiety and depression. *Journal of Abnormal Psychology, 102,* 304–311.

Mogg, K., Bradley, B., & Williams, R. (1995). Attentional bias in anxiety and depression: The role of awareness. *British Journal of Clinical Psychology, 34,* 17–36.

Murphy, H. B. M. (1982). *Comparative psychiatry.* Berlin: Springer Verlag.

Neff, J. A. & Hoppe, S. K. (1993). Race/ethnicity, acculturation, and psychological distress: Fatalism and religiosity as cultural resources. *Journal of Community Psychology, 21,* 3–20.

Nguyen, L. & Peterson, C. (1993). Depressive symptoms among Vietnamese-American college students. *Journal of Social Psychology, 133,* 65–71.

Okazaki, S. (1997). Sources of ethnic differences between Asian American and White American college students on measures of depression and social anxiety. *Journal of Abnormal Psychology, 186,* 52–60.

Ono, Y., Yoshimura, K., Sueoka, R., Yamauchi, K., Mizushima, H., Momose, T., Nakamura, K., Okonogi, K., & Asai, M. (1996). Avoidant personality disorder and taijin kyoufu: Social-cultural implications of the WHO/ADAMHA International Study of Personality Disorders in Japan. *Acta Psychiatrica Scandinavica, 93,* 172–176.

Paykel, E. S. (1992). *Handbook of affective disorders* (2nd edn.). New York: Guilford Press.

Rapee, R. & Heimberg, R. (1997). A cognitive-behavioral model of anxiety in social phobia. *Behaviour Research and Therapy, 35,* 741–756.

Rapee, R. & Lim, L. (1992). Discrepancy between self- and observer ratings of performance in social phobics. *Journal of Abnormal Psychology, 101,* 728–731.

Regier, D. A., Rae, D. S., Narrow, W. E., Kaelber, C. T., & Schatzberg, A. F. (1998). Prevalence of anxiety disorders and their comorbidity with mood and addictive disorders. *British Journal of Psychiatry, 173,* 24–28.

Robins, L. N. & Regier, D. A. (1991). *Psychiatric disorders in America: The Epidemiologic Catchment Area study.* New York: Free Press.

Sartorius, N., Jablensky, A., Gulbinat, W., & Ernberg, G. (1980) WHO collaborative study: Assessment of depressive disorders. *Psychological Medicine, 10,* 743–749.

Schneier, F. R., Johnson, J., Hornig, C. D., Liebowitz, M. R., & Weissman, M. M. (1992). Social phobia: Comorbidity and morbidity in an epidemiologic sample. *Archives of General Psychiatry, 49,* 282–288.

Seligman, M., Abramson, L., Semmel, A., & von Baeyer, C. (1979). Depressive attributional style. *Journal of Abnormal Psychology, 88,* 242–247.

Somervell, P. D., Leaf, P. J., Weissman, M. M., Blazer, D. G., & Bruce, M. L. (1989). The prevalence of major depression in black and white adults in five United States communities. *American Journal of Epidemiology, 130,* 725–735.

Sorenson, S. B. & Golding, J. M. (1988). Prevalence of suicide attempts in a Mexican-American population: Prevention implication of immigration and cultural issues. *Suicide and Life-Threatening Behavior, 18,* 322–333.

Stein, M. B., Tancer, M. E., Gelernter, C. S., Vittone, B. J., & Uhde, T. W. (1990). Major depression in patients with social phobia. *American Journal of Psychiatry, 147,* 637–639.

Stephan, W. G. & Stephan, C. W. (1989). Antecedents of intergroup anxiety in Asian-Americans and Hispanic-Americans. *International Journal of Intercultural Relations, 13,* 203–219.

Wallace, S. & Alden, L. E. (1997). Social phobia and positive social events: The price of success. *Journal of Abnormal Psychology, 106,* 416–424.

Watkins, P., Vache, K., Verney, S., Muller, S., & Mathews, A. (1996). Unconcious mood-congruent memory bias in depression. *Journal of Abnormal Psychology, 105,* 34–41.

Watson, D. & Clark, L. A. (1984). Negative affectivity: The disposition to experience aversive emotional states. *Journal of Abnormal Psychology, 96,* 465–490.

Watson, D., Clark, L. A., & Carey, G. (1988). Positive and negative affectivity and their relation to anxiety and depressive disorders. *Journal of Abnormal Psychology, 97,* 346–353.

Watson, D., Clark, L. A., Weber, K., Assenheimer, J. S., Strauss, M. E., & McCormick, R. A. (1995a). Testing a tripartite model: II. Exploring the symptom structure of anxiety and depression in student, adult, and patient samples. *Journal of Abnormal Psychology, 104,* 15–25.

Watson, D., Weber, K., Assenheimer, J. S., Clark, L. A., Strauss, M. E., & McCormick, R. A. (1995b). Testing a tripartite model: I. Evaluating the convergent and discriminant validity of anxiety and depression symptom scales. *Journal of Abnormal Psychology, 104,* 3–14.

Wells, J. E., Bushnell, J. A., Hornblow, A. R., Joyce, P. R., & Oakley-Browne, M. A. (1989). Christchurch Psychiatric Epidemiology Study: Methodology and lifetime prevalence for specific psychiatric disorders. *Australian and New Zealand Journal of Psychiatry, 23,* 315–326.

Williams, J. & Oaksford, M. (1992). Cognitive science, anxiety, and depression: From experiments to connectionism. In D. J. Stein & J. E. Young (Eds.), *Cognitive science and the clinical disorders* (pp. 107–123). San Diego: Academic Press.

Wittchen, H. & Vossen, A. (1995). Implications of comorbidity in anxiety disorders: A critical review. *Verhaltenstherapie, 5,* 120–133.

World Health Organization (1983). *Depressive disorders in different cultures.* Geneva, Switzerland: World Health Organization.

Xu, J. M. (1987). Some issues in the diagnosis of depression in China. *Canadian Journal of Psychiatry, 32,* 368–370.

Yanagida, E. & Marsella, A. J. (1978). The relationship between self-concept discrepancy and depression among Japanese American women. *Journal of Clinical Psychology, 34,* 654–659.

Ying, Y.-W. (1988). Depressive symptomatology among Chinese-Americans as measured by the CES-D. *Journal of Clinical Psychology, 44,* 739–746.

Zamanian, K., Thackrey, M., Starrett, R. A., & Brown, L. G. (1992). Acculturation and depression in Mexican-American elderly. *Clinical Gerontologist, 11,* 109–121.

Chapter 17

Interpersonal Perspectives on Social Phobia

Lynn E. Alden

CENTRAL THESIS
INTERPERSONAL FRAMEWORK
Social Pathogenesis
Relational Schema
Self-perpetuating Transaction Cycles
Social Motivation
Summary
EMPIRICAL EVIDENCE
Social Pathogenesis
The Relational Self
Maladaptive Transactional Cycles
   Biased social perceptions
   Behavioral patterns
   Others' reactions
   Documenting a cyclical pattern
Relatedness as a Social Goal
INTERPERSONAL CONTRIBUTIONS
Social Pathogenesis
The Relational Self
Others' Reactions
Social Motivation
The Interpersonal Process of Treatment
SUMMARY
REFERENCES

International Handbook of Social Anxiety: Concepts, Research and Interventions Relating to the Self and Shyness. Edited by W. Ray Crozier and Lynn E. Alden.
© 2001 John Wiley & Sons Ltd.

CENTRAL THESIS

At a fundamental level, social phobia is an *interpersonal* disorder. The characteristic symptoms of this condition, anxiety and self-doubt, arise when the individual contemplates interacting with other people and their most devastating effect is to impair the person's ability to develop satisfying personal and workplace relationships. Contemporary clinical research, on the other hand, is typically based on cognitive-behavioral formulations similar to those developed for other anxiety disorders. Although interpersonal factors are given a nod in these cognitive-behavioral theories, clinical studies have focused primarily on the individual's anxiety-related symptoms and behaviors rather than on the ways in which interpersonal processes contribute to the development and maintenance of this condition. In this chapter, we will examine social anxiety and social phobia through the lens of interpersonal theory to determine whether an interpersonal perspective contributes to our ability to understand and treat socially anxious patients.

The chapter will begin with a brief overview of the interpersonal perspective to outline the central tenets of this approach. I will then examine the empirical literature to determine whether research supports an interpersonal interpretation of social anxiety. Next, this model will be compared with contemporary cognitive-behavioral models of social phobia. Here, I will argue that the interpersonal model highlights factors that have been under-recognized in other approaches and points to new directions for research and treatment. My central thesis is that cognitive-behavioral formulations of social phobia would benefit from a more explicit inclusion of the role of interpersonal processes in the development and maintenance of this condition. Let us now turn to a description of the interpersonal framework.

INTERPERSONAL FRAMEWORK

Interpersonal models have emerged in a variety of contexts, most notably within psychodynamic, personality, and social psychological writings (e.g., Benjamin, 1993; Blatt & Zuroff, 1992; Coyne, 1976; Kiesler, 1983; Strupp & Binder, 1984) Although there are differences among the various theories, they share certain common elements, most notably that interpersonal behavior is interactive, in that one person's behavior exerts a "pull" on others' responses to them, and self-perpetuating, in that people tend to evoke responses from others that maintain their basic assumptions about the nature of their relationships with other people. In general, interpersonal writers assume that social behavior is best envisioned as a cycle of cognitive, emotional, and behavioral events that begin with one person and elicit complementary cognitive, emotional, and behavioral reactions from others. For purposes of this chapter, the interpersonal cycle can be depicted as a circular arrangement of several individual elements (see Figure 17.1).

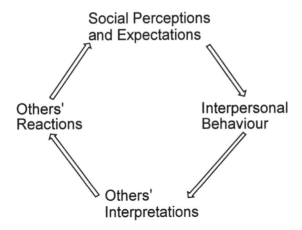

Figure 17.1 Interpersonal transaction cycle

Although there is variability among interpersonal writers that cannot be captured in this brief review, interpersonal models are generally based on several underlying assumptions. We will consider each of these in turn.

Social Pathogenesis

The first tenet of most interpersonal theories is that dysfunctional behavior develops from a pathological interpersonal environment, a process called social pathogenesis. Although interpersonal writers acknowledge that innate temperamental and physiological tendencies are the biological roots from which social behavior emerges, their primary interest is the way in which social processes shape and contribute to innate tendencies to form enduring interpersonal patterns. Thus, these writers assume that current social behavior reflects the person's developmental experiences, particularly his or her habitual transaction patterns with significant others (e.g., Benjamin, 1993; Strupp & Binder, 1994; Sullivan, 1953). According to interpersonal models, people develop their characteristic interpersonal strategies in order to deal with early relationships, and these strategies become self-perpetuating as people come to define themselves in terms of the specific relational roles they have assumed, for example, as one who must placate others or one who must take care not to give offense.

Relational Schema

Following from above, the second tenet of the interpersonal perspective is that early social relationships shape our enduring sense of self. Interpersonal writers propose that habitual patterns of interaction are distilled and stored in memory in the form of relational schemas, or structured cognitive representations that depict the relationships one had with significant others (Benjamin, 1993; Bowlby, 1977; Strupp & Binder, 1984). When we reflect on who we are, the information that comes most readily to mind is based on the concerns and fears we experienced and the behaviors we developed in the context of those early interactions. Interpersonal writers posit that contemporary social situations affect our experience of self because they bring to mind different relational schemas. For example, social cues that are reminiscent of an early negative relationship can elicit the concerns we experienced and the behavioral patterns we adopted in that earlier context, whereas cues reminiscent of a positive relationship will elicit a more positive sense of self.

Self-perpetuating Transaction Cycles

The third and most important tenet of the interpersonal model is that people establish interaction patterns that maintain their views of self and tendencies to adopt certain roles in relationships. As can be seen in Figure 17.1, there are at least four parts to the interaction cycle: how we perceive others, how we act toward them, how they interpret our actions, and how they respond to us in return. In particular, our perceptions and expectations of others are powerful determinants of our actions toward them and their actions in return. Interpersonal writers emphasize that our social perceptions are not always veridical, but can be biased by developmental experiences. Under some conditions, social cues bring to mind, or activate, specific relational schema that lead us to attribute qualities found in significant others in the past to people in the present (e.g., Strupp & Binder, 1984).

Such biases in the interpretation of interpersonal events influence the behavioral strategies we choose to manage those events. The traditional interpersonal position is that social cues that bring to mind past relationships lead people to resort to their habitual roles and thereby unwittingly re-enact the relationships they had with significant others (e.g., Strupp & Binder, 1984). However, some interpersonal writers take a broader view and suggest that the individual does not necessarily continue to play the same role. Benjamin (1993), for example, proposed that there are three general "copy processes", or ways in which early relationship patterns are transferred to current interactions. People may behave as though significant others are present (re-enactment); they can treat others as they have been treated (identification); or they can treat themselves as others have treated them (introjection). This view suggests greater variability in the way in which developmental experiences affect current behavior. Whatever form the pattern takes, interpersonal writers believe that there is an observable link between developmental experiences and people's behavior in important contemporary relationships.

The final and critical element in the cycle is that the behavioral patterns that are selected by people tend to pull reactions from others that confirm existing relational schema. Of course, others' responses reflect their own concerns and learning experiences as well any pressures that arise from our behavior. However, interpersonal writers believe that through our characteristic social behavior we exert a subtle force on other people that pulls for a complementary response, often a response that perpetuates our views of ourselves and our role in relationships (e.g., Kiesler, 1983). This concept of a self-perpetuating interactional cycle is at the heart of the interpersonal perspective.

Social Motivation

A fourth interpersonal tenet is the assumption that dysfunctional social behavior is an attempt, albeit ineffective, to maintain social connectedness (Benjamin, 1993). Humans are known to be inherently social beings who are highly motivated to build and maintain social relationships. Interpersonal writers posit that two basic goals drive social behavior: *attachment*, or closeness with others; and *differentiation*, or developing a sense of oneself as a separate, yet socially valued being. Developmentally, attachment is primary, and the infant's earliest social behaviors are directed toward eliciting closeness and nurturance from others (e.g., Bowlby, 1977; Sullivan, 1953). Once the child is assured of the availability of nurturing caretakers, the goal of asserting individual autonomy comes into play (e.g., Mahler, 1968). In ideal circumstances people develop behavioral strategies that allow them to maintain closeness with others yet assert individual desires. In adverse circumstances, on the other hand, people learn dysfunctional ways of maintaining closeness and asserting autonomy. Even here, however, what appear to be maladaptive interpersonal strategies are posited to represent strategic attempts to accomplish these same interpersonal goals. In particular, these writers believe that problematic interpersonal behavior reflects an underlying desire to maintain a sense of relatedness to others (Benjamin, 1993).

Summary

In summary, interpersonal writers posit that there are interpersonal themes that run through the person's life, linking past and present. Early experiences shape our sense of who we are and what we can expect from others. As we go through our lives, we continue to assign certain roles to ourselves and to others, even when it is not warranted, and our behavior tends to elicit responses from others that reinforce our pre-existing beliefs. Finally, no matter how maladaptive an individual's social behavior appears to others, the person's underlying goal is to maintain a sense of relatedness to significant others.

Although the interpersonal cycle is represented in Figure 17.1 as linear and unidirectional, most writers agree that bidirectional feedback loops between various elements of the cycle are also possible. One example of this is when people base their perceptions of a social event on their own feelings or behavior rather than on external information, such as others' reactions to them. Another example is when others' unsolicited behaviors confirm pre-existing relational schema without any input on our part. It should also be noted that different theorists emphasize different facets of the interpersonal model. For example, dynamic writers traditionally placed greater emphasis on developmental experiences, whereas interpersonal models of depression tend to underscore the impact of the person's behavior (e.g., reassurance-seeking) on others' responses (e.g., rejection; Coyne, 1976; Joiner & Meltalsky, 1995). Despite such differences, at the center of these various interpersonal theories lies the concept of a developmentally-based, self-perpetuating transactional cycle.

EMPIRICAL EVIDENCE

We turn now to an examination of the elements of our interpersonal model in the context of social anxiety and social phobia. In each section we will review empirical studies that speak to one of the interpersonal tenets discussed above. Our goal is to evaluate critically the available data to determine which of these tenets have empirical support and which do not.

Social Pathogenesis

If the interpersonal model is correct, the dysfunctional behavior of socially anxious people should result in part from the social environments in which they were raised. The biological underpinnings of social inhibition and anxiety have been amply documented (Kagan, Reznick, & Snidman, 1987; Plomin & Daniels, 1986; see also Schmidt, Polak, & Spooner, this volume, *Chapter 2*). Our question here is whether there is empirical support for the role of the social environment in shaping the expression of these biological factors.

The first evidence in favor of social pathogenesis can be found in the seminal studies of Jerry Kagan and his colleagues on behavioral inhibition. This work revealed that approximately one-quarter of children who were extremely timid at 21 months were no longer so at age 6 and, conversely, about one-quarter of children who were not inhibited at 21 months became inhibited by age 6 (Kagan, Reznick, Snidman, Gibbons, & Johnson, 1988). Although it is possible to posit two separate biological processes to explain these findings, another explanation is that a positive social environment can reduce innate behavioral inhibition, whereas an adverse social environment can produce inhibition in initially non-timid children. Consistent with this line of reasoning, patients who reported late onset shyness, as opposed to early onset shyness, were found to describe their parents as emotionally or physically abusive (Alden & Cappe, 1988; see also Stemberger, Turner, Beidel, & Calhoun, 1995).

Developmental researchers have attempted to identify those aspects of the social environment that moderate innate behavioral inhibition. These studies indicate that a number of parental behaviors are associated with shyness (see also Burgess, Rubin, Chea, & Nelson, this volume, *Chapter 7*). To take several examples: parental encouragement of open communication and involvement in social activities was associated with less shyness at both 12 and 24 months (Plomin & Daniels, 1986). Reductions in social inhibition were observed in temperamentally reactive infants whose mothers were not overly responsive to fretting and crying (Arcus, 1991). A six-year longitudinal study revealed that maternal responsiveness and personality characteristics predicted later shyness in girls, although not in boys (Engfer, 1993). In another longitudinal study, Rubin and his colleagues found greater shyness in children whose mothers responded to timid, unskilled child behavior with feelings of anger and disappointment and attempts to direct or control how the child behaved. Rubin concluded that a combination of temperamental factors and non-supportive parenting behavior interact to produce a negative self-schema that leads to shyness in social situations (Mills & Rubin, 1993; Rubin, LeMare, & Lollis, 1990). In an intriguing study of anxious children, some of whom had social phobia, Rapee and his colleagues found that parents tended to overprotect the anxious child during a laboratory task (Hudson & Rapee, 2000; see also Rapee & Sweeney, this volume, *Chapter 22*). Together, these studies indicate that parenting behaviors that calm the timid child and encourage engagement with life reduce the effects of innate inhibition, whereas excessive attempts at protection and control, and the expression of negative emotions exacerbate them.

Clinical researchers have examined this same issue, albeit retrospectively, by assessing patients' recollections of their parents' child-rearing attitudes and behaviors. Consistent with developmental studies, patients with social phobia viewed their parents as having been more controlling and less affectionate than did nonphobic controls (e.g., Arrindell, Emmelkamp, Monsma, & Brilman, 1983; Arrindell et al., 1989; Parker, 1979). These patients also described their parents as more concerned with others' opinions and more likely to use shame to discipline than did control subjects (Bruch & Heimberg, 1994). It is also notable that patients with more severe social fears were characterized by more pathogenic social environments. Patients with generalized social phobia reported more childhood social isolation and less family socializing than did patients with nongeneralized social phobia (Bruch & Heimberg, 1994). Finally, social phobics reported more negative behaviors in their parents than did patients with agoraphobia, a disorder that shares the anxiety-related aspects of social phobia, but with less prominent social fears (e.g., Arrindell et al., 1989; Bruch, Heimberg, Berger, & Collins, 1989). This association between degree of social developmental pathology and degree of contemporary interpersonal dysfunction is what interpersonal theories would predict. Although we cannot rule out the possibility of negative biases in retrospective reports of this type, the parental descriptions of social phobic adults are consistent with the type of parenting behavior observed to exacerbate behavioral inhibition in children (e.g., Hudson & Rapee, 2000; Rubin et al., 1990).

Less work has been devoted to the effects of peer relationships on social anxiety. Some studies indicate that socially anxious and inhibited individuals either reported or were observed to experience bullying and harassment from their peers (e.g., Olewus, 1993; Gilmartin, 1987; Ishiyama, 1984). However, the interpretation of these findings is limited by their cross-sectional or retrospective designs. One longitudinal study painted a more complex picture (Vernberg, Abwender, Ewell, & Beery, 1992). These researchers followed a group of early adolescents who had recently relocated. Social anxiety was found to predict less intimacy and companionship, but not direct peer rejection. Peer rejection, on the other hand, produced increases in social anxiety and fear of negative evaluation. These writers suggested that shyness interferes with friendship formation, but does not evoke rejection, whereas rejection can exacerbate the cognitive aspects of shyness (Vernberg et al., 1992).

Summary   Taken as a whole, these studies support the idea that early interpersonal experiences contribute to the problems of inhibited children. These studies suggest that the pathogenesis of social anxiety resides in an interaction of innate temperament and a family environment that either fails to help children overcome their innate timidity or exacerbates their fears through overprotection, control, or the expression of negative emotions. In addition, social anxiety appears to choke off the development of positive peer relationships that might temper these early experiences, while negative peer interactions intensify the child's self-doubts and evaluative fears. All in all, these studies are supportive of the concept of social pathogenesis proposed by interpersonal writers.

The Relational Self

According to the interpersonal perspective, the developmental experiences noted above shape the individual's sense of self, or self-schema. In particular, interpersonal writers propose that key information about the self concerns the person's role *vis-à-vis* significant others. Thus, how we see ourselves is based to a large extent on the nature of our habitual interactions with important others, which are distilled and stored in the form of relational schemas. If we have experienced different types of relationships with different significant others, our sense of self will be multifaceted, i.e., contain multiple relational schemas, any of which can become salient as social events bring to mind various significant relationships. If the interpersonal model is correct, the self-information critical to social anxiety should be of a relational nature, that is, concern the self in relation to significant others, not the self in isolation. In addition, the anxious person's sense of self should vary depending in part on which relational schema (e.g., positive or negative) are activated.

It is worth noting that many social-personality writers propose relational views of self (see Alden, Ryder, & Mellings, 2000). Schlenker and Leary's (1982) classic self-presentation theory postulates that people have a public, as well as a private, self (Leary & Kowalski, 1995; see also Leary, this volume, *Chapter 10*).

The public self is defined as our perception of others' impressions of us, and it is the decision that the public aspects of ourselves will fail to make the desired impression that triggers social anxiety. In a similar vein, Higgins and his colleagues posit that social anxiety arises when the person becomes aware of a discrepancy between knowledge structures representing the actual-self and the ought-other self, or the self one believes others think one ought to be (e.g., Higgins, Klein, & Strauman, 1985). The ought-other self is based on parental expectations and can therefore be seen as an internal store of information derived from experiences with significant others. Baldwin postulated that because socially anxious individuals have extensive experience with disapproving others, they develop elaborated negative relational schema (Baldwin, 1992; Baldwin & Main, in press). These negative schemas are then easily activated by social cues associated with early experiences and, once activated, lead to negative expectations in current social interactions and therefore to social anxiety (Baldwin & Main, in press). What is notable for our purposes is that all three theories postulate that it is the activation of relational information structures that precipitates social anxiety.

Is there any *empirical* support for the notion that information about the self is inherently connected to information about others? The best evidence comes from a series of ingenious studies by Baldwin in which he used experimental manipulations to activate different relational schema. In one set of studies, subjects were asked to envision either an accepting or critical significant other and then participate in a second allegedly unrelated task in which they rated their mood and self-esteem. Baldwin found that subjects who envisioned the critical other displayed a drop in mood and self-esteem (Baldwin, 1994, 1995). Other studies had subjects engage in paper–pencil tasks in the presence of photograph of a significant other that either depicted the person smiling or looking somber. The presence of the photograph produced changes in subjects' moods and self-evaluation (Baldwin, Carrell, & Lopez, 1990). These studies demonstrate that bringing to mind information about different significant others automatically alters one's experience of oneself as well. Additional support for these ideas are also found in several studies conducted by Higgins and Strauman, who demonstrated that priming procedures that increased awareness of discrepancies between the actual self and the ought-other self produced arousal (e.g., Higgins, Klein, & Strauman, 1985; Strauman & Higgins, 1987). Further work by Strauman indicated that patients with social phobia were characterized by larger discrepancies between the actual and ought-other self structures than were depressed patients (Strauman, 1989, 1992).

Summary   Although more work needs to be done to evaluate the concept of the relational self, these studies suggest that cognitive stores of information about self are intertwined with information about others' reactions to the self. These findings support the interpersonal notion of relational schema, or knowledge structures in which self and others are linked. Furthermore, the activation of negative *relational* information appears to precipitate social anxiety, a pattern consistent with the interpersonal perspective.

Maladaptive Transactional Cycles

At the heart of the interpersonal model is the concept of the self-perpetuating interpersonal cycle. As noted earlier, interpersonal writers propose that developmental experiences lead to biases in people's interpretations of contemporary social events, leading them to adopt behavioral patterns learned in earlier relationships. These behaviors, in turn, pull reactions from others that confirm people's pre-existing views of their role *vis-à-vis* other individuals. We will examine each aspect of the cyclical pattern by itself and then examine the evidence that the various elements of the cycle work together as postulated.

Biased Social Perceptions

As we have seen, developmental and clinical studies of childhood experiences indicate that the parents of socially anxious people may have been controlling, nonaffectionate, even angry, and shaming, and that peers may have bullied, harassed, or simply ignored them. If the interpersonal model is correct, socially anxious people should perceive contemporary significant others to have these same qualities and, equally important, their social interpretations should be inaccurate or biased.

Interpretative biases have been examined in two contexts: laboratory tasks and close relationships. Three studies found evidence for negative biases in laboratory social judgement tasks. Socially anxious subjects who read social scenarios expressed the belief that others would evaluate both themselves and other students negatively—a pattern the researchers interpreted as reflecting a generalized view of others as critical (Leary, Kowalski, & Campbell, 1988). In a similar vein, socially anxious students interpreted standardized facial expressions as conveying a more negative response to them than did nonanxious students (Pozo, Carver, Wellens, & Scheier, 1991). Finally, Lundh and Öst (1996) found that social phobic patients had better memory for pictures of negative faces than positive faces.

Other laboratory studies examined social perception during initial encounters. In a study of group interaction, shyness was correlated with negative perceptions of other group members on dimensions such as warmth and friendliness (Jones & Briggs, 1984). Several studies conducted in our lab found that patients with a social phobia who participated in a brief interaction rated their partners' liking for them lower than did control subjects. Furthermore, their perceptions of their partners were inaccurate in that they underestimated their partners' liking for them relative to their partners' actual responses (e.g., Alden & Wallace, 1995). There is also reason to believe that socially anxious subjects might selectively attend to certain types of social information. Rapee found that social phobics attended to negative as opposed to positive cues from members of an audience listening to their speeches, although the audience members were carefully trained to provide an equal number of positive and negative reactions (Veljaca & Rapee, 1998).

Jones and his colleagues examined biased interpretations in the context of close relationships. These researchers found that shy students rated their friends more negatively, i.e., as less considerate and courteous, than did non-shy students (Jones & Briggs, 1984). To determine whether this was due to an interpretative bias or to the selection of friends who actually had negative characteristics, a second study asked students and their best friends to rate themselves and each other. Although the shy students rated their friends negatively on attributes important to relational competence, the friends themselves did not—a finding the researchers interpreted as indicative of a negative bias in the social judgements of shy people (Jones & Carpenter, 1986).

Not all studies have found negative perceptual biases (e.g., Stopa & Clark, 1993; Alden & Wallace, 1995). However, one explanation for these inconsistent findings is that interpretative biases do not occur in all situations, but only when situational cues are reminiscent of significant earlier experiences (e.g., Strupp & Binder, 1984). Baldwin's work on the activation of relational schema supports this explanation. So too does a study by Alden and Bieling (1998), who found that manipulations that led socially anxious subjects to appraise their interaction partner as either potentially critical or accepting led to different interpretations of and reactions to the same partner behavior.

Summary Overall, this work indicates that although socially anxious people do not always perceive others negatively, in some situations they incorrectly interpret others' behavior as cold or unfriendly, and they display a tendency to selectively attend to negative social information. Thus, the evidence is largely, but not uniformly, supportive of the interpersonal notion of biased social interpretation.

Behavioral Patterns

According to the copy process theory proposed by Benjamin (1993), the behavior of socially anxious individuals should conform to one of three patterns: behaving as if a critical, controlling, nonaffectionate person were present (*re-enactment*), behaving in a nonaffectionate, critical, controlling manner toward others (*identification*), or behaving in a critical, controlling, and nonaffectionate way toward oneself (*introjection*). Although people with social anxiety and social phobia do not *always* display avoidant or maladaptive social behavior (e.g., Leary & Kowalski, 1995; Pilkonis, 1977; Rapee, 1995), certain situations tend to elicit responses that appear to be awkward and unskilled (e.g., Alden, Bieling, & Meleshko, 1995; Glass & Arnkoff, 1989; Glass & Furlong, 1990; Turner Beidel, Dancu, & Keys, 1986). The crucial test of the interpersonal model is whether these behaviors reflect significant developmental events in the predicted manner.

Empirical studies provide clear support for two of Benjamin's patterns, re-enactment and introjection. Faced with a critical, controlling person, one would likely attempt to deflect attention, avert one's eyes, talk less, disclose less, withdraw as soon as possible, and avoid future contact. Research suggests that these are typical behavioral responses of socially anxious and social phobic people (e.g.,

Glass & Arnkoff, 1989; Meleshko & Alden, 1993; Spence, Donovan, & Brechman-Toussaint, 1999; Turner et al., 1986). The research literature also indicates that socially anxious people are self-critical and hold themselves in low regard, behaviors that are consistent with the notion of introjecting a critical other (e.g., Cheek & Melchior, 1990; Glass, Merluzzi, Biever, & Larsen, 1982; Spence et al., 1999). The extent to which socially anxious people identify with critical others and become critical and controlling themselves is less clear. In support of this pattern, Jones and his colleagues found that shy people can be critical and nonaffectionate toward their friends and others (Jones & Briggs, 1984; Jones & Carpenter, 1986). In addition, recent work by Henderson indicated that some severely shy individuals are characterized by high levels of blaming others (see Henderson & Zimbardo, this volume, *Chapter 19*). Finally, we have found that some social phobic patients respond to their therapists with irritation and disapproval (Alden & Koch, 1999). On the other hand, some studies did not find this cold, critical pattern in social phobic patients (Alden & Wallace, 1995; Rapee & Lim, 1992; Stopa & Clark, 1993), and social anxiety is typically associated with nonassertive, not controlling, behavior. Thus, at present, support for a behavioral pattern reflecting identification with critical, controlling parents is mixed. It may be that this particular pattern of behavior characterizes relatively fewer socially anxious individuals than the more anxious and self-critical patterns. Certainly more study of the role of blame and other-directed criticism in social phobia is needed.

Summary   Overall, the behavioral patterns found in socially anxious and social phobic individuals are consistent with interpersonal proposals. Greater support was found for behavioral strategies reflecting reenactment and introjection of significant early relationships, but there are also suggestions that some socially anxious individuals may display identification with critical others. Although these patterns of contemporary behavior are similar to those found in developmental studies of the family interactions of shy children, it remains to be established whether these behaviors were actively adopted to manage early negative relationships, as suggested by interpersonal writers, or were simply the by-products of innate anxiety or inadequate opportunities to acquire social skills.

Others' Reactions

Another critical test of the interpersonal model is whether socially anxious individuals elicit negative responses from other people. Studies of shy and socially anxious individuals suggest that this is the case. Shy individuals were rated more negatively on a variety of interpersonal dimensions (e.g., warmth, relational competence, likability) by both objective interviewers and their best friends (e.g., Gough & Thorne, 1986; Jones & Briggs, 1984). Even more persuasive are several studies indicating that shy individuals are rated as less intelligent than non-shy people by peers during initial interactions, even though there is no actual association between social anxiety and intelligence (Gough & Thorne, 1986; Paulhus & Morgan, 1997). This finding suggests the presence of a global negative halo in others' perceptions of socially anxious people.

Studies conducted in our lab found that others were less likely to desire future interactions with socially anxious as opposed to nonanxious students following brief first-meeting conversations (e.g., Meleshko & Alden, 1993; Papsdorf & Alden, 1998). The social behavior of these anxious people apparently led others to disengage from the relationship. We also attempted to identify the exact behaviors that precipitate disengagement. Anxiety-related behavior (e.g., low eye contact, anxious mannerisms) was one factor, although this behavior displayed a relatively modest negative correlation with desire for future interaction. More significant were failing to reciprocate others' self-disclosures and self-focused, as opposed to other-focused, attention. These behaviors led others to perceive socially anxious targets as dissimilar to themselves and disinterested in them, factors that weighed heavily in their partners' decisions to disengage (Alden & Bieling, 1998; Alden & Mellings, 1999; Meleshko & Alden, 1993; Papsdorf & Alden, 1998). Other recent work indicated that children with social phobia were less likely than other children to receive positive outcomes from peers (Spence et al., 1999). Interestingly, there is reason to believe that others' negative reactions change with longer exposure to the socially anxious person. Spouses and long-term acquaintances typically rate shy people more positively than do strangers or recent acquaintances (e.g., Gough & Thorne, 1986).

Summary   Overall, it seems that socially anxious people evoke distinct reactions from other people, particularly in the early stages of relationship formation. Others interpret the behavior of anxious people as an expression of disinterest and dissimilarity and disengage from future contact, thereby choking off friendship development. Consistent with the interpersonal model, socially anxious people unwittingly produce the very response they fear—a lack of interest or even negative evaluation from others.

Documenting a Cyclical Pattern

To support an interpersonal model of social phobia, it must be demonstrated that these events are linked in the predicted cyclic pattern, specifically that biased perceptions produce dysfunctional behavior that, in turn, evoke negative social responses. Several studies have examined the links between these various events. In one such investigation, an experimental manipulation was used to alter subjects' appraisals of an upcoming interaction with an experimental confederate. When a critical-other schema was activated, socially anxious subjects engaged in self-protective behaviors, and these behaviors led to negative responses from their partner. In contrast, when an accepting-other schema was activated, the behavior of the socially anxious subjects did not differ from that of non-anxious controls and furthermore, their partners liked them as well as nonanxious controls (Alden & Bieling, 1998). A second study confirmed this pattern. Once again, self-protective behaviors, in particular avoidance of eye contact and lack of self-disclosure, produced lowered desire for future interactions (Papsdorf & Alden, 1998). These studies indicate that when socially anxious individuals interpret a situation as potentially negative, they adopt behavioral strategies that unwittingly produce the very outcomes they fear and, conversely, when they interpret others' motives more positively, they display proactive social responses.

Relatedness as a Social Goal

The interpersonal model assumes that dysfunctional behavior, such as the pattern noted above, represents a maladaptive attempt to relate to others. On the face of it, social phobics do not appear to be motivated by the desire to maintain closeness, as suggested by interpersonal writers. They tend to withdraw from or avoid social contact and have fewer friends than nonanxious people. Their behavior (little eye contact, less speech, low voice volume) often appears to reflect a desire to avoid rather than maintain closeness. Is there any reason to believe that this behavioral pattern is a strategic attempt, however inept, to maintain relatedness to others? If the interpersonal model is correct, two things should be true:

(1) the behaviors of social phobic people should be strategic, that is, designed to accomplish some goal rather than the result of other factors, such as skill deficits or conditioned anxiety;

(2) the ultimate goal of this behavioral pattern should be to maintain rather than avoid closeness with others.

According to social-personality writers, social behavior is motivated by a combination of acquisitive goals, the desire to garner positive outcomes such as attention and approval, and self-protective goals, the desire to avoid negative outcomes such as criticism and rejection (e.g., Schlenker & Leary, 1982; Arkin, Lake, & Baumgardner, 1986). Because socially anxious people chronically expect negative outcomes, they are said to direct their behavior, at least initially, toward self-protection. What is notable for our purposes is that both motive systems continue to operate. Thus, social anxiety is said to arise from a conflict between the desire for positive outcomes and the desire to avoid negative outcomes (Arkin, 1981). Moreover, the function of self-protective motivation is to maintain social relatedness. Self-protective concerns are said to motivate people to take steps to reduce the likelihood they will be rejected and excluded from the group, an outcome with considerable evolutionary survival value (see, for example, Leary, Tambor, Terdal, & Downs, 1995). One implication of this duality is that acquisitive goals should temper self-protective behavior and the desire to maintain closeness should be visible in the self-protective behavior of socially anxious people. Another implication is that the behavior of the socially anxious person should be flexible. If the salience of negative outcomes is reduced or the possibility of success is increased, anxious people should readily shift to acquisitive goals and prosocial behavior.

Empirical studies support some aspects of the dual motivational perspective. First, socially anxious individuals were found to subscribe to both acquisitive and protective motives. Whereas nonanxious control subjects displayed a predominance of acquisitive motivation, socially anxious and social phobic subjects displayed approximately equal amounts of both drives (Meleshko & Alden, 1993; Wallace & Alden, 1997). In addition, the relative strength of the various motivations changed in response to changes in the social situation. Social phobic patients displayed greater concern with gaining approval and less concern with avoiding disapproval when their conversational partner was friendly than when the partner was cool (Wallace & Alden, 1997; Arkin et al., 1986). Moreover, when there is a shift in goal orientation, socially anxious people readily engage in more effective social performance (Alden & Bieling, 1998; DePaulo, Epstein, & LeMay, 1990). These studies are consistent with the interpersonal notion that socially anxious people are motivated to maintain relatedness to others and when concern with disapproval is reduced, they readily direct their efforts toward doing so. However, one key aspect of the interpersonal model—that dysfunctional social behavior is an attempt to maintain closeness to significant others—has not been well studied. To establish this pattern, one would have to demonstrate that, consciously or unconsciously, the ultimate function of self-protective behavior is to maintain closeness with others. Some work provides hints that this may be the case. Socially anxious people do not always avoid or withdraw from social interactions. At times they display behaviors such as innocuous agreeableness, neutral conformity, or hovering on the periphery of social groups—strategies that allow them to remain in contact with others, while reducing the likelihood of negative outcomes (Arkin et al., 1986). Thus, it may be that the function of self-protective behaviors is to reduce the likelihood of exclusion.

Summary All in all, the behavioral flexibility of socially anxious people suggest that their behavior represents a strategic attempt to minimize negative outcomes, rather than a skill deficit or conditioned anxiety—factors that would be expected to exert a continuous effect on behavior, not the shifting behavioral strategies found in socially anxious people. In addition, the observation that socially anxious subjects readily work to gain attention and approval once self-protective concerns are reduced suggests that their ultimate goal is to relate to others, not to avoid closeness. Together these studies provide some support for the motivational views inherent in the interpersonal perspective outlined above.

INTERPERSONAL CONTRIBUTIONS

Having determined that social anxiety and social phobia can be conceptualized from an interpersonal perspective, we must now ask whether there are any advantages in doing so. There are many similarities between the cognitive-behavioral and interpersonal perspectives. Furthermore, many of the interpersonal tenets discussed above can be explained within the cognitive-behavioral framework, even if these events are not prominent features. The interpersonal model is complex and some elements, particularly related to internal events such as copy processes and the relational structure of the self-schema, require more scientific scrutiny. Before we consider incorporating elements of this model into cognitive-behavioral formulations, we must evaluate whether the benefits of doing so outweigh these disadvantages. A model is useful to the extent that it provides a better explanation for empirical findings than alternative theories, points to unrecognized or under-recognized phenomena, or offers new suggestions for intervention. Space does not permit a full analysis of each of the topics reviewed above; however, we will examine some of them to determine whether the interpersonal model meets these criteria.

Social Pathogenesis

Although cognitive-behavioral writers would be quick to agree that perceptual biases and dysfunctional behavior are learned responses, the interpersonal perspective more closely links social developmental experiences to current behavior and underscores the role of specific experiences in shaping the fears and behavioral patterns found in patients. Thus, an interpersonal perspective points to the importance of understanding the interpersonal histories of social phobic individuals. There is reason to believe that this understanding might be useful in treatment. First, reviewing significant interpersonal experiences can help the clinician to identify more quickly the specific interpersonal beliefs and behaviors that cause problems for individual patients. A discussion of such experiences can also be used to illustrate to patients that their social expectations were learned and are not a wholly accurate reflection of contemporary interactions. This understanding can then be used to encourage patients to look more objectively at current social events.

The interpersonal perspective also draws attention to variation in the developmental experiences of social phobic patients. When we look closely at childhood studies, we find a range of social environments: social isolation, parental shyness, parental failure to encourage communication and involvement, overcontrolling behavior, and expressions of anger and disappointment. Many clinicians have also encountered patients with social phobia and avoidant personality disorder who report childhood physical and sexual abuse or parental alcoholism. According to interpersonal writers, these experiences should be translated into different social fears and behavioral patterns. For example, one might expect that socially anxious people who had critical, abusive parents would display greater perceptual biases and distrust than those who grew up with socially isolated or shy but loving parents. Again, this points to researchable questions. Do different learning histories translate into different symptom patterns? If so, do these differences affect the process and outcome of treatment?

At least two studies examined variability in the fundamental nature of the patient's interpersonal behaviors and fears. One such study found that patients with avoidant personality disorder displayed a variety of interpersonal problem profiles as assessed by the Inventory of Interpersonal Problems-Circumplex Scales (Alden & Capreol, 1993; Alden, Wiggins, & Pincus, 1990). Some patients reported warm-submissive types of problems, such as excessive fears about hurting others' feelings and difficulties with assertiveness, whereas other patients reported cold-submissive types of problems, such as an inability to experience warm feelings toward others and uncertainty about the benefits of intimacy. Furthermore, patients with different patterns of interpersonal problems benefited from different cognitive-behavioral regimens (Alden & Capreol, 1993). Patients with warm-submissive behavior problems benefited from a behavioral regimen that focused on increasing self-disclosure and closeness to others. In contrast, avoidant patients with cold behavioral patterns responded better to a graduated exposure regimen that required them to increase their contact with other people. Apparently the warm avoidant patients were more capable or desirous of emotionally intimate relationships than were the cold avoidant patients. A second study found similar variability in the core interpersonal problems reported by group of patients with social phobia (Kachin, Newman, & Pincus, 2000). Although one must be cautious when drawing conclusions from so few studies, these results suggest that it may be useful to examine how interpersonal differences affect the clinical picture and treatment response of social phobic patients.

The Relational Self

For more than a hundred years, writers have observed that socially anxious individuals have negative self-concepts. Moreover, cognitive-behavioral theories include self-related processes such as self-focused attention and negative biases in self-related judgements. Is there anything to be gained by incorporating the somewhat cumbersome notion of the relational self in theories of social phobia?

The empirical literature suggests several advantages. First, the concept of a relational self provides a ready explanation for such findings as the automatic linkage between changes in thoughts of others and changes in mood and self-esteem (e.g., Baldwin, 1994, 1995). Our views of ourselves appear to change when we envision different interpersonal relationships. Second, relational information has been found to distinguish social anxiety from other emotional disorders. For example, both social phobic and depressed individuals have negative self-concepts and engage in dysfunctional self-related processes, such as self-focused attention and negative self-evaluation. However, social phobic individuals appear to use unique and distinctively interpersonal reference points to arrive at their negative self-judgements. For example, Strauman that found social phobia was uniquely associated with actual ought-other self discrepancies, whereas depression was associated with actual-ideal self discrepancies (e.g., Strauman, 1989, 1992). In a similar vein, Wallace and Alden (1995, 1997) found that socially anxious and social phobic patients displayed discrepancies between their ratings of self-efficacy and perceptions of others' standards, whereas depressed individuals displayed discrepancies between self-efficacy and personal standards. The social phobics appeared to judge themselves in light of their perceptions of what others expected, whereas depressed people judged themselves in light of their personal goals. Thus, although negative self-judgements do not discriminate the two conditions, relational information does.

All in all, this work suggests that when examining self-related processes in social phobia, it is necessary to consider the interpersonal nature of the self-schema. In particular, it would be useful to further delineate how interpersonal cues alter self-perception. Following from this, it may be possible to develop techniques that evoke positive relational schema, which could then be used to enhance the effects of cognitive-behavioral strategies such as exposure.

Others' Reactions

A key tenet of the interpersonal model is that others' responses are crucial to the maintenance of social anxiety. Similar ideas have been expressed by cognitive-behavioral writers (e.g., Clark & Wells, 1995), particularly those who espouse skill-deficit theories of social phobia (e.g., Turner, Beidel, Cooley, Woody, & Messer, 1994). What then does the interpersonal model add to these ideas?

First and foremost, an interpersonal perspective underscores the importance of understanding the specific nature of the interaction between socially anxious individuals and others. Different patients may alienate others in different ways. Again, this perspective points to the need to study variability in the interpersonal patterns established between different patients and those around them.

Another interpersonal contribution is the notion of using others' responses to identify the precise behaviors and qualities that evoke rejection. Studies following this strategy indicated that two important types of behavior are failure to reciprocate others' disclosures and self-preoccupation (e.g., Alden & Mellings, 1999; Meleshko & Alden, 1993; Papsdorf & Alden, 1998). Other studies suggest that socially anxious people are better received by those who have ongoing contact with them, perhaps because exposure allows others to rule out mistaken hypotheses about socially anxious people (e.g., Jones & Carpenter, 1986; Paulhus & Morgan, 1997). Findings such as these may be useful in treatment. First, these results could help patients to establish appropriate behavioral goals. For example, this information might be used to help patients to recognize that it is more important that they display interest in others and reciprocate others' disclosures than that they give a polished social "performance". Patients might also benefit from recognizing that they will fare better if they seek out social settings that allow repeated interactions with the same people. Not only does ongoing interaction increase the patients' comfort with others, it increases the likelihood that others will come to appreciate them as well (e.g., Paulhus & Morgan, 1997).

Social Motivation

The notion of self-protective motivation is strikingly similar to the concept of safety goals included in cognitive-behavioral models. For example, Clark and Wells (1995) proposed that social phobic patients adopt behaviors designed to prevent feared outcomes, thereby increasing their sense of safety, and research by these same writers underscores the importance of reducing safety behaviors when treating social phobic patients (Wells et al., 1995). In light of these similarities, what do we gain from an interpersonal approach?

The contribution of the interpersonal model here is the explicit recognition that social phobic patients are motivated by more than the pursuit of safety—they also desire closeness with others. Moreover, they are often capable of more effective social behavior than is initially apparent. It is helpful for clinicians to keep in mind that when the salience of negative outcomes is reduced, or the likelihood of success is increased, anxious people can readily shift to acquisitive goals and prosocial behavior because they are motivated to be close to others. Cognitive-behavioral treatment often involves behavioral rehearsal with video-taped feedback designed to help patients' improve their behavioral performance. Another approach might be to use such behavioral exercises to demonstrate to patients that their behavior is effective under certain conditions. For example, one often finds that patients with social phobia are more comfortable and effective with some types of people than with others. Thus, therapists might have patients rehearse the same situation while imagining different people as the recipient of their behavior, an exercise that can be used to illustrate how social cues lead them to anticipate different responses from others and adopt different roles. Another suggestion comes from Baldwin, who proposed that therapists experiment with procedures that prime positive and negative relational schema prior to social interactions (e.g., Baldwin, 1992).

The Interpersonal Process of Treatment

The final interpersonal contribution that we will consider here is the role of interpersonal processes in treatment. Interpersonal writers underscore the interpersonal nature of therapy, even if the treatment approach is cognitive-behavioral or pharmacological in orientation. By the very nature of their anxiety, patients with social phobia are particularly likely to be sensitive to interpersonal elements of treatment. Moreover, treatment sessions combine a number of features that are problematic for these patients—an ambiguous situation, an authority figure, subtle or not so subtle pressure to talk openly about personal failures. It is easy to see how treatment could evoke the same concerns and behavioral patterns that characterize these patients' daily social encounters. Consistent with these ideas, recent work at our clinic indicated that social phobic patients' perceptions of their relationship with their therapist predicted response to cognitive-behavioral treatment (Alden & Koch, 1999). Specifically, social phobic patients who perceived their therapist to be interested and concerned about them were more likely to complete homework assignments and to benefit from their treatment involvement than were patients for whom treatment evoked concerns about therapist disinterest. These findings indicate that interpersonal concerns influence behavior in treatment sessions and that therapists should be aware of potentially adverse interpersonal reactions.

SUMMARY

Our review indicated that the empirical literature supports the basic tenets of an interpersonal model of social phobia. We also identified some ways in which this framework contributes to existing clinical theories by drawing attention to under-recognized events, offering a better explanation for some empirical findings, and suggesting new directions for research and treatment. In particular, this framework more explicitly recognizes interpersonal variation in developmental experiences and in the beliefs and behavioral patterns derived from those experiences. It also suggests interesting possibilities about the nature of the self-schema and about the importance of understanding others' perceptions and responses to socially anxious people. These contributions suggest that an interpersonal perspective could be used to enrich current clinical theories of social phobia.

The purpose of this volume is to draw together research from a variety of fields, including developmental, social, personality, and clinical psychology. An over-arching advantage of the interpersonal perspective is that it provides a conceptual framework in which to integrate these various literatures because the model ties developmental experiences, self-schema, motivational goals, and current behavioral problems into a cohesive pattern. This integration not only enables cognitive-behavioral clinicians to draw on advances in child development, social cognition, and social psychology, it provides a common ground for researchers from all fields to meet and share their perspectives on social anxiety.

REFERENCES

Alden, L. E. & Bieling, P. M. (1998). Interpersonal consequences of the pursuit of safety. *Behaviour Research and Therapy, 36*, 1–9.

Alden, L. E., Bieling, P. J., & Meleshko, K. G. (1995). An interpersonal comparison of depression and social anxiety. In K. Craig & K. S. Dobson (Eds.), *Anxiety and depression in adults and children.* Thousand Oaks, CA: Sage Publications.

Alden, L. & Cappe, R. (1988). Prediction of treatment response in clients impaired by extreme shyness: Age of onset and public versus private shyness. *Canadian Journal of Behavioural Science, 20*, 40–49.

Alden, L. E. & Capreol, M. J. (1993). Interpersonal problem patterns in avoidant personality disordered outpatients: Prediction of treatment response. *Behavior Therapy, 24*, 356–376.

Alden, L. E. & Koch, W. J. (1999, November). *The process of cognitive-behavioral therapy with social phobia.* Paper presented at the Annual Meeting of the Association for the Advancement of Behavior Therapy. Toronto, Canada.

Alden, L. E. & Mellings, T. M. B. (1999). *Social anxiety and social information: Relative weight assigned to self and others.* Manuscript submitted for publication.

Alden, L. E., Ryder, A. G., & Mellings, T. M. B. (2000). Social phobia, social anxiety, and the self. In S. G. Hofmann, P. M. DiBartolo (Eds.), *From social anxiety to social phobia: Multiple perspectives* (pp. 370–390). New York: Allyn & Bacon.

Alden, L. E. & Wallace, S. T. (1995). Social phobia and social appraisal in successful and unsuccessful interactions. *Behaviour Research and Therapy, 33*, 497–506.

Alden, L. E., Wiggins, J. S., & Pincus, A. (1990). Construction of circumplex scales for the inventory of interpersonal problems. *Journal of Personality Assessment, 55,* 34–45.

Arcus, D. M. (1991). *The experiential modification of temperamental bias in inhibited and uninhibited children.* Unpublished doctoral dissertation. Harvard University, Cambridge, MA.

Arkin, R. M. (1981). Self-presentation styles. In J. T. Tedeschi (Ed.), *Impression management in social psychological research* (pp. 311–333). New York: Academic Press.

Arkin, R. M., Lake, E. A., & Baumgardner, A. H. (1986). Shyness and self-presentation. In W. H. Jones, J. M. Cheek, & S. R. Briggs (Eds.), *Shyness: Perspectives on research and treatment* (pp. 189–203). New York: Plenum Press.

Arrindell, W. A., Emmelkamp, P. M. G., Monsma, A., & Brilman, E. (1983). The role of perceived parental rearing practices in the etiology of phobic disorders: A controlled study. *British Journal of Psychiatry, 143,* 183–187.

Arrindell, W. A., Kwee, M. G. T., Methorst, G. J., Van Der Ende, J., Pol, E., & Moritiz, B. J. M. (1989). Perceived parental rearing styles of agoraphobic and socially phobic inpatients. *British Journal of Psychiatry, 155,* 526–535.

Baldwin, M. W. (1992). Relational schemas and the processing of social information. *Psychological Bulletin, 112,* 461–484.

Baldwin, M. W. (1994). Primed relational schemas as a source of self-evaluative reactions. *Journal of Social and Clinical Psychology, 13,* 380–403.

Baldwin, M. W. (1995). Relational schemas and cognition in close relationships. *Journal of Social and Personal Relationships, 12,* 547–552.

Baldwin, M. W., Carrell, S. E., & Lopez, D. F. (1990). Priming relationship schemas: My advisor and the Pope are watching me from the back of my mind. *Journal of Experimental Social Psychology, 26,* 435–454.

Baldwin, M. W. & Main, K. T. (in press). Social anxiety and the cued activation of relational knowledge. *Personality and Social Psychology Bulletin.*

Benjamin, L. W. (1993). *Interpersonal diagnosis and treatment of personality disorders.* New York: Guilford Press.

Blatt, S. J. & Zuroff, D. C. (1992). Interpersonal relatedness and self-definition: Two prototypes for depression. *Clinical Psychology Review. 12,* 527–562.

Bowlby, J. (1977). The making and breaking of affectional bonds. *British Journal of Psychiatry, 130,* 201–210.

Bruch, M. A. & Heimberg, R. G. (1994). Differences in perceptions of parental and personal characteristics between generalized and nongeneralized social phobics. *Journal of Anxiety Disorders, 8,* 155–168.

Bruch, M. A., Heimberg, R. G., Berger, P., & Collins, T. M. (1989). Social phobia and perceptions of early parental and personal characteristics. *Anxiety Research, 2,* 57–63.

Cheek, J. M. & Melchior, L. A. (1990). Shyness, self-esteem, and self-consciousness. In N. H. Leitenberg (Ed.), *Handbook of social and evaluative anxiety* (pp. 47–82). New York: Plenum Press.

Clark, D. M. & Wells, A. (1995). A cognitive model of social phobia. In R. G. Heimberg, M. Liebowitz, D. Hope, & F. Schneier (Eds.), *Social phobia: Diagnosis, assessment, and treatment* (pp. 69–93). New York: Guilford Press.

Coyne, J. C. (1976). Toward an interactional description of depression. *Psychiatry, 39,* 28–40.

DePaulo, B. M., Epstein, J. A., & LeMay, C. S. (1990). Responses of the socially anxious to the prospect of interpersonal evaluation. *Journal of Personality, 58,* 623–640.

Engfer, A. (1993). Antecedents and consequences of shyness in boys and girls: A 6-year longitudinal study. In K. H. Rubin & J. B. Asendorpf (Eds.), *Social withdrawal, inhibition, and shyness in childhood* (pp. 49–79). Hillsdale, NJ: Erlbaum.

Gilmartin, B. G. (1987). Peer group antecedents of severe love-shyness in males. *Journal of Personality, 55,* 467–489.

Glass, C. R. & Arnkoff, D. B. (1989). Behavioral assessment of social anxiety and social phobia. *Clinical Psychology Review*, *9*, 75–90.

Glass, C. R. & Furlong, M. (1990). Cognitive assessment of social anxiety: Affective and behavioral correlates. *Cognitive Therapy and Research*, *14*, 365–384.

Glass, C. R., Merluzzi, T. V., Biever, J. L., & Larsen, K. H. (1982). Cognitive assessment of social anxiety: Development and validation of a self-statement questionnaire. *Cognitive Therapy and Research*, *6*, 37–55.

Gough, H. & Thorne, A. (1986). Positive, negative and balanced shyness: Self-definitions and the reactions of others. In W. H. Jones, J. M. Cheek, & S. R. Briggs (Eds.), *Shyness: Perspectives on research and treatment* (pp. 205–225). New York: Plenum Press.

Higgins, E. T., Klein, R., & Strauman, T. (1985). Self-concept discrepancy theory: A psychological model for distinguishing among different aspects of depression and anxiety. *Social Cognition*, *3*, 51–76.

Hudson, J. L. & Rapee, R. M. (2000). The origins of social phobia. *Behavior Modification*, *24*, 102–129.

Ishiyama, R. J. (1984). Shyness, anxious social sensitivity, and self-isolating tendency. *Adolescence*, *19*, 903–011.

Joiner, T. E. & Metalsky, G. I. (1995). A prospective study of an integrative interpersonal theory of depression: A naturalistic study of college roommates. *Journal of Personality and Social Psychology*, *69*, 778–788.

Jones, W. H. & Briggs, S. R. (1984). The self-other discrepancy in social shyness. In R. Schwarzer (Ed.), *The self in anxiety, stress and depression* (pp. 93–107). Amsterdam: North Holland.

Jones, W. H. & Carpenter, B. N. (1986). Shyness, social behavior, and relationships. In W. H. Jones, J. M. Cheek, & S. R. Briggs (Eds.), *Shyness: Perspectives on research and treatment* (pp. 227–238). New York: Plenum Press.

Kachin, K. E., Newman, M. G., & Pincus, A. L. (2000). *A comparison of symptom-based and interpersonal approaches to the classification of social phobia subtypes.* Manuscript submitted for publication.

Kagan, J., Reznick, J. S., & Snidman, N. (1987). The physiology and psychology of behavioral inhibition in children. *Child Development*, *58*, 1459–1473.

Kagan, J., Reznick, J. S., Snidman, N., Gibbons, J., & Johnson, M. O. (1988). Childhood derivatives of inhibition and lack of inhibition to the unfamiliar. *Child Development*, *59*, 1580–1589.

Kiesler, D. J. (1983). The 1982 Interpersonal Circle: A taxonomy for complementarity in human transactions. *Psychological Review*, *90*, 185–214.

Leary, M. R. (1986). Affective and behavioral components of shyness: Implications for theory, measurement, and research. In W. H. Jones, J. M. Cheek, & S. R. Briggs (Eds.), *Shyness: Perspectives on research and treatment* (pp. 27–38). New York: Plenum Press.

Leary, M. R. & Kowalski, R. M. (1995). *Social anxiety.* New York: Guilford Press.

Leary, M. R., Kowalski, R. M., & Campbell, C. D. (1988). Self-presentational concerns and social anxiety: The role of generalized impression expectancies. *Journal of Research in Personality*, *22*, 308–321.

Leary, M. R., Tambor, E. S., Terdal, S. K., & Downs, D. L. (1995). Self-esteem as an interpersonal monitor: The sociometer hypothesis. *Journal of Personality and Social Psychology*, 68, 518–530.

Lundh, L. & Öst, L. (1996). Recognition bias for critical faces in social phobics. *Behaviour Research and Therapy*, *34*, 787–794.

Mahler, M. (1968). *On human symbiosis and the vicissitudes of individuation.* New York: International Universities Press.

Meleshko, K. A. & Alden, L. E. (1993). Anxiety and self-disclosure: Toward a motivational model. *Journal of Personality and Social Psychology*, *64*, 1000–1009.

Mills, R. S. L. & Rubin, K. H. (1993). Socialization factors in the development of social withdrawal. In K. H. Rubin & J. B. Asendorpf (Eds.), *Social withdrawal, inhibition, and shyness in childhood* (pp. 117–148). Hillsdale, NJ: Erlbaum.

Olewus, D. (1993). Victimization by peers: Antecedents and long-term outcomes. In K. H. Rubin & J. B. Asendorpf (Eds.), *Social withdrawal, inhibition, and shyness in childhood* (pp. 315–341). Hillsdale, NJ: Erlbaum.

Papsdorf, M. P. & Alden, L. E. (1998). Mediators of social rejection in socially anxious individuals. *Journal of Research in Personality*, *32*, 351–369.

Parker, G. (1979). Reported parental characteristics of agoraphobics and social phobics. *British Journal of Psychiatry*, *135*, 555–560.

Paulhus, D. L. & Morgan, K. L. (1997). Perceptions of intelligence in leaderless groups: The dynamic effects of shyness and acquaintance. *Journal of Personality and Social Psychology*, *72*, 581–591.

Pilkonis, P. A. (1977). The behavioral consequences of shyness. *Journal of Personality*, *45*, 596–611.

Plomin, R. & Daniels, D. (1986). Genetics and shyness. In W. H. Jones, J. M. Cheek, & S. R. Briggs (Eds.), *Shyness: Perspectives on research and treatment* (pp. 63–80). New York: Plenum Press.

Pozo, C., Carver, C. S., Wellens, A. R., & Scheier, M. F. (1991). Social anxiety and social perception: Construing others' reactions to the self. *Personality and Social Psychology Bulletin*, *17*, 355–362.

Rapee, R. M. (1995). Descriptive psychopathology of social phobia. In R. G. Heimberg, M. R. Liebowitz, D. A. Hope, & F. R. Schneier (Eds.), *Social phobia: Diagnosis, assessment and treatment* (pp. 41–66). New York: Guilford.

Rapee, R. M. & Lim, L. (1992). Discrepancy between self- and observer ratings of performance in social phobics. *Journal of Abnormal Psychology*, *101*, 728–731.

Rubin, K. H., LeMare, L., & Lollis, S. (1990). Social withdrawal in childhood: Developmental pathways to rejection. In S. R. Asher & J. D. Coie (Eds.), *Peer rejection in childhood* (pp. 217–249). New York: Cambridge University Press.

Schlenker, B. R. & Leary, M. R. (1982). Social anxiety and self-presentation: A conceptualization and model. *Psychological Bulletin*, *92*, 641–669.

Spence, S. H., Donovan, C., & Brechman–Toussaint, M. (1999). Social skills, social outcomes, and cognitive features of childhood social phobia. *Journal of Abnormal Psychology*, *108*, 211–221.

Stemberger, R. T., Turner, S. M., Beidel, D. C., & Calhoun, D. S. (1995). Social phobia: An analysis of possible developmental factors. *Journal of Abnormal Psychology*, *104*, 526–531.

Stopa, L. & Clark, D. M. (1993). Cognitive processes in social phobia. *Behaviour Research and Therapy*, *31*, 255–267.

Strauman, T. J. (1989). Self-discrepancies in clinical depression and social phobia: Cognitive structures that underlie emotional disorders? *Journal of Abnormal Psychology*, *98*, 14–22.

Strauman, T. J. (1992). Self-guides, autobiographical memory, and anxiety and dysphoria: Toward a cognitive model of vulnerability to emotional distress. *Journal of Abnormal Psychology*, *101*, 87–95.

Strauman, T. J. & Higgins, E. T. (1987). Automatic activation of self-discrepancies and emotional syndromes: When cognitive structures influence affect. *Journal of Personality and Social Psychology*, *53*, 1004–1014.

Strupp, H. H. & Binder, J. L. (1984). *Psychotherapy in a new key*. New York: Basic Books.

Sullivan, H. S. (1953). *The interpersonal theory of psychiatry*. New York: Norton.

Turner, S. M., Beidel, D. C., Cooley, M. R., Woody, S., & Messer, S. C. (1994). A multicomponent behavioural treatment for social phobia: Social effectiveness therapy. *Behaviour Research and Therapy*, *32*, 381–390.

Turner, S. M., Beidel, D. C., Dancu, D. V., & Keys, D. J. (1986). Psychopathology of social phobia and comparison to avoidant personality disorder. *Journal of Abnormal Psychology, 95*, 389–394.

Veljaca, K. A. & Rapee, R. M. (1998). Detection of negative and positive audience behaviours by socially anxious subjects. *Behaviour Research and therapy, 36*, 311–321.

Vernberg, E. M., Abwender, D. A., Ewell, K. K., & Beery, S. H. (1992). Social anxiety and peer relationships in early adolescence: A prospective analysis. *Journal of Clinical Child Psychology, 21*, 189–196.

Wallace, S. T. & Alden, L. E. (1995). Social anxiety and standard-setting following social success and failure. *Cognitive Therapy and Research, 19*, 613–631.

Wallace, S. T. & Alden, L. E. (1997). Social phobia and positive social events: The price of success. *Journal of Abnormal Psychology, 106*, 1–10.

Wells, A., Clark, D. M., Salkovskis, P. M. S., Ludgate, J., Hackmann, A., & Gelder, M. (1995). Social phobia: The role of in-situation safety behaviors in maintaining anxiety and negative beliefs. *Behavior Therapy, 26*, 153–161.

Chapter 18

A Cognitive Perspective on Social Phobia

David M. Clark

THE COGNITIVE MODEL
Processing in Social Situations
  Processing of the self as a social object
  Safety behaviours
  Somatic and Cognitive Symptoms
  Processing of External Social Cues
Processing before and after a Social Situation
EMPIRICAL STUDIES OF THE COGNITIVE MODEL
Hypotheses
Conclusions
A THEORY DERIVED COGNITIVE TREATMENT
Therapeutic Relationship
Deriving an Idiosyncratic Version of the Model
Manipulation of Self-focused Attention and Safety Behaviours
Video and Audio Feedback
Shift of Attention and Interrogation of the Social Environment
Dealing with Anticipatory and Post-event Processing
Dealing with Assumptions
EFFECTIVENESS OF THE COGNITIVE TREATMENT
ACKNOWLEDGEMENTS
REFERENCES

The persistence of social phobia is a puzzle. Individuals with other phobias such as claustrophobia, height phobia, and small animal phobias are able to success-fully avoid most encounters with their phobic object and it is generally thought

International Handbook of Social Anxiety: Concepts, Research and Interventions Relating to the Self and Shyness. Edited by W. Ray Crozier and Lynn E. Alden.
© 2001 John Wiley & Sons Ltd.

that this avoidance is the main reason for the persistence of their fears. In contrast, the nature of modern society is such that patients with social phobia often have to enter feared social situations. This distinction is recognized in recent versions of the *Diagnostic and Statistical Manual for Mental Disorders* (APA, 1987, 1994) where avoidance is necessary for the diagnosis of all phobias except for social phobia where it is specified that the phobia situation must be either "avoided *or* endured with intense distress" (APA, 1994, p. 417; emphasis added). Why does social phobia persist despite regular exposure to feared social situations? The present chapter provides an overview of a recent cognitive model of social phobia (Clark & Wells, 1995; Clark, 1997; Wells, 1997, 1998; Wells & Clark, 1997) that was specifically developed to explain such persistence.[1] Following a description of the model, research testing key aspects of the model is summarized, a treatment programme which aims to reverse the maintenance processes specified in the model is outlined, and preliminary evaluations of the treatment and its components are reviewed.

THE COGNITIVE MODEL

For the purpose of exposition, the model is divided into two parts. The first part concerns what happens when a social phobic enters a feared social situation. The second concerns what happens prior to entering, and after leaving a social situation.

Processing in Social Situations

Figure 18.1 illustrates the processes that Clark and Wells suggest occur when a social phobic enters a feared social situation. On the basis of early experience, patients with social phobia develop a series of assumptions about themselves and their social world. The assumptions can be divided into three categories:

- *Excessively high standards for social performance*, e.g., "I must not show any signs of weakness", "I must always sound intelligent and fluent", "I should only speak when other people pause", "I should always have something interesting to say".
- *Conditional beliefs concerning the consequences of performing in a certain way*, e.g., "If I disagree with someone, they will think I am stupid/will reject me", "If my hands shake/I blush/or show other signs of anxiety, people will think I am incompetent/odd/stupid", "If I am quiet, people will think I am boring", "If people get to know me, they won't like me".

---

[1] The Clark and Wells model draws heavily on the writings of earlier theorists, especially those of Beck, Emery, and Greenberg (1985), Butler (1985), Hartman (1983), Heimberg and Barlow (1988), Leary (1983), Salkovskis (1991), Teasdale and Barnard (1993), and Trower and Gilbert (1989), but is unique in the particular synthesis it proposes. If the reader views the synthesis as worthwhile, it is because its authors benefited from "standing on the shoulders of giants".

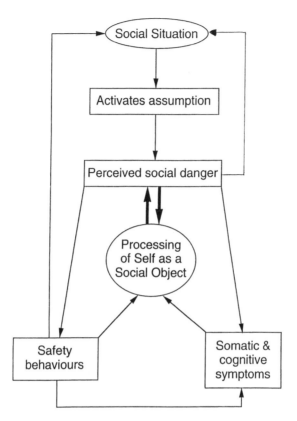

Figure 18.1 A model of the processes that occur when a social phobic enters a feared social situation (adapted from Clark & Wells, 1995)

- *Unconditional negative beliefs about the self*, e.g., "I'm odd/different", "I'm unlikeable/unacceptable", "I'm boring", "I'm stupid", "I'm different".

Such assumptions lead individuals to appraise relevant social situations as dangerous, to predict that they will fail to achieve their desired level of performance (e.g., "I'll shake, I'll make a fool of myself") and to interpret often benign or ambiguous social cues as signs of negative evaluation by others. Once a social situation is appraised in this way, the social phobic becomes anxious. Several interlinked vicious circles then maintain the individual's distress and prevent disconfirmation of the negative beliefs and appraisals.

Processing of the Self as a Social Object

A key factor is a shift in focus of attention and a particular type of negative self-processing. When individuals with social phobia believe they are in danger of negative evaluation by others, they shift their attention to detailed monitoring and observation of themselves. They then use the internal information made accessible by self-monitoring to infer how they appear to other people and what other people are thinking about them. In this way they become trapped in a closed system in which most of their evidence for their fears is self-generated and disconfirmatory evidence (such as other people's responses) becomes inaccessible or is ignored.

Three types of internal information are used to generate a negative self-impression. First, feeling anxious is equated with looking anxious. This can lead to marked distortions. For example, an individual may have a strong shaky feeling and assume that others must be able to see his or her hand shaking violently, when all that can be observed by others is a mild tremor or nothing at all. Second, many patients with social phobia appear to experience spontaneously occurring images in which they see themselves as if viewed from an observer's perspective. Unfortunately, what they see in the image is not what the observer would see but rather their fears visualized. For example, an individual who was concerned that she would appear stupid if she joined in a conversation with colleagues experienced marked tension around her lips before speaking. The tension triggered an image in which she saw herself with a contorted facial expression, looking like the "village idiot". Third, more diffuse types of "felt sense" can also contribute to the negative impression of one's social self. For example, the woman with the distorted image also felt "different and apart" from the other people she was sitting close to and wanted to talk to. This "felt" sense further reinforced her perception of herself as appearing stupid and uninteresting.

Safety Behaviours

When discussing phobias in general, Salkovskis (1991, 1996) suggested that patients often fail to benefit from the non-occurrence of a feared catastrophe when they are in a phobic situation because they engage in a variety of safety-seeking behaviours that are intended to prevent or minimize the feared catastrophe. If the catastrophe then fails to occur, patients ascribe the non-occurrence to the safety behaviour rather than inferring that the situation is less dangerous than they previously thought. Clark and Wells agree that safety behaviours operate in this fashion in social phobia and highlight several additional interesting features of social phobia-related safety behaviours.

First, although termed "behaviours", many safety-seeking acts are internal mental processes. For example, patients with social phobia who are worried that what they say may not make sense and will sound stupid, often report memorizing what they have said and comparing it with what they are about to say, while speaking. If everything goes well, patients are likely to think, "it only went well because I did all the memorizing and checking, if I had just been myself people would have realized how stupid I was".

Second, because there are often many levels to social phobics' fears, it is common for patients to engage in a large number of different safety behaviours while in a feared situation. Table 18.1 illustrates this point by summarizing the

Table 18.1 Safety behaviours associated with a patient's fear of blushing

Feared outcome	Safety behaviour intended to prevent feared outcome
"My face (and neck) will go red"	Keep cool (open windows, drink cold water, avoid hot drinks, wear thin clothes). Avoid eye contact. If in a meeting, pretend to be writing notes in order to look professional. Keep topic of conversation away from "difficult" issues. Tell myself the man isn't really attractive; "He's no more than a 2 (out of 10) for attractiveness".
"If I do blush, people will notice"	Wear clothes (scarf, high collar) that would hide part of blush. Wear make-up to hide the blush. Put hands over face; hide face with long hair. Stand in a dark part of the room. Turn away.
"If people notice, they will think badly of me"	Say something to suggest an alternative explanation for red face; viz. "It's hot in here", "I'm in a terrible rush today", "I'm recovering from flu", etc.

Adapted from Clark (1999, p. 58).

safety behaviours used by a patient who had a fear of blushing, especially while talking to men whom she thought other people would think were attractive. There were three components to her fear of blushing: fearing she would blush, fearing people would notice the blush, and fearing people would evaluate her negatively because of the blush. Several safety behaviours were used to try to prevent each feared outcome.

Third, safety behaviours can create some of the symptoms that social phobics fear. For example, trying to hide underarm sweating by wearing a jacket or keeping one's arms close to one's sides, produces more sweating. Similarly, memorizing what one has been saying makes it difficult to keep track of a conversation, triggering the thought "other people will think I'm boring/stupid".

Fourth, most safety behaviours have the consequence of increasing self-focused attention and self-monitoring, thus further enhancing the salience of one's negative self-image and reducing attention to others' behaviour.

Fifth, some safety behaviours can draw other people's attention to the patient. For example, a secretary who covered her face with her arms whenever she felt she was blushing discovered that colleagues in her office were considerably more likely to look at her when she did this than when she simply blushed. Similarly, a patient who intensely disliked being the centre of attention would speak quietly when trying to make a point in a meeting. The consequence of this manoeuvre was that people had difficulty hearing what she was saying and therefore stared at her.

Finally, some safety behaviours influence other people in a way which partly confirms the social phobic's fears. For example, social phobics' tendency to continually monitor what they have said and how they think they have been received often makes them appear distant and preoccupied. Similarly, their efforts to hide signs of anxiety and not show signs of weakness can make them appear aloof and unfriendly. Other people can interpret such behaviours as a sign that the phobic does not like them and, as a consequence, they respond to the phobic in a less warm and friendly fashion. In an observational study, Stopa and Clark (1993) confirmed that patients with social phobia can appear less outgoing and warm. Traditionally, this has been seen as a result of social skills deficits (Trower, Yardley, Bryant, & Shaw, 1978). In contrast to this point of view, Clark and Wells suggest that most social phobics have an adequate social skills capacity and their apparent social performance deficits are simply the observable side of their safety-seeking behaviours.

Somatic and Cognitive Symptoms

Social anxiety is accompanied by marked arousal. Patients are particularly concerned about the somatic and cognitive symptoms of anxiety that they think could be observed by others (e.g., sweating, feeling hot in the face, tremor, mental blanks) and interpret them as signs of impending or actual failure to meet their desired standards of social performance. Because of the perceived significance of arousal symptoms, patients are often hypervigilant for such symptoms. This hypervigilance tends to increase the subjective intensity of the somatic and cognitive symptoms. The symptoms can also be enhanced by a variety of safety behaviours (see sweating example above).

Processing of External Social Cues

The model by Clark and Wells places particular emphasis on self-focused attention and the use of internal information to construct a distorted, negative impression of one's observable self. Overall, it is thought that social anxiety is associated with reduced processing of external social cues. However, Clark and Wells also suggest that social phobics' (reduced) processing of the external social situation is likely to be biased in a negative direction. In particular, they may be more likely to notice and remember responses from others that they interpret as signs of disapproval. Given the relative paucity of overt negative reactions in most normal social interactions, many of the cues that are noticed and remembered may be ambiguous cues that can be interpreted negatively. This phenomenon may be particularly evident in public-speaking anxiety. Perhaps as a consequence of misapplying a rule about one to one social interactions ("when listening to another person, people should show that they are following the conversation by smiling/nodding, etc.") to lecturing situations, social phobics tend to interpret the absence of positive responses (no nods, no smiles), and the presence of ambiguous responses (looking down at one's notes, breaking eye contact) in an audience as signs of disapproval, when they could equally well be signs that the presentation is stimulating and thought provoking.

Processing before and after a Social Situation

Many social phobics experience considerable anxiety when anticipating a social event. Prior to the event they review in detail what they think might happen. As they start to think about the event, they become anxious and their thoughts tend to be dominated by recollections of past failures, by negative images of themselves during the event, and by other predictions of poor performance and rejection. Sometimes these ruminations lead the phobic to avoid the event completely. If this doesn't happen and the phobic participates in the event, he or she is likely to be already in a self-focused processing mode, expect failure, and be less likely to notice any signs of being accepted by other people.

Leaving or escaping from a social event does not necessarily bring to an immediate end the social phobic's negative thoughts and distress. There is no longer an immediate social danger and so anxiety rapidly declines. However, the nature of social interactions is such that the social phobic is unlikely to have received from others unambiguous signs of social approval, and for this reason it is not uncommon for him or her to conduct a "post-mortem" of the event. The interaction is reviewed in detail. During this review, the patient's anxious feelings and negative self-perception are likely to figure particularly prominently as they were processed in detail while the patient was in the situation, and hence would have been strongly encoded in memory. The unfortunate consequence of this is that the patient's review is likely to be dominated by his or her negative self-perception and the interaction is likely to be seen as much more negative than it really was. This may explain why some social phobics report a sense of shame that persists for a while after the anxiety has subsided. A further aspect of the post-mortem is the retrieval of other instances of perceived social failure. The recent interaction is then added to the list of past failures, with the consequence that an interaction which may have looked entirely neutral from an outside observer's perspective will have strengthened the patient's belief in his or her social inadequacy. Finally, some relatively minor aspects of the interaction can be subsequently appraised in a negative fashion and persistently ruminated about. For example, a patient at a dinner buffet mentioned how much he liked a bread and butter pudding. Later in the evening, he heard his hostess say she disliked bread and butter pudding. Afterwards, he thought his comment revealed he was unsophisticated and worthless.

EMPIRICAL STATUS OF THE COGNITIVE MODEL

The cognitive model outlined above comprises a series of testable hypotheses. Existing studies relevant to several of the key hypotheses are reviewed below. In some instances, the studies have used an analogue design in which high and low socially anxious non-patients are compared, rather than a clinical design in which patients with social phobia are compared with non-patients or with patients with another anxiety disorder. To avoid confusion, the effects observed in such studies are described as attributable to social anxiety rather than social phobia per se.

Hypotheses

Hypothesis 1: Social phobics interpret external social events in an excessively negative fashion   It has been suggested (Beck, Emery, & Greenberg, 1985; Clark & Beck, 1988; Clark & Wells, 1995) that at least two biases in the interpretation of external social events play a role in social phobia. First, patients with social phobia may have a tendency to interpret ambiguous social events in a negative fashion. Second, they may interpret unambiguous but mildly negative social events (e.g., mild criticism from an acquaintance) in a catastrophic fashion.

Amir, Foa, and Coles (1998) used a modification of a questionnaire originally developed by Butler and Mathews (1983) to assess interpretation of ambiguous events. Patients with generalized social phobia, patients with obsessive-compulsive disorder, and non-patient controls were presented with ambiguous social events (e.g., "someone you are dating says 'hello' to you") and ambiguous non-social events (e.g., "you receive a phone call from a clerk at your bank regarding your loan application"). After each event, three possible interpretations were presented and participants ranked the interpretations with respect their likelihood of coming into one's own mind or the mind of a "typical person" when in a similar situation. The results indicated that social phobia patients were more likely to make a negative interpretation of an ambiguous social event than either patients with obsessive-compulsive disorder or non-patient controls, and this effect only occurred in the self-relevant condition. In addition, the three groups did not differ in their interpretation of ambiguous non-social events.

Stopa and Clark (2000) confirmed and extended Amir et al.'s findings. Patients with generalized social phobia, equally anxious patients with other anxiety disorders, and non-patient controls were compared in terms of their interpretation of hypothetical ambiguous social events and mildly negative social events. For ambiguous events, patients with social phobia were more likely than both control groups to make, and believe, negative interpretations of social events but did not differ from other anxious patients in the likelihood of making, or believing, negative interpretations of non-social events. When presented with unambiguous, mildly negative events patients with social phobia were significantly more likely than both control groups to infer that the events would have catastrophic consequences.

Taken together, the questionnaire studies by Amir et al. (1998) and Stopa and Clark (2000) suggest that social phobia is associated with specific negative biases in the interpretation of self-referent social events. However, neither study assessed on-line interpretations, so it is unclear at this stage whether social phobics make the inferences identified in the studies on-line while observing external events in a social situation or whether they are more indirect inferences based on pre-existing beliefs and the contents of their negative self-impressions

(Stopa & Clark, 1993). A recent study of online processing in a text comprehension task (Hirsch & Mathews, 2000) provided data consistent with the latter possibility as non-patient controls showed a positive on-line inferential bias but social phobics failed to demonstrate positive or negative on-line emotional inferences. Further research is required to clarify this issue.

Hypothesis 2: Social phobics show enhanced self-focused attention when anxious in social situations The hypothesis that social phobia is associated with heightened self-focused attention has a long lineage and is well supported. Fenigstein, Scheier, and Buss (1975) defined public self-consciousness as attention to aspects of the self that might be observable to others and reported a significant positive correlation between public self-consciousness and social anxiety—a finding that was replicated by Hope and Heimberg (1988). Patients with social phobia have repeatedly been shown to score higher on the public self-consciousness scale than patients with other anxiety disorders and non-patients (Bruch, Heimberg, Berger, & Collins, 1989; Bruch & Heimberg, 1994; Saboonchi, Lundh, & Öst, 1999). Mellings and Alden (2000) studied attentional focus in social situations and found that high socially anxious individuals reported higher levels of self-focused attention than low socially anxious individuals.

Within the Clark and Wells model, self-focused attention increases the social phobic's awareness of interoceptive information that is likely to be taken as a sign that one is about to fail, or has failed, to convey an acceptable impression to others. As a consequence, it increases social anxiety. Woody (1996) provided direct support for the anxiety-inducing effects of self-focused attention by showing that an experimental manipulation of self-focus increased the anxiety levels of patients with generalized social phobia during a speech task.

Hypothesis 3: Social phobics show reduced processing of external social cues when anxious Mansell, Clark, Ehlers, and Chen (1999) used a modified dot-probe task to assess the hypothesis that social anxiety is associated with reduced processing of external social cues. Individuals scoring high and low on Fear of Negative Evaluation (FNE; Watson & Friend, 1969) were briefly presented with pairs of pictures, consisting of a face and a household object, under conditions of social-evaluative threat or no threat. As predicted, high socially anxious individuals showed an attentional bias away from faces when tested under conditions of social-evaluative threat, but not otherwise. More recently, using the same paradigm, Chen, Ehlers, Clark, and Mansell (2000) have reported that patients with social phobia also show reduced processing of faces.

Several memory studies have also provided results consistent with the diminished attention to external social cues hypothesis. If social phobics fail to attend to aspects of the external social situation, they should show reduced memory for such information. Kimble and Zehr (1982), Daly, Vangelisti, and Lawrence (1989), Hope, Heimberg, and Klein (1990) and Mellings and Alden (2000) all found that, compared to low socially anxious individuals, high socially anxious individuals had a poorer memory for details of a recent social interaction. As one might expect from the cognitive model, Mellings and Alden (2000) also found that recall of external social information (partner details) was poorest in individuals with the highest levels of self-focused attention during the interaction.

Hypothesis 4: Social phobics generate distorted observer-perspective images of how they think they appear to others when in feared social situations   Hackmann, Surawy, and Clark (1998) used a semistructured interview to assess the frequency and characteristics of spontaneous imagery in social anxiety-provoking situations. Consistent with the hypothesis, the majority (77%) of patients with social phobia reported experiencing negative, observer-perspective images, which they thought were at least partly distorted when they subsequently reflected on them. In contrast, only 10% of non-patient controls reported such images and their images were in general less negative. In a subsequent interview study, Hackmann, Clark, and McManus (2000) further explored the nature of social phobic imagery. Many images appeared to be recurrent, in the sense that they occurred in similar form in many different social situations. In addition, they often seemed to date back to a time close to the onset of the social phobia and to be linked to memories of criticism, humiliation, bullying and other adverse social events. These findings are consistent with the possibility that a mental image of the patient's observable, social self is laid down after early traumatic social experiences and the image is reactivated in subsequent social encounters without being markedly updated in the light of subsequent, more positive experience. Lack of updating could partly be a consequence of the social phobic's reduced attention to external social cues.

Hypothesis 5: Social phobics use the internal information made accessible by self-focused attention to make (erroneous) inferences about how they appear to others   Five studies (McEwan & Devins, 1983; Papageorgiou & Wells, 1997; Mansell & Clark, 1999; Mulkens, de Jong, Dobbelaar, & Bögels, 1999; Mellings & Alden, 2000) have provided evidence consistent with the hypothesis that socially anxious individuals use internal information to make excessively negative inferences about how they appear to others. In the first study, McEwan and Devins (1983) found that high socially anxious individuals who reported that they generally experience intense somatic sensations in social situations overestimated how anxious they appeared to their peers. In contrast, low socially anxious individuals and high socially anxious individuals who did not experience intense somatic sensations were accurate in their estimates of anxiety visibility. In an unpublished study, Papageorgiou and Wells (1997) found that high socially anxious individuals who were led to believe their heart rate was increasing just before a social-evaluative conversation later underestimated how well they came across to their conversation partner. Low socially anxious individuals did not show this effect.

Mansell and Clark (1999) required high and low socially anxious individuals to give a speech. Immediately afterwards, participants rated the extent to which they were aware of bodily sensations during the speech and how well they thought they appeared and performed. An independent assessor also rated participants' appearance and performance. Among high socially anxious individuals, there was a significant positive correlation between perceived bodily sensations and the extent to which the individuals overestimated negative aspects of their appearance (looking anxious, awkward, unconfident, etc.) Low socially anxious individuals did not show this effect.

Mulkens et al. (1999) required high and low fear of blushing individuals to engage in two social tasks which varied in embarrassingness. Objective measures of facial coloration and skin temperature indicated that the more embarrassing task produced more coloration but the two groups did not differ in objective coloration. However, subjective ratings indicated that the high fear of blushing group thought they had blushed more. Mulkens et al. suggest that the difference in subjective ratings between the high and low fearful groups arose because the former are likely to engage in more self-focused attention, which would enhance awareness of facial skin temperature. Finally, Mellings and Alden (2000) required high and low socially anxious individuals to have a conversation with a confederate. Compared to the judgements of an independent assessor, high socially anxious individuals overestimated the visibility of several anxiety-related behaviours and the amount of overestimation was positively correlated with self-focused attention during the interaction.

Hypothesis 6: In-situation safety seeking behaviours and self-focused attention prevent disconfirmation of social phobics' negative beliefs and maintain social phobia   Wells et al. (1995) tested the hypothesis that in-situation safety behaviours play a role in maintaining social phobia by comparing one session of exposure to a feared social situation with one session of similar exposure accompanied by the intentional dropping of safety behaviours. Although the two procedures did not differ in patients' credibility ratings, exposure and the dropping of safety behaviours produced significantly greater reductions in anxiety and belief ratings for feared outcomes in a behaviour test administered before and after the intervention. Morgan and Raffle (1999) obtained essentially similar results in a longer term study in which a three-week programme of "standard" group cognitive-behaviour therapy was compared with a three-week programme in which dropping safety behaviours manoeuvres were added to the standard protocol. Patients with social phobia whose treatment included dropping safety behaviours showed significantly greater improvements on the Social Phobia and Anxiety Inventory (Turner, Beidel, Dancu, & Stanley, 1989).

Most of the safety behaviours associated with social phobia have the effect of increasing self-focused attention. Wells and Papageorgiou (1998) assessed whether self-focused attention alone can maintain social anxiety by comparing one session of exposure to a feared social situation with one session of similar exposure accompanied by external focus of attention. Consistent with the hypothesis, exposure with external focus of attention produced significantly greater reductions in patients' anxiety and belief ratings in a subsequent behaviour test.

Hypothesis 7: In-situation safety behaviours and self-focused attention can contaminate social interactions by making social phobics less appealing to others
Several studies have found that patients with social phobia and other socially anxious individuals are less liked by conversational partners in first meeting situations and tend to be viewed as less likeable, less sympathetic or less easy to talk to by their friends (Alden & Wallace, 1995; Jones & Carpenter, 1986). Clark and Wells suggest that such effects are the unfortunate and unintended consequence of the safety-seeking behaviours that patients use in an attempt to prevent feared social catastrophes (e.g., making a fool of myself, seeming stupid). Examples of such safety behaviours include: rehearsing sentences before speaking, only speaking briefly, memorizing what one has said, self-monitoring, avoiding eye contact, and not talking about oneself. An alternative explanation is that social phobics are evaluated less positively because they have a general deficit in social skills development.

If the Clark and Wells hypothesis is correct, individuals' beliefs about whether other people are evaluating them negatively should have a marked effect on how they are perceived (because they will be more likely to engage in safety behaviours if they think they are being evaluated negatively). An elegant experiment by Curtis and Miller (1986) demonstrated this point. Students had a conversation with another person. After the conversation, they were given false feedback, indicating that the other person either liked or disliked them. They then had a second conversation with the same person. At the end of this conversation, that person was asked to rate the student. Students who were led to believe that the other person disliked them after the first conversation were rated as less warm, self-disclosing, and friendly after the second conversation and were less well liked.

Alden and Bieling (1998) provided more direct support for the safety behaviours hypothesis in an experiment in which high and low socially anxious individuals participated in a getting-acquainted task under conditions in which they were led to believe that the other person was particularly likely to appraise them positively or negatively. High socially anxious individuals used more safety behaviours and elicited more negative responses from others in the negative appraisal condition than in the positive appraisal condition.

Hypothesis 8: Social phobics' (reduced) processing of external social cues is biased in favour of detection and recall of cues that could be interpreted as signs of disapproval from others Three studies have reported results consistent with this hypothesis. Veljaca and Rapee (1998) required high and low socially anxious individuals to intentionally monitor and detect audience reactions while they were giving a speech. Compared to low socially anxious individuals, high socially anxious individuals were better at detecting negative audience behaviours (yawning, looking at watch, coughing) than positive audience behaviours (leaning forward, smiling, nodding). Gilboa-Schechtman, Foa, and Amir (1999) presented patients with social phobia and non-patient controls with a display of 12 faces and required them to detect the odd one out ("face-in-the-crowd paradigm"). Patients with social phobia were faster at detecting angry faces than happy faces in a neutral crowd. Non-patient controls did not show this effect. Lundh and Öst (1996) required patients with social phobia and non-patient controls to rate photographically presented faces as generally critical or accepting and shortly afterwards presented a surprise recognition test. Patients with social phobia showed a bias in favour of better recognition of faces they had categorized as critical than faces they had categorized as accepting. Non-patient controls did not show this effect.

Hypothesis 9: Social phobics engage in negatively biased anticipatory processing before entering feared social situations   Clark and Wells propose that social phobics engage in a variety of negatively biased cognitive processes in anticipation of feared social situations and that these processes increase anxiety and avoidance. One key process is selective recall of negative information about one's perceived, observable self. Mansell and Clark (1999) investigated recall of such information in an experiment in which high and low socially anxious students encoded positive and negative words in three different encoding conditions: public self-referent ("describes what someone who knows you, or who had just met you, would think of you"), private self-referent ("describes how you think about yourself") and other-referent ("describes your next door neighbour"). After encoding the words, participants were either threatened with giving a speech or not threatened. They were then asked to recall the words. Compared to low socially anxious individuals, high socially anxious individuals recalled fewer positive words and tended to recall more negative words. As predicted, this effect only occurred when individuals were anticipating giving a speech and was restricted to words encoded in terms of how they thought they would appear to other people (public self-referent condition). It therefore appears that a key aspect of anticipatory anxiety is selective retrieval of negative impressions of one's observable self.

Clark and Wells also suggest that social phobics selectively retrieve specific instances of past social failures when anticipating a stressful interaction. Hinrichsen and Clark (2000) reported a semistructured interview study that produced results consistent with this hypothesis. Compared to low socially anxious individuals, high socially anxious individuals were significantly more likely to report recalling and dwelling on past perceived social failures when anticipating a difficult social task. However, Mellings and Alden (2000) failed to observe a similar effect in an experimental study.

Hinrichsen and Clark's (2000) semistructured interview covered a wide range of possible anticipatory processes. As well as being more likely to report recalling past social failures, high socially anxious individuals were also more likely than low socially anxious individuals to: (1) dwell on ways of avoiding, or escaping from, the social situation; (2) catastrophize about what might happen in the situation; (3) engage in anticipatory safety behaviours (plan what they will say, mentally rehearse conversations, think of ways of putting things right if one makes a fool of oneself); and (4) generate negative, distorted, observer-perspective images about how they might appear in the situation. A second, experimental, study investigated whether the cognitive processes identified in the interview study played a role in maintaining anticipatory anxiety. Prior to giving a speech, individuals either engaged in the identified processes or performed a distraction task. Engaging in the mental processes that have been shown to be characteristic of high socially anxious individuals in the interview study produced more sustained elevations of anticipatory anxiety in both high and low socially anxious individuals, and led to higher levels of peak anxiety during the speech.

Hypothesis 10: Social phobics engage in prolonged, negatively biased, post-event processing   A novel aspect of the Clark and Wells model is the proposal that patients with social phobia engage in detailed post-event processing. No studies have investigated this hypothesis in patients. However, Rachman, Grüter-Andrew, and Shafran (2000) and Mellings and Alden (2000) both reported that high socially anxious individuals engage in more prolonged post-event processing than low socially anxious individuals. Rachman et al. (2000) noted that post-event processing involves recollections of the social event that tend to be recurrent and intrusive, interfering with concentration. Post-event processing was associated with greater subsequent avoidance of similar social situations. Mellings and Alden (2000) found that frequency of post-event rumination predicted recall of negative self-related information in a memory task performed one day after a stressful social interaction. Finally, Wells, Clark, and Ahmad (1998) and Wells and Papageorgiou (1999) investigated perspective taking in imagery recall of past anxiety-provoking situations and found that, compared to low socially anxious individuals, high socially anxious individuals and patients with social phobia were more likely to take an observer perspective in images of past social situations. Unfortunately, neither of these studies assessed the content of the images, so it is not known whether they were predominantly negative and distorted, as suggested by the model.

   Taken together, these four preliminary studies suggest that post-event processing occurs and has several of the characteristics highlighted in the Clark and Wells model.

Conclusions

The studies reviewed above provide encouraging support for most of the hypotheses embedded within the Clark and Wells model. However, for some of the hypotheses only analogue studies have so far been reported and it will be necessary to confirm their findings in studies with patients. In addition, several key aspects of the hypotheses remain to be assessed and the true causal status of several processes needs to be demonstrated by experimental manipulation of the relevant process.

A THEORY DERIVED COGNITIVE TREATMENT

Historically, some of the most effective cognitive-behavioural treatments for anxiety disorders have been developed by identifying the processes that normally prevent cognitive change and devising efficient procedures for reversing those maintaining processes (see Clark, 1997, 1999). With this in mind, Clark, Wells, and colleagues have devised a specialized cognitive treatment for social phobia which aims to reverse the maintaining processes specified in the model. As the model places particular emphasis on self-focused attention, negative self-processing, and safety behaviours, the treatment particularly emphasizes ways of reversing these features in order to reconfigure social phobics processing strategies in a way which will maximize opportunities for disconfirming negative beliefs by direct observation of the social situation, rather than oneself. A brief overview of the procedures is given below. Further expositions of the treatment can be found in Clark and Wells (1995), Wells and Clark (1997), Clark (1997), and Wells (1997, 1998).

Therapeutic Relationship

Social phobics pose particular problems for the therapeutic relationship. Therapy is itself a social interaction. For this reason, in the early stages of treatment patients may behave in therapy sessions in ways that are similar to how they behave in other feared social situations. First, they may employ fear-driven self-presentation manoeuvres (safety behaviours) that have the consequence of making them appear aloof, uninterested, or dismissive. It is important that therapists do not take offence or personalize these behaviours. Once patients start to make progress in therapy, their self-presentation can change dramatically and more open, relaxed individuals emerge. Second, some common therapist behaviours (leaning forward in one's chair, looking empathetically into patients' eyes when they appear anxious) can increase patients' self-consciousness, exacerbate mental blanks, and enhance their anxiety levels. For this reason, such manoeuvres should be used with caution in early sessions.

Deriving an Idiosyncratic Version of the Model

Therapy invariably starts by reviewing one or more recent, prototypical episodes of social anxiety. Careful questioning is used to develop an idiosyncratic version of the cognitive model. In order to reduce the patient's self-consciousness during questioning, and to help keep therapist and patient focused on the same parts of the episode, the model is usually developed on a white board. An example is shown in Figure 18.2. First, the patient's negative thoughts concerning feared outcomes and their perceived consequences are specified. Once the feared outcomes

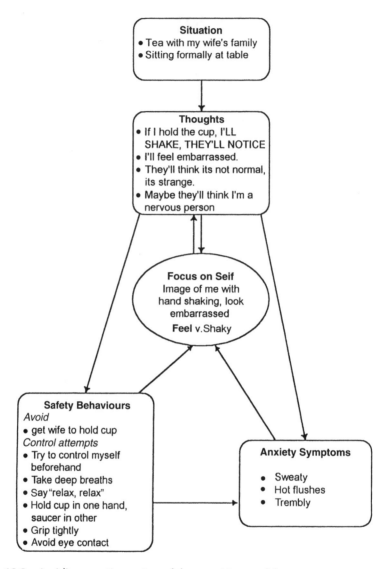

Figure 18.2   An idiosyncratic version of the cognitive model

have been identified, a comprehensive list of safety behaviours that are used to prevent different levels of outcome can be developed. Particularly useful questions include: "When you thought (specify the feared outcome) might/was happening, did you do anything to try to prevent it from happening? Did you do anything to try to prevent people from noticing?" and "Is there anything you do to try to ensure you come across well?". The shift to increased self-focused attention and the contents of patients' self-impressions are also identified. Useful questions for eliciting the self-impression include: "When you feel self-conscious, what are you aware of?", "Do you have an image of how you think you appear", "How do you feel you come across?". Typically, the self-impression contains one or more of the following elements: an observer-perspective image of how one might appear to others; awareness of anxious feelings that the patient thinks could be observable; and a felt sense of appearing different/deficient. The images often contain visible (or audible) distortions derived from interoceptive cues. For example, a warm forehead and slight sweating sensation can be transformed into a picture of rivulets of sweat running down the forehead. If the image is recurrent and seems to date from a much earlier traumatic social event, it can be helpful to clarify this point with patients in order to allow them to start to entertain the possibility that their self-impression is an excessively negative historical relic that has failed to update.

Manipulation of Self-focused Attention and Safety Behaviours

Once the patient and therapist have agreed a working version of the cognitive model, key elements of the model are manipulated. We have found that changing focus of attention and safety behaviours is often the best way to start. During a treatment session patients are asked to role-play a feared interaction under two conditions. In one condition, they are asked to focus attention on monitoring themselves and to use all of their normal safety behaviours. In the other condition, they are asked to drop their safety behaviours and focus their attention on the other person(s) in the interaction and on what is being said. After each role-play, patients rate how anxious they felt, how anxious they thought they appeared, and how well they thought they performed. By comparing these ratings several points can be established. First, to patients' considerable surprise, their previously habitual self-focus and safety behaviours seem to be associated with feeling more anxious, not less anxious. Second, ratings of how anxious patients think they appear and how well they think they performed closely follow the ratings of how they felt, indicating that they are using their feelings and other interoceptive information to infer how they appear to others.

Video and Audio Feedback

Once it is established that patients are using interoceptive information to infer how they appear to others, the next step is to obtain realistic information about how they actually appear. We have found video feedback to be a particularly effective way of doing this and routinely show patients the video of the focus of attention/safety behaviours experiment. In principle, video feedback allows patients to see their true, observable self directly. However, in our early explorations of the technique, we noticed that it could sometimes fail with patients continuing to view their video appearance more negatively than an impartial observer. Questioning indicated that one reason for this was that patients re-experienced feelings they had during the experiment while viewing the video. The feelings then influenced their perception in a negative direction. To resolve this problem, and to maximize perceived discrepancies between patients' self-image and the video, we now ask patients: (1) to visualize how they think they will appear before viewing the video, (2) to operationalize what their negative behaviours will look like ("How much will you shake? Please show me"; "How red is the blush? Please pick out a colour from the colour chart", etc.), and (3) to watch themselves as though they were watching a stranger, only drawing inferences from the visual and auditory information that would be available to any viewer, explicitly ignoring their feelings. With this cognitive preparation, video feedback usually helps patients to discover that they come across better than they think and, as a consequence, that their self-impression is misleading. Of course, they sometimes notice things that seem unsatisfactory as well. However, discussion often reveals that those behaviours are the consequence of a safety-seeking manoeuvre, and hence can be dropped. For example, a patient who was concerned that she would sound dysfluent and incoherent discovered that her speech was highly fluent but very slow. Questioning revealed that the slowness was an intentional strategy that could easily be dropped. Similarly, a patient who was concerned that his hand visibly shook while drinking with friends in a bar tended to turn his back to colleagues before drinking. Video feedback helped him see that the shaking was barely noticeable but the back turning looked strangely furtive.

Shift of Attention and Interrogation of the Social Environment

The next stage in therapy involves encouraging patients to shift to an external focus of attention and to drop their safety behaviours during social interactions in therapy sessions and homework assignments. The explicit rationale for this manoeuvre is that the evidence the patient normally uses to infer how he or she appears to others (i.e., the contents of their self-awareness) is inaccurate and it is necessary to focus more on the interaction and other people's responses in order to obtain a more accurate impression of how one appears.

As in other cognitive-behavioural programmes, patients are encouraged to systematically confront feared and avoided social events and tasks. However, the way exposure is conducted is rather different from the way that it is conducted in at least some of the traditional behavioural approaches. In particular, simple repetition of an exposure assignment is not considered to be helpful in itself. The guiding principle of treatment is not habituation per se, but rather a cognitive change framework in which exposure is explicitly used to test predictions the patient has about the danger in a particular situation.

Table 18.2 shows the way an exposure assignment is set up and afterwards processed in the cognitive treatment. The patient was a teacher who had difficulty joining in conversations with other teachers during coffee breaks. Ques-

Table 18.2 Record sheet for noting behavioural experiments

Date	Situation	Prediction (What exactly did you think would happen? How would you know?) (Rate belief 0–100%)	Experiment (What did you do to test the prediction?)	Outcome (What actually happened? Was the prediction correct?)	What I learned 1. Balanced view? (Rate belief 0–100%) 2. How likely is what you you predicted to happen in future (Rate 0–100%)?
Mon 7/8	Coffee break. Sitting with other teachers. Trying to join in the conversation.	If I just say things as they come into my mind, they'll think I'm stupid. 50%.	Say whatever comes into my mind and watch them like a hawk. Don't focus on myself. This only gives me misleading information (such as images of myself as the "village idiot"), and means I can't see them.	I did it and I watched the others. One of them showed interest and we talked. She seemed to quite enjoy it.	I am probably more acceptable than I think. 70%

Reproduced with permission from Clark (1999, p. S18).

tioning helped her to articulate the prediction: "If I just say the things that come into my mind, they will think I'm stupid." Normally she would think very carefully about all the clever things she could say and then choose one for the conversation (safety behaviour). The assignment helped her to discover that, contrary to her prediction, she was acceptable even without her frantic attempts at self-presentation.

As many social phobics have excessively high standards for social performance, it can be particularly helpful to encourage patients to behave in ways that they would consider unacceptable (given their rules) and observe others' responses. This exercise, which we have termed "widening the bandwidth" helps patients to discover that there are a wide range of acceptable ways of behaving in social situations. Such knowledge can be remarkably liberating as it means they no longer have to attempt to follow strict, and difficult to observe, rules. In order to maximize the impact of bandwidth-broadening experiments, it is important that patients specify in advance the ways in which other people would respond if the patient's predictions about the unacceptability of a particular behaviour were correct. For example, a patient who was excessively concerned about underarm sweating was encouraged to use water to dampen the armpits of his shirt before going into a shop and revealing his underarm to the shop assistant by pointing to an object on a high shelf. He predicted that the assistant would react with horror and this would be evident either by her being unable to look at his armpits (because she would be too embarrassed) or by her being unable to keep her eyes off them. Neither occurred, indicating that underarm perspiration had less significance to others than the patient had anticipated. Other common examples used to test particular rules include: introducing intentional pauses in mid-sentence or introducing um's and ah's in one's speech; intentionally shaking and spilling a drink; introducing a boring topic into a conversation, and expressing an opinion that you know others disagree with. A particular interesting feature of "widening bandwidth" exercises is that they allow patients to experientially discover many of the complexities of social interaction. For example, a patient who was afraid of boring other people often switched conversation topics. Questioning revealed that he used an internal clock to decide when to change topics. The clock seemed largely influenced by his feelings of discomfort, rather than by others' responses to the topic. As an experiment he was asked to continue with topics until the other person changed them. To his surprise he found that the slightly longer conversations that resulted were more fun and seemed more natural. In addition, he discovered that, in general, topic changing is nobody's specific responsibility. Instead, it has its own rhythm and happens fairly naturally, as long as you do not assume you are 100% responsible for it.

Surveys can be another excellent way of testing the negative predictions about what other people think of behaviours that patients are afraid of showing. For example, a social phobic who stuttered, and was concerned that other people would think she was stupid, was greatly reassured by a survey in which 15 people were asked what they thought of someone who stutters. To her surprise, nobody thought it was a sign of stupidity and respondents provided a wide range of explanations for why someone might stutter (mind on something else, thinking faster than she can think, a speech impediment, had been criticized as a child, etc.), none of which she considered threatening. Our survey questions tend to progress from general enquiries (i.e., "Why do you think people stutter?") to patients' specific negative predictions about the meaning of particular behaviours (i.e., "Do you think stuttering means someone is stupid?"). Responses to the latter provide the clearest disconfirmation of patients' beliefs. Of course, one cannot guarantee that an isolated individual might not concur with the negative evaluation. In such instances, it is useful to ask questions such as: "Is this person's opinion more valid than everyone else's?", "Does it matter if one person disapproves?", "Is it possible to please everyone all the time?", "If you disapproved of something similar in another person, would that make them deficient or worthless?".

Throughout the interrogation of the environment stage, the standard cognitive therapy discussion techniques (such as pie charts, conditional probability inverted pyramids, and decatastrophizing: see Clark, 2000) are used to help patients to maximize the benefit obtained from the behavioural experiments. Video feedback continues to be used to provide clear information about one's observable self and to try out different ways of behaving. Imagery transformation exercises in which patients access their negative self-images and transform them into more realistic images based on the video feedback, surveys and other experiments are also helpful (Hackmann, 1999).

Dealing with Anticipatory and Post-event Processing

The negatively biased pre- and post-event processing that is so characteristic of social phobia is also targeted in treatment. First, patients are helped to identify particular ways in which they think and behave before and after feared social events. The advantages and disadvantages of their anticipatory and post-event processing are discussed in detail, with the aim of establishing that the disadvantages predominate. The patient is then encouraged to experiment with banning these activities. Of course, sometimes patients indicate that they think preparation before an event is helpful. For formal presentations, this may well be true. However, most patients over-prepare and as a consequence find themselves trying to follow an exceptionally rigid script. To determine whether this is the case, behavioural experiments in which the amount of preparation is substantially reduced are used. Asking patients in a therapy session to speak off the cuff immediately after being given a topic such as "The advantages and disadvantages of the death penalty" or "Has Blair/Clinton been a good prime minister/president?" can be a particularly good way of doing this. For patients who initially find it difficult to ban their "post-mortems", shifting to a field perspective in the post-mortem, specifically focusing on information that may be inconsistent with their negative self-image and imaging themselves as they have appeared on therapy videos can be a helpful intermediate step.

Dealing with Assumptions

Excessively high standards of social behaviour and conditional assumptions about the consequences of behaving/appearing in a particular way are best dealt with by the bandwidth exercises and other behavioural experiments already outlined. Such manoeuvres often also change unconditional assumptions such as "I am weird/unlikeable". However, for some people these assumptions require additional cognitive manoeuvres, many of which were originally devised for the treatment of depression (Beck, Shaw, Rush, & Emery, 1979; Burns, 1980; Beck, 1995) or low self-esteem (Fennell, 1999).

Many negative self-beliefs are vague and poorly defined, and this is one reason why they persist. With this point in mind, it is often useful to start by asking patients to operationalize their negative self-belief before looking for evidence for and against it. For example, when challenging a belief such as, "I am weird" or "I am unlikeable", the therapist would start by asking the patient to list all the observable characteristics that could indicate that someone is unlikeable/weird and the converse. Once a full range of characteristics has been elicited, patients are encouraged to rate themselves and other people they know in terms of the extent to which they have each characteristic. Often, this helps patients see that they are not uniquely worse than others on the negative characteristics and they have many signs of being respected/likeable.

Of course, patients are prone to discount information that contradicts their negative self-beliefs. A particularly good way of circumventing this problem is Christine Padesky's Prejudice Model in which patients are asked to consider their negative beliefs as prejudices against themselves that are maintained by biases that are similar to those involved in the maintenance of other common prejudices (e.g., racial and sexual prejudices). Examples of such biases include: discounting, viewing as an exception, and ignoring evidence that is inconsistent with the prejudice. To help patients overcome such biases with respect to themselves, they are encouraged to keep a positive data log in which any event that *could* be seen as contradicting their negative self-belief is recorded. This technique can lead to a rapid accumulation of contrary data. Identifying early events and images that might explain how a negative self-belief arose can also be helpful, as are continua techniques for breaking down "all or nothing thinking". Finally, it is important for therapists to remember, and help patients to discover, that occasional negative responses from other people may have been triggered by the patient's safety behaviours, rather than being an indication that the other people view the patient as intrinsically unlikeable/unacceptable.

EFFECTIVENESS OF THE COGNITIVE TREATMENT

In order to obtain a preliminary estimate of the effectiveness of our theory-derived cognitive treatment, 15 consecutively referred patients with social phobia were given up to 16 sessions of treatment (Clark, 1999). The overall improvement was substantial. For example, on the Fear of Negative Evaluation Scale (Watson & Friend, 1969), there was a mean improvement of 11 points at post-treatment and 15 points at follow-up, with pre-post effect sizes being 2.7 and 3.7 respectively. These promising, preliminary results are now being followed by several controlled trials, the results of which are eagerly awaited. In the meantime, therapy experiments have confirmed the effectiveness of several key procedures in the overall treatment programme. Dropping safety behaviours (Wells et al., 1995) and shifting to externally focused attention (Wells & Papageorgiou, 1998) have both been shown to enhance the effectiveness of exposure to feared social situations. In addition, Harvey, Clark, Ehlers, and Rapee (2000) have shown that video feedback is more effective in correcting distorted self-impressions if preceded by the cognitive preparation outlined above.

ACKNOWLEDGEMENTS

The author's research is supported by the Wellcome Trust. Adrian Wells, Ann Hackmann, Freda McManus, Melanie Fennell, Anke Ehlers, Gillian Butler, Paul Salkovskis, Allison Harvey, and Warren Mansell provided invaluable clinical and theoretical contributions, which are gratefully acknowledged.

REFERENCES

Alden, L. E. & Bieling, P. (1998). Interpersonal consequences of the pursuit of safety. *Behaviour Research and Therapy, 36*, 53–65.

Alden, L. E. & Wallace, S. T. (1995). Social phobia and social appraisal in successful and unsuccessful social interactions. *Behaviour Research and Therapy, 33*, 497–505.

Amir, N., Foa, E. B., & Coles, M. E. (1998). Negative interpretation bias in social phobia. *Behaviour Research and Therapy, 36*, 945–957.

APA (1987). *Diagnostic and statistical manual of mental disorders* (3rd edition, revised). Washington, DC: American Psychiatric Association.

APA (1994). *Diagnostic and statistical manual of mental disorders* (4th edition). Washington, DC: American Psychiatric Association.

Beck, A. T., Emery, G., & Greenberg, R. L. (1985). *Anxiety disorders and phobias: A cognitive perspective.* New York: Basic Books.

Beck, A. T., Shaw, B., Rush, A. J., & Emery, G. (1979). *Cognitive therapy for depression.* New York: Guilford.

Beck, J. S. (1995). *Cognitive therapy: Basics and beyond.* New York: Guilford.

Bruch, M. A. & Heimberg, R. G. (1994). Differences in perceptions of parental and personal characteristics between generalized and nongeneralized social phobics. *Journal of Anxiety Disorders, 8*, 155–168.

Bruch, M. A., Heimberg, R. G., Berger, P. A., & Collins, T. M. (1989). Social phobia and perception of early parental and personal characteristics. *Anxiety Research, 12*, 57–65.

Burns, D. D. (1980). *Feeling good: The new mood therapy.* New York: William Morrow.

Butler, G. (1985). Exposure as a treatment for social phobia: Some instructive difficulties. *Behaviour Research and Therapy, 23*, 651–657.

Butler, G. & Mathews, A. M. (1993). Cognitive processes in anxiety. *Advances in Behaviour Research and Therapy, 5*, 51–63.

Chen, Y. P., Ehlers, A., Clark, D. M., & Mansell, W. (2000). *Social phobia and attentional avoidance of faces*. Manuscript submitted for publication.

Clark, D. M. (1997). Panic disorder and social phobia. In D. M. Clark & C. G. Fairburn (Eds.), *Science and practice of cognitive behaviour therapy* (pp. 119–153). Oxford: Oxford University Press.

Clark, D. M. (1999). Anxiety disorders: why they persist and how to treat them. *Behaviour Research and Therapy, 37*, S5–S27.

Clark, D. M. (2000). Cognitive behaviour therapy for anxiety disorders. In M. G. Gelder, J. Lopez-Ibor, & N. N. Andreason (Eds.), *New Oxford textbook of psychiatry*. Oxford University Press, Oxford.

Clark, D. M. & Beck, A. T. (1988). Cognitive approaches. In C. Last & M. Hersen (Eds.), *Handbook of anxiety disorders* (pp. 362–385). New York: Pergamon.

Clark, D. M. & Wells, A. (1995). A cognitive model of social phobia. In R. Heimberg, M. Liebowitz, D. A. Hope, & F. R. Schneier (Eds.), *Social phobia: Diagnosis, assessment and treatment*. (pp. 69–93). New York: Guilford Press.

Curtis, R. C. & Miller, K. (1986). Believing another likes or dislikes you: Behaviors making the beliefs come true. *Journal of Personality and Social Psychology, 51*, 284–290.

Daly, J. A., Vangelisti, A. L., & Lawrence, S. G. (1989). Self-focused attention and public speaking anxiety. *Personality and Individual Differences, 10*, 903–913.

Fennell, M. J. V. (1999). *Overcoming low self-esteem*. London: Robinson.

Fenigstein, F., Scheier, M. F., & Buss, A. K. (1975). Public and private self-consciousness: Assessment and theory. *Journal of Consulting and Clinical Psychology, 43*, 522–527.

Gilboa-Schechtman, E., Foa, E. B., & Amir, N. (1999). Attentional biases for facial expressions in social phobia: The face-in-the-crowd paradigm. *Cognition and Emotion, 13*, 305–318.

Hackmann, A. (1999). Working with images in clinical psychology. In P. Salkovskis (Ed.), *Comprehensive clinical psychology* (Vol. 6, pp. 301–318). Oxford: Elsevier.

Hackmann, A., Surawy, C., & Clark, D. M. (1998). Seeing yourself through others' eyes: A study of spontaneously occurring images in social phobia. *Behavioural and Cognitive Psychotherapy, 26*, 3–12.

Hackmann, A., Clark, D. M., & McManus, F. (2000). Recurrent images and early memories in social phobia. *Behaviour Research and Therapy, 38*, 601–610.

Harvey, A., Clark, D. M., Ehlers, A., & Rapee, R. M. (2000). Social anxiety and self-impression: cognitive preparation enhances the beneficial effects of video feedback following a stressful social task. *Behaviour Research and Therapy, 38*, 1183–1192.

Hartman, L. M. (1983). A metacognitive model of social anxiety: Implications for treatment. *Clinical Psychology Review, 3*, 435–456.

Heimberg, R. G. & Barlow, D. H. (1988). Psychosocial treatments for social phobia. *Psychosomatics, 29*, 27–37.

Hinrichsen, H. & Clark, D. M. (2000). *Anticipatory processing in social anxiety*. Manuscript submitted for publication.

Hope, D. A. & Heimberg, R. G. (1988). Public and private self-consciousness and social phobia. *Journal of Personality Assessment, 52*, 626–639.

Hope, D. A., Heimberg, R. G., & Klein, J. F. (1990). Social anxiety and the recall of interpersonal information. *Journal of Cognitive Psychotherapy, 4*, 185–195.

Hirsch, C. R. & Mathews, A. (2000). *Impaired positive inferential bias in social phobia*. Manuscript submitted for publication.

Jones, W. H. & Carpenter, B. N. (1986). Shyness, social behavior and relationships. In W. H. Jones, J. M. Cheek, & S. R. Briggs (Eds.), *Shyness: Perspectives on research and treatment* (pp. 227–238). New York: Plenum Press.

Kimble, C. E. & Zehr, H. D. (1982). Self-consciousness, information load, self-presentation, and memory in a social situation. *Journal of Social Psychology, 118*, 39–46.

Leary, M. R. (1983). *Understanding social anxiety*. Beverly Hills, CA: Sage.

Lundh, L. G. & Öst, L. G. (1996). Recognition bias for critical faces in social phobics. *Behaviour Research and Therapy*, *34*, 787–795.

Mansell, W. & Clark, D. M. (1999). How do I appear to others? Social anxiety and processing of the observable self. *Behaviour Research and Therapy*, *37*, 419–434.

Mansell, W., Clark, D. M., Ehlers, A., & Chen, Y. P. (1999). Social anxiety and attention away from emotional faces. *Cognition and Emotion*, *13*, 673–690.

McEwan, K. L. & Devins, G. M. (1983). Is increased arousal in social anxiety noticed by others? *Journal of Abnormal Psychology*, *92*, 417–421.

Mellings, T. M. B. & Alden, L. E. (2000). Cognitive processes in social anxiety: The effects of self-focus, rumination and anticipatory processing. *Behaviour Research and Therapy*, *38*, 243–257.

Morgan, H. & Raffle, C. (1999). Does reducing safety behaviours improve treatment response in patients with social phobia? *Australian and New Zealand Journal of Psychiatry*, *33*, 503–510.

Mulkens, S., de Jong, P. J., Dobbelaar, A., & Bögels, S. M. (1999). Fear of blushing: fearful preoccupation irrespective of facial coloration. *Behaviour Research and Therapy*, *37*, 1119–1128.

Papageorgiou, C. & Wells, A. (1997). *Social self-perception: Effects of false heart-rate feedback in socially anxious subjects*. Paper presented at the 25th Anniversary Conference of the British Association for Behavioural and Cognitive Psychotherapy. Canterbury, U.K.

Rachman, S., Grüter-Andrew, J., & Shafran, R. (2000). Post-event processing in social anxiety. *Behaviour Research and Therapy*, *38*, 611–617.

Rapee, R. M. & Lim, L. (1992). Discrepancy between self- and observer ratings of performance in social phobics. *Journal of Abnormal Psychology*, *101*, 728–731.

Saboonchi, F., Lundh, L. G., & Öst, L. G. (1999). Perfectionism and self-consciousness in social phobia and panic disorder with agoraphobia. *Behaviour Research and Therapy*, *37*, 799–808.

Salkovskis, P. (1991). The importance of behaviour in the maintenance of anxiety and panic: A cognitive account. *Behavioural Psychotherapy*, *19*, 6–19.

Salkovskis, P. M. (1996). The cognitive approach to anxiety: Threat beliefs, safety-seeking behavior and the special case of health anxiety and obsessions. In P. M. Salkovskis (Ed.), *Frontiers of cognitive therapy* (pp. 48–74). New York: Guilford.

Stopa, L. & Clark, D. M. (1993). Cognitive processes in social phobia. *Behaviour Research and Therapy*, *31*, 255–267.

Stopa, L. & Clark, D. M. (2000). Social phobia and interpretation of social events. *Behaviour Research and Therapy*, *38*, 273–283.

Teasdale, J. D. & Barnard, P. J. (1993). *Affect, cognition and change*. Hove, Sussex: Lawrence Erlbaum.

Turner S. M., Beidel D. C., Dancu C. V., & Stanley, M. A. (1989). An empirically derived inventory to measure social fears and anxiety: The social phobia and anxiety inventory. *Psychological Assessment*, *1*, 35–40.

Trower, P. & Gilbert, P. (1989). New theoretical conceptions of social anxiety and social phobia. *Clinical Psychology Review*, *9*, 19–35.

Trower, P., Yardley, K., Bryant, B., & Shaw, P. (1978). The treatment of social failure: a comparison of anxiety reduction and skills acquisition procedures on two social problems. *Behavior Modification*, *2*, 41–60.

Veljaca, K. & Rapee, R. M. (1998). Detection of negative and positive audience behaviours by socially anxious subjects. *Behaviour Research and Therapy*, *36*, 311–321.

Watson, D. & Friend, R. (1969). Measurement of social-evaluative anxiety. *Journal of Consulting and Clinical Psychology*, *33*, 448–457.

Wells, A. (1997). *Cognitive therapy of anxiety disorders: a practice manual and conceptual guide*. Chichester, Sussex: Wiley.

Wells, A. (1998). Cognitive therapy of social phobia. In N. Tarrier, A. Wells, & G. Haddock (Eds.), *Treating complex cases* (pp. 1–26). Chichester, Sussex: Wiley.

Wells, A. & Clark, D. M. (1997). Social phobia: A cognitive approach. In G. C. L. Davey (Ed.), *Phobias: A handbook of description, treatment and theory* (pp. 3–26). Chichester, Sussex: Wiley.

Wells, A., Clark, D. M., & Ahmad, S. (1998). How do I look with my minds eye: Perspective taking in social phobic imagery. *Behaviour Research and Therapy, 36*, 631–634.

Wells, A., Clark, D. M., Salkovskis, P., Ludgate, J., Hackmann, A., & Gelder, M. G. (1995). Social phobia: The role of in-situation safety behaviors in maintaining anxiety and negative beliefs. *Behavior Therapy, 26*, 153–161.

Wells, A. & Papageorgiou, C. (1998). Social phobia: Effects of external attention on anxiety, negative beliefs and perspective taking. *Behavior Therapy, 29*, 357–370.

Wells, A. & Papageorgiou, C. (1999). The observer perspective: Biased imagery in social phobia, agoraphobia, and blood/injury phobia. *Behaviour Research and Therapy, 37*, 653–658.

Woody, S. R. (1996). Effects of focus of attention on anxiety levels and social performance of individuals with social phobia. *Journal of Abnormal Psychology, 105*, 61–69.

Chapter 19

Shyness as a Clinical Condition: The Stanford Model

Lynne Henderson *and* Philip G. Zimbardo

DEFINITIONS, PREVALENCE, AND ETIOLOGY
Shyness Definition
Prevalence
Shyness Subtypes and Common Comorbid Problems
Etiology
SOCIAL FITNESS TRAINING
Treatment Philosophy
Assessment Procedures
   Intake interview and questionnaires
   Goal setting
   The hierarchy: Daily workouts for increasing behavioral and emotional fitness
   Assessing negative conditioning events
   Assessing maladaptive attributions: The Shyness Attribution Questionnaire
     (SAQ)
   Assessing blame: The Estimations of Others Scale (EOS)
   Assessing and Preventing Drop-out
TREATMENT PROCEDURES
Improving Behavioral Fitness
   Self-monitoring
   Behavioral fitness homework and self-rewards for workouts
   Telephone calls
   Motivation and compliance with an optimal training schedule
   Interpersonal skill training
   Empathy

International Handbook of Social Anxiety: Concepts, Research and Interventions Relating to the Self and Shyness. Edited by W. Ray Crozier and Lynn E. Alden.
© 2001 John Wiley & Sons Ltd.

Improving Mental Fitness
    Attributional and self-concept restructuring
Termination
Treatment Outcome
COMMON PROBLEMS
Medication to Enhance Social Performance and Comfort Level
Substance Use
Pessimism and Passivity
Difficulty Simulating Real-life
Secondary Gains that Accompany Passivity and Pessimism
SUMMARY
REFERENCES

Our interest in shyness grew out of Zimbardo's observations made in a mock prison study in 1971 in which normal college students were assigned to play either prisoners or guards (Zimbardo, 1977). The study was terminated because the students all too readily adapted to the roles they had been assigned. The student guards, in particular, displayed a sadistic use of power to subdue their "prisoners". While watching these changes, Zimbardo realized that the thinking of shy people combined the mentality found in the guard and prisoner roles—the guard-self imposes coercive control rules, which the prisoner-self ultimately accepts (Zimbardo, 1982). Zimbardo went on to study shyness as a social phenomenon. Lynne Henderson added to Zimbardo's theory by integrating concepts from social and personality psychology (Bandura, 1997; Mischel, 1999) with the psychodynamic theories of Lewis and Wurmser, who addressed shame affect in psychotherapy (Lewis, 1971; Wurmser, 1981), and developed the social fitness model. Together, these ideas led to the evolution of the Shyness Clinic, a program designed to treat individuals for whom shyness creates a self-induced prison.

In this chapter we present the unique features of the shyness program offered at our clinic. We begin by briefly considering the concept of shyness, its definition and epidemiology. Next, we describe our program philosophy, assessment procedures, and treatment techniques, placing an emphasis on those factors that distinguish our program from others. Finally, we consider common problems that arise in the treatment of shy clients and outline possible solutions to these problems.

DEFINITIONS, PREVALENCE, AND ETIOLOGY

Shyness Definition

Chronic shyness involves an excessive concern about negative evaluation and/or an avoidance of participation in social situations that would otherwise be pleasurable or important to one's professional or personal growth. Discomfort and non-participation must be severe enough to interfere with the pursuit of one's goals (Henderson, 1992). The experience of shyness is an approach/ avoidance conflict, distinguishable from natural introversion, a tendency to be quiet or reserved, but not overly concerned about social evaluation (Zimbardo, 1982).

We define chronic shyness in terms of the individual's goals because we wish to leave the definition in the hands of the person whose experience we are describing. We do this because we want to promote from the outset the idea that people can learn to define themselves in ways that either inhibit or promote social experimentation and constructive change. As social psychologists, we are well aware of the power of self-labeling, and chronically shy individuals generally lack a belief in their ability to achieve social goals. We believe that they can develop a sense of self-efficacy that will allow them to reappraise situations initially perceived as threatening to be challenging and manageable. As social psychologists, we are also skeptical about the use of external standards for defining shyness. Research in social psychology stresses the power of situational influences on behavior. For instance, socioeconomic status and cultural influences constrain what people are able to do, and those people who appear to be higher functioning due to higher status may be under-achieving in relation to their peer group (Henderson, Martinez, & Zimbardo, 1997). All in all, we feel that the individual's self-appraisal of shyness has greater value in treatment than any externally imposed judgement.

Prevalence

The prevalence of shyness in the general population is between 40 and 50% (Carducci & Zimbardo, 1995) and 61% in samples of adolescents (Henderson & Zimbardo, 1996). Gender ratios have been generally reported as equal in normative samples of shy college students (Cheek & Busch, 1981; Zimbardo, 1986). Data from the Shyness Clinic indicate that, of people seeking treatment for severe shyness, 60% are men and 40% are women.

Shyness Subtypes and Common Comorbid Problems

As we discuss later, we have been particularly interested in the role of causal attributions and self-blame in shyness. Samples of adolescents suggest that 30% of shy adolescents are self-blaming in social situations with negative outcomes. This subset scores significantly higher on measures of fear of negative evaluation and social anxiety than both non-shys and shy non-self-blamers (Henderson & Zimbardo, 1996).

Pilkonis (1977) distinguished between privately shy and publicly shy college students. The privately shy reported distress, but adequate social skill; the publicly shy reported difficulty with social behavior and inhibition. Zimbardo described shy extraverts as skilled, but socially anxious, and shy introverts as less skilled and inhibited (Zimbardo, 1977). We find that this distinction influences the choice of treatment techniques. In particular, the privately shy and the shy extraverts may need less work with social skills and more work with maladaptive thinking patterns and autonomic arousal. In contrast, the publicly shy patients generally benefit from skill training and techniques to increase emotional awareness and expression.

Our chronically shy clients are also distinguished by the presence of additional Axis I and II disorders. At the Shyness Clinic, 97% of our patients meet criteria for generalized social phobia and 57% meet criteria for at least one additional Axis I disorder. The most frequent Axis I disorders are dysthymia (29%) and generalized anxiety disorder (27%) (St. Lorant, Henderson, & Zimbardo, 1999).

According to the MCMI (Millon Clinical Multi-Axial Inventory), a striking 94% meet criteria for at least one additional Axis II disorder, most frequently the avoidant (67%), schizoid (35%) and dependent (23%) personality disorders. The MMPI (Minnesota Multiphasic Personality Inventory) further suggests the presence of compulsive (21%) and passive aggressive personality disorders (15%) (Greene, 1991). Our experience indicates that these personality features affect response to treatment. Those with avoidant personality disorder struggle with shame-based emotion and a reluctance to take risks without guarantees of acceptance. Those with dependent personality disorder tend to be submissive, but socially skilled and liked by other group members. The schizoid individuals usually struggle with fears of intimacy and intrusion, and have trouble persisting while relationships deepen. Passive aggressive clients resist treatment efforts and are more likely to alienate others.

Etiology

College students in treatment report an average age of onset for significant interference at 10 years, although many say they have been shy for as long as they can remember (Henderson et al., 1997). Developmental theory suggests that shyness is due to an interaction between temperament and environmental influences. The environmental influences that may be instrumental in the development of problematic shyness range from specific conditioning events, such as being teased or shamed by teachers or other children to emotional or physical abuse or neglect (Zimbardo, 1982). Observational learning, for example, viewing siblings or classmates who are humiliated or harshly treated, can also lead to shyness.

Parenting behaviors that may promote shyness are controlling, insensitive, or over-protective styles that involve frequent correction and shaming (Bruch, 1989). A particularly important issue is when and how parents should encourage or even push inhibited children so that they receive adequate socialization experiences. Many patients report minimal social interaction with peers, and a lack of family support for such interaction. Some also report little interaction with family, friends or relatives. Because extended family socializing predicts less shyness in young adults (Bruch, 1989), parental sociability in itself appears conducive to preventing shyness in children.

SOCIAL FITNESS TRAINING

We turn now to a discussion of our program, which we call *Social Fitness Training*. We will begin by considering the philosophy that underlies this approach and then describe the general goals of the treatment program. Following this we will discuss the intake assessment procedures used in our clinic and describe our treatment format. We will end this section by considering common problems that arise in the course of treatment.

Treatment Philosophy

The distinctive feature of our treatment philosophy is the concept of social fitness. Social fitness, like physical fitness, is a state of physiological, behavioral, emotional, and mental conditioning that implies adaptive functioning and a sense of well-being. A desired level of fitness usually requires exercise, practice, and consultation with experts. In the case of shyness, people seek professional help for specific skill development and the opportunity to practice in structured settings. We view problematic shyness as a state of mental and emotional fitness that is not optimal. We believe that a person can change behavior, thinking patterns, and attitudes, become more skilled at emotion regulation, or simply choose a more appropriate social niche in order to attain a state of improved conditioning. We also believe that, with effort and practice, most people can attain an adaptive state of social fitness in the same way that most people can attain an adaptive state of physical fitness.

In the social fitness model, we address four domains of shyness: (1) behavior, which is either inhibited or overactive; (2) physiological arousal that manifests in sweating, trembling, and increased heart rate; (3) maladaptive thinking patterns; and (4) negative emotions, such as embarrassment, shame, and guilt. In general, our treatment consists of behavioral exposure with cognitive restructuring, emphasizing specific attributional and self-concept restructuring, and interpersonal skill-building for initiating and deepening relationships. We believe that group therapy is the treatment of choice for chronic shyness. It is difficult for clients to carry out in-vivo exposures in the form of homework assignments, such as initiating conversations or asking people for dates, without the opportunity for exposure exercises and emotional support the group provides.

We take an educational approach that emphasizes goal formation, testable hypotheses and specific skill-building. Clients role-play desired behaviors in feared situations. They are conducted with the group and, where possible, with confederates who come in specifically for this purpose. Such role-plays are video-taped to provide immediate feedback to the client. They are also accompanied by challenges to habitual negative thinking patterns as therapists help clients to develop more adaptive ways of talking to themselves and of thinking about social situations. Within the cognitive component we place a great deal of emphasis on changing the tendency to assume too much responsibility for negative social out-comes (self-blame) and on challenging negative beliefs about the self.

A unique feature of our program is that we incorporate elements of an inter-personal short-term dynamic approach into an intimacy-building component. We do this because many clients have distorted ideas about interpersonal interac-tions based on early models and experiences with parents or peers. Sometimes they lack sufficient socialization experiences to have practiced behavior that others normally learned in elementary school and adolescence. Therapists link maladaptive behavioral patterns to early experiences, thereby helping clients to gain insight into particular coping styles. Recognizing the consequences of particular behavior patterns gives clients an increased sense of choice about experimenting with more adaptive ones.

Assessment Procedures

Although we include many of the same assessment procedures used by other treatment programs for social anxiety, we have also developed instruments to assess the cognitive factors that are particularly important to our model of shyness, namely attributions for social outcomes and the tendency to either blame oneself or others. We will begin by discussing the assessment procedures we share with other programs, including the identification of specific treatment goals and a behavioral hierarchy that is used for role-playing in sessions. We will then devote attention to the measures that are more specific to our program.

Intake Interview and Questionnaires

To establish clinical diagnoses, we use a structured clinical interview (ADIS-IV; DiNardo, Brown, & Barlow, 1994). To supplement this, we use several self-report measures of psychopathology, the Millon Clinical Multi-Axial Inventory (Millon, 1987) and the Minnesota Multiphasic Personality Inventory (Greene, 1991). Client profiles have been reported by Henderson (1997). We also use a variety of measures to assess various symptoms of shyness, including the Brief Fear of Negative Evaluation Questionnaire (Leary, 1983), the Coopersmith Self-esteem Inventory (Coopersmith, 1959) and the Beck Depression Inventory (Beck, Steer, & Garbin, 1988). Current behavior in feared situations is assessed using a BAT (behavior assessment test), which consists of a brief role-play or impromptu speech, usually videotaped, in front of a small audience. Finally, thought-listing forms are used to record negative thoughts that occur during the BAT (Cacioppo, Glass, & Merluzzi, 1970).

Goal Setting

At the end of the initial evaluation, which lasts between three and six or seven sessions, we focus on specific measurable goals. We find that goals tend to be vague and idealized when clients begin the evaluation and become more specific and realistic by the final session. Individual goals for six months of Social Fitness Training typically include increased social participation, better interpersonal communication, reduced physiological arousal, and increased emotional well-being. Goals generally imply more adaptive thinking in social situations, a more adaptive attribution style, and a more realistic view of the self. Increased participation may involve initiating more social contact or commenting in meetings. Reduced physiological arousal is defined as a reduction in SUDS level of at least 20 points in one or more challenging situations on the hierarchy. More adaptive thinking may involve fewer negative automatic thoughts and attributions or more consistent challenges to negative thoughts as they arise. Better interpersonal communication often involves saying what one thinks more frequently, identifying and expressing emotions, or appropriate self-disclosure.

The Hierarchy: Daily Workouts for Increasing Behavioral and Emotional Fitness

A hierarchy of 10 feared situations is constructed in cooperation with the client to be used as simulated exposures in the group sessions and to practice in-vivo during self-assigned behavioral homework between sessions. Clients are given copies of these hierarchies to guide their practice and to revise as goals are met or changed.

Assessing Negative Conditioning Events

We find that clients often fail to report traumatic events due to discomfort or because the significance of an event has not been recognized. For this reason, we ask clients to complete the Multi-modal Life History Questionnaire on a take-home basis. This procedure allows clients to record any stressful or traumatic events that may not have been discussed in the screening sessions (Lazarus, 1976).

Assessing Maladaptive Attributions: The Shyness Attribution Questionnaire (SAQ)

The Shyness Attribution Questionnaire (SAQ) (Henderson et al., 1997) is an instrument developed at our clinic to assess attribution of responsibility for social outcomes. The SAQ is administered by the therapist after the hierarchy is completed and consists of structured questions about attribution style and shame in the three most challenging situations from the client's hierarchy.

As noted earlier, we find that maladaptive attributional patterns and self-blame are important aspects of shyness and are associated with greater pathology. Shy clients who are generally fearful score significantly higher than those who are shy only on internal, global, stable, and self-blaming attributions on the SAQ. Studies with high school and college students also reveal that the trait of private self-consciousness (the tendency to focus on inner thoughts and feelings) significantly exacerbates the self-blaming tendency. Our evaluation studies indicate that one significant effect of treatment is to produce changes in these cognitive patterns. Shy and socially phobic college students who participated in eight-week treatment groups displayed significant reductions in negative attributions and shame on this questionnaire (Henderson et al., 1997). Similarly, data collected at the Shyness Clinic revealed that, following treatment, clients displayed significant reductions in global, stable, and self-blaming attributions and in the affective experience of shame. All of these findings support the usefulness of the SAQ in clinical populations.

We think these results are highly important. When clients are fearful and physiologically aroused, they can learn to use the energy, just as athletes and actors do, to give a good performance. After the situation, however, if they engage in self-blame, see themselves as inadequate, and experience shame, they want to withdraw and hide. They feel more vulnerable and less likely to want to initiate social contact.

We find that shame is more self-destructive than anticipatory physiological arousal in chronic shyness, particularly when avoidant personality disorder is present. Those diagnosed with avoidant personality disorder are more shame prone and more likely both to blame themselves *and* others. Moreover, shame in our clinic clients is a significant predictor of MCMI scores on self-defeating behavior and passive aggression and is correlated with resentment and antisocial attitudes on the MMPI (Henderson & Zimbardo, 1998).

Assessing Blame: The Estimations of Others Scale (EOS)

The EOS is an instrument developed at our clinic to measure the tendency to blame others. Henderson and Horowitz developed the measure using statements made by shyness clinic clients during treatment (Henderson & Horowitz, 1998). The scale shows good internal consistency in a college sample (Cronbach's Alpha = 0.91). Convergent validity is supported by correlations with suppressed anger items from the STAXI ($r = 0.38$) and with the social avoidance subscale of the Inventory of Interpersonal Problems (Horowitz, Rosenberg, Baer, Ureno, & Villasenor, 1988) ($r = 0.48$). Shy college students scored significantly higher than non-shy college students on the EOS, and shyness clinic clients scored significantly higher than the college sample.

Our clinical observations suggest that one way shy individuals reduce the debilitating pain of shame is to blame others. Unfortunately, blaming others leaves the client feeling alienated not only from the self, but also from potential sources of support (Henderson & Zimbardo, 1998). There is no safe place and no one with whom to experience emotional comfort and connection.

Research conducted at our clinic found that blaming others was the only significant negative predictor of perspective taking (the tendency to spontaneously adopt the psychological point of view of others) and empathic concern (other-oriented feelings of sympathy and concern for unfortunate others) in high school students (Davis, 1983; Henderson & Zimbardo, 1998). Empathy is associated with adaptive interpersonal functioning and may be one of the most important social skills that develops in middle childhood and adolescence (Davis, 1983). It is negatively related to aggressive/antisocial and externalizing behavior in both males and females (Miller & Eisenberg, 1988).

Given that shyness in adolescents is positively correlated with empathic concern, it may be only the tendency to blame the self or others that is responsible for the development of greater interpersonal problems, whether through inhibition or inappropriate responding. In our clinic, we use the EOS to help clients become aware of the tendency toward negative automatic thoughts about others. As they notice the pattern, they can begin to work toward a non-blaming problem-solving approach to social situations.

Assessing and Preventing Drop-out

Because shy clients display a strong tendency to drop out of treatment, behavior patterns that are likely to interfere with treatment are discussed with the client in the initial evaluation to anticipate the shame, resentment, and discouragement that trigger withdrawal. The chronically shy often do not see social exertion as a natural part of life. They tend to believe that other people "have it easier" and that things just come naturally to them. They are surprised when they discover that research suggests that shy college students do not report fear levels or experiences that are different from the non-shy (Maddux, Norton, & Leary, 1988). They also do not recognize the importance of commitment and the impact of dropping out on other members of the group.

Resentment and passive aggression are common in shy clients (Henderson & Zimbardo, 1998). With such individuals the therapist acknowledges the client's sense of exploitation and resentment. Together they explore ways that the client may express anger directly and use assertiveness techniques to ask directly for what is wanted so that the client can express negative feelings in ways that others can hear. The tendency to withdraw and self-sabotage is anticipated. The therapist asks for help from the client in facilitating continued participation in spite of mistrust and frustration. This may include writing to, or telephoning, the therapist to discuss the problem individually before it is brought up in the group. If someone will not make such an agreement with the therapist the prognosis is less optimistic. Clients must have an adequate alliance with the therapist to tolerate the anxiety and suspicion they feel with others.

With dependent clients, the therapist communicates understanding regarding the difficulty with self-assertion, and suggests specific behaviors the client can practice in the group, such as expressing genuine thoughts or feelings in spite of the risk of displeasing others. Clients suggest ways the therapist can facilitate these behaviors. In general, the assessment period is used to encourage clients to make a commitment to themselves, their therapists, and their group.

TREATMENT PROCEDURES

We turn now to a discussion of treatment techniques, beginning with the first stages of treatment and working through to termination. We will begin with techniques designed to increase clients' behavioral activity and fitness and then consider techniques designed to improve cognitive fitness. Following this description, we will present treatment evaluation data.

Improving Behavioral Fitness

Self-monitoring

When the initial evaluation is completed, clients begin the self-monitoring process. They record automatic thoughts in stressful situations and rate how positive or negative the outcome of a social situation was and how they assigned responsibility for the outcome. They begin to differentiate automatic thoughts regarding anticipated behavior and fears of rejection prior to a situation from negative attributions about the self and others that become salient after the situation has occurred. Clients also monitor their avoidance behavior and its relationship to their negative thoughts and beliefs.

Behavioral Fitness Homework and Self-rewards for Workouts

Homework is reviewed at the beginning of each group session and is assigned at the end of each session. Therapists help clients to set specific goals to encourage them to enter feared situations and practice new behaviors. Some assignments involve asking others to assist them with challenging maladaptive thoughts and beliefs when they are experiencing negative emotions like shame. They reward themselves in the form of enjoyable activities or by making check marks in notebooks provided for them in the first group session. They then pay themselves a self-determined amount of money for each check mark, usually at the end of the week or month. This money is used to purchase desired items.

Bragging sessions are encouraged during the homework period so that clients get in the habit of acknowledging their own work and sharing their pleasure with others. Because they tend to be envious, they are often afraid that people will envy them, so the group's enjoyment of their progress contributes to a sense of teamwork and camaraderie. Clients and therapists periodically rate how much working out the client is doing each week and the results are discussed in the session. Clients may fail to notice new behaviors that have become habitual. Reducing the difficulty of some homework or "chunking" it into smaller pieces is done if clients are "stuck".

Telephone Calls

Clients are assigned two telephone calls each week to other group members. This exercise gives them practice on the telephone and practice in forming acquaintances. Telephoning also helps them to develop group cohesiveness and support for each other.

Motivation and Compliance with an Optimal Training Schedule

Always salient, motivation and compliance are crucial in workouts. If clients do not work out they do not increase emotional and physical well-being. When clients make excuses, therapists emphasize choice. Excuses are part of the helpless role, and we have respect for clients' freedom to choose but resist self-conceptions of helplessness and lack of control. Clients are encouraged to do small things every day and to tackle one or two bigger challenges each week. It is like interval training in running or cycling. They must get to the top of their level of exertion ranges, then they can drop back to things that are easier.

Interpersonal Skill Training

Interpersonal skill training includes verbal and nonverbal communication, skillful listening, self-disclosure, trust-building, handling criticism, negotiation, and managing and expressing anger constructively. Most clients are more skilled than they believe they are. The benefit of the skills training component may derive more from the engagement with intimacy issues than from actual deficits in social skills.

Empathy

Empathy for the self and others is an ongoing focus in therapy. Chronically shy clients are self-conscious and critical of themselves and others. A critical focus on one's performance or an excessive focus on inner processes interferes with accurate perspective taking, i.e., seeing another's point of view or frame of reference. When clients begin to understand that an inward focus on a painful emotional state tends to have a negative influence on one's perceptions of the self and others they become more tolerant.

Improving Mental Fitness

Atributional and Self-concept Restructuring

A key feature of our cognitive approach is its focus on the specific restructuring of maladaptive attributions and negative biases about the self (Henderson et al., 1997). We emphasize attributional and self-concept restructuring to enable clients to recognize the tendency to blame the self in the face of negative social outcomes and to challenge negative self-schemas that operate outside awareness. Shy individuals reverse the self-enhancement bias; that is, they attribute their successes to external, temporary, and specific factors, and their failures to internal, stable, and global factors. Furthermore, they tend to dismiss positive feedback and positive change. What is more problematic, particularly when negative self-schemas are operational, is that they see small setbacks as evidence of basic inadequacy rather than as a natural aspect of learning.

Attributional and self-concept restructuring are particularly suited to self-defeating thinking patterns. It is important to distinguish between thoughts that are hypotheses that can be tested immediately, such as, "I won't be able to think of anything to say" from basic beliefs about the self. We find that if behavior changes, but beliefs about the self do not, clients return to a process of self-blame and shame at the first sign of frustration or disappointment, leaving them convinced that maladaptive self-schemas are accurate depictions of their personalities. Despite reluctance to acknowledge and discuss beliefs about inadequacy and powerlessness, shame-related emotions are expressed early in Social Fitness Training because we explicitly focus on shame-based self-schemas and self-blame. Openly expressing these emotions allows more opportunity for specific challenges to negative attributions.

Because self-concept distortions usually operate outside awareness, therapists present an information-processing model to help clients to understand how such distortions arise. Essentially this model states that when one blames the self in social situations, a state of shame is induced. Through a process of emotional reasoning, shame, in turn, elicits increased self-blame and distorted thinking about the self. As the process is repeated in the context of negative emotion and high self-awareness, highly articulated distorted beliefs about the self and others occurs. When there is a highly elaborated self-concept that is shame-based, that is, where the self is seen as socially inadequate, it serves as a powerful organizer of incoming information. Thus, information is organized around the concept of self as inadequate and others as contemptuous. To illustrate how this happens, therapists cite studies that show that people who label themselves as shy remember more negative than positive feedback even when they are given equal amounts of both (Smith & Sarason, 1975). The negative effect this has on motivation for the risk-taking necessary for social learning thus becomes apparent. The intent of this discussion is to help clients begin to recognize that all human beings continue to learn and develop through social interaction and that states of shyness are a normal part of life.

Therapists take emotional risks, at times explicitly disclosing their own negative attributions and beliefs about the self, acknowledging to clients the embarrassment or shame that accompanies these revelations. These risks help therapists to empathize with group members' experience, which is essential in working with shame. Clients hesitate to discuss shame and negative self-schemas with others, who they fear may be shocked or skeptical, particularly when a client appears to be functioning well on the surface. The therapist modeling and the group dialogue that follows helps to change these beliefs, which we believe cause a good deal of the suffering that accompanies problematic shyness.

These restructuring techniques are probably more applicable to shy individuals with long-standing difficulties than to those with more reactive and specific problems. However, working with these entrenched negative attitudes and beliefs serves to inoculate clients against their re-emergence after treatment when negative outcomes or ambiguous situations trigger them. Originally, it appeared that the specific focus on attribution style and self-concept distortions would be more applicable to a clinical population than to Stanford students and college students in general. However, in working with students, we found that self-blaming and self-concept distortions are quite prevalent in student treatment groups and in our community shyness seminars as well.

Termination

To determine readiness for termination, the therapist and client assess attributional style, shame, and current goal attainment and plan future goals. They also anticipate getting out of "social shape" and formulate plans to restart "workouts" on their own, or with support.

Treatment Outcome

We have conducted eight-week groups for Stanford students, 94% of whom met criteria for social phobia. Students showed significant reductions in social avoidance and anxiety, fear of negative evaluation, depression, shame, guilt, negative and self-blaming attributions, and general fearfulness, as measured by the questionnaires described earlier (Henderson et al., 1997). Progress is more arduous for most of our community clients due to long-standing avoidance and inhibited behavior and to the perceived lack of social opportunities and support. However, statistically and clinically significant reductions in the same variables are achieved in the 26-week community groups, in spite of the marked degree of comorbidity in this population. In addition, these clients generally obtain significantly lower scores on the Inventory of Interpersonal Problems (Horowitz et al., 1988), and the Anger In scale of the State-Trait Anger Inventory (STAXI) (Spielberger, 1979).

In 26 weeks of treatment, we typically see at least one significant relapse, based on a disappointing social interaction, and the return to self-blame, shame and negative beliefs about the self. Because we predict the relapses during the initial evaluation, and anticipate general discouragement in the group at about the 13th or 14th week of treatment, clients are better able to "climb back on their horses" and continue their social fitness workouts. Such experiences can be used to enhance understanding of the lethality of negative attributions and negative beliefs about the self and the importance of consistent effort and practice.

COMMON PROBLEMS

Our experience indicates that a number of problems commonly arise in the treatment of shy clients. We will consider a number of these below.

Medication to Enhance Social Performance and Comfort Level

Our clients sometimes use medication: benzodiazepines (e.g., Ativan, Xanax, and Klonopin), beta blockers (e.g., Inderol) or antidepressants (generally selective serotonin re-uptake inhibitors). Analogous to athletes taking steroids to improve performance, shy clients are afraid to be without their medication, hampering their faith in themselves and their long-term success. Clients usually attribute success to whatever medication they use, which interferes with a sense of self-efficacy. The use of antianxiety medication is also problematic because it buffers the experience of anxiety necessary for effective desensitization. Clients do not learn that they can manage their anxiety, reframing and channeling their arousal as an athlete does, to enhance perceptual acuity and behavioral performance.

Substance Use

We have a low incidence of substance dependence among our clients, but some clients use alcohol or cannabis to reduce social anxiety, often in relatively small quantities. If clients use alcohol during exposures (behavioral homework) they do not desensitize or learn that they can manage their anxiety. Sometimes they have not recognized that caffeine use exacerbates social anxiety. They are educated about the effects of alcohol and caffeine on social anxiety and performance.

Pessimism and Passivity

Learned pessimism and passivity are hallmarks of the chronically shy. Clients will seduce therapists into doing all the work. If this occurs, therapists become exhausted and angry, which interferes with treatment. In the end, clients who are expected to participate feel more empowered and efficacious. When they start "talking back" in the sessions, by challenging a comment a therapist has made, or rearranging an exposure to work better, they are participating more actively and making progress.

Difficulty Simulating Real Life

Sometimes it is difficult to simulate the exact experience a person is having at work or in social settings. For instance, a dominating male boss may be difficult. Often the client role-plays the boss first, to demonstrate the behavior. That can be instructive because different individuals respond differently to different personality styles. For instance, a manager was described as harsh, but when role-played actually sounded direct and even reasonable. Then the job becomes to help the client respond with reduced anxiety and increased assertiveness to inquiries about his work. In other cases, managers have been harsh and verbally abusive, and it can be difficult for clients and therapists alike to play these roles. Sometimes, due to age differences, group members, therapists, or confederates are not as threatening as potential dating or sexual partners. If a client can visualize the situation in sufficient detail, anxiety will usually be aroused. If not, the role-play serves as behavioral rehearsal or cognitive priming.

We find that when a person complains that the anxiety level is low, they often have subtle habits of avoidance. Sometimes the instruction to make more eye contact or to be more "present" helps. Intensifying the challenges during cognitive-restructuring may undermine defense mechanisms and reveal the underlying anxiety. However, this tactic may threaten the therapeutic alliance if excessive shame is experienced. Shame can promote withdrawal and reduced risk-taking both during the session and in homework activities between sessions.

Secondary Gains that Accompany Passivity and Pessimism

There are many secondary gains in chronic shyness. Others protect you, do things for you, pamper you, and are reluctant to exert pressure. In the groups, clients are helped to recognize that people who do not participate in their own lives become depressed, self-contemptuous, and experience a realistic sense of existential despair. Shame and guilt in small quantities stimulate growth. When clients take steps toward increased participation, demoralization is reduced and hope replaces despair. A kind of "tough love" usually develops in the group culture. Problems of shyness are not interpreted as illnesses to be cured, nor excuses to be given, but simply as human problems in living that can be overcome by appropriate strategies and group support.

SUMMARY

In this chapter, we have tried to provide a brief overview of the social fitness treatment program offered at the Shyness Clinic and to outline the common problems that therapists face as they work with shy clients. As we have seen, our program includes many of the elements found in the other treatment regimens described in this volume. However, we tend to place greater emphasis on the role of shame and blame in creating and maintaining shyness. Consistent with our social psychology backgrounds, we also focus on changing negative attributional patterns and distortions in self-concept. Finally, our program is firmly based on the notion of constructive collaboration. Together, students and instructors create a sense of community, which is the best antidote to shyness.

REFERENCES

Bandura, A. (1997). *Self-efficacy, the exercise of control.* New York: W. H. Freeman.

Beck, A. T., Steer, R. A., & Garbin, M. G. (1988). Psychometric properties of the Beck Depression Inventory: Twenty-five years of evaluation. *Clinical Psychology Review, 8,* 77–100.

Bruch, M. A. (1989). Familial and developmental antecedents of social phobia: Issues and findings. *Clinical Psychology Review, 9,* 37–47.

Cacioppo, J. T., Glass, C. R., & Merluzzi, T. V. (1970). Self-statements and self-evaluations: A cognitive response analysis of heterosocial anxiety. *Cognitive Therapy and Research, 3,* 249–262.

Carducci, B. J. & Zimbardo, P. G. (1995). Are you shy? *Psychology Today, November/December,* 34–40, 64, 66, 68.

Cheek, J. M. & Busch, C. M. (1981). The influence of shyness on loneliness in a new situation. *Personality and Social Psychology Bulletin, 7,* 572–577.

Coopersmith, S. (1959). A method for determining types of self-esteem. *Journal of Abnormal and Social Psychology, 59,* 87–94.

Davis, M. H. (1983). Measuring individual differences in empathy: Evidence for a multidimensional approach. *Journal of Personality and Social Psychology, 44,* 113–126.

DiNardo, P. A., Brown, T. A., & Barlow, D. H. (1994). *Anxiety disorders. Interview schedule for DSM-IV: Lifetime Version (ADIS-IV-L).* Albany, NY: Center for Stress and Anxiety Disorders, State University of New York at Albany.

Greene, R. L. (1991). *MMPI-2/MMPI: An Interpretive Manual.* Needham Heights, MA: Allyn & Bacon.

Henderson, L. (1992). Shyness groups. In M. McKay & K. Paleg (Eds.), *Focal group psychotherapy.* Oakland, CA: New Harbinger Press.

Henderson, L. (1997). MMPI Profiles of shyness in clinic patients. *Psychological Reports, 80,* 695–702.

Henderson, L. & Horowitz, L. M. (1998). *The Estimations of Others Scale (EOS).* Stanford University.

Henderson, L. & Horowitz, L. (1999, April). *Responses of high and low distress speakers telling a vulnerable story to rushed vs. attentive listeners.* Paper presented at the Society of Interpersonal Therapy and Research, Seattle.

Henderson, L., Martinez, A., & Zimbardo, P. G. (1997, July). *Social fitness training with attributional and self-concept restructuring; preliminary data with a college student population.* Paper presented at the International Conference on Shyness and Self-consciousness, Cardiff, Wales.

Henderson, L. M. & Zimbardo, P. G. (1996, March). *Shyness and control: Behavior? impression on others? "Second effort"?* Paper presented at the Stress, Trauma, and Anxiety: Impact on the Family. Anxiety Disorders Association of America 16th National Conference, Orlando, Florida.

Henderson, L. & Zimbardo, P. G. (1998, August). *Trouble in river city: Shame and anger in chronic shyness.* Paper presented at the American Psychological Association, 106th National Conference, San Francisco, CA.

Horowitz, L. M., Rosenberg, S. E., Baer, B. A., Ureno, G., & Villasenor, V. S. (1988). Inventory of interpersonal problems: Psychometric properties and clinical applications. *Journal of Consulting and Clinical Psychology, 56,* 885–892.

Lazarus, A. A. (1976). *Multi-modal behavior therapy.* New York: Springer.

Leary, M. (1983). A brief version of the fear of negative evaluation scale. *Personality and Social Psychology Bulletin, 9* (3), 371–375.

Lewis, H. B. (1971). *Shame and guilt in neurosis.* New York: International Universities Press.

Maddux, J. E., Norton, L., & Leary, M. R. (1988). Cognitive components of social anxiety: An investigation of the integration of self-presentation theory and self-efficacy theory. *Journal of Social and Clinical Psychology, 6,* 180–190.

Miller, P. A. & Eisenberg, N. (1988). The relation of empathy to aggressive and externalizing/antisocial behavior. *Psychological Bulletin, 103* (3), 324–344.

Millon, T. (1987). *The Millon Clinical Multi-Axial Inventory-II* (MCMI-II). Minneapolis, MN: National Computer Systems.

Mischel, W. (1999). *Introduction to personality.* New York: Harcourt Brace.

Pilkonis, P. A. (1977). Shyness, public and private, and its relationship to other measures of social behavior. *Journal of Personality, 45,* 585–595.

Smith, R. E. & Sarason, I. G. (1975). Social anxiety and the evaluation of negative interpersonal feedback. *Journal of Consulting and Clinical Psychology, 43* (3), 429.

Spielberger, C. D. (1979). *State-Trait Anger Expression Inventory (STAXI).* Odessa, FL: Psychological Assessment Resources, Inc.

St. Lorant, T., Henderson, L., & Zimbardo, P. (1999). Co-morbidity in a shyness clinic sample. (Submitted for publication.)

Wurmser, L. (1981). *The mask of shame.* Baltimore: Johns Hopkins University Press.

Zimbardo, P. G. (1977). *Shyness: What it is, what to do about it.* Reading, MA: Addison-Wesley.

Zimbardo, P. G. (1982). Shyness and the stresses of the human connection. In L. Goldberger & S. Breznitz (Eds.), *Handbook of stress: Theoretical and clinical aspects* (pp. 466–481). New York: Free Press.

Zimbardo, P. G. (1986). The Stanford shyness project. In W. H. Jones, J. M. Cheek, & S. R. Briggs (Eds.), *Shyness: Perspectives on research and treatment* (pp. 17–25). New York: Plenum Press.

Chapter 20

Cognitive-Behavioral Group Treatment for Social Phobia

Meredith E. Coles, Trevor A. Hart, *and* **Richard G. Heimberg**

COGNITIVE-BEHAVIORAL MODEL OF SOCIAL PHOBIA
Assessment of social phobia
BASICS OF COGNITIVE-BEHAVIORAL GROUP THERAPY FOR SOCIAL PHOBIA
EFFICACY OF COGNITIVE-BEHAVIORAL GROUP THERAPY
Empirical investigations of the efficacy of cognitive-behavioral group therapy
    for social phobia
FACTORS AFFECTING THE EFFICACY OF COGNITIVE-BEHAVIORAL INTERVENTIONS
LESSONS LEARNED FROM CLINICAL EXPERIENCE WITH COGNITIVE-BEHAVIORAL
    GROUP THERAPY
Difficulties during cognitive restructuring
Difficulties during in-session exposures
Difficulties with homework assignments
Difficulties with interpersonal dynamics
Difficulties with the demographic composition of groups
FUTURE DIRECTIONS
CONCLUSIONS
REFERENCES

Cognitive-Behavioral Group Therapy (CBGT; Heimberg & Becker, in press) was the first manualized treatment developed specifically for social phobia. Following the introduction of CBGT in a case series (Heimberg, Becker, Goldfinger, & Vermilyea, 1985), numerous controlled trials conducted in laboratories around the world have supported the clinical utility of CBGT and similar cognitive-behavioral protocols. This chapter begins with a presentation of a cognitive-behavioral model of social phobia and information on the assessment of patients

International Handbook of Social Anxiety: Concepts, Research and Interventions Relating to the Self and Shyness. Edited by W. Ray Crozier and Lynn E. Alden.
© 2001 John Wiley & Sons Ltd.

with social phobia. We then present the basic techniques of CBGT for social phobia and examine the empirical support for its efficacy. This is followed by a discussion of factors that may affect the efficacy of cognitive-behavioral interventions for social phobia. We share our reflections on lessons learned from nearly two decades of work with patients with social phobia and guidelines for clinicians based on this experience. Finally, future directions are discussed.

A COGNITIVE-BEHAVIORAL MODEL OF SOCIAL PHOBIA

Rapee and Heimberg's (1997) model is the most recent of the cognitive-behavioral models of social phobia, although other similar models exist (e.g., Clark & Wells, 1995, see David M. Clark, this volume, *Chapter 18*). Based on empirical research as well as clinical experience, Rapee and Heimberg (1997; see also Turk, Lerner, Heimberg, & Rapee, 2001) provide a broad explanatory framework for the etiology and maintenance of social phobia. In their model, people with social phobia may begin life with overprotective or overintrusive parents who reinforce the message that one is not competent to meet the social challenges of life. Parents may also convey the message that the evaluation of other people is important and model anxiety about how one is being evaluated. Such people thereby develop two major assumptions about themselves and others. The first assumption is that people tend to evaluate others in a critical and negative manner. The second is that it is extremely important to be appraised positively by others.

When approaching a social situation, the person with social phobia forms a mental representation of him- or herself as perceived by others. The mental representation comprises input from long-term memory, internal cues such as somatic sensations, and external cues such as others' facial expressions or tone of voice. Because the person with social phobia believes that the evaluation of others is so important, he or she attempts to predict the standards the other person(s) (the "audience") hold for him or her in the situation. The person with social phobia then attempts to determine if he or she is meeting those standards (i.e., attempts to determine whether the mental representation of him- or herself as perceived by others matches the predicted standards of the audience). However, this is a task doomed to failure because the mental representation of oneself as seen by others is negatively biased. Predicted failure to meet expected standards, as is common in social phobia, leads to expectations of negative evaluation by others and the prediction that negative (or even disastrous) social consequences will ensue. Negative expectations elicit further anxiety. Anxiety and negatively biased mental self-representations thereby reinforce each other in a vicious cycle.

The belief that the evaluation of others is extremely important and the negatively biased mental representation of the self as seen by others motivates hypervigilance for (i.e., preferential allocation of attention to) social threats and cues about potentially negative social outcomes. Preferential allocation of attention leads to the division of attentional resources among external social threats, threat-eliciting cues about one's behavior or appearance, and the demands of performing the current social task (e.g., having a conversation with an attractive other). Consequently, the individual may suffer from perceived or actual performance deficits, especially during tasks that require greater devotion of attentional resources. The socially anxious individual may also exhibit performance deficits because of subtle avoidance (e.g., avoiding eye contact or standing on the periphery of a group) and overt avoidance (not attending social gatherings). While avoidance behaviors are intended to decrease the potential of negative evaluation by others, these behaviors also inhibit social performance ("safety behaviors"; Wells et al., 1995). Performance deficits are interpreted as confirmation of predictions of failure, thus creating a self-fulfilling prophecy and maintenance of social anxiety.

CBGT aims to break the cognitive-affective-behavioral cycle of social phobia via two main techniques: exposure to feared situations (both in the group session and in the natural environment) and cognitive restructuring. Exposure to feared situations and cognitive restructuring provide a wide variety of opportunities for the patient, including (1) the opportunity to overcome avoidance and safety behaviors, (2) the opportunity for habituation to previously avoided situations or situations in which negative cognitions have previously over-ridden natural conditioning processes, (3) opportunities to improve the quality of one's behavior in avoided situations without the load of negative cognition, (4) opportunities to adjust mental representations of self as perceived by others, and (5) opportunities to gather information that may offer alternatives to negative predictions or beliefs about self and others in social situations. Cognitive-behavioral treatments also direct attention away from negative cues and toward the task at hand through the use of cognitive restructuring and goal-setting in association with exposures. The group format of CBGT may increase the potential for altering mental representations by providing additional sources of feedback about one's performance and by allowing more opportunities for positive and non-critical social interaction. The specific procedures of CBGT will be described in greater detail in a later section.

Assessment of Social Phobia

Formal assessment is an ongoing and essential part of CBGT for social phobia. Assessments provide valuable information as to the nature of each patient's concerns, assist the clinician in formulating exposures and cognitive-restructuring activities, and allow the clinician to observe changes in the patient's symptoms before, during, and after treatment. While the use of empirically validated assessment devices to examine the presence and severity of the symptoms of social phobia (e.g., diagnostic interviews, self-report measures, clinician-administered inventories) is critically important for the understanding and conceptualization of the individual patient and to index change across time in outcome research, space considerations prohibit a thorough examination of these instruments. In our clinic, we utilize the Anxiety Disorders Interview Schedule for DSM-IV: Lifetime Version (DiNardo, Brown, & Barlow, 1994) for diagnosis of social phobia and comorbid disorders. Other devices we employ include the self-report Social Interaction Anxiety Scale and Social Phobia Scale (Mattick & Clarke, 1998) and the clinician-administered Liebowitz Social Anxiety Scale (Heimberg et al., 1999; Liebowitz, 1987). The reader is referred to recent papers by Hart, Jack, Turk, and Heimberg (1999) and McNeil, Ries, and Turk (1995) for reviews of these and other social phobia assessment devices. Here we discuss the clinical use of assessment strategies that specifically inform CBGT therapists about potential treatment targets.

Behavioral and cognitive assessment methods provide valuable information about a patient's experience of anxiety and avoidance in feared situations as they begin treatment and throughout the treatment process. Behavioral assessments before and after CBGT in our clinic have consisted of either standardized or individualized role-plays. Standardized role-plays, in which all patients respond to the same stimuli (e.g., talking to a stranger or giving speech to a small audience), allow for the observation of differences across patients on each task. The information derived from these assessments helps the clinician to gauge the quality of the patient's performance in comparison to other patients, the degree of disruption of performance by anxiety or negative cognitions, and the potential need for remediation of deficits in social skills. However, individualized role-plays (i.e., the staging of situations specifically selected for relevance to the individual patient) may have greater external validity (Chiauzzi, Heimberg, Becker, & Gansler, 1985). The idiosyncratic fears of the individual patient may be incorporated into the role-play so that its impact on the patient's behavior can be determined. Thus, the relevance of the assessment situation to the patient may be maximized. Further, Coles and Heimberg (2000) suggest that the specific patterns of anxiety demonstrated during individualized behavioral assessments may be related to severity of social anxiety, independent of depressive symptoms, and that patients with different patterns of anxiety during pre-treatment behavioral assessment tasks may show differential response to CBGT.

Clinicians using CBGT may also benefit from the use of cognitive assessment tasks. Often used before and after role-plays, cognitive assessment tasks are helpful in identifying adaptive and maladaptive cognitions in feared situations. One of the most commonly used cognitive assessments is the thought-listing technique, which requires patients to record all of the thoughts that they can recall having had during a particular period of time (Cacioppo, Glass, & Merluzzi, 1979; Elting & Hope, 1995). Thought listing assessments allow clinicians to begin treatment armed with data on the thought content (i.e., the focus of specific negative cognitions) and thought processes (i.e., how one thought flows into another: does one negative thought lead to another, to another, etc., in an increasing spiral of negativity?) of each patient in an effort to maximize treatment relevance and impact.

Beyond the start of treatment, assessments continue to be an ongoing and essential part of CBGT. For example, patients are engaged in thought-listing exercises before each in-session exposure, and their degree of belief in specific negative cognitions is repeatedly assessed during cognitive-restructuring exercises. Subjective Units of Discomfort Scale ratings are collected during in-session exposures to provide information about patients' level of anxiety and responses to potential stressors (e.g., a pause in the conversation). Furthermore, the use of written homework assignments provides therapists with the opportunity to assess homework compliance as well as the adequacy of self-administered cognitive-restructuring skills.

BASICS OF COGNITIVE-BEHAVIORAL GROUP THERAPY FOR SOCIAL PHOBIA

CBGT is a multicomponent treatment that involves presentation of a cognitive-behavioral model of social phobia, training in cognitive-restructuring skills, repeated exposures to anxiety-provoking situations in sessions, and homework assignments for in-vivo exposures accompanied by self-administered cognitive-restructuring activities. CBGT is conducted in groups of six patients with two therapists. Sessions are typically held for approximately 2.5 hours weekly over a period of 12 weeks (although we are currently examining lengthier periods of treatment to determine if these might result in greater maintenance of gains for some patients or increase the total number of responding patients). In this section, we provide an overview of CBGT procedure and refer the reader to Heimberg and Juster (1995), Heimberg, Juster, Hope, and Mattia (1995) or Heimberg and Becker (in press) for a more thorough presentation of this topic. CBGT can be loosely divided into four parts: (1) an initial treatment orientation interview, (2) sessions 1 and 2, (3) sessions 3 through 11, and (4) the final (12th) session.

Before initiation of treatment, all patients participate in a treatment orientation interview. This interview has five goals. First, it allows the patient to become acquainted with one of the therapists, thereby serving to provide a familiar face at the first meeting of the group. Second, the therapist describes what will happen in treatment and answers any of the patient's questions. Third, the patient is introduced to the Subjective Units of Discomfort Scale (0 = no anxiety to 100 = the most anxiety ever experienced), which will be used throughout the treatment to quantify the patient's anxiety experience. Fourth, the therapist assists the patient in developing a fear and avoidance hierarchy that represents situations to be targeted in therapy. Fifth and finally, the treatment orientation interview allows for development of explicit treatment goals.

Following completion of the treatment orientation interview for each patient, group sessions begin. The first two sessions of CBGT are devoted to setting the stage for the remaining sessions and providing basic training in cognitive restruc-turing. During these sessions, the therapists take responsibility for the majority of the activity, allowing the group members time to become increasingly com-fortable in the group setting. The first session includes six activities: (1) intro-ductions of group members and therapists, (2) discussion of the group's ground rules (e.g., confidentiality), (3) sharing of individual social fears and treatment goals, (4) presentation of the cognitive-behavioral model of social phobia and the treatment rationale, (5) initial training in cognitive restructuring, focusing on identifying automatic thoughts, and (6) assignment of homework to record auto-matic thoughts during the following week. The second session continues where the first ended and emphasizes the development of basic skills needed for cog-nitive restructuring. Homework from the preceding week is reviewed, and auto-matic thoughts recorded for homework are used for further training in cognitive restructuring. Therapists use these thoughts (e.g., "I will not know what to say") to introduce the concept of thinking errors and to highlight thinking errors common in persons with social phobia (e.g., "fortune telling"). Therapists also introduce patients to the process of disputing their automatic thoughts (e.g., "Do I have a crystal ball that shows me that I will not know what to say?") and devel-oping rational responses (i.e., a statement summarizing the disputation of the patient's automatic thoughts (e.g., "I have done fine in conversations in the past. I'll just try my best"). The second session ends with the assignment of homework to label and dispute thinking errors in identified automatic thoughts.

Sessions 3 through 11 provide patients with repeated exposure to anxiety-provoking situations in which they can practice and hone their new cognitive-restructuring skills. After an initial homework review, patients take turns partic-ipating in exposures in session. Choice of exposure situations is guided by the fear and avoidance hierarchies developed during the treatment orientation inter-view and by additional clinical information collected during treatment. Initial exposures are typically chosen to elicit a Subjective Units of Discomfort Scale rating of approximately 50 (if the situation were to be experienced in real life). Efforts should be made to make exposures as realistic as possible through tech-niques such as the utilization of props, rearranging furniture, instructing role-players to behave in particular ways, and above all, by taking the time to specify which particular aspects of a situation elicit the patient's anxiety. Another criti-cal ingredient of CBGT is the coordination of exposures and cognitive restruc-turing. Once a patient is chosen to participate in an exposure, automatic thoughts regarding the situation are elicited, and thinking errors are labeled and disputed. This work is then summarized into a rational response for the patient to utilize during the exposure. Finally, observable, behavioral goals are set for the expo-sure. Patients may need help with setting goals and should be discouraged from setting unrealistic goals (e.g., "I won't be nervous"), goals that are difficult to quantify (e.g., "I'll make a good impression"), or goals that are dependent on the behavior of another person (e.g., "She'll accept my invitation to see a movie together"). Throughout the exposure, therapists prompt the patient each minute for his or her Subjective Units of Discomfort Scale ratings, which play an important part in later cognitive-restructuring activities. Repetition of rational responses at these times helps the patient to focus their attention and apply cognitive-coping skills during anxiety-provoking situations. Each exposure continues until the patient's anxiety begins to decrease or level off and behavioral goals are met (typically about 10 minutes). Debriefing following the exposure is comprised of five main components: (1) review of goal attainment and effective use of rational response(s), (2) review and disputation of any new automatic thoughts that occurred during or after the exposure, (3) review of the pattern of Subjective Units of Discomfort Scale ratings (i.e., how variations in experienced anxiety relates to events and/or thoughts during the exposure), (4) feedback from therapists and group members, and (5) reinforcement of the patient for facing a feared situation. During sessions 3 through 11, personalized homework assignments are developed for each patient. The therapists and patients work together to develop assignments that will allow the patient to confront situations similar to those practiced in the group. As in session, each patient is strongly encouraged to utilize cognitive-restructuring skills before, during, and after their homework exposures.

The first half of the final session allows time for additional exposures and associated cognitive-restructuring activities. The second half is devoted to reviewing each patient's progress over the course of treatment. Therapists also work with patients in identifying situations that may still be problematic and rational responses that may be useful in these situations and setting goals for continued work after the termination of formal treatment.

Treatment procedures are defined in step-by-step fashion for ease of administration of CBGT. Obviously, a firm understanding of these procedures is essential for the successful conduct of CBGT. Therapists interested in conducting CBGT will also greatly benefit from familiarity with social phobia, facility with cognitive-behavioral theory and case formulation, and experience in the administration of techniques of cognitive-behavior therapy, group treatment, and manualized treatments. It is important to keep in mind that this (and any) manualized treatment is not to be administered inflexibly but rather serves to keep the therapists on track and engaged in productive clinical activities and to support their attempts to work creatively within the bounds of the protocol. The reader is referred to an article by Kendall, Chu, Gifford, Hayes, and Nauta (1998) on the creative application of manualized treatments. Typical problems that may be encountered during CBGT and suggestions for remedying these situations will be considered later in this chapter.

EFFICACY OF COGNITIVE-BEHAVIORAL GROUP THERAPY

Since the introduction of social phobia in the third edition of the *Diagnostic and Statistical Manual of Mental Disorders* (DSM-III; American Psychiatric Association, 1980) there has been a surge of research addressing how to best treat this debilitating disorder. Within the domain of psychosocial treatments, efforts have been largely focused on cognitive-behavioral methods. These cognitive-behavioral methods typically combine systematic exposure to feared situations, behavioral experiments, and cognitive restructuring. Mounting evidence suggests that such interventions are effective at reducing social anxiety and related avoidance. Further, some studies suggest that treatment gains are maintained over time. Researchers have also begun to examine the factors that influence response to cognitive-behavioral interventions in an effort to increase efficacy of these procedures.

In the section to follow, we review the empirical evidence in support of the efficacy of CBGT. A comprehensive review of the efficacy of all cognitive-behavioral methods for the treatment of social phobia is beyond the scope of this chapter (see Juster & Heimberg, 1998; Turk, Coles, & Heimberg, in press). In focusing our attention on CBGT, we do not imply that CBGT is in any way superior to other similar cognitive-behavioral protocols developed by other investigators and clinicians. In fact, no study has yet to directly compare CBGT to another cognitive-behavioral approach, and meta-analyses (e.g., Feske & Chambless, 1995) do not suggest greater efficacy of CBGT.

Empirical Investigations of the Efficacy of Cognitive-Behavioral Group Therapy for Social Phobia

The clinical utility of CBGT was first demonstrated in a case series presented by Heimberg et al. (1985). The first controlled study was conducted by Heimberg et al. (1990), who examined the efficacy of CBGT in comparison to an attention-control treatment (educational-supportive group therapy; ES) in a sample of 49 patients who met DSM-III criteria for social phobia. Groups of patients were assigned to treatment conditions (CBGT or ES) as they appeared at the clinic, based on a predetermined random order. Each treatment was administered in 12 weekly 2-hour sessions. ES combined educational presentations about topics of relevance to social phobia and therapist-facilitated supportive group psychotherapy. Outcome expectancies and ratings of treatment credibility did not differ between CBGT and ES.

At post-treatment and six-month follow-up, both groups demonstrated significant reductions in clinician-rated phobic severity. However, those patients who had received CBGT were rated as significantly less severe. Both treatments also resulted in significant reductions in self-reported severity of social phobia from pre-treatment to post-treatment. However, only the CBGT group showed significant reductions from pre-treatment to six-month follow-up. At post-treatment, patients who had received CBGT reported less anxiety during both anticipatory and performance phases of a behavioral assessment than ES patients. Finally, Heimberg et al. (1990) calculated an index of the number of patients who manifested clinically significant improvement at post-treatment and follow-up. At post-treatment, 75% of CBGT patients, but only 40% of ES patients, were improved; at six-month follow-up, 81% of CBGT patients, but only 47% of ES patients, were improved.

After an interval of 4.5 to 6.25 years, 19 patients who had participated in the Heimberg et al. (1990) study completed a long-term follow-up assessment (Heimberg, Salzman, Holt, & Blendell, 1993). Comparison of patients who did and did not participate in the long-term follow up revealed that those who participated were less severely impaired at both pre-treatment and six-month follow-up and had rated the treatment they received as more credible at both assessment points. However, of those who did participate, pre-treatment differences were not evident between those who received CBGT and those who received ES. At the long-term follow-up assessment, both groups continued to demonstrate significant reductions in clinician-rated phobic severity from pre-treatment. Those who had received CBGT were rated as significantly less severe. As in Heimberg et al. (1990), an index of the number of patients who manifested clinically significant improvement was calculated and revealed that 89% of CBGT patients, but only 44% of ES patients, were improved at long-term follow-up assessment. The CBGT group was rated by independent assessors as barely symptomatic, while the mean for the ES group was above the clinical threshold for social phobia. CBGT patients continued to report significantly less severe symptoms than ES patients on numerous measures of social anxiety and tended to report lower levels of depressive symptoms. Finally, CBGT patients were rated as less anxious and more skilled during a behavioral assessment than ES patients at this long-term follow-up assessment.

CBGT has also been compared to cognitive-behavioral therapy based on identical procedures but delivered in individual sessions (ICBT). Lucas and Telch (1993) compared traditional CBGT, ICBT, and ES in a sample of 66 patients who met DSM-III-R (American Psychiatric Association, 1987) criteria for social phobia. CBGT and ICBT were both shown to be more effective than ES at reducing social anxiety. An index of cost-effectiveness was also calculated based on the number of patients in each condition who achieved reliable change per total therapist time per patient. This index suggested that CBGT was approximately 3 times more cost effective than ICBT and 2.5 times more cost effective than ES. While group cognitive-behavioral therapy is more cost effective, ICBT also has its own strengths, which include the initiation of treatment as soon as an individual patient is ready and allowing therapists to treat patients who may be unwilling to accept participation in a group because of their social anxiety.

In a recent multisite controlled trial, Heimberg et al. (1998) compared the efficacy of CBGT to that of the monoamine oxidase inhibitor phenelzine sulfate in 133 patients who met DSM-III-R criteria for social phobia. Groups of six patients were randomly assigned to one of four treatment conditions: CBGT, phenelzine, ES, and pill placebo. Heimberg et al. (1998) examined the efficacy of these four conditions over a 12-week period. At post-treatment (week 12), independent assessors classified a higher proportion of those receiving phenelzine (77%)

or CBGT (75%) as treatment responders (either markedly or moderately improved) relative to those who had received ES (35%) or pill placebo (41%). Phenelzine patients surpassed CBGT patients on a subset of measures, but patients who had received either CBGT or phenelzine generally outperformed patients in the control groups on a number of self-report and behavior test measures.

In order to examine the effects of maintenance treatment and durability of gains after termination of treatment, Liebowitz et al. (1999) followed the responders to either phenelzine or CBGT from the Heimberg et al. (1998) study for an additional 12 months. After week 12, these patients were entered into a six-month maintenance phase, and those who continued to respond throughout this period were entered into a six-month treatment-free follow-up phase. Patients who had received phenelzine in the first 12 weeks were somewhat less symptomatic at the onset of the maintenance phase of the study. Phenelzine patients who did not relapse maintained their superior gains throughout the maintenance and treatment-free phases. However, across the entire long-term follow-up (maintenance and follow-up phases), there was a trend toward greater relapse in the phenelzine group. Relapse rates were significantly worse for patients with generalized social phobia who had received phenelzine than patients with generalized social phobia who had received CBGT. The results of Heimberg et al. (1998) and Liebowitz et al. (1999) combine to suggest that while phenelzine may be associated with more rapid reductions in social anxiety, CBGT may produce more durable gains that are better maintained after treatment is withdrawn. While their long-term effects have not been studied, other medications have also been shown to produce similar symptom reductions at post-treatment. For example, Otto et al. (2000) compared clonazepam vs. CBGT for social phobia in 45 patients with DSM-III-R social phobia. Their results showed similar improvement across measures for both treatments at weeks 4, 8, and 12, although clonazepam patients were more improved on three self-report measures at week 12. See Hood and Nutt, this volume, *Chapter 21*, for more thorough coverage of pharmacological treatments for social phobia.

FACTORS AFFECTING THE EFFICACY OF COGNITIVE-BEHAVIORAL INTERVENTIONS

While effective psychosocial treatments for social phobia have been devised, not all patients are willing to enter treatment, complete treatment, or show adequate response. For instance, while Heimberg et al. (1998) showed that 75% of patients who completed a 12-week trial of CBGT were rated as responders, many had residual symptoms and many more failed to enter or complete treatment. While investigators have not devoted much attention to who enters treatment for social phobia (but see Juster, Heimberg, & Engelberg, 1995), several studies have examined predictors of response to cognitive-behavioral treatment among entering patients (e.g., Brown, Heimberg, & Juster, 1995; Chambless, Tran, & Glass, 1997; Hope, Herbert, & White, 1995; Scholing & Emmelkamp, 1999). A number of these studies focused specifically on CBGT.

Several of these studies have failed to identify strong predictors of outcome. In general, demographic characteristics have added little to the prediction of outcome of CBGT (Holt, Heimberg, & Hope, 1990; Juster, Heimberg, & Mattia, 1993). Some support for a predictive role of clinical characteristics in treatment outcome was reported by Holt et al. (1990), who found that patients with less severe symptoms, later onset, and shorter duration of symptoms were more likely to improve with CBGT. However, Juster et al. (1993) found no relationship between pre-treatment locus of control, or levels of social anxiety, general anxiety, or depression and response to CBGT. Studies examining social phobia subtype and comorbid avoidant personality disorder (APD) as potential predictors of treatment outcome (e.g., Brown et al., 1995; Hope et al., 1995; Turner, Beidel, Wolff, Spaulding, & Jacob, 1996) suggest that the generalized subtype and comorbid APD both predict lower end-state functioning, but these outcomes appear to be primarily related to higher levels of pre-treatment severity. Finally, an investigation of the effects of comorbid anxiety and depressive disorders in individuals with social phobia failed to show a significant moderating effect of comorbidity on outcome after 12 weeks of CBGT (Erwin, Heimberg, Juster, & Mindlin, 1999). In general, individuals with comorbid depressive disorders were more severely symptomatic than individals with no comorbid diagnoses or with only comorbid anxiety disorders both before and after treatment, while individuals with comorbid anxiety disorders were remarkably similar to individuals with social phobia alone. Chambless et al. (1997) found initial levels of depression to be the most consistent predictor of change between pre-test and post-test. Similarly, Scholing and Emmelkamp (1999) found that initial levels of depression significantly predicted the magnitude of improvement.

Process factors like expectancies for treatment outcome and compliance with CBGT homework assignments have proved to be stronger predictors of treatment outcome. Two studies found patient expectancy to be a unique predictor of outcome, even when other important variables such as pre-treatment severity were controlled (Chambless et al., 1997; Safren, Heimberg, & Juster, 1997). Homework compliance has also been shown to be associated with outcomes, with better compliance related to more positive outcome at both post-treatment (Leung & Heimberg, 1996) and six-month follow-up (Edelman & Chambless, 1995).

In conclusion, studies examining predictors of response to cognitive-behavioral interventions have identified factors that do and do not appear to be related to treatment outcome. Efforts to maximize factors related to positive gains may improve our treatment interventions. For example, techniques for modifying negative expectancies, or increasing homework compliance, may lead to better response. These studies further suggest that patients with particular profiles, such as patients with generalized social phobia or comorbid APD, may require longer or more intensive treatment.

LESSONS LEARNED FROM CLINICAL EXPERIENCE WITH COGNITIVE-BEHAVIORAL GROUP

While the CBGT manual clearly specifies the steps necessary for the conduct of sessions, years of clinical experience conducting CBGT have revealed common difficulties encountered in its implementation. This section addresses five types of problems that may arise in the conduct of CBGT: (1) difficulties during cognitive restructuring, (2) difficulties during exposure, (3) difficulties with homework assignments, (4) difficulties with interpersonal dynamics, and (5) difficulties with the demographic composition of groups. Our intention is to increase attention to these possible difficulties and provide suggestions for addressing these issues.

Difficulties during Cognitive Restructuring

Problems in the conduct of cognitive restructuring can arise on the part of both patients and therapists. Common problems presented by patients include a failure to report automatic thoughts, an inability or unwillingness to recognize thoughts as irrational or distorted, or a failure to grasp the central concepts of cognitive restructuring (e.g., an apparent inability to label thinking errors). When patients are unable to report automatic thoughts in the presence of high anxiety, it can be helpful to realize that the patient may be labeling his or her thoughts as feelings or reactions instead of thoughts. Prompts such as "what are you worried about?" or "what do you think might happen?" can often be helpful. Once automatic thoughts are elicited, some patients may be unable or unwilling to recognize these thoughts as distorted. Instead of arguing with the patient about whether thoughts are distorted or not, therapists may find it more useful to focus on whether the thoughts are adaptive and helpful in reaching the patient's goals. Finally, a small subset of patients are simply unable to master the central concepts of cognitive restructuring, and, in this case, we suggest that therapists try to reduce the complexity of the cognitive restructuring for these patients (e.g., by placing greater emphasis on self-statement substitution) and/or place a greater emphasis on repeated exposures.

While it is important to know how to address typical problems presented by patients, it is also useful for therapists to be aware of difficulties to which they may contribute. Some suggestions for the successful conduct of cognitive restructuring are as follows. First, therapists should avoid permitting patients to recount long and detailed stories about their anxious experiences as this may be an attempt to avoid potentially anxiety-provoking in-session exposure exercises. Second, therapists should focus on categorization and disputation of a representative sample of automatic thoughts, instead of trying to individually address each item on an exhaustive list. Attempts to address an exhaustive list of thoughts will generate more information than patients can retain, and patients will often find it difficult to keep their attention focused on cognitive-restructuring activities for the extended period required to address all thoughts. We have often observed that patients who experience significant anticipatory anxiety may experience a profound escalation in their anxiety as they focus on upcoming exposures more and cognitive-restructuring activities less. Therefore, it is far better to focus on a smaller sample of automatic thoughts and do a thorough job with them. Third, therapists should recognize that an exposure can begin before all cognitive-restructuring work is done. Therapists should guide the patient through the prescribed steps of cognitive restructuring before the in-session exposure, but it is unnecessary for the patient to thoroughly believe the alternatives to all his or her automatic thoughts before the exposure is begun. In-session exposures are often the most effective cognitive-restructuring tool. Fourth, therapists should address thoughts about specific negative consequences, rather than immediately confronting core maladaptive beliefs. For example, it is unlikely to be productive to challenge thoughts like "I'll be anxious" in the beginning stages of treatment. Although these thoughts may be quite exaggerated, thoughts about specific negative consequences of anxiety or poor performance may be more open for modification, and successful change in these beliefs may undermine the reasons that the patient predicts anxiety. Finally, above all, therapists should be patient and supportive of the patient's efforts at each stage of cognitive restructuring, avoiding telling the patient the "correct" answer or providing a rational response. Patients who do most of their own work will best develop and refine the skills necessary for enduring change. Lastly, therapists should be mindful of needlessly repeating what other therapists or patients have already said or of longwinded interventions that allow patients to become distracted or daydream while not the focus of attention.

Difficulties during In-Session Exposures

Problems can also arise in the conduct of in-session exposures. Patients may fail to report anxiety, role-players may perform in a less than desirable manner, or patients may fail to achieve goals. Therapists can successfully address each of these potential problems. If a patient fails to report anxiety during an exposure, therapists should: (1) assess whether the key anxiety-evoking aspects of the situation were incorporated, (2) assess whether the patient is experiencing anxiety but unwilling to report it, and (3) assess whether the patient engaged in disqualification of the exposure experience. Assessing these domains should reveal the source of the apparent discrepancy and allow for necessary modifications. To avoid less than desirable performance by role-players, the therapists should carefully select these individuals (particularly when using other group members) and provide them with detailed instructions as to what is expected of them. Finally, to avoid situations where the patient's worst fears do come true, it is best to take a graduated approach to exposures, having the patient attempt less difficult situations before more difficult ones.

Difficulties with Homework Assignments

As discussed earlier, homework compliance is related to better outcomes in CBGT (Edelman & Chambless, 1995; Leung & Heimberg, 1996). Therefore, addressing problems with homework completion is integral to the success of CBGT. Therapists should put serious thought into the development of appropriate homework assignments. This may be challenging in the case of more severely anxious or impaired patients who may have few opportunities for social interaction because of chronic avoidance of anxiety-provoking situations. For such patients, initial assignments may focus on the creation of future homework opportunities (e.g., join a social organization, enroll in a class, etc.). As a temporary solution, patients may also use visualization techniques to "engage" in their feared situations and complete cognitive restructuring around the visualized situation. Therapists should also be careful not to assign homework that the patient perceives as too difficult, as social fears may inhibit some patients from expressing disagreement with an assignment. To avoid this situation, therapists should actively involve patients in homework selection and should not consider a specific task as assigned until it is agreed to by the patient. Secondly, patients may fail to complete assignments. Procrastination arising from anxiety about the assigned task can result in failure to complete assignments. Therapists can circumvent patient procrastination if they assign: (1) cognitive restructuring homework in which the patient assesses the true dangerousness of the homework task, (2) another group member to serve as a homework "buddy" who will provide support and encouragement before the assignment is attempted, or (3) a situation that is less difficult or time-consuming. It is also important to keep in mind that, although completing homework assignments is an important step, completion does not ensure success. Patients can complete assignments in ways that are problematic or produce bad outcomes. Patients should be strongly encouraged to invest time and effort into preparatory cognitive restructuring, as failure to complete adequate cognitive restructuring may increase the probability of an unsatisfactory outcome. Patients should also be encouraged to set specific behavioral goals and to beware of disqualifying positive outcomes after completing assignments. Finally, patients occasionally may attempt a homework assignment and fail to achieve their goals. In these instances, it is important to help the patient adopt a problem-solving attitude about the failure and use it as a learning experience.

Difficulties with Interpersonal Dynamics

While difficulties can arise in the implementation of various components of CBGT, more general difficulties can also arise as a result of interpersonal dynamics between therapists and patients, among patients, or between therapists. Before the start of treatment, therapists should assess whether patients are appropriate for treatment in a group format. A patient who is overly verbose or insensitive to the concerns of other patients may inhibit the progress of the group. If this behavior is extreme, a referral for individual treatment may be preferable. If a patient who is verbose, or who attempts to dominate the attention of others, is enrolled in a group, therapists may wish to address these problems by suggesting behavioral goals for in-session exposures that will help the patient in interpersonal situations. For example, an exposure for a verbose man may include the goal of asking the role-player at least three open-ended questions and ask follow-up questions rather than talking about himself. Therapists may also wish to provide feedback as to how patients' behavior may be related to their anxiety in stressful situations. Further, some patients may have difficulty interacting with others based on their social fears. For example, a female patient with fears of talking to men may have difficulty interacting with male patients or therapists. Other patients with fears of authority figures may have difficulty interacting with the therapists. In these cases such interactions may become the focus of in-session exposures.

Difficulties with the Demographic Composition of Groups

Additional difficulties can arise if therapists are not cognizant of the demographic composition of each group. Some patients may feel uneasy about participating in a group entirely comprising patients and therapists of a different ethnic, cultural, or religious background (e.g., an African American patient in a group of otherwise exclusively Caucasian American patients and therapists). Similarly, patients may feel uncomfortable being the only man or only woman in the group. This may be especially important if the person of the minority gender is in treatment for fear of heterosexual interactions. In order to address these potential problems, we recommend making efforts to include patients from a variety of backgrounds and balancing the number of men and women in CBGT groups whenever possible. Further, clinicians should be careful not to assume that all patients in a group are heterosexual. CBGT therapists should therefore avoid asking questions that assume heterosexuality, such as asking a single woman with dating anxiety to "tell the group about your previous dates with men" before the patient has announced the gender of her dating partners.

In some instances patients will attempt to hide personal information (e.g., sexual orientation) or feel uncomfortable discussing concerns regarding potentially volatile topics (e.g., racial discomfort). In many cases, patients may be afraid to reveal their personal information or concerns specifically because of their social phobia. In these cases, we believe that these issues need to become a target of intervention as soon as possible. Support for the need to incorporate racial concerns into treatment plans is provided in a case study presented by Fink, Turner, and Beidel (1996). In this case, a 39-year-old African American woman reported fear of interacting with colleagues in the medical field. However, therapists later learned that her fears focused on interactions with Caucasian

Americans and incorporated these concerns into her treatment exercises. Fink et al. (1996) argued that it is unlikely that the long-term success realized by their patient would have been observed if her core concerns regarding cultural factors had not been addressed.

Beyond the need to develop appropriate treatment exercises, failure to disclose important information may also damage group cohesiveness. For example, imagine a situation in which a gay man masquerades as a straight man while saying he wants to develop dating relationships. If the "secret" is ultimately revealed after several weeks of treatment, other group members may feel betrayed, greatly impairing group cohesiveness. If therapists believe that a particular patient may be holding back, the therapists should meet privately with the patient and discuss the need to be open and honest in order to maximize treatment gains.

FUTURE DIRECTIONS

As stated above, CBGT has been shown to be an efficacious treatment for those suffering from social phobia. However, several issues in the implementation of CBGT have not yet received adequate empirical attention. Among these are (1) demonstration of CBGT effectiveness (as opposed to efficacy), (2) use of CBGT in private practice and hospital settings, (3) initiation of CBGT versus medication treatment, (4) use of medication in combination with CBGT, (5) use of CBGT versus ICBT, and (6) tailoring the length of treatment to the needs of different patients.

While CBGT has been shown to be efficacious in empirical trials, it is worthwhile to consider the distinction between efficacy and effectiveness. Efficacy typically refers to treatment outcomes obtained in controlled psychotherapy studies conducted within the confines of a laboratory, whereas effectiveness refers to treatment outcomes obtained in real-world clinic settings (Kazdin, 1998). Future studies need to assess the effectiveness of CBGT in non-research settings. Furthermore, although CBGT has been shown to decrease levels of symptom severity, future studies should examine whether CBGT returns patients to levels of functioning comparable to the general population (see Kendall, Marrs-Garcia, Nath, & Sheldrick, 1999). Finally, the ability of CBGT to improve general quality of life (e.g., job satisfaction, relationship satisfaction, health, etc.) should be further assessed. Safren, Heimberg, Brown, and Holle (1997) took a step in this direction and studied quality of life before and after CBGT in individuals with social phobia. Before treatment, individuals with social phobia judged their quality of life to be significantly poorer than normative samples. Although CBGT was shown to result in significant increases in patients' self-reported quality of life, the mean for the clinical sample was still lower than typical ratings for normative samples. Since Safren and colleagues were unable to include a follow-up assessment in their study, it is not possible to know whether improvements in quality of life continued after the end of formal treatment (e.g., after a brief treatment, a person who has never dated may have begun to do so, but he or she may not yet have developed a meaningful relationship with a potential life partner. The process may be in place but may take time to unfold before impacting quality of life.) Regardless, more research is needed to assess the ability of CBGT to return patients to levels of functioning consistent with normative samples in a variety of domains.

It also remains to be seen how effective CBGT will be in private practice and/or hospital settings. Many therapists may not have access to the predominantly academic settings where much of CBGT training for therapists occurs. While we hope that chapters such as this will be of service to those wishing to treat people with social phobia, greater efforts should be made in making CBGT training (or cognitive-behavioral training for many disorders, for that matter) more broadly accessible. For example, trained therapists may wish to consider setting up training workshops combined with multi-media long-distance training materials (e.g., videotape and computer-based media) and long-distance supervision of therapists who live too far away for face-to-face supervision. We hope that such efforts will be accompanied by research documenting the transportability of treatment using these and other training methods.

Clinicians should carefully weigh the benefits and drawbacks of using CBGT versus medication. While CBGT has the benefits of a lower relapse rate than at least one medication for social phobia (Liebowitz et al., 1999) and is not associated with side-effects such as dry mouth or sexual dysfunction, medication treatments may also have advantages. Medications are easier to administer than CBGT, and there are more clinicians able to administer medications than clinicians trained as cognitive-behavior therapists. Patients in rural areas may have difficulty locating a CBGT therapist and may prefer to go instead to a family physician for pharmacotherapy. Patients in rural and other areas in which no CBGT therapists are available may benefit from medications in tandem with self-help solutions (e.g., patient workbooks or computer programs) based on cognitive-behavioral principles. However, research is needed to demonstrate the efficacy of medications combined with self-help programs.

Further, we are interested in learning more about how to best combine medications with CBGT. We predict that the success of a combined medication–CBGT treatment would be maximized by the use of a team-based approach between physicians and therapists, whereby clinicians would actively communicate with each other about patient difficulties and progress in each treatment modality. In addition, we are curious as to the benefits of a staggered treatment plan whereby medication would begin before the commencement of CBGT and would terminate before the end of CBGT. Administration of medication before CBGT may increase the effectiveness of CBGT by reducing avoidance of feared situations (although this is likely to differ from medication to medication; e.g., there is evidence to suggest that exposure treatment for agoraphobia is compromised by the concurrent use of benzodiazepines; see Sartory, 1983). This staggered treatment would also allow the patient to have several weeks of treatment without medication to explore whether treatment-related reductions in anxiety and avoidance are attributable solely to the medication or to a combination of the medication and the patient's own personal efforts. CBGT may also be useful as relapse prevention after termination of medication.

Individual cognitive-behavioral treatment may also be used as an adjunct or instead of CBGT in the treatment of social phobia. Individual treatment as an adjunct to CBGT allows the therapist to spend more time on the patient's broader treatment goals and to address other issues that arise over the course of treatment (e.g., depression, anxiety problems not directly related to social phobia, relationship issues). As mentioned above, CBGT has been successfully adapted for individual treatment (ICBT; Lucas & Telch, 1993). ICBT obviates the need to wait until a group is assembled and allows for more scheduling flexibility. However, ICBT removes the automatic group social situation inherent in CBGT. ICBT also decreases the number of available role-players for exposures and eliminates opportunities for the patient to hear schema-discordant feedback from other group members about his or her performance.

Whether conducting therapy in a group or individual format, therapists may wish to consider issues regarding the length of treatment. The length of CBGT sessions as defined in the manual ($2^1/_2$ hours) may be difficult to fit into many therapists' or patients' schedules. Although the length of sessions can be decreased, therapists may then need to consider increasing the total number of sessions. However, this may need to be balanced with limitations on the overall number of sessions covered by each patient's health insurance. Therapists may also wish to consider tailoring the number of sessions depending on the clinical characteristics of the individual patient or patients. For example, patients with specific fears of public speaking will likely need fewer sessions than patients with more generalized concerns, and moderately impaired patients will likely need fewer sessions than severely impaired patients. Likewise, patients with comorbid depression tend to have more severe social anxiety (Erwin et al., in press) and may therefore benefit from more extended treatments relative to those with uncomplicated social phobia. When conducting group therapy instead of focusing on a time-limited treatment plan, therapists may also consider using open-ended groups that allow patients to terminate therapy as they reach their treatment goals.

CONCLUSIONS

This chapter highlights the progress that has been made in cognitive-behavioral interventions for social phobia. During the past two decades a treatment specifically designed for social phobia, CBGT, has been developed and refined. Further, numerous trials have supported the efficacy of CBGT and identified predictors of response to CBGT. This chapter presented a cognitive-behavioral model of social phobia, discussed recommendations for the assessment of patients with social phobia, and presented basic steps for the conduct of CBGT. Further, we presented potential difficulties in the conduct of CBGT and discussed methods for circumventing, or addressing, such difficulties. We hope that this chapter will not only aid clinicians in the treatment of social phobia, but will also serve as an impetus for further research on how to maximize treatment gains in a wide variety of clinical settings.

REFERENCES

American Psychiatric Association (1980). *Diagnostic and statistical manual of mental disorders* (3rd edn.). Washington, DC: Author.

American Psychiatric Association (1987). *Diagnostic and statistical manual of mental disorders* (3rd edn., revised). Washington, DC: Author.

Brown, E. B., Heimberg, R. G., & Juster, H. R. (1995). Social phobia subtype and avoidant personality disorder: Effect on severity of social phobia, impairment, and outcome of cognitive-behavioral treatment. *Behavior Therapy, 26*, 467–486.

Cacioppo, J. T., Glass, C. R., & Merluzzi, T. V. (1979). Self-statements and self-evaluations: A cognitive-response analysis of heterosocial anxiety. *Cognitive Therapy and Research, 3*, 249–262.

Chambless, D. L., Tran, G. Q., & Glass, C. R. (1997). Predictors of response to cognitive-behavioral group therapy for social phobia. *Journal of Anxiety Disorders, 11*, 221–240.

Chiauzzi, E. J., Heimberg, R. G., Becker, R. E., & Gansler, D. (1985). Personalized versus standard roleplays in the assessment of depressed patients' social skill. *Journal of Psychopathology and Behavioral Assessment, 7*, 121–133.

Clark, D. M. & Wells, A. (1995). A cognitive model of social phobia. In R. G. Heimberg, M. R. Liebowitz, D. A. Hope, & F. R. Schneier (Eds.), *Social phobia: Diagnosis, assessment, and treatment* (pp. 69–93). New York: Guilford Press.

Coles, M. E. & Heimberg, R. G. (2000). Patterns of anxious arousal during exposure to feared situations in individuals with social phobia. *Behaviour Research and Therapy, 38*, 405–424.

DiNardo, P. A., Brown, T. A., & Barlow, D. H. (1994). *Anxiety Disorders Interview Schedule for DSM-IV: Lifetime Version (ADIS-IV-L)*. Albany, NY: Graywind Publications.

Edelman, R. E. & Chambless, D. L. (1995). Adherence during sessions and homework in cognitive-behavioral group treatment of social phobia. *Behaviour Research and Therapy, 33*, 573–577.

Elting, D. T. & Hope, D. A. (1995). Cognitive assessment. In R. G. Heimberg, M. R. Liebowitz, D. A. Hope, & F. R. Schneier (Eds.), *Social phobia: Diagnosis, assessment, and treatment* (pp. 232–258). New York: Guilford Press.

Erwin, B. A., Heimberg, R. G., Juster, H., & Mindlin, M. (in press). Comorbid anxiety and mood disorders among persons with social anxiety disorder. *Behaviour Research and Therapy*.

Feske, U. & Chambless, D. L. (1995). Cognitive behavioral versus exposure only treatment for social phobia: A meta-analysis. *Behavior Therapy, 26*, 695–720.

Fink, C. M., Turner, S. M., & Beidel, D. C. (1996). Culturally relevant factors in the behavioral treatment of social phobia: A case study. *Journal of Anxiety Disorders, 10*, 201–209.

Hart, T. A., Jack, M. S., Turk, C. L., & Heimberg, R. G. (1999). Issues for the measurement of social anxiety disorder (social phobia). In H. G. M. Westenberg & J. A. den Boer (Eds.), *Social anxiety disorder: Recent trends and progress* (pp. 133–155). Amsterdam: Syn-Thesis Publishers.

Heimberg, R. G. & Becker, R. E. (in press). *Social fears and phobias: Nature and treatment*. New York: Guilford Press.

Heimberg, R. G., Becker, R. E., Goldfinger, K., & Vermilyea, J. A. (1985). Treatment of social phobia by exposure, cognitive restructuring, and homework assignments. *Journal of Nervous and Mental Disease, 173,* 236–245.

Heimberg, R. G., Dodge, C. S., Hope, D. A., Kennedy, C. R., Zollo, L. J., & Becker, R. E. (1990). Cognitive-behavioral group treatment of social phobia: Comparison to a credible placebo control. *Cognitive Therapy and Research, 14,* 1–23.

Heimberg, R. G., Horner, K. J., Juster, H. R., Safren, S. A., Brown, E. J., Schneier, F. R., & Liebowitz, M. R. (1999). Psychometric properties of the Liebowitz Social Anxiety Scale. *Psychological Medicine, 29,* 199–212.

Heimberg, R. G. & Juster, H. R. (1995). Cognitive-behavioral treatments: Literature review. In R. G. Heimberg, M. R. Liebowitz, D. A. Hope, & F. R. Schneier (Eds.), *Social phobia: Diagnosis, assessment, and treatment* (pp. 261–309). New York: Guilford Press.

Heimberg, R. G., Juster, H. R., Hope, D. A., & Mattia, J. I. (1995). Cognitive behavioral group treatment for social phobia: Description, case presentation and empirical support. In M. B. Stein (Ed.), *Social phobia: Clinical and research perspectives* (pp. 293–321). Washington, DC: American Psychiatric Press, Inc.

Heimberg, R. G., Liebowitz, M. R., Hope, D. A., Schneier, F. R., Holt, C. S., Welkowitz, L. A., Juster, H. R., Campeas, R., Bruch, M. A., Cloitre, M., Fallon, B., & Klein, D. F. (1998). Cognitive-behavioral group therapy versus phenelzine in social phobia: 12-week outcome *Archives of General Psychiatry, 55,* 1133–1141.

Heimberg, R. G., Salzman, D. G., Holt, C. S., & Blendell, K. A. (1993). Cognitive-behavioral group treatment for social phobia: Effectiveness at five-year follow-up. *Cognitive Therapy and Research, 17,* 325–339.

Holt, C. S., Heimberg, R. G., & Hope, D. A. (1990, November). *Success from the outset: Predictors of cognitive-behavioral therapy outcome among social phobics.* Paper presented at the annual meeting of the Association for Advancement of Behavior Therapy, San Francisco.

Hope, D. A., Herbert, J. D., & White, C. (1995). Diagnostic subtype, avoidant personality disorder, and efficacy of cognitive behavioral group therapy for social phobia. *Cognitive Therapy and Research, 19,* 285–303.

Juster, H. R. & Heimberg, R. G. (1998). Social phobia. In A. S. Bellack & M. Hersen (Eds.), *Comprehensive clinical psychology* (Vol. 6, pp. 475–498). Oxford: Pergamon.

Juster, H. R., Heimberg, R. G., & Engelberg, B. (1995). Self selection and sample selection in a treatment study of social phobia. *Behaviour Research and Therapy, 33,* 321–324.

Juster, H. R., Heimberg, R. G., & Mattia, J. I. (1993, November). *Judgment and prediction of response to cognitive-behavioral group therapy for social phobia.* Poster presented at the annual meeting of the Association for the Advancement of Behavior Therapy, Atlanta, GA.

Kazdin, A. E. (1998). *Research design in clinical psychology: 3rd edition.* Boston: Allyn & Bacon.

Kendall, P. C., Chu, B., Gifford, A., Hayes, C., & Nauta, M. (1998). Breathing life into a manual: Flexibility and creativity with manual-based treatments. *Cognitive and Behavioral Practice, 5,* 177–198.

Kendall, P. C., Marrs-Garcia, A., Nath, S. R., & Sheldrick, R. C. (1999). Normative comparisons for the evaluation of clinical significance. *Journal of Consulting and Clinical Psychology, 67,* 285–299.

Leung, A. & Heimberg, R. G. (1996). Homework compliance, perceptions of control, and outcome of cognitive-behavioral treatment of social phobia. *Behaviour Research and Therapy, 34,* 423–432.

Liebowitz, M. R. (1987). Social phobia. *Modern Problems of Pharmacopsychiatry, 22,* 141–173.

Liebowitz, M. R., Heimberg, R. G., Schneier, F. R., Hope, D. A., Davies, S., Holt, C. S., Goetz, D., Juster, H. R., Lin, S., Bruch, M. A., Marshall, R. D., & Klein, D. F. (1999).

Cognitive-behavioral group therapy versus phenelzine in social phobia: Long-term outcome. *Depression and Anxiety*, *10*, 89–98.

Lucas, R. A. & Telch, M. J. (1993, November). *Group versus individual treatment of social phobia*. Paper presented at the annual meeting of the Association for Advancement of Behavior Therapy, Atlanta, GA.

Mattick, R. P. & Clarke, J. C. (1998). Development and validation of measures of social phobia scrutiny fear and social interaction anxiety. *Behaviour Research and Therapy*, *36*, 455–470.

McNeil, D. W., Ries, B. J., & Turk, C. L. (1995). Behavioral assessment: Self-report, physiology, and overt behavior. In R. G. Heimberg, M. R. Liebowitz, D. A. Hope, & F. R. Schneier (Eds.), *Social phobia: Diagnosis, assessment, and treatment* (pp. 202–231). New York: Guilford Press.

Otto, M. W., Pollack, M. H., Gould, R. A., Wothington III, J. J., Heimberg, R. G., McArdle, E. T., & Rosenbaum, J. F. (2000). A comparison of the efficacy of clonazepam and cognitive-behavioral group therapy for the treatment of social phobia. *Journal of Anxiety Disorders*, *14*, 345–348.

Rapee, R. M. & Heimberg, R. G. (1997). A cognitive-behavioral model of anxiety in social phobia. *Behaviour Research and Therapy*, *35*, 741–756.

Safren, S. A., Heimberg, R. G., Brown, E. J., & Holle, C. (1997). Quality of life in social phobia. *Anxiety*, *4*, 126–133.

Safren, S. A., Heimberg, R. G., & Juster, H. R. (1997). Client expectancies and their relationship to pretreatment symptomatology and outcome of cognitive behavioral group treatment for social phobia. *Journal of Consulting and Clinical Psychology*, *65*, 694–698.

Sartory, G. (1983). Benzodiazepines and behavioral treatment of phobic anxiety. *Behavioural Psychotherapy*, *11*, 204–217.

Scholing, A. & Emmelkamp, P. M. G. (1999). Prediction of treatment outcome in social phobia: A cross validation. *Behaviour Research and Therapy*, *37*, 659–670.

Turk, C. L., Coles, M., & Heimberg, R. G. (in press). Psychological treatment of social phobia: A literature review. In D. J. Stein & E. Hollander (Eds.), *Textbook of anxiety disorders*. Washington, DC: American Psychiatric Press.

Turk, C. L., Lerner, J., Heimberg, R. G., & Rapee, R. M. (2001). An integrated cognitive-behavioral model of social anxiety. In S. G. Hofmann & P. M. DiBartolo (Eds.), *From social anxiety to social phobia: Multiple perspectives* (pp. 281–303). New York: Allyn & Bacon.

Turner, S. M., Beidel, D. C., Wolff, P. L., Spaulding, S., & Jacob, R. G. (1996) Clinical features affecting treatment outcome in social phobia. *Behaviour Research and Therapy*, *34*, 795–804.

Wells, A., Clark, D. M., Salkovskis, P., Ludgate, J., Hackmann, A., & Gelder, M. (1995). Social phobia: The role of in-situation safety behaviors in maintaining anxiety and negative beliefs. *Behavior Therapy*, *26*, 153–161.

Chapter 21

Psychopharmacological Treatments: An Overview

Sean D. Hood *and* **David J. Nutt**

MONOAMINE OXIDASE INHIBITORS
Introduction
Irreversible MAOIs
   Phenelzine
   Tranylcypromine
RIMAs
   Brofaromine
   Moclobemide
Conclusions
BENZODIAZEPINES
Introduction
   Alprazolam
   Clonazepam
   Bromazepam
Conclusions
SPECIFIC SEROTONIN REUPTAKE INHIBITORS
Introduction
   Fluvoxamine
   Sertraline
   Paroxetine
   Fluoxetine
   Citalopram
Conclusions
BETA BLOCKERS
OTHER
Tricyclic Antidepressants

International Handbook of Social Anxiety: Concepts, Research and Interventions Relating to the Self and Shyness. Edited by W. Ray Crozier and Lynn E. Alden.
© 2001 John Wiley & Sons Ltd.

Buspirone
Ondansetron
Bupropion
Clonidine
Nefazodone
Venlafaxine
Gabapentin
Pregabalin
Neuropeptides
Alcohol
CONCLUSIONS
REFERENCES

Social phobia (social anxiety disorder) has not customarily been viewed as a condition responsive to pharmacological treatment. In its generalized form it is often considered to be a type of extreme shyness or variant of avoidant personality disorder and thus enduring and resistant to change. The discrete subtype has been seen as akin to simple phobia and potentially responsive to behavioural therapies. The development of nosological systems, recognition of its high frequency and untreated morbidity, and the publication of promising case reports lead to the intensive examination of drug treatments of social phobia. This chapter critically evaluates the pharmacological regimens that have been used to treat social phobia.

MONOAMINE OXIDASE INHIBITORS

Introduction

Monoamine oxidase inhibitors (MAOIs) have been used in the treatment of depression since the 1960s, and by the mid 1980s researchers such as Liebowitz noted that atypical depressives with interpersonal hypersensitivity responded particularly well to phenelzine (Liebowitz et al., 1985). Open and control trials followed, which have confirmed the efficacy of MAOIs in the treatment of social phobia. Subsequently, reversible inhibitors of monoamine oxidase subtype A (RIMAs) that do not require a special diet have been developed, such as moclobemide (Fulton & Benfield, 1996) and brofaromine.

Irreversible MAOIs

Phenelzine

Following a promising open trial (Liebowitz et al., 1986), Liebowitz's group (Liebowitz et al., 1992) conducted a randomized controlled trial (RCT) comparing phenelzine and the beta-blocker atenolol in 74 completing DSM-III social phobics. Outcome measures included Clinical Global Improvement (CGI) and the Liebowitz Social Anxiety Scale (LSAS) as well as self-rating scales. Phenelzine was significantly more effective than both placebo and atenolol from week 8 onward according to observer ratings, although this did not reach significance on self-rating scales. Drug responders as measured by CGI (very much or much improved) were then entered into an 8-week maintenance phase, there was little clinical change in this period and numbers were small. A final discontinuation phase of 4 weeks lacked statistical power.

A second, rather complex double-blind study was undertaken in 65 DSM-III-R social phobic patients (Gelernter et al., 1991). All subjects received self-exposure therapy, and were randomized to phenelzine, alprazolam, cognitive and behavioural group therapy (CBGT) and placebo. Although those subjects treated with phenelzine or CBGT tended to maintain treatment gains for 2 months after therapy, there were no statistically significant differences between the four groups in the percentage of unequivocal responders or in other primary outcome measures.

There are a number of possible explanations for the lack of significance. First, the authors chose an exceptionally conservative response criterion—subjects were retrospectively classed as responding if they fell below the mean for the general population on the social phobia subscale of the Fear Questionnaire (FQ). Second, blind physician ratings were only completed for the medication groups, possibly confounding the results. Third, the pill placebo plus exposure therapy control group may not be a truly inactive comparison group. Fourth, the small sample size lacked adequate statistical power.

A double-blind, parallel group, flexible dose, placebo-controlled study of phenelzine and moclobemide was performed with 78 subjects with DSM-III-R social phobia (Versiani et al., 1992). Stringent exclusion criteria were used to minimize comorbidity, apart from avoidant personality disorder as measured on the Structured Clinical Interview for DSM-III-R (SCID) axis II. Phenelzine was superior to moclobemide on some measures by week 4, although the former suffered from more severe, frequent, and intractable side-effects. At the end of the 8-week treatment phase both phenelzine and moclobemide were significantly more effective than placebo on LSAS, CGI and the Social Avoidance and Distress Scale (SADS). The difference in onset between the active drugs may reflect the lower starting dose of moclobemide (200 mg/day until day 4, then 400 mg/day until end of week 4), as when this trial was performed the effective dose of moclobemide, generally 600 mg/day had not been established. Both drugs were still effective at week 16, although relapse was usual 8 weeks after stopping treatment. Avoidant personality disorder was common in all three groups at baseline (43/78 subjects), however by week 8 only 3 subjects on active drug (all moclobemide) still met the criteria, whereas 14 out of 16 in the placebo group continued to meet the SCID-II criteria.

An important trial addressed the comparative efficacy of drug and psychosocial treatments for social phobia (Heimberg et al., 1998). A four-cell design compared phenelzine, tablet placebo, CBGT and educational supportive group therapy (a credible psychosocial control (Heimberg et al., 1990)) in 133 patients from 2 sites over 12 weeks. One site was well known for pharmacological treatment (Liebowitz), the other for cognitive behavioural treatment (Heimberg) of anxiety disorders. A rationale for this design is discussed elsewhere (Liebowitz & Heimberg, 1996).

Phenelzine therapy and CBGT were superior to both placebo treatments across most measures after 12 weeks. Phenelzine response was more evident by 6 weeks, when 52% were classed as responders in contrast to 28% of patients undergoing CBGT. Overall, the magnitude of response effect was greater for phenelzine by 12 weeks, independent of site. There was a trend for reduction in the avoidant personality scores in *all* treatment groups. In the 6-month treatment-free follow up study (Liebowitz et al., 1999), 50% of subjects who had previously responded to phenelzine relapsed, compared with only 17% of CBGT subjects. Phenelzine non-relapsers continued to be more improved than CBGT non-relapsers throughout the study. Relapse on discontinuation was pronounced for patients with generalised social phobia. Thus, although phenelzine may have more immediate efficacy and potentially greater long-term effect, CBGT may confer greater protection against relapse.

Phenelzine has also been a successful treatment of selective mutism, a related condition, in reports of four children aged $5^1/_2$ to 7 years (Golwyn & Weinstock, 1990; Golwyn & Sevlie, 1999). One of these children had previously shown only minimal response to fluoxetine 16 mg/day.

Tranylcypromine

There have been no controlled trials of tranylcypromine in social phobia. An open trial of 32 patients with DSM-III social phobia looked at the effects of tranylcypromine over one year (Versiani, Mundim, Nardi, & Liebowitz, 1988). Improvement was measured according to discomfort in phobic situations and persistence in avoidant behaviour. At endpoint, 62% were markedly improved, 17% moderately so. Side-effects were common but only 4 patients ($12^1/_2$%) dropped out. This group also reported an 8-week open trial with 81 social phobic patients (Versiani, Nardi, & Mundim, 1989). Outcome measures included CGI, which improved significantly and LSAS, which improved substantially during this treatment. It is not clear if some patients participated in both trials.

RIMAs

Reversible inhibitors of monoamine oxidase subtype A (RIMAs) held much promise, potentially providing the efficacy of phenelzine without the restrictive dietary requirements needed to avoid tyramine hypertensive crises. Moclobemide is the prototype RIMA and brofaromine is an experimental drug that combines RIMA action with serotonin reuptake inhibition. Befloxatone, another RIMA, is a potential treatment of the future, having reached phase III trials in Europe and phase II in the USA for anxiety disorders.

Brofaromine

The first double-blind placebo-controlled trial of brofaromine in social phobia studied 21 females and 9 males over 12 weeks, with an additional 12-week continuation phase for responders (van Vliet, den Boer, & Westenberg, 1992). Brofaromine was more effective than placebo from week 8 onwards by LSAS and Hamilton Anxiety Rating Scale (HAM-A). Gains were maintained in the maintenance phase and the drug was well tolerated, although middle insomnia was reported in 73%.

The above report was the Dutch part of a two-country independent trial of brofaromine, the Swedish part ($n = 77$) was presented in 1995 (Fahlen, Nilsson, Borg, Humble, & Pauli, 1995). The primary efficacy results were similar in both studies, with 78% of brofaromine patients compared to 23% of placebo patients scoring much or very much improved on CGI at 12 weeks. Sleep disturbance was again a prominent side-effect, although this led to withdrawal from the study in only one subject. The brofaromine responders ($n = 22$) continued to improve during the 9-month single blind follow-up phase, whereas 6 of the 10 (60%) placebo responders relapsed.

The diagnosis of DSM-III-R avoidant personality disorder was examined in a subgroup of 57 patients compared with 58 controls (Fahlen, 1995). Although about 60% of both groups met diagnostic criteria before treatment, by 12 weeks this had significantly dropped to 20% in the brofaromine group in contrast to 44% in the control group.

A 12-week, 10-centre, placebo-controlled trial of brofaromine was undertaken in 102 outpatients with a primary DSM-III-R diagnosis of social phobia (Lott et al., 1997). Brofaromine-treated patients showed a significant although moderate reduction in LSAS, given that the mean endpoint score of 62.6 is still in the clinical range. Insomnia was noted in 7 of the 11 brofaromine patients who discontinued.

Moclobemide

A controlled trial comparing moclobemide and phenelzine with placebo (Versiani et al., 1992) is discussed above. Moclobemide showed similar but delayed efficacy in comparison to phenelzine, with better tolerability. Avoidant personality symptoms decreased with both active treatments.

A large ($n = 578$) multicentre, placebo-controlled, parallel group study set out to examine the efficacy and safety of moclobemide at doses of 300 and 600 mg/day over 12 weeks (Katschnig, Stein, & Buller, 1997). There were 445 completers, and attrition rates were similar among the three treatment groups. Moclobemide at 600 mg/day was significantly superior to placebo on primary and secondary efficacy measures. Moclobemide at 300 mg/day showed a trend towards efficacy on all outcome measures but achieved significance on about half of them. The magnitude of the response to moclobemide in this study was moderate; for instance, the LSAS total score dropped from 80.2 to 50.9 in the 600 mg/day group. Insomnia and headache were common adverse events, especially at the 600 mg/day dose. Post-hoc analyses showed that patients taking moclobemide 600 mg/day had a similar response regardless of the diagnosis of avoidant personality disorder, the duration of the illness, or the level of severity. Subjects with avoidant personality disorder responded less often to placebo.

In order to determine the efficacy and safety of different doses of moclobemide in the treatment of social phobia, a large ($n = 532$) 12-week fixed-dose study using 75, 150, 300 and 900 mg/day was undertaken in the United States (Noyes et al., 1997). At the end of the trial the response to moclobemide was indistinguishable from placebo. There was a trend towards greater efficacy of higher doses at week 8, which was not seen at week 12. The reason for this discrepant finding is not clear. It has been suggested that the study lacked sufficient statistical power once the dropout rate increased to over 30% between weeks 8 and 12 (Nutt & Montgomery, 1996); that using a categorical rather than dimensional primary outcome variable to measure responders would show a moderate effect (Blanco & Liebowitz, 1998); and the study authors commented on the high rate of placebo responders.

An open, naturalistic, 4–6-year study of moclobemide in DSM-III-R social phobia sought data on efficacy of long-term treatment and relapse, as well as identifying predictors of response (Versiani, Amrein, & Montgomery, 1997). All of the treatment phase completers (63.4%) responded, half improving by 8 weeks and two-thirds by 6 months. Absolute decreases in LSAS were greater in persons with generalized social phobia than circumscribed social phobia, however the relative reduction was similar (about 4% per month). Success was highest in patients without concomitant avoidant personality disorder and lowest in persons with concomitant alcohol abuse. During the no-treatment period 88% relapsed, there was no difference between gradual and abrupt withdrawal in terms of relapse. At post-study interview 63.2% were almost asymptomatic or better.

A subsequent single-centre, flexible dose study has confirmed the tolerability of moclobemide in social phobia but shown only limited clinical efficacy (Schneier et al., 1998). Seventy-seven non-placebo responders with DSM-III-R social phobia were randomized to moclobemide or placebo for 8 weeks of treatment, with CGI responders having the option to continue for an additional 8 weeks. Response rates at week 8 were modest, moclobemide was superior to placebo on only 2 of 10 primary outcome measures (LSAS subscales). Neither group showed significant changes on any continuous outcome measure from weeks 8 to 16. Despite a published criticism (Duffett, 1998), this article is notable for a balanced discussion of the differences in moclobemide efficacy between studies.

Conclusions

Irreversible MAOIs are the most thoroughly evaluated drug treatments for social phobia. Phenelzine's efficacy is unsurpassed to date in comparison with beta-blockers, benzodiazepines, RIMAs, and CBGT—at least in the short term (8–12 weeks). Long-term treatment may be needed, as relapse on discontinuation may be substantially higher than that seen with CBGT. The dietary restrictions required by this class, toxicity in overdose, and interaction with other drugs unfortunately limit the usefulness of these drugs in many settings.

The RIMAs brofaromine and moclobemide have failed to live up to their initial promise. Despite substantial efficacy in short-term trials, sleep disturbance was a persistent problem with brofaromine and it has been withdrawn for reasons unrelated to its effectiveness in social phobia. Moclobemide may not be a highly efficacious treatment for social phobia although the clinical evidence is contradictory. A long-term study was more promising; however, as this medication does not have a marketing indication in the United States its future seems bleak.

BENZODIAZEPINES

Introduction

Benzodiazepines augment the action of GABA, the major inhibitory neurotransmitter in the brain. Their rapid onset of action, favourable side-effect profile, and low risk for overdose fatality compared with the barbiturates has made them popular treatments. There is much concern, particularly in the lay press, of misuse and withdrawal problems with benzodiazepines although this is often exaggerated (Uhlenhuth, Balter, Ban, & Yang, 1995). Benzodiazepines are very effective, fast-acting anxiolytics, and the use of an anxiolytic to treat social phobia makes intuitive sense.

Alprazolam

An early case study described 4 patients who responded well to alprazolam (Lydiard, Laraia, Howell, & Ballenger, 1988). Another group examined 14 patients with DSM-III social phobia (Reich & Yates, 1988). Although 10 rated very much improved and four much improved by CGI, by one week after discontinuation all rating scales had returned to baseline. The comparative, randomized study of phenelzine, alprazolam, placebo and CBGT discussed above did not show any significant difference between treatments although there are methodological concerns (Gelernter et al., 1991). There was, however, a trend for alprazolam relapse after discontinuation and for superior efficacy of phenelzine.

Clonazepam

Clonazepam has been more extensively investigated as a treatment of social phobia. Versiani et al. treated 40 patients achieving significant improvement in LSAS (81.6 to 31.6) and CGI (5.0 to 2.1) after 8 weeks (Versiani et al., 1989). In a series of 5 patients, clonazepam was well tolerated and effective in all by CGI at week 8, with one patient remaining symptom free for 12 months after discontinuation (Ontiveros & Fontaine, 1990); 9 of 11 patients with generalized and specific social phobic variants responded to clonazepam in another report (Reiter, Pollack, Rosenbaum, & Cohen, 1990).

A placebo-controlled trial of clonazepam in 23 DSM-III-R social phobic subjects showed a significant benefit in the treatment group by week 8 on the LSAS, SAD, and FNE (Munjack, Baltazar, Bohn, Cabe, & Appleton, 1990). Initial sedation was usual in subjects receiving clonazepam, although it usually resolved spontaneously or with dose reduction.

Longer term data were reported in a 1- to 20-month open trial of clonazepam in 26 patients with social phobia (Davidson, Ford, Smith, & Potts, 1991). Only 15% failed to improve. Sedation, memory impairment and sexual dysfunction were the most frequently reported side-effects, however these were well tolerated with dose reduction. This study was followed by a randomized, controlled trial of clonazepam 0.5–3 mg/day in 75 patients with DSM-III-R social phobia (Davidson et al., 1993). Significant benefit was shown for clonazepam from as early as week 1 by CGI, with progressive and large magnitude reductions across most scales. At week 10 the response rate for clonazepam by CGI was 78.3% in contrast to 20.0% for placebo; LSAS dropped from 78.3 to 38.1. Side-effects were common but well tolerated, unsteadiness and dizziness were particularly frequent and persistent. A general maintenance of gains was found in 56 of these patients who were questioned two years after this trial (Sutherland, Tupler, Colket, & Davidson, 1996).

A controlled investigation of clonazepam discontinuation in 37 CGI responders to 6 months' open treatment compared continuation treatment with a gradual cessation (Connor et al., 1998). Slow discontinuation (0.25 mg/2 weeks) of clonazepam after 6 months' successful treatment of social phobia was well tolerated, although clinical response was modestly better in the group that took clonazepam for 11 months. Subjects randomised to continuation treatment underwent a rapid withdrawal over 3 weeks, which was not associated with significant change in clinical efficacy although post-hoc analysis showed more evidence of withdrawal symptoms than with the slow taper method. Despite this finding, no major withdrawal problems were seen with either regimen.

Bromazepam

There is one open trial of 10 patients who were treated for 8 weeks with bromazepam (Versiani et al., 1989). Significant improvement by CGI, LSAS, and Sheehan Disability Score (SDS) was seen, with LSAS decreasing from a mean of 69.3 to 15.8 by week 8. Somnolence was reported in all subjects.

Conclusions

Alprazolam and bromazepam have been investigated as treatments for social phobia; however the data for clonazepam are both more promising and complete.

Clonazepam is a well-tolerated treatment although side-effects such as unsteadiness and dizziness may be particularly persistent. Significant improvement after as little as one week is seen in some studies, and long-term gains of up to two years post-treatment have been shown. Major withdrawal problems are uncommon and may be minimized by a slow taper. Benzodiazepines may also be used on an as-required basis to aid confrontation of phobic situations. Long-term continuation treatment may be an effective strategy as there is a trend for loss of effect after stopping treatment. The potential for interaction with often comorbid alcoholism and the lack of antidepressant action should be carefully considered when choosing benzodiazepines.

SPECIFIC SEROTONIN REUPTAKE INHIBITORS

Introduction

Since the introduction of fluoxetine in the United States in 1988, specific serotonin reuptake inhibitor (SSRI) drugs have been widely prescribed as effective, well-tolerated and safe antidepressants. The nomenclature of these agents as "antidepressants" is increasingly outdated, as SSRIs have proven efficacy in a wide range of psychiatric conditions, including bulimia nervosa, obsessive-compulsive disorder (OCD), borderline personality disorder and dysthymia. Most recently, some SSRIs have obtained US Food and Drug Administration (FDA) approval for treatment of panic disorder (see Hood, Argyropoulos, & Nutt, 1999) and social phobia.

Fluvoxamine

In the first study of SSRI's in social phobia, fluvoxamine was shown to be superior to placebo in a small randomized-controlled trial (van Vliet, den Boer, & Westenberg, 1994; den Boer, van Vliet, & Westenberg, 1994). Thirty outpatients were treated with fluvoxamine, and at week 12 (measured by a 50% drop in LSAS anxiety subscale) fluvoxamine was significantly more effective (47%) than placebo (8%). Despite a gradual dose titration from 50 mg/day, anxiety was common (8/15) in the first few weeks of fluvoxamine treatment, as were nausea and sleep disturbance.

A subsequent multi-centre double-blind placebo-controlled trial investigated the effect of fluvoxamine (mean dose 202 mg/day) in 92 patients with DSM-IV social phobia (Stein et al., 1999a). Depressed patients were not explicitly excluded although most scored less than 10 on the HAM-D at onset. Fluvoxamine was superior to placebo on all social phobia rating scales from week 8 onwards, and at week 12 there were significantly more CGI responders in the fluvoxamine group (42.9%) than in the placebo group (22.7%). Side-effects, especially nausea and insomnia, led to discontinuation in one quarter on fluvoxamine, although sexual dysfunction in males was notably infrequent (11.4%).

Sertraline

The same group conducted an early open trial of sertraline in 22 patients with DSM-III-R social phobia over 8 weeks (Van Ameringen, Mancini, & Streiner, 1994). An 80% success rate by CGI was reported in 20 completers, although a high rate of comorbid depression may have inflated this figure. Subsequently, 11 social phobics without comorbid depression, substance abuse, or other anxiety disorder were enrolled in a 12-week open trial of sertraline (Munjack, Flowers, & Eagan, 1994). Five of seven completers responded significantly by week 6. A similar open trial ($n = 24$) that excluded comorbid social phobics found that 11 of 19 completers (58%) responded significantly in six weeks across primary and secondary outcome variables (Martins et al., 1994). Side-effects were common especially early in treatment, but no serious side-effects were seen. Finally, an open review of 11 patients treated with sertraline for at least 4 weeks showed that 63% were rated as much or very much improved by CGI (Czepowicz et al., 1995).

A double-blind, placebo-controlled, cross-over trial of sertraline in (DSM-III-R) social phobia was undertaken in 12 outpatients using flexible dosing (Katzelnick et al., 1995). Each arm lasted for 10 weeks with an intermediate 2-week taper. Half of the subjects receiving placebo were rated as either moderately or markedly improved in contrast to one patient (9%) taking placebo ($p < 0.03$). The mean reduction in LSAS during sertraline treatment was a substantial 22.0 in contrast to 5.5 in those taking placebo. Subjects taking sertraline first showed a non-significant tendency not to return to pretreatment levels while subsequently taking placebo.

Recently, 206 outpatients with generalized social phobia were randomized to 20 weeks' treatment of sertraline or placebo (Van Ameringen, Swinson, Walker, & Lane, 1999). Sertraline-treated patients showed significant improvement on all primary and secondary outcome measures, with 53% receiving sertraline versus 29% taking placebo responding by CGI.

A case series of seven children and adolescents with DSM-IV social phobia as a primary diagnosis included a 17-year-old girl who responded dramatically to sertraline 175 mg/day (Mancini, Van Ameringen, Oakman, & Farvolden, 1999).

Paroxetine

The earliest data were those of Ringold who reported two cases of patients with social phobia who appeared to show a preferential response to paroxetine 20 mg/day over fluoxetine and sertraline (Ringold, 1994).

Stein and colleagues undertook an 11-week open study of paroxetine (mean dose 47.9 mg/day) in 36 patients with DSM-IV generalized social phobia (Stein et al., 1996a). Although 79% also met criteria for avoidant personality disorder in this study, it is not stated if this diagnosis affected outcome. Substantial improvement was seen in 77% of 30 completers, rating much to very much improved on CGI. Mean LSAS score declined substantially from 75.1 to 37.2 at week 11. In a second phase of this study, 16 responders were randomized in a double-blind fashion to withdraw using paroxetine or placebo. There was a trend for placebo-substituted patients to fare worse, suggesting that early discontinuation of paroxetine results in high relapse rates.

The first published RCT of paroxetine in (generalized) DSM-IV social phobia assessed 187 patients across 14 North American centres over 12 weeks of treatment (Stein et al., 1998). The paroxetine group had significantly more dropouts than placebo (34% versus 23%, $p < 0.03$), largely due to dose-related adverse effects including delayed ejaculation (36% of males), headache, somnolence and nausea. Paroxetine was significantly superior to placebo on 5 of 6 efficacy measures, with a trend to improvement on the sixth. Mean LSAS scores declined from 78.0 to 47.5 in the active group, significantly favouring paroxetine. By CGI, 55.0% of persons taking paroxetine improved in contrast to 23.9% of those receiving placebo. A post-hoc analysis of this study to assess the relative efficacy of paroxetine in severe (LSAS > 82) or moderate (LSAS = 51–81) social phobia showed that while moderate social phobia responds well, severe social phobia responds even better (Montgomery, 1998). It has recently been reported that 90 completers from this study entered into a 24-week open phase with paroxetine followed by a one-week double blind randomization phase with paroxetine or placebo (Kumar, Pitts, & Carpenter, 1999). The number of CGI responders increased from 44% to 89% at the end of week 24 (63% taking note of 26 dropouts), with continuing improvement in LSAS. The re-randomization showed significant benefits for paroxetine by SADS and SDS work and family life items. Thus, 9 months of paroxetine treatment produced continuing symptomatic improvement.

A randomized, double-blind, placebo-controlled trial was undertaken in 290 patients with DSM-IV social phobia in South Africa (Stein et al., 1999b) and Europe over 12 weeks (Baldwin, Bobes, Stein, & Scharwachter, 1999). A one-week single-blind placebo phase excluded placebo responders and depressed patients (HAM-D ≥ 15). Thereafter subjects were randomized to flexible dosage paroxetine or placebo. In contrast to the previous trial, there was no overall difference in withdrawal rates between paroxetine (25%) and placebo (28%). Paroxetine-taking subjects had a significantly greater reduction in LSAS (87.6 to 58.2) and more CGI responders (65.7% versus 32.4%) than the placebo group from week 4 onwards. A statistically significant lessening of disability severity from moderate/marked to mild on SDS was also seen in the paroxetine group. Another RCT (Allgulander, 1999) examined the efficacy of paroxetine in 92 previously untreated patients with generalised social anxiety disorder over 12 weeks. The total LSAS score and response by CGI-I were primary outcome measures. The proportion of responders taking paroxetine (70.5%) was remarkably higher than the proportion taking placebo (8.3%). The reduction in LSAS in subjects taking paroxetine (70.4 to 37.0) was also significantly greater than in the placebo group. Paroxetine separated from placebo by week 4. All of the secondary outcome measures, including patient-rated visual analogue scores, significantly supported paroxetine by the end of the study. The comparatively high paroxetine and low placebo response rates are notable.

A large ($n = 384$) unpublished multicentre, dose-finding RCT (Liebowitz,

Stein, Tancer et al., 1999) showed that paroxetine was equally and significantly effective at doses of 20, 40 and 60 mg/day; as measured by CGI responders and decrease in LSAS.

The case series of children and adolescents with social phobia mentioned earlier included four girls (aged 11,16,17,18) and one boy (aged 7) who responded markedly to paroxetine treatment over 4–9 weeks (Mancini et al., 1999). Although doses ranged from 5 to 80 mg/day, only one subject reported any side-effect (somnolence).

Fluoxetine

The first report of the successful use of fluoxetine in social phobia described two patients with significant clinical improvement at doses of 20–40 mg/day (Sternbach, 1990). An open study of 12 patients with social phobia treated with fluoxetine lead to improvement lasting 6 weeks to 5 months in 67% by CGI (Schneier et al., 1992). Fluoxetine was also prescribed in an open study of 14 patients with generalized social phobia for up to 40 weeks (Black, Uhde, & Tancer, 1992). Seventy per cent taking fluoxetine alone responded. An additional case report of two co-incidental responses to fluoxetine in patients with primary depression and bulimia has been published (Berk, 1995). There is also a single case report of a response to fluoxetine 60 mg/day where paroxetine 40 mg/day and sertraline 200 mg/day had been ineffective (Taylor, 1997).

A 12-week open clinical trial of 16 patients with DSM-III-R social phobia examined the response to fluoxetine 20–60 mg/day (Van Ameringen, Mancini, & Streiner, 1993). An 11-point CGI rating scale was used rather than the standard 7-point scale, making comparisons difficult. Using this scale, 10 of 13 (76.9%) were responders—most had responded by seven weeks of treatment. Another open trial of 32 subjects treated with fluoxetine for 16 weeks showed 90% (26/29) of completers improved by CGI (Koponen, Lepola, & Juhani, 1995). An Italian study of 20 DSM-III-R social phobics with minimal comorbidity showed that 13 of 19 patients responded by CGI over 12 weeks of fluoxetine treatment (Perugi et al., 1994). Response was irrespective of a diagnosis of avoidant personality disorder, however, significantly more women (7/7) responded than men (6/13).

A number of studies involving children and adolescents with social anxiety deserve mention. An open study of 21 youths with treatment-resistant over-anxious disorders, social phobia, or separation anxiety disorder showed that 81% improved significantly by CGI at a mean fluoxetine dose of 25.7 mg/day (Birmaher et al., 1994). Subsequently, an open 9-week clinical trial of fluoxetine was undertaken in 16 children, 12 of whom had social phobia and were aged 10–17 (Fairbanks et al., 1997). Seven of 10 non-placebo-responding patients with social phobia were rated as much improved and one as very much improved after fluoxetine, and 50% of children with social anxiety no longer met DSM-III-R criteria. No patient worsened during fluoxetine treatment and the drug was well tolerated. A schedule of 5 mg/day initially, increasing by 5 mg daily each week, was used, although a dose of at least 20 mg/day was needed before any improvement was seen.

There are at least two reports of adolescent girls with fragile X syndrome and selective mutism in which a substantial improvement in severe shyness was noted with fluoxetine treatment (Hagerman et al., 1999; Linden et al., 1999). A 12-week double-blind controlled study of 15 placebo non-responding children with selective mutism who also met criteria for social phobia showed significant improvement in social anxiety by observer rating scales.

In an interesting study (Pallanti, Quercioli, Rossi, & Pazzagli, 1999), 12 schizophrenic patients with clozapine-induced social anxiety symptoms were subsequently treated with fluoxetine at doses of 20–50 mg/day. In 8 of these cases there was a significant reduction in LSAS total scores. The mean LSAS total score dropped from 83 to 60 with fluoxetine treatment.

Citalopram

There have been no RCT of citalopram in social phobia to date. A case report of 3 patients with social phobia first suggested that citalopram is an effective treatment (Lepola, Koponen, & Leinonen, 1994). These patients were resistant to other treatments and appear to have had a sustained improvement for at least 12 months. Citalopram was generally well tolerated (one patient developed retarded ejaculation), although benzodiazepines were used initially to minimize jitteriness.

An open, naturalistic trial of citalopram 40 mg/day was performed in 22 patients who had not responded to another SSRI or moclobemide (Bouwer & Stein, 1998). Comorbidity was high, with only 7 patients not having major depression (10/22) or panic disorder (5/22) at time of recruitment. Nevertheless, 86% of the subjects were classed as responders (CGI $\leq$ 2) by week 12. All patients completed the study, although side-effects such as insomnia, weight gain and decreased libido/delayed ejaculation were common.

Conclusions

The SSRIs have potential advantages over MAOIs and benzodiazepines in terms of dietary restrictions and dependence, respectively. They are efficacious in frequently comorbid conditions such as major depression or panic disorder, and are well tolerated in the medium to long-term treatment of these ailments.

In general, the effective SSRI dose in social phobia is higher than that used to treat major depression. Interestingly, the dose is often less than that needed in panic disorder (e.g., paroxetine 40 mg/day; Ballenger et al., 1998b). This may reflect differences in the neurobiology of these conditions, which to date has not been discerned. The evidence of the efficacy of SSRIs in social phobia is compromised by the lack of any head-to-head comparisons with established treatments such as MAOIs, benzodiazepines or CBGT. Additionally, many studies have examined generalized social phobics only, so the effectiveness of SSRIs in non-generalized social phobia is far less clear.

Within-group differences are difficult to discern, and a recent meta-analysis (van der Linden, Stein, & van Balkom, 2000) could find no statistical difference. Nevertheless from the clinical trials some tentative recommendations can be made. The most substantial evidence exists for paroxetine, even in severe social phobia. Sexual side-effects are seen in up to a third of men and may be more frequent with paroxetine and less frequent with fluvoxamine. Fluoxetine is the most studied SSRI in socially phobic children and adolescents and has shown good efficacy and tolerability in this group (see also Murphy, Bengston, Tan, Carbonell, & Levin, 2000). A premorbid diagnosis of avoidant personality disorder did not affect the outcome in one study, although the effect of SSRIs on avoidant personality disorder itself in social phobics has not been reported.

BETA BLOCKERS

Beta-adrenergic receptor antagonists, also known as beta-blockers, emerged in the late 1950s. The observation that these drugs are effective at blocking peripheral autonomic symptoms such as tachycardia, tremor, sweating, blushing, and dry mouth led to their use as anxiolytics. Beta-blockers are commonly used in the treatment of performance anxiety and studies generally show them to be effective, although it is impossible to know how many of these subjects actually met criteria for social phobia.

The earliest controlled study of a beta-blocker in social phobia examined 16 subjects treated with propanolol, all of whom also had social skills training (Fallon, Lloyd, & Harpin, 1981). There was no significant difference between groups. Atenolol was subsequently investigated because its poor ability to cross the blood–brain barrier provided a test of the hypothesis of a peripheral mechanism of social phobia, and it was potentially less likely to cause depression, sleep disturbance, or bronchoconstriction. Ten patients with DSM-III social phobia were treated in an open, 6-week trial (Gorman et al., 1985). Five patients showed a marked reduction of social phobic and avoidant symptoms and four a moderate reduction, with no distinction between generalized and non-generalized subtypes. This promising study was not confirmed in a comparative, controlled trial ($n = 74$) that confirmed the efficacy of phenelzine but showed that atenolol was no more effective than placebo (Liebowitz et al., 1992). Another placebo-controlled trial compared atenolol with flooding in 72 DSM-III-R social phobics (Turner, Beidel, & Jacob, 1994). Flooding was significantly more effective than atenolol and the latter was no more effective than placebo.

Overall it seems that beta-blockers are not effective in social phobia. A limited role in performance anxiety is indicated; however, one must exclude patients with asthma and many patients with chronic heart failure (Richie, 1995).

OTHER

Tricyclic Antidepressants

Observations that patients with atypical depression responded better to MAOIs than to tricyclic antidepressants (TCADs) led to tricyclics being largely ignored in recent studies of social phobia. Six of the tranylcypromine responders in Versiani et al.'s study had previously failed clomipramine trials of more than three months on doses of 175 to 250 mg/day.

A double-blind, placebo-controlled study of imipramine in 41 DSM-III-R social phobia subjects has been reported (Emmanuel et al., 1997). Response was determined by CGI improvement and a 50% drop in the Duke Social Phobia Scale. Only 21 patients completed 8 weeks of treatment, endpoint analysis showed no significant efficacy of imipramine. This lack of efficacy was confirmed by an 8-week study in 15 patients (Simpson et al., 1998). Six subjects (40%) dropped out due to adverse effects, and the overall response rate in completers was 22% by CGI with a mean reduction in LSAS of 18%.

Buspirone

Buspirone is a novel drug that is effective in the treatment of generalized anxiety disorder. Unlike the barbiturates and benzodiazepines it lacks hypnotic, anti-convulsant, and muscle-relaxant properties. Buspirone is a full agonist at soma-todendritic 5HT1A autoreceptors, a partial postsynaptic 5HT1A agonist, it binds modestly to dopamine receptors but not to the benzodiazepine–GABA binding site. A major metabolite has α2-andrenoceptor antagonistic properties.

A double-blind, placebo-controlled study of 34 musicians with performance anxiety and DSM-III-R social phobia compared buspirone with cognitive therapy over 6 weeks (Clark & Agras, 1991). Cognitive therapy was superior to buspirone and there was no significant benefit from combination treatment.

Subsequent open trials suggested that buspirone may have modest efficacy in social phobia. In one study, 17 non-placebo responders completed 2–12 weeks of open treatment (Schneier et al., 1993). At week 12, 47% had improved by CGI, with 67% of those tolerating a dose of at least 45 mg/day improving. Non-specific improvement was noted in an 8-week open trial of buspirone in 17 patients (Munjack, Bruns, & Baltazar, 1991). There is also a case report of a 16-year-old boy with social phobia and schizotypal personality traits responding well to a course of buspirone (Zwier & Rao, 1994).

The open trial findings were not supported in a 12-week randomized trial of 30 non-depressed DSM-IV social phobic patients (van Vliet et al., 1997). There were no statistically significant differences between buspirone 15–30 mg/day and placebo as measured by the Social Phobia Scale (SPS). Subscale analysis showed significant buspirone treatment effects for somatization and anxiety, which suggests a differential efficacy for generalized anxiety. Although it is possible that higher treatment doses may have improved the efficacy, only 1 of 15 patients treated with buspirone were rated as improved.

Buspirone may be effective in augmenting SSRI effect in social phobia. Van-Ameringen and colleagues found that 7 of 10 partial SSRI responding patients achieved a significant benefit from 8 weeks of buspirone augmentation (Van Ameringen, Mancini, & Wilson, 1996).

Buspirone thus does not have proven efficacy in social phobia, although the augmentation results are promising.

Ondansetron

Ondansetron, a 5HT3 antagonist, is a powerful antiemetic. Animal models suggested that low doses had anxiolytic properties. A 10-week, multi-centre, double-blind placebo-controlled trial of 275 social phobic patients showed that this drug was well tolerated at a dose of 0.25 mg twice daily and led to a small but significant reduction in the primary outcome measure (Bell & DeVeaugh-Geiss, 1999). Notably, this study was never published at full length in a peer-reviewed journal. Ondansetron is not being further developed for use in social phobia, although another 5HT3 antagonist (zatosetron) is currently in phase III trials for anxiety disorders in the US.

Bupropion

Bupropion is an antidepressant with a diverse mechanism of action, including norepinephrine and dopamine reuptake inhibition. It appears to be free of significant serotonergic activity and has minimal potential for sexual side-effects. There have been concerns about seizures with this agent, although it now seems that the risk is similar to that of the TCADs. There is a single published case report of a 29-year-old woman with a 6-month history of social blushing and avoidance who remitted with bupropion 300 mg/day (Emmanuel, Lydiard, & Ballenger, 1991).

Clonidine

Clonidine, an α2-andrenoceptor agonist, is a powerful antihypertensive agent that is used in the treatment of alcohol and opiate withdrawal, tic disorder and other psychiatric conditions. It is potentially useful in treating blushing in social phobia (Goldstein, 1987), however to date only anecdotal reports of efficacy exist, and this efficacy may be transient (Newcorn et al., 1998).

Nefazodone

Nefazodone is a novel antidepressant drug that has a complex mechanism of action including the blockade and down regulation of 5HT2A receptors and 5HT-reuptake inhibition. Unlike the SSRI's it exhibits an ascending dose–response curve, which may lead to greater effectiveness at higher doses. Nefazodone is well tolerated, can improve sleep and anxiety symptoms associated with depression, and has a low incidence of sexual side-effects.

Five patients with DSM-IV generalized social phobia were treated with nefazodone on an open basis over 12 weeks (Worthington et al., 1998). Although two patients discontinued after two months, there was a significant improvement in CGI, LSAS, and brief social phobia scale (BSPS). Another open trial of 23 patients with DSM-IV generalized social phobia examined the efficacy of nefazodone by self-report and clinical scales over 12 weeks (Van Ameringen et al., 1999). Sixteen (69.6%) responded by CGI, with significant improvement on measures of social anxiety, social phobic avoidance, depression, and social functioning by 9 weeks on average. One patient with alcohol dependence showed a substantial decrease in alcohol consumption. No patient withdrew due to side-effects, although two withdrew due to lack of efficacy. One girl, aged 15, was reported to respond substantially in a case series (Mancini et al., 1999), and although she reported visual accommodation problems at a dose of 400 mg/day this resolved when the dose was reduced to 350 mg/day.

Nefazodone thus holds promise as an effective treatment for social phobia, and controlled trials are indicated.

Venlafaxine

Venlafaxine is an antidepressant that inhibits (in decreasing orders of magnitude) serotonin, noradrenaline, and dopamine reuptake. In common with Nefazodone it exhibits a dose–response curve.

A case series of eight patients with SSRI-resistant social phobia showed substantial improvement with a course of venlafaxine (Kelsey, 1995). Recently, an open study evaluated the response to venlafaxine in 12 social phobic patients with particular reference to comorbid avoidant personality disorder (Altamura et al., 1999). Not only did venlafaxine significantly improve LSAS scores, but it also reduced avoidant personality symptomatology. Venlafaxine was tolerated moderately well, with nausea, headache and anxiety being the most frequent side-effects.

Gabapentin

Gabapentin is an anticonvulsant with a poorly understood mechanism of action. Preclinical work suggested an anxiolytic effect, and clinical studies of patients with epilepsy produced an improvement in mood and well-being. A recent study of gabapentin in panic disorder (Pande et al., 1999a) was disappointing, with a post-hoc evaluation required to show efficacy in a subgroup. A randomized controlled study of 69 patients with non-depressed DSM-IV social phobia over 14 weeks showed significant efficacy of gabapentin across all outcome measures (Pande et al., 1999b). The mean change in LSAS was from 87.4 to 60.3, withdrawal rates were similar for gabapentin and placebo groups. Although there is no dose–response data for gabapentin in social phobia, 64% of LSAS responders and 62% of CGI responders took 3,600 mg/day. Further trials of this drug are warranted.

Pregabalin

Pregabalin, a derivative of the neurotransmitter GABA and a relative of gabapentin, has been effective in preclinical and preliminary clinical studies (Feltner, Pande, Pollack et al., 2000) in the treatment of social phobia. A large, multi-centre, placebo- and comparator-controlled parallel-group, phase II trial is currently underway.

Neuropeptides

Neuropeptides have only recently begun to be investigated as anxiolytics, and results to date are mixed (Argyropoulos & Nutt, 2000). Cholecystokinin (CCK) is widely distributed in the brain, administration of its synthetic analogue penta-gastrin produces anxiety in social phobia and other conditions (van Vliet et al., 1997). Although CCK antagonists are therefore potentially anxiolytic, trials to date in panic disorder (Cowley et al., 1996) and generalized anxiety disorder (Adams et al., 1995) have been disappointing. Studies in social phobia are lacking. Neuropeptide Y (NPY) has anxiolytic effects, although it has been shown that under resting conditions plasma NPY levels do not differ between controls, social phobic and panic-disordered patients (Stein et al., 1996b). Although an adreno-corticotrophic hormone (ACTH) antagonist was found to be ineffective in social phobia (den Boer, van Vliet, & Westenberg, 1995), corticotrophin-releasing factor (CRF) antagonists are currently undergoing evaluation. This is a very active field of research, which has the potential to deliver a new class of social phobia treatments.

Alcohol

There is a complex relationship between alcohol and social phobia (Lepine & Pelissolo, 1998). Alcoholism is common in patients with social phobia, rates of 14–40% have been reported. Conversely, most studies report a prevalence of 10–20% of social phobia in persons with alcohol problems. These rates may be even higher for those with avoidant personality disorder (Stravynski, Lamontagne, & Lavallee, 1986).

Although alcohol is commonly thought of as a self-treatment for anxiety, few groups have attempted to determine objectively whether alcohol reduces social anxiety. A pilot study used a public-speaking challenge to examine response to alcohol in 18 socially phobic patients (Naftolowitz et al., 1994). The placebo drink contained a small amount of alcohol on the surface so subjects would smell and taste alcohol without actually receiving a significant amount. Alcohol consumption did not significantly decrease public-speaking anxiety in these patients. A recent study has extended this work, by examining a larger group of 40 subjects, administering a continuous public-speaking task, and differentiating the belief of receiving alcohol from actually receiving it (Himle et al., 1999). There was no

Table 21.1 Trials of irreversible MAOIs in social phobia

Type	Structure	Reference	N	Treatments	Outcomes
Open	2 wk. washout 1 wk. single blind 8 wk. treatment 8 wk. maintenance 4 wk. withdrawal	Liebowitz et al. (1986)	11	Phenelzine 45–90 mg/day	All responded, 7/11 markedly
RCT		Liebowitz et al. (1988, 1990, 1992)	74	1. Phenelzine 45–90 mg/day 2. Atenolol 50–100 mg/day 3. Placebo	Phenelzine 64% > atenolol 30% = placebo 23%* by week 8
RCT	12 wk. treatment (all subjects also received exposure therapy)	Gelernter et al. (1991)	65	1. Phenelzine 30–90 mg/day 2. Alprazolam 2.1–6.3 mg/day 3. CBGT 4. Placebo	Phenelzine 69%, alprazolam 38%, CBGT 24% and placebo 20% (trend) at wk. 12 Trend: Phenelzine & CBGT gains maintained 2 months after treatment
RCT	8 wk. treatment 8 wk. maintenance 3 wk. placebo crossover	Versiani et al. (1992)	78	1. Moclobemide 400–600 mg/day 2. Phenelzine 60–90 mg/day 3. Placebo	Phenelzine > placebo by week 4 Moclobemide > placebo by week 8 Avoidant PD Dx resolved with active treatments Both drugs still effective at 16 weeks, but relapse usual 8 weeks after stopping treatment
RCT (2 site)	12 wk. treatment (6 month maintenance and 6 month drug-free follow-up phase)	Heimberg et al. (1998) Liebowitz et al. (1999)	133	1. Phenelzine 60–90 mg/day 2. CBGT 3. Tablet Placebo 4. Educational Supportive Group Therapy (psychological placebo)	Phenelzine = CBGT > placebo by week 12 Phenelzine quicker onset and larger magnitude of effect Avoidant PD Sx reduced (trend) with all 4 treatments At 6 month drug-free followup, 50% of phenelzine-responders >17% of CBGT-responders relapsed. Phenelzine non-relapsers continued to exhibit a larger magnitude effect.
Case Report	(4 children aged 5½–7 years with selective mutism)	Golwyn et al. (1999, 1990)	4	Phenelzine 30–60 mg/day	Successful response, well tolerated 1 previous non-responder to fluoxetine 16 mg/day × 10 months
Open	1 year open	Versiani et al. (1988)	32	Tranylcypromine 40–60 mg/day	62% marked, 17% moderate, 21% no improvement over 1 year
Open	8 wk. open	Versiani et al. (1989)	81	Tranylcypromine 40–60 mg/day	Significant reduction in CGI-severity Trend reduction in LSAS

*Comparators indicate significance at p = 0.05.

Table 21.2 Trials of reversible MAOIs in social phobia

Type	Structure	Reference	N	Treatments	Outcomes
RCT	12 wk. treatment 12 wk. maintenance	van Vliet et al. (1992) Slaap et al. (1996)	30	1. Brofaromine 150 mg/day 2. Placebo	Brofaromine > placebo by week 8 Continued benefit in maintenance period ↑ blood pressure & heart rate predicted non-response
RCT	12 wk. treatment 12 wk. maintenance 9 month optional single blind follow-up	Fahlen et al. (1995) Fahlen (1995)	77 (57)	1. Brofaromine 150 mg/day 2. Placebo	78% Brofaromine > 23% placebo response by CGI at 12 weeks Brofaromine responders maintained long-term gains, 60% of placebo responders relapsed Reduction (60% → 20%) of DSM-III-R Avoidant Personality Disorder qualifiers in subgroup
RCT	1 wk. placebo washout 10 wk. treatment	Lott et al. (1997)	102	1. Brofaromine 50–150 mg/day 2. Placebo	Significant reduction in LSAS (mean 62.6) in brofaromine treated subjects
RCT	8 wk. treatment 8 wk. maintenance 3 wk. placebo crossover	Versiani et al. (1992)	78	1. Moclobemide 400–600 mg/day 2. Phenelzine 60–90 mg/day 3. Placebo	Phenelzine > placebo by week 4 Moclobemide > placebo by week 8 Avoidant PD Dx resolved with active treatments Both drugs still effective at 16 weeks, but relapse usual 8 weeks after stopping treatment
Open	12 wk. treatment	Bisserbe et al. (1994)	35	Moclobemide 300–600 mg/day	94% CGI improvement (18 completers) at wk. 12 LSAS improvement
RCT	1 wk. placebo run-in 12 wk. treatment	Katschnig et al. (1997)	578	1. Moclobemide 300 mg/day 2. Moclobemide 600 mg/day 3. Placebo	Moclobemide 600 mg/day well tolerated and superior to placebo on all measures Small magnitude effect Response to moclobemide 600 mg/day independent of avoidant personality disorder, duration or severity of illness
RCT	1 wk. placebo run-in 12 wk. treatment (fixed-dose) treatment	Noyes et al. (1997)	532	1. Moclobemide 75, 150, 300, 600, or 900 mg (fixed dose) 2. Placebo	Moclobemide (35%) = Placebo (33%) by CGI at 12 weeks (failed trial) Trend towards greater efficacy of higher doses at week 8
Open	(2 month washout) 2 years treatment >1 month no-treatment period up to 2 years re-treatment for recurrence > 1 month no-treatment period post-study follow-up 4–6 years after entry	Versiani et al. (1996, 1997)	101	Moclobemide 600–750 mg/day (mean = 730 mg/day)	All treatment completers (63%) responded, improving substantially on all scales Alcohol abuse highly predicted non-response, response better in non-avoidant personality disordered patients 88% relapsed during no-treatment period 63.2% almost asymptomatic at follow-up
RCT	1 wk. placebo run-in 8 wk. treatment 8 wk. maintenance (in CGI responders)	Schneier et al. (1998)	77	1. Moclobemide 200–800 mg/day (flexible) 2. Placebo	Moclobemide (17.5%) = placebo (13.5%) by CGI at 8 weeks (not significant) Small magnitude effect Moclobemide superior to placebo on 2 of 10 primary outcome measures

Table 21.3 Trials of benzodiazepines in social phobia

Type	Structure	Reference	N	Treatments	Outcomes
Case Report		Lydiard et al. (1988)	4	Alprazolam 3–8 mg/day	Marked reduction in symptomatology
Open	8 wk. treatment	Reich & Yates (1988)	14	Alprazolam 1–7 mg/day (78% received ≤ 3 mg/day)	All improved by CGI All relapsed by 1 week after cessation
RCT	12 wk. treatment (all subjects also received exposure therapy)	Gelernter et al. (1991)	65	1. Phenelzine 30–90 mg/day 2. Alprazolam 2.1–6.3 mg/day 3. CBGT 4. Placebo	Phenelzine 69%, alprazolam 38%, CBGT 24% and placebo 20% (trend) by week 12 Trend: Phenelzine & CBGT gains maintained 2 months after treatment
Open	8 wk. treatment	Versiani et al. (1989)	40	Clonazepam 1–6 mg/day	Significant improvement in CGI (5.0 → 2.1) and LSAS (81.6 → 31.6)
Open	8 wk. treatment	Ontiveros & Fontaine (1990)	5	Clonazepam 1–6 mg/day	All improved by CGI at week 8
Case Series		Reiter et al. (1990)	11	Clonazepam 0.75–3 mg/day	9/11 improved
RCT	8 wk. treatment	Munjack et al. (1990)	23	1. Clonazepam 1–6 mg/day 2. Placebo	Initial Sedation common (7/10) Clonazepam > placebo at week 8 by LSAS, SAD, FNE
Open	1–20 months' treatment	Davidson et al. (1991)	26	Clonazepam 0.5–5 mg/day	11/26 very much improved, 11/26 much improved
RCT	2 wk. washout 10 wk. treatment	Davidson et al. (1993)	75	1. Clonazepam 0.5–3 mg/day 2. Placebo	Clonazepam > placebo from week 1 by CGI, week 2 by LSAS and FNE, week 4 by SDS (work and social subscales) Clonazepam (78.3%) > placebo (20.0%) by CGI at week 10 LSAS reduction 78.3 → 38.1 at week 10
RCT	6 month open 5 month randomisation phase	Connor et al. (1998)	37	1. 5 months continuation treatment then rapid taper (3 wk.) 2. slow taper (0.25 mg/2 wk.) + placebo	Relapse: Placebo (21%) > continuation (0%), just significant Withdrawal Effects: Rapid > slow taper, although no major problems with either regimen
Open	8 wk. treatment	Versiani et al. (1989)	10	Bromazepam (mean dose 26.4 mg/day)	CGI improvement 5.0 → 1.3 LSAS reduction 69.3 → 15.8 Somnolence in 100%

Table 21.4 Trials of SSRIs in social phobia

Type	Structure	N	Treatments	Reference	Outcomes
RCT	10 wk. Drug A 2 week taper 10 wk. Drug B (crossover)	12	1. Sertraline 50–200mg/day 2. Placebo	Katzelnick et al. (1995)	Marked or Moderate improvement with sertraline (50%) > placebo (9%) LSAS reduction with sertraline (22.0) > placebo (5.5)
Open	8 wk. open	22	Sertraline 100–200 mg/day	Van Ameringen et al. (1994)	80% success by CGI in 16/20 completers High comorbid depression in sample?
Open	12 wk. open	11	Sertraline 50–200 mg/day	Munjack et al. (1994)	5/7 (non-comorbid) completers responded by week 6, having sertraline 100 mg/day for at least 2 weeks
Open	6 wk. open	24	Sertraline (unspecified dose)	Martins et al. (1994)	11/19 completers responded at week 6
Case Report	4 wk. open	11	Sertraline (at least 100 mg/day unless responding to lower dose)	Czepowicz et al. (1995)	7/11 much or very much improved by CGI
RCT	1 wk. placebo run-in 20 wk. treatment	206	Sertraline 50–200 mg/day	Van Ameringen et al. (1999)	Significant benefit of sertraline across all outcome measures Paroxetine (53%) > placebo (29%) by CGI Paroxetine (34.8%) > placebo (16.7%) by reduction in Duke Brief Social Phobia Scale (BSPS)
Case Report	(17 y.o. girl)	1	Sertraline 175 mg/day	Mancini et al. (1999)	Substantial response after 4 weeks
Case Report		3	Citalopram 20 mg/day	Lepola et al. (1994)	Well tolerated, benefits maintained for > 12 months
Open	12 wk. open	22	Citalopram 40 mg/day	Bower & Stein (1998)	86% responded by CGI All tolerated citalopram 40 mg/day, despite persistent side-effects Highly comorbid sample
Case Report		2	Paroxetine 20 mg/day	Ringold (1994)	Preferential response over fluoxetine and sertraline
Open	11 wk. open 12 wk. randomized withdrawal phase	36	Paroxetine 20–50 mg/day	Stein et al. (1996b)	77% responded by CGI Mean paroxetine LSAS improvement: 75.1 to 37.2 Withdrawal: 1/8 paroxetine relapsed, 5/8 placebo (trend)
Open	12 wk. open	18	Paroxetine 10–50 mg/day	Mancini & Van Ameringen (1996)	83.3% responded by CGI with improvement in all outcome measures
RCT	1 wk. placebo run-in 12 wk. treatment	187	1. Paroxetine 20–50mg/day 2. Placebo	Stein et al. (1998) Montgomery (1998)	Paroxetine > placebo on 5/6 outcome variables, with trend on the 6th. Paroxetine 55.0% > placebo 23.9% on CGI Mean LSAS declined significantly from 78.0 to 47.5 in paroxetine group More drop-outs in paroxetine group (34% vs. 23%). Delayed ejaculation noted in 36% males, although only 2/16 men with this symptom discontinued Response by severity (LSAS, CGI) Severe social phobia > moderate social phobia
Open	Stein et al. (1998) (above) completers 24 wk. open treatment 1 wk. re-randomization	90	Paroxetine 20–50 mg/day (Placebo used in re-randomization phase)	Kumar et al. (1999)	90 RCT completers entered open phase CGI responders at wk 24: 57/64 (89%) vs. 44/90 (44%) at week 1 Re-randomization phase: Paroxetine > placebo by SADS, SDS-work, SDS-family
RCT	1 wk. placebo run-in 12 wk. treatment 3 wk. withdrawal	290	1. Paroxetine 2. Placebo	Baldwin et al. (1999) Stein et al. (1999a)	Paroxetine (65.7%) > Placebo (32.4%) by CGI Paroxetine (87.6 to 58.2) > Placebo (86.1 to 70.5) by LSAS Equivalent drop-out rates

Design	Details	Reference	N	Drug/dose	Results
Case Report	(Children aged 7, 11, 116, 17, 18)	Mancini et al. (1999)	5	Paroxetine 5–80 mg/day	Dramatic improvement over 4–9 weeks. Only one patient reported any side-effect (somnolence)
RCT	1 wk. drug-free run-in 12 wk. treatment	Allgulander 1999	92	1. Paroxetine 20–50 mg/day 2. Placebo	Paroxetine (70.5%) > Placebo (8.3%) by CGI. Paroxetine (70.4 to 37.0) > Placebo (78.5 to 69.9) by LSAS. Primary outcomes significant by week 4, all measures significantly favoured Paroxetine by end of study.
RCT	12 wk. treatment	Liebowitz et al. (1999) (data on file)	384	1. Paroxetine 20 mg/day 2. Paroxetine 40 mg/day 3. Paroxetine 60 mg/day 4. Placebo	Paroxetine > Placebo by CGI (45%, 47%, 43% versus 28%). Paroxetine > Placebo by LSAS (−31, −24, −25 versus −15)
RCT	12 wk. treatment	van Vliet et al. (1994) den Boer et al. (1994)	30	1. Fluvoxamine 150 mg/day 2. Placebo	Week 12: Fluvoxamine (47%) > placebo (8%) by 50% improvement in LSAS-Anxiety. Initial anxiety, nausea, sleep disturbance common despite staring dose 50 mg/day
RCT	12 week treatment	Stein et al. (1999b)	92	1. Fluvoxamine 50–300 mg/day 2. Placebo	Fluvoxamine > placebo in all measures from week 8 onward. Week 12: Fluvoxamine (42.9%) > placebo (22.7%) by CGI. 25% subjects taking fluvoxamine withdrew due to side effects (esp. nausea, insomnia). Male sexual dysfunction low (11.4%)
Open	1 wk. single-blind placebo run-in 6 wk. single-blind treatment	DeVane et al. (1995, 1999)	10	Fluvoxamine 50–150 mg/day	Fluvoxamine > placebo by BSPS and HAM-A at end of treatment phase
Case Report		Sternbach (1990)	2	Fluoxetine 20–40 mg/day	Marked improvement noted in two treatment
Open		Schneier et al. (1992)	12	Fluoxetine 5–40 mg/day	67% improved by CGI
Open		Black et al. (1992)	14	Fluoxetine 10–100 mg/day	63% non-comorbid responders
Case Report		Berk (1995)	2	Fluoxetine 20 mg/day	Coincidental excellent response
Case Report		Taylor (1997)	1	Fluoxetine 60 mg/day	Preferential response over paroxetine and sertraline
Open	12 wk. treatment	Van Ameringen et al. (1993)	16	Fluoxetine 20–60 mg/day	76.9% (10/13) completers responded, mean time to response was 7 weeks
Open	16 wk. treatment	Koponen et al. (1995)	32	Fluoxetine	90% (26/29) completers improved by CGI
Open	12 wk. treatment	Perugi et al. (1994)	20	Fluoxetine 20–80 mg/day	68% (13/19) responded by CGI. All 7 women responded > 6/13 men. No impact of premorbid diagnosis of avoidant personality disorder on response
Open	(Adolescents with mixed anxiety disorders)	Birmaher et al. (1994)	21	Fluoxetine (mean dose 25.7 mg/day)	81% improved by CGI
Open	9 wk. treatment (children aged 9–17, 12 had social phobia unresponsive to psychotherapy)	Fairbanks et al. (1997)	12	Fluoxetine 5–80 mg	70% (7/10) improved by CGI. Significant ↓ in LSAS (modified) rated by child and mother after treatment. 50% (5/10) no longer met DSM-III-R social phobia criteria after treatment. Well tolerated, no disinhibition, doses >20 mg/day were effective
Open	12 wk. Treatment (schizophrenic patients with clozapine-induced social anxiety symptoms)	Pallanti et al. (1999)	12	Fluoxetine 30–50 mg/day	↓ in LSAS from 83 to 60. Significant improvement in 8 of 12.

Table 21.5 Trials of beta-blockers in social phobia

Type	Reference	Structure	N	Treatments	Outcomes
RCT	Fallon et al. (1981)	Treatment with both groups receiving social skills training	16	1. Propranolol 160–320 mg/day 2. Placebo	Non-significant difference between groups Both groups improved
Open	Gorman et al. (1985)	6 wk. open	10	Atenolol 50–100 mg/day	5/10 marked improvement 4/10 moderate improvement Generalized = Non-generalized outcome
RCT	Liebowitz et al. (1988, 1990, 1992)	2 wk. washout 1 wk. single blind 8 wk. treatment 8 wk. maintenance 4 wk. withdrawal	74	1. Phenelzine 45–90 mg/day 2. Atenolol 50–100 mg/day 3. Placebo	Week 8 (treatment) response Phenelzine (64%) > atenolol (30%) = placebo (23%)
RCT	Turner et al. (1994)	12 wk. treatment	72	1. Atenolol 25–100 mg/day 2. Flooding 3. Placebo	Flooding (89%) > atenolol (47%) = placebo (43%) by composite improvement index

Table 21.6 Trials of other drugs in social phobia

Type	Reference	Structure	N	Treatments	Outcomes
RCT	Emmanuel et al. (1997)	8 wk. treatment	41	1. Imipramine 50–300 mg/day 2. Placebo	21/41 (51%) completed No significant efficacy by CGI, Duke
Open	Simpson et al. (1998)	8 wk. open	15	Imipramine 250 mg/day	40% drop-out due to side-effects Mean ↓ LSAS 18% 22% improved by CGI
RCT	Clark & Agras (1991)	6 week treatment (musicians)	34	1. Buspirone 15–60 mg/day (mean dose 32 mg/day) 2. Placebo 3. 5 session CBGT with buspirone 4. 5 session CBGT with placebo	CBGT(100%) > buspirone (57%) No benefit in combination therapy

		N	Treatment	Author (year)	Results
Open	8 wk. open	17	Buspirone 35–60mg/day	Munjack et al. (1991)	82% (9/11) completers improved
Open	12 wk. open	21	Buspirone 15–60mg/day	Schneier et al. (1993)	47% improved by CGI at week 12 in 17 completers / 67% improved by CGI at week 12 of those treated with at least 45 mg/day
Case Report	(16 y.o. boy with social phobia and schizotypal traits)	1	Buspirone	Zweir & Rao (1994)	Substantial clinical improvement
RCT	12 wk. treatment	30	1. Buspirone 15–30mg/day 2. placebo	van Vliet et al. (1997)	Buspirone (1/15) = placebo (1/15) by SPS / Buspirone well tolerated
Case Report	(29 y.o. woman with social blushing and avoidance)	1	Bupropion 300mg/day	Emmanuel et al. (1991)	Remission of symptoms
Case Report	(25 y.o. man with social blushing)	1	Clonidine 0.1 mg (bd)	Goldstein (1987)	Social phobic with blushing responded to clonidine but not propranolol, phenelzine or alprazolam
Open	12 wk. treatment	5	Nefazodone 100–600mg/day (mean 370mg/day)	Worthington et al. (1998)	Significant improvement by LSAS, CGI, BSPS
Open	12 wk. treatment	23	Nefazodone 100–600mg/day	Van Ameringen et al. (1999)	21/23 completers / 16/23 (69.6%) responded by CGI / Significant improvement on most outcome measures
Case Report	(15 y.o. girl)	1	Nefazodone 350mg/day	Mancini et al. (1999)	Substantial improvement / Visual disturbance at dose of 400mg/day
Case Report		9	Venlafaxine	Kelsey (1995)	8 showed marked improvement / 8 had previous failed trials of SSRIs
Open	15 wk. treatment	12	Venlafaxine 112.5–187.5 mg/day	Altamura et al. (1999)	Significant improvement by LSAS / Significant reduction in avoidant symptoms
RCT	1 wk. placebo run-in 14 wk. treatment	69	1. Gabapentin 600–3,600 mg/day 2. Placebo	Pande et al. (1999)	Gabapentin > placebo by LSAS, CGI, SPIN / Gabapentin responders had 900–3,600 mg/day, 64% LSAS responders and 62% CGI responders were taking 3,600 mg/day
RCT (pilot)	Public speaking challenge	18	1. Alcohol 1.25 mg/kg 80 proof vodka 2. Placebo	Naftolowitz et al. (1994)	No significant decrease in speaking anxiety
RCT	Public speaking challenge 2 speeches	40	1. Alcohol 0.5 ml/kg 2. Placebo (All subjects received placebo before the first speech)	Himle et al. (1999)	No significant decrease in speaking anxiety / Belief in consuming an alcoholic drink increased anticipatory anxiety but buffered mid-performance anxiety

Table 21.7   Critical overview of psychopharmacological treatments in social phobia

Drug class	Drug	Suggested daily dose	Evidence*	Notes
MAOI	Phenelzine	60–90 mg	+++++	Tyramine free diet required
	Tranylcypromine	40–60 mg	++	Tyramine free diet required
RIMA	Brofaromine	150 mg	+++	Sleep disturbance common Withdrawn
	Moclobemide	600–800 mg	+++	May not be highly efficacious No license in USA
Benzodiazepine	Alprazolam	1–8 mg	+	Relapse after discontinuation common
	Clonazepam	1–6 mg	+++	Slow discontinuation well-tolerated, although relapse possible
	Bromazepam	26 mg	+	
SSRI	Sertraline	>100 mg	+++	
	Citalopram	20–40 mg	+	
	Paroxetine	20–50 mg	++++	Especially efficacious in severe social phobia Male sexual dysfunction uncommon
	Fluvoxamine	50–300 mg	++	Well tolerated and efficacious in open trials of children.
	Fluoxetine	20–80 mg	+	Start at 5 mg/day and proceed to at least 20 mg/day in children
Beta-Blocker	Propranolol	160–320 mg	–	Role limited to performance anxiety
	Atenolol	50–100 mg	– –	
Tricyclic	Imipramine		– –	Not effective
Other	Buspirone	30–45 mg	– –	
	Ondansetron	0.5 mg (bd)	?+	May have a role augmenting SSRI response
	Bupropion	300 mg	?	Small magnitude effect
	Clonidine	0.2 mg (bd)	?	Efficacy may be short-lived
	Nefazodone	100–600 mg	+	Promising open studies
	Venlafaxine	112.5–187.5 mg	+	Little data
	Gabapentin	900–3,600 mg	++	Promising single RCT
	Pregabalin			RCT currently underway
Neuropeptides			?	Significant ongoing research
Alcohol			– –	Not effective

* Strength of evidence key:

+++++   Very strong Randomized Controlled Trial (RCT) evidence for efficacy, including multiple substantiated RCT's with leading drugs in other classes.

++++   Strong RCT evidence for efficacy, no conflicting RCTs.

+++   Positive RCT evidence in multiple trials.

++   At least one sound RCT or large open trial supporting efficacy.

+   No RCT evidence, but open trials or case reports support efficacy.

?   Unclear efficacy.

–   Open trials or case reports suggest drug not efficacious.

– –   RCT show no significant effect of drug.

significant difference in anxiety between groups, however the belief that one received an alcoholic drink appeared to increase anticipatory anxiety but buffer mid-performance anxiety. Alcohol, thus, is not an effective treatment for social phobia.

CONCLUSIONS

Many drugs have been investigated as treatments of social phobia (social anxiety disorder). An overview of research to date is presented in Tables 21.1 to 21.7. The first conclusion to draw from these data is that some drugs are ineffective treatments of social phobia. Tricyclic antidepressants and alcohol are not effective. Beta-blockers may have a limited role in performance anxiety but their prescription for social phobia cannot now be justified. Buspirone may be a useful adjunct to SSRI treatment but is not in itself efficacious.

In contrast, other drug treatments are clearly very effective. The most robust data exist for the MAOI phenelzine, which is unsurpassed in comparison with beta-blockers, benzodiazepines, RIMAs and CBGT, although dietary restrictions hinder its usefulness. SSRIs are also proven treatments in social phobia, the best data exist for paroxetine, followed by sertraline and then fluvoxamine. A large magnitude effect, excellent tolerability in children and adults, and established efficacy in treating frequently comorbid conditions such as depression and panic disorder make it is understandable that SSRIs are recommended as first-line treatments of social phobia (Ballenger et al., 1998a). Although the RIMAs moclobemide and brofaromine are able treatments of social anxiety, they may have a smaller magnitude of effect than drugs such as phenelzine, and brofaromine is not now available. It is too early to determine the utility of drugs such as nefazodone and venlafaxine despite early studies suggesting effectiveness. Perhaps the most exciting future treatments include novel drugs such as pregabalin and gabapentin, and the developing class of neuropeptide agents. This is an area of intense current interest and we are likely to have some early results in the next few years.

Comparative efficacy of pharmacological treatments of social anxiety is, with the notable exception of phenelzine, largely lacking. There is an urgent need for comparative trials of SSRIs with effective drugs in other classes. Within-class randomized trials may also be of benefit, although taking the SSRIs as an example it seems likely that response is a class effect and that reports of differential SSRI response are probably idiosyncratic. Subtle differences in other aspects of drug therapy such as frequency of particular side-effects are emerging, although few generalizations can be made and drug choice on a case-by-case basis seems to be prudent.

A logical progression from comparative drug trials is comparison with effective non-drug treatments such as CBGT. Again, phenelzine leads in this area with promising results although relapse upon discontinuation is notable. Data for other drugs are lacking, although the child and adolescent SSRI trials offer us a clue here, as pharmacotherapy is not usually considered a first-line treatment in social anxiety in this group and thus the impressive gains reported were seen in non-responders to the conventional psychotherapy treatments. It is thus surprising that there has not been more interest in child and adolescent drug treatments in social phobia; controlled trials of SSRIs are especially indicated. A recent, extensive meta-analytic comparison of psychological and pharmacological therapies in social phobia (Fedoroff & Taylor, 2001) demonstrated that pharmacotherapies are the most effective treatments, at least in the short term

There are some caveats in interpreting the research data. Long-term data are patchy, and there is evidence of relapse after cessation. Recent randomized drug trials have concentrated on patients with the generalized social phobia subtype. The most obvious reason for this trend is that generalized social phobics score higher on outcome measures such as LSAS than those with the specific subtype, and thus it is easier to show a large magnitude treatment effect. As a consequence, the data for the efficacy of drug treatments in non-generalized social phobia are much less robust. Open and naturalistic reports, typically include a more diverse cohort in which response to drugs such as MAOIs and SSRIs in specific social phobia appears to be as effective as that seen in generalized social phobia. Depressed and panic-disordered patients are excluded from some social phobia trials, as it has been important to distinguish antidepressant and antipanic effect from a social phobia therapeutic effect. On the other hand, comorbidity is frequent in clinical practice and thus aids generalization of the research findings. There is good evidence, however, from both the more heterogeneous open trials and the controlled trials that did not exclude comorbid subjects that drug therapies work equally well in each group.

The impact of these medications on avoidant personality disorder symptoms is worth repeating. A comorbid diagnosis of avoidant personality disorder did not affect response to treatment with the three drugs in which the relationship was analysed: phenelzine, moclobemide, and fluoxetine. More striking is the consistent finding that successful treatment with drugs including phenelzine, tranylcypromine, moclobemide, brofaromine, atenolol, and venlafaxine lead to significant reduction in avoidant symptoms, often to the degree that the subject no longer met diagnostic criteria for avoidant personality disorder. This challenges the notion that these conditions (at least as defined by current instruments) are immutable, although the efficacy of these drugs in subjects with avoidant personality disorder but not social phobia has not been studied.

In summary, there are effective and well-tolerated drug treatments of social phobia. Drug therapy should be considered on a case-by-case basis as a first-line treatment of this condition.

REFERENCES

Adams, J. B., Pyke, R. E., Costa, J., Cutler, N. R., Schweizer, E., Wilcox, C. S., Wisselink, P. G., Greiner, M., Pierce, M. W., & Pande, A. C. (1995). A double-blind, placebo-controlled study of a CCK-B receptor antagonist, CI-988, in patients with generalized anxiety disorder. *Journal of Clinical Psychopharmacology, 15,* 428–434.

Allgulander, C. (1999). Paroxetine in social anxiety disorder: A randomized placebo-controlled study. *Acta Psychiatrica Scandinavica, 100,* 193–198.

Altamura, A. C., Pioli, R., Vitto, M., & Mannu, P. (1999). Venlafaxine in social phobia: a study in selective serotonin reuptake inhibitor non-responders. *International Clinical Psychopharmacology, 14,* 239–245.

Argyropoulos, S. & Nutt, D. (2000). Peptide receptors as targets for anxiolytic drugs. In M. Briley & D. Nutt (Eds.), *Anxiolytics: Milestones in drug therapy.* Basel: Verlag.

Baldwin, C. M., Bobes, J., Stein, D. J., & Scharwachter, I. (1999). Paroxetine in social phobia/social anxiety disorder. *British Journal of Psychiatry, 175,* 120–126.

Ballenger, J. C., Davidson, J. R., Lecrubier, Y., Nutt, D. J., Bobes, J., Beidel, D. C., Ono, Y., & Westenberg, H. G. (1998a). Consensus statement on social anxiety disorder from the International Consensus Group on Depression and Anxiety. *Journal of Clinical Psychiatry, 59* (Supplement 17), 54–60.

Ballenger, J. C., Wheadon, D. E., Steiner, M., Bushnell, W., & Gergel, I. P. (1998b). Double-blind, fixed-dose, placebo-controlled study of paroxetine in the treatment of panic disorder. *American Journal of Psychiatry, 155,* 36–42.

Bell, J. & DeVeaugh-Geiss, J. (1999). *Multicenter trial of a 5-HT$_3$ antagonist, ondansetron in social phobia.* Presented at the 39th Annual Meeting of the American College of Neuropsychopharmacology. San Juan, Puerto Rico.

Berk, M. (1995). Fluoxetine and social phobia [letter]. *Journal of Clinical Psychiatry, 56,* 36–37.

Birmaher, B., Waterman, G. S., Ryan, N., Cully, M., Balach, L., Ingram, J., & Brodsky, M. (1994). Fluoxetine for childhood anxiety disorders. *Journal of the American Academy of Child and Adolescent Psychiatry, 33,* 993–999.

Bisserbe, J. C. & Lepine, J. P. (1994). Moclobemide in social phobia: A pilot open study. GRP Group. Groupe de Recherche en Psychopharmacologie. *Clinical Neuropharmacology, 17* (Supplement 1), 88–94.

Black, B., Uhde, T. W., & Tancer, M. E. (1992). Fluoxetine for the treatment of social phobia [letter]. *Journal of Clinical Psychopharmacology, 12,* 293–295.

Blanco, C. & Liebowitz, M. R. (1998). Dimensional versus categorical response to moclobemide in social phobia [letter]. *Journal of Clinical Psychopharmacology, 18,* 344–346.

Bouwer, C. & Stein, D. J. (1998). Use of the selective serotonin reuptake inhibitor citalopram in the treatment of generalized social phobia. *Journal of Affective Disorders, 49,* 79–82.

Clark, D. B. & Agras, W. S. (1991). The assessment and treatment of performance anxiety in musicians [see comments]. *American Journal of Psychiatry, 148,* 598–605.

Connor, K. M., Davidson, J. R. T., Potts, N. L. S., Tupler, L. A., Miner, C. M., Malik, M. L., Book, S. W., Colket, J. T., & Ferrell, F. (1998). Discontinuation of clonazepam in the treatment of social phobia. *Journal of Clinical Psychopharmacology, 18,* 373–378.

Cowley, D. S., Adams, J. B., Pyke, R. E., Cook, J., Zaccharias, P., Wingerson, D., & Roy, B. P. (1996). Effect of CI-988, a cholecystokinin-B receptor antagonist, on lactate-induced panic. *Biological Psychiatry, 40,* 550–552.

Czepowicz, V. D., Johnson, M. R., Lydiard, R. B., Emmanuel, N. P., Ware, M. R., Mintzer, O. B., Walsh, M. D., & Ballenger, J. C. (1995). Sertraline in social phobia [letter]. *Journal of Clinical Psychopharmacology, 15,* 372–373.

Davidson, J. R., Ford, S. M., Smith, R. D., & Potts, N. L. (1991). Long-term treatment of social phobia with clonazepam. *Journal of Clinical Psychiatry, 52* (Supplement), 16–20.

Davidson, J. R. T., Potts, N., Richichi, E., Krishnan, R., Ford, S. M., Smith, R., & Wilson, W. H. (1993). Treatment of social phobia with clonazepam and placebo. *Journal of Clinical Psychopharmacology, 13* (6), 423–428.

den Boer, J. A., van Vliet, I. M., & Westenberg, H. G. M. (1994). Recent advances in the psychopharmacology of social phobia. *Progress in Neuro Psychopharmacology & Biological Psychiatry, 18* (4), 625–645.

den Boer, J. A., van Vliet, I. M., & Westenberg, H. G. M. (1995). Recent developments in the psychopharmacology of social phobia. *European Archives of Psychiatry and Clinical Neuroscience, 244* (6), 309–316.

DeVane, C. L., Ware, M. R., & Emmanuel, N. P. (1995). *The evaluation of the safety, efficacy, and physiological effects of fluvoxamine in social phobia.* Presented at the 24th Annual Meeting of the American College of Neuropsychopharmacology. San Juan, Puerto Rico.

DeVane, C. L., Ware, M. R., Emmanuel, N. P., Brawman-Mintzer, O., Morton, W. A., Villarreal, G., & Lydiard, R. B. (1999) Evaluation of the efficacy, safety and physiological effects of fluvoxamine in social phobia. *International Clinical Psychopharmacology, 14,* 345–351.

Duffett, R. (1998). Moclobemide in social phobia [letter]. *British Journal of Psychiatry, 172,* 451–452.

Emmanuel, N., Johnson, M., Villareal, G., Cosby, C., Czepowicz, V., Mintzer, O. B., Crawford, M., Book, S., Morton, A., Rubey, R., Amundsen, C., Roberts, J. M., Kapp, B., Jones, C., & Lydiard, R. B. (1997*). Imipramine in the treatment of social phobia: A double-blind study.* Presented at the 36th Annual Meeting of the American College of Neuropsychopharmacology. Kohala Coast, Hawaii.

Emmanuel, N. P., Lydiard, R. B., & Ballenger, J. C. (1991). Treatment of social phobia with bupropion [letter]. *Journal of Clinical Psychopharmacology, 11,* 276–277.

Fahlen, T. (1995). Personality traits in social phobia, II: Changes during drug treatment. *Journal of Clinical Psychiatry, 56,* 569–573.

Fahlen, T., Nilsson, H. L., Borg, K., Humble, M., & Pauli, U. (1995). Social phobia: The clinical efficacy and tolerability of the monoamine oxidase-A and serotonin uptake inhibitor brofaromine. A double-blind placebo-controlled study. *Acta Psychiatrica Scandinavica, 92,* 351–358.

Fairbanks, J. M., Pine, D. S., Tancer, N. K., Dummit, E. S., Kentgen, L. M., Martin, J., Asche, B. K., & Klein, R. G. (1997). Open fluoxetine treatment of mixed anxiety disorders in children and adolescents. *Journal of Child and Adolescent Psychopharmacology, 7,* 17–29.

Fallon, B., Lloyd, G. G., & Harpin, R. E. (1981). The treatment of social phobia: Real-life rehearsal with non-professional therapists. *Journal of Nervous and Mental Disorders, 169,* 180–184.

Fedoroff, I. C. & Taylor, S. (2001). Psychological and pharmacological treatments of social phobia: A meta-analysis. *Journal of Clinical Psychopharmacology, 21,* 311–324.

Feltner, D. E., Pande, A. C., Pollack, M. H. et al. (2000). A placebo-controlled study of pregabalin treatment of social phobia. *Program and Abstracts of the 20th National Conference of the Anxiety Disorders Association of America. NR-59.*

Fulton, B. & Benfield, P. (1996). Moclobemide. An update of its pharmacological properties and therapeutic use [published erratum appears in *Drugs,* 1996, Dec., *52* (6), 869], *Drugs, 52,* 450–474.

Gelernter, C. S., Uhde, T. W., Cimbolic, P., Arnkoff, D. B., Vittone, B. J., Tancer, M. E., & Bartko, J. J. (1991). Cognitive-behavioral and pharmacological treatments of social phobia. A controlled study. *Archives of General Psychiatry, 48,* 938–945.

Goldstein, S. (1987). Treatment of social phobia with clonidine. *Biological Psychiatry, 22,* 369–372.

Golwyn, D. H. & Sevlie, C. P. (1999). Phenelzine treatment of selective mutism in four prepubertal children. *Journal of Child and Adolescent Psychopharmacology, 9,* 109–113.

Golwyn, D. H. & Weinstock, R. C. (1990). Phenelzine treatment of elective mutism: A case report. *Journal of Clinical Psychiatry, 51,* 384–385.

Gorman, J. M., Liebowitz, M. R., Fyer, A. J., Campeas, R., & Klein, D. F. (1985).

Treatment of social phobia with atenolol. *Journal of Clinical Psychopharmacology*, *5*, 298–301.

Hagerman, R. J., Hills, J., Scharfenaker, S., & Lewis, H. (1999). Fragile X syndrome and selective mutism. *American Journal of Medical Genetics*, *83*, 313–317.

Heimberg, R. G., Dodge, C. S., Hope, D. A., Kennedy, C. R., Zollo, I., & Becker, R. E. (1990). Cognitive behavioral group treatment of social phobia: Comparison with a credible placebo control. *Cognitive Therapy and Research*, *14*, 1–23.

Heimberg, R. G., Liebowitz, M. R., Hope, D. A., Schneier, F. R., Holt, C. S., Welkowitz, L. A., Juster, H. R., Campeas, R., Bruch, M. A., Cloitre, M., Fallon, B., & Klein, D. F. (1998). Cognitive behavioral group therapy vs phenelzine therapy for social phobia—12-week outcome. *Archives of General Psychiatry*, *55*, 1133–1141.

Himle, J. A., Abelson, J. L., Haghightgou, H., Hill, E. M., Nesse, R. M., & Curtis, G. C. (1999). Effect of alcohol on social phobic anxiety. *American Journal of Psychiatry*, *15*, 1237–1243.

Hood, S. D., Argyropoulos, S., & Nutt, D. J. (1999). The efficacy of paxil (paroxetine) for panic disorder. *The Current Practice of Medicine*, *2*, 159–162.

Katschnig, H., Stein, M. B., & Buller, R. (1997). The International Multicenter Clinical Trial Group on Moclobemide in Social Phobia. Moclobemide in social phobia. A double-blind, placebo-controlled clinical study. *European Archives of Psychiatry and Clinical Neuroscience*, *247*, 71–80.

Katzelnick, D. J., Kobak, K. A., Greist, J. H., Jefferson, J. W., Mantle, J. M., & Serlin, R. C. (1995). Sertraline for social phobia: A double-blind, placebo-controlled crossover study. *American Journal of Psychiatry*, *152*, 1368–1371.

Kelsey, J. E. (1995). Venlafaxine in social phobia. *Psychopharmacology Bulletin*, *31*, 767–771.

Koponen, H., Lepola, U., & Juhani, L. E. V. (1995). *Fluoxetine in social phobia: A pilot study*. Presented at the 15th National Conference of the Anxiety Disorders Association of America. Pittsburgh, PA.

Kumar, R., Pitts, C. D., & Carpenter, D. (1999). Response to paroxetine is maintained during continued treatment in patients with social anxiety disorder. *European Neuropsychopharmacology*, *9*, S312–S313.

Lepine, J. P. & Pelissolo, A. (1998). Social phobia and alcoholism: A complex relationship. *Journal of Affective Disorders*, *50* (Supplement 1), S23–S28.

Lepola, U., Koponen, H., & Leinonen, E. (1994). Citalopram in the treatment of social phobia: A report of three cases. *Pharmacopsychiatry*, *27*, 186–188.

Liebowitz, M. R., Fyer, A. J., Gorman, J. M., Campeas, R., & Levin, A. (1986). Phenelzine in social phobia. *Journal of Clinical Psychopharmacology*, *6*, 93–98.

Liebowitz, M. R., Gorman, J., Fyer, A., Campeas, R., Levin, A., Davies, S., & Klein, D. F. (1985). Psychopharmacological treatment of social phobia. *Psychopharmacology Bulletin*, *21*, 610–614.

Liebowitz, M. R., Gorman, J. M., Fyer, A. J., Campeas, R., Levin, A. P., Sandberg, D., Hollander, E., Papp, L., & Goetz, D. (1988). Pharmacotherapy of social phobia: An interim report of a placebo-controlled comparison of phenelzine and atenolol. *Journal of Clinical Psychology*, *49*, 252–257.

Liebowitz, M. R. & Heimberg, R. G. (1996). Issues in the design of trials for the evaluation of psychopharmacological treatments for social phobia. *International Clinical Psychopharmacology*, *11* (Supplement 3), 49–53.

Liebowitz, M. R., Schneier, F. R., Campeas, R., Gorman, J., Fyer, A., Hollander, E., Hatterer, J., & Papp, L. (1990). Phenelzine and atenolol in social phobia. *Psychopharmacology Bulletin*, *26*, 123–125.

Liebowitz, M. R., Schneier, F. R., Campeas, R., Hollander, E., Hatterer, J., Fyer, A., Gorman, J., Papp, L., Davies, S., & Gully, R. (1992). Phenelzine vs atenolol in social phobia. A placebo-controlled comparison. *Archives of General Psychiatry*, *49*, 290–300.

Linden, M. G., Tassone, F., Gane, L. W., Hills, J. L., Hagerman, R. J., & Taylor, A. K. (1999).

Compound heterozygous female with fragile X syndrome. *American Journal of Medical Genetics, 83*, 318–321.

Liebowitz, M. R., Heimberg, R. G., Schneier, F. R., Hope, D. A., Davies, S., Holt, C. S., Goetz, D., Juster, H. R., Lin, S. H., Bruch, M. A., Marshall, R. D., & Klein, D. F. (1999). Cognitive-behavioral group therapy versus phenelzine in social phobia: Long-term outcome. *Depression & Anxiety, 10*, 89–98.

Liebowitz, M., Stein, M. B., Tancer, M. et al. (1999). A randomised double-blind, fixed-dose comparison of paroxetine and placebo in the treatment of generalised social anxiety disorder. *Study 454 (data on file).*

Lott, M., Greist, J. H., Jefferson, J. W., Kobak, K. A., Katzelnick, D. J., Katz, R. J., & Schaettle, S. C. (1997). Brofaromine for social phobia: A multicenter, placebo-controlled, double-blind study. *Journal of Clinical Psychopharmacology, 17*, 255–260.

Lydiard, R. B., Laraia, M. T., Howell, E. F., & Ballenger, J. C. (1988). Alprazolam in the treatment of social phobia. *Journal of Clinical Psychiatry, 49*, 17–19.

Mancini, C. & Van Ameringen, M. (1996). Paroxetine in social phobia. *Journal of Clinical Psychiatry, 57*, 519–522.

Mancini, C., Van Ameringen, M., Oakman, J. M., & Farvolden, P. (1999). Serotonergic agents in the treatment of social phobia in children and adolescents: A case series. *Depression and Anxiety, 10*, 33–39.

Martins, E. A., Pigott, T. A., Bernstein, S. E., Doyle, B. B., Sunderland, B., Smolka, V. M., & Dubbert, B. (1994). Sertraline in the treatment of patients with social phobia. *Anxiety, 1*, 291–297.

Montgomery, S. A. (1998). Implications of the severity of social phobia. *Journal of Affective Disorders, 50* (Supplement 1), S17–S22.

Munjack, D. J., Baltazar, P. L., Bohn, P. B., Cabe, D. D., & Appleton, A. A. (1990). Clonazepam in the treatment of social phobia: A pilot study. *Journal of Clinical Psychiatry, 51* (Supplement), S35–S40.

Munjack, D. J., Bruns, J., & Baltazar, P. L. (1991). A pilot study of buspirone in the treatment of social phobia. *Journal of Anxiety Disorders, 5*, 87–98.

Munjack, D. J., Flowers, C., & Eagan, T. V. (1994). Sertraline in social phobia. *Anxiety, 1*, 196–198.

Murphy, T. K., Bengtson, M. A., Tan, J. Y., Carbonell, E., & Levin, G. M. (2000). Selective serotonin reuptake inhibitors in the treatment of paediatric anxiety disorders: A review. [Review] [134 refs]. *International Clinical Psychopharmacology, 15 suppl 12*, S47–S63.

Naftolowitz, D. F., Vaughn, B. V., Ranc, J., & Tancer, M. E. (1994). Response to alcohol in social phobia. *Anxiety, 1*, 96–99.

Newcorn, J. H., Schulz, K., Harrison, M., DeBellis, M. D., Udarbe, J. K., & Halperin, J. M. (1998). Alpha 2 adrenergic agonists: Neurochemistry, efficacy, and clinical guidelines for use in children. *Pediatric Clinics of North America, 45*, 1099.

Noyes, R., Moroz, G., Davidson, J. R., Liebowitz, M. R., Davidson, A., Siegel, J., Bell, J., Cain, J. W., Curlik, S. M., Kent, T. A., Lydiard, R. B., Mallinger, A. G., Pollack, M. H., Rapaport, M., Rasmussen, S. A., Hedges, D., Schweizer, E., & Uhlenhuth, E. H. (1997). Moclobemide in social phobia: A controlled dose-response trial. *Journal of Clinical Psychopharmacology, 17*, 247–254.

Nutt, D. & Montgomery, S. A. (1996). Moclobemide in the treatment of social phobia. *International Clinical Psychopharmacology, 11* (Supplement 3), 77–82.

Ontiveros, A. & Fontaine, R. (1990). Social phobia and clonazepam. *Canadian Journal of Psychiatry, 35*, 439–441.

Pallanti, S., Quercioli, L., Rossi, A., & Pazzagli, A. (1999). The emergence of social phobia during clozapine treatment and its response to fluoxetine augmentation. *Journal of Clinical Psychiatry, 60*, 819–823.

Pande, A. C., Davidson, J. R. T., Jefferson, J. W., Janney, C. A., Katzelnick, D. J., Weisler, R. H., Greist, J. H., & Sutherland, S. M. (1999b). Treatment of social phobia with gabapentin: A placebo-controlled study. *Journal of Clinical Psychopharmacology, 19*, 341–348.

Pande, A. C., Pollack, M. H., Crockatt, J., Greiner, M., Chouinard, G., Lydiard, R. B., Taylor, C. B., Dager, S., & Shiovitz, T. (1999a). Placebo-controlled study of gabapentin treatment in panic disorder. Author.

Perugi, G., Nassini, S., Lenzi, M., Simonini, E., Cassano, G. B., & McNair, D. M. (1994). Treatment of social phobia with fluoxetine. *Anxiety*, *1*, 282–286.

Reich, J. & Yates, W. (1988). A pilot study of treatment of social phobia with alprazolam. *American Journal of Psychiatry*, *145*, 590–594.

Reiter, S. R., Pollack, M. H., Rosenbaum, J. F., & Cohen, L. S. (1990). Clonazepam for the treatment of social phobia. *Journal of Clinical Psychiatry*, *51*, 470–472.

Richie, J. L. (1995). ACC/AHA Task Force: Heart Failure Guidelines. *Journal of the American College of Cardiologists*, *26*, 1378–1398.

Ringold, A. L. (1994). Paroxetine efficacy in social phobia [letter; comment]. *Journal of Clinical Psychiatry*, *55*, 363–364.

Schneier, F. R., Chin, S. J., Hollander, E., & Liebowitz, M. R. (1992). Fluoxetine in social phobia [letter]. *Journal of Clinical Psychopharmacology*, *12*, 62–64.

Schneier, F. R., Goetz, D., Campeas, R., Fallon, B., Marshall, R., & Liebowitz, M. R. (1998). Placebo-controlled trial of moclobemide in social phobia. *British Journal of Psychiatry*, *172*, 70–77.

Schneier, F. R., Saoud, J. B., Campeas, R., Fallon, B. A., Hollander, E., Coplan, J., & Liebowitz, M. R. (1993). Buspirone in social phobia. *Journal of Clinical Psychopharmacology*, *13*, 251–256.

Simpson, H. B., Schneier, F. R., Campeas, R. B., Marshall, R. D., Fallon, B. A., Davies, S., Klein, D. F., & Liebowitz, M. R. (1998). Imipramine in the treatment of social phobia. *Journal of Clinical Psychopharmacology*, *18*, 132–135.

Slaap, B. R., van Vliet, I. M., Westenberg, H. G. M., & den Boer, J. A. (1996). Responders and non-responders to drug treatment in social phobia: Differences at baseline and prediction of response. *Journal of Affective Disorders*, *39*, 13–19.

Stein, D. J., Berk, M., Els, C., Emsley, R. A., Gittelson, L., Wilson, D., Oakes, R., & Hunter, B. (1999a). A double-blind placebo-controlled trial of paroxetine in the management of social phobia (social anxiety disorder) in South Africa. *South African Medical Journal*, *89*, 402–406.

Stein, M. B., Chartier, M. J., Hazen, A. L., Kroft, C. D., Chale, R. A., Coté, D., & Walker, J. R. (1996a). Paroxetine in the treatment of generalized social phobia: Open-label treatment and double-blind placebo-controlled discontinuation. *Journal of Clinical Psychopharmacology*, *16*, 218–222.

Stein, M. B., Fyer, A. J., Davidson, J. R., Pollack, M. H., & Wiita, B. (1999b). Fluvoxamine treatment of social phobia (social anxiety disorder): A double-blind, placebo-controlled study. *American Journal of Psychiatry*, *156*, 756–760.

Stein, M. B., Hauger, R. L., Dhalla, K. S., Chartier, M. J., & Asmundson, G. J. (1996b). Plasma neuropeptide Y in anxiety disorders: Findings in panic disorder and social phobia. *Psychiatry Research*, *59*, 183–188.

Stein, M. B., Liebowitz, M. R., Lydiard, R. B., Pitts, C. D., Bushnell, W., & Gergel, I. (1998). Paroxetine treatment of generalized social phobia (social anxiety disorder): A randomized controlled trial. *Journal of the American Medical Association*, *280*, 708–713.

Sternbach, H. (1990). Fluoxetine treatment of social phobia [letter]. *Journal of Clinical Psychopharmacology*, *10*, 230–231.

Stravynski, A., Lamontagne, Y., & Lavallee, Y. J. (1986). Clinical phobias and avoidant personality disorder among alcoholics admitted to an alcoholism rehabilitation setting. *Canadian Journal of Psychiatry*, *31*, 714–719.

Sutherland, S. M., Tupler, L. A., Colket, J. T., & Davidson, J. R. (1996). A 2-year follow-up of social phobia. Status after a brief medication trial. *Journal of Nervous and Mental Disorders*, *184*, 731–738.

Taylor, L. H. (1997). Fluoxetine efficacy in social phobia [letter]. *Journal of Clinical Psychiatry*, *58*, 124–125.

Turner, S. M., Beidel, D. C., & Jacob, R. G. (1994). Social phobia: A comparison of behavior therapy and atenolol. *Journal of Consultant Clinical Psychologists, 62,* 350–358.

Uhlenhuth, E. H., Balter, M. B., Ban, T. A., & Yang, K. (1995). International study of expert judgement on therapeutic use of benzodiazepines and other psychotherapeutic medications: II. Pharmacotherapy of anxiety disorders. *Journal of Affective Disorders, 35,* 153–162.

Van Ameringen, M., Mancini, C., & Oakman, J. M. (1999). Nefazodone in social phobia. *Journal of Clinical Psychiatry, 60,* 96–100.

Van Ameringen, M., Mancini, C., & Wilson, C. (1996). Buspirone augmentation of selective serotonin reuptake inhibitors (SSRIs) in social phobia. *Journal of Affective Disorders, 39,* 115–121.

Van Ameringen, M., Swinson, R. P., Walker, J. R., & Lane, R. M. (1999). A placebo-controlled study of sertraline in generalised social phobia. *The Journal of the European College of Neuropsychopharmacology, 9,* S235.

Van Ameringen, M., Mancini, C., & Streiner, D. (1994). Sertraline in social phobia. *Journal of Affective Disorders, 31,* 141–145.

Van Ameringen, M., Mancini, C., & Streiner, D. L. (1993). Fluoxetine efficacy in social phobia [see comments]. *Journal of Clinical Psychiatry, 54,* 27–32.

van der Linden, G. J., Stein, D. J., & van Balkom, A. J. (2000). The efficacy of the selective serotonin reuptake inhibitors for social anxiety disorder (social phobia): A meta-analysis of randomized controlled trials. *International Clinical Psychopharmacology, 15 Suppl 2,* S15–S23.

van Vliet, I. M., den Boer, J. A., & Westenberg, H. G. M. (1994). Psychopharmacological treatment of social phobia: A double blind placebo-controlled study with fluvoxamine. *Psychopharmacology, 115,* 128–134.

van Vliet, I. M., den Boer, J. A., & Westenberg, H. G. M. (1992). Psychopharmacological treatment of social phobia: Clinical and biochemical effects of brofaromine, a selective MAO-A inhibitor. *European Neuropsychopharmacology, 2,* 21–29.

van Vliet, I. M., den Boer, J. A., Westenberg, H. G. M., & Pian, K. L. (1997). Clinical effects of buspirone in social phobia: A double-blind placebo-controlled study. *Journal of Clinical Psychiatry, 58,* 164–168.

van Vliet, I. M., Westenberg, H. G. M., Slaap, B. R., den Boer, J. A., & Ho, P. K. (1997). Anxiogenic effects of pentagastrin in patients with social phobia and healthy controls. *Biological Psychiatry, 42,* 76–78.

Versiani, M., Amrein, R., & Montgomery, S. A. (1997). Social phobia: Long-term treatment outcome and prediction of response—a moclobemide study. *International Clinical Psychopharmacology, 12,* 239–254.

Versiani, M., Mundim, F. D., Nardi, A. E., & Liebowitz, M. R. (1988). Tranylcypromine in social phobia. *Journal of Clinical Psychopharmacology, 8,* 279–283.

Versiani, M., Nardi, A. E., & Mundim, F. D. (1989). Fobia social. *Jornal Brasileiro de Psiquiatria, 38,* 251–263.

Versiani, M., Nardi, A. E., Mundim, F. D., Alves, A. B., Liebowitz, M. R., & Amrein, R. (1992). Pharmacotherapy of social phobia. A controlled study with moclobemide and phenelzine. *British Journal of Psychiatry, 161,* 353–360.

Versiani, M., Nardi, A. E., Mundim, F. D., Pinto, S., Saboya, E., & Kovacs, R. (1996). The long-term treatment of social phobia with moclobemide. *International Journal of Clinical Psychopharmacology, 11* (Supplement 3), 83–88.

Worthington, J. J., Zucker, B. G., Fones, C. S., Otto, M. W., & Pollack, M. H. (1998). Nefazodone for social phobia: A clinical case series. *Depression and Anxiety, 8,* 131–133.

Zwier, K. & Rao, U. (1994). Buspirone use in an adolescent with social phobia and mixed personality disorder (cluster A type). *Journal of the American Academy of Child and Adolescent Psychiatry,* 1007.

Chapter 22

Social Phobia in Children and Adolescents: Nature and Assessment

Ronald M. Rapee *and* **Lynne Sweeney**

PSYCHOPATHOLOGY AND EPIDEMIOLOGY OF SOCIAL PHOBIA IN CHILDHOOD
Diagnosis and Clinical Correlates
Age of Onset and Prevalence
Comorbidity
ASSESSMENT TOOLS
Diagnostic Interviews
Self-report Measures
Psychophysiological Measures
Cognitive Measures
Family Functioning
Behavioural Measures
Experimental Studies
   Social skills
   Family interaction
CRITICAL CONSIDERATIONS IN ASSESSMENT
Social Desirability
Cross-informant Consistency
Developmental Sensitivity
Additional Assessment Issues
AETIOLOGY
SUMMARY AND CONCLUSIONS
REFERENCES

International Handbook of Social Anxiety: Concepts, Research and Interventions Relating to the Self and Shyness. Edited by W. Ray Crozier and Lynn E. Alden.
© 2001 John Wiley & Sons Ltd.

Social phobia is one of the most common anxiety disorders in children and adolescents (Verhulst, van der Ende, Ferdinand, & Jasius, 1997). About one in every five children presenting to a specialty anxiety clinic has significant social fears (Beidel & Turner, 1998). Social phobia is associated with a range of psychosocial impairments including social withdrawal and avoidant behaviour, social skill deficits, poor peer relationships, test anxiety and impairment in academic performance, and in more severe cases, depression, and alcohol and substance abuse (Vernberg, Abwender, Ewell, & Beery, 1992; Beidel & Turner, 1998; APA, 1994). Retrospective studies of adult anxiety patients have demonstrated that social phobia in the childhood years is predictive of anxiety in adulthood, with early diagnosis (that is, prior to 11 years of age) predictive of non-recovery in adulthood (Davidson, 1993, in Beidel & Turner, 1998).

Thus far, research on social phobia in child and adolescent populations has focused primarily on understanding the nature and maintenance of the disorder. Etiological explanations of social phobia are scant, while few publications have included detailed assessment protocols for diagnosis and treatment planning. With large numbers of children experiencing social fears and the evidence pointing to detrimental outcomes, research efforts to increase our understanding in these areas is imperative. This chapter will attempt to integrate available knowledge of diagnostic and assessment approaches to assist in the development of best practice with these fearful children. The first part of the chapter examines psychopathology and epidemiology of social phobia in childhood. Next we describe comprehensive and accurate assessment of social phobia in children, with a brief overview of etiology.

In this chapter we will use the words "childhood" and "children" to refer to both children and adolescents unless specifically referring to an adolescent population.

PSYCHOPATHOLOGY AND EPIDEMIOLOGY OF SOCIAL PHOBIA IN CHILDHOOD

Diagnosis and Clinical Correlates

Children with social phobia are fearful that they will embarrass or humiliate themselves in a social or performance situation. Exposure to the feared situation will almost always provoke an immediate anxiety response. This anxiety response in children may include crying, tantrums, freezing, or shrinking from social situations in addition to the fear more characteristic of adults. To meet diagnostic criteria, the child must show evidence of being able to have age-appropriate social relationships with familiar people and the social or performance fears must be present in situations involving peers and not just in adult interaction settings (DSM-IV; APA, 1994).

As mentioned above, children with social phobia experience a range of psychosocial impairments that can lead to detrimental effects in both the short and long term. School is the most common place where feared interactions occur. Beidel, Neal, and Lederer (1991) report that social phobic children experience, on average, about one feared interaction every other day, and that the most likely event is an unstructured encounter with a peer. Other commonly feared interactions include talking in front of others (e.g., reading aloud to the class), taking tests, and attending social events. It is not surprising to learn, then, that one study found that 30% of a group of school phobic children refused to go to school due to social fears (Last, Herzen, Kazdin, Finkelstein, & Strauss, 1991). In addition, Strauss and Last (1993) found that 64% of social phobic children reported a fear of school.

Age of Onset and Prevalence

Adult retrospective reports indicate that the average age of onset for social phobia is mid adolescence (APA, 1994; Liebowitz, Gorman, Fyer, & Klein, 1985; Turner, Beidel, Dancu, & Keyes, 1986), although one study using an adult sample reported that almost half of their sample had suffered with social phobia before 10 years of age (Schneier, Johnson, Hornig, Liebowitz, & Weissman, 1992). Studies using child samples have also reported earlier onsets. For example, Strauss and Last (1993) reported onset at a mean age of 12.3 years, whereas Beidel and Turner (1988) report that children as young as 8 can meet full criteria for a diagnosis of social phobia. Rapee (1995) suggests that data supporting an average age of onset for social phobia in mid adolescence may be misleading in that it overlooks the existence of social phobia and social evaluative concerns in younger children who may be at risk. Indeed, one study examining the prevalence of feared outcomes in children aged between 6 and 16 years reported a relatively constant fear of evaluative outcomes across all age groupings (Campbell & Rapee, 1994). It may be that social concerns are usually present from an early age, yet only become identified as a clinical disorder when they begin to cause interference in functioning—e.g., dating in adolescence.

Prevalence data are based largely on DSM-III-R criteria with rates of social phobia according to DSM-IV criteria expected to be even higher. Overall, changes in DSM-IV appear to have the benefit of restricting diagnostic possibilities for children with social fears to social phobia (Beidel & Turner, 1998). These changes will probably impact on prevalence rates and new estimates are likely to be a more accurate reflection of the true prevalence rates of social phobia in childhood.

Most studies cite prevalence of social phobia to be approximately 1–2% of the general child population (Anderson, Williams, McGee, & Silva, 1987; Kashani & Orvaschel, 1990; McGee et al., 1990). Anderson et al. (1987) sampled 11-year-old children and reported a 12-month prevalence rate of 0.9%, whereas Kashani and Orvaschel (1990) reported an overall prevalence rate of 1%. Only one study was found that used DSM-IV criteria. Using an adolescent sample, the six-month prevalence rate was 6.3% (Verhulst et al., 1997). This increase in prevalence rate is most likely accounted for by both changes in diagnostic categories from DSM-III-R to DSM-IV, and the sampling of older children.

Rates of social phobia in samples of children presenting to anxiety disorder clinics range from 15 to 18% (Last, Perrin, Hersen, & Kazdin, 1992; Albano, DiBartolo, Heimberg, & Barlow, 1995). Several studies of community samples have indicated a greater proportion of female to males who meet criteria for social phobia (e.g., Anderson et al., 1987). On the other hand, clinical sample studies have shown equal numbers of male and female social phobics seeking treatment (Last et al., 1992; Last, Strauss, & Francis, 1987; Strauss & Last, 1993). Given that parents and teachers are often the agents of referral for children, this discrepancy in gender ratios between community and clinical samples may point to differences in parental and community values for girls and boys. For example, a boy of Western cultural origin who actively avoids social situations (due to a fear of negative evaluation and over concern with saying or doing the wrong thing in social settings), may be more likely to cause distress to parents and teachers than a girl with similar problems, and thus be more likely to be referred.

Comorbidity

Based on data using DSM-III-R criteria, children rarely present with social phobia alone. Children are highly likely to meet criteria for at least one other anxiety diagnosis, with fewer children meeting diagnostic criteria for affective and externalising disorders. For example, Last et al. (1992) reported that 87% of children with social phobia met criteria for at least one other anxiety disorder, whereas Strauss and Last (1993) reported that 10% of children with social phobia met criteria for depression. A recent study of 25 socially phobic children based on DSM-IV criteria reported that 20% met criteria for specific phobia, 16% met criteria for generalized anxiety disorder, 16% had ADHD, 16% had learning difficulties, and 8% met criteria for depression (Beidel, Turner, & Morris, 1999).

ASSESSMENT TOOLS

Comprehensive and accurate assessment of social phobia (and child anxiety disorders, generally) is paramount to making clinical diagnoses, planning treatments, and evaluating outcomes. There is general agreement in the field that assessments of this nature are complex, depend on careful measurement, and benefit from including multiple informants in the assessment process (Schniering, Hudson, & Rapee, 2000). A recent review article described the assessment process with anxious children as a "daunting task". The authors went on to stress the importance of reliable and valid assessment tools that accurately determine the presence of symptoms across different domains, identify symptom clusters and symptom severity, include multiple informant options, and demonstrate sensitivity to outcome evaluations (March & Albano, 1998).

With large numbers of assessment instruments currently available for assessing anxiety disorders in children (see March & Albano, 1996), and mindful of the critical role assessment plays in diagnosis, treatment planning, treatment evaluation, and research, we now examine the utility of the various assessment tools to the evaluation of the socially phobic child.

Diagnostic Interviews

A number of structured and semistructured interviews have been developed for use with children to assist in establishing diagnostic status based on current classification systems. Generally, diagnostic interviews provide a means of quantifying clinical information in a standardized manner, thus increasing the reliability of clinical diagnosis while reducing the degree of interviewer bias (March & Albano, 1996). Structured interviews are relatively inflexible and require minimal interviewer judgements to arrive at a diagnosis, whereas semistructured interviews, although providing a standardized diagnostic questionnaire format, allow more flexibility and rely on interviewer judgement in determining final diagnostic status of the child.

The interviews available for use with children include the Diagnostic Interview Schedule for Children-Revised (DISC-R; Shaffer et al., 1993), the Kiddie Schedule for Affective Disorders and Schizophrenia—Present and Lifetime Version (K-SADS-PL; Kaufman, Birmaher, Brent, Rao, & Ryan, 1997); the Diagnostic Interview for Children and Adolescents (DICA; Herjanic & Reich, 1997), the Interview Schedule for Children (ISC; Kovacs, 1985), the Children's Assessment Schedule (CAS; Hodges, Cools, & McKnew, 1989), the Child and Adolescent Psychiatric Assessment (CAPA; Angold, 1997), and the Anxiety Disorders Interview Schedule for Children (ADIS-C; Silverman & Albano, 1995).

A detailed evaluation of each of these diagnostic interviews is beyond the scope of this paper. In brief, all interviews include both a parent and child component, span across the child and adolescent age range, and most are under revision to improve reliability or to match changing diagnostic classification systems (Schniering et al., 2000). Otherwise, the diagnostic interviews vary considerably in terms of structure, methods of administration, and how well they cover the anxiety disorders (see reviews by Silverman, 1991, 1994).

Of the aforementioned diagnostic interviews, the ADIS-IV-C (Silverman & Albano, 1995) offers a comprehensive and relevant assessment for a child with social phobia. In addition to assessing for all the anxiety disorders (including a new screening section for selective mutism), affective disorders, ADHD, and screening questions for a range of other disorders, the ADIS-IV-C includes questions about socialization and peer relationships that are particularly relevant for the child with social phobia. Also, the ADIS-IV-C opens with a series of questions about school thus enabling the socially anxious child time to settle before asking specifics about the child's worries (Beidel & Turner, 1998). The parent version includes the additional diagnostic categories of conduct disorder and oppositional defiant disorder as well as screening for a range of other disorders including enuresis, pervasive developmental disorders, and learning disorders.

While no reliability data have been published as yet on the ADIS-IV-C, a number of studies have reported acceptable reliabilities of both parent and child versions of the ADIS for DSM-III and DSM-III-R. For example, in a large study of 161 outpatients, Rapee, Barrett, Dadds, and Evans (1994) reported moderate to strong inter-rater reliability for the majority of childhood anxiety disorders (Kappas ranged from 0.59 to 0.82). On the other hand, utilizing the same sample, Rapee et al. (1994) reported inconsistent parent–child agreement for most diagnostic categories (Kappas ranged from 0.11 to 0.44). A number of factors have been proposed to account for this discrepancy including child's developmental stage, social desirability, and a tendency for anxious children to report a "larger number of more intense symptoms" than their parents (DiBartolo, Albano, Barlow, & Heimberg, 1998, p. 213). However, in cases where there is poor agreement between child and parent report, diagnosis is more frequently based on parent report (Rapee et al., 1994).

As an alternative diagnostic instrument, a version of K-SADS was specifically modified to improve assessment of the anxiety disorders and demonstrates good concordance rates with other structured diagnostic instruments for the anxiety disorders as well as other diagnostic categories (Last, 1986, cited in Beidel & Turner, 1998; Hodges, McKnew, Burbach, & Roebuck, 1987).

Self-report Measures

Whereas the structured or semistructured interview format is optimal for diagnosis, self-report measures provide a relatively quick method of assessment that allows children to report on a range of anxiety symptoms from their perspective. Given that anxiety is an internalizing disorder, children's self-report can reveal important elements of the symptom picture that are not readily observable to others. Additionally, self-report measures require minimal clinician time and contribute important normative data as well as treatment outcome data. There are many self-report measures that have been developed to assess general anxiety symptoms in the child population and several of these include a clear social anxiety subscale. Overall, these measures of anxiety appear to be reasonably reliable in children, can discriminate between anxious and non-anxious children (with less support shown for discriminant validity within the anxiety disorders), show utility in measuring the impact of change following treatment, and show relatively low cross-informant agreement between parent and child reports (similar to the findings of diagnostic interviews) (see Schniering et al., 2000, for a more detailed discussion).

In recent years, two self-report measures have emerged that have been designed specifically to assess social anxiety in children. The *Social Anxiety Scale for Children—Revised* (SASC-R; LaGreca & Stone, 1993) was developed to assess social fears in children by adapting two commonly used adult measures of social anxiety (*Social Avoidance and Distress Scale* and *Fear of Negative Evaluation*; Watson & Friend, 1969). The scale consists of 22 items that comprise three subscales: Social Avoidance and Distress in General, Social Avoidance and Distress in New Situations, and Fear of Negative Evaluation. In terms of reliability and validity of the SASC-R, La Greca and Stone (1993) report acceptable internal consistency for each of the three subscales ($r \geqslant 0.65$), and respectable concurrent validity in a sample of pre-adolescent children.

More recently, a second self-report measure of social phobia in children has been developed called the *Social Phobia and Anxiety Inventory for Children* (SPAI-C; Beidel, Turner, & Morris, 1995). The measure, designed for children between the ages of 8 and 14, consists of 26 items that comprise three factors: Assertiveness/General Conversation, Traditional Social Encounters, and Public Performance Factor. The authors report excellent internal consistency, high test–retest reliability across both short (2 weeks = 0.82) and longer (10 months = 0.63) periods, moderate correlations between the SPAI-C and other related constructs such as fear of criticism and general competence, and reasonable discriminant validity between children with social phobia from children with other anxiety disorders, externalizing disorders, and non-clinical controls (Beidel, Turner, & Fink, 1996). A parallel parent form is in the development stages.

Psychophysiological Measures

Despite reasonable interest in the area of physiological functioning in anxious children, few empirical investigations have been reported in the literature. Beidel and Turner (1998) report that people with social phobia show similar patterns of physiological responses to those with other anxiety problems. These authors further point out that people with social phobia experience a particular set of symptoms that implicate the beta-adrenergic system. These symptoms include heart palpitations, shaking, sweating, trembling, and blushing.

Generally, physiological assessments of anxious children most often include cardiovascular and electrodermal responding (see King, 1994, for a comprehensive review). While limited research has examined the utility and reliability of physiological measurement in anxious children, several findings that appear to be relevant to children with social anxiety have been reported. For example, Beidel (1988) reported that socially anxious children demonstrate increases in heart rate during a read-aloud behavioural avoidance test. Further, socially anxious children demonstrated increases in heart rate throughout the behavioural avoidance test compared with non-clinical controls who showed reductions in heart rate across the task suggesting habituation. Clearly, more research is needed in this area, however, availability, expense, and ease of using equipment, as well as general instability of certain responses appear to hinder both research investment in this area and inclusion of such measurement for assessment purposes.

Cognitive Measures

Research with adults on the role of cognition in the development and maintenance of anxiety has been extensive over the past several years. In the child domain, however, researchers have only recently begun to explore relationships between cognition and anxiety in children, with very limited research available that specifically examines cognitive features of children with social phobia.

Cognitive questionnaires for use with children are in their infancy. Several measures have been developed by modifying existing adult questionnaires. While there is some degree of support for the use of these measures in assessing cognition in children, research on the psychometric properties of these measures is fairly limited and the relevance of the items in the adult measures to cognitive components in child anxiety remains unexplored (see Schniering et al., 2000, for more details). Alternatively, measures developed specifically for use with children are few in number. The *Negative Affect Self-Statement Questionnaire* (NASSQ; Ronan, Kendall, & Rowe, 1994) was designed for children and includes specific anxiety items. The psychometric properties appear reasonable with anxious items discriminating between anxious and non-anxious groups of children, and the overall measures showing sensitivity to anxiety treatment (Ronan et al., 1994). In a recent study by Spence, Donovan, & Brechman-Toussaint (1999) a modified version of the *Subjective Probability* (*Social*) *Scale* (Lucock & Salkovskis, 1988) was used to assess children's perception of the probability of positive and negative social and non-social events. Three of the four scales demonstrated acceptable reliability (positive social, positive non-social, negative non-social), whereas the negative social subscale was a little lower thus suggesting caution in interpreting results based on this factor. This measure appears particularly relevant to the assessment of children with social phobia.

Finally, a measure of self-statements has recently been developed specifically for children based on interviews with several clinical groups (the *Children's Automatic Thoughts Scale*—CATS; Schniering & Rapee, 1999). Reported self-statements were listed and administered to both clinical and non-clinical children for rating. Factor analysis indicated four clear factors: hostility, loss, physical threat, and social threat. The social threat factor is especially relevant to social phobia, showing discrimination between socially anxious and non-clinical children.

In addition to self-report inventories, several recent studies have assessed cognitive features of children with social phobia by including behavioural avoidance tasks (see below).

Family Functioning

Studies that examine family functioning and the interaction patterns of anxious children and their families are a very recent addition to assessment protocols. To date, no studies have been conducted with children specifically diagnosed with social phobia. A number of self-report inventories and family assessment tests have been developed for use with children with anxiety, generally. Results from a limited number of studies suggest that anxious children and their families may experience unique patterns of interaction that may contribute to maintenance of anxious responding in the child. Although in the early stages, this line of research may provide relevant information to treatment planning and outcome evaluation.

A number of self- and parent-report inventories have been developed that assess various aspects of family interaction patterns in anxious children (see March & Albano, 1998). The range of aspects assessed include *family climate, structure, values* (dimensions of the Family Environment Scale; Moos & Moos, 1986), *family conflict issues* (Conflict Behaviour Questionnaire; Prinz, Foster, Kent & O'Leary, 1979), and *parents' expectancies* (Parent Expectancy Questionnaire; Eisen, Spasaro, Kearney, Albano, & Barlow, 1996). Reliability and validity of these measures appear to be reasonable in most cases, although applicability of certain measures to the assessment of anxious populations is still underway— e.g., Family Environment Scale. Overall, these measures appear to provide additional assessment information that bears relevance to treatment planning. Some measures have also shown sensitivity to treatment outcome—e.g., Conflict Behaviour Questionnaire (Prinz et al., 1979).

Several experimental studies have been devised that aim to evaluate constructed interactions between anxious children and their families. These studies include unstandardized behavioural assessment tasks and are discussed below.

Behavioural Measures

Behavioural assessment of anxiety includes the use of behavioural avoidance tests (BATs, also called *behavioural assessment tasks*) and behavioural observation (Dadds, Rapee, & Barrett, 1994). Although not widely used in the assessment of social phobia in children thus far, studies with adults, and recent research with children, indicate that these methods may provide information relevant to our understanding of the phenomenology of the disorder, treatment planning, and outcome evaluation. The main limitation of BATs and behavioural observations are that they are not well standardised, with the exception of BATs designed specifically for use in medical settings (March & Albano, 1998).

Beidel and Turner (1998) illustrate the importance of including behavioural measures in the assessment of socially anxious children. Based on anecdotal reports from their anxiety clinic, Beidel and Turner describe some referred children who fail to admit any concerns with anxiety or peer relationships, yet when asked to take part in a behavioural avoidance test of social skills and perfor- mance, these same children are unable to demonstrate friendship skills, maintain social interaction, or perform adequately on a social performance task. Thus, in these cases, the behavioural assessment task can identify important information regarding the child's presenting difficulties.

Experimental Studies

Social Skills

In a recent study by Spence et al. (1999) a behavioural assessment task and two behavioural observations were included (in addition to diagnostic interview and self- and parent-questionnaire data) to assess social features of children with social phobia. Using the Revised Behavioural Assessment Test for Children (BAT-CR; Ollendick, 1981—a modification of the Behavioural Assessment Test for Children—Bornstein, Bellack, & Hersen, 1977), children participated in 12 role-plays in social situations involving positive assertiveness in six of the role- plays and negative assertion in the remaining six. Three variables were derived to assess social performance across the 12 role-plays: eye contact, latency of response, and length of response. Two behavioural observations were included to assess social competence: a naturalistic school observation and an observation of assertiveness during the BAT-CR.

Results on these measures indicated that children with social phobia responded with fewer words during the role-paying tasks and were less assertive in role-play situations than control children (BAT-CR—behavioural observa- tion). Across *all* interactions, children with social phobia received fewer positive responses from peers and experienced more instances of being ignored than their non-anxious peers (school observation). Across interactions initiated by the socially anxious child, clinical children were more likely to be ignored than control children (school observation). These findings were consistent with both child and parent reports of social skills and social competence. That is, children with social phobia were rated by themselves and their parents as less socially skilled and as less socially competent than their non-anxious peers.

Interestingly, children with social phobia did not differ from their non-anxious peers on the amount of eye contact used or in the length of time to respond in the role-plays (BAT-CR). Also, when initiating a social exchange, children with social phobia did not differ from their non-anxious peers in the number of positive or negative outcomes they received.

Family Interaction

One study by Barrett, Rapee, Dadds, and Ryan (1996) included a *family* assess- ment task in which anxious children were presented with ambiguous situations and asked how they would respond. Next, parents were presented with the ambiguous situation and a brief family discussion ensued. Following this, children were asked a second time to report how they would respond. Interestingly, avoidant responding on the part of anxious children increased considerably following the brief family discussion, whereas oppositional and non-clinical children decreased their avoidant responses following the brief family discussion. Barrett and colleagues termed this phenomenon, the "FEAR" effect (Family Enhancement of Avoidant Responding). Although no studies have specifically examined children with social phobia, the use of this assessment technique with a focus on ambiguous, social, situations may be particularly relevant to the assessment of socially anxious children.

We have recently begun to include behavioural assessment tasks to address some of the limitations in the existing literature on parenting and anxiety (Hudson & Rapee, 1998; in press). For example, in one study, clinically anxious children were asked to complete two complex cognitive tasks while their mothers sat beside them with the solutions to the tasks. Mothers' instructions were to help only if they felt that the child really needed it. Blind raters scored the behaviour of the mother and child. Compared with mothers of non-clinical children, the mothers of anxious children were more likely to provide unsolicited help and were more generally intrusive in the task.

These results suggest that an over-involved style of parenting is associated with anxiety. The use of behavioural assessment tasks, albeit an unstandardized format, has produced potentially important information for the understanding and treatment of anxious children. The extent to which behavioural assessment tasks can be used in the assessment process awaits further research. In addition, research is needed to determine the extent to which these more general findings are relevant to children specifically diagnosed with social phobia.

CRITICAL CONSIDERATIONS IN ASSESSMENT

There are a number of critical issues in the assessment of children with social phobia, or anxiety more generally, that warrant discussion. These include *social desirability, cross-informant consistency, and developmental sensitivity.*

Social Desirability

Anxious children appear particularly primed for responding in socially desirable ways to assessment measures or tasks. Many researchers have noted anxious children's tremendous concerns with self-presentation and hypersensitivity to evaluation by others and have recognized that these behaviours are likely to result in socially desirable responses on assessment tasks (Kendall & Flannery-Schroeder, 1998; Schniering et al., 2000). Given the salience of fears of negative evaluation and poor social performance in children with social phobia, social desirability concerns may be even more relevant in this subgroup of anxious children. While measures have been developed that include lie scales—e.g., Revised Children's Manifest Anxiety Scale (Reynolds & Richmond, 1979)—these items rarely work with children. Interestingly, several empirical investigations that have examined relationships between social desirability and anxious symptoms in children have provided mixed results (e.g., Dadds, Perrin, & Yule, 1998). Further research is needed to clarify the precise relationships between anxiety and social desirability in socially anxious child populations.

Cross-informant Consistency

There have been sufficient studies to conclude that agreement between parent and child reports of anxiety in children is poor (Rapee et al., 1994; Kendall & Flannery-Schroeder, 1998), and these findings hold for questionnaire data as well as for diagnostic interviews. A recent study by DiBartolo et al. (1998) assessed cross-informant consistency in a sample of children with social phobia. Results indicated reasonable agreement between parent and child ratings on social fears, whereas parents reported much higher levels of social avoidance compared with child reports. Further analyses revealed that social desirability accounted, in part, for the low avoidance reports by the children.

Several explanations have been proposed to account for low cross-informant consistency in anxious children, including parental anxiety, over-reporting by parents to ensure their child's acceptance into treatment, items on self-report measures beyond the developmental level of the child, and social desirability. Concerns with cross-informant inconsistency may be addressed, in part, by including multiple methods of assessment for both parents and children. It should be noted however, that in certain circumstances, even young children have been found to be able to provide accurate predictions of their fear and avoidance levels (Cobham & Rapee, 1999). In fact, in some situations, these predictions may be even more accurate than that reported by their mothers.

Developmental Sensitivity

Developmental factors pose complex problems for the assessment of anxiety in children. Given that the majority of available measures are downward extensions of adult measures, the degree to which these actually measure the construct of interest remains unclear (see Campbell, Rapee, & Spence, 2001; McCathie & Spence, 1991). In this regard, the SPAI-C, an instrument designed specifically for children with social phobia, is recommended for use with children between ages 8 and 14 only. This reflects consideration of developmental relevance of the items of the SPAI-C to the population being assessed.

Furthermore, the development of children's understanding of emotion, their ability to introspect and to become self-aware is a process taking place during the childhood years. While research is limited, findings suggest that young children (<12 years of age) have not developed these concepts sufficiently to be able to answer some of the more complex questions about the experience of anxiety—e.g., questions about cause and effect (Schniering et al., 2000).

Additional Assessment Issues

Diagnostic comorbidity in children complicates assessment and treatment planning, as well as expectations for outcome. Children with social phobia often have an additional anxiety disorder or other psychiatric diagnosis. March and Albano (1998) highlight the need for assessors to consider both cross-sectional and longitudinal comorbidity in case formulation as this will impact on prognosis expectations and thus treatment planning and outcome evaluations.

Culture and gender are also important variables to consider in assessment practice. In brief, studies have shown that cultural factors can influence self-report measures of anxiety. For example, Chinese children have been found to report significantly more social fears than Western children (Dong, Yang, & Ollendick, 1994). In addition, assessment instruments may not include relevant items that capture certain fears found only in Asian cultures (Chang, 1984, in Beidel & Turner, 1998). In terms of gender, the finding that more female children have social phobia in the general population compared to equal numbers of male and female children with social phobia in clinical populations, suggests that further research is needed to improve our understanding of the factors responsible for the relatively lower numbers of female children with social phobia in clinical settings.

AETIOLOGY

Based on the assumption that socially anxious children develop into socially anxious adults (Caspi, Elder, & Bem, 1988), models of the development of social phobia in children would be expected to be identical to those for the development of social phobia in adults. Of course this conclusion is not entirely true since various factors are likely to have slightly different influences at different points along the course of development. For example, twin studies of anxiety in adults almost uniformly demonstrate a strong genetic involvement together with a strong involvement from non-shared environmental factors (Kendler, Neale, Kessler, Heath, & Eaves, 1992). In contrast, twin studies of anxiety in children show slightly less genetic influence together with some reasonable evidence for the role of shared environmental factors (Thapar & McGuffin, 1995). Nevertheless, the major influential components are likely to be consistent for both children and adults. For this reason, we will not provide a detailed discussion of the development of social phobia in children here, since most of the important factors have been elaborated elsewhere in this volume.

In brief, Rapee (2001) has described a comprehensive model of the development of generalized anxiety disorder that is most likely applicable to all of the anxiety disorders, including social phobia. According to this model, genetic factors as well as both shared and non-shared environmental factors all play a role in the development of anxiety. In addition, the model pays particular attention to gene–environment interactions as a central component in the development of the individual. While there are assumed to be several pathways to the development of anxiety, it is suggested that many individuals who later develop anxiety disorders, are characterized as temperamentally vulnerable. This temperamental style is characterized initially by high arousal and emotionality (Kagan & Snidman, 1991) and later by withdrawal behaviors (Rubin, Hymel, & Mills, 1989). The crucial issue is that this temperamental style influences much of the individual's environmental interactions that, in turn, have an influence on the individual's temperament. For example, one influential environmental factor in early childhood is believed to be the role of an overprotecting parent (Hudson & Rapee, 1998; Hudson & Rapee, in press; Rapee, 1997). While a small component of this parenting may be a result of the parent's own anxiety and hence emerge as a shared environmental influence, a large component is likely to be a reaction to the child's temperament in the first place, largely a gene–environment interaction. Specifically, we suggest that an emotional and withdrawn child will elicit over-involvement from a caring parent in order to avoid distress on the part of the child. Over time, the parent will begin to anticipate the child's distress and will intervene earlier and earlier. In turn, this will have the effect of maintaining and possibly increasing withdrawal and avoidance behaviors on the part of the child (Hudson & Rapee, in press).

We hypothesize that similar interactive processes affect the influence on the development of anxiety of other environmental factors such as parent socialization practices, peer socialization, non-specific stressors, and specific learning experiences (Hudson & Rapee, 2000; Rapee, 2001). In specific socially phobic populations, some retrospective evidence has pointed to the possible role of parent modelling, verbal instruction, and restricted family socialization (Bruch, Heimberg, Berger, & Collins, 1989; Rapee & Melville, 1997).

SUMMARY AND CONCLUSIONS

Epidemiological data indicate that social phobia is one of the most common anxiety disorders or problems in children and adolescents, that such problems are associated with a range of psychosocial impairments, and that it often follows a chronic course when left untreated. While there are a number of studies aimed at understanding the nature and maintenance of social phobia, little research has focused on aetiological explanations, assessment, or interventions designed specifically for the child with social phobia. Indeed research specifically on social phobia in children is still relatively uncommon.

Comprehensive and accurate assessment of children with social phobia requires the inclusion of standardized assessment tools that demonstrate acceptable reliability and validity. Also, assessments should include multiple informants and use multiple methods where possible. A sample assessment protocol that meets the above criteria may include parent, and child, self-report on a diagnostic interview, clinical rating scales, and several additional questionnaires that assess characteristics of children with social phobia such as cognitive features. Psychophysiological functioning, although often not assessed, is relatively easy to assess in some cases (e.g., heart rate) and can provide useful treatment and outcome data.

Very recently, experimental studies exploring parent interactions, parental overprotection, cognitive features and social skills have begun to emerge. However, the unstandardised nature of these assessment tasks and the absence of reliability and validity data preclude their inclusion in assessment protocols at present. Further research in this area is warranted. In addition, several issues need to be considered as part of the assessment of social phobia in children including social desirability, cross-informant consistency, developmental sensitivity, comorbidity, and gender and cultural issues. These issues highlight the complexity of factors that need to be considered in the assessment process from the selection of instrument, to the actual assessment, and interpretation thereafter. Certainly, it appears a "daunting task".

While few studies have examined aetiological factors in social phobia in children, several related areas of research such as social anxiety, shyness, social isolation, and social withdrawal may contribute to our developing understanding of the origins of the disorder. Based on the available research, we speculate that an inhibited and withdrawn temperament should be a central component in any model of the development of social phobia. In turn, several other influential factors, such as parenting styles, parent and peer socialization, learning experiences, and life events are likely to produce their effects in interaction with this temperamental component.

Focused research attention on anxiety disorders in children and adolescents is currently still a relatively new endeavour. While much of our knowledge of social phobia in adults is of relevance to an understanding of the disorder in children, there are likely to be several factors that differ across the lifespan. Future years will see increased understanding of the unique features of social phobia in young people.

REFERENCES

Albano, A. M., DiBartolo, P. M., Heimberg, R. G., & Barlow, D. H. (1995). Children and adolescents: Assessment and treatment. In R. G. Heimberg, M. R. Liebowitz, D. A. Hope, & F. R. Schneier (Eds.), *Social phobia: Diagnosis, assessment and treatment* (pp. 387–425). New York: Guilford Press.

Anderson, J. C., Williams, S., McGee, R., & Silva, P. A. (1987). DSM-III disorders in preadolescent children. Prevalence in a large sample from a general population. *Archives of General Psychiatry, 44*, 69–76.

Angold, A. (1997). The Child and Adolescent Psychiatric Instrument. In C. Thoarson (Ed.), *The instruments of psychiatric research* (pp. 271–304). Chichester, Sussex: Wiley.

APA (1994). *Diagnostic and Statistical Manual of Mental Disorders (4th Edn)*. Washington, DC: American Psychiatric Association.

Barrett, P. M., Rapee, R. M., Dadds, M. R., & Ryan, S. M. (1996). Family enhancement of cognitive style in anxious and aggressive children. Threat bias and the FEAR effect. *Journal of Abnormal Child Psychology, 24*, 187–203.

Beidel, D. C. (1988). Psychophysiological assessment of anxious emotional states in children. *Journal of Abnormal Psychology, 97*, 80–82.

Beidel, D. C., Neal, A. M., & Lederer, A. S. (1991). The feasibility and validity of a daily diary for the assessment of anxiety in children. *Behavior Therapy, 22*, 505–517.

Beidel, D. C. & Turner, S. M. (1998). *Shy children, phobic adults: Nature and treatment of social phobia.* Washington, DC: American Psychiatric Association.

Beidel, D. C., Turner, S. M., & Fink, C. M. (1996). The assessment of childhood social phobia: Construct, convergent and discriminative validity of the Social Phobia and Anxiety Inventory for Children (SPAI-C). *Psychological Assessment, 8*, 235–240.

Beidel, D. C., Turner, S. M., & Morris, T. L. (1995). A new inventory to assess childhood social anxiety and phobia: The Social Phobia and Anxiety Inventory of Children. *Psychological Assessment, 7*, 73–79.

Beidel, D. C., Turner, S. M., & Morris, T. L. (1999). The psychopathology of childhood social phobia. *Journal of the American Academy of Child and Adolescent Psychiatry, 38*, 643–650.

Bornstein, M. R., Bellack, A. S., & Hersen, M. (1977). Social skills training for unassertive children: A multiple baseline analysis. *Journal of Applied Behavior Analysis, 10*, 183–195.

Bruch, M. A., Heimberg, R. G., Berger, P., & Collins, T. M. (1989). Social phobia and perceptions of early parental and personal characteristics. *Anxiety Research, 2*, 57–65.

Campbell, M. A. & Rapee, R. M. (1994). The nature of feared outcome representation in children. *Journal of Abnormal Psychology, 22*, 99–111.

Campbell, M. A., Rapee, R. M., & Spence, S. (2001). Developmental changes in the interpretation of rating format on a questionnaire measure of worry. *Clinical Psychologist, 5*, 49–59.

Caspi, A., Elder, G. H., Jr., & Bem, D. J. (1988). Moving away from the world: Life-course patterns of shy children. *Developmental Psychology, 24*, 824–831.

Cobham, V. E. & Rapee, R. M. (1999). Accuracy of predicting a child's response to potential threat: A comparison of children and their mothers. *Australian Journal of Psychology, 51*, 25–28.

Dadds, M. R., Perrin, S., & Yule, W. (1998). Social desirability and self-reported anxiety in children: An analysis of the RCMAS Lie Scale. *Journal of Abnormal Child Psychology, 26*, 311–317.

Dadds, M. R., Rapee, R. M., & Barrett, P. M. (1994). Behavioural observation: In T. H. Ollendick, N. J. King, & W. Yule (Eds.), *International handbook of phobic and anxiety disorders in children and adolescents* (pp. 349–364). New York: Plenum Press.

DiBartolo, P. M., Albano, A. M., Barlow, D. H., & Heimberg, R. G. (1998). Cross-informant agreement in the assessment of social phobia in youth. *Journal of Abnormal Child Psychology, 26*, 213–220.

Dong, Q., Yang, B., & Ollendick, T. H. (1994). Fears in Chinese children and adolescents and their relations to anxiety and depression. *Journal of Child Psychology and Psychiatry and Allied Disciplines, 35*, 351–363.

Eisen, A. R., Spasaro, S. A., Kearney, C. A., Albano, A. M., & Barlow, D. H. (1996). Measuring parental expectancies in a childhood anxiety disorders sample: The Parental Expectancies Scale. *Behavior Therapist, 19*, 37–38.

Herjanic, B. & Reich, W. (1997). Development of a structured psychiatric interview for children: Agreement between child and parent on individual symptoms. *Journal of Abnormal Child Psychiatry, 25*, 21–31.

Hodges, K., Cools, J., & McKnew, D. (1989). Test–retest reliability of a clinical research interview for children: The Child Assessment Schedule (CAS). *Psychological Assessment: Journal of Consulting and Clinical Psychology*, *1*, 317–322.

Hodges, K., McKnew, D., Burback, D. J., & Roebuck, L. (1987). Diagnostic concordance between the Child Assessment Schedule (CAS) and the Schedule for Affective Disorders and Schizophrenia for School-Age Children (K-SADS) in an outpatient sample using lay interviewers. *Journal of the American Academy of Child and Adolescent Psychiatry*, *26*, 654–661.

Hudson, J. L. & Rapee, R. M. (1998). *Parent–child interactions and anxiety*. Paper presented at the World Congress of Behavioural and Cognitive Therapies, Acapulco, Mexico, July.

Hudson, J. L. & Rapee, R. M. (2000). The origins of social phobia. *Behavior Modification*, *24*, 102–129.

Hudson, J. L. & Rapee, R. M. (in press) Parent–child interactions and anxiety disorders: An observational study. *Behaviour Research and Therapy*.

Kagan, J. & Snidman, N. (1991). Infant predictors of inhibited and uninhibited profiles. *Psychological Science*, *2* (1), 40–44.

Kashani, J. H. & Orvaschel, H. (1990). A community study of anxiety in children and adolescents. *American Journal of Psychiatry*, *147*, 313–318.

Kaufman, J., Birmaher, B., Brent, D., Rao, U., & Ryan, N. (1997). Schedule for affective disorders and schizophrenia for school-age children—Present and lifetime version (K-SADS-PL): Initial reliability and validity data. *Journal of the American Academy of Child and Adolescent Psychiatry*, *36*, 980–988.

Kendall, P. C. & Flannery-Schroeder, E. C. (1998). Methodological issues in treatment research for anxiety disorders in youth. *Journal of Abnormal Child Psychology*, *26*, *1*, 27–38.

Kendler, K. S., Neale, M. C., Kessler, R. C., Heath, A. C., & Eaves, L. J. (1992). The genetic epidemiology of phobias in women: The interrelationship of agoraphobia, social phobia, situational phobia, and simple phobia. *Archives of General Psychiatry*, *49*, 273–281.

King, N. J. (1994). Physiological assessment. In T. H. Ollendick, N. J. King, & W. Yule (Eds.), *International handbook of phobic and anxiety disorders in children and adolescents* (pp. 365–379). New York: Plenum Press.

Kovacs, M. (1985). The interview schedule for children (ISC). *Psychopharmacology Bulletin*, *21*, 991–994.

LaGreca, A. M. & Stone, W. L. (1993). Social Anxiety for Children—Revised: Factor structure and concurrent validity. *Journal of Clinical Child Psychology*, *22*, 17–27.

Last, C. G., Hersen, M., Kazdin, A., Finkelstein, R., & Strauss, C. C. (1991). Anxiety disorders in children and their families. *Archives of General Psychiatry*, *48*, 928–937.

Last, C. G., Perrin, S., Hersen, M., & Kazdin, A. E. (1992). DSM-III-R anxiety disorders in children: Sociodemographic and clinical characteristics. *Journal of the American Academy of Child and Adolescent Psychiatry*, *31*, 928–934.

Last, C. G., Strauss, C. C., & Francis, G. (1987). Comorbidity among childhood anxiety disorders. *Journal of Nervous and Mental Disease*, *175*, 726–730.

Liebowitz, M. R., Gorman, J. M., Fyer, A. J., & Klein, D. F. (1985). Social phobia: Review of a neglected anxiety disorder. *Archives of General Psychiatry*, *42*, 669–677.

Lucock, M. P. & Salkovskis, P. M. (1988). Cognitive factors in social anxiety and its treatment. *Behaviour Research and Therapy*, *26*, 297–302.

March, J. & Albano, A. (1996). Assessment of anxiety in children and adolescents. In L. Dickstein, M. Riba, & M. Oldham (Eds.), *Review of Psychiatry XV* (Vol. 15, pp. 405–427). Washington, DC: American Psychiatric Association Press.

March, J. & Albano, A. (1998). New developments in assessing pediatric anxiety disorders. *Advances in Clinical Child Psychology*, *20*, 213–241.

McCathie, H. & Spence, S. H. (1991). What is the Revised Fear Survey Schedule for Children measuring? *Behaviour Research and Therapy*, *29*, 495–502.

McGee, R., Feehan, M., Williams, S., Partridge, F., Silva, P. A., & Kelly, J. (1990). DSM-III disorders in a large sample of adolescents. *Journal of American Academy of Child and Adolescent Psychiatry, 29*, 611–619.

Moos, R. H. & Moos, B. S. (1986). *Family Environment Scale manual*. Palo Alto, CA: Consulting Psychological Press.

Ollendick, T. H. (1981). Assessment of social interaction skills in school children. *Behavioral Counseling Quarterly, 1*, 227–243.

Prinz, R. J., Foster, S., Kent, R. N., & O'Leary, K. D. (1979). Multivariate assessment of conflict in distressed and nondistressed mother–adolescent dyads. *Journal of Applied Behavior Analysis, 12*, 691–700.

Rapee, R. (1995). Descriptive psychopathology of social phobia. In R. G. Heimberg, M. R. Liebowitz, D. A. Hope, & F. R. Schneier (Eds.), *Social phobia: Diagnosis, assessment and treatment* (pp. 41–66). New York: Guilford Press.

Rapee, R. M. (1997). Potential role of childrearing practices in the development of anxiety and depression. *Clinical Psychology Review, 17*, 47–67.

Rapee, R. M. (2001). The development of generalised anxiety. In M. W. Vasey & M. R. Dadds (Eds.), *The developmental psychopathology of anxiety* (pp. 481–503). New York: Oxford University Press.

Rapee, R. M., Barrett, P. M., Dadds, M. R., & Evans, L. (1994). Reliability of the DSM-III-R childhood anxiety disorders using structured interview: Interrater and parent–child agreement. *Journal of the American Academy of Child and Adolescent Psychiatry, 33*, 984–992.

Rapee, R. M. & Melville, L. F. (1997). Retrospective recall of family factors in social phobia and panic disorder. *Depression and Anxiety, 5*, 7–11.

Reynolds, C. R. & Richmond, B. O. (1979). What I Think and Feel: A revised measure of children's manifest anxiety. *Journal of Abnormal Child Psychology, 6*, 271–280.

Ronan, K. R., Kendall, P. C., & Rowe, M. (1994). Negative affectivity in children: Development and validation of a self-statement questionnaire. *Cognitive Therapy and Research, 18*, 509–528.

Rubin, K. H., Hymel, S., & Mills, R. S. L. (1989). Sociability and social withdrawal in childhood: Stability and outcomes. *Journal of Personality, 57*, 237–255.

Schaffer, D., Schwab-Stone, M., Fisher, P. W., Cohen, P., Piacentini, J., Davies, M., Conners, C. K., & Refier, D. (1993). The Diagnostic Interview Schedule for Children— Revised version (DISC-R): I Preparation, field testing, interrater reliability, and acceptability. *Journal of the American Academy of Child and Adolescent Psychiatry, 32*, 643–650.

Schneier, F. R., Johnson, J., Hornig, C. D., Liebowitz, M. R., & Weissman, M. M. (1992). Social phobia: Comorbidity and morbidity in an epidemiologic sample. *Archives of General Psychiatry, 49*, 282–288.

Schniering, C. A., Hudson, J. L., & Rapee, R. M. (2000). Issues in diagnosis and assessment of anxiety disorders in children and adolescents. *Clinical Psychology Review, 20*, 453–478.

Schniering, C. A. & Rapee, R. M. (1999). *Cognitive specificity in emotional disorders among children and adolescents*. Paper presented at 22nd AACBT National Conference, Perth, Australia, July.

Silverman, W. K. (1991). Diagnostic reliability of anxiety disorders in children using structured interviews [Special Issue: Assessment of childhood anxiety disorders]. *Journal of Anxiety Disorders, 5* (2), 105–124.

Silverman, W. K. (1994). Structured diagnostic interviews. In T. H. Ollendick, N. J. King, & W. Yule (Eds.), *International handbook of phobic and anxiety disorders in children and adolescents* (pp. 293–315). New York: Plenum Press.

Silverman, W. K. & Albano, A. M. (1995). *Anxiety disorders interview schedule for children*. San Antonio, TX: Psychological Corporation.

Spence, S. H., Donovan, C., & Brechman-Toussaint, M. (1999). Social skills, social outcomes and cognitive features of childhood social phobia. *Journal of Abnormal Psychology*, *108*, 211–221.

Strauss, C. C. & Last, C. G. (1993). Social and simple phobias in children. *Journal of Anxiety Disorders*, *1*, 141–152.

Thapar, A. & McGuffin, P. (1995). Are anxiety symptoms in childhood heritable? *Journal of Child Psychology and Psychiatry*, *36*, 439–447.

Turner, S. M., Beidel, D. C., Dancu, C. V., & Keys, D. J. (1986). Psychopathology of social phobia and comparison to avoidant personality disorder. *Journal of Abnormal Psychology*, *95*, 389–394.

Vernberg, E. M., Abwender, D. A., Ewell, K. K., & Beery, S. H. (1992). Social anxiety and peer relationships in early adolescence: A prospective analysis. *Journal of Clinical Child Psychology*, *21*, 189–196.

Verhulst, F. C., van der Ende, J., Ferdinand, R. F., & Jasius, M. C. (1997). The prevalence of DSM-III-R diagnoses in a national sample of Dutch adolescents. *Archives of General Psychiatry*, *54*, 329–336.

Watson, D. & Friend, R. (1969). Measurement of social-evaluative anxiety. *Journal of Consulting and Clinical psychology*, *33*, 448–457.

Chapter 23

Social Phobia in Children and Adolescents: Psychological Treatments

Lynne Sweeney *and* **Ronald M. Rapee**

TREATMENTS OF BROAD-BASED ANXIETY
Individual Treatments
Group Treatments
TREATMENT OF SOCIAL PHOBIA
Group Treatment: Uncontrolled Studies
Group Treatment: Controlled Studies
EARLY INTERVENTION AND PREVENTION
SUMMARY AND CONCLUSIONS
REFERENCES

Research into the psychological treatment of children with social phobia has received limited attention to date. Only a handful of studies have examined interventions designed specifically for the child or adolescent with social phobia. Epidemiological research has reported significant numbers of children suffering from social fears, while other research has shown that social anxiety and/or phobia in childhood may have detrimental effects on academic, social, and emotional functioning (see Chapter 22 for more details on the *nature* of social phobia in childhood). In light of this evidence, the development of effective treatment approaches is strongly indicated.

This chapter will review the available behavioural and cognitive-behavioural treatments for children with social phobia. We begin by examining treatments of broad-based anxiety in children where children with social phobia have been included. Next, we review treatment studies designed specifically for children

International Handbook of Social Anxiety: Concepts, Research and Interventions Relating to the Self and Shyness. Edited by W. Ray Crozier and Lynn E. Alden.
© 2001 John Wiley & Sons Ltd.

with social phobia. Following this, and in line with the recent increase in early intervention and prevention, we will discuss recent prevention research with children at risk for developing social phobia, including current research from our laboratory on anxiety prevention in preschool age children.

As in the previous chapter, we will use the words "childhood" and "children" to refer to both children and adolescents unless specifically referring to an adolescent population.

TREATMENTS OF BROAD-BASED ANXIETY

Individual Treatments

Three outcome studies of children with anxiety disorders that utilize an individual treatment approach have recently been published (Kendall, 1994; Barrett, Dadds, & Rapee, 1996; Kendall et al., 1997). Generally, these studies were similar in treatment approach—i.e., cognitive-behavioural treatment package (see Coping Cat manual for more details—Kendall, Kane, Howard, & Siqueland, 1990) with the exception of a parent management component included in the Barrett et al. (1996) study. Also, all three studies included children of similar ages (age range 7–14 years), with sample size smaller in the earlier Kendall study ($N = 47$) and larger in the latter two studies ($N = 79$, Barrett et al., 1996; $N = 94$, Kendall et al., 1997; see Table 23.1).

Overall, all three outcome studies reported similar results. At post-treatment, and at one-year follow-up, treatment conditions of all three studies demonstrated significant effects compared with waitlist control groups. That is, treated children were much more likely to be free of their initial diagnosis, and report fewer anxious symptoms, at post-treatment and follow-up than non-treated children. Barrett et al. (1996) reported greater improvement on several measures for the treatment group that included a parent component. Barrett et al. (1996) and Kendall et al. (1997) performed analyses to examine differential outcome by diagnosis. With few exceptions, findings indicated that treatment success was applicable for each diagnostic grouping.

Group Treatments

Several group treatment studies of broad-based anxiety disorders in children have been conducted recently (Barrett, 1998; Silverman et al., 1999; Rapee, 1996; Rapee, 2000). One study has also examined the relative efficacy of individual versus group administered cognitive-behavioural treatments for children with broad-based anxiety disorders (Flannery-Schroeder & Kendall, 2000; see Table 23.2).

In the first of these studies, Rapee (1996; 2000) conducted a group treatment (similar to Barrett et al.'s (1996) family treatment package) for children aged 7

Table 23.1 Summary table of treatment studies for children with broad-based anxiety disorders

Year	Authors	Type of study	Age range	Sample size	Duration/ type	Outcome
1994	Kendall	Individual/2 group comparison	9–13 years	Tx gp = 27 WI gp = 20	16 week CBT	Tx gp = 60% diagnosis free @ PT WI gp = 5% diagnosis free @ PT Tx gains maintained @ 12 mo. FU
1996	Barrett et al.	Individual/3 group comparison	7–14 years	CBT Tx gp = 28 CBT/FAM Tx gp = 25 WLC = 26	12 week	CBT gp = 57% diagnosis free PT CBT/FAM gp = 84% diagnosis free PT WLC gp = 26% diagnosis free PT Tx gains maintained @ 6, 12 mo. FU
1996/2000	Rapee	Group/2 group comparison	7–16 years	Tx gp = 95 WI gp = 15	9 session CBT	Significantly greater decrease in anxiety across Tx and follow-up in Tx vs. WI
1997	Kendall et al.	Individual/2 group comparison	9–13 years	Tx gp = 60 WLC gp = 34	16 week CBT	Tx gp = 53% diagnosis free PT WLC gp = 6% diagnosis free PT Tx gains maintained @ 12 mo. FU
1998	Barrett	Group/3 group comparison	7–14 years	CBT Tx gp = 23 CBT/FAM Tx gp = 17 WLC gp = 20	12 week	CBT gp = 56% diagnosis free @ PT; 65% @ FU CBTFAM gp = 71% diagnosis free @ PT; 85% @ FU WLC gp = 25% diagnosis free @ PT
1999	Silverman et al.	Group/2 group comparison	6–16 years	CBT Tx gp = 25 WLC gp = 16	10 week	CBT gp = 64% diagnosis free @ PT WLC gp = 13.4% diagnosis free @ PT Tx gains maintained @ 3, 6, & 12 mo. FU
2000	Flannery-Schroeder and Kendall	Group and individual/ 3 group comparison	8–14 years	Group gp = 12 Individ. gp = 13 WLC gp = 12	18 week	Group Tx = 50% diagnosis free @ PT Individ. Tx = 73% diagnosis free @ PT WLC gp = 8% diagnosis free @ PT Tx gains maintained @ 3 mo. FU

Note: CBT = cognitive-behavioural therapy; CBT/FAM = cognitive-behavioural therapy with a family component; PT = post treatment; Individ. = individual; WLC = waitlist control group; FU = follow-up.

Table 23.2 Summary table of treatment studies for children with a diagnosis of social phobia

Year	Authors	Type of study	Age range	Sample size	Duration/type	Outcome
1995	Albano et al.	Group/uncontrolled	Adolescent sample	N = 5	16 week CBT	• 4/5 subjects diagnosis free @ 3 mo. FU • 5/5 diagnosis free @ 12 mo. FU
1997	Beidel et al.	Group/uncontrolled	8–12 years	N = 16	24 sessions over 12 weeks	Child Report: sig. reduction in anxiety concerns @ PT Parent Report: sig. reduction in internalizing beh. @ PT
2000	Beidel et al.	Group/controlled	8–12 years	SET gp = 30 General gp = 20	12 week	SET gp = 67% diagnosis free @ PT General gp = 5% diagnosis free @ PT Tx gains maintained @ 6 mo. FU
2000	Spence et al.	Group/controlled	7–14 years	CBT Tx gp = 17 CBTFAM Tx gp = 19 WLC gp = 14	12 week	CBT gp = 58% diagnosis free @ PT CBTFAM gp = 87% diag. free @ PT WLC gp = 7% diagnosis free @ PT Tx gains maintained @ 6 mo. FU

to 16 years with broad-based anxiety disorders. Treatment was brief (9 sessions) and this, combined with the group format (around 6 families per group), resulted in a highly cost-effective delivery. Outcome showed good effects—treated children improved significantly more on both self and parent reports of anxious symptomatology than did waitlist children and continued to improve over the ensuing 12 months. Importantly, despite the change to a group format and the reduced number of sessions, effect sizes were similar to those found in earlier individual treatment programs (Barrett et al., 1996; Kendall, 1994). Examining differential outcome by diagnostic status, there was a tendency for children with principal diagnoses of social phobia and generalized anxiety to respond less at post-treatment than children with separation anxiety disorder. However, this trend was not seen at 12-month follow-up. These results seem to suggest that social phobia and generalized anxiety disorder may respond somewhat more slowly to treatment than does separation anxiety disorder.

Barrett (1998) conducted a three-group comparison comprising a cognitive-behavioural treatment group (CBTG: $N = 23$), a CBTG plus family component group (CBTGFAM: $N = 17$), and a waitlist control group (WLCG: $N = 20$). Both treatment groups showed significant change in diagnostic status and symptom measures at post-treatment and follow-up compared with the waitlist control group. Although differences between treatment groups were non-significant, the CBTGFAM treatment showed a trend towards greater improvement.

In a more recent trial, Silverman et al. (1999) treated 25 children and their parents using a cognitive-behavioural treatment program and compared the outcome with a waitlist group of children. At post-treatment, 64% of children in the treatment group no longer met primary diagnosis criteria compared with 12.5% of the waitlist control group. The success of treatment was also evident in clinical ratings of severity of anxiety and child and parent self-report measures. All treatment gains were maintained across 3-, 6- and 12-month follow-up. Analyses evaluating differential outcome by diagnostic group (social phobia, generalized anxiety disorder, and overanxious disorder) revealed no significant differences, thus supporting the applicability of this particular treatment package for children with social phobia (Silverman, personal communication, July, 1999).

Finally, Flannery-Schroeder and Kendall (2000) conducted a randomized clinical trial examining the relative efficacy of individual (ICBTG) versus group (GCBTG) administered cognitive-behavioural treatments for children with broad-based anxiety disorders. Results indicated that children in both the individual and group treatment conditions were significantly more likely to be free of their primary anxiety diagnosis and to show improvements on anxiety and coping measures at post-treatment and three month follow-up compared to children in the waitlist control group.

Although few in number, the above studies indicate that individual and group treatment of children with broad-based anxiety disorders (including social phobia) can be successful using a comprehensive cognitive-behavioural treatment package, and may be further enhanced with the inclusion of parents. More importantly to this paper, two of the three individual studies and two of the four group studies examined differential outcome by diagnosis and found that success of the treatments was equally applicable to children with a primary diagnosis of social phobia or avoidant disorder, thus providing preliminary support for the use of cognitive-behavioural treatment approaches for children with social phobia. An interesting finding from the Rapee (1996; 2000) study suggests that social phobia and generalized anxiety disorder may respond a little more slowly to cognitive-behavioural interventions, at least initially, compared to other diagnostic groups but the long-term results are equivalent.

TREATMENT OF SOCIAL PHOBIA

Group Treatment: Uncontrolled Studies

Two uncontrolled studies evaluated group treatment of children with a diagnosis of social phobia (Albano, Marten, Holt, Heimberg, & Barlow, 1995; Beidel, Turner, & Morris, 1997). In the first of these studies, Albano et al. (1995) presented findings from a pilot study of five adolescents with a principal diagnosis of social phobia. The study examined a 16-session multicomponent cognitive-behavioural group treatment package designed specifically for use with an adolescent population. The components of the treatment were largely drawn from successful treatment studies of adults with social phobia (see Heimberg, Salzman, Holt, & Blendall, 1993). In addition, specific skill-building strategies for adolescents were included, drawing largely from the work of Christoff, Scott, Kelley, Baer, and Kelly (1985). These treatment components comprised psychoeducation, social skills training, problem-solving and assertiveness training, cognitive restructuring, exposure techniques, and weekly homework assignments. Parental involvement was also an important part of the treatment package with the inclusion of parents at four "key" points in the 16-week treatment program.

At three months post-treatment, four of the five subjects no longer met diagnostic criteria for social phobia, whereas the remaining subject received only a provisional diagnosis of social phobia. At 12-month follow-up, all five subjects were free of a clinical diagnosis of social phobia with one subject receiving a "subclinical diagnosis of social phobia in partial remission" (Albano et al., 1995, p. 652).

This study, as a preliminary investigation, provides encouraging findings regarding the utility of a multicomponent cognitive-behavioural treatment package for adolescents with social phobia. However, the small sample size and absence of a control group make interpretations tentative. The authors are currently conducting a controlled trial comparing the effectiveness of this multicomponent cognitive behavioural treatment package with an educational control group for adolescents with a primary diagnosis of social phobia.

Using a younger sample of children with social phobia, Beidel et al. (1997) have reported preliminary findings using their own treatment program called *Social Effectiveness Therapy for Children*. As with the Albano et al. (1995) treatment package, Beidel and colleagues based their treatment program on intervention strategies that have been demonstrated to be effective in treating adults with social phobia. The pilot study, comprising 16 children between the ages of 8 and 12, consisted of 24 sessions over a 12-week period. The main treatment components were exposure and social skills training. Each week the children received one treatment session focused on exposure and the second treatment session on social skills training. Unique to this treatment program was the inclusion of a "peer-generalization component" (Beidel & Turner, 1998, p. 256). Following the weekly social skills training session, children with social phobia were paired with non-anxious peers for a 90-minute outing. This created natural opportunities for the child with social phobia to practise the newly learned social skill with a non-anxious peer.

The children reported significantly less social anxiety concerns at post-treatment on several measures. Similarly, parent reports indicated a significant reduction in internalizing behaviours from pre- to post-treatment. On behavioural tasks of reading aloud and role-playing, children were rated by independent and blind observers as significantly more skilled and with significantly less observable anxiety than pre-treatment ratings. These results are encouraging to the extent that they support continued evaluation of this particular treatment program for social phobia in adolescents. Multiple assessment modalities—i.e., questionnaire data and behavioural observations, as well as multiple informants—were used with all reports indicating reductions in social anxiety.

Group Treatment: Controlled Studies

Two controlled treatment outcome studies of children with social phobia provide further support for the utility of cognitive-behavioural approaches for treating this population (Spence, Donovan, & Brechman-Toussaint, 2000; Beidel, Turner, & Morris, 2000).

One study by Spence et al. (2000) compared the effectiveness of two different treatments (a cognitive-behavioural group [CBG; $N = 17$] versus a cognitive-behavioural group plus parent component [CBGPC; $N = 19$]), with a waitlist control group ($N = 14$). Children, ranging in age from 7 to 14 years, were randomly assigned to one of the three groups. Treated children received 12 weeks of weekly therapy sessions of 90 minutes' duration with two booster sessions at 3 months and 6 months post-treatment. Parents in the CBGPC received 12 weeks of weekly sessions of 30 minutes' duration, as well as observation of child sessions.

The treatment package consisted of social skills training, problem-solving, relaxation training, cognitive restructuring and exposure therapy (see Spence, 1995, for more details). The parent treatment component included instructions in parent management techniques particularly for socially anxious children as well as modelling and reinforcing of treatment objectives. Parents in the CBGPC also observed their child's sessions.

Significantly fewer children met criteria for a clinical diagnosis of social phobia at post-treatment in both active treatments compared with the waitlist control group: 87% diagnosis free in CBGPC; 58% in CBG; and 7% in the waitlist control group. These gains were maintained at follow-up. On measures of general and social anxiety, both treatments showed significant reductions at post-treatment compared with the waitlist group. Parent reports of children's social skills also increased for both treatment conditions compared with the control group. While there was a trend towards better results in the cognitive-behavioural treatment that included the parent component, this difference did not reach significance.

In a sample of 50 pre-adolescent children (8–12 years of age) diagnosed with social phobia, Beidel et al. (2000) compared the effectiveness of their Social Effectiveness Therapy for Children (SET-C; $N = 30$) with an active, but non-specific intervention ($N = 20$), primarily a test-taking and study-skills training program. Treatments were matched in terms of therapist contact time, group versus individual treatment time, the giving of homework, and number of weekly sessions.

Results were very encouraging. At post-treatment, 67% of the children in the SET-C group were free of their principal diagnosis of social phobia, compared with only 5% of children in the non-specific group. Furthermore, 52% of the SET-C group were judged to be treatment responders, while only 5% of the non-specific group achieved this classification. Similar to the Spence et al. (2000) study, improvements were also evident on other measures of social anxiety and social skills performance. All gains were maintained at 6 months post-treatment.

Overall, these preliminary studies support the utility of a multicomponent group cognitive-behavioural treatment approach for treating children with social phobia. The two controlled studies (Spence et al., 2000; Beidel et al., 2000) provide the most direct evidence of the efficacy of cognitive-behavioural interventions for children with social phobia, with exposure and social skills training the central treatment components in both studies.

Despite the promising results to date, several questions remain to be answered in future research. First, it is not clear from the current research which are the active or essential components to treatment. It is interesting to note that the studies that have been aimed specifically at treatment of social phobia have typically included some form of social skills training. An important question, then, is whether this is a necessary component of treatment for social phobia in children. The fact that treatment programs aimed at anxiety disorders in general in children do not include a strong social skills component and yet produce good effects, argues against this possibility. However, final decisions must await the conduct of treatment studies using a deconstruction methodology. It is also important to note that few of the treatment studies to date have focused on the treatment of social phobia in adolescents. It is possible that adolescents and younger children may have somewhat different needs and therefore, controlled outcome trials comparing techniques across different ages may be warranted. On this point, it should be noted that the study by Barrett et al. (1996) that was focused on anxiety disorders in general, showed a clear need for the inclusion of parents in younger children, but not for adolescents. Research that addresses other, more cost-efficient, forms of delivery, such as bibliotherapy may also be of value, as would research aimed at examining the application of treatment to difficult populations such as those with comorbid depression.

EARLY INTERVENTION AND PREVENTION

In line with the increasing trend towards *early intervention* and *prevention* in mental health, particularly in child populations, researchers have begun to evaluate the potential for cognitive-behavioural treatments to be used effectively as an early intervention or preventative approach with children who are anxious. Dadds, Spence, Holland, Barrett, and Laurens (1997) conducted a combined child- and parent-focused treatment for the prevention and early intervention of anxiety problems in children between the ages of 7 and 14. Of an initial cohort of 1,786 children, 128 met criteria for inclusion and agreed to participate in the school-based treatment. Children who met inclusion criteria were considered "at risk" based on a combination of child self-report of anxious symptoms, teacher ratings of shyness and anxiety, and parent report on a structured diagnostic instrument (see Dadds et al., 1997, for complete screening and inclusion details). The intervention was virtually identical to the treatment outlined above—i.e., *The Coping Koala*, Barrett et al. (1996), with minor modifications for administration in the school setting. Children were assigned to either the *Coping Koala* treatment program or a monitoring group.

Seventy-five per cent of the identified children met diagnostic criteria for an anxiety disorder. Hence, for these children, this study is another example of treatment for relatively mild anxiety disorders. Improvements were noted for both groups at post-treatment with significant differences between groups not emerging until 6-month follow-up. Longitudinal data were reported for 12- and 24-month follow-up in this sample (Dadds et al., 1999). Interestingly, at 12-month follow-up, differences between groups disappeared, whereas at 24-month follow-up, small but significant differences emerged again with children in the treatment group evidencing somewhat lower rates of anxiety disorders (20%) than did untreated children (39%).

The results of this study are of greater interest for the 25% of children who showed symptoms of anxiety without yet meeting criteria for an anxiety disorder. Only these children provide evidence relevant to early intervention. For these children, there was very little difference between treated and untreated children in the development of anxiety disorders two years following treatment. Most importantly, only 16% of the untreated children with anxiety symptoms at pre-treatment developed an anxiety disorder in the two years following treatment (compared with 11% of treated children). These results seriously question the assumption that children with moderate anxiety symptomatology are at dramatically increased risk for the later development of anxiety disorders and suggests that indicated prevention with mildly symptomatic anxious children may not be especially cost-effective.

An alternate model is to focus on selective prevention with children at high risk for the later development of anxiety disorders. One of the strongest demonstrated risk factors for anxiety disorders such as social phobia is a temperamental style labelled behavioural inhibition (Kagan, Reznick, & Gibbons, 1989, see Marshall & Stevenson-Hinde, this volume, *Chapter 3*). We are currently conducting a longitudinal prevention project with preschool age children who show early signs of anxiety, and their parents (Rapee & Sweeney, 1999). Our "at risk" group comprises 3.5–4.5-year-old children who are identified as behaviourally inhibited. We first ask parents of preschool age children to complete a questionnaire measure of temperament (Sanson, Smart, Prior, Oberklaid, & Pedlow, 1994). Children scoring in the upper range on the approach/withdrawal factor are then brought into the laboratory for an observational assessment of behavioral inhibition (BI; see Kagan et al., 1989). Parents of children who meet BI criteria are randomly assigned to either a 6-week cognitive-behavioural education group or a monitoring only group. The 6-week program (Rapee & Sweeney, 1998) educates parents in how to deliver cognitive restructuring and exposure to their children and teaches parent management strategies, as well as helping parents to become aware of their own anxieties and ways to manage them.

Pilot testing of this program has indicated very promising results (Rapee & Jacobs, 1998). Children whose parents underwent the education program showed a marked and significant decrease in both anxious symptomatology and, more impressively, temperament scores on withdrawal. Effects continued to increase to at least 6 months. Preliminary data in our larger, controlled trial are showing similar trends (Rapee & Sweeney, 1999). Children whose parents have been through the education program show a significantly greater decrease in parent-reported withdrawal at 6-month follow-up than do waitlist children (see Figure 23.1). To the extent that behavioural inhibition predicts the later development of anxiety disorders, including social phobia (Biederman et al., 1990), these results should lead to a reduced incidence of anxiety disorders in this population.

SUMMARY AND CONCLUSIONS

To date, few treatment studies have been conducted that include a specific focus on the treatment of socially phobic children. Nevertheless, results from these studies are encouraging and support the value of cognitive-behavioural treatments for children with social phobia.

There are a number of individual and group treatment studies for children with broad-based anxiety disorders, including social phobia. Generally, these studies have used a cognitive-behavioural treatment package, and in some cases, a family or parent component. The primary treatment components include education, cognitive restructuring and exposure therapy. Overall, results are encouraging showing significant reductions in the number of children maintaining a diagnosis at post-treatment and follow-up compared with waitlist control groups

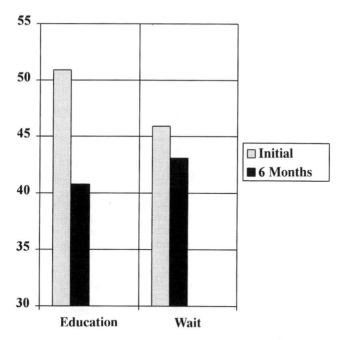

Figure 23.1   Changes in scores on withdrawal from initial assessment to 6-month follow-up in children whose parents have undergone an education program versus waitlist (N = 29)

as well as marked decreases in symptoms of general anxiety. These studies also show few differences in final outcome between children with social phobia and other anxiety disorders. Interestingly, results from our clinic suggest that children with a diagnosis of social phobia may respond a little more slowly to treatment than children with separation anxiety disorder (Rapee, 1996).

Two pilot studies and two very recent controlled treatment outcome studies have examined cognitive-behavioural treatment programs for children specifically diagnosed with social phobia. The two controlled studies provide the most direct evidence of the efficacy of cognitive-behavioural interventions for children with social phobia, with exposure and social skills training the central treatment components in both studies. Additional replication studies are needed. Future efforts with samples of children with social phobia should also focus on using deconstruction methodology to assist in evaluating the effectiveness of different treatment components, conducting studies with adolescents and assessing the usefulness of an individual treatment approach.

More recently, attention has begun to turn to the possible prevention of anxiety disorders such as social phobia. While indicated prevention for mildly symptomatic children may not be cost-effective, selective prevention programs with temperamentally at risk children may provide a valuable alternative. This exciting new development in the management of anxiety still requires considerable investigation. However, it may form the basis of a whole new direction in anxiety management, moving it into the realm of public health.

REFERENCES

Albano, A. M., Marten, P. A., Holt, C. S., Heimberg, R. G., & Barlow, D. H. (1995). Cognitive-behavioral group treatment for social phobia in adolescents: A preliminary study. *Journal of Nervous and Mental Disease*, *183*, 649–656.

Barrett, P. M. (1998). Evaluation of cognitive-behavioural group treatments for childhood anxiety disorders. *Journal of Clinical Child Psychology*, *27*, 459–468.

Barrett, P. M., Dadds, M. R., & Rapee, R. M. (1996). Family treatment of childhood anxiety: A controlled trial. *Journal of Consulting and Clinical Psychology*, *64*, 333–342.

Beidel, D. C. & Turner, S. M. (1998). *Shy children, phobic adults: Nature and treatment of social phobia*. Washington, DC: American Psychiatric Association.

Beidel, D. C., Turner, S. M., & Morris, T. L. (1997). *Social effectiveness therapy for children*. Paper presented at the annual meeting of the Anxiety Disorders Association of America, New Orleans, March.

Beidel, D. C., Turner, S. M., & Morris, T. L. (2000). Behavioral treatment of childhood social phobia. *Journal of Consulting and Clinical Psychology*, *68*, 1072–1080.

Biederman, J., Rosenbaum, J. F., Hirshfeld, D. R., et al. (1990). Psychiatric correlates of behavioral inhibition in young children and parents with and without psychiatric disorders. *Archives of General Psychiatry*, *47*, 21–26.

Christoff, K. A., Scott, W. O. N., Kelley, M. L., Baer, G., & Kelly, J. A. (1985). Social skills and social problem-solving training for shy young adolescents. *Behavior Therapy*, *16*, 468–477.

Dadds, M. R., Holland, D. E., Spence, S. H., Laurens, K. R., Mullins, M., & Barrett, P. M. (1999). Early intervention and prevention of anxiety disorders in children: Results at 2 year follow-up. *Journal of Consulting and Clinical Psychology*, *67*, 145–150.

Dadds, M. R., Spence, S. H., Holland, D. E., Barrett, R. M., & Laurens, K. R. (1997). Prevention and early intervention for anxiety disorders: A controlled trial. *Journal of Consulting and Clinical Psychology*, *65* (4), 627–635.

Flannery-Schroeder, E. C. & Kendall, P. C. (2000). Group and individual cognitive-behavioral treatments for youth with anxiety disorders: A randomised clinical trial. *Cognitive Therapy and Research*, *24*, 251–278.

Heimberg, R. G., Salzman, D. G., Holt, C. S., & Blendall, K. A. (1993). Cognitive-behavioural group treatment of social phobia: Effectiveness at 5 year follow-up. *Cognitive Therapy and Research*, *17*, 325–339.

Kagan, J., Reznick, J. S., & Gibbons, J. (1989). Inhibited and uninhibited types of children. *Child Development*, *60*, 838–845.

Kendall, P. C. (1994). Treating anxiety disorders in children. Results of a randomized clinical trial. *Journal of Consulting and Clinical Psychology*, *62*, 100–110.

Kendall, P. C., Flannery-Schroeder, E. C., Panichelli-Mindel, S., Southam-Gerow, M., Henin, A., & Warman, M. (1997). Therapy for youths with anxiety disorders: A second randomized clinical trial. *Journal of Consulting and Clinical Psychology*, *65*, 366–380.

Kendall, P. C., Kane, M., Howard, B., & Siqueland, L. (1990). *Cognitive-behavioral treatment of anxious children: Treatment manual*. Philadelphia, USA: Department of Psychology, Temple University.

Rapee, R. M. (1996). *Improved efficiency in the treatment of childhood anxiety disorders*. Paper presented at the 30th annual AABT convention. New York.

Rapee, R. M. (2000). Group treatment of children with anxiety disorders: Outcome and predictors of treatment response. *Australian Journal of Psychology*, *52*, 125–129.

Rapee, R. M. & Jacobs, D. (1998). *Prevention of anxiety disorders: A model and pilot treat-*

ment program. Paper presented at the World Congress of Behavioral and Cognitive Therapies, Acapulco, Mexico, July.

Rapee, R. M. & Sweeney, L. (1998). *PIP's Parent Education Program for Shy Preschoolers*. Unpublished manual. Macquarie University.

Rapee, R. M. & Sweeney, L. (1999). *Prevention of anxiety disorders: A model and pilot treatment program*. Paper presented at the Anxiety Disorders Association of America Annual meeting, San Diego.

Sanson, A. V., Smart, D. F., Prior, M., Oberklaid, F., & Pedlow, R. (1994). The structure of temperament from age 3 to 7 years: Age, sex, and sociodemographic influences. *Merrill–Palmer Quarterly, 40*, 233–252.

Silverman, W. K., Kurtines, W. M., Ginsburg, G. S., Weems, C. F., Lumpkin, P. W., & Carmichael, D. H. (1999). Treating anxiety disorders in children with cognitive-behavior therapy: A randomised clinical trial. *Journal of Consulting and Clinical Psychology, 67*, 995–1003.

Spence, S. H. (1995). *Social skills training: Enhancing social competence with children and adolescents*. Windsor, Berkshire: NFER-Nelson.

Spence, S. H., Donovan, C., & Brechman-Toussaint, M. (2000). The treatment of childhood social phobia: The effectiveness of a social skills training based cognitive-behavioral intervention, with and without parental involvement. *Journal of Child Psychology and Psychiatry, 41*, 713–726.

Author Index

Abe, K., 312
Abel, A., 303, 305, 312
Abelson, J. L., 488, 495
Abramson, L., 370
Abwender, D. A., 131, 388, 506
Achenbach, T. M., 161
Adamec, R. E., 32
Adams, J. B., 488
Adams, S., 168, 170
Adolfsson, R., 32
Afzelius, L., 286, 306, 312
Agras, W. S., 485, 494
Ahadi, S. A., 14, 108, 109, 111, 113, 339, 350
Ahmad, S., 264, 269, 271, 272, 418
Ainsworth, M., 39, 84, 86, 89, 91, 93, 140
Akselrod, S., 65
Albano, A. M., 508, 509, 510, 513, 516, 517, 530
Alberts, M., 312, 213, 314, 316
Albrecht, B., 341
Alden, L. E., 200, 201, 202, 203, 205, 226, 228, 230, 239, 246, 267, 291, 329, 370, 386, 388, 390, 391, 392, 393, 395, 396, 397, 398, 399, 413, 414, 415, 416, 417, 418
Alessandri, S., 102, 104
Alexander, A., 165
Alkon, A., 168, 170
Allan, S., 260, 261, 264, 274
Allen, J. J., 58
Allgulander, C., 474, 481
Alloy, L., 369
Allport, G., 108, 336
Alpert, J. E., 269, 361
Altamura, A. C., 487, 495

Altman, I., 196
Altman, S. A., 307
Alves, A. B., 473, 475, 489
Ameli, R., 36, 69
Amend, D., 25
American Psychiatric Association, 295, 316, 329, 330, 338, 339, 342, 343, 345, 346, 347, 348, 350, 359, 406, 455, 456, 457, 506, 507
Amies, P. L., 315
Amir, N., 370, 412, 416
Ammerman, R. T., 230
Amrein, R., 473, 475, 476, 489, 490
Amsterdam, B., 84, 85, 89, 91, 93, 103, 110
Amundsen, C., 484, 494
Andersen, S. M., 236, 249, 253
Anderson, C. A., 199, 228, 293
Anderson, J. C., 507, 508
Anderson, J. F., 164
Andersson, P., 286, 306, 312
Andrews, B., 189
Angleitner, A., 34, 337
Angold, A., 509
Appel, M. L., 64
Appelman, A. J., 228, 229
Appleton, A. A., 478, 491
Apsler, R., 292
Archer, D., 207
Arcus, D., 55, 177, 387
Arend, R. A., 140
Argyle, M., 85, 95, 192, 267
Argyropoulos, S., 479, 488
Arkin, R. M., 6, 121, 192, 202, 203, 212, 223, 225, 228, 229, 374, 394, 395
Arkowitz, H., 230

Arluke, A., 294, 309
Arnkoff, D. B., 198, 391, 392, 473, 477, 489, 491
Arnoult, L. H., 199, 228
Arnow, B., 239, 263
Aronson, E., 82
Arriaga, R. I., 70
Arrindell, W. A., 387
Arroyo, C. G., 364
Artenstein, M. S., 168
Asai, M., 365
Asche, B. K., 482, 493
Asendorpf, J. B., 13, 14, 15, 27, 78, 79, 80, 81, 82, 83, 84, 87, 90, 91, 93, 95, 122, 139, 141, 142, 152, 160, 162, 163, 171, 195, 197, 228, 284, 287, 290, 292, 293, 303, 313
Ashmore, R. D., 177
Asmundson, G. J., 368, 487, 492
Assenheimer, J. S., 373
Atherton, S. C., 226
Attili, G., 148, 153
Auerbach, J., 34, 42
Aune, K. S., 365
Aune, R. K., 365
Ayers, J., 163

Baak, K., 63, 65, 170
Bacon, M. K., 177
Baer, B. A., 438, 443
Baer, G., 530
Baerends, G. P., 54
Bahrick, L. E., 95
Bailey, K., 273
Baker, S. R., 306, 316
Balach, L., 482, 493
Baldwin, C. M., 481, 492

Baldwin, J. M., 120
Baldwin, M. W., 229, 230, 236, 241, 242, 243, 244, 245, 246, 247, 248, 249, 253, 389, 397, 399
Ball, D., 34
Ball, S. A., 341
Ballenger, J. C., 346, 361, 477, 480, 486, 491, 492, 495, 497, 483
Baltazar, P. L., 478, 485, 491, 495
Balter, M. B., 477
Ban, T. A., 477
Bandura, A., 432
Banerjee, R., 123, 125, 126, 127, 128, 130, 132, 288
Banon, E., 351
Barber, J. P., 329
Barger, A. C., 65
Barkow, J. H., 263, 265
Barlow, D. H., 282, 283, 285, 302, 316, 317, 346, 370, 373, 406, 436, 452, 508, 510, 513, 516, 530
Barnard, P. J., 406
Baron, R. M., 210
Baron-Cohen, S., 131, 264
Barone, P., 113, 228
Barrett, K. C., 8
Barrett, P. M., 510, 513, 514, 516, 533, 526, 529, 532, 533
Bartko, J. J., 473, 477, 489, 491
Bartlett, E. S., 79
Baruch, P., 368
Bates, A., 264, 274
Bates, G. W., 230
Bates, J. E., 137
Batten, N., 55
Battersby, S., 34
Baumeister, R. F., 220, 223, 225, 265, 267, 294, 296
Baumgardner, A. H., 121, 202, 394, 395
Bayles, K., 137
Bazzoui, W., 363
Beatty, M. J., 165
Beck, A. T., 245, 252, 266, 269, 274, 329, 363, 367, 369, 406, 412, 426
Beck, J. S., 426
Becker, L. A., 340, 341
Becker, R. E., 360, 370, 452, 449, 453, 456, 457, 474
Beech, J., 261, 269
Beery, S. H., 131, 388, 506
Beidel, D. C., 9, 12, 15, 64, 127, 331, 344, 386, 391, 392, 398, 415, 459, 463, 464, 484, 494, 497, 506, 507,

508, 510, 511, 513, 517, 530, 531, 532
Belfer, M. L., 168
Bell, I. R., 25, 38, 168, 170
Bell, J., 476, 486, 490
Bell, M. A., 35, 37, 59
Bellack, A. S., 344, 514
Belmaker, R. H., 33, 34, 42
Belsky, J., 143, 144, 151
Belyea, M., 269
Bem, D. J., 517
Bendall, D., 40
Benfield, P., 472
Bengel, D., 34, 42
Bengtson, M. A., 484
Benjamin, J., 34, 42, 45
Benjamin, L. S., 329
Benjamin, L. W., 382, 383, 384, 385, 391
Bennett, D. S., 137
Bennett, E. R., 33
Bennett, M., 125, 126, 288
Berger, P. A., 14, 198, 199, 204, 205, 387, 413, 518
Berger, R. D., 64
Bergeron, N., 26
Berglund, P., 360, 361, 362, 364
Bergman, E., 303, 305, 312
Bergner, R. M., 351
Berk, M. S., 236, 249, 253
Berk, M., 479, 482, 493
Berko, E., 211, 212
Bernet, Z., 369
Bernstein, D. P., 339
Bernstein, S. E., 480, 492
Berntson, G. G., 63, 64, 65, 66
Biederman, J., 15, 30, 534
Biederman, L., 54, 68
Bieling, P. M., 267, 391, 393, 395, 416
Bienert, H., 167
Biever, J. L., 198, 392
Bigelow, B. J., 130
Bille, B., 169
Binder, J. L., 239, 382, 383, 384, 391
Birch, H., 108, 109
Bird, H. R., 363
Birmaher, B., 482, 493, 509
Bishop, B., 65
Bisserbe, J. C., 490
Bissonnette, V., 206
Black, B., 482, 493
Blackburn, T., 127
Blaine, B., 228
Blaine, D., 33
Blais, M. A., 341
Blanco, C., 476
Bland, R. C., 360
Blatt, S. J., 382

Blazer, D. G., 360, 363
Blehar, M., 39, 140
Blendell, K. A., 457, 530
Blizard, D. A., 32
Bobes, J., 481, 492, 497
Bögels, S. M., 306, 312, 313, 314, 315, 316, 317, 415, 441
Bohn, P., 368
Bohn, P. B., 478, 491
Boissy, A., 32, 35
Boivin, M., 149
Bolduc, E. A., 15, 30
Bond, M. H., 147
Book, S., 478, 484, 491, 494
Boone, M., 368
Booth, C. L., 138, 140, 142
Borg, K., 475, 490
Borke, J., 102
Borkovec, T. D., 286
Bornstein, M. H., 148
Bornstein, M. R., 514
Borwick, D., 171
Boudewyns, P., 341
Bourgeois, J. P., 70
Bouton, M. E., 249
Bouwer, C., 483, 492
Bowers, K. S., 254
Bowlby, J., 236, 385
Boyce, W., 168, 170
Boyd, J. H., 360
Boyd, S., 341
Bradley, B., 368, 369
Bradley, M. M., 36
Bradley, S., 141
Bradshaw, S. D., 228
Bravo, M., 363
Brawell, L., 341
Brawman-Mintzer, O., 476, 493
Brazelton, T. B., 90, 95
Brechman-Toussaint, M., 209, 392, 392, 512, 514, 531, 532
Brene, S., 34
Brennan, K. A., 240
Brent, D., 509
Bretherton, I., 84, 86, 89, 91, 93
Brewerton, T. D., 361
Bridges, L. J., 140
Briggs, S. R., 9, 12, 13, 30, 78, 109, 191, 197, 206, 226, 328, 390, 391, 392
Brilman, E., 387
Britt, T. W., 286, 302, 303, 304, 305, 307, 308, 310, 311, 312, 318
Brodsky, M., 482, 493
Bronfenbrenner, U., 130
Bronson, G. W., 59
Brooks, J., 93
Brooks-Gunn, J., 89, 102, 103, 112

Brouillard, M., 253
Brown, E. B., 459
Brown, E. J., 452, 464
Brown, J. S., 69
Brown, L. G., 364
Brown, M., 137
Brown, T. A., 373, 436, 452
Bruce, M. L., 363
Bruch, M. A., 14, 196, 198, 197, 202, 204, 205, 207, 211, 212, 221, 225, 237, 282, 289, 292, 331, 387, 413, 434, 435, 457, 458, 465, 473, 489, 518
Bruns, J., 485, 495
Bryant, B., 192, 410
Buck, R. W., 286, 315
Budman, S., 341
Buescher, E. L., 168
Bugental, D., 141, 143, 174, 176
Bukowski, W., 141, 149
Buller, R., 475, 490
Burback, D. J., 510
Burger, J. M., 228, 229
Burgess, P. M., 230
Burgio, K. L., 240
Burnam, A. M., 364
Burnam, M. A., 360
Burnham, M., 123
Burns, D. D., 426
Burnstein, I. S., 260, 262
Burr, R., 340, 341, 342
Burroughs, E. I., 165
Busch, C. M., 433
Bushnell, J. A., 360
Bushnell, W., 481, 483, 492
Buss, A. H., 9, 10, 14, 25, 30, 38, 53, 78, 79, 80, 81, 87, 88, 95, 104, 105, 107, 108, 109, 111, 120, 121, 128, 162, 190, 191, 197, 221, 226, 240, 250, 288, 289, 302, 311, 328, 413
Buss, D. M., 260, 262, 350
Buss, E. H., 121, 311
Buss, K., 43, 61, 68
Buswell, B. N., 287, 292, 302, 303, 304, 307, 308, 309, 310, 312
Butler, G., 406, 412
Butterworth, G., 95, 124
Byer, A. L., 243
Byrne, A., 371
Byrne, D. F., 123
Byrne, R., 264
Bystritsky, A., 368

Cabe, D. D., 478, 491
Cacioppo, J. T., 63, 64, 65, 66, 273, 363, 436, 452

Cain, J. W., 476, 490
Cales, G., 317
Calhoun, D. S., 386
Calkins, S. D., 36, 37, 39, 59, 60, 63, 65, 66, 67, 138, 139, 140, 162
Cameron, D., 65
Cameron, O., 315
Camm, A. J., 66
Campbell, C., 230
Campbell, C. D., 200, 390
Campbell, E. K., 61
Campbell, I. M., 230
Campbell, K. B., 171
Campbell, M. A., 507, 516
Campbell, W., 369
Campeas, R., 329, 457, 458, 472, 473, 476, 482, 484, 485, 489, 490, 493, 494, 495
Campeau, S., 69, 70
Campos, J. J., 108
Cancienne, J., 369
Cane, D., 368
Canino, G. J., 363, 366
Cappe, R., 226, 291, 386
Capreol, M. J., 396, 397
Carbonell, E., 484
Carducci, B. J., 3, 281, 433
Carey, G., 373
Carey, W. B., 160
Carlson, E., 140
Carlson, J., 162
Carmichael, D. H., 526, 529
Carpenter, B. N., 391, 392, 398, 416
Carpenter, D., 481, 492
Carrell, S. E., 229, 244, 245, 389
Carroll, D., 33
Carter, L., 368
Carter, W. G., 130
Carver, C. S., 224, 239, 390
Caspi, A., 38, 138, 146, 197, 337, 517
Cassano, G. B., 482, 493
Castelfranchi, C., 78, 287, 302, 307, 308
Cattell, R. B., 328
Cen, G., 142, 148, 150
Chadwick, P., 270
Chale, R. A., 480
Chambless, D. L., 10, 329, 456, 459, 462
Chan, T., 349
Chance, M. R. A., 7
Chang, S. C., 365
Chapman, A. J., 95
Chapman, T. F., 366
Charney, D. S., 56
Chartier, M. J., 480, 487, 492

Cheah, C. S. L., 139, 144, 145, 146, 150, 152
Cheek, J. M., 9, 10, 13, 14, 30, 38, 78, 191, 197, 198, 210, 211, 221, 226, 237, 240, 282, 289, 290, 292, 328, 392, 433
Chen, E., 368
Chen, H., 142, 148, 150
Chen, X., 66, 137, 138, 141, 142, 143, 144, 146, 147, 148, 150, 152, 164, 174
Chen, Y. P., 413
Cherner, M., 55
Chesney, M., 168, 170
Chess, S., 53, 108, 109
Chesterman, B., 168, 170
Chiauzzi, E. J., 452
Chilamkurti, C., 12
Chin, S. J., 482, 493
Chiu, C., 111
Chorpita, B. F., 285, 373
Chouinard, G., 487
Christoff, K. A., 530
Chrousos, G. P., 43
Chu, B., 455
Chung, J., 168, 169, 170
Churchill, M. E., 230
Cicchetti, D., 112
Cicchetti, P., 31
Cimbolic, P., 473, 477, 489, 491
Clark, A. B., 54, 55, 68
Clark, D., 239, 367
Clark, D. B., 485, 494
Clark, D. M., 127, 239, 240, 250, 261, 264, 269, 270, 271, 272, 274, 316, 317, 391, 392, 298, 299, 406, 407, 409, 410, 412, 413, 414, 415, 417, 418, 419, 423, 425, 426, 427, 450, 451
Clark, L. A., 367, 373
Clarke, C., 63, 64, 138, 140
Clarke, J. C., 452
Clarkin, J. F., 340, 342, 347
Cleckley, H., 350
Cloitre, M., 369, 457, 458, 473, 489
Cloninger, C. R., 32, 33
Cobham, V. E., 516
Cohen, D. J., 33
Cohen, F., 168, 170
Cohen, L. S., 478, 491
Cohen, P., 339, 509
Cohen, R., 163
Cohen, R. J., 64, 65
Cohn, D. A., 39
Cohn, J. F., 40
Cole, S. W., 349
Coleman, K., 54, 55, 68

Coles, M., 370
Coles, M. E., 412, 452
Colket, J. T., 478, 491
Collins, A. C., 33
Collins, R. L., 33
Collins, T. M., 14, 198, 199, 204, 205, 387, 412, 518
Comadena, M. E., 164, 166, 167
Conger, A. J., 208
Connell, D., 40
Connell, J., 140
Conners, C. K., 509
Connor, J. M., 34
Connor, K. M., 478, 491
Contarello, A., 303, 313
Cook, J., 487
Cooley, C. H., 265
Cooley, M. R., 398
Coolidge, F. L., 340, 341
Cools, J., 509
Coopersmith, S., 436
Copeland, P., 32
Coplan, J., 485, 495
Coplan, R. J., 30, 37, 138, 139, 140, 162
Corbitt, E., 351
Corbitt, E. M., 338
Corley, R., 33
Cormack, C., 288
Coryell, W., 361
Cosby, C., 484, 494
Cosmides, L., 260, 262, 266
Costa, J., 487
Costa, P. T., 336, 337, 338, 340, 341, 342, 347, 350, 351
Costanzo, M., 207
Coté, D., 480
Cottle, M., 4
Cowley, D. S., 488
Cox, B. J., 261
Cox, D., 164
Coyne, J. C., 382, 386
Craske, M., 368
Crawford, M., 484, 494
Crnic, K., 130, 143, 144, 151
Crockatt, J., 487
Crocker, J., 228
Cromer, C. C., 130
Crook, J. H., 221
Crozier, W. R., 30, 121, 123, 219, 226, 288, 296, 314, 328
Csikszentmihalyi, I. S., 111
Csikszentmihalyi, M., 111, 113
Cully, M., 482, 493
Cummings, M., 143
Cummins, D. D., 260
Cupach, W. R., 210, 289, 290, 291, 292, 303, 309
Curlik, S. M., 476, 490

Curran, J. P., 207, 226
Curtis, G., 315
Curtis, G. C., 488, 495
Curtis, R. C., 416
Cuthbert, B. N., 36, 316
Cutler, B. L., 265
Cutler, N. R., 487
Cutlip, W. D. II, 286, 302, 303, 304, 305, 307, 308, 310, 311, 312, 318
Czepowicz, V., 480, 484, 492, 494
Czeschlik, T., 171

Dadds, M. R., 510, 513, 514, 516, 533
Dager, S., 487
Dalman, P., 317
Daly, A., 164
Daly, J. A., 164, 413
Dancu, C. V., 415, 507
Dancu, D. V., 391, 392
Daniels, D., 386, 387
Darby, B. W., 125, 129
Darwin, C., 87, 89, 95, 301, 302
Davidson, A., 476, 490
Davidson, J., 269, 346
Davidson, J. R. T., 360, 476, 478, 479, 487, 490, 491, 493, 495, 497
Davidson, R. J., 35, 36, 58, 59, 60, 70
Davies, M., 509
Davies, S., 329, 458, 465, 472, 482, 484, 489, 494
Davis, G. F., 164
Davis, K. L., 346
Davis, M., 31, 36, 42, 57, 59, 60
Davis, M. H., 439
Davis, R. D., 339, 340, 343, 347, 348
Dawson, G., 40
de Haan, M., 61
de Jong, P. J., 306, 308, 309, 312, 313, 314, 315, 316, 317, 414, 415
de Kloet, E. R., 61
de Raad, B., 338
de Waal, F. B. M., 307
de Wit, D. J., 3
Dean, J., 85, 95
Dearstyne, T., 55
Deary, I. J., 34
DeBellis, M. D., 486
DeBord, K. A., 243
Decarie, T. G., 82, 84, 85, 86, 87, 89, 90, 91, 93
DeFries, J. C., 32, 33
Del Medico, V. J., 362
Demby, A., 341

den Boer, J. A., 34, 42, 475, 479, 485, 487, 488, 490, 493, 495
Denton, K., 271
DePaola, S., 226
DePaulo, B. M., 225, 395
Derryberry, D., 70, 108
Deutch, A., 56
DeVane, C. L., 476, 493
DeVeaugh-Geiss, J., 486
DeVet, K., 108, 109, 171
Devins, G. M., 414
Devinsky, O., 286
Dhalla, K. S., 487, 492
Diamond, A., 70
Diamond, S., 166
DiBartolo, P. M., 508, 510, 516
Dibble, E., 33
DiBiase, R., 108, 111, 113, 288
Dickson, J. C., 103
Diekstra, R. F. W., 341
Dierker, L., 70
Digman, J. M., 336, 337, 338
Dikel, T., 70
DiLalla, L. F., 35, 53
Dill, J. C., 293
Dilsaver, S. C., 362
DiNardo, P. A., 436, 452
Dinnel, D. L., 365
Dirito, D. C., 340, 341
Dixon, A. K., 8, 267
Dobbelaar, A., 306, 314, 317, 414, 415
Dodge, C. S., 331, 360, 370, 456, 457, 474
Dong, Q., 517
Donnell, C., 369, 370
Donovan, C., 209, 392, 393, 512, 514, 531, 532
Donzella, B., 70
Dovidio, J. F., 248, 307
Downs, D. L., 10, 277, 394
Doyle, B. B., 480, 492
Draghi-Lorenz, R., 92, 93, 124
Drott, C., 317
Drummond, P. D., 286, 302, 305, 306, 313, 314, 315
Dryden, W., 274
Dubbert, B., 480, 492
Duggan, E. S., 240
Duijsens, I., 341
Dumas, J. E., 144
Dummit, E. S., 482, 493
Durham, R. L., 340, 341
Duval, S., 111, 265
Dweck, C. S., 111
Dyba, P., 165
Dyce, J. A., 341, 342

Eagan, T. V., 480, 492
Earls, F., 66
Eaton, W. W., 359, 360, 364
Eaves, L. J., 337, 517
Ebstein, R. P., 33, 34, 42
Edelman, R. E., 459, 462
Edelmann, R. J., 78, 86, 87, 93, 109, 239, 287, 291, 292, 295, 302, 303, 304, 305, 306, 307, 308, 309, 310, 311, 312, 313, 314, 315, 316, 317, 318
Edwards, M., 226
Ehlers, A., 316, 413, 427
Eibl-Eibesfeldt, I., 82, 84, 87, 93
Eisen, A. R., 513
Eisenberg, N., 14, 112, 160, 161, 439
Ekman, P., 285
Elder, G. H., 38, 146, 517
Eley, T. C., 32, 34
Elicker, J., 140
El-Islam, F., 363
Elkind, D., 311
Ellgring, H., 82
Ellis, A., 252
Ellis, P., 171
Ellis, S., 130
Ellyson, S. L., 307
Els, C., 479, 493
Elting, D. T., 452
Emerson, P. E., 130
Emery, G., 245, 252, 266, 269, 274, 406, 412, 426
Emmanuel, N. P., 476, 480, 485, 486, 492, 493, 494, 495
Emmelkamp, P. M., 316, 317, 387, 459
Emsley, R. A., 479, 493
Endicott, J., 361
Engelberg, B., 458
Engfer, A., 40, 146, 150, 163, 172, 173, 387
Enns, V., 242, 242
Entin, E., 204
Epstein, J. A., 225, 395
Epston, D., 252
Erhardt, D., 160, 161
Erikson, M. F., 141
Ernberg, G., 363
Erwin, B. A., 459, 466
Erwin, P. G., 131
Escobar, J. I., 360, 363
Eshleman, S., 3, 359
Essau, C. A., 361
Etcoff, N., 265, 272
Evans, L., 510, 516
Evans, M. A., 161, 162, 163, 164, 165, 166, 167, 168,

169, 179, 171, 175, 177, 290
Everett, J., 368
Ewell, K. K., 131, 388, 506
Eysenck, H. J., 108, 171, 337

Fabes, R. A., 14, 112, 160, 161
Fagin, S. S., 228
Fahlen, T., 331, 475, 490
Faholen, T., 317
Fairbanks, J. M., 482, 493
Fallon, B. A., 457, 458, 473, 476, 484, 485, 489, 490, 493, 494, 495
Falls, W. A., 69, 70
Faraone, S. V., 15, 30, 341
Farber, I. E., 69
Farooq, S., 363
Farvolden, P., 480, 481, 486, 492, 493, 495
Fava, M., 269, 361
Fedoroff, I. C., 477, 481, 498
Feehan, M., 507
Fehr, B., 242, 243
Feiring, C., 107
Feltner, D. E., 488
Fenichel, O., 329
Fenigstein, A., 128
Fenigstein, F., 413
Fennell. M. J. V., 274, 426
Fentress, J. C., 54
Ferdinand, R. F., 506, 508
Ferguson, L. R., 148
Ferrell, F., 478, 491
Feske, U., 456
Field, T., 40, 144
Field, T. M., 95
Fineberg, E., 34
Fink, C. M., 463, 464, 511
Fink, E. L., 309
Finkelstein, R., 507
Finn, J. D., 164
First, M. B., 343, 350
Fischer, A. R., 243
Fischer, K. W., 10, 187
Fischetti, M., 207, 226
Fisher, P. W., 509
Fiske, S. T., 238
Fitzsimmons, M., 164
Flannery-Schroeder, E. C., 515, 516, 526, 529
Fleeson, J., 39
Flicker, L., 282, 283, 302
Flint, J., 33
Flowers, C., 480, 482
Floyd, J., 82
Foa, E. B., 346, 370, 412, 416
Folkna, S., 168, 170
Fones, C. S., 486, 495
Fontaine, R., 478, 491

Foot, M., 36, 69
Ford, M. A., 162
Ford, S. M., 478, 491
Forde, D. R., 289
Foster, S., 513
Fowkes, F. G., 34
Fox, N. A., 30, 31, 35, 36, 37, 38, 39, 42, 58, 59, 60, 61, 63, 65, 67, 69, 112, 138, 139, 140, 144, 145, 146, 150, 152, 162, 286
Frances, A. J., 343, 344, 350, 351, 373
Francis, G., 508
Frazier, P., 243
Freeman, A., 329
Freeman, B., 34
Fremald, B., 261
Fridlund, A. J., 82
Friend, R., 413, 427, 511
Frijda, N., 225, 286
Fryer, M. R., 373
Frysinger, R. C., 31
Fuchs, M., 339, 340, 343, 347, 348
Fulker, D. W., 33
Fullard, W., 84, 89
Fulton, B., 472
Furlong, M., 199, 391
Furman, W., 166
Fyer, A. J., 329, 330, 331, 346, 365, 366, 472, 489, 472, 481, 482, 484, 493, 494, 507

Gahir, M. S., 363
Gaines, E., 228
Galassi, J. P., 198
Gale, A., 95
Gallagher, M., 31, 43
Gallup, G. G., Jr., 217, 218, 220
Gane, L. W., 482
Gansler, D., 452
Garcia, R., 40, 206
Garcia-Coll, C., 63, 64, 138, 140
Gardner, S., 177
Gardner, S. N., 95
Gaus, V., 265
Gelder, M., 261, 315, 329, 399, 451
Gelder, M. G., 415, 427
Gelernter, C. S., 362, 473, 477, 489, 491
Geller, V., 34, 42
Georgas, J., 303, 313
George, L. K., 360
Geppert, U., 102, 109
Gergel, I., 481, 483, 492
Gersten, M., 63, 65, 170, 177
Gest, S. D., 15

Geyer, M. A., 33
Giammarino, M., 262
Gibbons, J., 14, 53, 63, 65, 67, 386
Gifford, A., 455
Gilbert, P., 7, 189, 203, 205, 223, 260, 261, 262, 263, 264, 265, 266, 269, 270, 271, 273, 274, 275, 316, 317, 406
Gilboa-Schecthtman, E., 416
Gillingham, K., 126, 288
Gilmartin, B. G., 388
Ginsburg, G. S., 526, 529
Giordano-Beech, M., 265
Gittelson, L., 479, 493
Giuliano, T., 221, 224
Glabe, C., 34
Glass, C. R., 10, 198, 199, 291, 391, 392, 436, 452, 459
Glover, A., 55, 146, 153
Glowa, J. R., 31, 33
Gnepp, J., 129
Goetz, D., 458, 465, 476, 489, 490
Goffman, E., 5, 6, 105, 190, 222
Gold, P. W., 31, 33, 37, 38, 43, 61, 69
Golda, S., 526, 529
Goldberg, L. R., 336, 338
Goldberg, M. C., 42
Goldberg, S., 140, 141
Goldfinger, K., 449, 456
Goldfried, M. R., 371
Golding, J. M., 364
Goldman, D., 34
Goldman, M., 108, 109, 171
Goldman-Rakic, P. S., 70
Goldsmith, H. H., 53, 108
Goldstein, A. J., 329
Goldstein, S., 40, 486, 495
Goleman, D., 177
Golwyn, D. H., 474, 489
Goodnow, J. J., 141, 143
Goodwin, F. K., 43
Gordon, D., 65
Gordon, E., 164
Gorman, J. M., 329, 330, 331, 346, 347, 350, 472, 482, 484, 489, 493, 494, 507
Gorsky, J. M., 14, 198, 199, 204, 205
Gosling, S. D., 54
Goss, K., 264
Göthberg, G., 317
Gotlib, I., 368
Gottfried, A. W., 160
Gottman, J. M., 131
Gough, H., 392, 393
Gould, R. A., 458

Graham, P. W. A., 31
Grawe, J. M., 33
Gray, J. A., 33
Green, L. R., 308, 310, 312, 313
Greenberg, B. D., 34, 42, 45
Greenberg, J., 111
Greenberg, J. R., 236
Greenberg, M. T., 84, 89, 93
Greenberg, M., 1, 85, 91, 369
Greenberg, R. L., 266, 269, 274, 406, 412
Greene, R. L., 434, 436
Greene, R. W., 149
Greenspan, S. I., 140
Greiner, M., 487
Greist, J. H., 475, 480, 487, 490, 492, 495
Griffin, S., 228
Grillon, C., 36, 69, 70
Gritsenko, I., 34, 42
Grofer Klinger, L., 40
Gross, E., 303
Grossmann, K. E., 68
Grossmann, K., 68
Gruchow, H. A., 168
Grüter-Andrew, J., 418
Guarnaccia, P. J., 366
Guenther, D., 34
Guerin, D. W., 160
Guevara, L. M., 363
Guilford, J. P., 328
Guilford, R. B., 328
Guirgis, M., 26
Gulbinat, W., 363
Gully, R., 329, 472, 482, 494
Gunderson, J. G., 344, 347
Gunnar, M. R., 43, 61, 68
Gustavsson, J., 34
Guthrie, I. K., 14, 160, 161
Guy, L., 40

Haase, R. F., 211, 212
Hackmann, A., 261, 399, 414, 415, 425, 427, 451
Hadley, P., 165
Haemmerlie, F. M., 226
Hafler, D. A., 286
Hageman, W. J. J. M., 261
Hagerman, R. J., 483, 484, 493
Haghightgou, H., 488, 495
Halberstadt, A. G., 308, 310, 312, 313
Halperin, J. M., 486
Halpern, W. L., 163
Halverson, C. F., 337, 344
Hamer, D. H., 32, 34, 42, 45
Hamer, R. J., 198, 202, 221, 225
Hamerman, E., 31
Hammond, J., 163
Hampson, R. J., 287

Hampson, S. E., 86, 87, 93, 109, 302, 303, 307
Han, S., 160, 161
Hansell, S., 111
Harada, N., 365
Harker, L. A., 261
Harmar, A., 34
Harmon-Jones, E., 58
Harper, R. C., 260
Harpin, R. E., 484, 493
Harré, R., 284, 294
Harrington, G. M., 33
Harris, P. R., 79, 120, 284
Harrison, M., 486
Harrod, P. M. F., 166
Harrop, C., 261, 269
Hart, J., 61
Hart, T. A., 452
Hartman, L. M., 239, 406
Hartup, W. W., 41, 166
Harvey, A., 427
Haselton, J. R., 31
Hastings, P. D., 66, 137, 138, 141, 142, 143, 144, 146, 148, 150, 152, 174
Hatterer, J., 329, 472, 482, 494
Hauer, R., 167
Hauger, R. L., 487, 492
Hayes, C., 455
Hazan, C., 242
Hazen, A. L., 480
Healy, B., 40
Heath, A. C., 517
Hechenbleikner, N., 223, 227
Heckhausen, H., 102, 104
Hedges, D., 476, 490
Hegvik, R. L., 160
Heils, A., 34, 42
Heimberg, R. G., 127, 198, 202, 211, 221, 225, 246, 271, 274, 330, 331, 344, 360, 368, 369, 387, 370, 406, 413, 449, 450, 452, 453, 456, 457, 458, 459, 462, 464, 465, 466, 473, 474, 489, 508, 510, 516, 518, 530
Hellstrand, P., 286, 306, 312
Helmreich, R., 82
Henderson, H. A., 39, 59, 60, 66, 67, 138, 143, 144, 146, 152, 173, 174
Henderson, L., 127, 433, 434, 436, 437, 438, 439, 441, 443
Henin, A., 526
Henriques, J. B., 35
Herbert, J. D., 344, 459
Herjanic, B., 509
Hersen, M., 230, 507, 508, 514
Hershey, K. L., 14, 108, 109, 111, 113

Hertzig, M. E., 108, 109
Herzog, D. B., 361
Hesselman, S., 163
Hetherington, E. M., 40, 141
Hewitt, J. K., 33
Higgins, E. T., 224, 240, 242, 389, 397
Higley, J. D., 261
Higley, S., 261
Hildebrand, M., 316, 317
Hill, A. B., 368
Hill, D., 40
Hill, E. M., 488, 495
Hill, G. J., 207, 226
Hill, K., 303, 305, 312
Hill, L., 34
Hills, J., 482, 484, 493
Himle, J. A., 488, 495
Hinde, R. A., 53, 54, 137, 177
Hinds, L., 303, 305, 312
Hinrichsen, H., 417
Hinshaw, S. P., 160, 161
Hirsch, C. R., 413
Hirsch, J. A., 65
Hirschfeld, D. R., 15, 30, 534
Hirschfeld, R. M., 361
Hiruma, N., 365
Hitchcock, J., 31
Hitchcock, J. M., 36
Ho, P. K., 487, 490
Hodges, K., 509, 510
Hoffman, M. A., 228
Hofmann, S. G., 316
Holland, D. E., 533
Holland, P. C., 31, 43
Hollander, E., 329, 472, 482, 485, 493, 494, 495
Holle, C., 368, 464
Hollon, S. D., 371
Holmes, J. G., 244, 245, 246
Holt, C., 369
Holt, C. S., 331, 344, 457, 458, 459, 465, 473, 489, 530
Hong, Y., 111
Honig, A. S., 166
Hood, J., 141
Hood, S. D., 479
Hope, D. A., 127, 205, 221, 246, 265, 266, 331, 344, 360, 368, 413, 452, 453, 456, 457, 458, 459, 465, 473, 474, 479, 489
Hoppe, S. K., 364
Hornblow, A. R., 360
Horner, K. J., 452
Horney, K., 329
Hornig, C. D., 269, 331, 359, 360, 507
Horowitz, L. M., 438, 443
Horowitz, M. J., 236, 254

Horwath, E., 363
Hough, R. L., 360, 363
Howard, A., 248
Howard, B., 526
Howell, C. T., 161
Howell, E. F., 477, 491
Hrebickova, M., 338
Huber, A., 160, 161
Hudson, J. L., 387, 508, 511, 512, 515, 517, 518
Hughes, D. L., 360
Hughes, M., 3, 359
Humble, M., 475, 490
Hunt, A., 211
Hunter, B., 479, 493
Hyer, L., 341
Hymel, S., 41, 141, 146, 149, 164, 174, 518
Hyson, M. C., 78, 79, 80, 81, 83, 84, 87, 96, 189

Ianni, F., 351
Ickes, W., 206, 204, 206
Ingram, J., 482, 493
Ingram, R. E., 111, 271, 358, 367, 368, 369, 371, 373
Irwin, W., 58, 70
Iscoe, I., 121, 311
Ishiyama, F. I., 226
Ishiyama, R. J., 388
Iwata, J., 31
Iwawaki, S., 313
Izard, C. E., 78, 79, 80, 81, 83, 84, 87, 96, 102, 107, 189, 285, 294

Jablensky, A., 363
Jack, M. S., 452
Jackson, D., 58
Jackson, T., 226, 230, 290
Jacob, R. G., 459, 484, 494
Jacobs, D., 534
Jacobson, J. L., 39
Jaffe, J., 204
Jambor, T., 139
James, W., 78, 95, 328
Janet, P., 329
Jang, K. L., 33, 337
Janney, C. A., 487, 495
Jasius, M. C., 506, 508
Jaskir, J., 112
Jasnoski, M. L., 168, 170
Jefferson, J. W., 475, 480, 487, 490, 492, 495
John, O. P., 54, 337
Johnson, B., 248
Johnson, C., 248
Johnson, F., 363
Johnson, J., 269, 331, 359, 360, 363, 507

Johnson, K. A., 204, 205
Johnson, M., 484, 494
Johnson, M. O., 14, 53, 63, 65, 67, 1162, 168, 386
Johnson, M. R., 480, 492
Joiner, T. E., 373, 386
Jones, C., 484, 494
Jones, N. A., 35
Jones, R., 131
Jones, W. H., 30, 109, 226, 328, 390, 391, 392, 398, 416
Jonsson, E., 34
Jöreskog, K. G., 212
Joyce, P. R., 360
Juhani, L. E. V., 482, 493
Julia-Sellers, M., 168
Juster, H. R., 452, 453, 456, 457, 458, 459, 465, 466, 473, 489

Kachin, K. E., 397
Kaelber, C. T., 359, 360, 362
Kagan, J., 13, 14, 15, 24, 30, 35, 36, 37, 41, 44, 53, 54, 55, 57, 59, 61, 63, 64, 65, 66, 67, 69, 70, 78, 104, 107, 121, 138, 140, 141, 148, 160, 162, 168, 170, 237, 288, 386, 518, 534
Kahneman, D., 243
Kaiser, P., 168, 170
Kalin, N. H., 60
Kalish, H. I., 69
Kaloupek, D., 286
Kaltenbach, K., 84, 89
Kane, M., 526
Kaplan, D. A., 78, 82
Kaplan, M. S., 364
Kaplowitz, C., 103
Kapp, B., 484, 494
Kapp, B. S., 31
Karno, M., 360, 363
Kashani, J. H., 507
Kasniak, A., 25
Katschnig, H., 475, 490
Katz, M., 33
Katz, R. J., 475, 490
Katzelnick, D. J., 475, 480, 487, 490, 492, 495
Kaufman, J., 509
Kawakami, K., 248
Kazdin, A. E., 464, 507, 508
Kearney, C. A., 513
Kearsley, R. B., 141, 148
Keelan, J. P. R., 242, 243
Keenan, T. R., 130
Keller, M. B., 360, 361, 368, 371
Kelley, M. L., 530
Kelly, J., 507

Kelly, J. A., 530
Kelsey, J. E., 487, 495
Keltner, D., 8, 83, 84, 85, 86, 87, 91, 93, 94, 95, 261, 287, 292, 302, 303, 304, 307, 308, 309, 310, 312
Kemple, K., 160, 161
Kendall, P. C., 367, 369, 370, 371, 455, 464, 512, 515, 516, 526, 529
Kendler, K. S., 3, 359, 517
Kennedy, A., 139
Kennedy, C. R., 456, 457, 474
Kennedy, J. L., 34
Kenny, D. A., 210
Kenoya. M., 166
Kenrick, D. T., 260
Kent, J. M., 346, 349
Kent, R. N., 513
Kent, T. A., 476, 490
Kentgen, L. M., 482, 493
Kernberg, O. F., 344
Kessler, R. C., 3, 359, 360, 361, 362, 364, 517
Keys, D. J., 391, 392, 507
Kiecolt-Glaser, J. K., 263, 273
Kiesler, D. J., 239, 382, 385
Kihlstrom, J. F., 371
Kim, M., 69, 70
Kimble, C. E., 413
Kindlon, D., 66
King, A. Y. C., 147
King, D. S., 168, 170
King, N., 34
King, N. J., 511
Kinlaw, M. M., 340, 341
Klayman, J., 129
Klein, A. F., 330
Klein, D., 373
Klein, D. F., 329, 349, 351, 365, 457, 458, 465, 472, 473, 484, 489, 493, 494, 507
Klein, J. F., 127, 413
Klein, R., 389
Klein, R. G., 482, 493
Kleinknecht, E. E., 365
Kleinman, A., 363, 364
Klerman, G. L., 360, 361, 363
Knight, P. D., 204, 205
Knowles, T., 368
Knutson, B., 349
Kobak, K. A., 475, 480, 490, 492
Koch, E., 223, 227
Koch, W. J., 392, 399
Kochanska, G., 108, 109, 111, 113, 142, 144, 151, 171
Kodama, K., 34
Kohnstamm, G. A., 337, 344
Koh-Rangarajoo, E., 242, 243

Koopman, C., 346
Koplow, L., 166
Koponen, H., 482, 483, 492, 493
Kopp, C., 112
Kopp, C. B., 70
Korinek, J., 164
Korn, S., 108, 109
Koslowski, B., 90, 95
Kovacs, M., 509
Kovacs, R., 490
Kowal, A., 170
Kowalski, R. M., 200, 203, 209, 220, 222, 223, 226, 229, 230, 237, 246, 261, 266, 269, 282, 283, 285, 286, 287, 295, 305, 307, 388, 390, 391
Kozak, M. J., 346
Krakauer, I. D., 329
Kranzler, H. R., 341
Krasnoperova, E. N., 13, 30
Krebs, D. L., 271
Kretschmer, E., 329
Krishnan, R., 478, 491
Kriss, M., 371
Kroft, C. D., 480
Krull, D. S., 220
Kuczaj, S. A., 119, 121
Kuczkowski, R. J., 239
Kuczynski, L., 144
Kuhn, C., 40
Kuiper, N. A., 230
Kumakiri, C., 34
Kumar, R., 481, 492
Kuo, W., 363
Kurtines, W. M., 526, 529
Kuster, U., 109
Kwee, M. G. T., 261, 387

La Gaipa, J. J., 130
Ladd, G. W., 177
LaFreniere, P. J., 144
LaGreca, A. M., 127, 511
LaHoste, G. J., 34
Lake, E. A., 121, 202, 394, 395
Lambert, W. E., 165
Lamontagne, Y., 317, 488
Lance, J. W., 305
Landel, J. L., 291, 309
Landon, S. J., 163
Lane, R. M., 480, 495
Lang, P. J., 3, 36, 69, 316
Laplante, L., 368
Laraia, M. T., 477, 491
Larsen, K. H., 198, 392
Larsen, R. J., 267, 272
Larson, C., 58
Last, C. G., 507, 508
Last, K. A., 33
Laurens, K. R., 533

Lavallee, Y. J., 488
Lavori, P. W., 361
Lavy, E., 316, 317
Lawrence, S. G., 413
Lazarus, A. A., 437
Lazovik, A. D., 3
Leaf, P. J., 363
Leary, M. R., 6, 9, 10, 13, 121, 125, 129, 193, 197, 203, 204, 205, 209, 219, 220, 221, 222, 223, 225, 226, 227, 229, 230, 237, 246, 248, 250, 261, 263, 265, 266, 269, 282, 283, 285, 286, 287, 291, 293, 294, 295, 296, 302, 303, 304, 305, 307, 308, 309, 310, 311, 312, 313, 318, 328, 388, 390, 391, 394, 406, 437, 439
Lebra, T. S., 304
Lecrubier, Y., 497
Lederer, A. S., 507
LeDoux, J. E., 31, 57, 58, 70, 273
Ledwidge, B., 315
Lee, Y., 42
LeFan, J., 82
Leinonen, E., 482, 483, 492
LeMare, L., 140, 387
LeMay, C. S., 225, 395
Lemelin, S., 368
Lennox, R. D., 265
Lenzi, M., 482, 493
Leonard, H. L., 162
Lepine, J. P., 361, 488, 490
Lepola, U., 482, 483, 492, 493
Lerner, J., 450
Lerner, M., 34
Lesch, K. P., 34, 42
Leslie, A. M., 102
Leung, A., 459, 462
Levin, A., 472, 489
Levin, G. M., 484
Levin, J., 294, 309
Levine, J., 34, 42
Levitt, M., 103, 110
Lewin, M., 368
Lewis, C. E., 361
Lewis, H., 484, 493
Lewis, H. B., 432
Lewis, M., 78, 79, 80, 81, 84, 86, 87, 89, 91, 93, 94, 95, 101, 102, 103, 104, 107, 108, 109, 110, 111, 112, 113, 124, 284, 288, 303, 264, 270
Li, B., 147, 148
Li, L., 45
Lieberman, A. F., 140

Liebowitz, M. R., 269, 329, 330, 331, 344, 346, 347, 348, 349, 350, 359, 360, 365, 369, 452, 457, 458, 465, 467, 472, 473, 474, 475, 476, 481, 482, 484, 485, 489, 490, 492, 493, 494, 495, 507
Lim, H. K., 305
Lim, L., 370, 392
Lin, S., 458, 465
Lin, S. H., 489
Lindell, S. G., 261
Linden, M. G., 483
Lingsma, M. M., 261
Linnoila, M., 34, 261
Livesley, W. J., 33, 337, 340, 345
Lloyd, G. G., 484, 493
Loehlin, J. C., 337
Loiacono, D. M., 190
Lollis, S., 140, 387
Long, J., 34
Long, J. M., 37, 138
Lopez, D. F., 229, 244, 245, 389
Lord, C. G., 190
Lott, M., 475, 490
Loveland, K. A., 103
Lubin, B., 198
Lucas, R. A., 457, 466
Lucock, M. P., 230, 512
Ludgate, J., 261, 399, 415, 427, 451
Lumpkin, P. W., 526, 529
Lundh, L. G., 369, 390, 413, 417
Lydiard, R. B., 361, 476, 477, 480, 481, 484, 486, 487, 490, 491, 492, 493, 494, 495
Lykken, D. T., 350
Lyons, M. J., 341
Lyons-Ruth, D., 40

Maccoby, E. E., 40
MacDonald, K., 3, 147
MacLeod, A., 371
MacLeod, C., 367, 368
Maddocks, A., 361
Maddux, J. E., 226, 439
Magee, W. J., 359, 360, 364
Mahler, M., 385
Maidenberg, E., 368
Main, K., 230, 249, 253, 389
Main, M., 90, 95
Malhotra, A., 34
Malik, M., 66, 478, 491
Malliani, A., 66
Mallinger, A. G., 476, 490
Mallory, M. E., 304, 311, 312
Manassis, K., 141
Mancini, C., 15, 482, 486, 487

Mandler, G., 111
Mangelsdorf, S., 43, 61, 68, 140, 141, 146
Manning, P., 207, 208, 290
Mannu, P., 487, 495
Mannuzza, S., 365, 366
Mansell, W., 413, 414, 417
Manstead, A. S. R., 78, 282, 292, 309
Mantle, J. M., 480, 492
March, J., 509, 513, 517
Marcus, D. K., 287, 291
Mariotto, M. J., 208
Marks, G., 364
Marks, I. M., 241, 330
Markus, H., 224
Marrs-Garcia, A., 464
Marsella, A. J., 363
Marshall, P. J., 64, 66, 68, 70
Marshall, R. D., 458, 465, 476, 484, 489, 494, 490
Marshall, T. R., 36, 37, 59, 138
Marten, P. A., 530
Martin, B., 40, 141
Martin, J., 482, 493
Martin, J. A., 40
Martin, L. Y., 331
Martin, N. G., 337
Martin, R., 166
Martin, R. P., 337, 344
Martin, W. W., 95
Martinez, A., 433, 434, 437, 438, 441, 443
Martinez, R., 363
Martino, G. M., 38
Martins, E. A., 480, 492
Marvin, R. S., 84, 89, 93
Marvinney, D., 140, 141, 146
Masten, A., 163, 164
Masui, T., 312
Matas, L., 82, 83, 84, 93, 140
Matheny, A., 33, 109
Mathews, A., 367, 368, 369, 412, 413
Mathews, A. M., 241
Matias, R., 40
Matt, G., 369
Mattia, J., 368, 453, 459
Mattick, R. P., 452
Maynard Smith, J., 55
McArdle, E. T., 458
McCall, R. B., 53
McCann, C., 368
McCathie, H., 516
McClearn, G. E., 32
McClintic, S., 102, 104, 105
McConaughty, S. H., 161
McCormick, R. A., 373
McCrae, R. R., 336, 337, 338, 341, 342, 350

McCroskey, J. C., 162, 164
McCusker, G., 310
McDermid, B., 164
McDevitt, S. C., 160
McDonald, A. J., 58, 64, 70
McEwan, K. L., 414
McEwen, B. S., 31
McFall, R. M., 207
McGee, R., 507, 508
McGlashan, T. H., 346, 351
McGonagle, K. A., 3, 359, 360, 364
McGuffin, P., 517
McGuire, M., 260, 263, 273
McGuire, M. T., 7
McIntosh, B., 211
McKinnon, J., 140
McKnew, D., 509, 510
McLaughlin, S., 369
McLean, N. E., 269
McManus, F., 414
McNair, D. M., 482, 493
McNeil, D., 368
McNeil, D. W., 316, 452
McNichol, K., 137
Mead, G. H., 220, 221, 265
Meadows, S., 294, 302, 304, 306, 307, 309, 312, 313
Meares, R., 106
Mechanic, D., 111
Mednick, S. A., 53, 63
Mehlman, P. T., 261
Mehrabian, A., 166
Meier, G., 14, 163
Meier, V., 265, 266
Melamed, B. G., 316
Melchior, L. A., 10, 198, 226, 290, 392
Meleshko, K. A., 391, 392, 393, 395, 398
Meleshko, K. G. A., 202, 205, 226
Mellander, S., 286, 306, 312
Mellings, T. M. B., 388, 393, 398, 413, 414, 415, 417, 418
Melville, L. F., 518
Meredith, K. E., 38
Merikangas, K. R., 70
Merluzzi, T. B., 198
Merluzzi, T. V., 240, 392, 436, 452
Merry, J., 341
Mersch, P. P. A., 316, 317
Messer, S. C., 398
Metalsky, G. I., 386
Methorst, G. J., 387
Metts, S., 289, 291, 292, 303, 309
Meyer, D., 247
Mezzacappa, E., 66

Michalson, L., 102
Michela, J. L., 265
Millar, N., 369
Miller, J. W., 25
Miller, K., 416
Miller, P. A., 439
Miller, R. S., 9, 78, 82, 84, 89, 94, 189, 220, 223, 226, 281, 282, 283, 284, 285, 287, 289, 290, 291, 292, 293, 295, 302, 303, 304, 309, 310, 313
Miller, S., 33
Millon, C. M., 339, 340, 343, 347, 348
Millon, R. B., 339, 340, 343, 347, 348
Millon, T., 329, 339, 340, 343, 344, 345, 347, 348, 436
Mills, R. S. L., 40, 41, 131, 138, 140, 141, 142, 145, 148, 151, 152, 173, 175, 387, 518
Mindlin, M., 459, 466
Mineka, S., 368
Miner, C. M., 478, 491
Mintzer, O. B., 480, 484, 492, 494
Miranda, J., 358, 371, 373
Mischel, W., 432
Mitchell, S. A., 236
Mizushima, H., 365
Modigliani, A., 109
Moffitt, T., 310
Mogg, K., 368, 369
Momose, T., 365
Monroe, S. M., 196
Monsma, A., 387
Montgomery, R. L., 226
Montgomery, S. A., 476, 481, 490, 492
Moore, E. A., 349
Moos, B. S., 513
Moos, R. H., 513
Morgan, H., 415
Morgan, K. L., 190, 392, 398
Morgan, M. A., 70
Morison, P., 163, 164
Moritz, B. J. M., 387
Moroz, G., 476, 490
Morris, D. B., 111
Morris, P., 92, 93
Morris, T. L., 127, 508, 511, 530, 531, 532
Morrow, F. D., 38
Morse, J. Q., 329
Morton, A., 484, 494
Morton, W. A., 476, 493
Mosher, D. L., 78, 121, 285
Mougey, E. H., 168
Moyer, D., 90, 93, 95

Mueller, T. I., 361
Mulkens, S., 306, 313, 314, 315, 317, 414, 415
Muller, C. R., 34, 42
Muller, S., 369
Mullins, M., 533
Mundim, F. D., 473, 474, 475, 477, 478, 489, 490, 491
Munjack, D. J., 478, 480, 485, 491, 492, 495
Munson, P. A., 226
Murphy, B., 160, 161
Murphy, B. C., 14
Murphy, D. L., 34, 42, 45
Murphy, H. B. M., 365
Murphy, T. K., 484
Murray, K., 108, 109
Murray, P., 171
Myszka, M. T., 198

Nachmias, M., 43, 61, 68
Nader, K., 31
Naftolowitz, D. F., 488, 495
Nagle, R., 166
Nakamura, K., 365
Nardi, A. E., 473, 474, 475, 477, 478, 489, 490, 491
Narduzzi, K., 226, 230, 290
Narrow, W. E., 359, 360, 362
Nasby, W., 371
Nassini, S., 482, 493
Natale, M., 204
Nath, S. R., 464
Nauta, M., 455
Nawrocki, T., 40
Neal, A. M., 507
Neale, M. C., 517
Neely, J., 368
Neff, J. A., 364
Neidt, H., 34
Neisser, U., 95
Nelson, C., 70
Nelson, C. B., 3, 359
Nelson, L. J., 141, 142, 152
Nemanov, L., 33
Nesse, R., 4, 7, 260, 262, 315, 488, 495
Neto, F., 312, 313
Newcorn, J. H., 486
Newman, M. G., 316, 397
Newman, S. C., 360
Nguyen, L., 364
Nierenberg, A. A., 269
Nilsson, H. L., 475, 490
Noda, S., 34
Noethen, M. M., 34
Northman, E., 160
Norton, L., 439
Norton, L. W., 226
Norwood, R., 4, 188

Nothen, M., 34
Novick, D., 33
Noyes, R., 315, 476, 490
Nurius, P., 224
Nuss, S. M., 109
Nutt, D., 476, 479, 488, 497
Nyman, D., 331

O'Banion, K., 230
O'Brien, G., 286
O'Brien, G. T., 331
O'Connell, S., 263, 272
O'Connor, B. P., 341, 342
O'Leary, K. D., 513
O'Riordan, M. A., 131
Oakes, R., 479, 493
Oakley-Browne, M. A., 360
Oakman, J. M., 15, 480, 481, 486, 492, 493, 495
Oaksford, M., 367
Oberklaid, F., 137, 160, 534
Offord, D. R., 3
Ogborne, A., 3
Okada, S., 34
Okamoto, H., 34
Okazaki, S., 365
Okonogi, K., 365
Okyere, E., 363
Ollendick, T. H., 149, 514, 517
Olssen-Rex, L., 317
Olweus, D., 168, 388
Ono, Y., 365, 497
Ontiveros, A., 478, 491
Orn, H., 360
Orvaschel, H., 507
Osher, Y., 33
Öst, L. G., 369, 390, 413, 417
Oster, H., 92
Oswald, D. P., 149
Otto, M. W., 458, 486, 495
Oyebode, F., 363

Pagani, M., 66
Paget, K., 166
Pallanti, S., 483
Panagiotides, H., 40
Pande, A. C., 487, 488, 495
Panichelli-Mindel, S., 526
Papadopoulou, K., 292
Papageorgiou, C., 414, 415, 418, 427
Papp, L., 329, 472, 482, 494
Papsdorf, M. P., 393, 398
Parad, H. W., 262
Park, S., 143, 144, 151
Parke, R. D., 147, 286
Parker, G., 141, 142, 387
Parker, J., 141
Parker, J. G., 131
Parritz, R. H., 43, 61, 68

Parrott, W. G., 5, 282, 284, 303
Partridge, F., 507
Pastor, D., 141
Patrick, C. J., 350
Patterson, C., 45
Patterson, M. L., 223, 226, 230
Patton, K. M., 291, 309
Paulhus, D. L., 190, 392, 398
Pauli, U., 475, 490
Pava, J. A., 269
Paykel, E. S., 363
Pazzagli, A., 482
Pearl, L., 198, 199
Pearson, A., 129
Pedlow, R., 137, 160, 534
Pehl, J., 261
Pelham, B. W., 220
Pelissolo, A., 490
Pellegrini, A., 166
Pellegrini, D., 163, 164
Pelley, G., 162
Penn, D. L., 265, 266
Perner, J., 123
Perrin, S., 508, 516
Perry, J. C., 351
Perry, S., 40
Perugi, G., 482, 493
Perugini, M., 338
Peterson, C., 364
Peterson, J. M., 25
Petri, S., 34, 42
Petrovich, G. D., 70
Philbrick, P. B., 340, 341
Phillips, D., 329
Phillips, S. D., 196, 331
Piacentini, J., 509
Pian, K. L., 485, 495
Pickens, J., 40
Pickersgill, M. J., 261
Pierce, G. R., 10
Pierce, M. W., 487
Pierce, S., 61
Pigott, T. A., 480, 492
Pilkonis, P. A., 2, 4, 12, 13, 14,
     188, 226, 339, 340, 348,
     391, 433
Pincus, A., 396
Pincus, A. L., 397
Pincus, H. A., 338, 340, 341,
     350
Pine, D. S., 482, 493
Pines, A., 2
Pinto, S., 490
Pioli, R., 487, 495
Pitts, C. D., 481, 492
Plaisted, K., 131
Plant, R. W., 239
Plomin, R., 14, 30, 32, 33, 34,
     53, 108, 337, 386, 387
Plutchik, R., 102

Poggi, I., 78, 287, 302, 307, 308
Pol, E., 387
Poling, J. C., 341
Pollack, M. H., 458, 476, 478,
     479, 486, 488, 490, 491, 495
Pollack, W. S., 347
Pollans, C. H., 331
Porges, S. W., 37, 63, 65, 138,
     144
Porter, R., 2
Potts, N. L. S., 478, 491
Powell, J. L., 230
Pozo, C., 239, 390
Predmore, S., 228
Price, J. M., 177
Price, J. S., 261
Priel, B., 33
Prinz, R. J., 513
Prior, M., 137, 160, 534
Prisbell, M., 207, 208
Pritchard, D., 170
Propping, P., 34
Prusank, D. T., 164, 166, 167
Pryor, J. B., 240
Putman, S., 143, 144, 151, 171
Putman, S. P., 108, 109
Pyke, R. E., 487
Pyszczynski, T., 111

Qamar, A. B., 362
Quercioli, L., 482
Quigley, K. S., 65

Rachman, S., 418
Radl, S. L., 161, 162
Rae, D. S., 359, 360, 362
Raffle, C., 415
Rahe, D., 166
Raine, A., 53, 63
Rakic, P., 70
Ramanaiah, N. V., 340
Ramsay, D., 102, 109, 112
Ranc, J., 488, 495
Rao, U., 485, 495, 509
Rapaport, M., 476, 490
Rapee, R. M., 271, 274, 368,
     370, 387, 390, 391, 392,
     416, 427, 450, 507, 508,
     510, 511, 512, 513, 514,
     515, 516, 517, 518, 526,
     529, 532, 533, 534, 535
Rasmussen, S. A., 476, 490
Ray, G., 207, 208, 290
Recchia, S., 102, 104, 105
Reddy, V., 90, 92, 93, 124
Reed, M. A., 70
Refier, D., 509
Regehr, C., 241
Regier, D. A., 359, 360, 362
Regino, R., 34

Reich, J., 315, 477, 491
Reich, W., 509
Reis, D. J., 31
Reiter, S. R., 478, 491
Reith, W., 316
Rejeski, W. J., 286
Ren, R., 307
Renken, B., 140, 141, 146
Renneberg, B., 329
Reynolds, C. R., 516
Reznick, J. S., 14, 15, 24, 30, 35,
     37, 53, 61, 63, 64, 65, 67,
     78, 107, 138, 140, 160, 162,
     168, 170, 237, 288, 386, 534
Ricard, M., 82, 84, 85, 86, 87,
     89, 90, 91, 93
Rice, J., 361
Rice, M., 165
Richards, J. E., 65
Richey, H., 167
Richey, M., 167
Richichi, E., 478, 491
Richie, J. L., 484
Richmond, B. O., 516
Richmond, V. P., 162, 165
Rickman, M., 35, 60
Ridge, B., 137
Ridgeway, D., 119, 121
Riemann, R., 34, 337
Ries, B., 368
Ries, B. J., 452
Riggio, R. E., 207, 226, 290
Rimoldi, O., 66
Ringold, A. L., 480, 492
Riordan, L., 65, 66
Riso, L. P., 373
Ritts, V., 223, 226
Rivet, K. M., 211
Roberts, J. M., 484, 494
Robin, R., 34
Robins, C., 371
Robins, L. N., 359
Roebuck, L., 510
Rogers, T. B., 230
Rogoff, B., 130
Romanski, L. M., 70
Ronan, K., 369, 370
Ronan, K. R., 512
Rose-Krasnor, L., 41, 138, 140,
     141, 142
Rosen, J. B., 31, 36, 43, 57, 62
Rosenbaum, J. F., 15, 30, 269,
     361, 458, 478, 491, 534
Rosenberg, A., 63, 65, 168, 170
Rosenberg, S. E., 438, 443
Rossi, A., 482
Roth, W. T., 316
Rothbart, M. K., 14, 53, 91,
     108, 109, 111, 113, 339, 350
Rounsaville, B. J., 341

Rowe, D. C., 33
Rowe, M., 512
Roy, B. P., 487
Rubey, R., 484, 494
Rubin, K. H., 27, 30, 37, 39, 40,
    41, 59, 60, 67, 61, 66, 69,
    131, 137, 138, 139, 140,
    141, 142, 143, 144, 145,
    146, 147, 148, 149, 150,
    151, 152, 162, 163, 164,
    171, 173, 174, 176, 196,
    387, 518
Rubin, W. W., 42
Rubio-Stipec, M., 363, 366
Ruff, H. A., 91
Ruffman, T., 130
Rush, A. J., 426
Russell, D., 314
Rutter, M., 32, 34
Ryan, N., 482, 493, 509
Ryan, R. M., 239
Ryan, S. M., 514
Ryder, A. G., 388

Saarni, C., 288
Sabini, J., 5
Sabol, S. Z., 34, 42
Saboonchi, F., 413
Saboya, E., 490
Sabshin, M., 351
Safran, J. D., 236, 239
Safren, S. A., 452, 459, 464
Sakaguchi, A., 31
Salkovskis, P. M., 230, 261, 399,
    406, 408, 415, 427, 451, 512
Salzman, D. G., 457, 530
Sandberg, D., 40
Sanderman, R., 261
Sanderson, C. J., 329, 340, 342,
    343, 347
Sanislow, C. A., 346, 351
Sankis, L. M., 349, 351
Sanson, A., 137, 160
Sanson, A. V., 534
Santana, F., 360
Saoud, J. B., 485, 495
Sapolsky, R. M., 261, 273
Sarason, B. R., 10
Sarason, I. G., 10, 442
Sartorius, N., 363
Sartory, G., 465
Sartre, J.-P., 265
Sato, T., 34
Sattler, J. M., 307
Saucier, G., 336
Saul, J. P., 64, 65, 66
Scarpa, A., 53, 63
Schachter, S., 219, 225
Schaettle, S. C., 475, 490
Schaffer, D., 509

Schaffer, H. R., 130
Schanberg, S., 40
Scharfenaker, S., 484, 493
Scharwachter, I., 481, 492
Schatzberg, A. F., 359, 360, 362
Scheff, T. J., 5, 265
Scheier, M. F., 128, 191, 239,
    224, 250, 390, 413
Schlenker, B. R., 6, 13, 121,
    125, 127, 129, 193, 197,
    203, 219, 222, 223, 225,
    237, 248, 250, 283, 285,
    293, 388, 394
Schmidt, L. A., 25, 30, 35, 37,
    38, 39, 42, 59, 60, 61, 67,
    286
Schneider, B., 162
Schneider, B. H., 26, 148, 153
Schneider-Rosen, K., 112
Schneier, F. R., 269, 328, 329,
    331, 359, 360, 452, 457,
    458, 465, 467, 472, 473,
    482, 484, 485, 489, 490,
    493, 494, 495, 507
Schniering, C. A., 508, 511,
    512, 515, 517
Scholing, A., 316, 317, 459
Schroeder, J. E., 208
Schudson, M., 5, 7
Schulkin, J., 25, 31, 37, 38, 42,
    43, 57, 61, 62, 69
Schulman, A. H., 103
Schulz, K., 486
Schuster, B., 262
Schvaneveldt, R. W., 247
Schwab-Stone, M., 509
Schwartz, G. E., 25, 38
Schweizer, E., 476, 487, 490
Scott, J. C., 261
Scott, M. D., 164
Scott, W. O. N., 530
Sedikides, C., 218, 220
Sedvall, G. C., 34
Segal, Z. V., 358, 371, 373
Segrin, C., 209, 210
Selhub, J., 25
Seligman, C. R., 165
Seligman, M., 370
Selman, R. L., 123, 128, 288
Semel, E. M., 163
Semin, G. R., 78, 282, 292, 309
Semmel, A., 370
Sennett, R., 5
Serlin, R. C., 480, 492
Sesman, M., 363
Sevlie, C. P., 474, 489
Shackelford, T. K., 267, 272
Shafran, R., 418
Shannon, D., 65, 66
Shannon, D. C., 65, 66

Sharkey, W. F., 292, 304, 309
Sharpe, J. P., 340
Shaver, P. R., 242
Shaw, B., 426
Shaw, P., 410
Shaw, P. M., 315
Shea, C. A., 291
Shea, T., 361
Shear, M. K., 346, 347, 350
Shearn, D., 303, 305, 312
Sheikh, A. J., 363
Sheldon, W. H., 168
Sheldrick, R. C., 464
Shepard, S. A., 14, 160, 161
Shepperd, J. A., 6, 223, 225,
    228, 229
Sherling, G., 261, 269, 270, 275
Shields, S. A., 304, 311, 312,
    313
Shimizu, E., 34
Shiovitz, T., 487
Shirasawa, H., 34
Shouldice, A., 53, 54
Shrout, P. E., 363
Shulman, S., 140
Siani, M. W., 38
Siegel, J., 476, 490
Siever, L. J., 346
Sigler, K. D., 265, 266
Sigueland, L., 526
Silva, P. A., 138, 507, 508
Silver, M., 5
Silverman, W. K., 509, 526, 529
Simon, A., 304, 311, 312, 313
Simonini, E., 482, 493
Simons, A. D., 196
Simpson, A. E., 177
Simpson, H. B., 485, 494
Simpson, J. A., 260
Sims, J., 33
Sinclair, L., 241
Sitcoske, M., 31
Skov, V., 306, 312, 313
Skowronski, J. J., 218, 220
Slaap, B. R., 487, 490
Sladeczek, I. E., 162
Slaughter, J., 228
Smallbone, A., 95
Smart, D. F., 534
Smith, B., 128
Smith, C., 61, 69
Smith, C. C., 37, 42
Smith, G. E., 286
Smith, J. M., 64
Smith, R. D., 478, 491
Smith, R. E., 442
Smith, R. S., 252
Smith, S. F., 282, 284, 303
Smith, S. L., 171
Smith, T. G., 109, 191, 226

Smith, T. W., 369, 370
Smolka, V. M., 480, 492
Snidman, N., 14, 15, 24, 30, 35,
36, 37, 53, 55, 57, 59, 61,
63, 64, 65, 66, 67, 69, 70,
78, 107, 138, 140, 160, 162,
168, 170, 237, 386, 518, 534
Snyder, M., 132
Soldz, S., 341
Solyom, C., 315
Solyom, L., 315
Somervell, P. D., 363
Sommers, R. K., 163
Sörbom, D., 212
Sorenson, S. B., 364
Southam-Gerow, M., 526
Spasaro, S. A., 513
Spaulding, S., 459
Spence, S., 516
Spence, S. H., 209, 392, 512,
514, 516, 531, 532, 533
Spiegel, D., 346
Spieker, S., 40
Spielberger, C. D., 331, 443
Spinath, F. M., 34
Spitzberg, B. H., 210, 290
Spitzer, R. L., 343, 344
Spivack, G., 164
Spratt, G., 95
Spyer, K. M., 62
Srivastava, S., 337
Sroufe, L. A., 39, 82, 83, 84, 93,
140, 141, 146
St. Lorant, T., 434
Stafford, L., 304, 309
Stahl, S. M., 346, 349
Stanger, C., 78, 84, 87, 93, 94,
95, 102, 103, 104, 109, 110,
113, 124, 288
Stanley, M. A., 415
Stansbury, K., 61
Starrett, R. A., 364
Stasson, M. F., 228
Staton-Spicer, A., 166
Stein, D. J., 479, 481, 483, 492,
493
Stein, M. B., 289, 360, 361, 362,
364, 368, 475, 481, 488,
490, 492, 493
Steiner, M., 483
Stelmack, R. M., 171
Stemberger, R. T., 386
Stephan, C. W., 365
Stephan, W. G., 365
Stern, D. N., 90, 95, 236, 239,
253
Sternbach, H., 482, 493
Sternberg, E., 61, 69
Sternberg, E. M., 33, 37
Stevens, S. S., 168

Stevenson, J., 55
Stevenson-Hinde, J., 53, 54, 55,
64, 66, 68, 70, 146, 153, 177
Stewart, S., 37
Stewart, S. L., 30, 66, 137, 138,
139, 141, 142, 143, 144,
146, 148, 150, 152, 162, 174
Stifter, C. A., 65, 90, 93, 85
Stiles, W. B., 294
Stillwell-Barnes, R., 54
Stini, W. A., 25
Stinson, L., 206
Stipek, D. J., 102, 104, 105
Stone, G. P., 304
Stone, N., 286
Stone, V., 131
Stone, W. L., 127, 511
Stonehouse, C. M., 289
Stopa, L., 239, 250, 391, 392,
410, 412, 413
Stouthamer-Loeber, M., 310
Strauman, T. J., 389, 397
Strauss, C. C., 507, 508
Strauss, M. E., 373
Stravynski, A., 488
Street, R., 167
Streiner, D. L., 480, 482, 492,
493
Strelau, J., 34
Strickland, R., 269
Strupp, H. H., 239, 382, 383,
384, 391
Sturmer, P. J., 198, 199
Suarez, S. D., 218, 220
Sueoka, R., 365
Sullivan, H. S., 383, 385
Sullivan, M. W., 78, 84, 87, 93,
94, 95, 288, 102, 103, 104,
109, 110, 113, 124
Sun, Y., 148
Sunderland, B., 480, 492
Sunohara, G. A., 34
Suomi, S. J., 32, 261
Surawy, C., 414
Sutherland, S. M., 478, 487, 495
Sutton, S., 368
Sutton, S. K., 59
Svrakic, N. M., 32
Swann, W. B., Jr., 220, 228
Swanson, J. M., 34
Swanson, L. W., 70
Sweeney, L., 534
Swift, M. S., 164
Swinson, R. J., 261
Swinson, R. P., 141, 480, 495
Szarota, P., 338

Tajima, N., 112
Takahashi, L. K., 42, 60
Talbert, S., 341

Tambor, E. S., 394
Tan, J. Y., 484
Tancer, M. E., 362, 473, 477,
482, 488, 489, 491, 493,
495
Tancer, N. K., 163, 482, 493
Tangney, J. P., 10, 187, 282, 283,
284, 285, 302, 303
Tassone, F., 482
Tata, P., 368
Taub, D. M., 261
Taylor, A. K., 482
Taylor, C. B., 239, 253, 487
Taylor, D. A., 196
Taylor, K. L., 265
Taylor, L., 368
Taylor, L. H., 482, 493
Taylor, S., 477, 481, 498
Taylor, S. E., 238
Teasdale, J. D., 406
Tedlow, J. R., 269
Tee, K., 246
Teglasi, H., 228
Telaranta, T., 317
Telch, M., 253
Telch, M. J., 457, 466
Templeton, J. L., 286, 302, 303,
304, 305, 307, 308, 310,
311, 312, 318
Tennen, H., 341
Terdal, S. K., 394
Teschuk, M., 246
Thackrey, M., 364
Thapar, A., 517
Thomas, A., 53, 108, 109, 164
Thompson, R. A., 140
Thomson, S., 125, 126, 288
Thorne, A., 392, 393
Throckmorton, B., 226
Thyer, B., 315
Tice, D. M., 223, 294
Timbers, D. M., 360
Timms, M. W. H., 304, 317
Tinbergen, N., 54
Tomarken, A. J., 35, 36
Tomblin, J. B., 165
Tooby, J., 260, 262, 266
Tooke, W., 204, 206
Topol, D. A., 162
Totusek, P., 166
Tout, K., 61
Townsley, R. M., 9, 12, 331,
344
Towson, S., 226, 230, 290
Trabasso, T., 129
Trainor, L. J., 35
Tran, G. Q., 459
Trevarthen, C., 95, 96
Troisi, A., 263
Tronick, E. Z., 40

Trower, P., 7, 192, 203, 205, 223, 260, 261, 267, 269, 273, 275, 316, 317, 406, 410
Trull, T. J., 340, 341, 342, 347, 351
Tschann, J. M., 168, 170
Tsuang, M. T., 341
Tucker, G. R., 165
Tucker, W. B., 168
Tupler, L. A., 478, 491
Turk, C., 368
Turk, C. L., 450, 452, 456
Turnball, C., 269
Turner, J. R., 33
Turner, S. M., 9, 12, 15, 127, 331, 344, 362, 386, 391, 392, 398, 459, 463, 464, 484, 494, 506, 507, 508, 510, 511, 513, 517, 530, 531, 532
Turovsky, J., 285
Tversky, A., 243
Twentyman, C. T., 207
Tylec, A., 34
Tyson, M. C., 1

Ubel, F. A., 65
Uchino, B. N., 63, 64, 66, 263, 273
Udarbe, J. K., 486
Uebelacker, L. A., 269
Uereno, G., 438, 443
Uhde, T. W., 362, 473, 477, 482, 489, 491, 493
Uhlenhuth, E. H., 476, 477, 490
Umansky, R., 33
Urbanek, M., 34

Vache, K., 369
van Ameringen, M., 15, 480, 481, 482, 486, 487, 492, 493, 495
van Balkom, A. J., 484
van Der Ende, J., 387
van der Linden, G. J., 484
van der Molen, H. T., 82, 261, 282, 286, 290
van Hoof, J., 307
van Hout, W. J. P. J., 316, 317
van Kleek, A., 167
van Vliet, I. M., 475, 479, 485, 488, 490, 493, 495
van Zullen, M. H., 339, 340, 343, 347, 348
Vangelisti, A. L., 413
Vasey, M. W., 130
Vaughn, B. V., 488, 495
Vazquez, C., 369
Vega-Lahr, N., 40

Velez, N., 339
Veljaca, K. A., 390, 416
Venables, P. H., 53, 63
Verhulst, F. C., 506, 508
Vermigly, P., 148, 153
Vermilyea, J. A., 370, 449, 456
Vernberg, E. M., 131, 388, 506
Verney, S., 369
Vernon, P. A., 33
Versiani, M., 473, 474, 475, 476, 477, 478, 489, 490, 491
Vickers, J., 261
Victor, J., 286
Villanueva, C., 303, 313
Villareal, G., 476, 484, 493, 494
Villasenor, V. S., 438, 443
Vincent, A., 368
Vincent, P., 368
Virkkunen, M., 34
Vitto, M., 487, 495
Vittone, B. J., 362, 473, 477, 489, 491
von Baeyer, C., 370
Vossen, A., 361
Vrana, S. R., 316

Wadeson, R., 26
Wakefield, J. C., 262, 351
Walker, B. A., 309
Walker, E., 363
Walker, J. R., 289, 480, 495
Wall, S., 39, 140
Wallace, S. T., 200, 201, 202, 203, 230, 239, 370, 390, 391, 392, 395, 397, 416
Wallander, J. L., 208, 226
Walsh, M. D., 480, 492
Walters, K. S., 205
Wang, Y., 160, 161
Wara, D., 168, 170
Ward, D., 208
Ware, M. R., 476, 480, 492, 493
Ware, W. B., 198
Warman, M., 526
Warnke, S., 161, 170, 175, 177
Waterman, S., 482, 493
Waternaux, C. M., 341
Waters, E., 39, 82, 83, 84, 93, 119, 121, 140
Watkins, P., 369
Watson, A. K., 13
Watson, D., 367, 373, 413, 427, 511
Watson, K., 139
Weber, K., 373
Weems, C. F., 526, 529
Wegner, D. M., 221, 224
Weiner, B., 111, 200
Weinraub, M., 84, 89
Weinstock, R. C., 474, 489

Weisler, R. H., 487, 495
Weiss, M., 78, 84, 87, 93, 94, 95, 102, 103, 104, 109, 110, 124
Weissberg, H. W., 207
Weissman, M. M., 269, 331, 338, 359, 360, 363, 507
Weist, M. D., 149
Welkowitz, L. A., 457, 458, 473, 489
Wellens, A. R., 239, 390
Wells, A., 127, 239, 240, 261, 264, 267, 269, 270, 271, 272, 274, 316, 317, 398, 399, 406, 407, 412, 414, 415, 418, 419, 427, 451
Wells, J. E., 360
Welty, R., 32
Wenger, A., 339, 340, 343, 347, 348
Werner, E. E., 252
West, K., 341
Westen, D., 236
Westenberg, H. G. M., 12, 34, 42, 475, 479, 485, 487, 488, 490, 493, 495, 497, 493
Wheadon, D. E., 483
Wheeler, R. W., 3
White, B. B., 78, 121, 285
White, C., 459
White, M., 252
Whiteman, M. C., 34
Wicklund, R. A., 111, 265
Widiger, T. A., 336, 338, 339, 340, 341, 342, 343, 344, 345, 347, 349, 351, 373
Wigal, S., 34
Wigal, S. B., 34
Wigal, T., 34
Wiggins, J. S., 338, 340, 341, 396
Wiig, L., 163
Wiita, B., 479, 493
Wilcox, C. S., 487
Wilkinson, M., 143
Wille, D. E., 39
Willerman, B., 82
Williams, G. C., 262
Williams, J., 367
Williams, J. B. W., 343, 344
Williams, L., 34
Williams, R., 368, 369
Williams, S., 507, 508
Wilpers, S., 195, 293
Wilson, C., 486
Wilson, D., 479, 493
Wilson, D. S., 54, 55, 68
Wilson, R. S., 109
Wilson, W. H., 478, 491
Wingerson, D., 487
Winnicott, D. W., 253
Winton, E. C., 239

Wisselink, P. G., 487
Wittchen, H., 359, 360, 361, 364
Wittchen, H.-U., 3, 361
Wolfe, R. N., 265
Wolff, P. L., 15, 459
Wolkowitz, O. M., 349
Wolpe, J., 3
Wood, J. V., 265
Woody, S., 398
Woody, S. R., 10, 413
Wordern, T. J., 331
World Health Organization, 363
Worthington, J. J., 269, 458, 487, 495
Wright, D. M., 243
Wright, J. C., 262
Wurmser, L., 432

Xu, J. M., 364

Yamanouchi, N., 34
Yamauchi, K., 365
Yanagida, E., 363
Yang, B., 517
Yang, K., 477
Yardley, K., 410
Yates, W., 315, 477, 491
Yeung, A. S., 341
Ying, Y-W., 363
Yoshimura, K., 365
Yost, J. H., 190
Young, G., 84, 85, 86, 91
Young, J. W., 148
Young, R. C., 307, 308, 309
Younger, A., 148, 153
Younger, A. J., 26, 162
Youngstrom, E. A., 285, 294
Yuill, N., 119, 123, 125, 126, 128, 129, 130, 132, 288
Yule, W., 516

Zaccharias, P., 487
Zahn-Waxler, C., 142
Zamanian, K., 364
Zammuner, V., 303, 313
Zehr, H. D., 413
Zelazo, P. R., 148
Zhao, S., 3, 359
Zigler, E., 364
Zimbardo, P. G., 2, 3, 4, 30, 82, 161, 162, 165, 167, 177, 188, 190, 328, 331, 432, 433, 434, 437, 438, 439, 441, 443
Zimmerman, E., 40
Zollo, L. J., 456, 457, 474
Zucker, B. G., 486, 495
Zuckerman, M., 198
Zunz, M., 54
Zuroff, D. C., 382
Zwier, K., 485, 495

Subject Index

academic achievement and shyness, 164–165
adrenocortical activity, 43, 340
age of onset
  blushing, 311
  depression, 360, 362
  shyness, 434
  social phobia, 289, 360, 507–508
aggression, 259, 260, 262, 263, 267, 275, 276, 434, 439
agonic mode of behaviour, 7, 224
agoraphobia, 3, 253, 387, 465
Ainsworth Strange Situation test, 27, 61–62, 68, 140
alcohol and public speaking anxiety, 488
alcohol problems, 3, 11, 331, 361, 444, 479, 487, 488
allergies, 25, 168, 170
alprazolam, 473, 477, 478
ambivalence, 83–87
amygdala, 24, 31–32, 35, 42–43, 56–58, 60, 62–65, 70
anxiety disorders clinic, 15
Anxiety Disorders Interview Schedule for Children, 509–510
Anxiety Disorders Interview Schedule for DSM-IV: Life-time Version, 452
anxious self-preoccupation, 197, 291
appeasement, 8, 78, 224, 292, 307–308, 310
arousal, 285, 314, 267, 270, 275, 373, 410, 434–438
assertiveness, 141, 142, 143, 148, 171, 261, 267, 274, 275, 340, 392, 396, 439, 445, 511, 514, 530
assessment of family functioning, 513, 514–515
assessment of social anxiety, 436, 451–453
  in children and adolescents, 505–519
atenolol, 473, 484, 498
attachment, 27, 30, 39, 41, 44, 120, 139–141, 240, 242–244, 253, 385
  attachment status and inhibition, 61, 68–69

theory, 23, 27, 39, 140, 242
attention deficit hyperactivity disorder (ADHD), 34, 508, 509
attention processes, 239, 368–369, 390–391, 407–411
attractiveness, 260–23, 265–266, 269–272, 274–276
Attribution Style Questionnaire, 370
attribution, 199–200, 227–229, 245, 270, 370, 433, 435–438
  restructuring, 435, 441–443
automatic thoughts, 252, 440, 454, 460, 461, 512
availability heuristic, 243
avoidant personality disorder, 12, 328–332, 338–352, 365, 396–397, 438, 472
  cross-cultural studies, 337–338
  pharmacological treatment, 473, 475, 476, 480, 482, 484, 488
  and social phobia, 339, 342–358

bandwidth broadening technique in therapy, 424, 426
barbiturates, 477, 485
bashfulness, 79, 83, 87, 90, 96, 107, 120
Beck Depression Inventory, 436
bed nucleus of stria terminalis, 70
befloxatone, 474
behavioural avoidance test, 513
behavioural inhibition
  and anxiety disorder, 15, 534
  and attachment, 139–141
  definition, 53, 138–139
  impact of programme of research, 14, 16–17, 23–24
  and parenting, 141–147, 177, 386–387
  related to shyness, 11, 121, 197, 219
  as culture bound construct, 148
  neurobiological model, 55–57, 67
  physiological correlates, 25, 35–38, 54–71, 168
  temporal stability of, 53–54, 60

benzodiazepines, 444, 465, 476, 477–479, 483, 485, 497
beta-adrenergic receptor agonists (beta blockers), 444, 473, 476, 484, 497
beta-adrenergic receptors, 286, 306, 511
blame, 392, 438, 439, 445
  see also self-blame
blush
  classic, 305
  creeping, 305
blushing, 11, 13, 87, 190–191, 270, 286–287, 301–318, 366
  and affiliation, 308–310
  age differences, 311–312
  chronic, 294–295, 302, 305, 306, 311, 314, 315–318
  cultural differences, 303, 304, 313
  and embarrassment, 81, 88, 101, 109, 121, 291, 302–311, 313–316
  fear of, 415
  gender differences, 312
  individual differences, 311–315
  physiology of, 302, 305–306, 314–315, 316
  propensity, 306, 313–316
  and safety behaviours, 409–410
  and self-attention, 10, 190
  and self-conscious shyness, 88
  situations evoking, 303–305
  and social phobia, 315–318, 345, 406, 422, 511
  theories of, 307–311
  treatments for anxiety about, 317–318
blushing, pharmacological intervention, 484, 486
Blushing Propensity Scale, 306, 312–315
Brief Social Phobia Scale, 487
brofaromine, 472, 474–475, 477, 497, 498
bromazepam, 478
bullying, 269, 292, 388, 390, 414
bupropion, 486
buspirone, 485–486, 497

C-attachment status, 140–141, 146
Child and Adolescent Psychiatric Assessment, 509
Child Behavior Questionnaire, 14
child-rearing, 104
  see also parenting
Children's Assessment Schedule, 509
Children's Automatic Thoughts Scale, 512
children's conceptions
  embarrassment, 126
  self-presentation, 126–130
  shyness, 119–134
  social anxiety, 125–126
    individual differences in, 126–132
cholecystokinin, 488
citalopram, 483
classroom behaviour and shyness, 165–168, 196, 209
  and social phobia, 507

Clinical Evaluation of Language Functioning, 163
Clinical Global Improvement scale (CGI), 473, 474, 476, 477, 478, 480, 481, 482, 487
clomipramine, 485
clonazepam, 458, 477–479
clonidine, 486
closeness with others, 385, 394–395, 397, 399
cognitive behaviour group therapy, 330, 449–467, 473, 474, 483, 497
  for children's broad-based anxiety, 526–530
  for children's social phobia, 530–533
cognitive behaviour therapy, 332, 395–399, 419–422, 449–460, 464, 466, 473
  for children's broad-based anxiety, 526–530
  for children's social phobia, 531–532
  family component, 534–535
cognitive distortion, 271
cognitive interference, 208
cognitive overload, 271
cognitive priming technique, 241–242, 244–246, 249, 253, 254, 389, 399, 445
cognitive representation, 384
cognitive restructuring, 252, 441–443, 451, 453–456, 530, 531, 534
cognitive schema, 329, 367, 371–373, 384
  see also relational schema, self-schema
cognitive therapy, 274, 419–427, 435, 485
collectivist society and shyness, 147–148
Colorado Child Temperament Inventory, 14
comorbidity
  anxiety and mood disorders, 362
  avoidant personality disorder and social phobia, 331, 459, 473, 480, 487, 498
  in children, 508, 517
  depression and shyness, 434
  depression and social anxiety, 358–366, 459, 466, 480, 483, 508
  implications for pharmacological research, 497–498
  rates for depression and social phobia, 359, 361
  shyness and generalized social phobia, 434
  shyness and generalized anxiety disorder, 434
  shyness and dysthymia, 434
  shyness and Axis II disorders, 434
Conflict Behaviour Questionnaire, 513
conspicuousness, 88, 104, 107, 109, 121, 162, 282, 289
conversation
  anxiety about, 265, 422–424
  appropriate responsiveness, 287, 290, 410
  attractiveness to partner, 416
  hesitation and reticence, 14, 24, 203
  in vivo exposure, 435
  negative self-statements in, 198
  perceived as competitive, 266
  performance demands, 451
  physiological response to, 316, 414
  rules of, 261

shyness and verbal content, 204–205
skills, 168, 192, 207, 208–209, 226, 270, 511
Coopersmith Self-Esteem Inventory, 436
coping behaviour, 16, 17, 44, 61, 112, 174, 190, 273, 295, 315, 436, 455, 529
Coping Koala treatment programme, 533
copy process theory, 384, 391
corticosterone, 33, 42
corticotrophin, 488
cortisol, 24, 37, 38, 42–43, 56, 60–62, 112–113, 168, 273
cosmetics
as attractiveness enhancement, 265
to mask blushing, 310
cost effectiveness of treatment, 457, 529, 533, 535
coyness, 26, 79–82, 84–96, 124
cross-cultural studies
depression, 360, 362–364
shyness, 2
social phobia, 4, 364–366
see also cultural differences
cross-situational consistency, 160–161, 516
cultural differences in
blushing, 303, 304, 313
expression, 82, 84, 86, 87
meaning of shyness and inhibition, 147–149
parental beliefs and values, 148–149
cultural factors in assessment, 517
cultural values, 147

Darwin's influence, 301, 302, 307, 318
decatastrophizing, 425
defence system, 203–204, 265, 267, 270, 274, 275
definition issues, 8–9, 16, 79–82, 119, 122, 138–139, 207, 219, 432–433
depression, 3, 11, 34, 35, 38, 40–41, 42, 43, 44, 82, 142–143, 150, 197, 261, 264, 269, 271, 273, 275, 331–332, 339, 358–375, 386, 397, 426, 445, 459, 466
and acculturation, 364
age of onset, 360, 362
cross-cultural studies, 360, 362–364
degree of impairment, 359–360
and pharmacological interventions for social phobia, 472, 479, 480, 482–484, 486, 497–498
Devereux Elementary School Behaviour Rating Scale, 164
Diagnostic and Statistical Manual of Mental Disorders (DSM), 11, 331
see also separate editions (DSM-I, etc.)
Diagnostic Interview for Children and Adolescents, 509
Diagnostic Interview Schedule for Children—Revised, 509
diagnostic interviews, 509, 510, 519
diathesis–stress model, 30, 41–44, 196
difficult temperament, 137
dominance, 203, 205, 224, 260, 304, 308

dopamine, 33–34, 485, 487
dot probe task, 368, 413
drop out rates in treatment, 439, 474, 476, 481, 485
drug use/abuse, 331, 361, 444, 480
DSM-I, 329
DSM-II, 329
DSM-III, 3, 329, 330, 343, 359, 373, 455, 456, 473, 474, 477, 510
DSM-III-R, 330, 331, 340, 344, 406, 457, 458, 473, 475, 476, 478, 480, 482, 484, 485, 507–508, 510
DSM-IV Anxiety Disorders Group, 348
DSM-IV, 11–12, 316, 338–339, 342, 344, 345, 347, 348, 350, 365, 366, 372, 374, 406, 452, 480, 481, 485, 486, 487, 506, 507–508
DSM-V, 346–347
Duke Social Phobia Scale, 485
Dynamic Interaction Paradigm, 204, 205–206, 212
dysthymia, 479

early-appearing shyness, *see* fearful shyness
EAS Temperament Survey, 14
eating disorders, 361, 479, 482
eczema, 168
educational-supportive group therapy (ES), 456–458, 474
EEG measures of frontal cortex, 35–38, 56–60
elective mutism, 162, 163, 474, 483, 509
embarrassability, 192, 289, 290, 294, 295, 310, 313, 314
embarrassment, 101–115
antecedents, 282–284
in avoidant personality disorder, 339–340, 343
children's understanding of, 126, 128, 132
and depression, 362
as emotion, 9, 10, 11, 30, 435
empathic, 248, 288
evaluation type, 26, 80–81, 88–89, 95, 106–107, 114
exposure type, 26, 80–81, 88–89, 95, 103, 104, 105–115
facial expression, 26, 82, 96
Goffman's theory, 5
individual differences, 107–114, 289–291
at mirror image, 89, 103–104, 109–110, 113
of mother about child, 40, 142, 175, 176
non-verbal behaviour, 8, 287–289, 291
phenomenology, 284–286
physiology, 286–287
and self-consciousness, 121, 124–126, 128, 264, 336
and self-presentation, 5, 223
and shame, 106, 115
and social phobia, 3, 343, 367, 420, 424, 506
and shyness, 6, 81, 105, 107, 114, 115, 190, 280–296
and temperament, 25, 108, 110–111
see also blushing

empathy in therapy, 441
endoscopic transthoracic sympathectomy, 317–318
Epidemiological Catchment Area study, 359–364
epidemiological studies of social phobia, 3
Estimation of Others Scale, 438
evolutionary perspective on social anxiety, 7–8, 54–55, 223, 259–276, 294, 308
    implications for therapy, 274–275
exposure treatment, 16, 422, 435, 451, 453, 454, 460, 461, 463, 473, 530, 531, 534, 535
Expressive One Word Picture Vocabulary Test, 163
extraversion, 11, 168, 178, 269, 336–338, 342, 434
eye contact, 206, 393, 410, 445, 514
eye contact avoidance, 261, 262, 267, 270, 271, 416, 451

facial expression of shyness, 80, 83–96, 102, 208, 287
    in infancy, 86, 87, 89, 90–96
Family Enhancement of Avoidant Responding, 515
Family Environment Scale, 513
father's behaviour, 147, 171, 174, 177
fear, 35, 43, 70, 86, 103, 107, 109, 115, 120, 139, 142, 143, 144, 152, 170, 219, 220, 235, 260, 294, 367, 384, 387, 408, 438, 439
fear of negative evaluation, 289, 290, 293, 210, 313, 433, 508
Fear of Negative Evaluation Scale, 261, 413, 427, 478, 511
    Brief Form, 436
Fear Questionnaire, 473
fear system, 31–32, 39, 41, 42, 43, 44, 56
fearful shyness, 25, 80–81, 88, 92, 120–123, 125, 127, 133, 288, 293, 328
Fears Questionnaire, 241
Five Factor model of personality, 191, 195, 335–338
flooding technique, 484
fluoxetine, 481–483, 498
fluvoxamine, 479, 483, 497
Fragile X syndrome, 482
freezing, 42, 506
friends, 391–392, 394, 416
friendship formation, 131, 171, 196, 260, 263, 266, 273, 274, 388

GABA, 485, 487
gabapentin, 487, 497
gaze aversion, 8, 13, 26, 83–84, 88, 90–92, 109, 124, 199, 205, 210, 219, 262, 287, 307–308
gaze return, 84
gender as factor in assessment of children's social phobia, 517
gender differences, 13, 138
    in blushing, 313
    in emotional expressiveness, 211–212

in moderating influence of temperament on conscience, 108
in prevalence of children's social phobia, 508
in shy child's relationship with parents, 146, 148–149, 177–178, 387
in shyness, 40–41, 146
generalized anxiety disorder, 434, 485, 518, 529
generalized social phobia, 12, 330, 331, 344–348, 360, 370, 387, 412, 434, 458, 476, 480–484, 486, 497
genetic basis, 31–34, 41, 44, 55, 269, 517–518
giggling, 109
group belonging, 260

Hamilton Anxiety Rating Scale (HAM-A), 475
Hamilton Depression Rating Scale (HAM-D), 479
hand movements, 83, 86–87, 199, 270
hay fever, 168
head movement, 26, 83, 86–87, 90, 287, 307
heart period variability, 24, 42, 56, 64–66
heart period, 24, 27, 56, 62–64
heart rate, 9, 11, 33, 37, 38, 42, 43, 121, 286, 316, 414, 435, 511–512, 519
    see also heart period
hedonic mode, 7, 224
hemisphere asymmetry, 24, 35–37, 40, 42
heritability, 35, 54, 288
hippocampus, 31, 57
humour, 292
hypervigilance, 410, 450–451
hypothalamic-pituitary-adrenal system (HPA), 42–43, 57, 60, 168
hypothalamus, 42, 56, 60–62, 64, 70

idea of me, 101, 103, 106
illness and childhood shyness, 168–170
imipramine, 484
individual differences
    in blushing propensity, 311–315
    in shyness, 191–192, 197–212, 219, 225, 226–230, 241, 289–291
inhibited behaviour, 90, 163, 172, 219, 223, 225, 231, 261, 262, 270, 292, 296, 434, 435
    as criterion of avoidant personality disorder, 342, 345, 347
    and maternal responsiveness, 387
inhibited children, 107–108, 114, 161, 162, 174, 388
intelligence, 163–165, 392
internalizing behaviour, 138, 142, 151, 152, 161, 173, 531
International World Health Organization/U.S. Alcohol, Drug Abuse and Mental Health Administration Composite International Diagnostic Interview Field Trial, 361
Interpersonal Perception Task, 207
interpersonal script, 238, 240, 247–248, 251, 253, 254

interpretation bias, 239, 241, 390–391, 410, 412–413, 416–417
Interview Schedule for Children, 509
introversion, 168, 171, 197, 243, 340, 351, 434
Inventory of Interpersonal Problems, 438, 443
Inventory of Interpersonal Problems— Circumplex Scales, 396
irreversible MAOIs, 472–474

Kiddie Schedule for Affective Disorders and Schizophrenia—Present and Lifetime Version, 509–510

language competence, 162, 163
    deficits, 163
    vocabulary test performance, 163
lexical decision task, 247, 368
Liebowitz Social Anxiety Scale (LSAS), 452, 473, 474, 475, 476, 477, 478, 480, 481, 487, 498
limbic sites/system, 31, 35, 37, 42, 57
loneliness, 149, 210, 293
Louisville Twin Study, 33

maternal behaviour
    anger, 387
    control/over-control, 142–146, 148, 150, 152, 173, 174, 176, 387
    criticism, 173
    directive, 142, 144, 173, 175, 387
    disappointment, 387
    encouragement, 150, 175
    intrusive, 146
    influenced by child's temperament, 44
    not accepting, 148
    over-solicitous, 145, 174
    positive affect, 174
    power assertive, 148, 173, 175
    protective, 148, 150, 151, 174
    monitoring, 173
    punishment, 173
    rejection, 150
    responsiveness, 174, 387
    rewarding, 39
    sensitivity, 39, 43, 140, 150
    support, 146
    warmth, 150–153, 174
maternal beliefs, 40, 151, 152–153
Mead's theory of self, 188, 192, 220, 221, 275
memory processes, 236, 246–249, 251–252, 369, 389, 383–384, 413–414, 417–418, 442, 450
mental representation of self, 450, 451
meta-representation, 101–104
migraine, 169–170
Millon Clinical Multi-Axial Inventory, 434, 436, 438
mind reading, 264, 275, 276
Minnesota Multiphasic Personality Inventory, 434, 436, 438

mirror self-recognition paradigm, 92, 93, 103, 104, 109, 112, 217, 288
moclobemide, 472, 473, 474, 475–477, 483, 497, 498
modesty, 104, 105, 132, 365
monoamine oxidase inhibitors (MAOIs), 457, 472–477, 483, 497
mother's depression, 40
mother's personality, 27, 40–41
mother's shyness, 151
Multi-modal Life History Questionnaire, 437
Multiple Affect Adjective Checklist, 198

National Comorbidity Study, 3, 359–364
nefazodone, 486–487, 497
Negative Affect Self-Statement Questionnaire, 512
negative self-statements, 198–199, 203, 254
negative thought pattern, 420–421, 436–440, 442, 452
neuropeptides, 488, 497
neuroticism, 11, 33, 34, 41, 42, 150, 336–338, 340, 342, 349, 351
neurotransmitters, 33, 34, 42, 488
New York Longitudinal Study, 24
NIMH Collaborative Study of the Psychobiology of Depression, 361
non-verbal behaviour, 203, 205–206, 208–209, 262, 287–289, 291, 309
    see also facial expression
norepinephrine, 485
novelty seeking, 33–34
novelty/novel situations
    and behavioural reactivity, 34–35, 140
    clothes, 172
    and fearful shyness, 81, 88, 107, 120, 133
    food, 171
    and inhibition, 59, 143, 151, 162
    parent reluctance to let child explore, 145
    parent strategy to reduce upset, 175
    and shyness, 78, 81, 162
    as theme in research, 13, 159

objective self-awareness, 88, 95, 111, 112
observer–perspective image, 414, 421
ondansetron, 486
over-controlled behaviour, 138, 139, 161

paradoxical intervention treatment for blushing, 317
parasympathetic nervous system, 62–66, 144, 286, 305
Parent Expectancy Questionnaire, 513
parental behaviour
    abusive, 396
    acceptance, 143, 148, 152
    affection, 143, 237, 387, 390
    alcoholism, 396
    anger, 390, 396
    anxiety, 516, 518

calming, 387
coldness, 397
concern with others' opinions, 387
control/over-control, 141–145, 147–149, 176,
    237, 387, 390, 392, 396, 434, 450
criticism, 145, 392, 396
directive, 142–144, 176
disappointment, 396
disapproval, 145
encouragement, 148, 150, 152, 387, 396, 434
expression of negative emotion, 387
insensitivity, 27, 176, 434
intrusiveness, 143, 450
model anxiety, 450, 518
negative behaviours, 387
over-involvement, 143, 515
over-solicitous, 145, 149
power assertive, 143, 173
protection/overprotection, 176, 177, 387, 434,
    518
punishment, 292
rejection, 152
sensitivity, 27, 30, 40, 44, 143, 149, 152
shyness, 396
sociability, 435
supportive, 143, 387
use of shame, 237, 387, 390, 434
warmth, 397
parent–child relationship, 138, 140
parenting beliefs, 138, 141–143, 148, 149, 151,
    152
  perceptions of child's shyness, 142
parenting, 172–178
  and gender of shy child, 177–178
Parkinson's Disease, 25
paroxetine, 349, 480–482, 484, 497
pathological shyness, 82, 328, 332
Peabody Picture Vocabulary Test, 163
peer rejection, 139, 149, 169, 388
peer relationships, 130–131, 134, 139, 14, 143,
    144, 161, 165, 171, 288–289, 387–388, 434
perspective taking, 123–125, 128, 220–222, 244,
    288, 307, 439
pharmacological treatment, 16, 17, 332, 346–349,
    351, 465–466
  for children, 474, 480–483, 487, 497
phenelzine, 346, 457–458, 472–473, 474, 475, 476,
    477, 484, 497, 498
physical attractiveness, 211, 226
physiological correlates of shyness, 34–39
Piaget's theory of perspective taking, 123
positive experience of shyness, 77–79, 92,
    147–148
pregabalin, 488, 497
Prejudice Model, 426
prevalence
  avoidant personality disorder, 338–339
  shyness, 331, 433
  social phobia, 359
  social phobia in children, 507–508

private self, 388
private self-awareness, 221
private self-consciousness, 128, 314, 328, 438
private shyness, 433–434
processing of information, 238–245, 406–411,
    413–414, 416–418
propanolol, 484
protective self-presentation, 192, 202–205, 212,
    225, 228–9, 393–395, 398–399
psychoanalysis, 27, 39
psychopathy, 350
public self, 388–389
public self-awareness, 121
public self-consciousness, 128, 191, 221, 230, 246,
    250–251, 289, 314, 328, 413
public shyness, 433–434
public speaking, 9, 12, 304, 305, 343, 360, 361,
    410, 414, 425, 452, 488
pumpkinseed sunfish, 54

quietness in new situations, 53
  see also reticence

reactivity, 34–35, 36–37, 59, 108, 112, 113, 140,
    168–169, 177, 387
regulation of emotion, 31, 35
relational evaluation, 223–227
relational schema, 189, 191, 229–230, 235–255,
    329, 383–386, 388–389, 399
relational self, 388–389, 397–398
respiratory infection, 169
respiratory sinus arrhythmia (RSA), 65–66
reticence
  as component of shyness, 13, 82, 172, 219,
      223, 225, 285
  content of speech, 162, 204–206
  as criterion for diagnosis of social phobia,
      345
  frequency and duration of speech acts, 14, 15,
      162, 163, 171, 203–206, 394, 514
  interacting with strangers, 15, 53
  latency of speech acts, 14, 24, 162, 203, 422
  and neuroticism, 340
  and parents' behaviour, 144, 146, 149
  self-perceived dysfluency, 422
  and self-presentation, 225, 231, 285
  and social withdrawal, 139, 145
  in school, 163, 170, 171
reversible inhibitors of monoamine oxidase
    subtype A (RIMAs), 472, 474–477, 497
Revised Behavioural Assessment Test for
    Children, 514
Revised Children's Manifest Anxiety Scale,
    516
Revised Infant Temperament Questionnaire,
    109
role taking, 123, 128, 531

safety behaviour, 6, 16, 239, 261, 270, 274,
    398–399, 407–410, 415–424, 426–427

safety system, 205, 273
schema accessibility, 241, 243, 252, 253
schema activation, 241–242, 246–249, 25, 254, 391
school
  and children's social phobia, 507, 510
  and shyness, 27, 163–168
school refusal, 507
selective mutism, *see* elective mutism
selective serotonin reuptake inhibitor (SSRI), 349, 444, 474, 479–483, 486–487, 488, 497
self-appraisal, 200–202
self-attention, 107, 218, 221
self-awareness, 108–109, 110, 112, 189, 218, 221, 222, 224, 246, 422, 442
self-blame, 12, 432, 434, 435, 437–443, 445
self-concept, 101, 114, 226–227, 229, 240, 397, 442, 445
  restructuring, 441–443
self-confidence, 145
self-conscious emotions, 101, 102, 104, 109, 124, 133, 134, 189
self-conscious shyness, 25, 80–81, 120–125, 128, 133–134, 288, 290, 293, 328
self-consciousness
  and blushing, 306, 314
  cognitive component of social anxiety, 12–13
  and embarrassment, 104, 105
  emergence, 25–26, 80, 89, 124–128, 288, 311
  individual differences, 113, 313
  interpersonal basis, 96
  as facet of neuroticism, 336, 340, 342
  as reaction to therapist, 419
  and self-conscious emotions, 10
  and self-focused attention, 111, 239, 421
  and shyness, 6, 79, 126, 133, 166, 441
  and social anxiety, 17, 127, 348, 350
  and theory of mind, 264, 270, 276
self-criticism, 241, 248, 370, 441
self-disclosure, 205, 239, 391–393, 397, 437, 441
self-efficacy, 201, 218, 226, 397, 433, 444
self-esteem
  and accessibility of relational schemas, 241, 242, 245, 389, 397
  and avoidant personality disorder, 331
  cultural differences, 363
  as focus of therapy, 274, 426
  influence on perception of embarrassment and shyness, 218, 226, 227, 290, 436
  and social anxiety, 227, 240, 261, 265
self-evaluation, 104, 108, 159, 218, 242, 244, 246, 247, 251, 264, 310, 397
self-focused attention, 10, 43, 111, 224, 245–246, 265, 274, 314, 393, 397, 409, 410, 413–416, 419, 420, 423
self-identity, 265, 271, 272
self-labelling, 433
self-monitoring, 10, 132, 408, 409, 416, 421, 440
self-perception, 226–227, 411, 424

self-perpetuating transaction cycle, 384–386, 390–391
self-preoccupation, 398
self-presentation
  appropriateness of, 222
  change following therapy, 419
  children's understanding, 125–134
  concerns, 127, 128, 133, 223, 307, 515
  damage limiting, 261, 266, 271, 274
  in development of shyness, 125–134
  display of emotion, 124
  motivation, 129, 222–225
  skill, 122, 209, 285
  standards, 224
  strategies, 132, 225, 228
  task, 37–38, 285
  and theory of mind, 270
self-presentational model of social anxiety, 5, 6, 188, 197, 203, 222–225, 248–250, 388
self-recognition, 102, 109, 110–113
self-reflection, 217–218, 220, 224
self-regard, 149, 392
self-regulation, 145, 218, 224
self-schema, 16, 238, 240, 248, 263, 387–388, 395, 397, 442
self-worth, 30, 38, 145, 290
serotonin (5-HTT), 34, 41–43, 273
sertraline, 480, 482, 497
sexual partner, 264, 267, 269, 445
sexual relationship, 260, 263, 266
shame, 4, 5, 8, 9, 10, 26, 30, 108, 265, 269, 270, 272
  blushing in, 303
  display, 86, 261–262, 287
  development, 102–104, 264
  versus embarrassment, 106, 115
  parents' use in discipline, 237, 262, 434
  in shyness, 435, 437–443, 445
  in psychotherapy, 432, 445
  in social phobics, 411
Sheehan Disability Score, 478
sheepishness, 79, 84, 90, 107, 288
shyness at home, 27, 170–178
Shyness Attribution Questionnaire, 437–438
shyness sub-types, 210–211, 433–434
side effects of treatment, 473, 474, 475, 477, 478, 479, 480, 481, 486, 487, 497
sleep disturbances, 170, 367, 475, 477, 479, 483, 484, 495, 496
smile control, 84–86, 93, 94, 287
smiling, 25, 84–86, 89, 90–95, 109, 124, 287, 307–308, 410, 416
sociability, 40, 107, 218
Social Anxiety Scale for Children—Revised, 127, 511
social attention, 307
social avoidance, 261, 274, 275, 366, 391, 418, 440, 451
Social Avoidance and Distress Scale, 478, 511
social comparison, 261

social competence, 38, 39–40, 44, 140, 141, 143, 147, 148, 172, 260, 291, 514
Social Effectiveness Therapy for Children, 530, 532
social evaluation concerns, 13, 15, 81, 264, 288
social fitness model, 432, 435–446
social groups, 260
social hierarchy, 260, 261, 262
Social Interaction Anxiety Scale, 261, 452
social isolation, 139
social judgment task, 390
social norms, 291
social pathogenesis, 383, 386–388, 396–397
Social Phobia and Anxiety Inventory, 415
Social Phobia and Anxiety Inventory for Children, 127, 511, 516
Social Phobia Scale, 452, 485
social phobia
  and behavioural inhibition, 15
  blushing, 295, 306, 315–318
  in children, 209, 393
  as clinical syndrome, 328–330, 332
  cognitive behaviour group therapy, 449–467
  cognitive perspective, 405–430
  diathesis–stress model, 42
  gender differences, 364–365
  interpersonal perspectives, 332, 387–400
  interpersonal process of treatment, 399
  non-generalized, 12, 330, 360, 387, 484
  and public self-consciousness, 221
  public speaking form, 360, 361
  relational schemas, 239, 240
  and self-appraisal, 201
  and self-attention, 10
  and self-presentation, 6, 127, 203
  and shyness, 11, 119
  and submissive strategies, 275
  see also generalized social phobia
social rank, 260–261, 266, 269, 270, 271
social rejection, 237, 239, 267, 269, 272, 292, 294, 386, 394
social rules, 4, 5, 260–261, 262, 310, 424
Social Self-Presentation Style Scale, 202–203
social skills
  assessment, 452
  and cognitive distortion, 272
  coaching children in, 167–158
  deficits, 192, 206–210, 226, 246, 339, 344, 346, 394, 398, 410
  deficits in children, 209–210, 514, 519
  development of, 44, 275, 439
  parental influence on acquisition, 39–40, 141–145, 237
  peer-generalization component in training, 531
  and shyness, 290, 433, 434
  training, 192, 274, 435, 441, 484, 530, 531, 532, 535

social withdrawal, 11, 42, 43, 44, 58, 138–149, 151–153, 172, 175, 219, 225, 231, 394, 518, 519
sociometer, 10, 227
solitary behaviour, 139
solitary play, 89, 172
solitary-active behaviour, 139
solitary-passive behaviour, 139, 151
speech disturbances, 87, 88
stage fright, 119
Stanford Agoraphobia Exposure Protocol, 253
Stanford Shyness Clinic, 328, 432–446
Stanford Shyness Survey, 3, 4, 12, 13
startle response, 35–37, 42–43, 57, 69–70
State–Trait Anger Inventory, 438, 443
strangers
  anxiety, 79, 350
  in assessment of behavioural inhibition, 68
  in assessment of social phobia, 452
  and behavioural inhibition, 14, 83, 151
  development of anxiety, 59, 80, 90, 93, 95, 176, 265
  and fearful shyness, 15, 81, 120, 121, 133
  fear of, 15, 95, 107, 119, 265
  opinions of, and social evaluation, 294
  physiological responses to, in laboratory, 35, 65, 144
  and shyness, 161, 171, 202, 204
Stroop task, 368
Structured Clinical Interview for DSM-III-R, 473
stuttering, 424–425
Subjective Probability (Social) Scale, 512
Subjective Units of Discomfort Scale (SUDS), 437, 453, 454–455
submissive behaviour, 259, 261, 262, 266, 270, 274, 275, 286, 307–308, 434
suicide ideation, 360, 363, 367
suicide, 358, 360
sympathetic nervous system, 9, 12, 62–66, 286, 340

taijin-kyofu-sho, 365
teachers' interventions for shyness, 166–168
teasing, 131, 289, 434
temperament, 104–114, 434, 518, 534
temporal stability
  behavioral inhibition, 24, 25, 53–54, 138
  five personality factors, 336–337
  reticence, 145
  shyness, 38, 160–161
thalamus, 56, 57
theory of mind, 123, 124, 188, 260, 263–265, 269, 270
therapeutic relationship, 419, 442, 452
thinking errors, 454, 460
thumb sucking, 171
timidity, 33, 261, 262, 275, 336, 338, 339, 386–388
Toddler Temperament Scale, 109
transgression of social rules, 290

transitional object, 253
tranylcypromine, 474, 485, 498
tricyclic antidepressants, 484, 488, 497
tripartite model of social anxiety and
    depression, 373–374
twin studies, 32, 33, 35, 53, 55, 337, 517
tyramine, 474

unfamiliar people and situations, 14, 24, 33, 53,
    62, 144, 159, 162, 172, 185, 189
US Food and Drug Administration, 479

vagal tone, 144, 173
vagus, 56, 63
venlafaxine, 487, 497, 498
video feedback in therapy, 421–422, 425, 427,
    436

wariness, 53, 81, 138, 139, 140, 143, 144, 146, 147,
    148, 149, 171, 174, 175, 176, 259, 294
Wechsler Intelligence Scale—Revised, 163
World Health Organization, 363
worry, 12, 13, 282, 286, 289, 294, 373–374